Family in Transition

Tenth Edition

Arlene S. Skolnick
University of California, Berkeley
Jerome H. Skolnick
University of California, Berkeley

 LONGMAN

An imprint of Addison Wesley Longman, Inc.

New York • Reading, Massachusetts • Menlo Park, California • Harlow, England
Don Mills, Ontario • Sydney • Mexico City • Madrid • Amsterdam

Editor-in-Chief : Priscilla McGeehon
Marketing Manager: Megan Galvin
Project Coordination, Text Design, Art Studio, and Electronic Page Makeup:
   Thompson Steele Production Services
Cover Design/Manager: Nancy Danahy
Cover Photo: © PhotoDisc, Inc.
Full Service Production Manager: Eric Jorgensen
Print Buyer: Denise Sandler
Printer and Binder: The Maple-Vail Book Manufacturing Group
Cover Printer: The Lehigh Press, Inc.

Library of Congress Cataloging-in-Publication Data

Family in transition / [edited by] Arlene S. Skolnick, Jerome H.
   Skolnick. — 10th ed.
      p.   cm.
   Includes bibliographical references.
   ISBN 0-321-03434-1 (alk. paper)
   1. Family. I. Skolnick, Arlene S.   II. Skolnick,
Jerome H.
HQ518.F336 1998
306.85—dc21   98-22506
                                                        CIP

Please visit our website at http://longman.awl.com

ISBN 0-321-03434-1

12345678910—MA—01009998

Contents

Part Four   Families in Society   257

Preface

"May you live in interesting times" is said to be an ancient Chinese curse. The two decades we have been editing this book have certainly been interesting times to be studying the family. Family life has changed dramatically, and the meaning of these changes is fiercely debated, both in the field of family studies and in the public arena. Fears over the "breakdown of the family" have become a national obsession and a central issue in American politics. As a result, the importance of having basic knowledge about the family is more than academic.

As in previous editions, we have had three aims in this version. First, we have tried to describe current trends in family life, and place them in historical context. Second, we have tried to include articles representing the cutting edge of family scholarship, and yet balance them with excellent older ones. Third, we have tried to select articles that are scholarly, and yet understandable to an audience of undergraduates.

The 15 new readings include the following:

- Matthew Guttman's study of changing gender roles in Mexico and the decline of "machismo."
- Beth Bailey's inquiry into the different aspects of the sexual revolution of the 1960s and 70s.
- Frank Furstenberg's look into the future of marriage, and at what has to be done to ensure that it has one.
- Rosanna Hertz's study of three different ways parents organize the care of their young children.
- Janet Giele's analysis of conservative, liberal, and feminist views of the changing family.

In addition to the new articles, the book has been reorganized in the interests of clarity and coherence. We have added a new chapter on public debates on the family.

A test bank, providing multiple choice, true/false, and essay questions for each reading has been developed by Rifat Salam.

Finally, a word of thanks to all the people over the years who have helped us with suggestions for this book. Thanks also to Rifat Salam, of the NYU Sociology department, whose literature searches, valuable suggestions, and general helpfulness made this edition possible.

Last but not least, thanks to the following reviewers who offered many good ideas for this edition:

Robin Franck	Southwestern College
Lynda Dickson	University of Colorado at Colorado Springs
William Egelman	Iona College
Peter Adler	University of Denver
Michael Goslin	Tallahassee Community College
Allan Johnson	Hartford College for Women
Sandra French	Indiana University Southeast
Kathleen Tiemann	University of North Dakota
Lisa Waldner	University of Houston-Downtown
Carol Brooks-Gardner	Indiana University
David Gay	University of Central Florida
Barbara Bollman	Community College of Denver
Jacqueline Troup	Cerritos College

Arlene J. Skolnick
Jerome H. Skolnick

INTRODUCTION: FAMILY IN TRANSITION

C loning. Cyberspace. The Internet. Genetic engineering. The global economy. It is clear that in the closing decades of the twentieth century, the world has been massively transformed. "Every once in a while," states the introduction to *Business Week*'s issue on the 21st century, "the established order is overthrown. Within a span of decades, technological advances, organizational innovations, and new ways of thinking transform economies."

Although the state of the American family has been the subject of great public attention in recent years, the discussion of family has been strangely disconnected from talk of the other transformations we are living through. Instead, family talk is suffused with nostalgia and confusion—what happened, we wonder, to the fifties family of Ozzie and Harriet? Or as one prominent politician put it, "Why do we have all these problems we didn't have in 1955?"

The readings in this book show why this nostalgic approach to understanding the American family is seriously flawed. Of course family life has changed massively since the 1950s, and too many children and families are beset by serious stresses and troubles. But we can't understand these changes and problems without understanding the impact of large-scale changes in society on the small worlds of everyday family life. All the advanced industrialized nations have experienced the same changes the United States has—a transformation in women's roles, rising divorce rates, lower marriage and birth rates, and an increase in single-parent families. In no other country, however, has family change been so traumatic and divisive as ours.

To many Americans it has seemed as if "an earthquake had shuddered through the American family" (Preston, 1984). Divorce rates first skyrocketed, then stabilized at historically high levels. Women have surged into the work-

1

place. Birth rates have declined. The women's movement has changed the way men and women think and act toward one another, both inside the home and in the world at large. Furthermore, social and sexual rules that once seemed carved in stone have crumbled away: unmarried couples now live together openly; unmarried mothers keep their babies. Abortion has become legal. Remaining single and remaining childless, thought to be highly deviant once (though not illegal), have both become acceptable lifestyle options.

Today most people live in ways that do not conform to the cultural ideal that prevailed in the 1950s. The traditional breadwinner/housewife family with minor children today represents only a small minority of families. The "typical" American family is now likely to be one of four other kinds: the two-wage-earner family, the single-parent family, the "blended" family of remarriage, or the "empty nest" couple whose children have grown up and moved out. Apart from these variations, large numbers of people will spend part of their lives living apart from their families—as single young adults, as divorced singles, as older people who have lost a spouse.

The changes of recent decades have affected more than the forms of family life; they have been psychological as well. A major study of American attitudes over two decades revealed a profound shift in how people think about family life, work, and themselves (Veroff, Douvan, and Kulka, 1981). In 1957 four-fifths of respondents thought that a man or woman who did not want to marry was sick, immoral, and selfish. By 1976 only one-fourth of respondents thought that choice was bad. Summing up many complex findings, the authors conclude that America underwent a "psychological revolution" in the two decades between surveys. Twenty years earlier, people defined their satisfaction and problems—and indeed themselves—in terms of how well they lived up to traditional bread-winner/housewife and mother roles. More recently, people have become more introspective, more attentive to inner experience. Fulfillment has come to mean finding intimacy, meaning, and self-definition.

Ever since the 1970s the mass media have been serving up stories and statistics seemingly showing that the family is disintegrating, falling apart, on the verge of disappearing. In the 1990s, the public discussion of family issues turned into a polarized, often angry political debate. In the 1992 election, then Vice President Dan Quayle set off a firestorm by attacking the fictional television character Murphy Brown for having a child without being married. The show, according to Quayle, made a mockery of "the importance of fathers" and revealed "a poverty of values." The public clearly preferred candidate Clinton's focus on "the economy, stupid" and his definition of "family values" as "valuing families"—no matter what their form—traditional, two parent, one parent, extended.

Yet less than a year after the election, "Dan Quayle was right" became the new national consensus. A sudden blizzard of newspaper columns, magazine articles, and talk show "experts" warned that divorce and single parenthood are inflicting serious damage on children and on society in general. This family structure, they argue, whether it results from divorce or unmarried motherhood, is the single biggest problem facing the country, because it is the root cause of all the rest—poverty, crime, drugs, school failure, youth violence, and other social ills.

The proposed solution? Restore the traditional two-parent family. "Traditionalists" propose a national campaign, much like the campaign against cigarette smoking, to make divorce and single parenthood socially unacceptable once again. In addition, these "traditionalists" support the successful effort to do away with welfare and to make divorces more difficult to obtain.

The traditionalists' argument is based on family research, and indeed, a few family scholars, most of them political conservatives, have been actively involved in the campaign to promote these views to the general public. But putting social science into the middle of the "argument culture" (Tannen, 1998) that dominates our media and politics these days, is not an effective way to deal with the complexities of either the research or family life itself.

Deborah Tannen points out that in the U.S. there is currently a pervasive warlike mentality that portrays any issue as a battle between two—and only two—opposing sides (1998). Popular political talk shows like *Crossfire*, *Equal Time*, and *Hardball*, which often amount to little more than shouting matches, are the most extreme examples. Such shows typically feature the most assertive advocates from each side. In general, arguments are regarded as newsworthy, while calm discussions of an issue are not. None of the media are immune, including newspapers and magazines. Howard Kurtz, a media critic, observes that "the middle ground, the sensible center, is dismissed as too squishy, too dull, too likely to send the audience channel-surfing (1996, p. 4)."

It's not surprising then, that public debate about the family often sinks to the level of a "food fight" as it lurches from one hot topic to another—single mothers, divorce, gay marriage, nannies, and working mothers. Each issue has only two sides: Are you for or against the two-parent family? Is divorce bad for children? Should mothers of young children work or not? Is the family "in decline" or not?

The "two-sides" approach makes it difficult to discuss realistically the issues and problems facing the country. It doesn't describe the range of views among family scholars, and it doesn't fit the research evidence. For example, if someone takes the position that "divorce is damaging to children" the argument culture leads us to assume that there are people on the other "side" who will argue just the opposite—in other words, that divorce is "good," or at least, not harmful. But as researcher Paul Amato suggests, the right question to ask is "Under what circumstances is divorce harmful or beneficial to children?" (1994) In most public debates about divorce, however, that question is never asked, and the public never hears the useful information they should. Moreover, the public never gets to hear what researchers have found out about what helps and what hurts children in divorced and single-parent families.

Still another problem with popular discourse about the family is that it exaggerates the extent of change. For example, we sometimes hear that the traditional nuclear family no longer exists, or has shrunk to a tiny percentage of the population. But that statement depends on a very narrow definition of family—two biological parents, in their first marriage, with a full-time breadwinner husband and a full-time homemaker, and two or three children under the age of 18. Of course that kind of family has declined—for the simple reason that most wives and mothers now work outside the home. It has also declined because there are more married couples with grown children than there used to be.

Similarly, we hear that divorce rates have shot up since the 1950s, but we are not told that the trend towards higher divorce rates started in the nineteenth century, with more marital breakups in each succeeding generation. Nor do we hear that despite the current high divorce rates (actually down from 1979), the United States has the highest marriage rates in the industrial world. About 90 percent of Americans marry at some point in their lives, and virtually all that do either have, or want to have, children. Further, surveys repeatedly show that family is central to the lives of most Americans. They find family ties their deepest source of satisfaction and meaning, as well as the source of their greatest worries (Mellman, Lazarus, and Rivlin, 1990). In sum, family life in America is a complex mixture of both continuity and change.

While the transformations of the past three decades do not mean the end of family life, they have brought a number of new difficulties. For example, most families now depend on the earnings of wives and mothers, but the rest of society has not caught up to the new realities. There is still an earnings gap between men and women. Employed wives and mothers still bear most of workload in the home. For both men and women, the demands of the job are often at odds with family needs.

UNDERSTANDING THE CHANGING FAMILY

During the same years in which the family was becoming the object of public anxiety and political debate, a torrent of new research on the family was pouring forth. The study of the family had come to excite the interest of scholars in a range of disciplines—history, demography, economics, law, psychology. As a result of this research, we now have much more information available about the family than ever before. Ironically, much of the new scholarship is at odds with the widespread assumption that the family had a long, stable history until hit by the social "earthquake" of the 1960s and 1970s. We have learned from historians that the "lost" golden age of family happiness and stability we yearn for never actually existed.

Because of the continuing stream of new family scholarship, as well as shifts in public attitudes toward the family, each edition of *Family in Transition* has been different from the one before it. When we put together the first edition of this book in the early 1970s, the first rumblings of change were beginning to be felt. The youth movements of the 1960s and the emerging women's movement were challenging many of the assumptions on which conventional marriage and family patterns had been based. The mass media were regularly presenting stories that also challenged in one way or another traditional views on sex, marriage, and family. There was talk, for example, of "the population explosion" and of the desirability of "zero population growth." There was a growing perception that the ideal of the three-, four-, or five-child family of the 1950s was not necessarily good for the country as a whole, or for every couple.

Meanwhile, Hollywood movies were presenting a new and cynical view of marriage. It was almost taken for granted that marriages were unhappy, particularly if the spouses were middle class, middle aged, or affluent. Many people were openly defying conventional standards of behavior: College girls were beginning to live openly with young men, unwed movie actresses were publicizing rather than hiding their pregnancies, and homosexuals were beginning openly to protest persecution and discrimination.

It seemed as if something was happening to family life in America, even if there were no sharp changes in the major statistical indicators. People seemed to be looking at sex, marriage, parenthood, and family life in new ways, even if behavior on a mass scale was not changing very noticeably.

In putting together the readings for that first edition of *Family in Transition*, we found that the professional literature of the time seemed to deny that change was possible. An extreme version of this view was the statement by an anthropologist that the nuclear family (mother, father, and children) "is a biological phenomenon . . . as rooted in organs and physiological structures as insect societies" (LaBarre, 1954, p. 104). Any changes in the basic structure of family roles or in child rearing were assumed to be unworkable, if not unthinkable.

The family in modern society was portrayed as a streamlined, more highly evolved version of a universal family. According to the sociological theorist Talcott Parsons and his followers (1951, 1954), the modern family, with sharply contrasting male and female roles, had become more specialized. It transferred work and educational roles to other agencies and specialized in child rearing and emotional support. No less important for having relinquished certain tasks, the modern family was now the only part of society to carry out such functions.

The family theories of the postwar era were descriptively correct insofar as they portrayed the ideal middle-class family patterns of a particular society at a particular historical period. But they went astray in elevating the status quo to the level of a timeless necessity. In addition, the theories did not acknowledge the great diversity among families that has always existed in America. For example, the working-mother or single-parent family could be seen only as deviant. Ethnic differences also received very little attention, or were considered undesirable variations from the mainstream, middle-class norm.

Still another flaw in the dominant view was its neglect of internal strains within the family, even when it was presumably functioning as it was supposed to. Paradoxically, these strains were vividly described by the very theorists who idealized the role of the family in modern society. Parsons, for example, observed that when home no longer functioned as an economic unit, women, children, and old people were placed in an ambiguous position. They became dependent on the male breadwinner and were cut off from society's major source of achievement and status.

Parsons saw women's roles as particularly difficult: even at the height of the June Cleaver era, being a housewife was not seen as a real occupation; it was vaguely defined, highly demanding, yet not considered real work in a society that measures achievement by the size of one's paycheck. The combination of existing strains and the demystifying effects of the challenges to the family status quo seems to have provided, as Judith Blake (1978, p. 11) pointed out, a classic set of conditions for social change.

Part of the confusion surrounding the current status of the family arises from the fact that the family is a surprisingly problematic area of study; there are few if any self-evident facts, even statistical ones. Researchers have found, for example, that when the statistics of family life are plotted for the entire twentieth century, or back into the nineteenth century, a surprising finding emerges: Today's young people—with their low marriage, high divorce, and low fertility rates—appear to be behaving in ways consistent with long-term historical trends (Cherlin, 1981; Masnick and Bane, 1980). The recent changes in family life only appear deviant when compared to what people were doing in the 1940s and 1950s. But it was the postwar generation that married young, moved to the suburbs, and had three, four, or more children that departed from twentieth-century trends. As one study put it, "Had the 1940s and 1950s not happened, today's young adults would appear to be behaving normally" (Masnick and Bane, 1980, p. 2).

Thus, the meaning of change in a particular indicator of family life depends on the time frame in which it is placed. If we look at trends over too short a period of time—say ten or twenty years—we may think we are seeing a marked change, when, in fact, an older pattern may be reemerging. For some issues, even discerning what the trends are can be a problem.

For example, whether or not we conclude that there is an "epidemic" of teenage pregnancy depends on how we define adolescence and what measure of illegitimacy we use. Contrary to the popular notion of skyrocketing teenage pregnancy, teenaged childbearing has actually been on the decline during the past two decades (Luker, this volume). It is possible for the *ratio* of illegitimate births to all births to go up at the same time as there are declines in the *absolute number* of births and in the likelihood that an individual will bear an illegitimate child. This is not to say that concern about teenage pregnancy is unwarranted; but the reality is much more complex than the simple and scary notion an "epidemic" implies. Given the complexities of interpreting data on the family, it is little wonder that, as Joseph Featherstone observes (1979, p. 37), the family is a "great intellectual Rorschach blot."

1. The Myth of the Universal Nuclear Family

To say that the family is the same everywhere is in some sense true. Yet families vary in organization, membership, life cycles, emotional environments, ideologies, social and kinship networks, and economic and other functions. Although anthropologists have tried to come up with a single definition of family that would hold across time and place, they generally have concluded that doing so is not useful (Geertz, 1965; Stephens, 1963).

Biologically, of course, a woman and a man must unite sexually to produce a child—even if only sperm and egg meet in a test tube. But no social kinship ties or living arrangements flow inevitably from biological union. Indeed, the definition of marriage is not the same across cultures. Although some cultures have weddings and notions of monogamy and permanence, many cultures lack one or more of these attributes. In some cultures, the majority of people mate and have children without legal marriage and often without living together. In other societies, husbands, wives, and children do not live together under the same roof.

In our own society, the assumption of universality has usually defined what is normal and natural both for research and therapy and has subtly influenced our thinking to regard deviations from the nuclear family as sick or perverse or immoral. As Suzanne Keller (1971) once observed:

> The fallacy of universality has done students of behavior a great disservice. By leading us to seek and hence to find a single pattern, it has blinded us to historical precedents for multiple legitimate family arrangements.

2. The Myth of Family Harmony

To question the idea of the happy family is not to say that love and joy are not found in family life or that many people do not find their deepest satisfactions in their families. Rather, the happy-family assumption omits important, if unpleasant, aspects of family life. Western society has not always assumed such a sentimental model of the family. From the Bible to the fairy tale, from Sophocles to Shakespeare, from Eugene O'Neill to the soap opera, there is a tragic tradition of portraying the family as a high-voltage emotional setting, charged with love and hate, tenderness and spite, even incest and murder.

There is also a low-comedy tradition. George Orwell once pointed out that the world of henpecked husbands and tyrannical mothers-in-law is as much a part of the Western cultural heritage as is Greek drama. Although the comic tradition tends to portray men's discontents rather than women's, it scarcely views the family as a setting for ideal happiness.

Social theorists have not always portrayed the family as harmoniously fulfilling the needs of its members and society. Around the turn of the century, the founders of sociology took for granted that conflict was a basic part of social life and that individuals, classes, and social institutions would struggle to promote their own interests and values. They argued that intimate relations inevitably involve antagonism as well as love. This mixture of strong positive and negative feelings sets close relationships apart from less intimate ones.

In recent years, family scholars have been studying family violence such as child abuse and wife beating to understand better the realistic strains of family life. Long-known facts about family violence have recently been incorporated into a general analysis of the family. More police officers are killed and injured dealing with family fights than in dealing with any other kind of situation; of all the relationships between murderers and their victims, the family relationship is most common. Studies of family violence reveal that it is much more widespread than had been assumed, cannot easily be attributed to mental illness, and is not confined to the lower classes. Family violence seems to be a product of psychological tensions and external stresses that can affect all families at all social levels.

The study of family interaction has also undermined the traditional image of the happy, harmonious family. About three decades ago, researchers and therapists began to bring mental patients and their families together to watch how they behaved with one another. Oddly, whole family groups had not been systematically studied before.

At first the family interactions were interpreted as pathogenic: a parent expressing affection in words but showing nonverbal hostility; alliances being made between different family members; families having secrets; one family member being singled out as a scapegoat to be blamed for the family's troubles. As more and more families were studied, such patterns were found in many families, not just in those families with a schizophrenic child. Although this line of research did not uncover the cause of schizophrenia, it made an important discovery about family life: So-called normal families can often be, in the words of one study, "difficult environments for interaction."

3. The Myth of Parental Determinism

The kind of family a child grows up in leaves a profound, lifelong impact. But a large body of recent research shows that early family experience is not the all-powerful, irreversible influence it has sometimes been thought to be. An unfortunate childhood does not doom a person to an unhappy adulthood. Nor does a happy childhood guarantee a similarly blessed future (Macfarlane, 1964; Emde and Harmon, 1984; Rubin, 1996).

First, children come into this world with their own temperamental and other individual characteristics. As parents have long known, child rearing is not like molding clay or writing on a blank slate. Rather, although parents are far more powerful, it's a two-way process in which both parent and child try to shape each other. Further, children are active perceivers and interpreters of the world. Finally, parents and children do not live in a social vacuum; children are also influenced by the world around them and the people in it—the kin group, the neighborhood, other children, the school, the media.

4. The Myth of a Stable, Harmonious Past

Laments about the current state of decay of the family imply some earlier era when the family was more stable and harmonious. But unless we can agree what earlier time should be chosen as a baseline and what characteristics of the family should be specified, it makes little sense to speak of family decline. Historians have not, in fact, located a golden age of the family.

Recent historical studies of family life also cast doubt on the reality of family tranquillity. Historians have found that premarital sexuality, illegitimacy, generational conflict, and even infanticide can best be studied as a part of family life itself rather than as separate categories of deviation. For example, William Kessen (1965), in his history of the field of child study, observes:

> Perhaps the most persistent single note in the history of the child is the reluctance of mothers to suckle their babies. The running war between the mother, who does not want to nurse, and the philosopher-psychologists, who insist she must, stretches over two thousand years (pp. 1–2).

The most shocking finding of the recent wave of historical studies is the prevalence of infanticide throughout European history. Infanticide has long been attributed to primitive peoples or assumed to be the desperate act of an unwed mother. It now appears that infanticide provided a major means of population control in all societies lacking reliable contraception, Europe included, and that it was practiced by families on legitimate children.

Rather than being an instinctive trait, having tender feelings toward infants—regarding a baby as a precious individual—seems to emerge only when infants have a decent chance of surviving and adults experience enough security to avoid feeling that children are competing with them in a struggle for survival. Throughout many centuries of European history, both of these conditions were lacking.

Another myth about the family is that of changelessness—the belief that the family has been essentially the same over the centuries, until recently, when it began to come apart. Family life has always been in flux; when the world around them changes, families change in response. At periods when a whole society undergoes some major transformation, family change may be especially rapid and dislocating.

In many ways, the era we are living through today resembles two earlier periods of family crisis and transformation in American history (see Skolnick, 1991). The first occurred in the early nineteenth century, when the growth of industry and commerce moved work out of the home. Briefly, the separation of home and work disrupted existing patterns of daily family life, opening a gap between the way people actually lived and the cultural blueprints for proper gender and generational roles (Ryan, 1981). In the older pattern, when most people worked on farms, a father was not just the head of the household, but also boss of the family enterprise. Mother and children and hired hands worked under his supervision. But when work moved out, father—along with older sons and daughters—went with it, leaving behind mother and the younger children. These dislocations in the functions and meaning of family life unleashed an era of personal stress and cultural confusion.

Eventually, a new model of family emerged that not only reflected the new separation of work and family, but glorified it. No longer a workplace, the household now became idealized as "home sweet home," an emotional and spiritual shelter from the heartless world outside. Although father remained the head of the family, mother was now the central figure in the home. The new model celebrated the "true woman's" purity, virtue, and selflessness. Many of our culture's most basic ideas about the family in American culture, such as "women's place is in the home," were formed at this time. In short, the family pattern we now think of as traditional was in fact the first version of the modern family.

Historians label this model of the family "Victorian" because it became influential in England and Western Europe as well as in the United States during the reign of Queen Victoria. It reflected, in idealized form, the nineteenth-century middle-class family. However, the Victorian model became the prevailing cultural definition of family. Few families could live up to the ideal in all its particulars; working-class, black, and ethnic families, for example, could not get by without the economic contributions of wives, mothers, and daughters. And even for middle-class families, the Victorian ideal prescribed a standard of perfection that was virtually impossible to fulfill (Demos, 1986).

Eventually, however, social change overtook the Victorian model. Beginning around the 1880s, another period of rapid economic, social, and cultural change unsettled Victorian family patterns, especially their gender arrangements. Several generations of so-called new women challenged Victorian notions of femininity. They became educated, pursued careers, became involved in political causes— including their own—and created the first wave of feminism. This ferment culminated in the victory of the women's suffrage movement. It was followed by the 1920s' jazz-age era of flappers and flaming youth—the first, and probably the major, sexual revolution of the twentieth century.

To many observers at the time, it appeared that the family and morality had broken down. Another cultural crisis ensued, until a new cultural blueprint emerged—the companionate model of marriage and the family. The new model was a revised, more relaxed version of the Victorian family; companionship and sexual intimacy were now defined as central to marriage.

This highly abbreviated history of family and cultural change forms the necessary backdrop for understanding the family upheavals of the late twentieth century. As in earlier times, major changes in the economy and society have destabilized an existing model of family life and the everyday patterns and practices that have sustained it. We have experienced a triple revolution: first, the move toward a postindustrial service and information economy; second, a life course revolution brought about by the reductions in mortality and fertility; and third, a psychological transformation rooted mainly in rising educational levels.

Although these shifts have profound implications for everyone in contemporary society, women have been the pacesetters of change. Most women's lives and expectations over the past three decades, inside and outside the family, have departed drastically from those of their own mothers. Men's lives today also are different from their fathers' generation, but to a much lesser extent.

THE TRIPLE REVOLUTION

The Postindustrial Family

The most obvious way the new economy affects the family is in its drawing women, especially married women, into the workplace. A service and information economy produces large numbers of jobs that, unlike factory work, seem suitable for women. Yet as Jessie Bernard (1982) once observed, the transformation of a housewife into a paid worker outside the home sends tremors through every family relationship. It creates a more "symmetrical" family, undoing the sharp contrast between men's and women's roles that marks the bread-winner/housewife pattern. It also reduces women's economic dependence on men, thereby making it easier for women to leave unhappy marriages.

Beyond drawing women into the workplace, shifts in the nature of work and a rapidly changing globalized economy have unsettled the lives of individuals and families at all class levels. The well-paying industrial jobs that once enabled a blue-collar worker to own a home and support a family are no longer available. The once secure jobs that sustained the "organization men" and their families in the 1950s and 1960s have been made shaky by downsizing, an unstable economy, corporate takeovers, and a rapid pace of technological change.

The new economic climate has also made the transition to adulthood increasingly problematic. The reduction in job opportunities is in part responsible for young adults' lower fertility rates and for women flooding into the workplace. Further, the family formation patterns of the 1950s are out of step with the increased educational demands of today's postindustrial society. In the post-war years, particularly in the United States, young people entered adulthood in one giant step—going to work, marrying young and moving to a separate household from their parents, and having children quickly. Today, few young adults can afford to marry and have children in their late teens or early twenties. In an economy where a college degree is necessary to earn a living wage, early marriage impedes education for both men and women.

Those who do not go on to college have little access to jobs that can sustain a family. Particularly in the inner cities of the United States, growing numbers of young people have come to see no future for themselves at all in the ordinary world of work. In middle-class families, a narrowing opportunity structure has increased anxieties about downward mobility for offspring, and parents as well. The "Hamlet syndrome" or the "incompletely launched young adult syndrome" has become common: Young adults deviate from their parents' expectations by failing to launch careers and become successfully independent adults, and may even come home to crowd their parents' empty nest (Schnaiberg and Goldenberg, 1989).

The Life Course Revolution

The demographic transformations of the twentieth century are no less significant than the economic ones. We cannot hope to understand current predicaments of family life without understanding how radically the demographic and social circumstances of twentieth-century Americans have changed. In earlier times, mortality rates were highest among infants, and the possibility of death from tuberculosis, pneumonia, or other infectious diseases was an ever-present threat to young and middle-aged adults. Before the turn of this century, only 40 percent of women lived through all the stages of a normal life course—growing up, marrying, having children, and surviving with a spouse to the age of 50 (Uhlenberg, 1980).

Demographic and economic change has had a profound effect on women's lives. Women today are living longer and having fewer children. When infant and child mortality rates fall, women no longer have to have five or seven or nine children to make sure that two or three will survive to adulthood. After rearing children, the average woman can look forward to three or four decades without maternal responsibilities. Since traditional assumptions about women are based on the notion that they are constantly involved with pregnancy, child rearing, and related domestic concerns, the current ferment about women's roles may be seen as a way of bringing cultural attitudes in line with existing social realities.

As people live longer, they can stay married longer. Actually, the biggest change in twentieth-century marriage is not the proportion of marriages disrupted through divorce, but the potential length of marriage and the number of years spent without children in the home. By the 1970s the statistically average couple would spend only 18 percent of their married lives raising young children, compared with 54 percent a century ago (Bane, 1976). As a result, marriage is becoming defined less as a union between parents raising a brood of children and more as a personal relationship between two individuals.

A Psychological Revolution

The third major transformation is a set of psychocultural changes that might be described as "psychological gentrification" (Skolnick, 1991). That is, cultural advantages once enjoyed only by the upper classes—in particular, education—have been extended to those lower down on the socioeconomic scale. Psychological gentrification also involves greater leisure time, travel, and exposure to information, as well as a general rise in the standard of living. Despite the persistence of poverty, unemployment, and economic insecurity in the industrialized world, far less of the population than in the historical past is living at the level of sheer subsistence.

Throughout Western society, rising levels of education and related changes have been linked to a complex set of shifts in personal and political attitudes. One of these is a more psychological approach to life—greater introspectiveness and a yearning for warmth and intimacy in family and other relationships (Veroff, Douvan, and Kulka, 1981). There is also evidence of an increasing preference on the part of both men and women for a more companionate ideal of marriage and a more democratic family. More broadly, these changes in attitude have been described as a shift to "postmaterialist values," emphasizing self-expression, tolerance, equality, and a concern for the quality of life (Inglehart, 1990).

The multiple social transformations of our era have brought both costs and benefits: Family relations have become both more fragile and more emotionally rich; mass longevity has brought us a host of problems as well as the gift of extended life. Although change has brought greater opportunities for women, persisting gender inequality means women have borne a large share of the costs of these gains. But we cannot turn the clock back to the family models of the past.

Paradoxically, after all the upheavals of recent decades, the emotional and cultural significance of the family persists. Family remains the center of most people's lives and, as numerous surveys show, a cherished value. While marriage has become more fragile, the parent-child relationship—especially the mother-child relationship—remains a core attachment across the life course (Rossi and Rossi, 1990). The family, however, can be both "here to stay" and beset with difficulties. There is widespread recognition that the massive social and economic changes we have lived through call for public and private-sector policies in support of families. Most European countries have recognized for some time that governments must play a role in supplying an array of supports to families—health care, children's allowances, housing subsidies, support for working parents and children (such as child care, parental leave, and shorter work days for parents), as well as an array of services for the elderly.

Each country's response to these changes, as we've noted earlier, has been shaped by its own political and cultural traditions. The United States remains embroiled in a cultural war over the family; many social commentators and political leaders have promised to reverse the recent trends and restore the "traditional" family. In contrast, other Western nations, including Canada and the other English-speaking countries, have responded to family change by establishing policies aimed at mitigating the problems brought about by economic and social changes. As a result of these policies, these countries have been spared much of the poverty and social disintegration that has plagued the United States in the last decade.

Looking Ahead

The world at the end of the twentieth century is vastly different from what it was at the beginning, or even the middle. Families are struggling to adapt to new realities. The countries that have been at the leading edge of family change still find themselves caught between yesterday's norms, today's new realities, and an uncertain future. As we have seen, changes in women's lives have been a pivotal factor in recent family trends. In many countries there is a considerable difference between men's and women's attitudes and expectations of one another. Even where both partners accept a more equal division of labor in the home, there is often a gap between attitudes and behavior. In no country have employers, the government, or men fully caught up to the changes in women's lives.

But a knowledge of family history reveals that the solution to contemporary problems will not be found in some lost golden age. Families have always struggled with outside circumstances and inner conflict. Our current troubles inside and outside the family are genuine, but we should never forget that many of the most vexing issues confronting us derive from benefits of modernization few of us would be willing to give up—for example, longer, healthier lives, and the ability to choose how many children to have and when to have them. There was no problem of the aged in the past, because most people never aged; they died before they got old. Nor was adolescence a difficult stage of the life cycle when children worked, education was a privilege of the rich, and a person's place in society was determined by heredity rather than choice. And when most people were hungry illiterates, only aristocrats could worry about sexual satisfaction and self-fulfillment.

In short, there is no point in giving in to the lure of nostalgia. There is no golden age of the family to long for, nor even some past pattern of behavior and belief that would guarantee us harmony and stability if only we had the will to return to it. Family life is bound up with the social, economic, and ideological circumstances of particular times and places. We are no longer peasants, Puritans, pioneers, or even suburbanites circa 1955. We face conditions unknown to our ancestors, and we must find new ways to cope with them.

A Note on "the Family"

Some family scholars have suggested that we drop the term "the family" and replace it with "families" or "family life." The problem with "the family" is that it calls to mind the stereotyped image of the Ozzie and Harriet kind of family—two parents and their two or three minor children. But those other terms don't always work. In our own writing we use the term "the family" in much the same way we use "the economy"—as an abstract term that refers to a mosaic of forms and practices in the real world.

REFERENCES

Amato, P.R., Life span adjustment of children to their parents' divorce. *The Future of Children* 4, no 1. (Spring, 1994)

Bane, M. J. 1976. *Here to Stay.* New York: Basic Books.

Bernard, J. 1982. *The Future of Marriage.* New York: Bantam.

Blake, J. 1978. Structural differentiation and the family: A quiet revolution. Presented at American Sociology Association, San Francisco.

Cherlin, A. J. 1981. *Marriage, Divorce, Remarriage.* Cambridge, Mass.: Harvard University Press.

Demos, John. 1986. *Past, Present, and Personal.* New York: Oxford University Press.

Emde, R. N., and R. J. Harmon, eds. 1984. *Continuities and Discontinuities in Development.* New York: Plenum Press.

Featherstone, J. 1979. Family matters. *Harvard Educational Review* 49, no. 1: 20–52.

Geertz, G. 1965. The impact of the concept of culture on the concept of man. In *New Views of the Nature of Man,* edited by J. R. Platt. Chicago: University of Chicago Press.

Haggard, M. 1982. Are the Good Times Really Over for Good? Song copyright 1982.

Inglehart, Ronald. 1990. *Culture Shift.* New Jersey: Princeton University Press.

Keller, S. 1971. Does the family have a future? *Journal of Comparative Studies,* Spring.

Kessen, W. 1965. *The Child.* New York: John Wiley.

LaBarre, W. 1954. *The Human Animal.* Chicago: University of Chicago Press.

Lasch, C. 1978. *Haven in a Heartless World.* New York: Basic Books.

Macfarlane, J. W. 1964. Perspectives on personality consistency and change from the guidance study. *Vita Humana* 7: 115–126.

Malinowski, B. 1930. Parenthood, the basis of the social order. In *The New Generation*, edited by Calverton and Schmalhousen, New York: Macauley Company.

Masnick, G., and M. J. Bane. 1980. *The Nation's Families: 1960–1990*. Boston: Auburn House.

Mellman, A., E. Lazarus, and A. Rivlin. 1990. Family time, family values. In *Rebuilding the Nest*, edited by D. Blankenhorn, S. Bayme, and J. Elshtain. Milwaukee: Family Service America.

Norton, A. J., and P. C. Glick. 1986. One-parent families: A social and economic profile. *Family Relations* 35: 9–17.

Parsons, T. 1951. *The Social System*. Glencoe, Ill.: Free Press.

Parsons, T. 1954. The kinship system of the contemporary United States. In *Essays in Sociological Theory*. Glencoe, Ill.: Free Press.

Preston, S. H. 1984. Presidential address to the Population Association of America. Quoted in *Family and Nation* by D. P. Moynihan (1986). San Diego: Harcourt Brace Jovanovich.

Rossi, A. S., and P. H. Rossi. 1990. *Of Human Bonding: Parent-Child Relations Across the Life Course*. Hawthorne, New York: Aldine de Gruyter.

Rubin, L. 1996. *The Transcendent Child*. New York: Basic Books.

Ryan, M. 1981. *The Cradle of the Middle Class*. New York: Cambridge University Press.

Schnaiberg, A., and S. Goldenberg. 1989. From empty nest to crowded nest: The dynamics of incompletely launched young adults. *Social Problems* 36, no. 3 (June) 251–69.

Skolnick, A. 1991. *Embattled Paradise: The American Family in an Age of Uncertainty*. New York: Basic Books.

Stephens, W. N. 1963. *The Family in Cross-Cultural Perspective*. New York: World.

Tannen, D. 1998. *The Argument Culture*.

Uhlenberg, P. 1980. Death and the family. *Journal of Family History* 5, no. 3: 313–20.

Veroff, J., E. Douvan, and R. A. Kulka. 1981. *The Inner American: A Self-Portrait from 1957 to 1976*. New York: Basic Books.

PART ONE

THE CHANGING FAMILY

◆

INTRODUCTION

The study of the family does not belong to any single scholarly field; genetics, physiology, archaeology, history, anthropology, sociology, psychology, and economics all touch upon it. Religious and ethical authorities claim a stake in the family, and troubled individuals and families generate therapeutic demands on family scholarship. In short, the study of the family is interdisciplinary, controversial, and necessary for the formulation of social policy and practices.

Interdisciplinary subjects present characteristic problems. Each discipline has its own assumptions and views of the world, which may not directly transfer into another field. Some biologists and physically oriented anthropologists, for example, analyze human affairs in terms of individual motives and instincts; for them, society is a shadowy presence, serving mainly as the setting for biologically motivated individual action. Many sociologists and cultural anthropologists, in contrast, perceive the individual as an actor playing a role written by culture and society. According to this view, the individual has no wholly autonomous thoughts and impulses. One important school of psychology sees people neither as passive recipients of social pressures nor as creatures driven by powerful lusts, but as information processors trying to make sense of their environment. There is no easy way to reconcile such perspectives. Scientific paradigms—characteristic ways of looking at the world—determine not only what answers will be found, but what questions will be asked. This fact has perhaps created special confusion in the study of the family.

"We speak of families," R. D. Laing has observed, "as though we know what families are. We identify, as families, networks of people who live together over time, who have ties of marriage or kinship to one another" (Laing, 1971, p. 3).

There is the assumption that family life, so familiar a part of everyday experience, is easily understood. But familiarity may breed a sense of destiny—what we experience is transformed into the "natural":

> One difficulty in the psychological sciences lies in the familiarity of the phenomena with which they deal. A certain intellectual effort is required to see how such phenomena can pose serious problems or call for intricate explanatory theories. One is inclined to take them for granted as necessary or somehow "natural." (Chomsky, 1968, p. 21)

The selections in Part One examine the myths, realities, and meaning of "family." John Gillis debunks many current beliefs about the family in times past. He argues that nostalgia for some lost time when families were more loving and stable has been a constant theme in modern times, but we should not confuse our cozy images of the family in earlier eras with the families that previous generations actually lived in. Family life in the past was no freer of problems and dilemmas than it is today. Gillis also points out that many of the family rituals we celebrate today are relatively recent inventions, rather than traditions handed down from the distant past.

Idyllic images of the family in earlier times typically omit the high mortality rates that prevailed before the twentieth century. Death could strike at any age, and was a constant threat to family stability. Arlene Skolnick's article reveals the profound impact of high mortality on family relationships, and how new problems arose from the lengthening of the life span over the course of the twentieth century.

Stephanie Coontz points to flaws in our nostalgic assumptions about the families of a more recent era—the 1950s—the era that Americans are most likely to think of as a golden age of family. People living at the time did not see it that way. Yet, Coontz argues, in many ways, because of a strong economy and governmental policies like the GI Bill of Rights, the country really was a better place for families than it is today.

The readings in Chapter Two are concerned with the meaning of family in modern society. David Rosen also examines the legal system as it struggles to define family in a time of change and uncertainty. He looks at how the courts in recent years have dealt with the diverse kinds of family arrangements that come before them, and how the law is evolving to accommodate them.

Helen Ragoné examines the meaning of family through surrogate motherhood—a practice that seems a radical departure from traditional understandings of motherhood, fatherhood, and biological relatedness. She finds, however, that all participants in the process try to define their actions in terms of traditional values. For example, surrogate mothers explain that by having a child for a childless couple they are "giving the gift of life," and not simply getting pregnant in exchange for money. The surrogate mother and a woman who will adopt her child often form an emotional bond with one another, and the adoptive mother sees herself as conceiving the child "in her heart" before it was formed in the surrogate's body. In short, all the participants in surrogacy emphasize the importance of traditional values such as love of children and family.

REFERENCES

Chomsky, N. 1968. *Language and Mind.* New York: Harcourt, Brace and World.
Laing, R. D. 1971. *The Politics of the Family.* New York: Random House.

◆

CHAPTER 1

FAMILIES PRESENT
AND PAST

R E A D I N G

1

Myths of Family Past

JOHN GILLIS

> This acute awareness of tradition is a modern phenomenon that reflects a
> desire for custom and routine in a world characterized by constant change and
> innovation. Reverence for the past has become so strong that when traditions
> do not exist, they are frequently invented.
>
> —Witold Rybczynski, *Home*

Much about modern family life is changing, but one thing that never seems to
change is the notion that family is not what it used to be. Families past are
presented to us not only as more stable but as more authentic than families
present. We imagine their times to have been the days when fathers were really
fathers, mothers true mothers, and children still children. Families past are
invariably portrayed as simpler, less problematic. We imagine them not only as
large but as better integrated, untroubled by generational divisions, close to kin,
respectful of the old, honoring the dead. Families past are imagined as rooted
and centered, identified with particular places and loyal to their own pasts. We
think of them as "traditional," not only because they belong to the past but
because they were supposedly more attached to it. And because we imagine
previous generations to have been such dedicated keepers of custom, we regard
all our own family occasions in the same light in which we regard the old furniture passed down from generation to generation—as having seen better days.

From *A World of Their Own Making: Myth, Ritual, and the Quest for Family Values.* Copyright
1996. Published by Basic Books, a division of Harper Collins.

But like antiques, family traditions have actually acquired their value by the passage of time and are far more treasured today than when they were new. It comes as a considerable surprise to most people that our cherished family traditions are of relatively recent origins, few older than the mid-nineteenth century. It was the European and American Protestant middle classes, the Victorians, who were the first to value the old as such. They invented the modern notion of antiques and were also the first to assign the past that quality of authenticity we so readily accept. The more things change, the more we desire to keep them the same. Never has the old silver shown brighter or custom been kept in such mint condition. No period in human history has been so devoted to preservation, restoration, and reenactment as our own. In earlier times, the past belonged only to elites, who kept heritage just as they kept offices and land—for themselves. Today the past has been democratized and we all must have our own history. What was once a luxury has become a necessity. What was once a privilege is now a right.

It is the present that endows antiques with their current value, and it is the present that has given family past its huge significance. The unity, continuity, rootedness, and traditionalism ascribed to families past, first by the Victorians and then by each succeeding modern generation, parallels the way in which community is seen as being in a perpetual state of disintegration. On both sides of the Atlantic there has been a tendency to pick a particular time and place as the epitome of community—for Americans the New England town, for Swedes the villages of the Darlana region, for Germans the small walled city, for the English the villages of the so-called Home Countries—and to designate it the epitome of the traditional community, causing everything that followed to be seen in terms of destruction and loss.

When we talk about family in terms of tradition, the result is the same. In projecting a static image of family onto a particular past time and place, we immediately begin to describe change in terms of "decline" or "loss." Ironically, we are also in the habit of updating the traditional community and family periodically so that the location of the golden age is constantly changing. For the Victorians, the traditional family, imagined to be rooted and extended, was located sometime before industrialization and urbanization, but for those who came of age during the First World War, tradition was associated with the Victorians themselves; today we think of the 1950s and early 1960s as the location of the family and community life we imagine we have lost.

Summoning images from the past is one of the ways we generate the hope and energy necessary to strive for better communities and families in the future. But when the remembered past becomes an end in itself, becoming "mere nostalgia, it degenerates into a terminal bubble of the past that closes one off from the living spontaneity of the present and denies the possibility of a future." Either way, the notion of the traditional family is a myth many families live by.

Looking back from the 1990s, and preoccupied with rising divorce and illegitimacy rates, we perceive the 1950s as a rock of stability. But that was a decade gripped by anxiety about family life, and especially about the threat posed by the new youth cultures. The 1950s version of the traditional family was an idealized image of the Depression family, which was imagined as holding on by holding tight to one another. But those who lived through the 1920s and 1930s would not have recognized themselves in the myths that later generations made of them, for these were the same people who saw themselves to be in the midst of a sexual revolution. The so-called Lost Generation felt wholly cut off from a past they imagined to have been as stable as their present was chaotic. For them, the Victorian family was tradition. But as we have seen, the Victorians were by no means sure of themselves when it came to family matters. They were deeply anxious about the loss of community resulting from rapid urbanization and no more secure in their family life than we are. In 1851 the American Horace Bushnell looked back with regret on the passing of the days when families were "harnessed, all together, into the producing process, young and old, male and female, from the boy who rode the plough-horse to the grandmother knitting under her spectacles."

The European middle classes were also believers in progress, but like their American counterparts, they saw the good family life as behind rather than in front of them. Nostalgia was not unknown before this time, but it had always been focused more on place than on the past as such. It was not until the Victorian age that Western cultures began to associate paradise with origins rather than with destinations and to transform the past, particularly childhoods past, into an ideal. God has given us each our own Paradise, our own old childhood, over which the old glories linger—to which our own hearts cling, as all we have ever known of Heaven upon earth," wrote James Anthony Froude in 1849, establishing a precedent for the yearning for times past that has been particularly pronounced in Western middle-class cultures, especially among middle-class males, ever since.

The Victorians—or more specifically, the Protestant middle classes—were the first to experience the pastness of the past. Feeling themselves ravaged by time, they exempted earlier generations from history, calling them "traditional" and imputing to them a static and naturalized status. They imagined earlier families to have been large and cohesive, inclusive of kin as well as multiple generations, rooted in place and tradition, and more deeply religious than themselves. From those sturdy foundations all else descended, or more accurately, degenerated, because for the Victorians, as for us, the past offered the authentic original of family life, so perfect that they could do no better than build on it. As in all subsequent versions of the traditional family, the Victorian version included fathers and mothers who were always larger than life, and children who were always devoted and obedient.

Middle-class Victorians were not necessarily the first to invent a usable family past. For centuries, those pretending to aristocratic or patrician status had been creating pedigrees for themselves. But prior to the nineteenth century, genealogy had been a very exclusive enterprise; very few families were conscious of their own origins, much less interested in the history of family generally. The working classes were anything but nostalgic about their pasts. Until very recently, their family stories were about hard times, and their memories of childhood often bitter. Middle-class Victorians started by inventing traditions for their own families, but they quickly became advocates of tradition in general. By 1900 they had founded hundreds of genealogical and historical societies in Europe and North America. Enthusiasm for family traditions was slower to arrive at other social levels, but by the 1970s the search for roots had become a mass preoccupation, and today everyone is a family historian. Children learn to value family history in school, magazines tell us how to refurbish our family traditions, and software programs make it even easier to construct the family tree. Today every family wants its own history and its own traditions. Arising alongside the new familism is a new ethnicity, which stresses the uniqueness of every group's identity based on the uniqueness of its particular history.

Yet despite all the diversity, there is a certain uniformity: the "traditional family" imagined by WASPS is strikingly like that conjured up by Jews, Germans, and Mexican Americans. All these visions of family past emphasize stability and unity, rootedness and continuity. When they remember earlier generations as more cooperative and caring, African Americans are no different than Asian or Irish Americans. Cross-national comparisons show a similar uniformity. The images of the old homestead held by Swedes and Poles are not all that different from those held by Californians and Australians. It turns out that we are all seeking essentially the same thing, namely, a reassuring myth of family past that can serve our present needs and future aspirations.

We must be careful not to confuse the family past we live by with the families that previous generations actually lived with. Until quite recently, historians also failed to make this distinction, but in the last two decades demographic and social history research has revealed a very different picture of families past, one that suggests much more continuity between families past and present in actual behavior than anyone would have imagined. It seems that the fragmentation, instability, and discontinuity that we feel so keenly today has been part of the European experience of family life since at least the late Middle Ages. Europeans who came to the Americas carried a dream of caring and cooperation with them but were unable to realize it in the new land. Throughout the seventeenth and eighteenth centuries, family unity and continuity remained elusive on both sides of the Atlantic, and, in the great industrial and political upheavals of the nineteenth century, it became even more so.

Human reproduction has never been straightforward, and no society has found a way to eliminate its contradictions. Different peoples have found a bewildering variety of ways of coping; over time it is not the problems that have changed but the answers. The questions that Western civilization has had to face over the centuries are to some degree the same as those that every preindustrial society has to confront, namely, how to manage the fragmenting effects of high levels of mortality and fertility along with low levels of very unevenly distributed resources. Until our own century, no part of the world was able to control death or birth rates or produce the levels of affluence that would have given hope that all families might share in roughly the same resources.

We know that Europe, and particularly northwestern Europe, departed from the preexisting domestic practices of both the classical Mediterranean world and Germanic peoples beginning in the Middle Ages, setting it on a course of development different from most parts of the world. At the core of the unique European family system, and distinguishing it from the family systems of Africa, Asia, and the pre-Columbian Americas, was the single-family household established by monogamous marriage. The first "rule" was that marriage should not take place without the couple first having established a basis of economic independence. "When thou art married, if it may be, live of thyself with thy wife, in a family of thine own," was the advice offered to English young people by William Whateley in 1624. Colonial settlers also heeded his maxim that "the mixing of governours in a household, or subordinating or uniting of two Masters, or two Dames under one roof, doth fall out most times, to be a matter of unquietness to all parties."

Multiple-family households continued to predominate in southern and eastern Europe, but in northwestern Europe and those parts of the world its peoples settled, the single-family household contributed to a second unique characteristic: a relatively high age of marriage. From at least the fourteenth century onward, the marriage age of men averaged about twenty-six years, and women generally married at twenty-three. In contrast to other world regions, these ages were both remarkably high and relatively evenly matched. European marriage age did not fall significantly until the late eighteenth century, but even then it remained high by world standards. And today it seems to be returning to its old levels once again, confirming a pattern that has lasted for almost six centuries.

The linkage between late age of marriage and household formation led to two more unique features of the Western family system. The late age of marriage gave rise to a very large pool of unmarried young people. Most of them hoped to gain a household and marry eventually, but given the straitened circumstances of the medieval and early modern economies, not all would have this opportunity. Rates of lifetime celibacy therefore never fell below 10 percent and sometimes went as high as 20 percent, in sharp contrast to other world regions where some form of marriage was virtually universal. Wedlock did not become universal in the West until the twentieth century; now, as we approach a new millennium, the old pattern of late marriage and low marriage rates seems to be reasserting itself.

Only the wealthy and powerful were ever guaranteed access to marriage, but even they could not escape the effects of the high mortality rates that prevailed right up to the present century. Mortality before the twentieth century was catastrophic by any standard. The average life expectancy was the midforties for both sexes, mortality was distributed across the age spectrum, and rates of infant mortality ranged from 15 to 30 percent for the first year of life. By the age of twenty, a half or more of the birth cohort was deceased, and life remained very uncertain throughout middle age as well. It was not until the twentieth century that mortality declined significantly: two-thirds of the longevity gains in the entire history of the human race have been attained in the last one hundred years.

High rates of mortality have always been associated with high rates of fertility. Simply to replace the children who died, women in the past had to devote their entire married life to childbearing. From the fourteenth through the nineteenth centuries, married women had an average of four to six children. They might have had more had not the age of marriage been so high and so many women either died or reached the limits of their physical capacity to have children. In any case, population growth in Europe and North America remained moderate by the standards of today's Third World, where early marriage combines with lengthening life expectancies to produce very high birth rates.

Despite the relatively moderate nature of European population growth, families in the past had difficulty rearing all their children, partly owing to parental mortality: in England prior to the midnineteenth century, 17 percent of children were fatherless by age ten, and 27 percent by age fifteen. Peter Laslett has estimated that one-half to two-thirds of all young women had lost their fathers by the time they married in their midtwenties. Given this very high level of orphanage, it is not surprising that children lived elsewhere than in their natal homes. What is astonishing is that even children with two parents moved out of the natal house at a very young age in large numbers. Some did so as mere children, but the greatest exodus happened in the midteens, when virtually all young people lived and worked in another dwelling for shorter or longer periods of time. David Herlihy has estimated that in late medieval and early modern Europe, two-thirds to three-quarters of the entire population spent some part of their childhood and youth living away from their families of birth. In England, one-fifth of all rural people in the early modern period were living in households other than their own.

Extrafamilial residents included not only orphaned children but large numbers of unmarried servants and apprentices, plus a fair number of married adults who were forced by poverty or other circumstances to work away from home. On the death of a marriage partner, it was common for the surviving spouse to remarry immediately so as to maintain the household, but when he or she was unable to remarry, the household was likely to disperse, with widows and widowers constituting a large part of the adults living apart from their families of birth and marriage.

Thus, contrary to myth, the three-generation household was relatively rare. Throughout the late medieval and early modern periods, the two groups least likely to be living with their own kin were children in their teens and old persons. The young were accommodated by the institutions of apprenticeship and servanthood, which had been fixtures in the West since at least the fourteenth century. The elderly were taken care of by a combination of poor relief and arrangements worked out when they were no longer able to sustain their own households. While some old folks made out "retirement" contracts with their own families, a surprising number lived in the households of nonrelatives. Most, especially those whose children had predeceased them, had little choice, but others chose such a living arrangement because it sustained some small part of their independence.

Today we are so used to thinking of the poor as having the greatest numbers of children that it comes as a shock to learn that, before the nineteenth century, the largest households were those of the wealthy. Not only were the wealthy better able to afford to keep more of their own children, but they actively recruited the largest numbers of servants and live-in workers. In the household economy that prevailed from the fourteenth to the nineteenth centuries, the "big houses" benefited from the surplus labor of their less fortunate neighbors, whose own residences were not ordinarily dignified with the word *house*, much less the word *home*. The upward circulation of young people in their teens and twenties also benefited poorer families by relieving them of feeding and housing costs, and thus there functioned a unique system of exchange of children that sustained the economic, social, and political order of Europe and North America until the nineteenth century.

Even moderately well-off families regularly ceded their rights over their children through apprenticeship contracts that ensured good treatment of youngsters in return for their loyalty to their masters and mistresses. Parental rights were socially and legally rather than naturally defined. The social order was understood to depend on a hierarchy of households, with each head of house, starting with the monarchy, exercising parental (usually patriarchal but sometimes matriarchal) authority over all the inhabitants, related or not. In this multitiered system, only a minority of families could rely solely on their own reproduction to form and sustain a household. All families, rich and poor, were dependent on one another to some degree. And this central fact of economic, social, and political life was contingent on the ability of everyone to imagine family as something other than that constituted by birth or marriage. For most of its history, therefore, the Western family system has functioned with an imaginary that has enabled individuals to form familial relations with strangers and to feel at home away from home.

Our myths of family past tell us that people used to be more monogamous and that sex was always contained within marriage, but here again the historical reality proves to be quite different. It took a very long time for the church to assert its control over marriage and divorce, and, even as late as the nineteenth century, common-law nuptials and folk customs of divorce were common in both Europe and North America. Until then, the line between married and unmarried persons was often somewhat indistinct. While illegitimacy rates remained moderate in most places throughout the centuries, premarital pregnancy rates were somewhat higher, never falling below 10 percent and sometimes rising to 30 percent.

In the agrarian and rural manufacturing economies that prevailed until the nineteenth century, there were never enough resources to afford everyone access to a farm or a trade and thus to marry and have a family of their own. But this fact did not prevent people from establishing intimate relationships outside the single-family household system. The distinction between the big house and the little house had its parallel in the distinction between big weddings, solemnized by the church and recognized in law, and the little marriages that people conducted to sustain ties that did not receive the same official or even social recognition. Prior to the church's regulation of marriage in the twelfth century, Europeans had legitimated their sexual unions and the resulting children in all kinds of rituals of their own making. Wells, bridges, and prominent natural features served as altars where vows were exchanged. Rings and other love tokens predated church marriage, which ultimately, but somewhat reluctantly, incorporated these pagan symbols into its ceremonies. For a very long time the church itself accepted the consent of the parties as sufficient validation of a marriage. Its own rites did not triumph completely until the nineteenth century.

We may like to think of the big church wedding as traditional, but it too is of very recent origin. Before the nineteenth century, no great fuss was made about premarital pregnancy or even illegitimate birth as long as the community was assured that it would not be unduly burdened by the child. Merely having a child did not change a person's social status. In eighteenth-century Maine, Martha Ballard's son Jonathan continued living with his mother as her son even though he was the father of Sally Pierce's child. And Sally remained with her own family until, some four months after the birth, she married the reluctant Jonathan. Yet the couple lived with both the Ballards and the Pierces for another month before they "went to housekeeping." Only when they had their own household did Jonathan take his place among the town fathers of Hallowell. His rite of passage was quite public and formal. He became a man of the town when, along with six other recently married men, he was initiated into the mock office of "hog reeve."

The rites of female passage were typically less public, but we can be fairly sure that having her own house changed Sally's status from girl to woman. It surprises us that giving birth to a child was not the transformative event then that it is today, but prior to the nineteenth century, motherhood, fatherhood, and childhood were all socially rather than biologically defined statuses. Mothers were those women, including many who had not given birth, who were engaged in the tasks of mothering; fathers were those men, including bachelors, who headed households. The various tasks of mothering were shareable and separable from childbearing. Wet-nursing was common on both sides of the Atlantic, and infants were often removed from the birth family for long periods. In households where mothers were either busy or absent, older daughters frequently acted as "little mothers" to their younger siblings.

Indeed, child-rearing was by no means exclusively the domain of women: prior to the midnineteenth century, fathers were expected to be at least as involved as mothers with the raising of children. Fatherhood, like motherhood, was defined socially rather than biologically. Fathering meant much more than inseminating: it was understood as a well-defined set of domestic skills—provisioning, hospitality, and child-rearing—that male heads of households were expected to acquire and share with other men. Many a bachelor head of house had "his own family" in the eighteenth century, and over a lifetime the German *Hausvater* would be father to many children not his own, while his children were being fathered elsewhere.

Today we think of motherhood, fatherhood, and childhood as natural conditions inherent in the biological relationship itself, a conception quite the opposite of these earlier understandings of mothering and fathering as skills to be acquired, used, and then set aside. Even children were expected to learn to be children, for until the midnineteenth century, domestic advice manuals were directed as much to them as to their parents. Treated as a social role rather than as a biologically defined age category, both childhood and youth were something to adjust to. In fact, all family relationships were achieved rather than natural. Social definitions of family invariably prevailed over biological definitions. The social father, the *pater*, took precedence over the natural father, the *genitor*, just as natural mothers gave pride of place to social mothers in a world where a child's survival often depended on having a variety of nurturers, male as well as female.

The economic necessity that compelled young people to postpone and even forgo marriage and forced parents to give up their children was made palatable by a contemporary understanding of family flexible and capacious enough to provide everyone with surrogate family relations of one kind or another. Origins did not matter much to the very large part of the population who, because of mortality or mobility, were cut off from their pasts.

Prior to the nineteenth century, families on both sides of the Atlantic had little of the stability and continuity we now want to attribute to them. In the Old Country as well as in the New World, families rarely dwelled in one place (much less the same house) for even two generations. Farms and townhouses had an identity of their own independent of the succession of families who inhabited them. Places gave their names to people, not vice versa. Elite families were sometimes referred to as "houses" only because the house defined the family. The term "family" still meant all the members of the house—servants, boarders, live-in employees, as well as resident blood relations. In those days, even visitors were regarded as part of the family.

This constant changeover was built into a hierarchical social order in which everyone knew his or her place, even if they knew little of their pasts. The rich could claim not only the productive and reproductive capacity of the poor but their very identities. This prerogative was most evident in slave-holding regions, where the big house claimed rights superior to those of the natural families under its purview by forbidding slave marriages and refusing to legitimate slave offspring. Such patriarchy was not confined to plantations, however, for all masters claimed the right to the loyalty of those who lived under their roofs, including the right to forbid the marriages of servants and apprentices. What millions of African Americans were forced to do by enslavement, the European poor were compelled to do by the terms of their bonded labor.

Only a small number of families could claim a past and a future. The relative lack of surnames prior to the seventeenth and eighteenth centuries testifies to how little family name meant to any but those at the highest levels of European and American society. It was not uncommon for slaves and poor people to adopt their masters' names and family identities. In eighteenth-century Virginia, "blacks and whites were in one family, by blood and by adoption," according to Mechal Sobel. There the big houses initially housed both slaves and masters. The latter talked about the former as family, calling them "uncle," "aunt," and "mammy." In return, slaves took the master's name and adopted his family history as their own, often using this fictive kinship as a defense against the inhumanity of slavery. In Europe, live-in servants and journeymen were also "family" and became equally adept at manipulating the patriarchal ideology to serve their own purposes.

In effect, most people lived for much of their lives according to the rhythms and the spaces of families other than their own by birth or marriage. In Virginia, slaves celebrated births and mourned the deaths of the members of their masters' families. Nobody prior to the nineteenth century would have entertained our notion that every natural family deserves its own rituals and myths, its own history, its own roots. Medieval Catholicism placed the family of origin furthest from its divine archetype, and the Protestant emphasis on life being a journey that leads to union with God further limited the importance of family and place of origin. Until the early nineteenth century, Western culture was far more concerned with endings than beginnings, with destinations rather than starting points.

Until the midnineteenth century, most Americans and Europeans still located themselves spatially in the Great Chain of Being rather than temporally in the Great Line of Progress. It was through place rather than history that they made themselves at home in the world. We who have lost that sense of place depend much more on time for our bearings, and specifically on origins, which we believe give meaning and value to both things and people. A person, a family, a nation—nothing without a past can have meaning or substance. But apart from the genealogies of the aristocratic elites, premodern knowledge of ancestors did not extend back more than two generations. Most would neither have known nor cared where their forefathers were buried. Except for the elites, nobody tended family graves or organized formal anniversaries. Ralph Josselin, a seventeenth-century English clergyman, showed little interest in his forebears; he thought of himself and his wife as the trunk of a tree and his children as its branches. What is striking is that Josselin's family tree had no roots.

Such an attitude does not fit with our cherished myths of family past, through which we project our obsession with ancestors onto earlier generations. Partly because of communication difficulties and partly because of employment conditions, family reunions were rare before the nineteenth century, though family members were usually dispersed over only a ten- or twenty-mile distance. But there is also little evidence that anyone cared to come together in a regular, ritualized way. Baptisms, weddings, and funerals, which we imagine to have been bigger family events in the past than they are now, were rarely attended by kin and often not even by the immediate family. Baptisms were often hurried affairs that took place while mothers were still confined to the house by the prescribed lying-in period. Betrothal largely ended the family role in marriage, and the bride was escorted to the church by a raucous crowd, not by her father. Parents played a very minor role in premodern weddings. Gifts came from the community rather than from family and kin, and it was also the community that gave the dead their final send-off. Only in the nineteenth century did funerals become family occasions.

In the language of preindustrial Europe and colonial America, the distinctions between kin, and between kin and nonkin, were much more ambiguous than they are today. Before the nineteenth century, no one made a sharp distinction between friendship, by implication a matter of choice, and kinship, with its sense of obligation. Families past were not especially familiar with their relatives, especially those who lived at a distance, and they did not distinguish clearly between their various in-laws. The terms "mother-in-law" and "stepmother" were often used interchangeably, and grandmothers and grandfathers could be any older female or male relative, or sometimes a familiar older person. The more intimate language of "grandma" and "grandpa" did not emerge until the middle of the eighteenth century and was not popularly adopted until much later. The term "friend" was used for relatives, neighbors, and members of the same religious faith. In turn, the familial idiom was extended to guilds, confraternities, monasteries, and the military—groups that today we would not call families.

The language of family was kept open and fluid for good reason. Parents taught their children not to be too reliant on blood ties alone, and New England Puritans reminded themselves constantly not to love their spouses and children too much, for doing so might detract from their love of God. "Look not for Perfection in your relations. God reserves that for another state where marriage is not needed," they told themselves. Parenthood, childhood, and marriage were all terminated at death. Thomas Hooker wrote that there would be "no marrying in heaven," for, as he and his contemporaries imagined Paradise, everyone would be "as dear to another, as if all relations of husbands and wives, of parents, and children, and friends, were in every one of them." Until well into the nineteenth century, heaven was represented not as a community of families but as one large community of friends.

Prior to the nineteenth century, when it was place, not past, that gave people their sense of identity, almost everyone lived in a household. In parts of New England, it was illegal to live on one's own, while in Europe longstanding household and hostel systems kept the number of those living alone to a minimum. Home was the place that sheltered you at the moment, not the one special place associated with childhood or family of origin.

Contrary to what we have come to believe, our ancestors were not more sessile. Nor were they attached to particular houses; the moves we find traumatic, they took in stride. The Maine midwife Martha Ballard made a record in her diary, on April 21, 1791, of leaving a place where she had been resident for twelve years: "We removed from the mills to the house which was Old Leut Howards, and Peter went to the mills with his family." The notation for the next read: "At home. Began my gardin." As Laurel Thatcher Ulrich notes, "Her story of the transition from one house to another is told almost inadvertently, in the course of a quiet chronicle of daily work." For Martha Ballard, home was simply the here and now, a work site like any other, with no sentiment attached to it. Her diary entry also suggests that home was a destination rather than a place of return, another difference that separates her world from ours.

We assume that homemaking skills have degenerated over time, but once again a common belief turns out to be an illusion. In fact, the old households were very difficult to domesticate, for they were busy places of work and heavy traffic that resisted the strenuous efforts of even the most dedicated housekeeper. Houses in the eighteenth century seemed to have a will of their own, defying their owners to bring peace and order to their interiors. Houses sheltered people but did not comfort them. Martha Ballard sometimes found her household so much "up in arms" that even her strong will was defeated, and she had little good to say about her domestic space, as opposed to her garden.

No doubt, Martha Ballard was using the image of the unruly house to express her own sense of declining powers, but it was typical of eighteenth-century people to think of the space around them as alive, as something they had to make peace with. They had a personal relationship to the places where they lived, but they attached their sentiments to land- and townscapes rather than to particular houses. Old houses meant much less to them than they do to us. Their dwellings were on the whole less permanent than ours, and they had no compunctions about tearing them down or moving them when circumstances required.

Our ancestors were anything but homebodies. They had a stronger sense of place and felt more at home in the world at large than we do. They moved easily in and out of one another's households, for the ancient traditions of hospitality were by no means dead; the presence of strangers in the household was still perceived as an enhancement to status. In the eighteenth century, comfort had not yet triumphed over generosity; for instance, William Byrd II, the head of one of Virginia's great families, was either visited or visited others on more than three-quarters of the days of the year. At a humbler level, it seems that visiting enhanced vital bonds of community, creating interdependencies that were invaluable in time of illness or hardship. Some visits were brief, but others, especially those of young people, could be quite extended. In big as well as little houses, the constant traffic of people precluded the cozy home life we imagine to have existed in the past.

In eighteenth-century North America, women may well have done more moving about than men. They referred to this as "gadding"; it has little of the formal, ritualistic character that the Victorians associated with female visiting. People entered without knocking, even without acknowledgment, and seated themselves at the hearth or the table with an air of familiarity that we would find quite astonishing and disturbing. Even the middle classes moved between households so frequently that it was often difficult to tell which family belonged where. The house had yet to become a strictly private space associated exclusively with the nuclear family. It was still the primary place of work and the meeting place of different classes, genders, and ages. Little about it conforms to the myth of the old homestead as a peaceful refuge, the original home sweet home.

We must also dispense with the notion that families past were more concerned with maintaining custom and tradition, and that they maintained the "quality time" we see as so threatened in our own day and age. By and large, premodern Europeans and Americans were less concerned with the economy of time than with the economy of space. Households took their time together pretty much for granted, allowing it to be governed by the rhythms of work and leisure and not setting apart any strictly family times. As we shall see, they lived by an entirely different culture of time than we do. The past had not yet taken on that quality of irrecoverable pastness that causes us so much anguish. Even the dead were within reach in the village graveyard, and people were more likely to be haunted by them, troubled by their presence. It is we, rather than they, who are ancestor worshipers.

The eighteenth century did not think of generations as we do. The term itself simply meant the offspring of a common parent and implied sameness rather than difference. By this definition, all generations occupied the same capacious present. The young were not necessarily identified with the future, nor the old with the past. In the premodern economy of time all ages were conceived of as equidistant from death, and the age differences we make so much of today mattered much less.

People then may have been less obsessed with temporal differences than we are now, and less aware of age than we are, but when it came to sharing space, trouble could erupt. This was precisely what happened when Martha Ballard was forced to share her house with her son Jonathan and his wife Sally. It was common under such circumstances for the parties to draw up an agreement about the rationing of space and resources so as to avoid strife. The Ballards made such an agreement, but it was not sufficient to prevent tensions between Martha and her daughter-in-law.

Contrary to another of our favorite images of families past, the desire for closeness for closeness' sake was notably absent. Families usually gathered to work or to pursue communally organized leisure, not to have family occasions as such. Most such gatherings were returns to community rather than to family as such, and the nostalgia we associate with family occasions was entirely missing. No graves were visited or ancestors remembered. In the premodern economy of time, no rupture between past and present was visible, and there was no compelling need to connect with other generations or to memorialize the dead.

Given the separation and loss that resulted from the demographic and economic realities of the preindustrial era, it is no wonder that our ancestors regarded forgetfulness as a kind of blessing. We like to think of our ancestors as having better memories, but like so many of our ideas about the past, this belief is more a projection of our fears of forgetting than a true reflection of what was important to them. Montaigne was convinced that "an excellent memory is often conjoined with the weakest intellects." In premodern Europe and North America, people were under no religious obligation to remember earthly things, not even their own families. "The things and relationships of this life are like prints in the Sand, there is not the least appearance of remembrance of them," declared Thomas Hooker. "The King remembers not his Crown, the Husband the Wife, the Father the child." It was God, not man, who remembered.

We want to believe that families past were less fragmented, discontinuous, and divided than families now, but historical reality is anything but reassuring on this point. Lawrence Stone has calculated that the proportion of marriages broken up by death in earlier centuries is just about the same as the proportion broken up by divorce today. Of course, one kind of separation is involuntary and the other is a choice, but it is hard to argue that fragmentation and loss of family ties are anything new, or that we are facing today a situation unprecedented in the history of Western civilization. What has changed are the cultural resources that different periods have had at their disposal to cope with the perpetual challenge of creating a sense of continuity and permanence. Propagating the myth of families past as more stable and united than families present is contemporary culture's way of achieving this result.

It is imperative that we disabuse ourselves of our misconceptions of family past, but we must not stop there. Those who would simply debunk the myths of family past seem to think that we can transcend myth entirely. Marina Warner is right to warn us that "pleas for a return to reason, for simply stripping away illusion, ignore the necessity and the vitality of mythical material in the consciousness as well as unconsciousness." We are no more able to live without our imagined families than were our ancestors. The only difference lies in the fact that their myths, rituals, and icons were provided by religion and community, while ours are self-generated. We will not understand our own engagement with myth and ritual until we understand how earlier generations engaged with theirs. In this way, we can use the past to throw light on the present.

The Life Course Revolution

ARLENE SKOLNICK

Many of us, in moments of nostalgia, imagine the past as a kind of Disneyland— a quaint setting we might step back into with our sense of ourselves intact, yet free of the stresses of modern life. But in yearning for the golden past we imagine we have lost, we are unaware of what we have escaped.

In our time, for example, dying before reaching old age has become a rare event; about three-quarters of all people die after their sixty-fifth birthday. It is hard for us to appreciate what a novelty this is in human experience. In 1850, only 2 percent of the population lived past sixty-five. "We place dying in what we take to be its logical position," observes the social historian Ronald Blythe, "which is at the close of a long life, whereas our ancestors accepted the futility of placing it in any position at all. In the midst of life we are in death, they said, and they meant it. To them it was a fact; to us it is a metaphor."

This longevity revolution is largely a twentieth-century phenomenon. Astonishingly, two-thirds of the total increase in human longevity since prehistoric times has taken place since 1900—and a good deal of that increase has occurred in recent decades. Mortality rates in previous centuries were several times higher than today, and death commonly struck at any age. Infancy was particularly hazardous; "it took two babies to make one adult," as one demographer put it. A white baby girl today has a greater chance of living to be sixty than her counterpart born in 1870 would have had of reaching her first birthday. And after infancy, death still hovered as an ever-present possibility. It was not unusual for young and middle-aged adults to die of tuberculosis, pneumonia, or other infectious diseases. (Keats died at twenty-five, Schubert at thirty-one, Mozart at thirty-five.)

These simple changes in mortality have had profound, yet little-appreciated effects on family life; they have encouraged stronger emotional bonds between parents and children, lengthened the duration of marriage and parent-child relationships, made grandparenthood an expectable stage of the life course, and increased the number of grandparents whom children actually know. More and more families have four or even five generations alive at the same time. And for the first time in history, the average couple has more parents living than it has children. It is also the first era when most of the parent-child relationship takes place after the child becomes an adult.

In a paper entitled "Death and the Family," the demographer Peter Uhlenberg has examined some of these repercussions by contrasting conditions in 1900 with those in 1976. In 1900, for example, half of all parents would have experienced the death of a child; by 1976 only 6 percent would. And more than half of all children who lived to the age of fifteen in 1900 would have experienced the death of a parent or sibling, compared with less than 9 percent in 1976. Another outcome of the lower death rates was a decline in the number of orphans and orphanages. Current discussions of divorce rarely take into account the almost constant family disruption children experienced in "the good old days." In 1900, 1 out of 4 children under the age of fifteen lost a parent; 1 out of 62 lost both. The corresponding figures for 1976 are, respectively, 1 out of 20 and 1 out of 1,800.

Because being orphaned used to be so common, the chances of a child's not living with either parent was much greater at the turn of the century than it is now. Indeed, some of the current growth in single-parent families is offset by a decline in the number of children raised in institutions, in foster homes, or by relatives. This fact does not diminish the stresses of divorce and other serious family problems of today, but it does help correct the tendency to contrast the terrible Present with an idealized Past.

Today's children rarely experience the death of a close relative, except for elderly grandparents. And it is possible to grow into adulthood without experiencing even that loss. "We never had any deaths in my family," a friend recently told me, explaining that none of her relatives had died until she was in her twenties. In earlier times, children were made aware of the constant possibility of death, attended deathbed scenes, and were even encouraged to examine the decaying corpses of family members.

One psychological result of our escape from the daily presence of death is that we are ill prepared for it when it comes. For most of us, the first time we feel a heightened concern with our own mortality is in our thirties and forties when we realize that the years we have already lived outnumber those we have left.

Another result is that the death of a child is no longer a sad but normal hazard of parenthood. Rather, it has become a devastating, life-shattering loss from which a parent may never fully recover. The intense emotional bonding between parents and infants that we see as a sociobiological given did not become the norm until the eighteenth and nineteenth centuries. The privileged classes created the concept of the "emotionally priceless" child, a powerful ideal that gradually filtered down through the rest of society.

The high infant mortality rates of premodern times were partly due to neglect, and often to lethal child-rearing practices such as sending infants off to a wet nurse* or, worse, infanticide. It now appears that in all societies lacking reliable contraception, the careless treatment and neglect of unwanted children acted as a major form of birth control. This does not necessarily imply that parents were uncaring toward all their children; rather, they seem to have practiced "selective neglect" of sickly infants in favor of sturdy ones, or of later children in favor of earlier ones.† In 1801 a writer observed of Bavarian peasants:

> The peasant has joy when his wife brings forth the first fruit of their love, he has joy with the second and third as well, but not with the fourth. . . . He sees all children coming thereafter as hostile creatures, which take the bread from his mouth and the mouths of his family. Even the heart of the most gentle mother becomes cold with the birth of the fifth child, and the sixth, she unashamedly wishes death, that the child should pass to heaven.

Declining fertility rates are another major result of falling death rates. Until the baby boom of the 1940s and 1950s, fertility rates had been dropping continuously since the eighteenth century. By taking away parents' fear that some of their children would not survive to adulthood, lowered early-childhood mortality rates encouraged careful planning of births and smaller families. The combination of longer lives and fewer, more closely spaced children created a still-lengthening empty-nest stage in the family. This in turn has encouraged the companionate style of marriage, since husband and wife can expect to live together for many years after their children have moved out.

Many demographers have suggested that falling mortality rates are directly linked to rising divorce rates. In 1891 W. F. Willcox of Cornell University made one of the most accurate social science predictions ever. Looking at the high and steadily rising divorce rates of the time, along with falling mortality rates, he predicted that around 1980, the two curves would cross and the number of marriages ended by divorce would equal those ended by death. In the late 1970s, it all happened as Willcox had predicted. Then divorce rates continued to increase before leveling off in the 1980s, while mortality rates continued to

---

*Wet-nursing—the breastfeeding of an infant by a woman other than the mother—was widely practiced in premodern Europe and colonial America. Writing of a two-thousand-year-old "war of the breast," the developmental psychologist William Kessen notes that the most persistent theme in the history of childhood is the reluctance of mothers to suckle their babies, and the urgings of philosophers and physicians that they do so. Infants were typically sent away from home for a year and a half or two years to be raised by poor country women, in squalid conditions. When they took in more babies than they had milk enough to suckle, the babies would die of malnutrition.

The reluctance to breast-feed may not have reflected maternal indifference so much as other demands in premodern, precontraceptive times—the need to take part in the family economy, the unwillingness of husbands to abstain from sex for a year and a half or two. (Her milk would dry up if a mother became pregnant.) Although in France and elsewhere the custom persisted into the twentieth century, large-scale wet-nursing symbolizes the gulf between modern and premodern sensibilities about infants and their care.

†The anthropologist Nancy Scheper-Hughes describes how impoverished mothers in northeastern Brazil select which infants to nurture.

decline. As a result, a couple marrying today is more likely to celebrate a fortieth wedding anniversary than were couples around the turn of the century.

In statistical terms, then, it looks as if divorce has restored a level of instability to marriage that had existed earlier due to the high mortality rate. But as Lawrence Stone observes, "it would be rash to claim that the psychological effects of the termination of marriage by divorce, that is by an act of will, bear a close resemblance to its termination by the inexorable accident of death."

THE NEW STAGES OF LIFE

In recent years it has become clear that the stages of life we usually think of as built into human development are, to a large degree, social and cultural inventions. Although people everywhere may pass through infancy, childhood, adulthood, and old age, the facts of nature are "doctored," as Ruth Benedict once put it, in different ways by different cultures.

The Favorite Age

In 1962 Phillipe Ariès made the startling claim that "in medieval society, the idea of childhood did not exist." Ariès argued not that parents then neglected their children, but that they did not think of children as having a special nature that required special treatment; after the age of around five to seven, children simply joined the adult world of work and play. This "small adult" conception of childhood has been observed by many anthropologists in preindustrial societies. In Europe, according to Ariès and others, childhood was discovered, or invented, in the seventeenth and nineteenth centuries, with the emergence of the private, domestic, companionate family and formal schooling. These institutions created distinct roles for children, enabling childhood to emerge as a distinct stage of life.

Despite challenges to Ariès's work, the bulk of historical and cross-cultural evidence supports the contention that childhood as we know it today is a relatively recent cultural invention; our ideas about children, child-rearing practices, and the conditions of children's lives are dramatically different from those of earlier centuries. The same is true of adolescence. Teenagers, such a conspicuous and noisy presence in modern life, and their stage of life, known for its turmoil and soul searching, are not universal features of life in other times and places.

Of course, the physical changes of puberty—sexual maturation and spurt in growth—happen to everyone everywhere. Yet, even here, there is cultural and historical variation. In the past hundred years, the age of first menstruation has declined from the mid-teens to twelve, and the age young men reach their full height has declined from twenty-five to under twenty. Both changes are believed to be due to improvements in nutrition and health care, and these average ages are not expected to continue dropping.

Some societies have puberty rites, but they bring about a transition from childhood not to adolescence but to adulthood. Other societies take no note at all of the changes, and the transition from childhood to adulthood takes place simply and without social recognition. Adolescence as we know it today appears to have evolved late in the nineteenth century; there is virtual consensus among social scientists that it is "a creature of the industrial revolution and it continues to be shaped by the forces which defined that revolution: industrialization, specialization, urbanization . . . and bureaucratization of human organizations and institutions, and continuing technological development."

In America before the second half of the nineteenth century, youth was an ill-defined category. Puberty did not mark any new status or life experience. For the majority of young people who lived on farms, work life began early, at seven or eight years old or even younger. As they grew older, their responsibility would increase, and they would gradually move toward maturity. Adults were not ignorant of the differences between children and adults, but distinctions of age meant relatively little. As had been the practice in Europe, young people could be sent away to become apprentices or servants in other households. As late as the early years of this century, working-class children went to work at the age of ten or twelve.

A second condition leading to a distinct stage of adolescence was the founding of mass education systems, particularly the large public high school. Compulsory education helped define adolescence by setting a precise age for it; high schools brought large numbers of teenagers together to create their own society for a good part of their daily lives. So the complete set of conditions for adolescence on a mass scale did not exist until the end of the nineteenth century.

The changed family situations of late-nineteenth- and early-twentieth-century youth also helped make this life stage more psychologically problematic. Along with the increasing array of options to choose from, rapid social change was making one generation's experience increasingly different from that of the next. Among the immigrants who were flooding into the country at around the time adolescence was emerging, the generation gap was particularly acute. But no parents were immune to the rapid shifts in society and culture that were transforming America in the decades around the turn of the century.

Further, the structure and emotional atmosphere of middle-class family life was changing also, creating a more intimate and emotionally intense family life. Contrary to the view that industrialization had weakened parent-child relations, the evidence is that family ties between parents and adolescents intensified at this time: adolescents lived at home until they married, and depended more completely, and for a longer time, on their parents than in the past. Demographic change had cut family size in half over the course of the century. Mothers were encouraged to devote themselves to the careful nurturing of fewer children.

This more intensive family life seems likely to have increased the emotional strain of adolescence. Smaller households and a more nurturing style of child rearing, combined with the increased contact between parents, especially mothers, and adolescent children, may have created a kind of " 'Oedipal family' in middle class America."

The young person's awakening sexuality, particularly the young male's, is likely to have been more disturbing to both himself and his parents than during the era when young men commonly lived away from home. . . . There is evidence that during the Victorian era, fears of adolescent male sexuality, and of masturbation in particular, were remarkably intense and widespread.

Family conflict in general may have been intensified by the peculiar combination of teenagers' increased dependence on parents and increased autonomy in making their own life choices. Despite its tensions, the new emotionally intense middle-class home made it more difficult than ever for adolescents to leave home for the heartless, indifferent world outside.

By the end of the nineteenth century, conceptions of adolescence took on modern form, and by the first decades of the twentieth century, *adolescence* had become a household word. As articulated forcefully by the psychologist G. Stanley Hall in his 1904 treatise, adolescence was a biological process—not simply the onset of sexual maturity but a turbulent, transitional stage in the evolution of the human species: "some ancient period of storm and stress when old moorings were broken and a higher level attained."

Hall seemed to provide the answers to questions people were asking about the troublesome young. His public influence eventually faded, but his conception of adolescence as a time of storm and stress lived on. Adolescence continued to be seen as a period of both great promise and great peril: "every step of the upward way is strewn with the wreckage of body, mind and morals." The youth problem—whether the lower-class problem of delinquency, or the identity crises and other psychological problems of middle-class youth—has continued to haunt America, and other modern societies, ever since.

Ironically, then, the institutions that had developed to organize and control a problematic age ended by heightening adolescent self-awareness, isolating youth from the rest of society, and creating a youth culture, making the transition to adulthood still more problematic and risky. Institutional recognition in turn made adolescents a more distinct part of the population, and being adolescent a more distinct and self-conscious experience. As it became part of the social structure of modern society, adolescence also became an important stage of the individual's biography—an indeterminate period of being neither child nor adult that created its own problems. Any society that excludes youth from adult work, and offers them what Erikson calls a "moratorium"—time and space to try out identities and lifestyles—and at the same time demands extended schooling as the route to success is likely to turn adolescence into a "struggle for self." It is also likely to run the risk of increasing numbers of mixed-up, rebellious youth.

But, in fact, the classic picture of adolescent storm and stress is not universal. Studies of adolescents in America and other industrialized societies suggest that extreme rebellion and rejection of parents, flamboyant behavior, and psychological turmoil do not describe most adolescents, even today. Media images of the youth of the 1980s and 1990s as a deeply troubled, lost generation beset by crime, drug abuse, and teenage pregnancy are also largely mistaken.

Although sexual activity and experimenting with drugs and alcohol have become common among middle-class young people, drug use has actually declined in recent years. Disturbing as these practices are for parents and other adults, they apparently do not interfere with normal development for most adolescents. Nevertheless, for a significant minority, sex and drugs add complications to a period of development during which a young person's life can easily go awry—temporarily or for good.

More typically, for most young people, the teen years are marked by mild rebelliousness and moodiness—enough to make it a difficult period for parents but not one of a profound parent-child generation gap or of deep alienation from conventional values. These ordinary tensions of family living through adolescence are exacerbated in times of rapid social change, when the world adolescents confront is vastly different from the one in which their parents came of age. Always at the forefront of social change, adolescents in industrial societies inevitably bring discomfort to their elders, who "wish to see their children's adolescence as an enactment of the retrospectively distorted memory of their own. . . . But such intergenerational continuity can occur only in the rapidly disappearing isolation of the desert or the rain forest."

If adolescence is a creation of modern culture, that culture has also been shaped by adolescence. Adolescents, with their music, fads, fashions, and conflicts, not only are conspicuous, but reflect a state of mind that often extends beyond the years designated for them. The adolescent mode of experience—accessible to people of any age—is marked by "exploration, becoming, growth, and pain."

Since the nineteenth century, for example, the coming-of-age novel has become a familiar literary genre. Patricia Spacks observes that while Victorian authors looked back at adolescence from the perspective of adulthood, twentieth-century novelists since James Joyce and D. H. Lawrence have become more intensely identified with their young heroes, writing not from a distance but from "deep inside the adolescence experience." The novelist's use of the adolescent to symbolize the artist as romantic outsider mirrors a more general cultural tendency. As Phillipe Ariès observes, "Our society has passed from a period which was ignorant of adolescence to a period in which adolescence is the favorite age. We now want to come to it early and linger in it as long as possible."

The Discovery of Adulthood

Middle age is the latest life stage to be discovered, and the notion of mid-life crisis recapitulates the storm-and-stress conception of adolescence. Over the course of the twentieth century, especially during the years after World War II, a developmental conception of childhood became institutionalized in public thought. Parents took it for granted that children passed through ages, stages, and phases: the terrible twos, the teenage rebel. In recent years the idea of development has been increasingly applied to adults, as new stages of adult life are discovered. Indeed much of the psychological revolution of recent years—the tendency to look at life through psychological lenses—can be understood in part as the extension of the developmental approach to adulthood.

In 1976 Gail Sheehy's best-selling *Passages* popularized the concept of mid-life crisis. Sheehy argued that every individual must pass through such a watershed, a time when we reevaluate our sense of self, undergo a crisis, and emerge with a new identity. Failure to do so, she warned, can have dire consequences. The book was the most influential popular attempt to apply to adults the ages-and-stages approach to development that had long been applied to children.

Ironically, this came about just as historians were raising questions about the universality of those stages.

Despite its popularity, Sheehy's book, and the research she reported in it, have come under increasing criticism. "Is the mid-life crisis, if it exists, more than a warmed-over identity crisis?" asked one review of the research literature on mid-life. In fact, there is little or no evidence for the notion that adults pass through a series of sharply defined stages, or a series of crises that must be resolved before passing from one stage to the next.

Nevertheless, the notion of a mid-life crisis caught on because it reflected shifts in adult experience across the life course. Most people's decisions about marriage and work are no longer irrevocably made at one fateful turning point on the brink of adulthood. The choices made at twenty-one may no longer fit at forty or fifty—the world has changed; parents, children, and spouses have changed; working life has changed. The kind of issue that makes adolescence problematic—the array of choices and the need to fashion a coherent, continuous sense of self in the midst of all this change—recurs throughout adulthood. As a Jules Feiffer cartoon concludes, "Maturity is a phase, but adolescence is forever."

Like the identity crisis of adolescence, the concept of mid-life crisis appears to reflect the experience of the more educated and advantaged. Those with more options in life are more likely to engage in the kind of introspection and reappraisal of previous choices that make up the core of the mid-life crisis. Such people realize that they will never fulfill their earlier dreams, or that they have gotten what they wanted and find they are still not happy. But as the Berkeley longitudinal data show, even in that segment of the population, mid-life crisis is far from the norm. People who have experienced fewer choices in the past, and have fewer options for charting new directions in the future, are less likely to encounter a mid-life crisis. Among middle Americans, life is dominated by making ends meet, coping with everyday events, and managing unexpected crises.

While there may be no fixed series of stages or crises adults must pass through, middle age or mid-life in our time does have some unique features that make it an unsettled time, different from other periods in the life course as well as from mid-life in earlier eras. First, as we saw earlier, middle age is the first period in which most people today confront death, illness, and physical decline. It is also an uneasy age because of the increased importance of sexuality in modern life. Sexuality has come to be seen as the core of our sense of self, and sexual fulfillment as the center of the couple relationship. In mid-life, people confront the decline of their physical attractiveness, if not of their sexuality.

There is more than a passing resemblance between the identity problems of adolescence and the issues that fall under the rubric of "mid-life crisis." In a list of themes recurring in the literature on the experience of identity crisis, particularly in adolescence, the psychologist Roy Baumeister includes: feelings of emptiness, feelings of vagueness, generalized malaise, anxiety, self-consciousness. These symptoms describe not only adolescent and mid-life crises but what Erikson has labeled identity problems—or what has, of late, been considered narcissism.

Consider, for example, Heinz Kohut's description of patients suffering from what he calls narcissistic personality disorders. They come to the analyst with vague symptoms, but eventually focus on feelings about the self—emptiness, vague depression, being drained of energy, having no "zest" for work or anything else, shifts in self-esteem, heightened sensitivity to the opinions and reactions of others, feeling unfulfilled, a sense of uncertainty and purposelessness. "It seems on the face of it," observes the literary critic Steven Marcus, "as if these people are actually suffering from what was once called unhappiness."

The New Aging

Because of the extraordinary revolution in longevity, the proportion of elderly people in modern industrial societies is higher than it has ever been. This little-noticed but profound transformation affects not just the old but families, an individual's life course, and society as a whole. We have no cultural precedents for the mass of the population reaching old age. Further, the meaning of *old age* has changed—indeed, it is a life stage still in process, its boundaries unclear. When he came into office at the age of sixty-four, George Bush did not seem like an old man. Yet when Franklin Roosevelt died at the same age, he did seem to be "old."

President Bush illustrates why gerontologists in recent years have had to revise the meaning of "old." He is a good example of what they have termed the "young old" or the "new elders"; the social historian Peter Laslett uses the term "the third age." Whatever it is called, it represents a new stage of life created by the extension of the life course in industrialized countries. Recent decades have witnessed the first generations of people who live past sixty-five and remain healthy, vigorous, alert, and, mostly due to retirement plans, financially independent. These people are "pioneers on the frontier of age," observed the journalist Frances Fitzgerald, in her study of Sun City, a retirement community near Tampa, Florida, "people for whom society had as yet no set of expectations and no vision."

The meaning of the later stages of life remains unsettled. Just after gerontologists had marked off the "young old"—people who seemed more middle-aged than old—they had to devise a third category, the "oldest old," to describe the fastest-growing group in the population, people over eighty-five. Many if not most of these people are like Tithonus, the mythical figure who asked the gods for eternal life but forgot to ask for eternal youth as well. For them, the gift of long life has come at the cost of chronic disease and disability.

The psychological impact of this unheralded longevity revolution has largely been ignored, except when misconstrued. The fear of age, according to Christopher Lasch, is one of the chief symptoms of this culture's alleged narcissism. But when people expected to die in their forties or fifties, they didn't have to face the problem of aging. Alzheimer's disease, for example, now approaching epidemic proportions, is an ironic by-product of the extension of the average life span. When living to seventy or eighty is a realistic prospect, it makes sense to diet and exercise, to eat healthy foods, and to make other "narcissistic" investments in the self.

Further, "the gift of mass longevity," the anthropologist David Plath argues, has been so recent, dramatic, and rapid that it has become profoundly unsettling in all postindustrial societies: "If the essential cultural nightmare of the nineteenth century was to be in poverty, perhaps ours is to be old and alone or afflicted with terminal disease."

Many people thus find themselves in life stages for which cultural scripts have not yet been written; family members face one another in relationships for which tradition provides little guidance. "We are stuck with awkward-sounding terms like 'adult children' and . . . 'grandson-in-law.' " And when cultural rules are ambiguous, emotional relationships can become tense or at least ambivalent.

A study of five-generation families in Germany reveals the confusion and strain that result when children and parents are both in advanced old age—for example, a great-great-grandmother and her daughter, who is herself a great-grandmother. Who has the right to be old? Who should take care of whom? Similarly, Plath, who has studied the problems of mass longevity in Japan, finds that even in that familistic society the traditional meaning of family roles has been put into question by the stretching out of the life span. In the United States, some observers note that people moving into retirement communities sometimes bring their parents to live with them. Said one disappointed retiree: "I want to enjoy my grandchildren; I never expected that when I was a grandparent I'd have to look after my parents."

R E A D I N G

3

What We Really Miss About the 1950s

STEPHANIE COONTZ

In a 1996 poll by the Knight-Ridder news agency, more Americans chose the 1950s than any other single decade as the best time for children to grow up. And despite the research I've done on the underside of 1950s families, I don't think it's crazy for people to feel nostalgic about the period. For one thing, it's easy to see why people might look back fondly to a decade when real wages grew more in any single year than in the entire ten years of the 1980s combined, a time when the average 30-year-old man could buy a median-priced home on only 15–18 percent of his salary.

But it's more than just a financial issue. When I talk with modern parents, even ones who grew up in unhappy families, they associate the 1950s with a yearning they feel for a time when there were fewer complicated choices for kids or parents to grapple with, when there was more predictability in how people formed and maintained families, and when there was a coherent "moral order" in their community to serve as a reference point for family norms. Even people who found that moral order grossly unfair or repressive often say that its presence provided them with something concrete to push against.

I can sympathize entirely. One of my most empowering moments occurred the summer I turned 12, when my mother marched down to the library with me to confront a librarian who'd curtly refused to let me check out a book that was "not appropriate" for my age. "Don't you *ever* tell my daughter what she can and can't read," fumed my mom. "She's a mature young lady and she can make her own choices." In recent years I've often thought back to the gratitude I felt toward my mother for that act of trust in me. I wish I had some way of earning similar points from my own son. But much as I've always respected his values, I certainly wouldn't have walked into my local video store when he was 12 and demanded that he be allowed to check out absolutely anything he wanted!

Still, I have no illusions that I'd actually like to go back to the 1950s, and neither do most people who express such occasional nostalgia. For example, although the 1950s got more votes than any other decade in the Knight-Ridder poll, it did not win an outright majority: 38 percent of respondents picked the 1950s; 27 percent picked the 1960s or the 1970s. Voters between the ages of 50 and 64 were most likely to choose the 1950s, the decade in which they themselves came of age, as the best time for kids; voters under 30 were more likely to choose the 1970s. African Americans differed over whether the 1960s, 1970s, or 1980s were best, but all age groups of blacks agreed that later decades were definitely preferable to the 1950s.

Nostalgia for the 1950s is real and deserves to be taken seriously, but it usually shouldn't be taken literally. Even people who *do* pick the 1950s as the best decade generally end up saying, once they start discussing their feelings in depth, that it's not the family arrangements in and of themselves that they want to revive. They don't miss the way women used to be treated, they sure wouldn't want to live with most of the fathers they knew in their neighborhoods, and "come to think of it"—I don't know how many times I've recorded these exact words—"I communicate with my kids *much* better than my parents or grandparents did." When Judith Wallerstein recently interviewed 100 spouses in "happy" marriages, she found that only five "wanted a marriage like their parents'." The husbands "consciously rejected the role models provided by their fathers. The women said they could never be happy living as their mothers did."

People today understandably feel that their lives are out of balance, but they yearn for something totally *new*—a more equal distribution of work, family, and community time for both men and women, children and adults. If the 1990s are lopsided in one direction, the 1950s were equally lopsided in the opposite direction.

What most people really feel nostalgic about has little to do with the internal structure of 1950s families. It is the belief that the 1950s provided a more family-friendly economic and social environment, an easier climate in which to keep kids on the straight and narrow, and above all, a greater feeling of hope for a family's long-term future, especially for its young. The contrast between the perceived hopefulness of the fifties and our own misgivings about the future is key to contemporary nostalgia for the period. Greater optimism *did* exist then, even among many individuals and groups who were in terrible circumstances. But if we are to take people's sense of loss seriously, rather than merely to capitalize on it for a hidden political agenda, we need to develop a historical perspective on where that hope came from.

Part of it came from families comparing their prospects in the 1950s to their unstable, often grindingly uncomfortable pasts, especially the two horrible decades just before. In the 1920s after two centuries of child labor and income insecurity, and for the first time in American history, a bare majority of children had come to live in a family with a male breadwinner, a female homemaker, and a chance at a high school education. Yet no sooner did the ideals associated with such a family begin to blossom than they were buried by the stock market crash of 1929 and the Great Depression of the 1930s. During the 1930s domestic violence soared; divorce rates fell, but informal separations jumped; fertility plummeted. Murder rates were higher in 1933 than they were in the 1980s. Families were uprooted or torn apart. Thousands of young people left home to seek work, often riding the rails across the country.

World War II brought the beginning of economic recovery, and people's renewed interest in forming families resulted in a marriage and childbearing boom, but stability was still beyond most people's grasp. Postwar communities were rocked by racial tensions, labor strife, and a right-wing backlash against the radical union movement of the 1930s. Many women resented being fired from wartime jobs they had grown to enjoy. Veterans often came home to find that they had to elbow their way back into their families, with wives and children resisting their attempts to reassert domestic authority. In one recent study of fathers who returned from the war, four times as many reported painful, even traumatic, reunions as remembered happy ones.

By 1946 one in every three marriages was ending in divorce. Even couples who stayed together went through rough times, as an acute housing shortage forced families to double up with relatives or friends. Tempers frayed and generational relations grew strained. "No home is big enough to house two families, particularly two of different generations, with opposite theories on child training," warned a 1948 film on the problems of modern marriage.

So after the widespread domestic strife, family disruptions, and violence of the 1930s and the instability of the World War II period, people were ready to try something new. The postwar economic boom gave them the chance.

The 1950s was the first time that a majority of Americans could even *dream* of creating a secure oasis in their immediate nuclear families. There they could focus their emotional and financial investments, reduce obligations to others that might keep them from seizing their own chance at a new start, and escape the interference of an older generation of neighbors or relatives who tried to tell them how to run their lives and raise their kids. Oral histories of the postwar period resound with the theme of escaping from in-laws, maiden aunts, older parents, even needy siblings.

The private family also provided a refuge from the anxieties of the new nuclear age and the cold war, as well as a place to get away from the political witch-hunts led by Senator Joe McCarthy and his allies. When having the wrong friends at the wrong time or belonging to any "suspicious" organization could ruin your career and reputation, it was safer to pull out of groups you might have joined earlier and to focus on your family. On a more positive note, the nuclear family was where people could try to satisfy their long-pent-up desires for a more stable marriage, a decent home, and the chance to really enjoy their children.

THE 1950s FAMILY EXPERIMENT

The key to understanding the successes, failures, and comparatively short life of 1950s family forms and values is to understand the period as one of *experimentation* with the possibilities of a new kind of family, not as the expression of some longstanding tradition. At the end of the 1940s, the divorce rate, which had been rising steadily since the 1890s, dropped sharply; the age of marriage fell to a 100-year low; and the birth rate soared. Women who had worked during the depression or World War II quit their jobs as soon as they became pregnant, which meant quite a few women were specializing in child raising; fewer women remained childless during the 1950s than in any decade since the late nineteenth century. The timing and spacing of childbearing became far more compressed, so that young mothers were likely to have two or more children in diapers at once, with no older sibling to help in their care. At the same time, again for the first time in 100 years, the educational gap between young middle-class women and men increased, while job segregation for working men and women seems to have peaked. These demographic changes increased the dependence of women on marriage, in contrast to gradual trends in the opposite direction since the early twentieth century.

The result was that family life and gender roles became much more predictable, orderly, and settled in the 1950s than they were either twenty years earlier or would be twenty years later. Only slightly more than one in four marriages ended in divorce during the 1950s. Very few young people spent any extended period of time in a nonfamily setting: They moved from their parent's family into their own family, after   just a brief experience with independent living, and they started having children soon after marriage. Whereas two-thirds of women aged 20-24 were not yet married in 1990, only 28 percent of women this age were still single in 1960.

Ninety percent of all the households in the country were families in the 1950s, in comparison with only 71 percent by 1990. Eighty-six percent of all children lived in two-parent homes in 1950, as opposed to just 72 percent in 1990. And the percentage living with both biological parents—rather than, say, a parent and stepparent—was dramatically higher than it had been at the turn of the century or is today: 70 percent in 1950, compared with only 50 percent in 1990. Nearly 60 percent of kids—an all-time high—were born into male bread-winner-female homemaker families; only a minority of the rest had mothers who worked in the paid labor force.

If the organization and uniformity of family life in the 1950s were new, so were the values, especially the emphasis on putting all one's emotional and financial eggs in the small basket of the immediate nuclear family. Right up through the 1940's, ties of work, friendship, neighborhood, ethnicity, extended kin, and voluntary organizations were as important a source of identity for most Americans, and sometimes a *more* important source of obligation, than marriage and the nuclear family. All this changed in the postwar era. The spread of suburbs and automobiles, combined with the destruction of older ethnic neighborhoods in many cities, led to the decline of the neighborhood social club. Young couples moved away from parents and kin, cutting ties with traditional extrafamilial networks that might compete for their attention. A critical factor in this trend was the emergence of a group of family sociologists and marriage counselors who followed Talcott Parsons in claiming that the nuclear family, built on a sharp division of labor between husband and wife, was the cornerstone of modern society.

The new family experts tended to advocate views such as those first raised in a 1946 book, *Their Mother' Sons*, by psychiatrist Edward Strecker. Strecker and his followers argued that American boys were infantalized and emasculated by women who were old-fashioned "moms" instead of modern "mothers." One sign that might be that dreaded "mom," Strecker warned women, was if you felt you should take your aging parents into your own home, rather than putting them in "a good institution . . . where they will receive adequate care and comfort." Modern "mothers" placed their parents in nursing homes and poured all their energies into their nuclear family. They were discouraged from diluting their wifely and maternal commitments by maintaining "competing" interests in friends, jobs, or extended family networks, yet they were also supposed to cheerfully grant early independence to their (male) children—an emotional double bind that may explain why so many women who took this advice to heart ended up abusing alcohol or tranquilizers over the course of the decade.

The call for young couples to break from their parents and youthful friends was a consistent theme in 1950s popular culture. In *Marty*, one of the most highly praised TV plays and movies of the 1950s, the hero almost loses his chance at love by listening to the carping of his mother and aunt and letting himself be influenced by old friends who resent the time he spends with his new girlfriend. In the end, he turns his back on mother, aunt, and friends to get his new marriage and a little business of his own off to a good start. Other movies, novels, and popular psychology tracts portrayed the dreadful things that happened when women became more interested in careers than marriage or men resisted domestic conformity.

Yet many people felt guilty about moving away from older parents and relatives; "modern mothers" worried that fostering independence in their kids could lead to defiance or even juvenile delinquency (the recurring nightmare of the age); there was considerable confusion about how men and women could maintain clear breadwinner-homemaker distinctions in a period of expanding education, job openings, and consumer aspirations. People clamored for advice. They got it from the new family education specialists and marriage counselors, from columns in women's magazines, from government pamphlets, and above all from television. While 1950s TV melodramas warned against letting anything dilute the commitment to getting married and having kids, the new family sitcoms gave people nightly lessons on how to make their marriage or rapidly expanding family work—or, in the case of *I Love Lucy*, probably the most popular show of the era, how *not* to make their marriage and family work. Lucy and Ricky gave weekly comic reminders of how much trouble a woman could get into by wanting a career or hatching some hare-brained scheme behind her husband's back.

At the time, everyone knew that shows such as *Donna Reed, Ozzie and Harriet, Leave It to Beaver,* and *Father Knows Best* were not the way families really were. People didn't watch those shows to see their own lives reflected back at them. They watched them to see how families were *supposed* to live—and also to get a little reassurance that they were headed in the right direction. The sitcoms were simultaneously advertisements, etiquette manuals, and how-to lessons for a new way of organizing marriage and child raising. I have studied the scripts of these shows for years, since I often use them in my classes on family history, but it wasn't until I became a parent that I felt their extraordinary pull. The secret of their appeal, I suddenly realized, was that they offered 1950s viewers, wracked with the same feelings of parental inadequacy as was I, the promise that there were easy answers and surefire techniques for raising kids.

Ever since, I have found it useful to think of the sitcoms as the 1950s equivalent of today's beer ads. As most people know, beer ads are consciously aimed at men who *aren't* as strong and sexy as the models in the commercials, guys who are uneasily aware of the gap between the ideal masculine pursuits and their own achievements. The promise is that if the viewers on the couch will just drink brand X, they too will be able to run 10 miles without gasping for breath. Their bodies will firm up, their complexions will clear up, and maybe the Swedish bikini team will come over and hang out at their place.

Similarly, the 1950s sitcoms were aimed at young couples who had married in haste, women who had tasted new freedoms during World War II and given up their jobs with regret, veterans whose children resented their attempts to reassert paternal authority, and individuals disturbed by the changing racial and ethnic mix of postwar America. The message was clear: Buy these ranch houses, Hotpoint appliances, and child-raising ideals; relate to your spouse like this; get a new car to wash with your kids on Sunday afternoons; organize your dinners like that—and you too can escape from the conflicts of race, class, and political witch-hunts into harmonious families where father knows best, mothers are never bored or irritated, and teenagers rush to the dinner table each night, eager to get their latest dose of parental wisdom.

Many families found it possible to put together a good imitation of this way of living during the 1950s and 1960s. Couples were often able to construct marriages that were much more harmonious than those in which they had grown up, and to devote far more time to their children. Even when marriages were deeply unhappy, as many were, the new stability, economic security, and educational advantages parents were able to offer their kids counted for a lot in people's assessment of their life satisfaction. And in some matters, ignorance could be bliss: The lack of media coverage of problems such as abuse or incest was terribly hard on the casualties, but it protected more fortunate families from knowledge and fear of many social ills.

There was tremendous hostility to people who could be defined as "others": Jews, African Americans, Puerto Ricans, the poor, gays or lesbians, and "the red menace." Yet on a day-to-day basis, the civility that prevailed in homogeneous neighborhoods allowed people to ignore larger patterns of racial and political repression. Racial clashes were ever-present in the 1950s, sometimes escalating into full-scale antiblack riots, but individual homicide rates fell to almost half the levels of the 1930s. As nuclear families moved into the suburbs, they retreated from social activism but entered voluntary relationships with people who had children the same age; they became involved in PTAs together, joined bridge clubs, went bowling. There does seem to have been a stronger sense of neighborly commonalities than many of us feel today. Even though this local community was often the product of exclusion or repression, it sometimes looks attractive to modern Americans whose commutes are getting longer and whose family or work patterns give them little in common with their neighbors.

The optimism that allowed many families to rise above their internal difficulties and to put limits on their individualistic values during the 1950s came from the sense that America was on a dramatically different trajectory than it had been in the past, an upward and expansionary path that had already taken people to better places than they had ever seen before and would certainly take their children even farther. This confidence that almost everyone could look forward to a better future stands in sharp contrast to how most contemporary Americans feel, and it explains why a period in which many people were much worse off than today sometimes still looks like a better period for families than our own.

Throughout the 1950s, poverty was higher than it is today, but it was less concentrated in pockets of blight existing side-by-side with extremes of wealth, and, unlike today, it was falling rather than rising. At the end of the 1930s, almost two-thirds of the population had incomes below the poverty standards of the day, while only one in eight had a middle-class income (defined as two to five times the poverty line). By 1960, a majority of the population had climbed into the middle-income range.

Unmarried people were hardly sexually abstinent in the 1950s, but the age of first intercourse was somewhat higher than it is now, and despite a tripling of nonmarital birth rates between 1940 and 1958, more then 70 per cent of nonmarital pregnancies led to weddings before the child was born. Teenage birth rates were almost twice as high in 1957 as in the 1990s, but most teen births were to married couples, and the effect of teen pregnancy in reducing further schooling for young people did not hurt their life prospects the way it does today. High school graduation rates were lower in the 1950s than they are today, and minority students had far worse test scores, but there were jobs for people who dropped out of high school or graduated without good reading skills—jobs that actually had a future. People entering the job market in the 1950s had no way of knowing that they would be the last generation to have a good shot at reaching middle-class status without the benefit of postsecondary schooling.

Millions of men from impoverished, rural, unemployed, or poorly educated family backgrounds found steady jobs in the steel, auto, appliance, construction, and shipping industries. Lower middle-class men went further on in college during the 1950s than they would have been able to expect in earlier decades, enabling them to make the transition to secure white-collar work. The experience of shared sacrifices in the depression and war, reinforced by a New Deal—inspired belief in the ability of government to make life better, gave people a sense of hope for the future. Confidence in government, business, education, and other institutions was on the rise. This general optimism affected people's experience and assessment of family life. It is no wonder modern Americans yearn for a similar sense of hope.

But before we sign on to any attempts to turn the family clock back to the 1950s, we should note that the family successes and community solidarities of the 1950s rested on a totally different set of political and economic conditions than we have today. Contrary to widespread belief, the 1950s was not an age of laissez-faire government and free market competition. A major cause of the social mobility of young families in the 1950s was that federal assistance programs were much more generous and widespread than they are today.

In the most ambitious and successful affirmative action program ever adopted in America, 40 percent of young men were eligible for veterans' benefits, and these benefits were far more extensive than those available to Vietnam-era vets. Financed in part by a federal income tax on the rich that went up to 87 percent and a corporate tax rate of 52 percent, such benefits provided quite a jump start for a generation of young families. The GI bill paid most tuition costs for vets who attended college, doubling the percentage of college students from prewar levels. At the other end of the life span, Social Security began to build up a significant safety net for the elderly, formerly the poorest segment of the population. Starting in 1950, the federal government regularly mandated raises in the minimum wage to keep pace with inflation. The minimum wage may have been only $1.40 as late as 1968, but a person who worked for that amount full-time, year-round, earned 118 percent of the poverty figure for a family of three. By 1995, a full-time minimum-wage worker could earn only 72 percent of the poverty level.

An important source of the economic expansion of the 1950s was that public works spending at all levels of government comprised nearly 20 percent of total expenditures in 1950s as compared to less than 7 percent in 1984. Between 1950 and 1960, nonmilitary, nonresidential public construction rose by 58 percent. Construction expenditures for new schools (in dollar amounts adjusted for inflation) rose by 72 percent; funding on sewers and waterworks rose by 46 percent. Government paid 90 percent of the costs of building the new Interstate Highway system. These programs opened up suburbia to growing numbers of middle-class Americans and created secure, well-paying jobs for blue-collar workers.

Government also reorganized home financing, underwriting low down payments and long-term mortgages that had been rejected as bad business by private industry. To do this, government put public assets behind housing lending programs, created two new national financial institutions to facilitate home loans, allowed veterans to put down payments as low as a dollar on a house, and offered tax breaks to people who bought homes. The National Education Defense Act funded the socioeconomic mobility of thousands of young men who trained themselves for well-paying jobs in such fields as engineering.

Unlike contemporary welfare programs, government investment in 1950s families was not just for immediate subsistence but encouraged long-term asset development, rewarding people for increasing their investment in homes and education. Thus it was far less likely that such families or individuals would ever fall back to where they started, even after a string of bad luck. Subsidies for higher education were greater the longer people stayed in school and the more expensive the school they selected. Mortgage deductions got bigger as people traded up to better houses.

These social and political support systems magnified the impact of the postwar economic boom. "In the years between 1947 and 1973," reports economist Robert Kuttner, "the median paycheck more than doubled, and the bottom 20 percent enjoyed the greatest gains." High rates of unionization meant that blue-collar workers were making much more financial progress than most of their counterparts today. In 1952, when eager home buyers flocked to the opening of Levittown, Pennsylvania, the largest planned community yet constructed, "it took a factory worker one day to earn enough money to pay the closing costs on a new Levittown house, then selling for $10,000." By 1991, such a home was selling for $100,000 or more, and it took a factory worker *eighteen weeks* to earn enough money for just the closing costs.

The legacy of the union struggle of the 1930s and 1950s, combined with government support for raising people's living standards, set limits on corporations that have disappeared in recent decades. Corporations paid 23 percent of federal income taxes in the 1950s as compared to just 9.2 percent in 1991. Big companies earned higher profit margins than smaller firms, partly due to their dominance of the market, partly to America's postwar economic advantage. They chose (or were forced) to share these extra earnings, which economists call "rents," with employees. Economists at the Brookings Institution and Harvard University estimate that 70 percent of such corporate rents were passed on to workers at all levels of the firm, benefiting secretaries and janitors as well as

CEOs. Corporations routinely retained workers even in slack periods, as a way of ensuring workplace stability. Although they often received more generous tax breaks from communities than they gave back in investment, at least they kept their plants and employment offices in the same place. AT&T, for example, received much of the technology it used to finance its postwar expansion from publicly funded communications research conducted as part of the war effort, and, as current AT&T chairman Robert Allen puts it, there "used to be a life-long commitment on the employee's part and on our part." Today, however, he admits, "the contract doesn't exist anymore.

Television trivia experts still argue over exactly what the fathers in many 1950s sitcoms did for a living. Whatever it was, though, they obviously didn't have to worry about downsizing. If most married people stayed in long-term relationships during the 1950s, so did most corporations, sticking with the communities they grew up in and the employees they originally hired. Corporations were not constantly relocating in search of cheap labor during the 1950s; unlike today, increases in worker productivity usually led to increases in wages. The number of workers covered by corporate pension plans and health benefits increased steadily. So did limits on the work week. There is good reason that people look back to the 1950s as a less hurried age: The average American was working a shorter workday in the 1950s than his or her counterpart today, when a quarter of the work-force puts in 49 or more hours a week.

So politicians are practicing quite a double standard when they tell us to return to the family forms of the 1950s, while they do nothing to resolve the job programs and family subsidies of that era, the limits on corporate relocation and financial wheeling-dealing, the much higher share of taxes paid by corporations then, the availability of union jobs for noncollege youth, and the subsidies for higher education such as the National Defense Education Act loans. Furthermore, they're not telling the whole story when they claim that the 1950s was the most prosperous time for families and the most secure decade for children. Instead, playing to our understandable nostalgia for a time when things seemed to be getting better, not worse, they engage in a tricky chronological shell game with their figures, diverting our attention from two important points. First, many individuals, families, and groups were excluded from the economic prosperity, family optimism, and social civility of the 1950s. Second, the all-time high point of child well-being and family economic security came not during the 1950s but *at the end of the 1960s*.

◆

CHAPTER 2

THE MEANING(S)
OF FAMILY

READING

4

What Is a Family? Nature, Culture, and the Law

DAVID M. ROSEN

Throughout the United States, courts are grappling with the problem of how to define family and kinship relationships. Until recently, this appeared to be a relatively straightforward issue. The only family relationships given legal or jural recognition were those based upon blood ties, marriage, or adoption. But the emergence of new forms of domestic relationships, especially domestic relationships between gay and lesbian partners, has forced courts to decide whether traditional legal concepts of family relations should be extended to include new relationships that otherwise have no basis in law. In this article, I argue that deeply-rooted concepts of kinship underlie legal decision-making in this area, and define the boundaries of judicial discretion to modify the basic concepts of family law.[1]

To demonstrate this I analyze three recent cases in which New York courts have adopted three distinct strategies for meeting the legal challenges of new families. These strategies are:

1. The outright application of traditional family law concepts to new family arrangements.

From *Marriage and Family Review*, vol. 17, No. 112. © 1991 by The Haworth Press, Inc. All rights reserved.

2. The rejection of family law concepts as applicable to new family arrangements.

3. The rejection of the application of family law concepts to new families, coupled with the substitution of non-family-law legal concepts so as to provide judicial relief to the parties involved.

FIRST LEGAL STRATEGY: APPLICATION OF FAMILY LAW TO NEW FAMILY ARRANGEMENTS

An example of the first strategy is found in the New York case of *Braschi* v. *Stahl Associates Co.* (1989) in which the New York State Court of Appeals ruled that the term "family" applied to a gay couple who had lived together for ten years. The practical issue involved was whether under New York law the survivor of a long-term domestic relationship had the right to possession of a rent-controlled apartment which the couple shared. In New York, this is a significant property right. The court, in upholding the right of the surviving partner, declared that protection against eviction "should find its foundation in the reality of family life. In the context of eviction, a . . . realistic, and certainly valid, view of a family includes two adult life-time partners whose relationship is long-term and characterized by an emotional and financial commitment and interdependence."

This decision of the court prompted the New York Division of Housing and Renewal to redefine the concept of family to include long-term gay and lesbian relationships. Although lesbian and gay couples will benefit greatly by these actions, the greatest beneficiaries are expected to be a wide range of non-traditional families, especially families of the poor.

SECOND LEGAL STRATEGY: REJECTION OF FAMILY LAW CONCEPTS IN REFERENCE TO NEW FAMILY ARRANGEMENTS

The second strategy is exemplified by the case of *Alison D.* v. *Virginia M.* (1990) in which a New York Appellate Division ruled that the term "parent" applied solely to biological relationships, and denied a former lesbian partner visitation rights to a child she and the biological mother of the child had parented together. In this case, the two women began living with each other in 1978. In 1980, they decided to raise a family, and Virginia M. was artificially inseminated. A boy was born, and the two women shared in the care of the child and jointly assumed all parenting responsibilities. In 1983, the relationship between the women ended, and Alison D. moved out of their home. Initially, she enjoyed regular visitation, but her former partner cut off all visitation in 1987. The Court's decision of May 1990 left Alison D. without any legal rights to see the child.

THIRD LEGAL STRATEGY: DENIAL OF THE FAMILY-LAW MODEL, BUT APPLICATION OF OTHER LEGAL THEORIES TO PROVIDE RELIEF TO THE PARTIES

An example of the third strategy lies in the case titled *The Estate of Steven Szabo* (1990) decided in July 1990. Here a New York Surrogate's Court determined that the term "spouse" did not apply to a gay life-partner, and denied the partner any inheritance rights in his deceased partner's estate. In this case, the two men had lived together for eighteen years before Mr. Szabo died. After his death, a will was probated. The will predated the relationship between the parties, and made no mention of the surviving partner.

Under New York law, a spouse cannot be disinherited, and if the spouse is unnamed in a will, he or she can by law obtain up to one half of the deceased's estate. In this case, had the surviving partner been deemed a "spouse" he would have been able to obtain a large share of the estate. Of particular importance was the cooperative apartment in which the couple had lived, but to which the deceased partner held title. The Court rejected the plaintiff's claim that he was a spouse, but it was willing to entertain his claims to the estate based upon proof of the financial arrangements between the partners during their lifetime together.

These instances show that these three terms in American kinship and law—family, parent, and spouse—have been treated in markedly different ways by New York Courts. While the decisions in all these cases involve complex legal reasoning, underlying these decisions are key concepts of American kinship, especially the concepts of "nature" and "culture." In brief, I argue that when "new" family relationships are modeled on traditional relationships grounded in "nature," the law is less likely to recognize the "new" relationship. Conversely, the more a "new" family relationship is modeled on a traditional relationship grounded in culture, the more likely it is that the law will legally recognize the new relationship. Consequently, kin terms such as "parent," "mother" or "father," which in American kinship are understood as involving cultural and legal recognition of an existing biological fact, are not readily transferred to new family relationships. A term like "family," which incorporates multiple relationships grounded in both nature and culture, is more easily applied to new family relationships. Finally, terms such as "spouse," "husband" or "wife," straddle the boundaries between nature and culture, and evoke a hybrid response from the courts.

THE ORDER OF NATURE, THE ORDER OF CULTURE AND THE ORDER OF LAW

Kinship terms are cultural constructs which derive their meaning from their relationships with other concepts. In American kinship, as Schneider (1980) has pointed out, the world of relatives is constructed out of deeply felt assumptions about nature and culture.[2] Schneider has termed the distinction between nature and culture as the "order of nature" and the "order of law." Both of these orders are culturally constructed; that is, what is considered "nature" is itself culturally defined. Schneider's usage of the order of nature refers to the belief that some persons are considered relatives because they share a common heredity or blood. They are biogenetically connected. Schneider uses the "order of law" to refer to the belief that other persons are relatives because they are bound together by law or custom. For the purpose of this article, I distinguish between the order of nature, the order of culture and the order of law. All of these orders are culturally constructed, but they refer to specific ways in which human experience is symbolized.[3]

By the "order of nature" I mean that system of symbols that tends to define certain human characteristics as inherent. The symbolism of nature may describe the make up of persons, relations, or even sentiments, to the extent that these are perceived as arising from "nature."

By the "order of culture," I mean a system of symbols that stands for the world of customary beliefs, codes of conduct, and traditions created and imposed by human beings to serve as guidelines for action. The "order of law" is defined as a symbolic subdomain of the order of culture, which refers specifically to those codes of conduct created by judges, courts, legislatures and other law-making bodies in society.

In American kinship, the primary use of natural symbolism is found in the belief that some relatives are natural relatives because they share in a common substance: blood or heredity. But it is also the case that social actions and social relationships can be symbolized as more or less natural. For example, former United States Supreme Court Justice Burger, in his concurring opinion in the case of *Bowers* v. *Hardwick* (1985), resurrected with approval the commentaries of the eighteenth century English jurist Blackstone, that sodomy is "a crime against nature . . . the very mention of which is a disgrace to human nature" (p. 197). With this rhetorical flourish, a Georgia statute criminalizing homosexual relations was upheld as constitutional, and homosexuality was banished from the world of nature to the world of deviant culture.

Though Supreme Court Justices may see the distinction between nature and culture as relatively fixed, anthropologists have usually been of the mind that these categories are far more elastic. Some time ago, Ortner (1974) pointed out that the dichotomy between nature and culture was frequently used to define the relationship between male and female. Similarly, Barnes (1977) has demonstrated that the kin category of "mother" is usually more closely identified with nature than is the category of "father," even though both father and mother are equal participants in the genetic make-up of the child. All this suggests that the symbolism of nature and culture enters into human experience in a variety of predictable and unpredictable ways.

The orders of nature, culture and law combine to create American ideas of kinship. The primary elements are the combination of the order of nature and the order of culture. The combination of these two creates the world of relatives as these are understood in American kinship. The order of law may or may not recognize these relatives. That is, the relationships as they exist in nature,

TABLE 5.1 "Nature" and "culture" as components of family relationships.

Nature		Culture	
sperm donors	father	husband	fictive kin
"illegitimate" children	mother	wife	adopted children

culture, or some combination thereof may or may not have any legally defined rights or obligations. Table 5.1 illustrates how the world of kinship is created through the intersection of nature and culture.

At the far left side of the chart are relatives that exist primarily in the order of nature and may include so-called "illegitimate children," as well as the offspring of sperm donors. These are relatives to whom an individual may be related "by blood," but for whom no significant relationship in culture or in law exists.

At the far right of the chart are relatives who exist by virtue of culture alone. These include all the various fictive kin relationships that exist in American culture. Fictive aunts and uncles, brothers and sisters, and adopted children. These may exist only in culture, as in the case of fictive "brothers" and "sisters," or they may exist in both culture and in law, as in the case of adopted children.

Finally, in the middle are two categories of relatives that exist in both nature and culture. These are relatives for whom the order of nature appears to be reified by the order of culture. Relatives such as father and mother exist both in nature and in culture because the code of conduct expressed in culture is understood as a symbolic reenactment or replication of inherent ties. Thus for Americans, much of what is called kinship is symbolized as a cultural recognition of biological or natural facts. Many of these relationships, (e.g., mother and father) also exist in the order of law, in that law-making bodies have created a special symbolic code for governing these relationships. Other relationships, such as the relationships between second or third cousins, do not necessarily exist in the order of law. These are relatives solely in nature and culture. In this paper, I place the husband and wife relationship in the orders of nature and culture. Obviously, husbands and wives are not usually "blood" relatives, but in American culture, the relationship is seen as arising out of the nature of male-female relationships and the natural desire of men and women to mate and reproduce. In addition, it is sometimes remarked that the husband-wife relationship involves an exchange of fluids (i.e., semen) which gives this relationship a natural quality mimicking that of blood. Moreover, one practically universal basis for the annulment of marriage in American law is the failure of this exchange of fluids to take place. An annulment is conceptually different from a divorce, in that while divorce terminates a marriage, an annulment decrees that a marriage never existed. Thus the essence of a marital relationship is a blend of nature and culture.

In addition, there is tension between nature and culture which pervades American thinking about kinship. For example, the literature on step-parenting indicates that stepmothers have far more difficulty in integrating themselves into reconstituted families than do stepfathers, because of the cultural perception that relationships between mothers and children are more deeply imbedded in nature than in culture. Stepfathers seem to more easily assume the more culturally defined father role (Johnson, Klee and Smith, 1988).

The tension between nature and culture is even more apparent in adoption. By law, adoption severs all the rights of the biological mother and father to the child. All these rights and duties are transferred to the adopting parents. Yet nature looms as an ever-present danger to the adopting parents, and a host of devices exist to keep nature at bay. In the not-so-distant past, the fact of adoption was kept a secret, to be withheld from a child until he or she was "old enough to know"; that is old enough so that the cultural definition of the parent could resist the "pull" of the biological parent. The fear that someday the biological mother might come to successfully reclaim the love and loyalty linked to blood is not far from the minds of many adoptive parents, even though this fearsome scenario rarely occurs in fact.

Adopting parents also use geographic and cultural distance as ways of keeping nature at bay. Children are frequently adopted from foreign countries or distant states. Language also plays a role in the process. In current adoption jargon, the biological mother is now called the "birth mother" while the adopting mother is now "the mother." Adoption literature is also careful to spell out that a child "was" adopted, rather than "is" adopted, so as to signify that adoption is a way of coming into a family rather than an eternal condition. And, a pregnant woman seeking to find an adoptive family for her baby is termed a "situation," a term that clearly distances the adopting parents from the compelling fact of biological kinship.

Finally, the innumerable personal and procedural barriers placed in the way of so-called "open" adoptions are clearly linked to the fears of adopting parents and the law of the powerful claim of the biological mother. At the root of these feelings lies the primordial fear that culture cannot triumph over nature.

The Law Grapples with Redefining Family Relationships

A more detailed look at the legal decisions described above will illustrate how the tensions between nature and culture manifest themselves in legal decision-making. It is important to note that in all these cases, none of the kin or family terms are defined by statute or regulation. It fell to the courts to provide the definitions.[4]

What Is a Family?   In the case of *Braschi* v. *Stahl Associates Co.* (1989), the question was whether Miguel Braschi would be able to remain as a tenant in the apartment he had shared with his domestic partner Leslie Blanchard for more than ten years. At issue was the Court's interpretation of New York City Rent and Eviction regulations which provided that upon the death of a tenant in a rent controlled apartment, the landlord may not dispossess "either the surviving spouse of the deceased tenant or some other family member of the deceased tenant's *family* who has been living with the tenant" (p. 206). The Court of

Appeals specifically focused upon the meaning of the term "family." It did not address the issue of the term "spouse."

The Court rejected the idea that the term "family member" should be construed consistently with New York's intestacy laws, which regulate the inheritance of property, to mean relationships of blood, consanguinity, or adoption (p. 209). Instead, the Court argued that the non-eviction provisions are not designed to govern succession to property, but to protect certain occupants from the loss of their homes. In light of this, the Court argued that the term "family" should not be "rigidly restricted to those people who have formalized their relationship by obtaining, for instance, a marriage certificate or adoption order. The intended protection against sudden eviction should not rest on fictitious legal distinctions or genetic history, but instead should find its foundation in the reality of family life" (p. 211). The Court proceeded to provide a distinctly cultural view of family as "a group of people united by certain convictions or common affiliation" or as a "collective body of persons who live in one house under one head or management." Finally, the Court added that in using the term "family" the legislature had "intended to extend protection to those who reside in households having all of the normal familial characteristics" (p. 211). Indeed, the Court went on at length to describe how much the relationship between Braschi and Blanchard fit the facts of family life. As the Court put it:

> Appellant and Blanchard lived together as permanent life partners for more than 10 years. They regarded one another, and were regarded by friends and family, as spouses. The two men's families were aware of the nature of the relationship, and they regularly visited each other's families and attended family functions together, as a couple. Even today, appellant continues to maintain a relationship with Blanchard's niece, who considers him an uncle. (p. 213)

It is of considerable significance that the Court characterized the relationship between the parties as factually equivalent to a spousal relationship. Yet the issue of whether the parties were spouses to each other was apparently never raised or addressed. By resting his case on a cultural definition of family, Mr. Braschi obtained a favorable decision. Exactly how he would have fared had he relied on the idea that he was Blanchard's spouse cannot be ascertained from this case. However, the next case, *The Estate of Steven Szabo*, suggests that he would have had a more difficult time.

What Is a Spouse?   In the *Estate of Steven Szabo* (1990), the plaintiff presented a number of theories under which he should prevail. Each was predicated on the same set of facts, namely, that he and the deceased were gay life partners since 1970, and that they had agreed from the outset of their relationship to share living expenses and quarters, although they had signed no written agreement. According to the surviving partner, the financial arrangements between them were that he would give his entire monthly paycheck to Szabo, who then subtracted the cost of monthly household expenses, including the maintenance of the cooperative apartment that they shared. The balance of the money was placed in a savings account, and Szabo gave the plaintiff an allowance for weekly personal expenses. As seen earlier, when Szabo died, a will was probated, which predated the relationship and did not mention the plaintiff. In addition, there were no joint bank accounts, nor was the surviving partner the beneficiary of any life insurance policy. Title to the cooperative apartment in which they had lived together was also apparently held solely in the name of Szabo (p. 31).

It is easy to see, from the plaintiff's point of view, that this was a long-term relationship, like a marriage, in which the surviving partner was about to be evicted from the cooperative apartment he shared with the deceased without any of the money they had saved together for nearly twenty years. The plaintiff's most novel theory was that a gay life-partner is equivalent to a spouse. As previously stated, under New York law, a surviving spouse who is unnamed in a will is entitled to up to one-half of the net estate of the deceased partner. Therefore, if he were declared a spouse, he could obtain a substantial share of the estate solely by virtue of his spousal relationship and without having to prove any of the facts about their financial relationship.

However, the Court rejected this claim. Instead, the Court held that, by definition, a spouse means the person to whom one is legally married, and that the law made no provision for a marriage between persons of the same sex. "Marriage," the Court stated, "is and always has been a contract between a man and a woman" (p. 31). Here, of course the Court is emphasizing that marriage is a creation of both nature and culture. On the one hand, marriage is a contract, a cultural construction or transaction consisting of a series of mutual promises. On the other hand, it is grounded in nature, in that the only persons entitled to enter into such a contract are those persons who are heterosexual.

But the Court is able to separate the natural and cultural elements. For while nature and culture must come together in the creation of a marriage, and while the issue of inheritance flows from the natural side of the marriage, the financial relationships between the parties lie primarily in the world of culture. As a result, the Court allowed the plaintiff to proceed on two alternative theories; first on a claim for "money had and received," and old Common Law theory, which asserts that Szabo, and now his estate, received money that in equity and good conscience belong to the plaintiff; second, on the claim of "constructive trust," namely, that the estate has legal title to property in violation of some essential principal of equity. Under this theory the plaintiff would be permitted to show that the parties, by reason of their close relationship, were fiduciaries to each other, and that Szabo (and now, his estate) had a duty to act for his partner's benefit in connection with the money he had saved for him. These alternative theories find their bases in the world of business and commerce. They belong primarily to the world of culture. They derive from transactions into which all people, regardless of their natural connection to each other, can freely choose to enter.

What Is a Parent?   In *Alison D.* v. *Virginia M.* (1990) the Court was called upon to define the meaning of parent under New York's Domestic Relations law. At issue in this case was whether Alison D. had visitation rights to a child she and her former lesbian lover had parented together. Her basic claim was that she stood *in loco parentis* to the child, namely that the relationship the partners created gave her all the rights, duties, and responsibilities of a parent. As in the previous cases, the language of the law does not specifically define the term parent. Thus, the Court was asked to adopt the concept of parent as one standing *in loco parentis* (p. 23).

The Court saw no connection between the issues in *Braschi* v. *Stahl Associates Co.* and this case, but did not detail any reason why. The Court admitted that Alison D. and the child had a close and loving relationship, but it framed the entire dispute as one between a parent and a non-parent with respect to visitation of the child. Pronouncing Alison D. a "biological stranger," it chose to follow a line of cases which grants rights to non-parents only under extraordinary circumstances such as the unfitness of the biological parent.

Justice Kooper, who dissented in this case rejected the Court's reliance upon biology. She argued for a cultural definition of parenthood. In particular, she asserted that like the term "family," the term "parent" should be subject to a "frank inquiry into the realities of the relationship involved" (p. 24).

Interestingly, in this case the Court could have solved the problem by adopting the theory of equitable estoppel. Equitable estoppel is a vague legal concept which allows the Court to do justice by preventing a person from asserting a right he or she might otherwise have had. It is often used when the voluntary conduct of one party induces another to act in such a way that it is unjust for the party who does the misleading to assert his or her legal rights. Thus, in this case, the Court could have accepted the view that Virginia M. induced Alison D. into a long-term parental relationship and as a result, she should be barred from asserting the legal claim that Alison D. was not a parent. In this way, the Court would have done justice without actually having to redefine the concept of parent.

Significantly, this doctrine has sometimes been used to suppress biological claim to kinship. The classic example is where a woman becomes pregnant as a result of an adulterous relationship. Should she and her husband ultimately divorce, she will ordinarily be prevented from proving that the husband was not the biological father of their child. The doctrine of equitable estoppel creates the unrebuttable legal fiction that the child of a lawful marriage is the child of the husband and wife.

It might also be argued that adoption provides another model upon which the decision could have been based. After all, once adoption takes place, the issue of nature becomes legally irrelevant. Adoption could stand for the principle that a cultural-legal relationship can override a natural relationship even in parent-child relationships. A similar principle could be applied to lesbian and gay life-partner situations. This scenario is unlikely in the immediate future, since adoption was created through legislative action, rather than through judicial interpretation.

It is also clear that, adoption aside, parent-child relationships are one of the most difficult to redefine in the order of culture. Denmark, for example, allows for marriage-like unions for gay and lesbian couples which involve virtually all the rights and duties of marriage, but does not grant such couples the right to adopt or obtain joint custody of a child (Rule, 1989). The limited legal recognition of domestic partnerships in cities such as New York and San Francisco cannot deal with the issue of children.

The tension between the order of nature and the order of culture will continue to inform the domain of American family law. That the categories are undergoing constant revision is clear. In a recent surrogate mother case, a California Superior Court awarded full custody of the child to her genetic parents, and denied any rights to the surrogate mother, in whom a fertilized egg had been implanted after in-vitro fertilization. Whereas the New York Court dubbed Alison D. a "biological stranger," the California Court declared the surrogate mother a "genetic stranger." In making the decision, the Court was eventually forced to define the womb and the umbilical connection between the surrogate mother and the child as culture, analogizing it to a "fosterparent" relationship and a "home" for the embryo (Mydans, 1990).

CONCLUSION

Beginning in the 1930s, American law began to develop around the theory of legal realism. Legal realism was not as much a philosophical theory as it was an attitude. It called for an instrumental utilitarian use of law which rejected legal fictions. Law was a social tool (Friedman, 1985). In this light, it has sometimes been noted that family law has historically been the least amenable to legal realism and has been the most preoccupied with conscious creation of the symbolism of family life (Melton, 1987; Melton and Wilcox, 1989).

Certainly, the cases discussed in this article show some attempt to develop a more "realistic" view of family relationships. Nevertheless, it is clear that "realism," in the context of family law, requires a fundamental reordering of rather basic concepts of American kinship. This may be harder to accomplish than in other areas of law, where realism has triumphed. As this article has shown, the categories of nature and culture remain prime symbolic vehicles through which issues of family and kinship are addressed. "Adjudication," as Fiss puts it, "is interpretation . . . it is neither wholly discretionary nor . . . wholly mechanical" (Fiss, 1988). Judges will continue to bend and shape these categories, but they are not so easily abandoned. Judges will continue to make use of the cultural tools at hand to craft legal decisions.

NOTES

1. By family law, I mean the entire body of law which defines the rights and duties of kin. These laws may fall under the gloss of family law, domestic relations law, estate law, the law of wills, etc.

2. The following paragraphs constitute an extended dialogue with Schneider's text.

3. My use of the term symbol follows that of Clifford Geertz (1973). As to the specific issue of the symbolism of law, I take the view that law makes use of ideas and concepts that cut across all forms of social action, although in some societies law also makes use of a rather specialized vocabulary. For a fuller discussion of these issues see Geertz (1983) and Rosen (1989).

4. It is important to note that legal proceedings in the United States are shaped primarily by the parties to the issue and not the Court. Each side, plaintiff and defendant, comes to court with various theories as to why he or she should prevail. The theories must be offered by the parties themselves and the court will usually not substitute its own theories for those of the litigants. Moreover, litigants may present alternative and even inconsistent theories. The litigants usually try to present as many theories as possible under which their side could prevail. The Court will normally have the opportunity to choose among a variety of legal justifications for its decision.

REFERENCES

Barnes, J. A. (1977). "Genetrix:genitor::nature:culture?", in J. Goody (Ed.), *The character of kinship*, Cambridge: Cambridge University Press.

Fiss, Owen (1988). "Objectivity and interpretation," in S. Levinson & S. Maillauz (Eds.) *Interpreting law and literature* (pp. 229–249) Evanston: Northwestern University Press.

Friedman, Lawrence (1985). *A history of American law* (pp. 688–89). New York: Simon and Schuster.

Geertz, Clifford (1973). *The interpretation of culture*. New York: Basic Books.

Geertz, Clifford (1983). Local knowledge: fact and law in comparative perspective, in his *Local Knowledge* (pp. 167–234). New York: Basic Books.

Johnson, C. E., Klee, L., and Schmidt, C. (1988). Conceptions of parenthood and kinship among children of divorce. *American Anthropologist*, 90:136–144.

Melton, Gary B. (1987). The clashing of symbols: prelude to child and family policy, *American Psychologist*, 42:345–54.

Melton, Gary B. and Wilcox, Brian (1989). Changes in family law and family life, *American Psychologist* 44:1213–1216.

Mydans, Seth. Surrogate denied custody of child. (1990, October 23) *New York Times* p. A-14.

Ortner, Sherry (1974). Is female to male as nature is to culture?, in M. Rosaido and L. Lamphere (Eds.), *Women, culture and society*, Stanford: Stanford University Press.

Rosen, Lawrence (1989). *The anthropology of justice*. Cambridge: Cambridge University Press.

Rule, Sheila. Rights for gay couples in Denmark. (1989, October 2) *New York Times* p. A-19.

Schneider, David (1980). *American kinship: a cultural account*. Chicago: University of Chicago Press.

LIST OF CASES

In re *Alison D.* v. *Virginia M.*, (1990, March 9) *New York Law Journal*, p. 21

Bowers v. *Hardwick*, 478 U.S. 186, 197 (1985)

Braschi v. *Stahl Associates Co.*, 74 N.Y. 2d 201 (1989)

The Estate of Steven Szabo, (1990, July 16) *New York Law Journal*, p. 31

R E A D I N G

5

Chasing the Blood Tie: Surrogate Mothers, Adoptive Mothers, and Fathers

HELENA RAGONÉ

An election that's about ideas and values is also about philosophy, and I have one. At the bright center is the individual, and radiating out from him or her is the family, the essential unit of closeness and love. For it's the family that communicates to our children, to the 21st century, our culture, our religious faith, our traditions, and our history. —George Bush, Presidential Nomination Acceptance Speech, 1989

In the wake of publicity created by the Baby M Case,[1] it seems unlikely that any in the United States can have remained unfamiliar with surrogate motherhood or have yet to form an opinion. The Baby M Case raised, and ultimately left unanswered, many questions about what constitutes motherhood, fatherhood, family reproduction, and kinship. Much of what has been written about surrogate motherhood has, however, been largely speculative or polemical in nature; it ranges from the view that surrogate motherhood is symptomatic of the dissolution of the American family[2] and the sanctity of motherhood, to charges that it reduces or assigns women to a breeder class structurally akin to prostitution (Dworkin 1978), or that it constitutes a form of commercial baby selling (Annas 1988; Neuhaus 1988).

In recent years a plethora of studies on reproduction has emerged in the field of anthropology (Browner 1986; Delaney 1986; 1991; Dolgin 1993; Ginsburg 1987, 1989; Martin 1987; Modell 1989; Newman 1985; Ragoné 1991, 1994; Rapp 1987, 1988, 1990; Scrimshaw 1978; Strathern 1991, 1992a, 1992b).[3] Not since the "virgin birth" controversy have so many theorists turned their attention to the subject (Leach 1967; Spiro 1968). Many of these studies represent a response to the interest generated by the emergence of what are collectively called assisted reproductive technologies, such as in vitro fertilization, surrogate motherhood, amniocentesis, and ultrasound. Much of the relevant research examines how these technologies are affecting the relationship between "Procreative beliefs and the wider context (worldview, cosmology, and culture)" (Delaney 1986:495), as exemplified by concepts and definitions of personhood and knowledge (Strathern 1991, 1992a). There nevertheless remains a paucity of

From: *Situated Lives: Gender and Culture in Everyday Life* edited by Louise Lamphere, Helena Ragoné and Patricia Zavella. Copyright 1997. Published by Routledge.

ethnographic material about these technologies—in particular about surrogate motherhood, the subject of this article, which is based on fieldwork conducted at three different surrogate mother programs from 1988 to the present.

Historically there have been three profound shifts in the Western conceptualization of the categories of conception, reproduction, and parenthood. The first occurred in response to the separation of intercourse from reproduction through birth control methods (Snowden and Snowden 1983), a precedent that may have paved the way for surrogate motherhood in the 1980s (Andrews 1984:xiii). A second shift occurred in response to the emergence of assisted reproductive technologies and to the subsequent fragmentation of the unity of reproduction, when it became possible for pregnancy to occur without necessarily having been "preceded by sexual intercourse" (Snowden and Snowden 1983:5). The third shift occurred in response to further advances in reproductive medicine that called into question the "organic unity of fetus and mother" (Martin 1987:20). It was not, however, until the emergence of reproductive medicine that the fragmentation of motherhood became a reality; with that historical change, what was once the "single figure of the mother is dispersed among several potential figures, as the functions of maternal procreation— aspects of her physical parenthood—become dispersed" (Strathern 1991:32). As will be shown in the following section, the a priori acceptance of surrogates' stated motivations has often produced an incomplete profile of surrogate mothers.

SURROGATE MOTIVATIONS

When I began my field research in 1988, surrogate mother programs and directors had already become the subject of considerable media attention, a great deal of it sensationalized and negative in character. At that time there were ten established surrogate mother programs in the United States; in addition, there were also a number of small, part-time businesses (none of which were included in the study) in which lawyers, doctors, adoption agents, and others arranged occasional surrogate mother contracts.[4] In order to obtain as stable a sample as possible, I chose to include only firmly established programs in my study. The oldest of the programs was established in approximately 1980, and none of the programs included in my study had been in business for fewer than ten years as of 1994.

There are two types of surrogate mother programs: what I call "open" programs, in which surrogate and couple select one another and interact throughout the insemination and the pregnancy, and "closed" program, in which couples select their surrogates from information—biological and medical information and a photograph of the surrogate—provided to them by the programs. After the child is born in a "closed" program, the couple and surrogate meet only to finalize the stepparent adoption.[5] I formally interviewed a total of 28 surrogates, from six different programs. Aside from these formal interviews I also engaged in countless conversations with surrogates, observing

them as they interacted with their families, testified before legislative committees, worked in surrogate programs, and socialized at program gatherings with
directors and others. Quite often I was an invited guest at the homes of program
directors, a situation that provided me with a unique opportunity to observe
directors interacting with their own spouses and children, with couples and
surrogates, and with members of their staffs. The opportunity to observe the
daily working of the surrogate mother programs provided me with invaluable
data on the day-to-day operations of the programs. At one program, I attended
staff meetings on a regular basis and observed consultations in which prospective couples and surrogates were interviewed singly by members of the staff such
as the director, a psychologist, a medical coordinator, or the administrative coordinator.

A review of the literature on surrogate motherhood reveals that, until now,
the primary research focus has been on the surrogate mother herself, and that
there have been no ethnographic studies on surrogate mother programs and
commissioning couples. Studies of the surrogate population tend to focus, at
times exclusively, on surrogates' stated motivations for becoming surrogate
mothers (Parker 1983). Their stated reasons include the desire to help an infertile couple start a family, financial remuneration, and a love of pregnancy
(Parker 1983:140). As I began my own research I soon observed a remarkable
degree of consistency or uniformity in surrogates' responses to questions about
their initial motivations for becoming surrogates; it was as if they had all been
given a script in which they espoused many of the motivations earlier catalogued
by Parker, motivations that also, as I will show, reflect culturally accepted ideas
about reproduction, motherhood, and family and are fully reinforced by the
programs.[6] I also began to uncover several areas of conflict between professed
motivations and actual experiences, discovering, for example, that although
surrogates claim to experience "easy pregnancies" and "problem-free labor," it
was not unusual for surrogates to have experienced miscarriages, ectopic pregnancies, and related difficulties, as the following examples reveal. Jeannie, age
36, divorced with one child and employed in the entertainment industry,
described the ectopic pregnancy she experienced while she was a surrogate in
this manner: "I almost bled to death: I literally almost died for my couple."
Nevertheless, she was again inseminating a second time for the same couple. As
this and other examples demonstrate, even when their experiences are at odds
with their stated motivations, surrogates tend not to acknowledge inconsistencies between their initially stated motivations and their subsequent experiences.
This reformulation of motivation is seen in the following instance as well. Fran,
age 27, divorced with one child and working as a dog trainer, described the difficulty of her delivery in this way: "I had a rough delivery, a C-section, and my
lung collapsed because I had the flu, but it was worth every minute of it. If I were
to die from childbirth, that's the best way to die. You died for a cause, a good
one." As both these examples illustrate, some surrogates readily embrace the
idea of meaningful suffering, heroism, or sacrifice, and although their stated
motivations are of some interest they do not adequately account for the range of
shifting motivations uncovered in my research.

One of the motivations most frequently assumed to be primary by the casual observer is remuneration, and I took considerable pains to try to evaluate its influence on surrogates. In the programs, surrogates receive between $10,000 and $15,000 (for three to four months of insemination and nine months of pregnancy, on average), a fee that has changed only nominally since the early 1980s.[7] As one program psychologist explained, the amount paid to surrogates is intentionally held at an artificially low rate by the programs so as to screen out women who might be motivated solely by monetary gain. One of the questions I sought to explore was whether surrogates were denying the importance of remuneration in order to cast their actions in a more culturally acceptable light, or whether they were motivated in part by remuneration and in part by other factors (with the importance of remuneration decreasing as the pregnancy progresses, the version of events put forth by both program staff and surrogates).

The opinion popular among both scholars and the general population, that surrogates are motivated primarily by financial gain, has tended to result in oversimplified analyses of surrogate motivations. The following are typical of surrogate explanations for the connection between the initial decision to become a surrogate and the remuneration they receive. Dismissals of the idea that remuneration serves as a primary source of motivation for surrogates of the kind expressed by Fran were frequent: "It [surrogacy] sounded so interesting and fun. The money wasn't enough to be pregnant for nine months."

Andrea, age 29, was married with three children. A high school graduate who worked as a motel night auditor, she expressly denied the idea that remuneration motivates most surrogates. As she said here, "I'm not doing it for the money. Take the money: that wouldn't stop me. It wouldn't stop the majority."

Sara, age 27, who attended two years of college, was married with two children and worked part-time as a tax examiner. Here she explains her feelings about remuneration:

> What's 10,000 bucks? You can't even buy a car. If it was just for the money you will want the baby. Money wasn't important. I possibly would have done it just for expenses, especially for the people I did it for. My father would have given me the money not to do it.

The issue of remuneration proved to be of particular interest in that, although surrogates do accept monetary compensation for their reproductive work, its role is a multifaceted one. The surrogate pregnancy, unlike a traditional pregnancy, is viewed by the surrogate and her family as work; as such, it is informed by the belief that work is something that occurs only within the context of paid occupations (Ferree 1984:72). It is interesting to note that surrogates rarely spend the money they earn on themselves. Not one of the surrogates I interviewed spent the money she earned on herself alone; the majority spend it on their children—as a contribution to their college education funds, for example—while others spend it on home improvement, gifts for their husbands, a family vacation, or simply to pay off "family debts."

One of the primary reasons that most surrogates do not spend the money they earn on themselves alone appears to stem from the fact that the money serves as a buffer against and/or reward to their families—in particular to their husbands, who make a number of compromises as a result of the surrogate arrangement. One of these compromises is obligatory abstention from sexual intercourse with their wives from the time insemination begins until a pregnancy has been confirmed (a period of time that lasts on average from three to four months in length, but that may be extended for as long as one year).

Surrogacy is viewed by surrogates as a part-time job in the sense that it allows a woman, especially a mother, to stay at home—to have, as one surrogate noted, "the luxury of staying home with my children," an idea that is also attractive to their husbands. The fact that a surrogate need not leave home on a routine basis or in any formalized way to earn money is perceived by the surrogate and her husband as a benefit; the surrogate, however, consequently spends less time with her family as a result of a new schedule that includes medical appointments, therapy sessions, social engagements with the commissioning couple. Thus surrogates are able to use the monetary compensation they receive as a means of procuring their husbands' support when and if they become less available to the family because of their employment.

The devaluation of the amount of the surrogate payment by surrogates as insufficient to compensate for "nine months of pregnancy" serves several important purposes. First, this view is representative of the cultural belief that children are "priceless" (Zelizer 1985); in this sense surrogates are merely reiterating a widely held cultural belief when they devalue the amount of remuneration they receive. When, for example, the largest and one of the most well-established surrogate mother programs changed the wording of its advertising copy from "Help an Infertile Couple" to "Give the Gift of Life," the vastly increased volume of response revealed that the program had discovered a successful formula with which to reach the surrogate population. With surrogacy, the gift is conceptualized as a child, a formulation that is widely used in Euro-American culture-for example, in blood (Titmuss 1971) and organ donation (Fox and Swazey 1992).

The gift formulation holds particular appeal for surrogates because it reinforces the idea that having a child for someone is an act that cannot be compensated for monetarily. As I have already mentioned, the "gift of life" theme is further enhanced by some surrogates to embrace the near-sacrifice of their own lives in childbirth.

Fran, whose dismissal of the importance of payment I have already quoted, also offered another, more revealing account of her decision to become a surrogate mother: "I wanted to do the ultimate thing for somebody, to give them the ultimate gift. Nobody can beat that, nobody can do anything nicer for them." Stella, age 38, married with two children, noted that the commissioning couples "consider it [the baby] a gift and I consider it a gift." Carolyn, age 33, married with two children and the owner of a house-cleaning company, discussed her feelings about remuneration and having a surrogate child in these terms: "It's a gift of love. I have always been a really giving person, and it's the ultimate way to give. I've always had babies so easily. It's the ultimate gift of love."

As we can see, when surrogates characterize the child they reproduce for couples as a "gift," they are also suggesting tacitly that mere monetary compensation would never be sufficient to repay the debt incurred. Although this formulation may at first appear to be a reiteration of the belief that children are culturally priceless, it also suggests that surrogates recognize that they are creating a state of enduring solidarity between themselves and their couples-precisely as in the practice of exogamy, where the end result is "more profound than the result of other gift transactions, because the relationship established is not just one of reciprocity, but one of kinship" (Rubin 1975:172). As Rubin summarizes Mauss's pioneering work on this subject, "The significance of gift giving is that [it] expresses, affirms, or creates a social link between the partners of exchange . . . confers upon its participants a special relationship of trust, solidarity and mutual aid" (1975:172).

Thus when surrogates frame the equation as one in which a gift is being proffered, the theme serves as a counterpoint to the business aspect of the arrangement, a reminder to them and to the commissioning couple that one of the symbolically central functions of money—the "removal of the personal element from human relationships through it(s) indifferent and objective nature" (Simmel 1978:297)—may be insufficient to erase certain kinds of relationships, and that the relational element may continue to surface despite the monetary exchange.

This formation of surrogacy as a matter of altruism versus remuneration has also proved to be a pivotal issue in legislative debates and discussions. Jan Sutton, the founder and spokeswoman of the National Association of Surrogate Mothers (a group of more than 100 surrogates who support legislation in favor of surrogacy), stated in her testimony before an information-gathering session of the California state legislature in 1989: "My organization and its members would all still be surrogates if no payment was involved" (Ragoné 1989). Her sentiment is not unrepresentative of those expressed by the surrogates interviewed for this study. Interestingly enough, once Sutton had informed the committee of that fact, several of the members of the panel who had previously voiced their opposition to surrogacy in its commercial form began to express praise for Sutton, indicating that her testimony had altered their opinion of surrogacy.

In direct response to her testimony, the committee began instead to discuss a proposal to ban commercial surrogacy but to allow for the practice of noncommercial surrogacy. In the latter practice the surrogate is barred from receiving financial compensation for her work, although physicians and lawyers involved are allowed their usual compensation for services rendered. In Britain, where commercial surrogacy has been declared illegal, the issue was framed often in moral terms: "The symbol of the pure surrogate who creates a child for love was pitted against the symbol of the wicked surrogate who prostitutes her maternity" (Cannell 1990:683). This dichotomous rendering in which "pure" surrogates are set in opposition to "wicked" surrogates is predicated on the idea that altruism precludes remuneration. In the Baby M Case, for example, the most decisive issue was the one concerning payment to the surrogate (Hull 1990:155).

Although surrogates overwhelmingly cast their actions in a traditional light, couching the desire to become a surrogate in conservative and traditionally feminine terms, it is clear that in many respects surrogate motherhood represents a departure from traditional motherhood. It transforms private motherhood into public motherhood, and it provides women with remuneration for their reproductive work—work that has in American culture been done, as Schneider has noted, for "love" rather than for "money" (Schneider 1968). It is this aspect that has unintendedly become one of the primary foci of consideration in state legislatures throughout the United States. Of the 15 states that now have surrogacy laws in place, the "most common regulations, applicable in 11 states . . . are statutes voiding paid surrogacy contracts" (Andrews 1992:50). The overwhelming acceptance of the idea of unpaid or noncommercial surrogacy (both in the United States and in Britain) can be attributed to the belief that it "duplicates maternity in culturally the most self-less manner" (Strathern 1991:31).

But what is perhaps even more important, the corresponding rejection of paid or commercial surrogacy may also be said to result from a cultural resistance to conflating the symbolic value of the family with the world of work to which it has long been held in opposition. From a legal perspective, commercial surrogacy has been viewed largely by the courts as a matter of "merg[ing] the family with the world of business and commerce" (Dolgin 1993:692), a prospect that presents a challenge to American cultural definitions in which the family has traditionally represented "the antithesis of the market relations of capitalism; it is also sacralized in our minds as the last stronghold against the state, as the symbolic refuge from the intrusion of a public domain that consistently threatens our sense of privacy and self determination" (Collier et al. 1982:37).

Resistance in U.S. society to merging these two realms, the domestic and the public, may be traced to the entrenched belief that the

> private realm [is] where women are most in evidence, where natural functions like sex and bodily functions related to procreation take place, where the affective content of relations is primary and [thatl a public realm [is] where men are most in evidence, where culture is produced, where one's efficiency at producing goods or services takes precedence. [Martin 1987:15–16]

With the introduction of the phenomenon of public motherhood in the form of surrogacy, however, the separation of family and work has been irrevocably challenged. Over time it became clear to me that many of the women who chose to become surrogate mothers did so as a way to transcend the limitations of their domestic roles as wives, mothers, and homemakers while concomitantly attesting to the importance of those roles and to the satisfaction they derived from them. That idea indeed accounted for some of their contradictory statements. Surrogates, who are for the most part from predominantly working-class backgrounds, have, for example, often been denied access to prestigious roles and other avenues for attaining status and power. Surrogacy thus provides them with confirmation that motherhood is important and socially valued.[8] Surrogacy also introduces them to a world filled with social interaction with people who are deeply appreciative of the work that they do, and in this way surrogates receive validation and are rewarded for their reproductive work through their participation in this new form of public motherhood.

Of all the surrogates' stated motivations, remuneration proved to be the most problematic.[9] On a symbolic level, remuneration detracts from the idealized cultural image of women/mothers as selfless, nurturant, and altruistic, an image that surrogates have no wish to alter. Then, too, if surrogates were to acknowledge money as adequate compensation for their reproductive work, they would lose the sense that theirs is a gift that transcends all monetary compensation.[10] The fact that some surrogates had experienced difficult pregnancies and deliveries and were not thereby dissuaded from becoming surrogate mothers, coupled with their devaluation of remuneration and their tendency to characterize the child as a gift, suggested that current theories about surrogate motivations provided only a partial explanation for what was clearly a more complex phenomenon.

From the moment she places a telephone call to a surrogate mother program to the moment she delivers the child, the balance of power in a surrogate's personal life is altered radically. Her time can no longer be devoted exclusively to the care and nurture of her own family because she has entered into a legal and social contract to perform an important and economically rewarded task: helping an infertile couple to begin a family of their own. Unlike other types of employment, this activity cannot be regarded as unfeminine, selfish, or nonnurturant. As I have previously mentioned, the surrogate's husband must sign a consent form in which he agrees to abstain from sexual intercourse with his wife until a pregnancy has been confirmed. In so doing he agrees to relinquish both his sexual and procreative ties to his wife and thus is understood to be supporting his wife's decision to conceive and gestate another man's child (or another couple's child, in the case of gestational surrogacy). Once a surrogate enters a program, she also begins to recognize just how important having a child is to the commissioning couple. She sees with renewed clarity that no matter how much material success the couple has, their lives are emotionally impoverished because of their inability to have a child. In this way the surrogate's fertility serves as a leveling device for perceived, if unacknowledged, economic differences—and many surrogates begin to see themselves as altruistic or heroic figures who can rectify the imbalance in a couple's life.

FATHERS, ADOPTIVE MOTHERS, AND SURROGATE MOTHERS

Studies on surrogate motherhood have tended to characterize the couple's motivations as lacking in complexity; in other words, it is assumed that the primary motivation is to have a child that is biologically related to at least one member of the couple (in this case the father and, in the case of donor insemination, the mother) (Glover 1990). A tendency on the part of earlier researchers to accept this theory at face value may be said to stem from the influence of Euro-American kinship ideology, particularly from its emphasis on the centrality of biogenetic relatedness, and perhaps secondarily from the fact that researchers have not had ready access to this population. Biological relatedness thus continues to be accepted as a given, "one way of grounding the distinctiveness of kin relations . . . the natural facts of life that seem to lie prior to everything else" (Strathern 1992a:19).[11]

While genetic relatedness is clearly one of the primary motivations for couples' choice of surrogate motherhood, this view is something of a simplification unless one also acknowledges that surrogacy contradicts several cultural norms, not the least of which is that it involves procreation outside marriage. The case of surrogate motherhood requires that we go beyond the parameters that until now have delineated domains such as reproduction and kinship, to "pursue meaning[s] where they lead" (Delaney 1986:496). Although couples may be motivated initially by a desire to have a child that is biologically related to at least one of the partners, the fact that this can be achieved only by employing the services of a woman other than the wife introduces a host of dilemmas.

Fathers and adoptive mothers resolve the problems posed by surrogate motherhood through various and separate strategies. Their disparate concerns stem not only from the biogenetic relationship the father bears to the child and from the adoptive mother's lack of such a relationship, but also from the pressures of having to negotiate the landscape of this novel terrain. For the father the primary obstacle or issue posed by surrogate motherhood is that a woman other than his wife will be the "mother" of his child. The following quotations from fathers illustrate the considerable degree of ambiguity created by surrogate motherhood. They also reveal the couples' shared assumptions about American kinship ideology and how it is that "biological elements have primarily symbolic significance . . . [whose] meaning is not biology at all" (Schneider 1972:45).

Tom and his wife, for example, had experienced 17 years of infertility. Initially opposed to surrogate motherhood out of concern that his wife would feel "left out," Tom described his early reactions: "Yes, the whole thing was at first strange. I thought to myself; here she [the surrogate] is carrying my baby. Isn't she supposed to be my wife?"

Ed, a 45-year-old college professor, described a similar sense of confusion: "I felt weird about another woman carrying my child, but as we all got to know one another it didn't seem weird. It seemed strangely comfortable after a while."

Richard, age 43, a computer engineer, described similar feelings of awkwardness about the child's biological tie to the surrogate:

> Seeing Jane [the surrogate] in him [his son], it's literally a part of herself she gave. That's fairly profound. I developed an appreciation of the magnitude of what she did and the inappropriateness of approaching this as a business relationship. It didn't seem like such a big thing initially for another woman to carry my baby, a little awkward in not knowing how to relate to her and not wanting to interfere with her relationship with her husband. But after Tommy was born I can see Jane in his appearance and I had a feeling it was a strange thing we did not to have a relationship with Jane. But it's wearing off, and I'm not struck so much with: I've got a piece of Jane here.

Questions such as Tom's "Isn't she supposed to be my wife?" reflect the concern and confusion experienced by husbands, their ambivalence underscoring the continued symbolic centrality of sexual intercourse and procreation in

American kinship, both of which continue to symbolize unity and love (Schneider 1968). The father's relationship to the surrogate, although strictly noncoital, is altered by the fact that it produces what was always, until the recent past, the product of a sexual union—namely, a child. Feelings of discomfort or "awkwardness," and concerns as to how to behave toward the surrogate and the surrogate's husband, stem from the idea that the father-surrogate relationship may be considered adultery by those unfamiliar with the particulars of the surrogate arrangement. For example, one program reported that a client from the Middle East arrived at the program office with the expectation that he would engage in sexual intercourse with the surrogate. One surrogate remarked on this ambivalence: "The general public thinks I went to bed with the father. They think I committed adultery!"

In addition to concerns about his relationship to the surrogate vis-a-vis the child, a father is aware that the child bears no genetic tie to his wife. The husband thus gains his inclusivity in the surrogate relationship through his biological contribution vis-a-vis the surrogate: he is both the genitor and pater; but it is the surrogate, not his wife, who is the genetrix. One of the primary strategies employed by both couples and surrogates is to deemphasize the husband's role precisely because it is the surrogate-father relationship that raises the specter of adultery or, more accurately, temporary polygandry and temporary polygyny. They also downplay the significance of his biological link to the child, focusing instead on the bond that develops between the adoptive and the surrogate mother.

THE SURROGATE AND ADOPTIVE MOTHER BOND

The adoptive mother attempts to resolve her lack of genetic relatedness to the child through what I have labeled her "mythic conception" of the child—that is, the notion that her desire to have a child is what first makes the surrogate arrangement a possibility. Cybil, an adoptive mother, explained the mythic conception in this way: "Ann is my baby; she was conceived in my heart before Lisa's [the surrogate's] body." Lucy, an adoptive mother, described the symbiotic relationship that developed between herself and her surrogate in a slightly different way: "She [the surrogate] represented that part of me that couldn't have a child."

The adoptive mother also experiences what can be described as a "pseudo-pregnancy" through which she experiences the state of pregnancy by proxy as close to the experience as an infertile woman can be. As one surrogate said of this relationship, "I had a closeness with Sue [the adoptive mother] that you would have with your husband. She took Lamaze class and went to the delivery room with me." In fact, when geographical proximity permits, it is expected in the open programs that adoptive mothers will accompany surrogates to all medical appointments and birthing classes, in addition to attending the delivery of the child in the hospital (where the biological father and the surrogate's husband are also present whenever possible).

Together, the surrogate and the adoptive mother thus define reproduction as "women's business," often reiterating the idea that their relationship is a natural and exclusive one. As Celeste, a surrogate mother, pointed out: "The whole miracle of birth would be lost if she [the adoptive mother] wasn't there. If women don't experience the birth of their children being born they would be alienated and they would be breeders." Mary, a surrogate whose adoptive mother gave her a heart-shaped necklace to commemorate the birth of the child, said, "I feel a sisterhood to all women of the world. I am doing this for her, looking to see her holding the baby."[12] Both of the adoptive mother's strategies, her mythic conception of the child and her pseudopregnancy, are—as these quotations demonstrate—greatly facilitated by the surrogate, who not only deemphasizes the importance of her physical pregnancy but also disavows the importance of her own biological link to the child. Celeste summed up the sentiment expressed by many surrogates when she stated, "She [the adoptive mother] was emotionally pregnant, and I was just *physically pregnant*" (emphasis added).

Without exception, when surrogates are asked whether they think of the child as their own, they say that they do not.[13] Kay, a surrogate, age 35 and divorced with two children, explained her feelings in this way: "I never think of the child as mine. After I had the baby, the mother came into the room and held the baby. I couldn't relate that it had any part of me."

Mary, age 37, married with three children, similarly stated, "I don't think of the baby as my child. I donated an egg I wasn't going to be using." Jeannie, yet another surrogate, described herself as having no connection to the child: "I feel like a vehicle, just like a cow; it's their baby, it's his sperm."

The surrogate's ability to deemphasize her own biological link to the child is made possible in part by her focus upon the folk theory of procreation in which paternity is viewed as the "primary, essential and creative role" (Delaney 1986:495). Even though in the realm of scientific knowledge women have long been identified as cocreators, "in Europe and America, the knowledge has not been encompassed symbolically. Symbols change slowly and the two levels of discourse are hardly ever brought into conjunction" (Delaney 1986:509).

With the "dominant folk theory of procreation in the West," paternity has been conceptualized as the "power to create and engender life" (Delaney 1986:510), whereas maternity has come to mean "giving nurturance and giving birth" (Delaney 1986:495). Surrogates, therefore, emphasize the importance of nurturance and consistently define that aspect of motherhood as a choice that one can elect to make or not make. This emphasis on nurturance is embraced readily by the surrogate and adoptive mother alike since "one of the central notions in the modern American construct of the family is that of nurturance" (Collier et al. 1982:34). In the United States nurturance until now has been considered "natural to women and [the] basis of their cultural authority" (Ginsburg 1987:629). Like other kinds of assisted reproduction, surrogate motherhood is understood to "fall into older cultural terrains, where women interpret their options in light of prior and contradictory meanings of pregnancy and childbearing" (Rapp 1990:41).

For this reason surrogates underplay their own biological contribution in order to bring to the fore the importance of the social, nurturant role played by the adoptive mother. The efforts of surrogates and adoptive mothers to separate social motherhood from biological motherhood can be seen to represent a reworking of the nature/culture dichotomy. A primary strategy an adoptive mother may employ in order to resolve her lack of genetic relatedness to the child is her use of the idea of intentionality, specifically of "conception in the heart"—that is, the idea that in the final analysis it is the adoptive mother's desire to have a child that brings the surrogate arrangement into being and ultimately results in the birth of a child. The surrogate thus devalues her own genetic/physical contribution while highlighting the pseudopregnancy of the adoptive mother and the importance of the latter's role as nurturer. In this way motherhood is reinterpreted as primarily an important social role in order to sidestep problematic aspects of the surrogate's biogenetic relationship to the child and the adoptive mother's lack of a biogenetic link. This focus upon intentionality and nurturance by both surrogates and adoptive mothers is reflected in the following statement by Andy, a 39-year-old surrogate, who is the mother of two children and a full-time nurse:

> Parents are the ones who raise the child. I got that from my parents, who adopted children. My siblings were curious and my parents gave them the information they had and they never wanted to track down their biological parents. I don't think of the baby as mine; *it is the parents, the ones who raise the child*, that are important (emphasis added).

The adoptive mother and father of the child attempt to resolve the tensions inherent in the surrogate arrangement, in particular its rearrangement of boundaries through the blurring of the distinctions between pregnancy and motherhood, genetic relatedness and affective bonds, wife and mother, wife and husband, and wife and surrogate mother. The surrogate's role in achieving these goals is nevertheless essential. Through the process in which pregnancy and birth are defined as being exclusively women's business, the father's role is relegated to secondary status in the relational triangle. The surrogate plays a primary role in facilitating the adoptive mother's role as mother of the child, something that is made possible by her refusal to nurture the child to which she gives birth. In the interest of assisting this process the surrogate consistently devalues her biological contribution or genetic relationship to the child.

In this process of emphasizing the value of nurturance, surrogates describe motherhood as a role that one can adopt or refuse, and this concept of nurturance as choice is for them the single most important defining aspect of motherhood. Surrogates believe that, in the case of surrogacy, motherhood is comprised of two separable aspects: first, the biological process (insemination, pregnancy, and delivery); and second, the social process (nurturance). They reason that a woman can either choose to nurture—that is, to accept the role of social mother—or choose not to nurture, thereby rejecting the role of social mother.[14]

As we have seen, surrogates, couples, and surrogate mother programs work in concert to create a new idea of order and appropriate relations and boundaries by directing their attention to the sanctity of motherhood as it is illustrated in the surrogate and adoptive mother bond. The surrogate and adoptive mother work in unison, reinforcing one another's view that it is social rather than biological motherhood that ultimately creates a mother. Nurture, they reason together, is a far more important and central construct of motherhood than nature. The decision on the part of the surrogate not to nurture the child nullifies the value of biological motherhood, while the adoptive mother's choice to nurture activates or fully brings forth motherhood.

Because of the emphasis couples place on having a child that is biologically related to at least one partner, I was initially perplexed to learn that less than five percent of couples chose to have a paternity test performed once the child had been born (although this option is offered to every couple); surrogate contracts specifically state that the couple is under no obligation to accept the child until such a test has been performed. In view of the fact that couples spend between $40,000 and $45,000 in fees to have a child who is biologically related to them, such a lack of interest in the paternity test is initially perplexing. When asked about paternity testing, wives and husbands typically give responses such as these: "We knew she was ours from the minute we saw her," or "We decided that it really didn't matter; he was ours no matter what."

While these statements may initially appear to contradict the stated purpose of pursuing a partially biogenetic solution to childlessness, they can also be understood to fulfill two important purposes. From the wife's perspective, an element of doubt as to the child's paternity introduces a new variable that serves to equalize the issue of relatedness. The husband is of course aware that he has a decisive advantage over his wife in terms of his genetic relatedness to the child. Although paternal doubt is always present for males, in the case of surrogate motherhood paternal doubt is thereby culturally enhanced. Allowing paternal certainty to remain a mystery represents an attempt to redress symbolically the imbalance created between wife and husband through the surrogate arrangement. Before the advent of these reproductive technologies, the "figure of the mother provided a natural model for the social construction of the 'natural' facts" (Strathern 1991:5); motherhood was seen as a single, unified experience, combining both the social and biological aspects—unlike fatherhood, in which the father acquired a "double identity." With the separation of the social and biological elements, however, motherhood has, in the context of surrogacy, also acquired this double identity (Strathern 1991:4-5). In this way, surrogate motherhood thus produces the "maternal counterpart to the double identity of the father, certain in one mode and uncertain in another" (Strathern 1991:4).

All the participants in the surrogate motherhood triad work to downplay the importance of biological relatedness as it pertains to women. They tend to reinforce the idea of motherhood as nurturance so that the adoptive mother's inability to give birth or become a genetrix (both wife and mother) is of diminished importance. At the same time, the husband's relationship to the surrogate vis-a-vis the child, and his biological relationship to the child, is also deemphasized. The idea that the adoptive mother is a mother by virtue of her role as nurturer is frequently echoed by all parties concerned. In this sense motherhood, as it pertains to surrogacy, is redefined as a social role. This occludes the somewhat problematic issues of the surrogate's biogenetic relationship to the child and the adoptive mother's lack of such a relationship.

Thus the decision not to have a paternity test performed provides additional reinforcement for the idea of parenthood as a social construct rather than a biological phenomenon. The importance of the bond that develops between the surrogate and the adoptive mother is twofold: it merges the adoptive mother (or mater) and the surrogate (or genetrix) into one by reinforcing and maintaining the unity of experience, erasing the boundaries that surrogacy creates; and, at the same time, it establishes and maintains new boundaries as they are needed between surrogate and father.

I have attempted here to show that surrogates' stated motivations for choosing surrogate motherhood represent only one aspect of a whole complex of motivations. While surrogates do, as they say, enjoy being pregnant, desire to help an infertile couple to start a family of their own, and value the compensation they receive, there are other equally good—if not more—compelling reasons that motivate this unique group of women to become surrogate mothers. Biological relatedness is both the initial motivation for and the ultimate goal of surrogacy, and it is also that facet of surrogacy that makes it most consistent with the biogenetic basis of American kinship ideology. Nevertheless, it must be deemphasized—even devalued—by all the participants in order to make surrogacy consistent with American cultural values about appropriate relations between wives and husbands. In addition to broadening the scope of our understanding about the motivations of the couples who choose to pursue a surrogate solution, I hope that this article has illuminated the complexity of the couples' decision-making process as well as their motivation.

As we have seen, surrogates as a group tend to highlight only those aspects of surrogacy that are congruent with traditional values such as the importance of family. Like the couples, they also tend to deemphasize those aspects of the surrogate relationship that represent a departure from conventional beliefs about motherhood, reproduction, and the family. Interspersed with surrogates' assertions that surrogate motherhood is merely an extension of their conventional female roles as mother, however, are frequent interjections about the unique nature of what they are doing. The following quotation, for example, reflects surrogates' awareness of the radical, unusual, and adventurous nature of their actions: "Not everyone can do it. It's like the steelworkers who walk on beams ten floors up. Not everyone can do it; not everyone can be a surrogate."

It is thus not surprising, in view of their socialization, their life experiences, and their somewhat limited choices, that surrogates claim that it is their love of children, pregnancy and family, and their desire to help others that motivates them to become surrogates. To do otherwise would be to acknowledge that there may be inconsistencies within, and areas of conflict between, their traditional female roles as wives, mothers, and homemakers and their newfound public personae as surrogate mothers.

In conclusion, it can be said that all the participants involved in the surrogacy process wish to attain traditional ends, and are therefore willing to set aside their reservations about the means by which parenthood is attained. Placing surrogacy inside tradition, they attempt to circumvent some of the more difficult issues raised by the surrogacy process. In this way, programs and participants pick and choose among American cultural values about family, parenthood, and reproduction, now choosing biological relatedness, now nurture, according to their needs.

NOTES

This article has benefited greatly from the comments, suggestions, and encouragement of many individuals. I would like to express my gratitude to the late David Schneider for his support of my work, and for his pioneering work on American kinship without which my own research would have been considerably less complete. I would also like to thank Marilyn Strathern for her encouragement. Many thanks to my anonymous reviewers for their incisive comments. Special thanks are due also to the following individuals: Robbie Apfel, William Beeman, Carole Browner, Sarah Franklin, Lina Fruzzetti, Louise Lamphere, Lucile Newman, Rayna Rapp, Susan Scrimshaw, Bennet Simon, and June Starr.

1. A couple, Willliam and Elizabeth Stern, contracted with a surrogate, Mary Beth Whitehead, to bear a child for them because Elizabeth Stern suffered from multiple sclerosis, a condition that can be exacerbated by pregnancy. Once the child was born, however, Whitehead refused to relinquish the child to the Sterns, and in 1987, William Stern, the biological father, filed suit against Whitehead in an effort to enforce the terms of the surrogate contract. The decision of the lower court to award custody to the biological father and to permit his wife to adopt the child was overturned by the New Jersey Supreme Court, which then awarded custody to William Stern, prohibiting Elizabeth Stern from adopting the child while granting visitation rights to Mary Beth Whitehead. These decisions mirrored public opinion about surrogacy (Hull 1990:154).
2. See Rapp (1978:279) and Gordon (1988:3) for a historical analysis of the idea of the demise of the American family.
3. For a more extensive review of the literature, see, for example, Ginsburg and Rapp 1991.
4. As of 1994, only seven of the original ten are now in existence. I have changed the names of programs, surrogates, couples, and directors in order to protect their identities.
5. Over the years I have interviewed surrogates who had been employed by closed programs, interviewed the administrative assistant at the largest closed program, and spoken with program directors who arrange either a closed or open arrangement (depending upon the couple's choice). Many of the data presented in this article were collected in the open programs.
6. See, for example, Ragoné 1994 for a detailed account of the role of the surrogate mother program.
7. One of the programs has, however, recently increased its rate to $15,000. Surrogates also receive an allowance for maternity clothing, remuneration

for time lost from work (if they have employment outside of the home), and reimbursement for all babysitting fees incurred as a result of surrogate-related activities.

8. The quantifiable data reveal that surrogates are predominantly white, an average of 27 years of age, high school graduates, of Protestant or Catholic background, and married with an average of three children. Approximately 30 percent are full-time homemakers, and those surrogates who are employed outside the home tend to be employed in the service sector. A comparison of surrogate and couple statistics reveals pronounced differences in educational background, occupation, and income level. The average combined family income of commissioning couples is in excess of $100,000, as compared to $38,000 for married surrogates.

9. For example, Gullestad (1992) observed that girls who worked as babysitters in Norway tended to emphasize the extent to which their work was motivated by nurturance, deemphasizing the importance of the remuneration they received.

10. Surrogate motivations are diverse and overlapping, and surrogates express empathy for infertile couples as well as joy experienced during pregnancy.

11. Commissioning couples consistently articulate the belief that surrogacy is a superior alternative to adoption Many couples have attempted to adopt, only to discover the shortage of healthy white infants and age limit criteria of adoption agencies: see Ragoné 1994. Surrogacy not only provides them with the highly desirable partial genetic link (through the father), but it also permits them to meet and interact with the biological mother—something that is usually not possible with adoption.

12. When Robert Winston, a pioneer in assisted reproductive technologies in Britain, revealed that he had facilitated a surrogate arrangement that involved two sisters, the case tended to elicit from the public "strong and sentimental approval" (Cannell 1990:675).

13. Prospective surrogates who find themselves unwilling to dismiss their biological link to a child frequently opt for gestational surrogacy rather than abandon the idea of surrogate motherhood altogether, even though the risk of medical complication is thereby greatly increased. Over a three-year period I observed that the rate of gestational surrogacy had increased from less than five percent to close to fifty percent at the largest of the surrogate mother programs and at another well-established program. I am currently in the process of researching gestational surrogacy.

14. Giddens' theory of structuration is understood as a corrective to both the exclusively rigid structuralist worldview (which tends to eliminate agency) and phenomenologists, symbolic interactionists, and enthnomethodologists who overemphasize the plasticity of society (Baber 1991:220). Giddens has articulated the view that "all structural properties of social systems are enabling as well as constraining" (1984:177), a phenomenon that can be seen in surrogate arrangements when surrogates and couples focus upon certain elements or aspects of parenthood while deemphasizing others. The way in which these different idioms of nature and nurture are emphasized

and deemphasized also parallels and substantiates Strathern's observations (1992c) about the selective weight of nature/nurture in the kinship context.

REFERENCES

Annas, George. 1988. Fairy Tales Surrogate Mothers Tell. *In* Surrogate Motherhood: Politics and Privacy. Larry Gostin, ed. Pp. 43–55. Bloomington: Indiana University Press.

Andrews, Lori. 1984. New Conceptions A Consumer's Guide to the Newest Infertility Treatments. New York: Ballantine. 1992. Surrogacy Wars. California Lawyer 12(10): 42–49.

Baber, Zaheer. 1991. Beyond the Structure/Agency Dualism: An Evaluation of Giddens' Theory of Structuration. Sociological Inquiry 61(2):219–230

Browner, Carole. 1986. The Politics of Reproduction in a Mexican Village. Signs 11:710–724.

Cannell, Fenella. 1990. Concepts of Parenthood: The Warnock Report, the Gillick and Modern Myths. American Ethnologist 17:667–686.

Collier, Jane, Michelle Rosaldo, and Sylvia Yanagisako. 1982. Is There a Family? New Anthropological Views. *In* Rethinking the Family: Some Feminist Questions. Barrie Thorne and Marilyn Yalom, eds. Pp. 25–39. New York: Longman.

Delaney, Carol. 1986. The Meaning of Paternity and the Virgin Birth Debate. Man 24 (3):497–513. 1991. The Seed and the Soil: Gender and Cosmology in a Turkish Village Society. Berkeley: University of California Press.

Dolgin, Janet. 1993. Just a Gene: Judicial Assumptions about Parenthood. UCLA Law Review 40(3).

Dworkin, Andrea. 1978. Right-Wing Women. New York: Perigee Books.

Ferree, Myra. 1984. Sacrifice, Satisfaction and Social Change: Employment and the Family. *In* My Troubles Are Going to Have Trouble with Me. Karen Sacks and Dorothy Remy, eds. Pp. 61–79. New Brunswick, NJ: Rutgers University Press.

Fox, Reneé, and Judith Swazey. 1992. Spare Parts: Organ Replacement in American Society. Oxford: Oxford University Press.

Giddens, Anthony. 1984. The Constitution of Society. Berkeley: University of California Press.

Ginsburg, Faye. 1987. Procreation Stories: Reproduction, Nurturance and Procreation in Life Narratives of Abortion Activists. American Ethnologist 14(4):623–636. 1989. Contested Lives: The Abortion Debate in an American Community. Berkeley: University of California Press.

Ginsburg, Faye, and Rayna Rapp. 1991. The Politics of Reproduction. Annual Review of Anthropology 20:311–343.

Glover, Jonathan. 1990. Ethics of New Reproductive Technologies: The Glover Report to the European Commission. DeKalb: Northern Illinois Press.

Gordon, Linda. 1988. Heroes of Their Own Lives. New York: Viking.

Gullestad, Marianne. 1992. The Art of Social Relations. Oslo, Norway: Scandinavian Press.

Hull, Richard. 1990. Gestational Surrogacy and Surrogate Motherhood. *In* Ethical Issues in the New Reproductive Technologies. Richard Hull, ed. Pp. 150–155. Belmont, CA: Wadsworth Publishers.

Leach, Edmund R. 1967. Virgin Birth. *In* Proceedings of the Royal Anthropological Institute for 1966. Pp. 39–49. London: RAI.

Martin, Emily. 1987. The Woman in the Body: A Cultural Analysis of Reproduction. Boston: Beacon Press.

Modell, Judith. 1989. Last Chance Babies: Interpretations of Parenthood in an In Vitro Fertilization Program. Medical Anthropology Quarterly 3(2):124–138.

Neuhaus, Robert. 1988. Renting Women, Buying Babies and Class Struggles. Society 25(3):8–10.

Newman, Lucile, ed. 1985. Women's Medicine: A Cross-Cultural Study of Indigenous Fertility Regulations. New Brunswick, NJ: Rutgers University Press.

Parker, Philip. 1983. Motivation of Surrogate Mothers: Initial Findings. American Journal of Psychiatry 140:117–119.

Ragoné, Helena. 1989. Proceedings from an information-gathering committee to the California State Legislature. Unpublished notes. 1991. Surrogate Motherhood in America. Ph.D. dissertation, Brown University. 1994. Surrogate Motherhood: Conception in the Heart. Boulder, CO, and Oxford: Westview Press/Basic Books.

Rapp, Rayna. 1978. Family and Class in Contemporary America: Notes toward an Understanding of Ideology. Science and Society 42(3):278–300. 1987. Moral Pioneers: Women, Men and Fetuses on a Frontier of Reproductive Technology. Women and Health 13(1/2):101–116. 1988. Chromosomes and Communication: The Disclosure of Genetic Counseling. Medical Anthropology Quarterly 2:143–157. 1990. Constructing Amniocentesis: Maternal and Medical Discourses. *In* Uncertain Terms: Negotiating Gender in American Culture. Faye Ginsburg and Anna Lowenhaupt Tsing, eds. Pp. 28–42. Boston: Beacon Press.

Rubin, Gayle. 1975. The Traffic in Woman: Notes on the Political Economy of Sex. *In* Toward an Anthropology of Women. Rayna Reiter, ed. Pp. 157–210. New York: Monthly Review Press.

Schneider, David. 1968. American Kinship: A Cultural Account. Englewood Cliffs, NJ: Prentice Hall. 1972 What Is Kinship All About? *In* Kinship Studies in the Morgan Centennial Year. Priscilla Reining, ed. Pp. 32–63. Washington, DC: Anthropological Society of Washington.

Scrimshaw, Susan. 1978. Infant Mortality and Behavior in the Regulation of Family Size. Population Development Review 4:383–403.

Simmel, Georg. 1978. The Philosophy of Money. London: Routledge and Kegan Paul.

Snowden, R. G. Mitchell, and E. Snowden. 1983. Artificial Reproduction: A Social Investigation. London: Allen and Unwin.

Spiro, Melford. 1968 Virgin Birth, Parthenogenesis, and Physiological Paternity: An Essay in Cultural Interpretation. Man (n.s.) 3:242–261.

Strathern, Marilyn. 1991. The Pursuit of Certainty: Investigating Kinship in the Late Twentieth Century. Paper presented at the 90th American Anthropological Association Annual Meeting, Chicago. 1992a. Reproducing the Future. New York: Routledge. 1992b. The Meaning of Assisted Kinship. *In* Changing Human Reproduction. Meg Stacey, ed. Pp. 148–169. London: Sage Publications. 1992c. After Nature: English Kinship in the Late Twentieth Century. Cambridge: Cambridge University Press.

Titmuss, Richard. 1971. The Gift Relationship: From Human Blood to Social Policy. New York: Pantheon Books.

Zelizer, Vivian. 1985. Pricing the Priceless Child. New York: Basic Books.

P A R T   T W O

THE SEXES

INTRODUCTION

American society has experienced both a sexual revolution and a gender revolution. The first has liberalized attitudes toward erotic behavior and expression; the second has changed the roles and status of women and men in the direction of greater equality. Both revolutions have been brought about by the rapid social changes in recent years, and both revolutions have challenged traditional conceptions of marriage.

The traditional idea of sexuality defines sex as a powerful biological drive continually struggling for gratification against restraints imposed by civilization. The notion of sexual instincts also implies a kind of innate knowledge: A person intuitively knows his or her own identity as male or female, he or she knows how to act accordingly, and he or she is attracted to the "proper" sex object—a person of the opposite gender. In other words, the view of sex as biological drive pure and simple implies "that sexuality has a magical ability, possessed by no other capacity, that allows biological drives to be expressed directly in psychological and social behaviors" (Gagnon and Simon, 1970, p. 24).

The whole issue of the relative importance of biological versus psychological and social factors in sexuality and sex differences has been obscured by polemics. On the one hand, there are the strict biological determinists who declare that anatomy is destiny. On the other hand, there are those who argue

83

that all aspects of sexuality and sex-role differences are matters of learning and social construction.

There are two essential points to be made about the nature-versus-nurture argument. First, modern genetic theory views biology and environment as interacting, not opposing forces. Second, both biological determinists and their opponents assume that if a biological force exists, it must be overwhelmingly strong. But the most sophisticated evidence concerning both gender development *and* erotic arousal suggests that physiological forces are gentle rather than powerful. Despite all the media stories about a "gay gene" or "a gene for lung cancer," the scientific reality is more complicated. As one researcher wrote recently "they have identified a number of genes that may, under certain circumstances, make an individual more or less susceptible to the action of a variety of environmental agents" (cited in Berwick, 1998, p. 4).

In terms of scholarship, the main effect of the sex-role and sexual revolutions has been on awareness and consciousness. For example, much early social science writing was revealed to have been based on sexist assumptions. Many sociologists and psychologists took it for granted that women's roles and functions in society reflect universal physiological and temperamental traits. Since in practically every society women were subordinate to men, inequality was interpreted as an inescapable necessity of organized social life. Such analysis suffered from the same intellectual flaw as the idea that discrimination against nonwhites implies their innate inferiority. All such explanations failed to analyze the social institutions and forces producing and supporting the observed differences. In approaching the study of either the physical or the social relations between the sexes, it is therefore important to understand how traditional stereotypes have influenced both popular and professional concepts of sexuality and sex differences.

William J. Goode's article develops this theme by examining how men's views of male-female relations are shaped by their position as a dominant or "superordinate" social group, and how stereotyping influences and sets limits on male and female socialization. These limits rob both men and women of a broader potential—for example, closeness to their children for men, achievement for women. Stereotyping thus diminishes the capacity of both women and men to fulfill a broader potential than traditional sex roles dictate.

As Matthew Guttmann demonstrates in his article, gender relations are changing even in Mexico, a culture long seen as one of the most "macho." Five-year-old boys in nursery school are now willing to play with dolls; grandfathers who never changed their own children's diapers have learned how to do so for their grandchildren. Guttman links these shifts to a host of changes in society: women becoming educated and working outside the home, and the influence of the women's movement, television, and even some churches. Men and women are still far from equal, but the changes in Mexico show that even the most deeply rooted traditions of male-female relations are capable of change.

The transformation of gender is intertwined with changes in sex and marriage. In her article, Beth Bailey presents an historian's overview of the most recent sexual revolution. She finds that it was composed of at least three separate strands. First, there has been a gradual increase, over the course of the twentieth century, in sexual imagery and openness about sexual matters in the media and in public life generally. Second, in the 1960s and 1970s, premarital sex, which had always been part of dating, came to include intercourse, and even living together before or without marriage. The flamboyant sex radicals of the sixties' counter-culture were the loudest but the least numerous part of the sexual revolution.

The sexual revolution raises questions about the nature of human sexuality and the meaning of "normality." One way to look for answers is to examine the anthropological evidence. Burton Pasternak, and Carol and Melvin Ember reveal the great variation that exists in sexual attitudes and practices of different cultures around the world. Some are more permissive than the United States today, some are far more restrictive. Some regard sex as a duty, some as a pleasure, and some regard it as dangerous and fearful. Some societies deny homosexuality exists, others tolerate it, still others actually prescribe homosexual relationships between boys and older men. These authors also discuss some of the explanations anthropologists have offered to explain such widely divergent customs.

To many Americans, the recent changes in sexual norms and behavior are prime symptoms of moral decay. Public anxiety about the future of marriage, as Frank Furstenberg points out in his article, sometimes approaches hysterical levels. He argues that recent changes are not signs that marriage is disappearing or in a severe state of crisis, but that there *is* cause for concern. The traditional marriage bargain, he explains, in which women exchanged their domestic services for financial support, is no longer valid. Now that women work outside the home, they are no longer as dependent on men as they used to be. Further, most men no longer have jobs that pay enough to support a family. Both men and women say they believe in greater equality in marriage, but in practice, most women still do the lion's share of housework and child care.

While people in all walks of life are grappling with new expectations of gender equality, for many young adults with low incomes, marriage has become a luxury item. Furstenberg finds that people still value marriage, but that living together or single parenthood has become "the budget way to start a family." Restoring marriage to its former status will require moving towards a society that provides secure jobs and better child-care options.

What would a truly equal marriage look like? Are there any couples with genuinely egalitarian relationships? In her article, Pepper Schwartz reports on her study of "peer marriages"—couples who believe strongly in equality and who share the childrearing, housework, and control over money. She found that there is no single blueprint for a successful peer marriage, but keeping such a marriage going takes a lot of effort in a society that does not offer much support for these nontraditional arrangements.

Along with the sexual revolution, the sharp increase in divorce rates since the 1960s has given rise to public alarm about the future of the family, and even proposals to make divorces harder to get. But as the article by Mavis Hetherington and colleagues shows, divorce is not a single event, but a long process. It is a complex chain of events and life experiences that begins long before the divorce itself and continues long after. Although divorce is an emotionally wrenching process for all concerned, it's difficult to make blanket statements about its long-term effects. Divorce tends to be a different experience for men, women, and children; and individual reactions to it vary enormously (we discuss the impact of divorce on children in Chapter 7).

One frequent outcome of a divorce is remarriage by one or both spouses. Such remarriages generate interesting and problematic kinship structures and relationships that have scarcely been studied and for which we may not even have names. We know something about stepparents and stepchildren, but is there a difference between the way a father acts with his own children of his first marriage who live part of the time with his first wife, and the children of his second marriage who live full-time with him and his second wife? What of half-brothers and -sisters? What of the relationship between a father's first-marriage children, his second wife's first-marriage children, and the children of the second marriage? The selection by Constance R. Ahrons and Roy H. Rodgers discusses the family complexities generated by divorce and modern remarriage.

Despite all its difficulties, marriage is not likely to go out of style in the near future. Ultimately we agree with Jessie Bernard (1982), who, after a devastating critique of traditional marriage from the point of view of a sociologist who is also a feminist, said this:

> The future of marriage is as assured as any social form can be. . . . For men and women will continue to want intimacy, they will continue to want to celebrate their mutuality, to experience the mystic unity which once led the church to consider marriage a sacrament. . . . There is hardly any probability such commitments will disappear or that all relationships between them will become merely casual or transient. (p. 301)

REFERENCES

Bernard, Jessie. 1982. *The Future of Marriage*. New York: World.

Berwick, Robert C. 1998. The doors of perception. *The Los Angeles Times Book Review*. March 15.

Gagnon, J. H., and W. Simon. 1970. *The Sexual Scene*. Chicago: Aldine/Transaction.

Money, J., and A. A. Ehrhardt. 1972. *Man and Woman, Boy and Girl*. Baltimore: Johns Hopkins University Press.

◆

CHAPTER 3

CHANGING GENDER ROLES

R E A D I N G

6

Why Men Resist

WILLIAM J. GOODE

For many women, the very title of my essay is an exercise in banality, for there is no puzzle. To analyze the peculiar thoughtways of men seems unnecessary, since ultimately their resistance is that of dominant groups throughout history: they enjoy an exploitive position that yields them an unearned profit in money, power, and prestige. Why should they give it up?

That answer contains, of course, some parts of the truth, but we shall move more effectively toward equality only if we grasp much more of the truth than that bitter view reveals. If it were completely true, then the great power of men would have made all societies male-vanity cultures, in which women are kept behind blank walls and forced to work at productive tasks only with their sisters, while men laze away their hours in parasitic pleasure. In fact, one can observe that the position of women varies a good deal by class, by society, and over time, and no one has succeeded in proving that those variations are only the result of men's exploitation.

Indeed, there are inherent socioeconomic contradictions in any attempt by males to create a fully exploitative set of material advantages for all males. Moreover, there are inherent emotional contradictions in any effort to achieve full domination in that intimate sphere.

From *Rethinking the Family*, 1992. Barrie Thorne and Marilyn Yalom (Eds.). Boston: Northeastern University Press.

As to the first contradiction, women—and men, too, in the same situation, who are powerless, slavish, and ignorant are most easily exploitable, and thus there are always some male pressures to place them in that position. Unfortunately, such women (or men) do not yield much surplus product. In fact, they do not produce much at all. Women who are freer and are more in command of productive skills, as in hunting and gathering societies and increasingly in modern industrial ones, produce far more, but they are also more resistant to exploitation or domination. Without understanding that powerful relationship, men have moved throughout history toward one or the other of these great choices, with their built-in disadvantages and advantages.

As to emotional ties, men would like to be lords of their castle and to be loved absolutely—if successful, this is the cheapest exploitative system—but in real life this is less likely to happen unless one loves in return. In that case what happens is what happens in real life: men care about the joys and sorrows of the women to whom they are attached. Mutual caring reduces the degree to which men are willing to exploit their wives, mothers, and sisters. More interesting, their caring also takes the form of wanting to prevent other men from exploiting these women when they are in the outside world. That is, men as individuals know that they are to be trusted, and so should have great power, but other men cannot be trusted, and therefore the laws should restrain such fellows.

These large sets of contrary tensions have some effect on even those contemporary men who do not believe that the present relations between men and women are unjust. Both sets, moreover, support the present trend toward greater equality. In short, men do resist, but these and other tensions prevent them from resisting as fully as they might otherwise, and not so much as a cynical interpretation of their private attitudes would expect. On the other hand, they do resist somewhat more strenuously than we should predict from their public assertion in favor of, for example, equal pay, or slogans like "liberty and justice for all."

Why is that resistance so strenuous? My attempt here to answer that question is necessarily limited. Even to present the latest data on the supposed psychological traits of males would require more space than is available here. I shall try to avoid the temptation of simply describing men's reactions to the women's movement, although I do plan to inform you of men's attitudes toward some aspects of equality. I shall try to avoid defending men, except to the extent that explaining them may be a defense. And, as is already obvious, I shall not assert that we are on the brink of a profound, sudden change in sex-role allocations in the direction of equality, for we must never underestimate the cunning or the staying power of those in charge. Finally, because we are all observers of men, it is unlikely that we can bring forward many findings that are entirely unknown to you. At best, I can suggest some fruitful, perhaps new, ways of looking at male roles. Within these limitations, I shall focus on the following themes:

1. As against the rather narrow definition of men's roles to be found in the current literature on the topic, I want to remind you of a much wider range of traditionally approved roles in this and other cultures.

2. As against the conspiracy theory of the oppression of women, I shall suggest a modest "sociology of the dominant group" to interpret men's behavior and thinking about male roles and thus offer some robust hypotheses about why they resist.

3. I shall point to two central areas of role behavior, occupations and domestic tasks, where change seems glacial at present and men's resistance strong.

4. As against those who feel that if utopia does not arrive with the next full moon, we should all despair, I shall point to some processes now occurring that are different from any in recorded history and that will continue to press toward more fundamental changes in men's social positions and role in this as well as other countries of the world.

THE RANGE OF SEX ROLES

Let me begin by reminding you of the standard sociological view about the allocation of sex roles. First, although it is agreed that we can, with only small error, divide the population into males and females, the biological differences between the two that might affect the distribution of sex roles—which sex is supposed to do which social tasks, which should have which rights—are much too small to determine the large differences in sex-role allocation within any given society or to explain the curious doctrines that serve to uphold it. Second, even if some differences would give an advantage to men (or women) in some tasks or achievements, the overlap in talent is so great that a large minority of women (or men)—perhaps even a majority—could do any task as well as could members of the other sex. Third, the biological differences are too fixed in anatomy and physiology to account for the wide diversity of sex-role allocation we observe when we compare different societies over time and cultures.

Consequently, most of the sex-role allocation must be explained by how we rear children, by the sexual division of labor, by the cultural definitions of what is appropriate to the sexes, and by the social pressures we put on the two sexes to keep each in its place. Since human beings created these role assignments, they can also change them. On the other hand, these roles afford large advantages to men (e.g., opportunity, range of choices, mobility, payoffs for what is accomplished, cultivation of skills, authority, and prestige) in this and every other society we know. Consequently, men are likely to resist large alterations in roles. They will do so even though they understand that in exchange for their privileges, they have to pay high costs in morbidity, mortality, and failure.[1] As a consequence of this fact about men's position, it can be supposed that they will resist unless their ability to rig the system in their favor is somehow reduced. It is my belief that this capacity is in fact being undermined somewhat, though not at a rapid rate.

A first glance at descriptions of the male role, especially as described in the literature on mass media, social stereotypes, family roles, and personality attributes, suggests that the male role is definite, narrow, and agreed upon. Males, we are told, are pressed into a specific mold. For example, "the male role prescribes that men be active, aggressive, competitive, . . . while the female role prescribes that women should be nurturant, warm, altruistic . . . and the like."[2] The male role requires the suppression of emotion: "the male role, as personally and socially defined, requires men to appear tough, objective, striving, achieving, unsentimental. . . . If he weeps, if he shows weakness, he will likely be viewed as unmanly." Or: "Men are programmed to be strong and 'aggressive.' "[3] Those statements were published some time ago, but the flood of books since then has only elaborated that description.

We are so accustomed to reading such descriptions that we almost believe them, unless we stop to ask, first, how many men do we actually know who carry out these social prescriptions (i.e., how many are emotionally anesthetized, aggressive, physically tough and daring, unwilling or unable to give nurturance to a child)? Second, and this is the test of a social role, do they lose their membership cards in the male fraternity if they fail in these respects? If socialization and social pressures are so all-powerful, where are all the John Wayne types in our society? Or, to ask a more searching question, how seriously should we take such sex-role prescriptions if so few men live up to them? The recent creation of male groups chanting around a campfire, searching for the lost primitive hunter within each bosom, suggests that our generation can not even play the role anymore without a great deal of coaching.

The key fact is not that many men do not live up to such prescriptions; that is obvious. They never did. Rather, many other qualities and performances have always been viewed as acceptable or admirable, and this is true even among boys, who are often thought to be strong supporters of sex stereotypes. The macho boy is admired, but so is the one who edits the school newspaper, who draws cartoons, or who is simply a warm friend. There are at least a handful of ways of being an admired professor. Indeed, a common feminist complaint against the present system is that women are much more narrowly confined in the ways they are permitted to be professors, or members of any occupation.

But we can go further. A much more profound observation is that oppressed groups are *typically* given narrow ranges of social roles, while dominant groups afford their members a far wider set of behavior patterns, each qualitatively different but each still accepted or esteemed in varying degrees. One of the privileges granted, or simply assumed, by ruling groups, is that they can indulge in a variety of eccentricities while still demanding and getting a fair measure of authority or prestige. Consider in this connection, to cite only one spectacular example, the crotchets and quirks cultivated by the English upper classes over the centuries.

Moreover, if we enlarge our vision to encompass other times and places, the range becomes even greater. We are not surprised to observe Latin American men embrace one another, Arab or Indian boys walk together hand in hand, or seminary students being gentle. The male role prescriptions that commonly appear in the literature do not describe correctly the male ideal in Jewish culture, which embodies a love of music, learning, and literature; an avoidance of physical violence; an acceptance of tears and sentiment, nurturance, and a sensitivity to others feelings. In the South that I knew half a century ago, young rural boys were expected to nurture their younger siblings, and male-male relations were ideally expected to be tender, supporting, and expressed occasionally by embraces. Among my own kin, some fathers then kissed their school-age sons; among Greek Americans in New York City, that practice continues many decades later. Or, to consider England once more, let us remember the admired men of Elizabethan England. True enough, one ideal was the violent, daring Sir Francis Drake and the brawling poet Ben Jonson. But men also expressed themselves in kissing and embracing, writing love poems to one another, donning decorative (not to say gaudy and flamboyant) clothing, and studying flowers as well as the fiery heavens.

I assert, then, that men manage to be in charge of things in all societies but that their very control permits them to create a wide range of ideal male roles, with the consequence that large numbers of men, not just a few, can locate rewarding positions in the social structure. Thereby, too, they considerably narrow the options left for feminine sex roles. Feminists especially resent the narrowness of the feminine role in informal interaction, where they feel they are dealt with only as women, however this may be softened by personal warmth or affection. . . .

THE SOCIOLOGY OF SUPERORDINATES

That set of relationships is only part of the complex male view, and I want to continue with my sketch of the main elements in what may be called the "sociology of superordinates." That is, I believe there are some general principles or regularities to be found in the relationships between superordinates—here, the sex-class called males—and subordinates, in this instance women. Those regularities do not justify, but they do explain in some degree, the modern resistance of men to their social situation.[4] Here are some of them:

1. The observations made by either men or women about members of the other sex are limited and somewhat biased by what they are most interested in and by their lack of opportunity to observe behind the scenes of each others' lives.[5] However, far less of what men do is determined by women; what men do affects women much more. As a consequence, men are often simply less motivated to observe carefully many aspects of women's behavior and activity because women's behavior does not affect as much what men propose to do. By contrast, almost everything men do will affect what women *have* to do, and thus women are motivated to observe men's behavior as keenly as they can.

2. Since any given cohort of men know they did not create the system that gives them their advantages, they reject any charges that they conspired to dominate women.

3. Since men, like other dominants or superordinates, take for granted the system that gives them their status, they are not aware of how much the social structure, from attitude patterns to laws, pervasively yields small,

cumulative, and eventually large advantages in most competitions. As a consequence, they assume that their greater accomplishments are actually the result of inborn superiority. Dominants are never satisfied with their rule unless they can also justify it.

4. As a corollary to this male view, when men weigh their situation, they are more aware of the burdens and responsibilities they bear than of their unearned advantages.

5. Superiors, and thus men, do not easily notice the talents or accomplishments of subordinates, and men have not in the past seen much wisdom in giving women more opportunities for growth, for women, in their view, are not capable of much anyway, especially in the areas of men's special skills. As is obvious, this is a self-validating process. Thus, few women have embarrassed men in the past by becoming superior in those areas. When they did, their superiority was seen, and is often still seen, as an odd exception. As a consequence, men see their superior position as a just one.

6. Men view even small losses of deference, advantages, or opportunities as large threats and losses. Their own gains, or their maintenance of old advantages, are not noticed as much.[6]

Although the male view is similar to that of superordinates generally, as the foregoing principles suggest, one cannot simply equate the two. The structural position of males is different from that of superordinate groups, classes, ethnic populations, or castes. Males are, first, not a group, but a social segment or a statistical aggregate within the society. They share much of a common destiny, but they share few if any group or collective goals (within small groups they may be buddies, but not with all males). Second, males share with certain women whatever gain or loss they experience as members of high or low castes, ethnic groups, or classes. For example, women in a ruling stratum share with their men a high social rank deference from the lower orders, and so on; men in a lowly Indian caste share that rank with their women, too. In modern societies, men and women in the same family are on a more or less equal basis with respect to "inheritance, educational opportunity (at least undergraduate), personal consumption of goods, most rights before the law, and the love and responsibility of their children."[7] They are not fully equal, to be sure, but much more equal than are members of very different castes or social classes.

Moreover, from the male view, women also enjoy certain exemptions: "freedom from military conscription, whole or partial exemption from certain kinds of heavy work, preferential courtesies of various kinds." Indeed, men have generally believed, on the whole, that their own lot is the more difficult one.[8]

It is possible, however, that feminist cries of indignation have touched their hearts, and those of women too, in recent years. Without giving a breakdown by gender, Gallup announced "a remarkable shift of opinion" in 1989: almost half those polled asserted that men "have a better life" than women, compared with only 32 percent in 1975. Almost certainly many women have been convinced, since nearly two-thirds of younger women felt that way.[9] Fifty-nine percent of a 1990 *Times Mirror* sample of women aged eighteen to twenty-four agreed, but so did 65 percent of the men. . . .

DOMESTIC DUTIES AND JOBS

So far, the opinion data give some small cause for optimism. Nevertheless, all announcements of the imminent arrival of utopias are premature. Although men's approval of more equality for women has risen, the record in two major areas of men's roles—the spheres of home and occupation—gives some reason for optimism, but little for rejoicing. Here we can be brief, for though voluminous and complex data exist, the main conclusions can easily be summarized.[10] Changes have occurred, but they are not great if we consider the society as a whole and focus on changes in behavior. In short, men have gained great credit (in conformity with their higher ranking) for a few modest steps toward equality.

Let us consider first the domestic role of men. The many complex studies done during the past decade have at least shown how difficult it is to pin down the causes of the present division of labor in the home. Thus, a simple summary is not adequate, but I note some salient findings here.

Women who work full-time have reduced the hours they spend on household tasks—in some studies, by almost half, while the reduction is substantial even if only routine tasks are included.[11] Husbands do not do much more housework if their wives are employed full time; nevertheless, over time men have increased their contribution (especially in child care), although the increase must be measured by a few minutes per day. White men and men with high incomes are least likely to increase their contribution. About half of both husbands and wives believe they ought to share equally; four-fifths think this of child care.[12] This represents a substantial change among wives, since until the end of the 1970s only about one-fourth of wives stated that they thought their husbands should work more, while the vanguard of opinion was led by the young, the educated, and African Americans.[13]

I have sometimes suggested that men generally decide if they must contribute more equally to housework, then they begin to feel the seduction of doing it in a quicker, more slovenly fashion. One study of a highly educated sample suggests this relationship: both spouses at least express more satisfaction when the division is equal, but the two want different things. The man wants to spend only a few hours in household work, while the women wants the traditional chores (laundry, shopping, cooking) to be shared.[14] In the United States, as in other countries, men are quicker to express support for equality in that sphere than actually to practice it. They may be wise in doing so, for that is surely less costly, at least for the present.

Of course, there are some differences. If a child two years or younger is in the house, the father does more, especially in child care. Better-educated husbands do a bit more, and so do younger husbands. But the indisputable fact is that men's domestic contribution does not change much whether or not they work, and whether or not their wives work.

With reference to the second large area of men's roles, holding jobs, we observe two further general principles of the relations between superordinates and those at lesser ranks. One is that men do not, in general, feel threatened by competition from women if they believe that the competition is fair and that women do not have an inside track. (To be sure, against overwhelming evidence, many do believe women enjoy that preference, while many whites believe that Blacks also have the inside track.) Men still feel that they are superior and will do better if given the chance. Since no society has actually tried the radical notion of genuinely fair competition, they have little reason to fear as yet. Except in a few occupations, they have lost very little ground. Women's position (by some measures) did improve during the 1970s, but changed very little in the 1980s.[15]

The second general principle of superordination noted here is that those who hold advantaged positions in the social structure (men, in this case) can perceive or observe that they are being flooded by people they consider their inferiors—women, Blacks, or the lower classes—while the massive statistical fact is that only a few such people are rising by much. There are several causes of this seeming paradox.

First, the new arrivals are more visible, by being different from those who have held the jobs up to this time. The second cause is our perception of relative numbers. Since there are far fewer positions at higher job levels, only a few new arrivals constitute a fair-size minority of the total at that level. Third, the mass media emphasize the hiring of women in jobs that seem not to be traditional for them, for that is considered news. Men's structural position, then, causes them to perceive radical change here even when little has taken place, and they resist it.

Nevertheless, the general conclusion does not change much. There is progress, but it is not at all clear-cut. After all, as long as the entrance of a few women into good jobs is news, the reality is less rosy than one might hope. Here are a few details:

> The number of businesses owned by women increased by 63 percent between 1982 and 1987.[16]
> The percentage of physicians who were women rose to 20 percent by 1988, an increase of two-thirds from 1980.
> Women made almost no inroads into the skilled crafts.
> Women made up almost one-half of all bakers, but nearly all simply put the dough through the final process in retail stores.
> As buyers and as administrators or managers in education, auditing, personnel, and training, women occupied about one-half of the jobs by 1988. However, they made up only about 3 percent of the top executives in large U.S. companies by 1991, almost no change from 1980. In general, their earnings in this group of managerial jobs were about two-thirds of male salaries.[17]
> As bus drivers and bartenders, women had almost half of the jobs.
> Over the decade, women's salaries rose; instead of making two-thirds of men's wages, they were making 72 percent.

The strongest variable that determines the lower wages of women is occupational segregation by sex, and that changed very little in the 1980s.[18] The blunt fact is that women have been able to enter a given occupation easily only if men longer defend that territory. Or, more dramatically, the common pattern of "feminization" in most occupations is simple: They are rising on an elevator in a crumbling building. The job itself is being downgraded. They get better wages than other women, perhaps, but lower wages than men once made in those occupations.

Although the mass figures are correct, we need not discount all our daily observation either. We do see women entering formerly masculine jobs, from garbage collecting to corporate management. That helps undermine sex stereotypes and thereby becomes a force against inequality. Although occupational segregation continues to be strong, it did decline in most professions (e.g., engineering, dentistry, science, law, medicine). That is, the percentage of women in those professions did rise. Generally they doubled or trebled in the period 1970–88.[19] Of course, the absolute percentages of women in such professions remain modest (4–22 percent), because in occupations where almost everyone was once male, it is not possible to recruit, train, and hire enough women to achieve equality within even a generation. Still, the trend seems clear.

A secondary effect of these increasing numbers should be noted. Percentages are important, but so are absolute numbers. When women lawyers increase from about seven thousand to more than a hundred thousand, they become a much larger social force, even though they still form no more than about 22 percent of the total occupation. When women medical students, while remaining a minority in their classes, increase in number so that they can form committees, petition administrators, or give solidarity to one another against any traditional masculine badgering and disesteem, they greatly increase their influence on discriminatory attitudes and behavior. That is, as their rise in numbers permits the formation of real groups in any occupation, their power mounts faster (except at the very start) than the numbers or the percentages. Thus, changes occur even when the percentage of the occupation made up of women is not really large.

BASES OF PRESENT CHANGES

Most large-scale, objective measures of men's roles show little change over the past decade, but men do feel now and then that their position is in question, and their security somewhat fragile. I believe they are right, for they sense a set of forces that lie deeper and are more powerful than the day-to-day negotiation and renegotiation of advantage among individual husbands and wives, fathers and children, or bosses and those who work for them. Men are troubled by this new situation.

The conditions we live in are different from those of any earlier civilization, and they give less support to men's claims of superiority than perhaps any other historical era. When these conditions weaken that support, men can rely only on previous tradition, on power, or on their attempts to socialize their children to shore up their faltering advantages. Such rhetoric is not likely to be successful against the new objective conditions and the claims of aggrieved women. Thus, men are correct when they feel they are losing some of their privileges, even if many continue to smile at the rhetoric of the women's liberation movement.

The new conditions can be listed concretely, but I shall also give you a theoretical formulation of the process. Concretely, because of the increased use of various mechanical gadgets and devices, fewer tasks require much strength. As to those that still require strength, most men cannot do them either. Women can now do more household tasks that men once felt only they could do, and still more tasks are done by repair specialists called in to do them. With the development of modern warfare, there are few if any important combat activities that only men can do. Even now, their "auxiliary" tasks take them in and around battle zones as a matter of course. Women are much better educated than before.

With each passing year, psychological and sociological research reduces the areas in which men are reported to excel over women and discloses far more overlap in talents, so that even when males still seem to have an advantage, it is but slight. It is also becoming more widely understood that the top posts in government and business are not best filled by the stereotypical aggressive male but by the people, male or female, who are sensitive to others' needs, adept at obtaining cooperation, and skilled in social relations. Indeed, had male management in a number of U.S. industries followed that truth over the past decade, their failure to meet Japanese competition would surely have been less. Finally, in one sphere after another, the number of women who try to achieve rises, and so does the number who succeed.

Although the pressure of new laws has its direct effect on these conditions, the laws themselves arise from an awareness of the foregoing forces. Phrased in more theoretical terms, the underlying shift is toward the decreasing marginal utility of males, and this I suspect is the main source of men's resistance to women's liberation. That is, fewer people believe that what the male does is indispensable, is nonsubstitutable, or adds such a special value to any endeavor that it justifies his extra "price" or reward. In past wars, for example, males enjoyed a very high value not only because it was felt that they could do the job better than women but also because they might well make the key or marginal difference between being conquered and remaining free. In many societies, their marginal utility came from their contribution of animal protein through hunting. As revolutionary heroes, explorers, hunters, warriors, and daring capitalist entrepreneurs, men felt, and doubtless their women did too, that their contribution was beyond anything women could do. Without question, this would not be true of all men, but it would have been true of men as a distinct group. Men thereby earned extra privileges of rank, authority, and creature services.

It is not then as individuals, as persons, that males will be deemed less worthy in the future or their contributions less needed. Rather, they will be seen as having no claims to extra rewards solely because they are members of the male sex-class. This is part of a still broader trend of our generation, which will also increasingly deny that being white or upper-class produces a marginally superior result and thus justifies extra privileges.

The relations of individuals are subject to continuous renegotiation as people try to gain or keep advantages or cast off burdens. They fail or succeed in part because one or the other person has special resources or deficits that are unique to that individual. Over the long run, however, the outcome of those negotiations depends on the deeper social forces I have been describing, which ultimately determine which qualities or performances are more or less valued.

Men now perceive that they may be losing some of their advantages and that more aspects of their social roles are subject to public challenge and renegotiation than in the past. They resist these changes, and we can suppose they will continue to do so. In all such changes, there are gains and losses. Commonly, when people at lower social ranks gain freedom, those at higher ranks lose some power or centrality. When those at the lower ranks also lose some protection, some support, those at the higher ranks lose some of the burden of responsibility. It is also true that the care or help given by any dominant group in the past was never as much as their members believed, and their loss in political power or economic rule was never as great as they feared.

On the other hand, I know of no instance when a group or social stratum gained its freedom or moved toward more respect and then its members decided that they did not want it. Therefore, although men will not joyfully give up their rank, in spite of its burdens, neither will women decide that they would like to get back the older feminine privileges, accompanied by the lack of respect and material rewards that went with those courtesies.

I believe that men perceive their roles as being under threat in a world that is different from any in the past. No society has yet come even close to equality between the sexes, but the modern social forces described here did not exist before, either. At the most cautious, we must concede that the conditions favoring a trend toward more equality are more favorable than at any previous time in history. If we have little reason to conclude that equality is at hand, let us at least rejoice that we are still marching in the right direction.

NOTES

1. Herbert Goldberg, *The Hazards of Being Male* (New York: Nash, 1976), and Patricia C. Sexton, *The Feminized Male: Classrooms, White Collars, and the Decline of Manliness* (New York: Random House, 1969). On the recognition of disadvantages, see J. S. Chafetz, *Masculine/Feminine or Human?* (Itasca, Ill.: Peacock, 1974), 56 ff.

2. Joseph H. Pleck, "The Psychology of Sex Roles: Traditional and New Views," in *Women and Men: Changing Roles, Relationships, and Perceptions*, ed. Libby A. Cater and Anne F. Scott (New York: Aspen Institute for Humanistic Studies, 1976), 182. Pleck has carried out the most extensive research on male roles, and I am indebted to him for special help in this inquiry.

3. Sidney M. Jourard, "Some Lethal Aspects of the Male Role," in *Men and Masculinity*, ed. Joseph H. Pleck and Jack Sawyer (Englewood Cliffs, N.J.:

Prentice-Hall, 1974), 22, and Irving London, "Frigidity, Sensitivity, and Sexual Roles," in *Men and Masculinity*, ed. Pleck and Sawyer, 42. See also the summary of such traits in I. K. Braverman et al., "Sex-Role Stereotypes: A Current Appraisal," in *Women and Achievement*, ed. Martha T. S. Mednick, S. S. Tangri, and Lois W. Hoffman (New York: Wiley, 1974), 32–47.

4. Robert Bierstedt's "The Sociology of the Majority," in his *Power and Progress* (New York: McGraw-Hill, 1974), 199–220, does not state these principles, but I was led to them by thinking about his analysis.

5. Robert K. Merton, in "The Perspectives of Insiders and Outsiders," in his *The Sociology of Science* (Chicago: University of Chicago Press, 1973), 99–136, has analyzed this view in some detail.

6. This general pattern is noted at various points in my monograph *The Celebration of Heroes: Prestige as a Social Control System* (Berkeley and Los Angeles: University of California Press, 1979).

7. Erving Goffman, "The Arrangement between the Sexes," *Theory and Society* 4 (1977): 307.

8. Hazel Erskine, "The Polls: Women's Roles," *Public Opinion Quarterly 35* (Summer 1971).

9. Linda DeStefano and Diane Colasanto, Gallup Organization press release, 5 February 1989. For the *Times Mirror* sample, see Times Mirror Center for the People and the Press, press release, September 1990, 5.

10. By now, the research data on household tasks are voluminous, their conclusions complex, and by the time they are published they may be somewhat dated. For comparison with other countries, see Jonathan Gershuny and John P. Robinson, "Historic Changes in the Household Division of Labor," *Demography* 25 (1988): 537–52. See also Linda Thompson and Alexis J. Walker, "Gender in Families: Women and Men in Marriage, Work, and Parenthood," *Journal of Marriage and the Family* 51 (1989): 845–71; Mary H. Benin and Joan Agostinelli, "Husbands' and Wives' Satisfaction with the Division of Labor," *Journal of Marriage and the Family* 50 (1988): 349–61; and Beth A. Shelton, "The Distribution of Household Tasks," *Journal of Family Issues* 11 (1990): 115–35. Joseph Pleck was a leader in these studies during the 1970s and 1980s.

11. Shelton, "Distribution of Household Tasks," table 2, p. 124; Gershuny and Robinson, "Historical Changes," 550.

12. Thompson and Walker, "Gender in Families," 857.

13. Arland Thornton and Deborah S. Freedman, "Changes in the Sex Role Attitudes of Women, 1962–1977," *American Sociological Review* 44 (1979): 833.

14. Benin and Agostinelli, "Husbands' and Wives' Satisfaction," 360.

15. For an excellent analysis of the many complex processes involved in these changes, see Barbara F. Reskin and Patricia A. Roos, *Job Queues, Gender Queues* (Philadelphia: Temple University Press, 1990).

16. U.S. Department of Commerce, Bureau of the Census, *Statistical Abstract of the United States, 1991* (Washington, D.C.: GPO, 1992).

17. These and other related data were published in *U.S. News and World Report*, 17 June 1991, from a study of the "glass ceiling" conducted for the Department of Labor but not officially issued.

18. Reskin and Roos, *Job Queues, Gender Queues*, tables 1.7, 1.8. See especially the case studies of changes in occupational segregation in ibid., part 2. In the usual case of "desegregation," women move into men's jobs (bartending, in-store baking, bus driving, banking) when those jobs are downgraded, usually technologically, so that the wages no longer attract men. Most of the expansion of women's jobs has occurred in "female" jobs, service jobs at lower levels.

19. Ibid., 19. On the earlier period, see also Victor R. Fuchs, "A Note on Sex Segregation in Professional Occupations," *Explorations in Economic Research* 2, no. 1 (Winter 1975): 105–11.

R E A D I N G

7

The Meanings of Macho: Changing Mexican Male Identities

MATTHEW C. GUTMANN

By 1992, most of the five-year-old boys in the San Bernabé Nursery School in Col. Santo Domingo cheerfully participated in the game called *"el banño de la muñeca,"* "the doll bath." Aurora Muñoz, the director of the Nursery, noted that the boys also now swept up, watered the plants, and collected the trash. When she began working at San Bernabé in 1982, however, many of the boys would protest: "Only *viejas* do that!" (similar to "That's girls' work!"). Aurora Muñoz attributed the changes to the fact that, as the boys themselves reported, their older brothers and fathers often did these things now, so why shouldn't they? In the *colonia popular* neighborhood of Santo Domingo on the southside of Mexico City, where I began conducting ethnographic fieldwork on male identities in 1992, grandfathers sometimes remark on the changes in men and women in

From: *Situated Lives: Gender and Culture in Everyday Life* edited by Louise Lamphere, Helena Ragoné and Patricia Zavella. Copyright 1997. Published by Routledge.

their lifetimes. When they were young, for instance, only girls were sent shopping for food, while today being allowed for the first time to go buy fresh tortillas marks a rite of passage for boys as well as girls.

In social science as well as popular literature the Mexican male, especially if he is from the lower classes, is often portrayed as the archetype of "machismo," which, however defined, invariably conjures up the image of virulent sexism (see Gilmore; 1990; Mernissi, 1975/1987; Paz, 1950/1992; Ramos, 1934/1992; Stevens, 1973). On the face of it, the classifications "Mexican men" or "Spanish-speaking men" are anachronisms. Such general categories negate important differences which exist within regions, classes, age cohorts, and ethnic groups in Mexico and throughout Latin America and Spain. Yet Brandes is still one of the few scholars to point to this variety: "Over the years, I acquired an image of Tzintzuntzan, and the Lake Patzcuaro region as a whole, as deviating from the usual social-science portrait of Mexican machismo" (1988:30).

As this paper will show, the diversity of male identities in the neighborhood of Col. Santo Domingo alone is enormous. Nonetheless, despite this diversity of male identities, at the same time certain important similarities exist among men who share particular sociocultural and historical experiences. Here, in order to examine Mexican male identities and to determine whether and how they may be transforming, I will explore intergenerational differences in what *ser hombre*, to be a man, means today in a lower class area of Mexico's capital city.

The history of Col. Santo Domingo makes it a good place to examine what, if any, are some of the changes in gender relations occurring today in Mexican society, and specifically, how male gender attitudes and behavior may be experienced and perceived differently today by both women and men. Before 1971, Santo Domingo was a wasteland of volcanic rocks, caves, shrubs, snakes, and scorpions. With migration from the impoverished countryside and other parts of the capital exacerbating the housing shortage in the cities, in one 24-hour period in early September 1971, nearly 5,000 families "parachuted" into the inhospitable yet uninhabited lava fields of Santo Domingo. It still stands as the largest single land invasion in Latin American history.

In the period since the invasion, as in many other urban and rural areas of Latin America, popular movements for social services (water, electricity, schools, sewage, and so on) have been a major political force in the area. In these popular struggles, the women of Col. Santo Domingo have generally been among the most active participants, and sometimes the leaders, including an opposition to continued government attempts to stop or coopt the independent organization of the residents of Col. Santo Domingo.

CHANGED "BY NECESSITY"

To a great extent this activity on the part of women has reflected the fact that most men can find jobs only outside the *colonia*, and that in many families it has been at least implicitly understood that women more than men had the job of trying to resolve day-to-day deprivations in the neighborhood. In addition, while Col. Santo Domingo was struggling into existence during the 1970s and

1980s, another change was occurring in the broader Mexican society that greatly affected men's relations with women, and therefore men's own identities: women in unprecedented numbers began to work outside the home.

The most common explanation offered by men and women of varying ages in Col. Santo Domingo as to why so many men are now taking greater responsibility for various household duties that previously were the rather exclusive duties of women is *"por necesidad,"* by necessity, because they have to. What they usually mean is that in many families, especially since the economic crisis of 1982, it has become economically necessary for both husband and wife to have paid work, and that this has often required the husband to do some of the household tasks that previously may have been done by the wife alone. What few men state, but what many women discuss with a certain relish, is that *por necesidad* can refer also to men being forced by the women with whom they live to take on some of these responsibilities. That is, in terms of changes in cultural attitudes regarding housework, quite regularly it is women who change first and then make—or at least try to make—their men change.

Women's participation in remunerated employment is significantly higher in Mexico City than in any other part of the country; thus one important result of migration from the rural *campo* to this sprawling metropolis of 20,000,000 inhabitants is a change in many women's occupational patterns (see Table 3.1).

While in Mexico City in 1990, around 30 percent of women worked for money, this figure was slightly less than 20 percent for the country overall. Statistics by age groups reveal an even starker contrast between Mexico City and the country as a whole: over 40 percent of women between the ages of 40 and 44 in the Federal District were still "economically active" in 1900. Only 22 percent of women in Mexico in the same age category were registered as having remunerated employment (see Table 3.2).

While I sat one day on a stool in his kitchen admiring the masonry work in his brick walls, Marcos washed the morning dishes. I asked Marcos if he had always done this chore. He paused for a moment, thinking, and then turning around to face me, shrugged and said: "I began doing it regularly four years, two months ago." Skeptical by nature and more than mildly surprised by the precision of his response, I inquired how he could so clearly remember his initiation into this task. "Quite simple, really," he replied with a grin—he knew exactly

TABLE 3.1 Women's and Men's Participation in the Economically Active Population (as Percentage of Total Population over 12 years old) for Mexico City and Mexico in 1990

	Mexico City (%)	Mexico (%)
Women	30.66	19.58
Men	66.81	68.01
Total	47.63	43.04

Source: *Estados Unidos , Mexicanos, Resumen General, XI Censo General de Población y Viviendo*, 1990: Cuadro 27, p. 310. Mexico City: Instituto de Estadística. Geografía e Informática.

TABLE 3.2 Women's and Men s participation in the Economically Active Population, by Selected age Groups (as percentage of Total Population over 12 years old for Mexico City and Mexico in 1990

	Women	Men	Total
Mexico City			
20–24 years	40.14	69.61	54.28
25–29 years	44.85	88.97	65.96
30–34 years	43.94	94.48	67.75
15–39 years	43.22	95.42	67.71
40–44 years	41.06	94.93	66.37
Mexico			
20–24 years	29.10	77.10	52.02
25–29 years	28.42	89.32	57.43
30–34 years	26,87	92.11	58.10
35–39 years	24.85	92.18	57.35
40–44 years	22.56	91.17	56.00

Source: *Estados Unidos Mexicanos. Resumen General, XI Censo General de Población y Vivienda,* 1990. Cuadro 27, p.316. Mexico City Instituto Nacional de Eseadística. Geografía e Informática.

what I was driving at with my questions about men doing housework—"that's when my *vieja* began working full time. Before that she was around the house a lot more."

Gilberto Echeverría, a sixty-eight-year-old grandfather, offered his own experience. "Things used to be much more simple. For 40 years, I earned the family money as an *albañil* [laborer in construction], and my wife, before she died, she was responsible for everything in the home." "Now," he mused in a meditative tone, "now it's a wonder you can tell who's who. My daughter is also making money and my son-in-law helps [*ayuda*] her all the time in the house." Doña Berta says that her husband, who is still working on the line in the same factory after 20 years, used to get ridiculed by his brother when their five children were young, because Don Antonio would hold the children, change their diapers, and in general help a lot in raising them. Her brother-in-law's attitude was fairly typical of his generation. Now, she reports with a certain satisfied look, the tables have turned a lot and "the father who doesn't do these things is more likely to be the one being ridiculed."

It is not uncommon for husbands and fathers in their 20s and 30s in Col. Santo Domingo to wash dishes, sweep, change diapers, and go shopping on a regular basis. They will tell you about it if you ask, as will some of their wives, mothers, and sisters, and you will see them in their homes, in front of their houses, and in the neighhborhood markets. One friend boasted to me one day. "Why sometimes I'm the one buying my daughters their sanitary pads. And, I'll tell you, I've got no problem with this as some guys still do. Well, so long as they tell me what brand to buy. After all, I'm not going to stand there like an asshole just gaping at all the feminine hygiene products!" It is certainly more common now than at any time in the past for men in Col. Santo Domingo to participate in most chores involved in running the household.

One exception to this is cooking, which among older and younger men—and not a few women—in various classes in Mexico City is still commonly seen as the consummately female task. Therefore, rare is the man who prepares his or others' meals on a regular basis. Many men do cook when their wives or other women are not around, though this generally takes the form of reheating food which the women have left for them. And a lot of men like to cook for fiestas and on festive occasions, often having a special, signature meat dish (like calf brain tacos or a spicy goat stew). When asked about their not cooking more, some men explain that their wives will not let them enter the kitchen area, much less cook. Some of these same wives clarified for me that the real issue was that their husbands are far better at giving excuses than working.

The partial and relatively recent changes within the division of labor in some households in the *colonia* are not simply a reflection of economic transformations, for example, women working outside the home, but also relate to cultural changes in what it means to be a man today in at least some working class neighborhoods of Mexico City. It is a further indication of the actual duties performed and of the cultural values still placed on these household tasks, by women as well as by men, that the expression used by nearly all to describe men's activities in the home is *ayudar a la esposa*, helping the wife. Men generally do not equally share in these responsibilities, in word or deed, and the cultural division of labor between women is still regarded as important and therefore enforced by many. The female *doble jornada*, second shift (literally double day), is an ongoing and significant feature of life for many households in Santo Domingo. In addition, and related to their often privileged position in Mexican society, men in particular sometimes admit to trying to take advantage of the situation, by attributing greater natural energy to women and greater natural *florjera* (laziness) to men.

FATHERS AND SON

Even more than housework, cooking, and shopping, parenting is considered by some scholars as a habitually and often exclusively feminine domain, and the extent of shared parenting between women and men is deemed a key test of the degree of gender equality in societies (see, for example, Chodorow, 1978; Ruddick, 1989). At the same time, Margaret Mead once defined the distinctively human aspect as lying "in the nurturing behavior of the male, who among human beings everywhere helps provide food for women and children" (1949/1975, p. 188). If not nearly measuring up to Mead's idyllic classification, in various *colonias populares* in Mexico City, as in other parts of Mexico today and historically, there exists a tremendous variety in patterns of parenting, specifically with reference to the roles played by men in raising children, which may challenge findings based more exclusively on certain U.S. middle class settings.

True enough, in Col. Santo Domingo it is certainly the case that women usually spend more time with the children than men do, and in the minds of a lot of women and men there, children, especially young children, belong with their mother or other women. And it is still the case that a majority of women in *clases populares* list as their work *hogar* and *ama de casa*, housework and housewife; clearly they are still in most households the adults most responsible for parenting day in and day out. Yet historically, in certain rural regions of Mexico, for instance, men have often played a special role in raising boys, particularly after they have reached an age when they are finally deemed mature enough to help with, or at least not get in the way of, their fathers' work in the fields (see Lewis, 1951/1963; Romney & Romney, 1963).

In the cities today, some men speak with great pleasure about having jobs that allow them to spend time with their children while they are working, like those furniture repairmen or cobblers who have little workshops in their houses, or others like car mechanics who work in the street in front of their homes. In addition, while family sizes are growing smaller, in households with older children it is common to find older girls, and increasingly older brothers and male cousins, caring for younger siblings, for example, after school when parents and other adults may still be working.

Some men in their 70s today who took part in the invasion of Santo Domingo 20 years ago, after their children were already grown, talk about having had a lot of responsibilities for raising their boys in particular. In formal interviews conducted with men and women in Col. Santo Domingo, a common theme among older men is that their parenting role with their boys included two particular dimensions. One, frequently these men relate that they usually took the boys with them when they went out on errands or to visit friends during their "free time," especially on weekends. Two, they were responsible more than the boys' mothers for teaching the boys technical skills (a trade) that would be necessary in fulfilling their later, adult masculine responsibilities as economic providers. Significantly, older women and men both report having shared in providing moral instruction and discipline for the boys. At least with the older generation, girls were more exclusively raised by women.

Alejandra Sánchez, a mother of two teenage girls, is convinced that the main reason her husband has never taken much responsibility for the children is because they have no sons. She laments that had there been two boys instead, he would have had "to buck up," and life for her would have been very different. Her situation is felt by neighbors to be rather typical of old-fashioned relations between mothers and fathers, and in this sense more exceptional in a community that has undergone innumerable changes in cultural relations, including those between men and women. Whether she is right is impossible to say, but her perception that with boys her irresponsible husband would have been at least culturally pressured if not obligated to take on certain accepted male parenting duties is certain.

A division of labor, fathers-sons and mothers-daughters, still pertains in some younger families in Col. Santo Domingo, but many men with small children today like to claim as a point of pride that they treat their boys and girls the same. If they spend more time with the boys outside the home, they sometimes explain, it is because it simply works out that way, because it is more convenient for both the father and mother, or because the boys want to spend time with them more than the girls do. To this must be added the fact that mothers—more than fathers—are often reluctant to have their girls go out with the men. Despite the fact that men carry and walk their daughters, it remains the case that from very early on boys are shepherded off with their fathers by their mothers in a way that girls seldom are.

Changing economic conditions in Mexico, especially since 1982, have impelled further changes among broad sectors of the male population. Some older men in Col. Santo Domingo are being laid off from jobs they have held for decades, and thus find themselves unemployed (and semiemployable at best) at the age of 60. They frequently report having more daily contact with their grandchildren than they ever had with their own children, a situation only some find agreeable. Among intellectuals in the middle classes, tougher economic times have sometimes necessitated doing without the live-in maid/nanny who was ubiquitous only a short time ago. Therefore men in these strata find themselves caring for their children far more than ever in the past, and the expression *"Estoy de Kramer,"* "I'm Kramering," has come into vogue, meaning "I've got the kids," recalling the U. S. movie Kramer vs. Kramer, and pointing to certain U. S. cultural influences regarding modern family values and practices.

All in all, it is difficult in the case of Col. Santo Domingo to argue that in terms of attitudes and behavior parenting is identified exclusively with women. To some extent historically and without question today, for a variety of reasons, active, consistent, and long-term parenting is a central ingredient there for numerous, though obviously not all, men and women in what it means to be a man.

MACHOS ARE NOT WHAT THEY USED TO BE

It is common to hear women and men in Col. Santo Domingo say that while there used to be a lot of macho men, they are not as prevalent today. Some people who make this comment are too young to know anything firsthand about the old days, but regardless, they are sure there was more machismo before. If some oldtimers like to divide the world of men into machos and *mandilones* (meaning female-dominated men), it is far more common for younger men in Col. Santo Domingo to define themselves as belonging to a third category, the "nonmacho" group, *"ni macho, ni mandilón,"* "neither macho nor *mandilón."* Though others may define a friend or relative as "your typical Mexican macho," the same man will frequently reject the label for himself, describing all the things he does to help his wife around the home, pointing out that he does not beat his wife (one of the few generally agreed on attributes of machos), and so on. What is most significant is not simply how the terms macho and machismo are variously defined—there is little consensus on their meanings—but more, that today the terms are so routinely regarded by men in the working class in Col. Santo Domingo, Mexico City, as pejorative and not worthy of emulation.

Further, while many men in Col. Santo Domingo have (re)considered the relative merits of being macho, fewer have changed the way they refer to a group of men that, for them, is beyond the pale, that is, the *maricones*, queers, homosexuals, who thus constitute an especially marginalized fourth category of Mexican masculinities.

Sociocultural changes directly involving women have propelled new ways of thinking and acting among men with regard to machismo. Such changes among women have required reevaluations and changes among men, for if womanhood no longer is so closely tied to motherhood, manhood too must be at least partially recast. As a single (and still childless!) young man of 27 explained, "For me, having a lot of kids to prove you're really macho is a bunch of bullshit. That stuff went out four decades ago." Not all would agree with his periodization, but the sentiment is more widespread than the conventional wisdom—that Mexican males need confirmation of their virility through procreation—would allow.

In 1970, the average number of children per woman (out of the female population over 12 years old) in Mexico as a whole was 4.5 and for Mexico City 2.6. In 1990, the figure for Mexico City was 2.0, while for the country two years earlier it had dropped to 2.5 (see Table 3.3). The drop in birthrates in the last 20 years in Mexico as a whole, and its urban centers in particular, has been dramatic. This decline has not necessarily led to direct changes in parenting attitudes and behavior on the part of men, but it certainly reflects changes in cultural practices by women regarding an area long closely identified with their gender identities.

Another sign of changes in gender identities in Col. Santo Domingo, especially in the last decade, has to do with women's alcohol consumption and adultery. While no precise figures are available, male and female residents of the neighborhood uniformly agree that women are drinking alcohol and "*saliendo*," "going out" (in the sense of cheating on their spouses), in far higher numbers than ever before. There is disagreement as to whether men are drinking and

TABLE 3.3 Birthrates in Mexico from 1900 to 1988: Average Number of Children per Woman over 12 years old

Year	(at any given time)
1900	5.0
1940	4.6
1960	4.5
1970	4.5
1977	3.8
1981	3.4
1983	3.1
1985	2.8
1988	2.5

Source: Adapted from Zavala de Cosío, 1992, pp.26, 222, 282.

cheating more. People are also divided, and of significance not neatly along gender lines, as to whether these developments among women are good or bad in the long run. Regardless of different individuals' opinions about how women today are "altering the rules," the changes have contributed, among other things, to the initiation of numerous discussions within families and among friends about the meaning of terms like equality when applied to gender relations.

WOMEN ARE "NATURAL LEADERS" IN COL. SANTO DOMINGO

Aurora Muñoz of the San Bernabé Nursery School says that women "tend to be natural leaders in Santo Domingo because of the needs of the *colonia*." From the beginning of the neighborhood in 1971, women led in the fights to acquire water for all residents. Then for electricity and schools. Only recently, in 1992, were streets being torn up to lay sewage pipes for the over 150,000 residents of Col. Santo Domingo.

Older women and men seem to have an easier time responding to questions about what difference it might make to grow up in an area in which women are community organizers and leaders, as opposed to one in which even if women work outside the home they certainly do not play an integral role in the political campaigns and protests of the neighborhood. For those who have grown up in Col. Santo Domingo, or in other areas of Mexico City where "popular urban movements" have taken place in the past 15 years, it is far more difficult to even imagine a situation in which women are not community activists.

Few questions are received by younger adults in the *colonia* as being so absurd (to the point of provoking chuckles) as those which inquire about the *mujer sumisa* or *mujer abnegada*, the submissive or self-sacrificing woman. It is not that people do not recognize her to exist; everyone can point to a neighbor or aunt whom they will characterize in this way. And it is true that the disdainful laugh of some men at the question about submissive women barely conceals a defensiveness regarding their own behavior toward women. Yet even when people identify *la mujer sumisa* as a relic from the provinces, that is, a migrant from another part of the country, people commonly point out to the inquiring ethnographer that this really is not an accurate description of women in many of the villages of Mexico either.

"Sure," Manuel Ramos points out to me, "these women exist and have always existed, but with all the moving around people have done in the last 30 years do you think this has left everything the way it was once between women and men? Impossible."

Further, as Fidel Aguirre, a technician working in a laboratory outside the *colonia* took pains to explain, "with women working outside the home it's not just a question of them having their own money now, as important as this has been. What's also involved is that women have met all sorts of different people, which has changed them forever. And this has meant that the men have changed, for if they don't, more and more they're getting left behind by women. Let me tell you, this is what's happening."

In addition to these changes in the sociocultural landscape, several others have of course greatly contributed to the questioning and challenging of gender relations among people in Col. Santo Domingo. Chief among these must be listed the fact that through at least the early years of college, the numbers of females and males are today roughly equivalent, and thus expectations of women themselves (and frequently, of parents for their daughters, husbands for their wives, and so on) are quite different from what they were with earlier generations. Television, and within this the cultural reach of the U.S., has had a profound impact. Some government family centers and some churches have developed forums in which such information has been disseminated as well. A grandfather of eight grinned when he said that while he had never changed the diapers on his own children he had since learned how to do it for the next generation. Where did he learn this? From a program in his church.

Finally, the women's movement and the struggles for homosexual rights have had important, if more indirect, influences in Col. Santo Domingo on the self-conceptions that women of all ages, and to a lesser extent men of especially the younger generations, have concerning being women and men. This influence is realized in a number of ways, from women's health care workers who have been active in the community for over 10 years, to feminist magazines which at times have reached a mass circulation in some of the *colonial populares.*

CHANGING MEN

In Mexico in the last 20 years, precisely the period in which Col. Santo Domingo has come into being, the entire society has witnessed rapid and widespread upheavals involving the economy, gender roles, struggles over ethnic identity, regional development and stagnation, ecological catastrophes, international migration, and political insurgency and repression. For most of this century there was a sense among even the poor that times would get better. Now, for many, the mood is more akin to the postmodernist malaise that has struck indeterminate others around the globe.

Each of these sociocultural factors has its own particular timetable and trajectory, and it is far from clear, in the case of gender relations for example, where things are truly heading. But while we must therefore be particularly cautious in our attempt to analyze changes in these phenomena, we must also guard against a perhaps even more debilitating contemporary notion that nothing ever does change, especially when it comes to life between women and men.

The changes in attitudes and behavior on the part of men and women in Col. Santo Domingo are deeply felt, and evidently part of a developing process of transforming gender relations throughout Mexico. They are not, however, uniformly experienced or acknowledged. The ethnographic research reported in this paper has been conducted primarily in a lower class urban milieu, and secondarily among middle class merchants and professionals in Mexico City.

Lomnitz and Pérez-Lizaur (1987) conducted an ethnographic study of an elite Mexican family for 7 years. As the focus of their investigation concerned kinship networks, their findings are quite pertinent here. They write that among the elites studied, the father's "participation in raising children is indirect; he may occasionally play with his small children or, when they grow up, gradually introduce his sons to certain aspects of a man's world. Child rearing is the direct and formal responsibility of the mother" (p. 210).

For at least many fathers in Col. Santo Domingo, this is hardly the situation. Simply to note the greater responsibilities that women in both elite and popular classes have in parenting misses the enormous differences in the content of fathering in each context. Fathers in Col. Santo Domingo to a far greater extent appear to be integral in all stages of their children's lives, though to be sure in practice they are present more in the evenings and on weekends, commonly more with their boys than with their girls, and more with children over 3 or 4 years old. But beyond a merely quantitative, time-allocation difference in fathers' attention to their children, men in at least certain *colonias populares* define their own and others' masculinity in part in terms of their active role in parenting.

Of course, as important as fathering may be to numerous men in Col. Santo Domingo, it is not all there is to being a man. In a conversation with an older couple on what had changed between women and men in their lifetimes, the woman (whom neighbors like to describe as a classic *mujer abnegada*) offered, "Why, the liberation of the woman!" She did not care to expand on this opinion except to add that it has been women who had changed the most since her youth, implying that the men were lagging behind. Her husband, a straight-talking character, dismissed his wife's comment with a wave of his hand and countered that what was different was that: "Today there're a lot of queers who've stopped being men." Clearly the directions in which changes have occurred are not uniform, either between women and men or between generations.

As a sign of continuing subordination of women to men, and despite the greater financial liberty brought to women by earning their own salaries, far more women are still economically dependent on men than men on women in Col. Santo Domingo. Talking with women who have endured years of battering from their husbands with no end yet in sight, this point is made repeatedly.

Birthrates have dropped, and contraceptives are used more than ever before, yet it is still most common to find women being held mainly responsible for birth control: a woman from Col. Santo Domingo went to get condoms at a state health service and was told by a male government doctor that prophylactics were only for promiscuous women, and that since they are not comfortable for men anyway, she should give her husband a break and use an I.U.D.

And while the boys in the San Bernabé Nursery School today play "girls' games" and, with the girls, help to clean up more than they used to, most of the girls, when they remember, are still careful to not get their clothes dirty, and most of the boys are still embarrassed when they cry, because their mothers and fathers are still teaching them that girls don't play like that and boys don't cry.

The developments and transformations in Col. Santo Domingo do not indicate full equality, cooperation, and mutual respect suddenly blossoming in gender relations there. Nonetheless, as part of the broader society and because of certain specific conditions pertaining in this largely self-built community, the "Mexican macho" stereotypes so common in the social sciences are today inappropriate and misleading in understanding large sections of men in this area, how they see themselves and how the women with whom they share their lives see them, their history, and their future.

REFERENCES

Arizpe, L. (1989). *Cultura y desarrollo: Una etnografía de las creencias de una comunidad mexicana.* Mexico City: Porrua/Universidad Nacional Autónoma de México.

Bartra, R. (1987). *La jaula de la melancolia: Identidad y metamorfosis del Mexicano.* Mexico City: Grijalbo. (In English: *The Cage of Melancholy: Identity and Metamorphosis of the Mexican.* Christopher J. Hall, trans. New Brunswick: Rutgers University Press, 1992.)

Brandes, S. (1988). *Power and persuasion: Fiestas and social control in rural Mexico.* Philadelphia: University of Pennsylvania Press.

Chodorow, N. (1978). *The reproduction of mothering: Psychoanalysis and the sociology of gender.* Berkeley: University of California Press.

de Barbieri, T. (1990). Sobre géneros, practicas y valves: notas acerca de posibles erosiones del machismo en Mexico. In J. M. Ramírez Sáiz (Ed.), *Normas y prácticas: morales y cívicas en la vida cotidiana* (pp. 83–106). Mexico City: Universidad Nacional Autónoma de *México.*

García, B., Muñoz, H., and de Oliveira, O. (1982). *Hogares y trabajadores en la Ciadad de Mexico.* Mexico City: El Colegio de México/Universidad Nacional Autónoma de México.

Gilmore, D. (1990). *Manhood in the making: Cultural concepts of mascunlinity.* New Haven: Yale University Press.

Lewis, O. (1951/1963). *Life in a Mexican village: Tepoztlán restudied.* Urbana: University of Illinois Press.

Lomnitz, L., and Perez-Lizaur, M. (1987). *A Mexican elite family: 1820–1980.* Princeton: Princeton University Press.

Mead, M. (1949/1975). *Male and female: A study of the sexes in a changing world.* New York: Wm. Morrow.

Mernissi, F. (1975/1987). *Beyond the veil: Male-female dynamics in modern Muslim society.* Bloomington: Indiana University Press.

Paz, O. (1950/1992). *El laberinto de la soledad. Mexico City:* Fondo de Cultura Economica. (In English: *The Labyrinth of Solitude: Life and Thought in Mexico.* Lysander Kemp, trans. New York: Grove, 1961.)

Ramos, S. (1934/1992). *El perfil del hombre y la cultura en México.* Mexico City: Espasa-Calpe Mexicana. (In English: *Profile of man and culture in Mexico.* Peter G. Earle, trans. Austin: University of Texas Press, 1962.)

Romney, K., and Rornney, R. (1963). The Mixtecans of Juxtlahuaca, Mexico. In B. Whiting (Ed.), *Six cultures: Studies in child rearing* (pp. 541–691). New York: John Wiley.

Ruddick, S. (1989). *Maternal thinking: Toward a politics of peace.* Boston: Beacon.

Stevens, E. (1973). *Marianismo:* The Other Face of *Machismo* in Latin America. In A. Pescatello (Ed.), *Male and Female in Latin America* (pp. 90–101). Pittsburgh: University of Pittsburgh Press.

Zavala de Cosío, M. E. (1992). *Cambios de fecundidad en México y políticas de población.* Mexico City: El Colegio de Mexico.

CHAPTER 4

◆

SEXUALITY AND

SOCIETY

READING

8

Sexual Revolution(s)

BETH BAILEY

In 1957 America's favorite TV couple, the safely married Ricky and Lucy Ricardo, slept in twin beds. Having beds at all was probably progressive—as late as 1962 June and Ward Cleaver did not even have a bedroom. Elvis's pelvis was censored in each of his three appearances on the *Ed Sullivan Show* in 1956, leaving his oddly disembodied upper torso and head thrashing about on the TV screen. But the sensuality in his eyes, his lips, his lyrics was unmistakable, and his genitals were all the more important in their absence. There was, likewise, no mistaking Mick Jagger's meaning when he grimaced ostentatiously and sang "Let's spend some *time* together" on *Ed Sullivan* in 1967. Much of the audience knew that the line was really "Let's spend the night together," and the rest quickly got the idea. The viewing public could see absence and hear silence— and therein lay the seeds of the sexual revolution.

What we call the sexual revolution grew from these tensions between public and private—not only from tensions manifest in public culture, but also from tensions between private behaviors and the public rules and ideologies that were meant to govern behavior. By the 1950s the gulf between private acts and public norms was often quite wide—and the distance was crucial. People had sex outside marriage, but very, very few acknowledged that publicly. A woman who married the only man with whom she had had premarital sex still worried years later: "I was afraid someone might have learned that we had intercourse before

From: *The Sixties: From Memory to History* edited by David Farber. Copyright 1994. Published by The University of North Carolina Press.

marriage and I'd be disgraced." The consequences, however, were not just psychological. Young women (and sometimes men) discovered to be having premarital sex were routinely expelled from school or college; gay men risked jail for engaging in consensual sex. There were real penalties for sexual misconduct, and while many deviated from the sexual orthodoxy of the day, all but a few did so furtively, careful not to get "caught."

Few episodes demonstrate the tensions between the public and private dimensions of sexuality in midcentury America better than the furor that surrounded the publication of the studies of sexual behavior collectively referred to as the "Kinsey Reports." Though a dry, social scientific report, *Sexual Behavior in the Human Male* (1948) had sold over a quarter of a million copies by 1953, when the companion volume on the human female came out. The male volume was controversial, but the female volume was, in *Look* magazine's characterization, "stronger stuff." Kinsey made it clear that he understood the social implications of his study, introducing a section on "the pre-marital coital behavior of the female sample which has been available for this study" with the following qualification: "Because of this public condemnation of pre-marital coitus, one might believe that such contacts would be rare among American females and males. But this is only the overt culture, the things that people openly profess to believe and do. Our previous report (1948) on the male has indicated how far publicly expressed attitudes may depart from the realities of behavior—the covert culture, what males actually do."

Kinsey, a biologist who had begun his career with much less controversial studies of the gall wasp, drew fire from many quarters, but throughout the criticism is evident concern about his uncomfortable juxtaposition of public and private. "What price biological science . . . to reveal intimacies of one's private sex life and to draw conclusions from inscriptions on the walls of public toilets?" asked one American in a letter to the editor of *Look* magazine.

Much of the reaction to Kinsey did hinge on the distance between the "overt" and the "covert." People were shocked to learn how many men and women were doing what they were not supposed to be doing. Kinsey found that 50 percent of the women in his sample had had premarital sex (even though between 80 percent and 89 percent of his sample disapproved of premarital sex on "moral grounds"), that 61 percent of college-educated men and 84 percent of men who had completed only high school had had premarital sex, that over one-third of the married women in the sample had "engaged in petting" with more than ten different men, that approximately half of the married couples had engaged in "oral stimulation" of both male and female genitalia, and that at least 37 percent of American men had had "some homosexual experience" during their lifetimes.

By pulling the sheets back, so to speak, Kinsey had publicized the private. Many people must have been reassured by the knowledge that they were not alone, that their sexual behaviors were not individual deviant acts but part of widespread social trends. But others saw danger in what Kinsey had done. By demonstrating the distance between the overt and the covert cultures, Kinsey had further undermined what was manifestly a beleaguered set of rules. *Time* magazine warned its readers against the attitude that "there is morality in numbers," the *Chicago Tribune* called Kinsey a "menace to society," and the *Ladies' Home Journal* ran an article with the disclaimer: "The facts of behavior reported . . . are not to be interpreted as moral or social justification for individual acts."

Looking back to the century's midpoint, it is clear that the coherence of (to use Kinsey's terms) covert and overt sexual cultures was strained beyond repair. The sexual revolution of the 1960s emerged from these tensions, and to that extent it was not revolutionary, but evolutionary. As much as anything else, we see the overt coming to terms with the covert. But the revision of revolution to evolution would miss a crucial point. It is not historians who have labeled these changes "sexual revolution"—it was people at the time, those who participated and those who watched. And they called it that before much of what we would see as revolutionary really emerged—before gay liberation and the women's movement and Alex Comfort's *The Joy of Sex* (1972) and "promiscuity" and singles' bars. The term was in general use by 1963—earlier than one might expect.

To make any sense of the sexual revolution, we have to pay attention to the label people gave it. Revolutions, for good or ill, are moments of danger. It matters that a metaphor of revolution gave structure to the myriad changes taking place in American society. The changes in sexual mores and behaviors could as easily have been cast as evolutionary—but they were not.

Looking back, the question of whether or not the sexual revolution was revolutionary is not easy to answer; it depends partly on one's political (defined broadly) position. Part of the trouble, though, is that the sexual revolution was not one movement. It was instead a set of movements, movements that were closely linked, even intertwined, but which often made uneasy bedfellows. Here I hope to do some untangling, laying out three of the most important strands of the sexual revolution and showing their historical origins, continuities, and disruptions.

The first strand, which transcended youth, might be cast as both evolutionary and revolutionary. Throughout the twentieth century, picking up speed in the 1920s, the 1940s and the 1960s, we have seen a sexualization of America's culture. Sexual images have become more and more a part of public life, and sex—or more accurately, the representation of sex—is used to great effect in a marketplace that offers Americans fulfillment through consumption. Although the blatancy of today's sexual images would be shocking to someone transported from an earlier era, such representations developed gradually and generally did not challenge more "traditional" understandings of sex and of men's and women's respective roles in sex or in society.

The second strand was the most modest in aspect but perhaps the most revolutionary in implication. In the 1960s and early 1970s an increasing number of young people began to live together "without benefit of matrimony," as the phrase went at the time. While sex was usually a part of the relationship (and probably a more important part than most people acknowledged), few called on concepts of "free love" or "pleasure" but instead used words like "honesty," "commitment," and "family." Many of the young people who lived together could have passed for young marrieds and in that sense were pursuing fairly traditional arrangements. At the same time, self-consciously or not, they challenged the tattered remnants of a Victorian epistemological and ideological system that still, in the early 1960s, fundamentally structured the public sexual mores of the American middle class.

The third strand was more self-consciously revolutionary, as sex was *actively claimed* by young people and used not only for pleasure, but also for power in a new form of cultural politics that shook the nation. As those who threw themselves into the "youth revolution" (a label that did not stick) knew so well, the struggle for America's future would take place not in the structure of electoral politics, but on the battlefield of cultural meaning. Sex was an incendiary tool of a revolution that was more than political. But not even the cultural revolutionaries agreed on goals, or on the role and meaning of sex in the revolution.

These last two strands had to do primarily with young people, and that is significant. The changes that took place in America's sexual mores and behaviors in the sixties were *experienced* and *defined* as revolutionary in large part because they were so closely tied to youth. The nation's young, according to common wisdom and the mass media, were in revolt. Of course, the sexual revolution was not limited to youth, and sex was only one part of the revolutionary claims of youth. Still, it was the intersection of sex and youth that signaled danger. And the fact that these were often middle-class youths, the ones reared in a culture of respectability (told that a single sexual misstep could jeopardize their bright futures), made their frontal challenges to sexual mores all the more inexplicable and alarming.

Each of these strands is complex, and I make no pretense to be exhaustive. Thus, rather than attempting to provide a complete picture of changes in behaviors or ideologies, I will examine several manifestations of seemingly larger trends. The sexualization of culture (the first strand) is illustrated by the emergence of *Playboy* and *Cosmo* magazines. For the "modest revolutionaries" (the second strand), I look to the national scandal over a Barnard College junior's "arrangement" in 1968 and the efforts of University of Kansas students to establish a coed dormitory. Finally, the cultural radicals (the third strand) are represented by the writings of a few counterculture figures.

By focusing on the 1960s, we lose much of the "sexual revolution." In many ways, the most important decade of that revolution was the 1970s, when the "strands" of the 1960s joined with gay liberation, the women's movement, and powerful assertions of the importance of cultural differences in America. Yet, by concentrating on the early years of the sexual revolution, we see its tangled roots—the sexual ideologies and behaviors that gave it birth. We can also understand how little had been resolved—even begun—by the end of the 1960s.

BEFORE THE REVOLUTION: YOUTH AND SEX

Like many of the protest movements that challenged American tranquility in the sixties, the sexual revolution developed within the protected space and intensified atmosphere of the college campus. An American historian recalls returning to Harvard University in 1966 after a year of postgraduate study in England. Off balance from culture shock and travel fatigue, he entered Harvard Yard and knew with absolute certainty that he had "missed the sexual revolution." One can imagine a single symbolic act of copulation signaling the beginning of the revolution (it has a nicely ironic echo of "the shot heard round the world"). The single act and the revolution complete in 1966 are fanciful constructions; not everything began or ended at Harvard even in those glory years. But events there and at other elite colleges and universities, if only because of the national attention they received, provide a way into the public intersections of sex, youth and cultural politics.

Harvard had set a precedent in student freedom in 1952, when girls (the contemporary term) were allowed to visit in Harvard men's rooms. The freedom offered was not supposed to be sexual—or at least not flagrantly so. But by 1963 Dean Jon Monro complained that he was "badly shaken up by some severe violations," for a once "pleasant privilege" had come to be "considered a license to use the college rooms for wild parties or sexual intercourse." The controversy went public with the aid of *Time* magazine, which fanned the flames by quoting a senior's statement that "morality is a relative concept projecting certain mythologies associated with magico-religious beliefs." The Parietals Committee of the Harvard Council for Undergraduate Affairs, according to the *Boston Herald*, concluded that "if these deep emotional commitments and ties occasionally lead to sexual intercourse, surely even that is more healthy than the situation a generation ago when 'nice girls' were dated under largely artificial circumstances and sexual needs were gratified at a brothel." Both justifications seemed fundamentally troubling in different ways, but at least the controversy focused on men. The sexual double standard was strong. When the spotlight turned on women, the stakes seemed even higher.

The media had a field day when the president of Vassar College, Sarah Blanding, said unequivocally that if a student wished to engage in premarital sex, she must withdraw from the college. The oft-quoted student reply to her dictum chilled the hearts of middle-class parents throughout the country: "If Vassar is to become the Poughkeepsie Victorian Seminary for young Virgins, then the change of policy had better be made explicit in admissions catalogs."

Such challenges to authority and to conventional morality were reported to eager audiences around the nation. None of this, of course, was new. National audiences had been scandalized by the panty raid epidemic of the early 1950s; the antics and petting parties of college youth had provided sensational fodder for hungry journalists in the 1920s. The parents—and grandparents—of these young people had chipped away at the system of sexual controls themselves. But they had not directly and publicly denied the very foundations of sexual morality. With few exceptions, they had evaded the controls and circumvented the rules, climbing into dorm rooms through open windows, signing out to the library and going to motels, carefully maintaining virginity in the technical sense while engaging in every caress known to married couples. The evasions often succeeded, but that does not mean that the controls had no effect. On the contrary, they had a great impact on the ways people experienced sex.

There were, in fact, two major systems of sexual control, one structural and one ideological. These systems worked to reinforce one another, but they affected the lives of those they touched differently.

The structural system was the more practical of the two but probably the less successful. It worked by limiting opportunities for the unmarried to have intercourse. Parents of teenagers set curfews and promoted double dating, hoping that by preventing privacy they would limit sexual exploration. Colleges, acting in loco parentis, used several tactics: visitation hours, parietals, security patrols, and restrictions on students' use of cars. When Oberlin students mounted a protest against the college's policy on cars in 1963, one male student observed that the issue was not transportation but privacy: "We wouldn't care if the cars had no wheels, just so long as they had doors."

The rules governing hours applied only to women and, to some extent, were meant to guarantee women's safety by keeping track of their comings and goings. But the larger rationale clearly had to do with sexual conduct. Men were not allowed in women's rooms but were received in lounges or "date rooms," where privacy was never assured. By setting curfew hours and requiring women to sign out from their dormitories, indicating who they were with and where they were going, college authorities meant to limit possibilities for privacy. Rules for men were not deemed necessary—because of a sexual double standard, because men's safety and well-being seemed less threatened in general, and because the colleges and universities were primarily concerned with controlling their own populations. If women were supervised or chaperoned and in by 11:00 P.M., the men would not have partners—at least, not partners drawn from the population that mattered.

Throughout the 1950s, the structural controls became increasingly complex; by the early 1960s they were so elaborate as to be ludicrous. At the University of Michigan in 1962, the student handbook devoted nine of its fifteen pages to rules for women. Curfews varied by the night of the week, by the student's year in college, and even, in some places, by her grade point average. Students could claim Automatic Late Permissions (ALPs) but only under certain conditions. Penalties at Michigan (an institutional version of "grounding") began when a student had eleven "late minutes"—but the late minutes could be acquired one at a time throughout the semester. At the University of Kansas in the late 1950s, one sorority asked the new dean of women to discipline two women who had flagrantly disregarded curfew. The dean, investigating, discovered that the women in question had been between one and three minutes late signing in on three occasions.

The myriad of rules, as anyone who lived through this period well knows, did not prevent sexual relations between students so much as they structured the times and places and ways that students could have sexual contact. Students said extended good-nights on the porches of houses, they petted in dormitory lounges while struggling to keep three feet on the floor and clothing in some semblance of order, and they had intercourse in cars, keeping an eye out for police patrols. What could be done after eleven could be done before eleven, and sex need not occur behind a closed door and in a bed—but this set of rules had a profound impact on the *ways* college students and many young people living in their parents homes *experienced sex*.

The overelaboration of rules, in itself, offers evidence that the controls were beleaguered. Nonetheless, the rules were rarely challenged frontally and thus they offered some illusion of control. This system of rules, in all its inconsistency, arbitrariness, and blindness, helped to preserve the distinction between public and private, the coexistence of overt and covert, that defines midcentury American sexuality.

The ideological system of controls was more pervasive than the structured system and probably more effective. This system centered on ideas of difference: men and women were fundamentally different creatures, with different roles and interests in sex. Whether one adopted a psychoanalytic or an essentialist approach, whether one looked to scholarly or popular analysis, the final conclusion pointed to *difference*. In sex (as in life), women were the limit setters and men the aggressors.

The proper limits naturally depended on one's marital status, but even within marriage sex was to be structured along lines of difference rather than of commonality. Marital advice books since the 1920s had the importance of female orgasm, insisting that men must satisfy their wives, but even these calls for orgasm equality posited male and female pleasure as competing interests. The language of difference in postwar America, which was often quite extreme, can be seen as a defensive reaction to changing gender roles in American society.

One influential psychoanalytic study, provocatively titled *Modern Woman: The Lost Sex*, condemned women who tried to be men and argued the natural difference between men and women by comparing their roles in sexual intercourse. The woman's role is "passive," the authors asserted. "[Sex] is not as easy as rolling off a log for her. It is easier. It is as easy as being the log itself. She cannot fail to deliver a masterly performance, by doing nothing whatever except being duly appreciative and allowing nature to take its course." For the man, in contrast, sexuality is "overt, apparent and urgent, outward and ever-present," fostered by psychological and physiological pressures toward orgasm. Men might experiment sexually with few or no consequences and no diminution of pleasure. Women, on the other hand, could not: "The strong desire for children or lack of it in a woman has a crucial bearing on how much enjoyment she derives from the sexual act. . . . Woman cannot make . . . pleasure an end in itself without inducing a decline in the pleasure."

These experts argued from a psychoanalytic framework, but much less theoretical work also insisted on the fundamental difference between men and women, and on their fundamentally different interests in sex. Texts used in marriage courses in American high schools and college typically included chapters on the difference between men and women—and these difference were not limited to their reproductive systems.

Woman did in fact have a different and more imperative interest in controlling sex than men, for women could become pregnant. Few doctors would fit an unmarried woman with a diaphragm, though one might get by in the anonymity of a city with a cheap "gold" ring from a drugstore or by pretending to be preparing for an impending honeymoon. Relying on the ubiquitous condom in the wallet was risky and douching (Coca-Cola had a short-lived popularity) even more so. Abortion was illegal, and though many abortions took place, they were dangerous, expensive, and usually frightening and degrading experiences. Dependable and *available* birth control might have made a difference (many would later attribute "the sexual revolution" to the "pill"), but sexual behaviors and sexual mores were not based simply on the threat of illegitimate pregnancy. Kinsey found that only 44 percent of the women in his sample said that they "restricted their pre-marital coitus" because of fear of pregnancy, whereas 80 percent cited "moral reasons." Interestingly, 44 percent of the sample also noted their "fear of public opinion."

Women who were too "free" with sexual favors could lose value and even threaten their marriageability. In this society, a woman's future socioeconomic status depended primarily on her husband's occupation and earning power. While a girl was expected to "pet to be popular," girls and women who went "too far" risked their futures. Advice books and columns from the 1940s and 1950s linked girls' and womens' "value" to their "virtue," arguing in explicitly economic terms that "free" kisses destroyed a woman's value in the dating system: "The boys find her easy to afford. She doesn't put a high value on herself." The exchange was even clearer in the marriage market. In chilling language, a teen adviser asked: "Who wants second hand goods?"

It was not only the advisers and experts who equated virtue and value. Fifty percent of the male respondents in Kinsey's study wanted to marry a virgin. Even though a relatively high percentage of women had intercourse before marriage, and a greater number engaged in "petting," most of these women at least *expected* to marry the man, and many did. Still, there might be consequences. Elaine Tyler May, who analyzed responses to a large, ongoing psychological study of married couples in the postwar era, found that many couples struggled with the psychological burdens of premarital intimacy for much of their married lives. In the context of a social/cultural system that insisted that "nice girls don't," many reported a legacy of guilt or mistrust. One woman wrote of her husband: "I think he felt that because we had been intimate before marriage that I could be as easily interested in any man that came along."

Of course, sexual mores and behaviors were highly conditioned by the sexual double standard. Lip service was paid to the ideal of male premarital chastity, but that ideal was usually obviated by the notion, strong in peer culture and implicitly acknowledged in the larger culture, that sexual intercourse was a male rite of passage. Middle-class boys pushed at the limits set by middle-class girls, but they generally looked elsewhere for "experience." A man who went to high school in the early 1960s (and did not lose his virginity until his first year of college) recalls the system with a kind of horror: "You slept with one kind of woman, and dated another kind, and the women you slept with, you didn't have much respect for, generally."

The distinction was often based on class—middle-class boys and men had sex with girls and women of the lower classes, or even with prostitutes. They did not really expect to have intercourse with a woman of their own class unless they were to be married. Samuel Hynes, in his memoir of coming of age as a navy flier during World War II, describes that certain knowledge: "There were nice girls in our lives, too. Being middle-class is more than a social station, it's kind of destiny. A middle-class boy from Minneapolis will seek out nice middle-class girls, in Memphis or anywhere else, will take them out on middle-class dates and try to put their hand inside their middle-class underpants. And he will fail. It was all a story that had already been written."

Dating, for middle-class youth, was a process of sexual negotiation. "Good girls" had to keep their virginity yet still contend with their own sexual desires or with boys who expected at least some petting as a "return" on the cost of the date. Petting was virtually universal in the world of heterosexual dating. A 1959 *Atlantic* article, "Sex and the College Girl," described the ideal as having "done every possible kind of petting without actually having intercourse."

For most middle-class youth in the postwar era, sex involved a series of skirmishes that centered around lines and boundaries: kissing, necking, petting above the waist, petting below the waist, petting through clothes, petting under clothes, mild petting, heavy petting. The progression of sexual intimacy had emerged as a highly ordered system. Each act constituted a stage, ordered in a strict hierarchy (first base, second base, and so forth), with vaginal penetration as the ultimate step. But in their attempts to preserve technical virginity, many young people engaged in sexual behaviors that, in the sexual hierarchy of the larger culture, should have been more forbidden than vaginal intercourse. One woman remembers: "We went pretty far, very far; everything but intercourse. But it was very frustrating. . . . Sex was out of the question. I had it in mind that I was going to be a virgin. So I came up with oral sex. . . . I thought I invented it."

Many young men and women acted in defiance of the rules, but that does not make the rules irrelevant. The same physical act can have very different meanings depending on its emotional and social/cultural contexts. For America's large middle class and for all those who aspired to "respectability" in the prerevolutionary twentieth century, sex was overwhelmingly secret or furtive. Sex was a set of acts with high stakes and possibly serious consequences, acts that emphasized and reinforced the different roles of men and women in American society. We do not know how each person felt about his or her private acts, but we do know that few were willing or able to publicly reject the system of sexual controls.

The members of the generation that would be labeled "the sixties" were revolutionary in that they called fundamental principles of sexual morality and control into question. The system of controls they had been inherited and lived within was based on a set of presumptions rooted in the previous century. In an evolving set of arguments and actions (which never became thoroughly coherent or unified), they rejected a system of sexual controls organized around concepts of difference and hierarchy.

Both systems of control—the structural and the ideological—were firmly rooted in a Victorian epistemology that had, in most areas of life, broken down by the early twentieth century. This system was based on a belief in absolute truth and a passion for order and control. Victorian thought, as Joseph Singal has argued persuasively, insisted on "preserving absolute standards based on a radical dichotomy between that which was deemed 'human' and that regarded as 'animal.'" On the "human" side were all forces of civilization; on the "animal," all instincts, passions, and desires that threatened order and self-control. Sex clearly fell into the latter category. But the Victorian romance was not restricted to human versus animal, civilized versus savage. The moral dichotomy "fostered a tendency to see the world in polar terms." Thus we find rigid dichotomous pairs not only of good and evil, but of men and women, body and soul, home and world, public and private.

Victorian epistemology, with its remarkably comfortable and comforting certainties and its stifling absolutes, was shaken by the rise of a new science that looked to "dynamic process" and "relativism" instead of the rigid dichotomies of Victorian thought. It was challenged from within by those children of Victorianism who "yearned to smash the glass and breathe freely," as Jackson Lears argued in his study of antimodernism. And most fundamentally, it was undermined by the realities of an urban industrial society. American Victorian culture was, as much as anything, a strategy of the emerging middle classes. Overwhelmed by the chaos of the social order that had produced them and that they sought to manage, the middling classes had attempted to separate themselves from disorder and corruption. This separation, finally, was untenable.

The Victorian order was overthrown and replaced by a self-consciously "modern culture." One place we point to demonstrate the decline of Victorianism is the change in sexual "manners and mores" in the early twentieth century. Nonetheless, sex may be the place that Victorian thought least relinquished its hold. This is not to say that prudishness reigned—the continuity is more subtle and more fundamental. Skirts rose above the knee, couples dated and petted, sexologists and psychologists acknowledged that women were not naturally "passionless," and the good judge Ben Lindsey called for the "companionate marriage." But the systems of control that regulated and structured sex were Victorian at their core, with science replacing religion to authorize absolute truth, and with inflexible bipolar constructions somewhat reformulated but intact. The system of public controls over premarital sex was based on rigid dichotomous pairings: men and women, public and private. This distinction would be rejected—or at least recast—in the cultural and sexual struggles of the sixties.

REVOLUTIONARIES

All those who rejected the sexual mores of the postwar era did not reject the fundamental premises that gave them shape. *Playboy* magazine played an enormously important (if symbolic) role in the sexual revolution, or at least in preparing the ground for the sexual revolution. *Playboy* was a men's magazine in the tradition of *Esquire* (for which its founder had worked briefly) but laid claim to a revolutionary stance partly by replacing *Esquire's* airbrushed drawings with airbrushed flesh.

Begun by Hugh Hefner in 1953 with an initial print run of 70,000, *Playboy* passed the one million circulation mark in three years. By the mid-1960s Hefner had amassed a fortune of $100 million, including a lasciviously appointed forty-eight-room mansion staffed by thirty Playboy "bunnies" ("fuck like bunnies" is a phrase we have largely left behind, but most people at the time caught the allusion). Playboy clubs, also staffed by large-breasted and long-legged women in bunny ears and cottontails, flourished throughout the country. Though *Playboy* offered quality writing and advice for those aspiring to sophistication, the greatest selling point of the magazine was undoubtedly its illustrations.

Playboy, however, offered more than masturbatory opportunities. Between the pages of coyly arranged female bodies—more, inscribed in the coyly arranged female bodies—flourished a strong and relatively coherent ideology. Hefner called it a philosophy and wrote quite a few articles expounding it (a philosophy professor in North Carolina took it seriously enough to describe his course as "philosophy from Socrates to Hefner").

Hefner saw his naked women as "a symbol of disobedience, a triumph of sexuality, an end of Puritanism." He saw his magazines as an attack on "our ferocious anti-sexuality, our dark antieroticism." But his thrust toward pleasure and light was not to be undertaken in partnership. The Playboy philosophy, according to Hefner, had less to do with sex and more to do with sex roles. American society increasingly "blurred distinctions between the sexes . . . not only in business, but in such diverse realms as household chores, leisure activities, smoking and drinking habits, clothing styles, upswinging homosexuality and the sex-obliterating aspects of togetherness," concluded the "Playboy Panel" in June 1962. In Part 19 of his extended essay on the Playboy philosophy, Hefner wrote: "PLAYBOY stresses a strongly heterosexual concept of society—in which the separate roles of men and women are clearly defined and compatible."

Read without context, Hefner's call does not necessarily preclude sex as a common interest between men and women. He is certainly advocating heterosexual sex. But the models of sex offered are not partnerships. Ever innovative in marketing and design, *Playboy* offered in one issue a special "coloring book" section. A page featuring three excessively voluptuous women was captioned: "Make one of the girls a blonde. Make one of the girls a brunette. Make one of the girls a redhead. It does not matter which is which. The girls' haircolors are interchangeable. So are the girls."

Sex, in the Playboy mode, was a contest—not of wills, in the model of the male seducer and the virtuous female, but of exploitative intent, as in the playboy and the would-be wife. In *Playboy's* world, women were out to ensnare men, to entangle them in a web of responsibility and obligation (not the least of which was financial). Barbara Ehrenreich has convincingly argued that *Playboy* was an integral part of a male-initiated revolution in sex roles, for it advocated that men reject burdensome responsibility (mainly in the shape of wives) for lives of pleasure through consumption. Sex, of course, was part of this pleasurable universe. In *Playboy*, sex was located in the realm of consumption, and women were interchangeable objects, mute, making no demands, each airbrushed beauty supplanted by the next month's model.

It was not only to men that sexual freedom was sold through exploitative visions. When Helen Gurley Brown revitalized the traditional women's magazine that was *Cosmopolitan* in 1965, she compared her magazine to *Playboy*—and *Cosmo* did celebrate the pleasures of single womanhood and "sexual and material consumerism." But before Brown ran *Cosmo*, she had made her contribution to the sexual revolution with *Sex and the Single Girl*, published in May 1962. By April 1963, 150,000 hard-cover copies had been sold, garnering Brown much media attention and a syndicated newspaper column, "Woman Alone."

The claim of *Sex and the Single Girl* was, quite simply, "nice, single girls *do.*" Brown's radical message to a society in which twenty-three-year-olds were called old maids was that singleness is good. Marriage, she insisted, should not be an immediate goal. The Single Girl sounds like the Playboy's dream, but she was more likely a nightmare revisited. Marriage, Brown advised, is "insurance for the worst years of your life. During the best years you don't need a husband." But she quickly amended that statement: "You do need a man every step of the way, and they are often cheaper emotionally and more fun by the dozen." That fun explicitly included sex, and on the woman's terms. But Brown's celebration of the joys of single life still posed men and women as adversaries. "She need never be bored with one man per lifetime," she enthused. "Her choice of partners is endless and they seek *her* . . . Her married friends refer to her pursuers as wolves, but actually many of them turn out to be lambs—to be shorn and worn by her."

Brown's celebration of the single "girl" actually began with a success story—her own. "I married for the first time at thirty-seven. I got the man I wanted," begins *Sex and the Single Girl*. Brown's description of that union is instructive: "David is a motion picture producer, forty-four, brainy, charming and sexy. He was sought after by many a Hollywood starlet as well as some less flamboyant but more deadly types. And I got him! We have two Mercedes-Benzes, one hundred acres of virgin forest near San Francisco, a Mediterranean house overlooking the Pacific, a full-time maid and a good life."

While Brown believes "her body wants to" is a sufficient reason for a woman to have an "affair," she is not positing identical interests of men and women in sex. Instead, she asserts the validity of women's interests—interests that include Mercedes-Benzes, full-time maids, lunch ("Anyone can take you to lunch. How bored can you be for an hour?"), vacations, and vicuna coats. But by offering a female version of the Playboy ethic, she greatly strengthened its message.

Unlike the youths who called for honesty, who sought to blur the boundaries between male and female, *Playboy* and *Cosmo* offered a vision of sexual freedom based on difference and deceit, but within a shared universe of an intensely competitive market economy. They were revolutionary in their claiming of sex as a legitimate pleasure and in the directness they brought to portraying sex as an arena for struggle and exploitation that could be enjoined by men and women alike (though in different ways and to different ends). Without this strand, the sexual revolution would have looked very different. In many ways *Playboy* was a necessary condition for "revolution," for it linked sex to the emerging culture of consumption and the rites of the marketplace. As it fed into the sexual reconfigurations of the sixties, *Playboy* helped make sex more—or less—than a rite of youth.

In the revolutionary spring of 1968, *Life* magazine looked from the student protests at Columbia across the street to Barnard College: "A sexual anthropologist of some future century, analyzing the pill, the drive-in, the works of Harold Robbins, the Tween-Bra and all the other artifacts of the American Sexual Revolution, may consider the case of Linda LeClair and her boyfriend, Peter Behr, as a moment in which the morality of an era changed."

The LeClair affair, as it was heralded in newspaper headlines and syndicated columns around the country, was indeed such a moment. Linda LeClair and Peter Behr were accidental revolutionaries, but as *Life* not so kindly noted, "history will often have its little joke. And so it was this spring when it found as its symbol of the revolution a champion as staunch, as bold and as unalluring as Linda LeClair." The significance of the moment is not to be found in the actions of LeClair and Behr, who certainly lacked revolutionary glamour despite all the headlines about "Free Love," but in the contest over the meaning of those actions.

The facts of the case were simple. On 4 March 1968 the *New York Times* ran an article called "An Arrangement: Living Together for Convenience, Security, Sex." (The piece ran full-page width; below it appeared articles on "How to Duck the Hemline Issue" and "A Cook's Guide to the Shallot.") An "arrangement," the author informs us, was one of the current euphemisms for what was otherwise known as "shacking up" or, more innocuously, "living together." The article, which offers a fairly sympathetic portrait of several unmarried student couples who lived together in New York City, features an interview with a Barnard sophomore, "Susan," who lived with her boyfriend "Peter" in an off-campus apartment. Though Barnard had strict housing regulations and parietals (the curfew was midnight on weekends and ten o'clock on weeknights, and students were meant to live either at home or in Barnard housing), Susan had received permission to live off campus by accepting a job listed through Barnard's employment office as a "live-in maid." The job had, in fact, been listed by a young married woman who was a good friend of "Susan's."

Not surprisingly, the feature article caught the attention of Barnard administrators, who had little trouble identifying "Susan" as Linda LeClair. LeClair was brought before the Judiciary Council—not for her sexual conduct, but for lying to Barnard about her housing arrangements. Her choice of roommate was certainly an issue; if she had been found to be living alone or, as one Barnard student confessed to the *Times*, with a female cat, she would not have been headline-worthy.

Linda, however, was versed in campus politics, and she and Peter owned a mimeograph machine. She played it both ways, appearing for her hearings in a demure, knee-length pastel dress and churning out pamphlets on what she and Peter called "A Victorian Drama." She and Peter distributed a survey on campus, garnering three hundred replies, most of which admitted to some violation of Barnard's parietals or housing regulations. Sixty women were willing to go public and signed forms that read: "I am a student of Barnard College and I have violated the Barnard Housing Regulations. . . . In the interest of fairness I request that an investigation be made of my disobedience."

Linda LeClair had not done anything especially unusual, as several letters from alumnae to Barnard's president, Martha Peterson, testified. But her case was a symbol of change, and it tells us much about how people understood the incident. The president's office received over two hundred telephone calls (most demanding LeClair's expulsion) and over one hundred letters; editorials ran in newspapers, large and small, throughout the country. Some of the letters were vehement in their condemnation of LeClair and of the college. Francis Beamen of Needham, Massachusetts, suggested that Barnard should be renamed "BARNYARD"; Charles Orsinger wrote (on good quality letterhead), "If you let Linda stay in college, I can finally prove to my wife with a front page news story about that bunch of glorified whores going to eastern colleges." An unsigned letter began: "SUBJECT: Barnard College—and the kow-tow to female 'students' who practice prostitution, PUBLICLY!"

Though the term "alley cat" cropped up more than once, a majority of the letters were thoughtful attempts to come to terms with the changing morality of America's youth. Many were from parents who understood the symbolic import of the case. Overwhelmingly, those who did not simply rant about "whoredom" structured their comments around concepts of public and private. The word *flaunt* appeared over and over in the letters to President Peterson. Linda was "flaunting her sneering attitude"; Linda and Peter were "openly flaunting their disregard of moral codes"; they were "openly flaunting rules of civilized society." Mrs. Bruce Bromley, Jr., wrote her first such letter on a public issue to recommend, "Do not let Miss LeClair attend Barnard as long as she flaunts immorality in your face." David Abrahamson, M.D., identifying himself as a former Columbia faculty member, offered "any help in this difficult case." He advised President Peterson, "Undoubtedly the girl's behavior must be regarded as exhibitionism, as her tendency is to be in the limelight which clearly indicates some emotional disturbance or upset."

The public-private question *was* the issue in this case—the letter writers were correct. Most were willing to acknowledge that "mistakes" can happen; many were willing to allow for some "discreet" sex among the unmarried young. But Linda LeClair *claimed* the right to determine her own "private" life; she rejected the private—public dichotomy *as it was framed around sex*, casting her case as an issue of individual right versus institutional authority.

But public response to the case is interesting in another way. When a woman wrote President Peterson that "it is time for these young people to put sex back in its proper place, instead of something to be flaunted" and William F. Buckley condemned the "delinquency of this pathetic little girl, so gluttonous for sex and publicity," they were not listening. Sex was not what Linda and Peter talked about. Sex was not mentioned. Security was, and "family." "Peter is my family," said Linda. "It's a very united married type of relationship—it's the most important one in each of our lives. And our lives are very much intertwined."

Of course they had sex. They were young and in love, and their peer culture accepted sex within such relationships. But what they claimed was partnership—a partnership that obviated the larger culture's insistence on the difference between men and women. The letters suggesting that young women would "welcome a strong rule against living with men to protect them against doing that" made no sense in LeClair's universe. When she claimed that Barnard's rules were discriminatory because Columbia men had no such rules, that "Barnard College was founded on the principle of equality between women and men," and asked, "If women are able, intelligent people, why must we be supervised and curfewed?" she was denying that men and women had different interests and needs. Just as the private-public dichotomy was a cornerstone of sexual control in the postwar era, the much-touted differences between men and women were a crucial part of the system.

Many people in the 1960s and 1970s struggled with questions of equality and difference in sophisticated and hard-thought ways. Neither Peter Behr nor Linda LeClair was especially gifted in that respect. What they argued was commonplace to them—a natural language and set of assumptions that nonetheless had revolutionary implications. It is when a set of assumptions becomes natural and unself-conscious, when a language appears in the private comments of a wide variety or people that it is worth taking seriously. The unity of interests that Behr and LeClair called upon as they obviated the male-female dichotomy was not restricted to students in the progressive institutions on either coast.

In 1969 the administration at the University of Kansas (KU), a state institution dependent on a conservative, though populist, legislature for its funding, attempted to establish a coed dormitory for some of its scholarship students. KU had tried coed living as an experiment in the 1964 summer session and found students well satisfied, though some complained that it was awkward to go downstairs to the candy machines with one's hair in curlers. Curlers were out of fashion by 1969, and the administration moved forward with caution.

A survey on attitudes toward coed housing was given to those who lived in the scholarship halls, and the answers of the men survive. The results of the survey go against conventional wisdom about the provinces. Only one man (of the 124 responses recorded) said his parents objected to the arrangement ("Pending further discussion," he noted). But what is most striking is the language in which the men supported and opposed the plan. "As a stereotypical answer," one man wrote, "I already am able to do all the roleplaying socially I need, and see communication now as an ultimate goal." A sophomore who listed his classification as both "soph." and "4-F I hope" responded: "I believe that the segregation of the sexes is unnatural. I would like to associate with women on a basis other than dating roles. This tradition of segregation is discriminatory and promotes inequality of mankind." One man thought coed living would make the hall "more homey." Another said it would be "more humane." Many used the word "natural." The most eloquent of the sophomores wrote: "[It would] allow them to meet and interact with one another in a situation relatively free of sexual overtones; that is, the participating individuals would be free to encounter one another as human beings, rather than having to play the traditional stereotyped male and female roles. I feel that coed living is the only feasible way to allow people to escape this stereotypical role behavior."

The student-generated proposal that went forward in December 1970 stressed these (as they defined them) "philosophical" justifications. The system "would NOT be an arrangement for increased boy-meets-girl contact or for convenience in finding dates," the committee insisted. Instead, coed living would "contribute to the development of each resident as a full human being." Through "interpersonal relationships based on friendship and cooperative efforts rather than on the male/female roles we usually play in dating situations" students would try to develop "a human concern that transcends membership in one or the other sex.

While the students disavowed "'boy-meets-girl' contact" as motivation, no one seriously believed that sex was going to disappear. The most cogently stated argument against the plan came from a young man who insisted: "[You] can't ignore the sexual overtones involved in coed living; after all, sex is the basic motivation for your plan. (I didn't say lust, I said sex)." Yet the language in which they framed their proposal was significant: they called for relationships (including sexual) based on a common humanity.

Like Peter Behr and Linda LeClair, these students at the University of Kansas were attempting to redefine both sex and sex roles. Sex should not be negotiated through the dichotomous pairings of male and female, public and private. Instead, they attempted to formulate and articulate a new standard that looked to a model of "togetherness" undreamed of and likely undesired by their parents. The *Life* magazine issue with which this essay began characterized the "sexual revolution" as "dull." "Love still makes the world go square," the author concluded, for the revolutionaries he interviewed subscribed to a philosophy "less indebted to *Playboy* than Peanuts, in which sex is not so much a pleasure as a warm puppy." To his amusement, one "California girl" told him: "Besides being my lover, Bob is my best friend in all the world," and a young man insisted, "We are not sleeping together, we are living together."

For those to whom *Playboy* promised revolution, this attitude was undoubtedly tame. And in the context of the cultural revolution taking place among America's youth, and documented in titillating detail by magazines such as *Life*, these were modest revolutionaries indeed, seeming almost already out of step with their generation. But the issue, to these "dull" revolutionaries, as to their more flamboyant brothers and sister, was larger than sex. They understood that the line between public and private had utility; that the personal was political.

In 1967, The Summer of Love

It was a "holy pilgrimage," according to the Council for a Summer of Love. In the streets of Haight-Ashbury, thousands and thousands of "pilgrims" acted out a street theater of costumed fantasy, drugs and music and sex that was unimaginable in the neat suburban streets of their earlier youth. Visionaries and revolutionaries had preceded the deluge; few of them drowned. Others did. But the tide flowed in the vague countercultural yearnings, drawn by the pop hit "San

Francisco (Be Sure to Wear Flowers in Your Hair)" and its promise of a "love-in," by the pictures in *Life* magazine or in *Look* magazine or in *Time* magazine, by the proclamations of the underground press that San Francisco would be "the love-guerilla training school for drop-outs from mainstream America . . . where the new world, a human world of the 21st century is being constructed." Here sexual freedom would be explored; not cohabitation, not "arrangements," not "living together" in ways that looked a lot like marriage except for the lack of a piece of paper that symbolized the sanction of the state. Sex in the Haight was revolutionary.

In neat suburban houses on neat suburban streets, people came to imagine this new world, helped by television and by the color pictures in glossy-paper magazines (a joke in the Haight told of "bead-wearing *Look* reporters interviewing bead-wearing *Life* reporters"). Everyone knew that these pilgrims represented a tiny fraction of America's young, but the images reverberated. America felt itself in revolution.

Todd Gitlin, in his soul-searching memoir of the sixties, argues the cultural significance of the few:

> Youth culture seemed a counterculture. There were many more weekend dope-smokers than hard-core "heads"; many more readers of the *Oracle* than writers for it; many more co-habitors than orgiasts; many more turners-on than droppers-out. Thanks to the sheer number and concentration of youth, the torrent of drugs, the sexual revolution, the traumatic war, the general stampede away from authority, and the trend-spotting media, it was easy to assume that all the styles of revolt and disaffection were spilling together tributaries into a common torrent of youth and euphoria, life against death, joy over sacrifice, now over later, remaking the whole bleeding world.

Youth culture and counterculture, as Gitlin argues so well, were not synonymous, and for many the culture itself was more a matter of lifestyle than revolutionary intent. But the strands flowed together in the chaos of the age, and the few and the marginal provided archetypes that were read into the youth culture by an American public that did not see the lines of division. "Hippies, yippies, flippies," said Mayor Richard Daley of Chicago. "Free Love," screamed the headlines about Barnard's Linda LeClair.

But even the truly revolutionary youths were not unified, no more on the subject of sex than on anything else. Members of the New Left, revolutionary but rarely countercultural, had sex but did not talk about it all the time. They consigned sex to a relatively "private" sphere. Denizens of Haight-Ashbury lived a Dionysian sexuality, most looking nowhere but to immediate pleasure. Some political-cultural revolutionaries, however, claimed sex and used it for the revolution. They capitalized on the sexual chaos and fears of the nation, attempting to use sex to politicize youth and to challenge "Amerika."

In March 1968 the *Sun*, a Detroit people's paper put out by a "community of artists and lovers" (most notably John Sinclair of the rock group MC5), declared a "Total Assault on the Culture." Sinclair, in his "editorial statement," disavowed any prescriptive intent but informed his readers: "We *have* found that there are three essential human activities of the greatest importance to all persons, and that people are well and healthy in proportion to their involvement in these activities: rock and roll, dope, and fucking in the streets. . . . We suggest the three in combination, all the time."

He meant it. He meant it partly because it was outrageous, but there was more to it. "Fucking" helps you "escape the hangups that are drilled into us in this weirdo country"—it negates "private lives," "feels good," and so destroys an economy of pain and scarcity. Lapsing into inappropriately programmatic language, Sinclair argued:

> Our position is that all people must be free to fuck freely, whenever and wherever they want to, or not to fuck if they don't wanna—in bed, on the floor, in the chair, on the streets, in the parks and fields, "back seat boogie for the high school kids" sing the Fugs who brought it all out in the open on stage and on records, fuck whoever wants to fuck you and everybody else do the same. America's silly sexual "mores" are the end-product of thousands of years of deprivation and sickness, of marriage and companionship based on the ridiculous misconception that one person can "belong" to another person, that "love" is something that has to do with being "hurt," sacrificing, holding out, "teardrops on your pillow," and all that shit.

Sinclair was not alone in his paean to copulation. Other countercultural seekers believed that they had to remake love and reclaim sex to create community. These few struggled, with varying degrees of honesty and sincerity, over the significance of sex in the beloved community.

For others, sex was less a philosophy than a weapon. In the spring of 1968, the revolutionary potential of sex also suffused the claims of the Yippies as they struggled to stage a "Festival of Life" to counter the "Death Convention" in Chicago. "How can you separate politics and sex?" Jerry Rubin asked with indignation after the fact. Yippies lived by that creed. Sex was a double-edged sword, to be played two ways. Sex was a lure to youth; it was part of their attempt to tap the youth market, to "sell a revolutionary consciousness." It was also a challenge, "flaunted in the face" (as it were) of America.

The first Yippie manifesto, released in January 1968, summoned the tribes of Chicago. It played well in the underground press, with its promise of "50,000 of us dancing in the streets, throbbing with amplifiers and harmony . . . making love in the parks." Sex was a politics of pleasure, a politics of abundance that made sense to young middle-class whites who had been raised in the world without limits that was postwar America.

Sex was also incendiary, and the Yippies knew that well. It guaranteed attention. Thus the "top secret" plans for the convention that Abbie Hoffman mimeographed and distributed to the press promised a barbecue and lovemaking by the lake, followed by "Pin the Tail on the Donkey," "Pin the Rubber on the Pope," and "other normal and healthy games." Grandstanding before a crowd of Chicago reporters, the Yippies presented a city official with an official document wrapped in a *Playboy* centerfold inscribed, "To Dick with love, the Yippies." The *Playboy* centerfold in the Yippies' hands was an awkward nexus

between the old and the new sexuality. As a symbolic act, it did not proffer freedom so much as challenge authority. It was a sign of disrespect—to Mayor
Richard Daley and to straight America.

While America was full of young people sporting long hair and beads, the
committed revolutionaries (of cultural stripe) were few in number and marginal
at best. It is telling that the LeClair affair could still be a scandal in a nation that
had weathered the Summer of Love. But the lines were blurred in sixties
America. One might ask with Todd Gitlin, "What was marginal anymore, where
was the mainstream anyway?" when the Beatles were singing, "Why Don't We
Do It in the Road?"

CONCLUSION

The battles of the sexual revolution were hard fought, its victories ambiguous,
its outcome still unclear. What we call the sexual revolution was an amalgam of
movements that flowed together in an unsettled era. They were often at odds
with one another, rarely well thought out, and usually without a clear agenda.

The sexual revolution was built on equal measures of hypocrisy and honesty,
equality and exploitation. Indeed, the individual strands contain mixed motivations and ideological charges. Even the most heartfelt or best intentions did not
always work out for the good when put into practice by mere humans with physical and psychological frailties. As we struggle over the meaning of the "revolution" and ask ourselves who, in fact, *won*, it helps to untangle the threads and
reject the conflation of radically different impulses into a singular revolution.

R E A D I N G

9

Culture Channels Sexuality

BURTON PASTERNAK, CAROL EMBER, MELVIN EMBER

Although sexuality is part of human nature, no society leaves it to nature alone;
all have rules and attitudes channeling proper conduct. When it comes to how
much and what sorts of sexual activity societies allow or encourage before
marriage, outside marriage, and even within marriage, there is considerable variation. Societies also differ in their tolerance of homosexual sexuality. We also

From *Sex, Gender and Kinship: A Cross-Cultural Perspective.* Copyright 1997. Published by
Prentice-Hall.

find that restrictions of one sort or another may not apply throughout life, or to all aspects of sex. Moreover, the various cultural rules governing sexual behavior are not haphazard; within societies there seems to be some consistency among them. For example, societies that frown on sexual expression in young children are also likely to punish premarital and postmarital sex.

Customs may also change over time. In our own society, attitudes were becoming more permissive until the AIDS epidemic. During the 1970s, American behavior and attitudes suggested that acceptance and frequency of premarital sex had increased markedly since Kinsey's surveys in the 1940s. Surprisingly, attitudes toward extramarital sex had not changed much from the 1940s to the 1970s; the vast majority surveyed in the 1970s still objected to it. More recent surveys in the 1990s indicate a large drop in the frequency of both extramarital and premarital sex.

What do we know about how sexuality and sexual relations are regulated cross-culturally? How uniform or varied are customs governing childhood sexuality, premarital sex, and sex after marriage? Do people everywhere disapprove of sexual relations among persons of the same sex? It is to these questions that we now turn. As many of our examples illustrate, acceptance of sexuality is not an all-or-nothing matter; societies differ in the sorts of heterosexual relationships they tolerate (or encourage), and with whom such relationships are proper. So in our discussion of attitudes toward sexuality, it will be useful to consider various kinds of sexuality separately.

It is important to keep in mind that the customs of a society may be reported by an ethnographer as of the time she or he was there, but often (if the culture had been severely disrupted) the ethnography pertains to an earlier time, such as before the people were confined to a reservation. So the customs of a society may have changed substantially after the ethnographic report which we refer to in our discussion.

CHILDHOOD SEXUALITY

One thing we know is that the sexual curiosity of children is not worrisome to all people; in many societies people greet it with tolerance and openness. An ethnographer working among the Aymara of Peru described a people for whom sexual relations in general were considered "normal, natural, and pleasurable." From early childhood the sexes were unsegregated and related easily and freely. Children slept near their parents and were, from early childhood, aware of adult sexuality. The Aymara viewed the sex play of young children with tolerant amusement. Masturbation was not actively disapproved and evoked neither guilt nor shame. Heterosexual activity on the part of children, too, was generally ignored, and if noted, evoked only amusement or mild ridicule. Girls and boys alike usually had considerable sexual experience by the time they reached puberty—in this society virginity had no special value.

Similarly, the Cubeo Indians of the northwest Amazon considered masturbation and sex play between same sex children neither shameful nor worthy of discouragement. We are told that Cubeo boys sometimes indulged in mutual masturbation, while girls might stroke one another's nipples to produce erection. While younger people participated in this "mild form of homosexual eroticism," however, "true homosexuality" was rare.

Not all societies are so permissive when it comes to sex in general or to masturbation in particular. Consider the people of East Bay, a South Pacific island, who exhibited "great concern for sexual propriety." They discouraged children from touching their genitalia in public—the boys through good-natured ridicule, the girls by scolding. By age five, children had learned to avoid all physical contact with the opposite sex and had become highly sensitive to lapses in modesty. Girls and boys were careful to maintain proper distance at all times. Among the Ashanti of Ghana, a father warned his son against the evils of masturbation, of "making a pestle of his penis." And among the Chinese of Taiwan, masturbation was also greeted with strong disapproval:

> If a child is discovered masturbating he is severely scolded and beaten. He is threatened with what will happen if he continues; he will be unable to urinate, or he will go crazy. Children are also expected to conceal their genitalia from the eyes of others. If a boy urinates outside, he must use his hand to conceal his genitals, while girls past the age of four are expected to use the privacy of the benjo [toilet] where no one can see them. They are reprimanded with slaps and scoldings if they expose themselves.

Childhood sexuality is not just about allowing or encouraging children to be autoerotic or sexual with others of their own age. We should also consider attitudes about sexuality involving adults and children. In our society most people consider any sexual behavior involving an adult and child to be child abuse and strongly condemn it. But some societies are more tolerant of sexual behavior between adults and children. We are told that Thai mothers often tickled their sons' genitalia while feeding or playing with them, for example. Among the Kogi of Colombia, mothers taught their sons how to masturbate, using this method from about age five to calm them and make them sleep. What is especially interesting about the Kogi is that fathers' attitudes toward masturbation were very different from mothers'. Fathers considered masturbation a serious transgression and punished it harshly. They were especially concerned about it because of the belief that a child's masturbation endangered the father's health:

> A father condemns in general the manifestations of infantile sexuality in both sexes, but a mother does not. She, in addition to masturbating her son, shows a lively interest in the erotic pleasures which her daughter derives from her body and takes a certain pride in the fact that this instinct is developing in her children. Both parents nevertheless try to avoid having the children observe the sexual activities of the adults, since these are carried out almost solely at night and outside the house, the children evidently do not have any occasion to learn about them.

Some societies also allowed older people special license with respect to sex with young children. Here, for example, is a description of a practice among the Truk of the South Pacific:

> Among older people no longer able for physical or social reasons to have heterosexual liaisons, two practices are reported by a number of informants. Older men not infrequently perform cunnilingus on preadolescent girls; both are said to enjoy this,

the men because it is their only sexual outlet and the girls because it is so gentle . . . [the Trukese refer to such behavior] with tolerant amusement over the dilemma of these old people who have to resort to such devices in order to obtain sexual satisfaction.

While this description might suggest that any sexuality was permitted, the Trukese were much less permissive about certain kinds of sex. When children three or four years in age were observed masturbating they were crossly told to stop, although reproofs did not go beyond "mild pats and somewhat angry sounding remarks." They believed that heterosexual activity made children sick, and that notion extended to masturbation. Yet, as the ethnographers pointed out,

> we may be fairly sure that the prohibition does not reflect disapproval of masturbation as such for this activity is permitted adults with only the restrictions of modesty which apply, for example, to urination, provided the people nearby are of the same sex.

As we have seen, people are not always consistent regarding the kinds of sexual activities allowed infants and children. However, there is a general tendency for societies that allow children to express their sexuality with each other before puberty to be fairly tolerant of premarital and extramarital intercourse as well. Such societies also tend not to insist on modesty in dress and do not constrain their talk about sex around children. Still, no society is entirely free and open about sex. Even the most permissive societies do not allow sexual intercourse between parents and children or between brothers and sisters.

HETEROSEXUALITY IN ADOLESCENCE

Do relatively permissive societies alter their attitudes toward sexuality when pregnancy becomes possible? Mostly they do not; as we have seen, tolerance of childhood sexuality generally predicts tolerance for premarital sex. Many societies permissive of childhood sexuality get girls to marry before or shortly after puberty, so premarital pregnancy is not usually a problem. Some make a clear distinction between sexual play and intercourse before marriage. For example, among the Kikuyu of Kenya, premarital sex was traditionally encouraged as long as intercourse was avoided. Adolescents practiced *ngweko* which involved "platonic love and fondling." Girls wore an *apron* over their genitals and adults taught them, and the boys, how to intertwine legs so as to enjoy sex without intercourse. Traditionally, they learned to do this after initiation into an age-set, but now that the initiation and age-set system has broken down, the practice of ngweko has diminished. Sexual activity has not decreased, however, and premarital pregnancy is not now unusual.

More permissive than the Kikuyu were the Trobriand Islanders who permitted sexual intercourse before marriage. Girls were expected to have sex with boys visiting from other villages, and could have as many lovers as they wished. This was still the case during the 1970s and 1980s when Annette B. Weiner did fieldwork among the Trobriand Islanders. As she describes it,

> in the Trobriands, adultery is a crime, but premarital love affairs are not. For unmarried young people, each decorative element is carefully chosen to catch the eye of a

possible lover, as each use of magic is calculated to "make someone want to sleep with you." Attraction and seduction are adolescent pursuits, and the presence of young people walking through Losuia, laughing, singing, and teasing, made Saturdays almost as celebratory as traditional yam harvest feasts.

Even while involved in the daily village routine, young people are preoccupied with their own plans and negotiations. Throughout the day, lovers send messages back and forth to arrange evening meeting places. Conversations between young people are filled with sexual metaphors that express a person's intention. Questions such as "Can I have a coconut to drink?" or "Can I ride your bicycle?" are Trobriand ways to say, "Will you sleep with me?" Dabweyowa once told me, "Women's eyes are different than men's. When I talk to a girl I watch her eyes. If she looks straight at me, I know she wants me." Young women are just as assertive and dominant as men in their pursuit or refusal of a lover.

Given the frequency of premarital sex among the Trobrianders, Malinowski was puzzled about why there was so little premarital pregnancy. Whiting et al. suggest its rarity was perhaps due to adolescent subfecundity—Trobriand girls remained unmarried for only about three years after puberty. Trobriand Islanders believed that pregnancy was unrelated to copulation, perhaps because the frequent sex did not often result in pregnancy.

Among the Tikopia of the Pacific, masturbation was an acceptable alternative to intercourse for the young of both sexes. Their only reservation was that masturbation makes the hands unclean for food preparation. In the case of men, masturbation could involve self or mutual stimulation, and a girl might masturbate herself if she

> cannot get a man to have intercourse with her, or is too shy to ask the one she wants. It is said that only women who have already tasted sex pleasure will act thus. Such a woman "remembers the male organ," and with her finger, or a manioc root, or a peeled banana, rubs herself. She does so with increasing energy as her desire climbs up. It is because of the force used that it is customary to peel the banana; otherwise her genitals would become sore.

Allowing premarital sex does not always mean that anxiety about sex is absent. For example, even though premarital sex on the Micronesian island of Truk was allowed during the late 1940s and early 1950s, courting usually involved trysts in the bush and secret visits at night to the girl's home. Discovery evoked teasing, even if there was no punishment. The Trukese believed men should initiate sex. But for young men, getting a sexual relationship started, and keeping it going, could be quite stressful. For one thing, it was not easy to find unmarried women with whom to "practice" because girls married early, usually around the time of puberty. It was easier to establish illicit relationships with married women. That was always a bit risky; if discovered, such relationships could be embarrassing, especially for the young man. Courting an unmarried (or married) woman usually required skill at writing love letters. Gladwin and Sarason noted: "It is ironic that, in terms of quantity at least, the most important use to which the art of writing has been put by the Trukese since it was taught them so painfully by missionaries and administration alike is the writing of love letters." A woman could pick and choose among potential lovers, who struggled and competed to satisfy her sexual needs:

Sexual intercourse, without which a lover's relationship has no meaning for the Trukese, by its very nature requires the expression of strong emotion not only by the man, but also by the woman. In some societies the occurrence or nonoccurrence of female orgasm is not considered of major importance; on Truk, however, it is important, particularly for more accomplished or serious lovers, and its occurrence is a function of the contribution of both partners to the relationship. For the man it determines the success or failure of his performance: If he reaches his climax before the woman he not only leaves her in some degree unsatisfied, but more importantly from his standpoint has "lost" in the contest.

The woman could also exert some control over her lover by virtue of the fact that she possessed his letters, by their nature clear evidence of his intent to consummate a sexual liaison. Their purpose was unambiguous, and by answering a letter a woman essentially agreed to sex. Were she later to become displeased with her lover, she could publicize the letters to his discomfort. All-around, sexual liaisons were far more difficult and sensitive for the man (although not less exciting for that reason):

> It is the woman whose position is at every turn secure and the man who exposes himself to hazards. A man has committed himself by writing the first letter; the woman holds and can expose the incriminating document. With the entry into the house and his approach to the woman it is again the man who runs the risk: of being discovered or of being rejected. And finally during the intercourse itself it is the man who stands to "lose" if he ejaculates too soon; it must furthermore be noted that it is under these circumstances that the type of intercourse least likely to produce rapid orgasm in the woman is used.

Not all peoples are as tolerant of premarital sex as those we have been describing. The Chinese certainly valued premarital chastity and wifely fidelity after marriage. They traditionally took pains to control the perambulation of women, and to limit their contact with the opposite sex. These efforts were not always successful. Constant watchfulness notwithstanding, girls did (and do) have affairs and even get pregnant before marriage, courting discovery, punishment, shame, and possibly reducing bride-wealth value. It was a heavy burden for any family to discover, after a son's marriage, that his bride was not a virgin. But, as one of Pasternak's Taiwan informants put it, "rice already cooked cannot be returned to the storage bin." Such a family usually tries to contain and hide their discovery, but the daughter-in-law can expect to pay for her indiscretion.

Watchfulness was essential among the Tepoztlan of Mexico as well, where a girl's life became "crabbed, cribbed, confined" from her first menstruation. From then on she was not to speak to or encourage boys in the least way. It was a mother's burden to guard her daughters' chastity and reputation. One mother confided to the ethnographer that she wished her fifteen-year-old daughter would marry soon because it was inconvenient to "spy" on her all the time. Indeed, virginity at marriage was (and often still is) important in many cultures. In many Muslim societies, it used to be customary to display blood-stained sheets after the wedding night as proof of a bride's virginity.

With increased education, attitudes toward female/male relationships are often relaxed. In the small Moroccan town of Zawiya, adolescent girls and boys can now walk to school and study together, although dating is still taboo and marriages are still largely arranged (as of the mid–1980s). In the previous generation, just talking together was considered shameful. Even now a girl risks her reputation if people see her too often in a boy's company; they invariably suspect the worst. And a boy might well eliminate as potential mate any girl who has kissed him before. Zawiya town clearly has a double standard, constraining girls more than boys. But surprisingly it is not common for societies to have a double standard regarding premarital sex.

What sorts of societies are more accepting of premarital sex than others, and why? Comparative research work by Suzanne G. Frayser provides some indications. To begin with, her research revealed that more societies allow premarital sex for one or both sexes than do not, and that where there are restraints, they are considerably more likely to apply to sex before marriage than to extramarital sex. Further, societies that restrict sex before marriage are likely to restrict extramarital sex as well. When the rules differ for women and men, it is always in the direction of allowing greater freedom to males. As Frayser put it, "the double standard operates only in one direction."

But why should there be more interest in restricting women's sexual relationships, or in confining them to the reproductive context (to marriage) in some societies but not in others? In this connection, Frayser draws our attention to the fact that women are more obviously linked to their offspring than men, through childbirth, nursing, and the like. For men, the linkage must be assured in other ways:

> If a man has a continuing relationship with a woman who confines her sexual relations exclusively to him, he can more easily identify any children she bears as his own. Therefore, a man indirectly affirms his physical link to his child by creating a close, social bond with the woman whose children he wishes to claim as his own. Cultural beliefs about his role in conception and the restriction of the woman's sexual relations to him further strengthen the basis for his connection with the child.

Still, why are some people more concerned about paternity than others? It is clear that societies vary in the degree to which social groups have an interest in the reproductive potential of women. Consider two examples Frayser provides, one a society in which there is little interest, the other in which interest is considerable.

Among the Kimam, inhabitants of an island off New Guinea, women may have premarital sex and even take the initiative in that regard. There is considerable extramarital liberty as well, for women as well as men. It is not that having children is of no concern; everyone wants sons to work the gardens and to provide support in old age. They need daughters, too, to exchange for daughters-in-law. Interest in childbirth is so strong that a man can divorce or kill his wife for aborting her child.

Although the Kimam appreciate the biological contribution women and men make to childbearing, they base rights to children on other considerations. As Frayser puts it, "conceiving or giving birth to a child is not sufficient reason to claim the right of parenthood; people acquire this right by taking care of the child." For that reason, a barren woman need not fear shame or retribution. Adoption provides an easy solution; few refuse to give a child. Establishment of paternity may not be so much an issue because adoption is acceptable. A man helps support his sister's children and has the right to adopt the sister's child.

Consider now the Kenuzi Nubians, on Egypt's Nile River, among whom strict control over women's sexuality begins early. When a girl is three or four, the custom is to remove her clitoris and practically seal her vaginal opening to guarantee virginity at marriage. And once married she can have sex only with her husband, who often spends long periods working far from home. Husbands sometimes insist that their wives' vaginas be sewn up during long absences. A husband may kill his wife at the slightest suspicion of infidelity, so conception during his absence is to be avoided at all cost.

Like the Kimam, the Kenuzi want children; women to ensure continuation of marriage (and husband's economic support), men to provide for continuity of their descent groups. In fact, reproduction is so much a group concern among the Kenuzi that a man is under pressure to remarry if his wife bears no sons. (This is a source of considerable anxiety for wives, especially given that one-third to one-half of Kenuzi children die young.) Sons, as in all patrilineal societies, belong to the kin groups of their father. For these reasons, men may feel it important to establish paternity and they attempt to do so by strictly controlling the sexuality of women. However, societies that emphasize the mother in kinship (matrilineal societies) have no comparable problem. Identification of the mother is critical for access to kin group resources but maternity is hardly problematic. Knowing the identity of the father is not vital, so controlling his sexuality is probably not as necessary in societies that have kin groups oriented around women.

Where descent is traced through women, then, establishing paternity may be less vital. There, a man's responsibility is to his sister's children; children belong to their mother's group, which is also that of the mother's brother. A man's own offspring belong to a different group—to that of his wife. Thus, a husband's contribution to reproduction can be relatively brief and limited. The link between mother and child is crucial, but motherhood requires no special confirmation.

Is the patterning of kinship crucial to the control of sexuality, then? Frayser's data do confirm that patrilineal systems are more likely to restrict women's sexual relations, and confine their reproductive potential to one man, than matrilineal systems. We find the opposite where descent is traced through women: low confinement of women's sexual and reproductive relationships to one man.

But what of societies in which descent is not traced exclusively through women or men, or in which there are no descent groups at all? Such societies, like patrilineal ones, also tend to emphasize father-child bonds. Frayser suggests this may be because most of these societies require a woman to live with or near her husband's family (patrilocally) when she marries:

> Paternity would be most important in patrilocal groups, because it is the only residence pattern whereby an individual's postmarital residence depends upon where the person's father lives. In addition, patrilocal residence means that the raw materials for community organization consist of clusters of related males.

The comparative evidence confirms that patrilocality is significantly related to restrictions on women's sexual and reproductive relationships. It is even more strongly related to such restrictions than patrilineal descent is related to such restrictions. In fact, patrilineal societies may have these constraints because they are usually also patrilocal.

The nature of kinship organization clearly has an impact, but environmental factors too may play a role. The Circum-Mediterranean area is especially restrictive when it comes to female sexuality, with strong prohibitions against both premarital and extramarital sex. Divorces are difficult to obtain, and where granted the basis is usually barrenness. Remarriage after divorce or death of a husband is difficult. And, as Jane Schneider has pointed out, considerable attention is given in this region to matters of honor, shame, and virginity. There is also considerable competition for pastoral and agricultural resources, resulting in conflict within and between groups, and weak political integration. In the face of competition and social fragmentation, family and descent groups are unstable. Lacking effective political controls, codes of honor and shame provide some degree of social control. In Frayser's view, there may be good reason for women to abide by these codes as well:

> In Circum-Mediterranean societies, a woman's contribution to subsistence relative to a man's is lowest in comparison with all other world areas. Therefore, if a woman's husband divorces her, her consequent economic deprivation would be of major proportions. This economic loss could over-shadow a woman's temptation to violate the regulations placed upon her sexual or reproductive relationships.

Are similar sorts of societies likely, then, to be more or less permissive when it comes to premarital sex? Indeed, in societies where property and other rights are passed to children through males (patrilineal descent) and where married couples live with or near the husband's parents (patrilocal residence), premarital pregnancies tend to evoke considerable disapproval.

In such societies, an unmarried woman who becomes pregnant puts her child at a severe economic as well as social disadvantage. However, if rights to property pass through the mother (matrilineal descent) and women live with or near their own kin when they marry (matrilocal residence), then illegitimate children usually enjoy access to resources.

Societies with dowry, goods and money given by the bride's family to the bride or the couple, are also likely to be restrictive of premarital sex. And, as we will see in the chapter on getting married, dowry is common in socially stratified societies, where families often use large dowries to attract high-status sons-in-law. That strategy may well fail, however, if a daughter has had sex with and become pregnant by a low-status male. So, one reason families guard daughters may be to defend against social climbers attempting to use seduction and pregnancy to force a marriage.

Cross-cultural studies do indicate that complex societies—those with political hierarchies, part- or full-time craft specialists, cities and towns, and class stratification—are especially likely to restrict premarital sex. Perhaps with increasing social inequality, parents become increasingly concerned about their children avoiding marriage with people "beneath them." Permissive premarital sex could complicate matters if it leads to inappropriate emotional attachments.

Even worse, unsuitable liaisons resulting in pregnancy could make it difficult or impossible for a girl to marry well. Consistent with this notion, we find that societies with little premarital sex also tend to have arranged marriages.

The degree to which premarital and extramarital sexuality are regulated in society are clearly not matters of chance or accident. These customs and practices are related to each other, to characteristics of kinship and political organization, and perhaps to ecological adaptations as well. Our understanding of the connections is still rudimentary, however, and much more research still needs to be done.

HOMOSEXUALITY

We discuss homosexuality separately because societal attitudes toward it are apparently unrelated to those governing heterosexuality. Because many societies deny homosexuality exists and many ethnographers have ignored it, the incidence or prevalence of homosexuality cross-culturally is difficult to estimate. It is easier simply to determine whether a society permits or prohibits homosexuality. We know less about female homosexuality (less often discussed in ethnographies), but we do know that if it is permitted for adolescent girls, it is almost always also permitted for adolescent boys. We are also aware that permissiveness of homosexuality in adolescence almost always predicts tolerance of it in adulthood.

The consensus now is that homosexuality is not a unitary phenomenon. Some researchers suggest that different types of male homosexuality should be distinguished. In some societies, for example, homosexuality is *mandatory* during a phase of the life cycle. This is the case in parts of Melanesia, where homosexuality is commonly associated with the initiation rites which all adolescent boys undergo. Here, younger participants receive semen from older men in homosexual episodes. They subsequently become the inseminators of younger boys. Later still, they marry heterosexually and have children. Some examples follow.

Among the Big Nambas of Malekula, an island in eastern Melanesia, boys become lovers of older men. The custom is that, after a decision to hold circumcision rites, fathers find guardians for their sons, guardians who will possess exclusive sexual rights over the boys. The guardian becomes the boy's "husband," in a relationship that is very close and usually monogamous. (Chiefs are different; they may take many boy lovers just as they may have many wives.) The boy accompanies his guardian everywhere, and should one die, the survivor would mourn him deeply.

Homosexual liaisons elsewhere in Melanesia are not as intimate or monogamous as among the Big Nambas. Those of the Keraki, in the Trans-Fly area of Papua New Guinea, are more transitory. With respect to the Keraki, Creed tells us that

> sodomy was fully sanctioned by male society, universally practiced, and . . . homosexuality was actually regarded as essential to a boy's bodily growth. Boys are initiated at the bull-roarer ceremony at about the age of thirteen. On the night of the ceremony the initiate is turned over to a youth of the previous group of initiates who

introduces the boy to homosexual intercourse. In all cases . . . the older youth was the mother's brother's son or the father's sister's son of the new initiate. After this, the boy is available to fellow villagers or visitors of the opposite moiety who wish to have homosexual relations with him. During this time the initiates live together in a seclusion hut for several months, during which they are supposed to grow rapidly with the aid of homosexual activities. At the end of the seclusion the youth becomes a "bachelor." He associates more freely with the elders and shows an increased interest in hunting, but he continues to play the passive role in homosexual relations for a year or so.

Initiates then go through a ceremony during which lime is poured down their throats. People believe the burns which result ensure that the boys have not become pregnant as a result of their homosexual relationships. From that time sexual passivity is over; newly initiated youths now become the inseminators of other boys until, in time, they marry heterosexually.

The expectation that all boys will engage in homosexual relationships with older men is not limited to Melanesia. Other societies have this custom as well. For example, the Siwans of Egypt expected all unmarried males to have homosexual relations, which their fathers arranged. The custom was not entirely permissive, however, since it limited a man to one boy. Although the government eventually prohibited Siwan homosexuality, it was practiced quite openly until 1909. Almost all older men reported having had homosexual relationships as boys. Later, between sixteen and twenty years of age, they invariably married girls. As in Melanesia, then, homosexuality was a phase in every man's life.

The mandatory homosexuality we have been describing usually involves relationships between older men and boys. But homosexuality finds acceptance even in societies where it is not mandatory; some researchers suggest that it commonly occurs as a form of adolescent experimentation. As we noted in our earlier discussion of childhood sexuality, some societies allow casual homosexual play. Still others have special times when homosexuality can be expressed. For example, the Papago of the southwestern United States had "nights of saturnalia," during which males could have brief homosexual relationships. Quite a few North American Indian societies also accommodated male transvestites, commonly referred to as *berdaches*. These men assumed the dress, occupations, and many of the behaviors of women. But whether they were homosexual as well is not clear. The evidence in the ethnographic literature suggests quite a bit of variability. In some societies, like the Papago, Crow, Mohave, and Santee, berdaches reportedly did engage in homosexual behavior. However, informants denied they were homosexual among the Flathead, Pima, Plains Cree, Chiracahua Apache, and Bella Coola. Also variable was the extent to which berdaches married. Where they did, in some societies they customarily married nonberdache men and assumed a woman's role; in other cases they married women and established heterosexual relationships.

In some native North American societies, females too could adopt transvestite roles, but this was much less often accepted. One survey found reports of female transvestites in 30 native North American societies, compared to 113 with male transvestites. And in societies with both female and male berdaches, the females were usually far less common than their male counterparts. Female berdaches often cross-dressed and took up some male pursuits, like hunting. Homosexuality is mentioned in connection with them in some North American societies, but in others their sexual proclivities are not clearly described.

Sexuality is not necessarily either heterosexual or homosexual. The notion of gender does not invariably involve just two categories—female and male— and berdache-like roles are not limited to North America. In a survey of 186 societies, Richley H. Crapo found such statuses in 41 or 22 percent of them, and about half were outside North America. Only eight societies (3 percent) provided evidence of female berdaches. Just as accounts more often describe male berdaches, so do they more often report male homosexuality than lesbianism. Without more research on lesbianism in societies around the world, there is no way to know whether it is reported less often than male homosexuality because it really is so, or because ethnographers have neglected to investigate the phenomenon and the members of many societies are more reluctant to discuss it.

The fact that societies accepting homosexuality in childhood are generally also tolerant of it in adulthood does not imply that expectations about sexual behavior do not change in adulthood. Reproduction requires heterosexual relationships, so it is hardly surprising that, once individuals are able to reproduce, societies expect and prefer them to do so. Indeed, even in societies where most or all individuals have homosexual experiences during an early stage of their lives, most adults marry and have heterosexual intercourse. And even where people may adopt roles atypical for their sex, such individuals are rare. There are actually very few societies in which people prefer homosexuality over heterosexuality in adulthood. The Etoro of New Guinea were one such society. Although most men married and had heterosexual sex, the Etoro actually prohibited heterosexual sex for as many as 260 days a year, and never allowed it in or near the house or gardens. There were no restrictions on male homosexuality, however; the Etoro believed it made crops flourish and boys strong.

While people tolerate homosexuality in most societies, in some they condemn or ridicule it, or consider it incomprehensible. A few societies even eliminate persons discovered engaging in homosexual acts. For example, the Eastern Apache executed homosexuals, considering them dangerous witches. However, they did not consider cross-dressing synonymous with homosexuality; they ridiculed berdaches, but did not execute them unless they were homosexual as well. Among the Azande of the Sudan, too, the reaction was severe. Lesbianism among women in princely households was punishable by death, flogging the likely response in poorer families.

Several cross-cultural studies have attempted to discover why some societies are more accepting of homosexuality than others. The findings, unfortunately, have been contradictory. Part of the problem may be that most researchers have not distinguished different kinds of male homosexuality. If degree of acceptance varies according to type, then failing to make such distinctions could well obscure the results. Nonetheless, an intriguing study by Dennis Werner found that societies with evidence of population pressure on resources, and therefore with reason to limit reproduction, are more likely to tolerate male homosexuality.

The presumption is, of course, that more homosexuality translates into less heterosexuality and, therefore, a lower reproductive rate. By way of contrast, societies that forbid abortion and infanticide for married women (most permit these practices for illegitimate births) are likely to disapprove of male homosexuality, suggesting that it may be less acceptable in societies struggling to increase their populations. These societies may discourage any behavior that inhibits population growth. Widespread homosexuality would have that effect to the extent that it decreased heterosexual relations. Another bit of evidence in support of the population pressure interpretation is that societies with famines and severe food shortages, indirect indicators of excess population, are also more likely to allow homosexuality.

Policy changes in the former Soviet Union were consistent with this interpretation. In 1917, during the turmoil of revolution, the government encouraged people to have fewer children, and also revoked laws prohibiting abortion and homosexuality. Later, when a pronatalist policy emerged (1934–1936), the Soviet government rewarded mothers with many children, and once again declared abortion and homosexuality illegal.

Population pressure may not be the only inducement to more relaxed attitudes toward homosexuality. We know, for example, that societies with customary rites of passage from boyhood to manhood (usually including genital operations) are also more likely to condone or encourage homosexuality, although the reasons are unclear. It is important to keep in mind, as well, that while problems of population growth (too little or too much) may have something to do with *societal* attitudes toward homosexuality, such problems cannot explain why certain *individuals* become homosexual.

Let us return, now, to the matter of types. Have comparative studies thrown any light on the conditions under which different forms of homosexuality are more or less likely to occur? In one study, Richley H. Crapo compared mandatory intergenerational homosexuality (which he calls mentorship homosexuality) with voluntary same generation homosexuality, and found that they occur in different types of societies. The mentorship variety appears in societies with male-centered kin groups, a good deal of segregation of the sexes in childhood, and clear role distinctions between males and females.

This is consistent with earlier suggestions that mentorship homosexuality is part of a larger syndrome reflecting strong male power and authority. Where older men exercise strong control over women and younger males, institutionalizing homosexuality for younger males may increase their prospects of acquiring multiple wives. If this is so, mentorship homosexuality may have more to do with control than with some fundamental homosexual orientation or desire. Societies with voluntary same generation homosexuality (or at least a tolerance of male transvestites) may be different. Although early theorists thought that male transvestism was a way for some males to escape oppressive sex-role requirements (such as aggressive warrior roles), subsequent research by Munroe, Whiting, and Hally found that male transvestism was actually more likely where sex-role distinctions are *minimal.* In societies that emphasize female-male role differences, people seem to consider transvestism less acceptable.

We have been talking about the degree to which societies allow or tolerate different kinds of sex, but we have not yet considered how people *think* of sex—as desirable and pleasurable, or as a duty and perhaps even frightening? Just because a society allows a certain type of sex with a certain type of person does not mean people generally desire it. On the other hand, even forbidden sex may be illicitly enjoyed by some. When it comes to attitudes toward sexuality, too, we find considerable variation, as the following examples will show.

Sex, according to the Chukchee of Siberia, was the "best thing" in the world, while for the Cayapa of Ecuador it was "a little like work." And earlier in this chapter, we discussed the Aymara and Trukese, who clearly also considered sex pleasurable and desirable. Where people think of sex as pleasurable, it is not necessarily so for one sex alone. This was clearly the case on Truk, where men went to great lengths to ensure orgasm in their partners. And among the Bemba of Africa,

> puberty is eagerly looked forward to by the girls. They and their parents watch the growth of their breasts with interest and excitement and openly discuss the approach of womanhood. Girls are enthusiastic about the prospect of marriage and are taught that sex relations are pleasant and that it is their duty to give pleasure to their husbands. They do not seem to fear the first act of intercourse or to apprehend that it will be painful.

Malinowski tells us that for Trobriand Islanders the most important idea about sex was that it is "purely a source of pleasure." Here is an informant's account, a description of lovemaking which clearly conveys the pleasure derived by women and men alike:

> When I sleep with Dabugera I embrace her, I hug her with my whole body, I rub noses with her. We suck each other's lower lip, so that we are stirred to passion. We suck each other's tongues, we bite each other's noses, we bite each other's chins, we bite cheeks and caress the armpit and the groin. Then she will say: "O my lover, it itches very much . . . push on again, my whole body melts with pleasure . . . do it vigorously, be quick, so that the fluids may discharge . . . tread on again, my body feels so pleasant."

In some societies men take special pains to assure the pleasure of their sex partners. This was clearly also the case among the Toradja, a people of Central Celebes, according to the account provided by Adriani and Kruyte:

> for the purpose of increasing sensual pleasure, the penis is sometimes mutilated. . . . One man from there even claimed that someone whose penis is not mutilated is not desired by the women. This mutilation is done by inserting under the skin of the glans of the penis little marbles of about five millimeters in diameter, which are ground from shells. The men of Kawanga had this operation done in a woods located between this place and Moengkoe-lande. The skin of the glans of the penis is pinched in a split piece of wood, so that it protrudes above. Then the skin is pierced and the little balls are pushed into the cut, after which this is rubbed with horse manure. These little marbles are called *kandoekoe* (*makamloekoe,* "uneven, bumpy"). At each operation two or three little balls are inserted, up to seven in all. (It is said

that there are girls who inquire about the number of kandoekoe that a young man who asks to marry them has, with the words: "How many guests do you have" (*bara sangkoedja linggonamoe*). They are said to be inserted in such a way that, when the penis is limp, the little marbles are on the under side of it, and with an erection they come to lie on the upper side. The operation takes place without any ceremony. When the wound has healed, the person must not eat any peas (*tibesi*), fern greens (*bate'a*), or slimy vegetables; otherwise the little marbles will fall out.

While many people consider sex pleasurable, there are also those who find it dangerous and fearful. The Mae Enga, in Highland New Guinea, are an example of a society in which men are afraid to have sex with women, even in marriage. Before and after heterosexual sex, men engage in various rituals to protect themselves against harm. Mervyn Meggitt described the situation as follows:

> Each act of coitus increases a man's chances of being contaminated . . . copulation is in itself detrimental to male well-being. Men believe that the vital fluid residing in a man's skin makes it sound and handsome, a condition that determines and reflects his mental vigor and self-confidence. This fluid also manifests itself as his semen. Hence, every ejaculation depletes his vitality, and over-indulgence must dull his mind and leave his body permanently exhausted and withered.

We do not have research yet on why some societies think of sex as a pleasure versus a duty, but we do know quite a bit about the conditions under which men will fear sex with women. Relatively few societies express fears as strong as the Mae Enga, but we find evidence of a milder fear of sex in many societies around the world. During planting, sex may spoil the harvest; dreams about sex can bring bad luck; sex before sports may result in losing the game. Carol R. Ember has conducted cross-cultural research to evaluate four explanations of men's fear of sex with women. She limited herself to men's attitudes only because women's views are not often described in ethnographies.

One explanation, suggested by Meggitt on the basis of data from various places in New Guinea, is that men may fear sex with women if they usually obtain wives from their enemies, as the Mae Enga did (along with many other societies in Papua New Guinea's Western Highlands.) On the other hand, fear of sex with women is likely to be absent if marriage is not with traditional enemies (as in the Central Highlands of Papua New Guinea).

A second hypothesis Ember tested was that of Shirley Lindenbaum, who proposed that fear of sex with women may be a cultural device that serves to restrain population growth where resources are endangered. If Lindenbaum is right, fear of sex with women should be found in the presence of population pressure.

Beatrice B. Whiting suggested a third possibility: If men are conflicted about their sexual identity, they are likely to exhibit exaggerated masculine behavior as well as antagonism toward, and fear of, women. We might expect problems of sexual identity where there is an initial unconscious feminine identification and a subsequent (more conscious) identification with men. That sequence is likely where, early in life, boys have almost exclusive contact with mothers who exert almost complete control over them. That situation could lead to an initial feminine identification. When they later become aware that men actually control the society's important resources, boys might shift their identification to men. Accordingly, men's fear of sex with women should be particularly likely where they initially have a cross-sex identification.

The fourth proposal Ember tested was that of William N. Stephens, who suggested that some societies may produce an exaggerated *Oedipus complex*, which in turn is conducive to a fear of sex with women. The idea here is that anxiety about heterosexual sex should emerge where we find an unconscious equation of *mother* with *sex partner*. If a boy's sexual interest in his mother were heightened for some reason, he would be especially frightened because of the incest taboo (fearing retaliation by the father). Under what circumstances might the Oedipus complex be exaggerated? Stephens suggests this might occur where custom frustrates a mother's sexual expression, causing her to redirect some of her sexual interest toward her son. This could happen, for example, where there is a long postpartum sex taboo (a mother avoiding sex for a year or more after she gives birth). But whatever the reason, the closer the relationship between mother and son, and the more contact between them, the more likely his Oedipal impulses will be enhanced, and the more likely he will fear sex with women (generalizing from his fear of sex with his mother).

When Ember tested the predictive value of these four hypotheses cross-culturally, she found support for all four. The more a society marries its enemies, the more likely men will fear sex with women. The more evidence of population pressure (food shortages or famine), the more likely men will be afraid of sex with women. Where mothers sleep closer to their infants than to their husbands *and* live with or near their husbands' families when they marry (a combination that presumably produces conflict over male sex identity), men tend to fear sex with women. As for the Oedipal interpretation, duration of the postpartum sex taboo does not by itself predict that men will fear sex with women, but Ember did find that men are likely to fear sex with women in societies where mothers customarily sleep closer physically (in the same bed or room) to their babies than to their husbands. Because all of the hypotheses tested were supported, Ember suggests the following theory to integrate them:

> "Marrying enemies" (with food shortage as a partial cause) creates emotional distance (including sleeping distance) between husbands and wives. This in turn may exaggerate a boy's unconscious sexual interest in his mother, which becomes frightening in view of the incest taboo. Given the incest taboo, this exaggerated interest may result in a general fear of sex with women.

Reanalyzing Ember's data, Michio Kitahara has offered a different interpretation. He suggests that food shortages may have a more direct effect on men's fear of sex than Ember supposed; anxiety about food itself may inhibit sexual desire. (The Embers now speculate that, lacking an adequate diet, people might experience dizziness and weakness during and after sex, reactions that could lead to the conclusion that sex is dangerous.) Societies in which men fear sex with women may have considerable stress of one kind or another. Food shortage is only one kind of stress; there are others. For example, if people find mates in nearby villages with which they are periodically at war, marriage with women from enemy villages might well promote sexual anxiety. We should keep in mind, however, that the risk of famine and marriage with enemies are likely to be stressful for both parties, for the women as well as the men. If Kitahara's theory is right, then, we would expect both genders to fear heterosexual sex. Unfortunately, we do not yet have comparative research that might enable us to confirm or refute this theory. One reason may be that ethnographic accounts are generally deficient about women's thoughts on sexual attitudes, probably because most of them have been written by men.

Fear of women is not only manifested in reluctance to have sex. The Mae Enga also believe that menstrual blood is dangerous, that contact with it can "sicken a man and cause persistent vomiting, turn his blood black, corrupt his vital juices so that his skin darkens and wrinkles as his flesh wastes, permanently dull his wits, and eventually lead to a slow decline and death." The Onge of Little Andaman are also among those who refrain during menses, believing that swelling of the arms and legs would follow. Among the Chinese, too, sex is prohibited during menstruation; women in this state are considered polluting, as they are for one month after childbirth, when sex would "endanger the health of all concerned."

The notion that menstrual blood is dangerous is actually fairly common around the world, and most often the danger is to men or to the community at large. Rarely are risks to women mentioned in ethnographic accounts. This raises the possibility that men's fear of sex with women, and fear of menstrual blood, may both be part of a more general pattern of husband-wife avoidance and aloofness. It should also be noted that societies in which sex is enjoyable rather than frightening, and in which marital relationships are likely to be inti-mate, are generally also those in which social organization does not center on men. We will return to the issue of marital intimacy and aloofness later, in our chapter on marital relationships. But first let us shift gears to pursue at greater length a matter only vaguely suggested thus far. At a number of points in this chapter, we noted that societies vary in terms of how sharply they define differ-ent roles for women and men. Just what is the relationship between sex and social roles, or between them and characteristics of personality? It is to these questions that we will turn in the next chapter.

CHAPTER 5

◆

MARRIAGE, DIVORCE, REMARRIAGE

R E A D I N G

10

The Future of Marriage

FRANK P. FURSTENBERG, JR.

It's clear that the institution of family is undergoing a major overhaul. Perhaps you've recently been to a wedding where the bride and groom have invited their former spouses to join the festivities. Or maybe a family member told you that your 37-year-old unmarried cousin is pregnant by artificial insemination. Or you heard that your 75-year-old widowed grandfather just moved in with his 68-year-old woman friend. To those of us who grew up in the 1950s, the married-couple family is beginning to look like the Model T Ford.

Public concern over changes in the practice of marriage is approaching hysteria. An avalanche of books and articles declares that the American family is in a severe state of crisis. Yet little agreement exists among experts on what the crisis is about, why it has occurred, or what could be done to restore confidence in matrimony. I believe that the current situation falls somewhere between those who embrace the changes with complete sanguinity and an increasingly vocal group who see the meltdown of the so-called traditional family as an unmitigated disaster.

Social scientists agree that we have seen a startling amount of change in nuptial practices in the past half century. The shift is producing an especially striking contrast from the 1940s, because the period just after World War II was a time of remarkable domestication. The post-war period followed several

From *American Demographics*, June 1996. Copyright 1996.

Frank F. Furstenberg, Jr., is the Zellerbach Family Professor of Sociology at the University of Pennsylvania, and author of Divided Families: *What Happens to Children When Parents Part.*

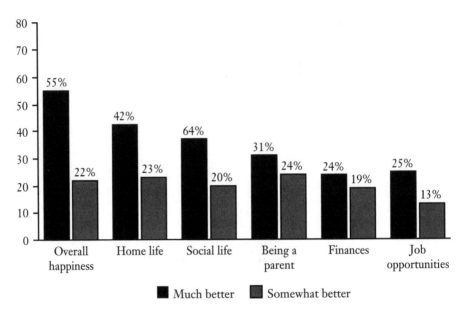

Percent of separated women who say selected aspects of their life are
somewhat or much better than the year before they separated, 1992-93

■ Much better   ▨ Somewhat better

FIGURE 5.1 The Trade-Offs of Ending a Marriage. Recently separated women are
more likely to perceive improvement in their parenting and social lives than in their
financial well-being. *Note:* Separated women are those who split from their husbands
since the last survey was taken in 1987–88. *Source:* National Survey of Families and
Households, 1992–93.

decades of turbulence in marriage patterns initiated by rapid urbanization
during World War I, and the Great Depression.

Many of the complaints about family life in the 1990s sound an awful lot like
those voiced in the 1950s, an era we look upon with nostalgia. We often forget
that the current gold standard of family life—the family built upon an intimate
marital relationship—was regarded with great suspicion when it made its debut.
The middle-class nuclear family that became the norm at mid-century was a
stripped-down version of the extended families of previous decades. Kingsley
Davis observed that a host of social ills could be traced to this new form of
family: " . . . The family union has been reduced to its lowest common denomi-
nator—married couple and children. The family aspect of our culture has
become couple-centered with only one or two children eventually entering the
charmed circle," he wrote.

Ernest Burgess, one of the most respected sociologists of his generation,
wrote in 1953 that urbanization, greater mobilization, individualization,
increased secularization, and the emancipation of women had transformed the
family from an institution based on law and custom to one based on companionship and love. Despite believing that the changes taking place in the family were

largely beneficial to society, Burgess acknowledged that enormous pressure would be placed on the marital relationship to meet new expectations for intimacy. Burgess and Davis correctly predicted that divorce would rise because of the tremendous strain placed on couples to manage the growing demands for congeniality and cooperation.

Marriage is not in immediate danger of extinction, though. In 1960, 94 percent of women had been married at least once by age 45. The share in 1994 was 91 percent. In other words, the vast majority of Americans are still willing to try marriage at some point. What has changed from the 1960s is when, how, and for how long.

The median age at marriage has risen from a low of 20.3 for women and 22.5 for men in 1960, to 24.5 for women and 26.7 or men in 1994. The proportion of women never married by their late 20s tripled from a historical low of 11 percent in 1960 to a high of 33 percent in 1993. The divorce rate among ever-married women more than doubled between the early 1960s and late 1980s, although it has since leveled off.

The number of children living in married-couple families dropped from 88 percent in 1960 to 69 percent in 1994. Divorce plays a role in this decline, but much of the rise in single-parent families results from the sharp increase in nonmarital childbearing. The proportion of births occurring out of wedlock jumped from 5 percent in 1960 to 31 percent in 1993. While some of these births occur among couples who are living together, the vast majority are to single parents.

The increase in single-parenthood due to divorce and out-of-wedlock births may be the most telling sign that Americans are losing confidence in marriage. Ironically, some of today's most vitriolic political rhetoric is directed toward gay couples who want the right to marry, just as the cultural legitimacy of marriage has been declining.

WHAT WE GET OUT OF MARRIAGE

What has transformed societal attitudes toward marriage so that young people delay it, older people get out of it, and some skip it altogether? Before attempting to answer these questions, a few cautions are in order. Demographers and sociologists, like climatologists, are pretty good at short-term forecasts, but have little ability to forecast into the distant future. In truth, no one can predict what marriage patterns will look like 50 years from now.

Virtually no one foresaw the "marriage rush" of the 1940s that preceded the baby boom. And few predicted the sudden decline of the institution in the 1960s. If our society alternates periods of embracing and rejecting marriage, then we could be poised on the cusp of a marriage restoration. It's doubtful, however, because most of the forces that have worked to reduce the strength of marital bonds are unlikely to reverse in the near future.

The biggest stress on marriage in the late 20th century is a transition from a clearcut gender-based division of labor to a much less focused one. For a century or more, men were assigned to the work force and women to domestic duties.

Labor force participation rate of mothers with children younger than age 6 at home for all women aged 16 and older and for married women, 1975-94

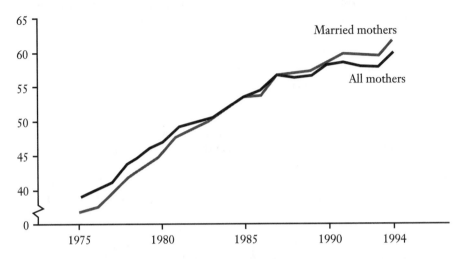

FIGURE 5.2   Mom Learns to Juggle. Married mothers of preschoolers are more likely than all mothers to be in the labor force. *Source:* Bureau of Labor Statistics.

This social arrangement is becoming defunct. Women are only moderately less likely than men to be gainfully employed. Even women with young children are more likely than not to be working. In 1994, 55 percent of women with children under age 6 were currently employed, compared with 19 percent in 1960.

Women's participation in the labor force has reduced their economic dependency on men. The traditional bargain struck between men and women— financial support in exchange for domestic services—is no longer valid. Men now expect women to help bring home the bacon. And women expect men to help cook the bacon, feed the kids, and clean up afterward. In addition, the old status order that granted men a privileged position in the family is crumbling.

These dramatic alterations in the marriage contract are widely endorsed in theory by men and women alike. The share of both who say their ideal marriage is one in which spouses share household and work responsibilities has increased since the 1970s, according to the 1995 Virginia Slims Opinion Poll. Yet in practice, moves toward gender equality have come with a price. Both men and women enter marriage with higher expectations for interpersonal communication, intimacy, and sexual gratification. If these expectations are not met, they feel freer than they once did to dissolve the relationship and seek a new partner.

Being out of marriage has its downside, too, of course. About four in ten recently separated women say they are worse off financially than they were while married, according to the 1992–93 National Survey of Families and Households. This longitudinal study asked women who separated from their husbands since the previous survey in 1987–88 to evaluate several aspects of their lives. At the same time, 43 percent of separated women say their finances are better than during marriage.

Ending an unhappy marriage obviously brings about other positive changes. If it didn't, people wouldn't divorce. Being a single parent isn't easy. Yet more than half of separated women say that being a parent is better than before their split-up; 52 percent say care of children is better. Sixty-five percent say their overall home life is better, and 49 percent say their leisure time has improved. This may not mean they have more leisure time than while married, but perhaps the quality of that time is more fulfilling.

The increase in the share of women who work is not the only reason why Americans readily leave marriages that don't suit them. Legal reform and social trends have made divorce and nonmarital childbearing easier and more acceptable. Safe, affordable contraception enables couples to engage in sex outside of marriage with minimal risk of pregnancy. Women's college-enrollment rates have risen sharply in the past two decades, while public policies and societal attitudes have helped increase their involvement in politics and government. These changes have spurred women to greater autonomy. Each has affected marriage in a different way, but they have all worked in concert toward the same result: to make marriage less imperative and more discretionary.

Some Americans vigorously object to this "take-it-or-leave-it" approach to marriage on moral grounds, hoping to reverse the course of recent history by restoring "traditional" family values. Yet changes in the practice of marriage are not peculiar to the U.S. The decline of marriage as it was practiced in the 1940s in the United States has occurred in virtually all Western societies.

MARRIAGE AS A LUXURY ITEM

The rise of delayed marriage, divorce, and out-of-wedlock childbearing disturbs the moral sensibilities of many observers. Others may not object on moral grounds, but they fear that the byproducts of intimate relationships—children— are no longer safeguarded by the family. Their fears are well-founded. A great deal of research shows that children are disadvantaged by our society's high level of marital flux.

A wealth of data shows that married men and women have lower incidences of alcohol related problems and other health risks than do divorced and widowed people. Men especially seem to enjoy health benefits from marriage. Experts believe this is because wives often monitor health behavior, and because marriage provides incentives for men to avoid high-risk behaviors.

Marriage gives all parties involved an economic boost. In fact, stable marriages could be perpetuating the growing division in American society between the haves and have-nots. Marriage, quite simply, is a form of having. Children growing up with both of their biological parents are likely to be more educated, and to have better job skills and a more secure sense of themselves. Thus, they enter adulthood with greater chances of success and a greater likelihood of finding a mate with a similar profile.

This does not mean, however, that children are better off with married parents. Some think that men and women today lack the capacity to sacrifice for children as they did a generation ago. Maybe they do. But if sacrifice means remaining in stressful, hostile, and abusive environment, it's not necessarily worth it. Even so, I doubt if failure to compromise one's own needs for the good of others is the main reason why fewer couples are getting married and staying married.

In my research on low-income families, I hear men and women talking about the virtues of marriage. Nearly all endorse the idea that children are better off when they grow up with both biological parents, although this is probably said in the context of assuming that the marriage is a "good" one.

Plenty of young people have seen "bad" marriages as they've grown up, which has given them an understandable fear of committing themselves and children to such a situation. "Most of my girlfriends, they got married when they was 20," says one woman. "Now they divorced. They got children. Fathers don't do nothing for them, so then, it was a toss-up. Either to go ahead and start out on the wrong foot or get on the right foot and then fall down." In other words, if you plan to have children, it may not matter too much whether you get married first, because you may not get anything out of the marriage, either financially or emotionally.

Although women may not depend on men's economic support as much as they used to, they still expect something out of the bargain. Young adults in low-income populations feel that they don't have the wherewithal to enter marriage. It's as if marriage has become a luxury consumer item, available only to those with the means to bring it off. Living together or single-parenthood has become the budget way to start a family. Most low-income people I talk to would prefer the luxury model. They just can't afford it.

Marriage is both a cause and a consequence of economic, cultural, and psychological stratification in American society. The recent apparent increase in income inequality in the U.S. means that the population may continue to sort itself between those who are eligible for marriage and a growing number who are deemed ineligible to marry.

There is little to suggest that marriage will become more accessible and enduring in the next century. The unpredictability and insecurity of the job market is likely to have an unsettling effect on marriage in the short term by making marriage a risky proposition, and in the long term by generating larger numbers of people who are the products of unstable family situations. Men are making some progress in taking on household tasks, including child care, but women still shoulder most of the burden in families, causing continued marital stress.

While this may sound unduly pessimistic, marriage may change for the better if people are committed to making the institution work, albeit in a new format. The end of the 20th century may eventually be recognized as the period when this new form of family—the symmetrical marriage—first appeared.

It's no longer noteworthy to see a man pushing a stroller or for preschoolers to be just as curious about mommy's job as daddy's. As with many social trends,

Percent distribution of respondents' ideal lifestyle, by sex, 1974 and 1995

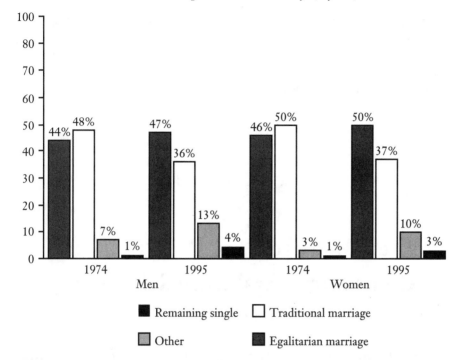

FIGURE 5.3   The Perfect Family, 1974–95. Both men and women are more likely now than 20 years ago to say an egalitarian marriage is ideal, but they are also more likely to favor alternatives to marriage. *Source:* Virginia Slims Opinion Poll.

well-educated couples appear to be leading the way in developing marriages based on equal sharing of economic and family responsibilities. It may be a little easier for them, too, because they are more likely to have the resources to hire people to do the things they choose not to do themselves.

The move toward symmetry may be more challenging for average Americans of more modest means. Couples who work split shifts because they can't afford child care may be sharing the economic and household load, but they don't spend much time with their spouses.

Single parents who have no one with whom to share the load might have little sympathy for couples who argue about whose turn it is to do the dishes, but at least they are spared the arguing. Single people supporting themselves may feel that their finances are strapped, but when a married person loses his or her job, more than one person is adversely affected.

I am often struck by the fact that we have generous ways—both public and private—of aiding communities beset by natural disasters. Yet we do practically nothing for the same communities when a private industry abandons them, or when their young people can't find work, no matter how hard they look. Restoring marriage to an institution of enduring, compassionate relationships will require more than sanctimonious calls for traditional, communitarian, and family values. We should back up our words with resources. This includes moving toward a society that offers secure, remunerative jobs, as well as better child-care options and more flexible schedules so people can accept those jobs. Otherwise, the institution of marriage as we knew it in this century will in the 21st century become a practice of the privileged. Marriage could become a luxury item that most Americans cannot afford.

R E A D I N G

11

Peer Marriage: What Does It Take to Create a Truly Egalitarian Relationship?

PEPPER SCHWARTZ

When I told people that I was beginning a research study of couples who evenly divided parenting and housework responsibilities, the usual reaction was mock curiosity—how was I going to find the three existing egalitarian couples in the universe? Despite several decades of dissecting the sexism and inequities inherent in traditional marriage, as a society, we have yet to develop a clear picture of how more balanced marital partnerships actually work. Some critics even argue that the practice of true equality in marriage is not much more common today than it was 30 years ago. In fact, authors like Arlie Hochschild have suggested that women's liberation has made prospects for equity worse. The basic theme of her provocative book, *The Second Shift*, is that women now have two jobs—their old, traditional marital roles and their new responsibilities in the work force. A look at the spectacular divorce rates and lower marriage rate for successful women provides further fuel for the argument that equality has just brought wives more, not less, burdens.

All of this figured heavily in my own commitment to exploring the alternative possibilities for marital partnership. Ten years ago this began with *American Couples: Money, Work and Sex*, a study I did with Phillip Blumstein that compared

From *The Family Therapy Networker*, September/October 1994, pp. 57–61. Copyright 1994. Published by the Family Therapy Network.

Pepper Schwartz, Ph.D., is a professor of sociology and an author. Address: University of Washington, Seattle, Washington, 98195. Her latest book is *Peer Marriage: How Love Between Equals Really Works* (Free Press, 1994).

more than 6,000 couples—married, cohabitating, gay males and lesbians—looking for, among other things, what aspects of gendered behavior contributed to relationship satisfaction and durability. This study contained within it a small number of egalitarian couples, who fascinated and inspired me. We discussed them rather briefly in the book, but our editor encouraged us to make them the subject of a second study that would examine how couples manage to sustain an egalitarian partnership over time. Unfortunately, my co-author was not able to continue the project and it was not until three years ago that I began the research on what I came to call Peer Marriage. I began looking for couples who had worked out no worse than a 60–40 split on childrearing, housework and control of discretionary funds and who considered themselves to have "equal status or standing in the relationship."

I started out interviewing some of the couples originally studied for *American Couples* and then, using what sociologists call a "snowball sample," I asked those couples if they knew anyone else like themselves that I could interview. After talking to a few couples in a given network, I then would look for a different kind of couple (different class, race, educational background, etc.) in order to extend the range of my sample. I interviewed 57 egalitarian couples, but even after the formal study was over, I kept running into couples that fit my specifications and did 10 more partial interviews.

While initially my design included only Peer Marriages, I also began to interview a lot of couples who others thought to be egalitarian, but who did not meet my criteria. Instead of throwing them out of the sample, I used them as a base of comparison, dividing them into two additional categories: "Traditionals" and "Near Peers." Traditionals were couples in which the man usually had veto power over decision-making (except with the children) and in which the wife felt that she did not have—nor did she want—equal status. The Near Peers were couples who, while they believed in equality, felt derailed from their initial goal of an egalitarian marriage because of the realities of raising children and/or the need or desire to maximize male income. As a result, the husband could not be anywhere near as participatory a father as the couple had initially envisioned. These two groups proved to be a fortuitous addition to the design. It is sometimes hard to understand what peer couples are doing that allows them to fulfill an egalitarian agenda without understanding what keeps other couples from doing the same.

Even though I consider myself to be in a Peer Marriage, I found many surprises among the Peer Couples I studied. Of course, as a researcher, one is never supposed to extrapolate from one's own experience, but it is almost impossible not to unconsciously put one's presuppositions into the hypothesis phase of the research. Clearly, people make their marital bargains for many different reasons, and face different challenges in sustaining them. Here are some of the discoveries I made that I thought might be of use to therapists.

I assumed most couples would, like myself, come to egalitarianism out of the women's movement or feminist ideology. Nevertheless, while approximately 40 percent of the women and about 20 percent of the men cited feminism and a desire to be in a nonhierarchical relationship, the majority of couples mentioned other reasons. These included a desire to avoid parental models that they found oppressive in their own upbringing, the *other* partner's strong preference for an egalitarian marriage, some emotional turmoil that had led to their rethinking their relationship, or an intense desire for co-parenting. Women in particular often mentioned their own parents as a negative model. One woman said, "I want a husband who knows how to pack his own suitcase, who puts away his own clothes, who can't tell me to shut up at will . . . My mother may have been happy with this kind of marriage, but I'm still angry at my father for treating my mother like that—and angry at her for letting him." A 25-year-old husband told me, on a different theme, "My main objective in having an equal relationship was not to be the kind of father I had. I want my kids to know me before they are adults. I want them to be able to talk to me. I want them to run to me if they hurt themselves. I want our conversations to be more than me telling them they could do better on a test or that I was disappointed they didn't make the team. I want to be all the things to my kids that my dad was not. I want us to have hugged many, many times and not just on birthdays or their wedding day."

Quite a few men in Peer Marriages said they really had no strong feelings about being in either traditional or egalitarian marriages, but had merely followed their wives' lead. Typical of this group was a high school basketball coach who said he had had a very traditional first marriage because that was the only arrangement that he and his wife could envision even when it wasn't working. But when he met his current wife, a policewoman who had been single quite a while, her demands for equality seemed perfectly reasonable to him. He just, more or less, fell into line with his future wife's ideas about the relationship. Many of these men told me they had always expected a woman to be the emotional architect of a relationship and were predisposed to let her set the rules.

Most of the couples, however, did have strong ideas about marriage and placed particular emphasis on equity and equality. Even if they didn't start out with a common agenda, most ended up sharing a high degree of conscious purpose. People's particular personal philosophies about marriage mattered less than the fact that their philosophies differentiated their family from a culture that reinforced the general belief that equality is neither possible nor even in the long-term interests of couples. Many people talked about how easy it is to slide into old and familiar roles or follow economic opportunities that started to whittle away at male participation in childrearing. It takes an intense desire to keep a couple on the nontraditional track and a clear sense of purpose to justify the economic sacrifices and daily complications it takes to co-parent. As one wife of 10 years said, "We always try to make sure that we don't start getting traditional. It's so easy to do. But we really want this extraordinary empathy and respect we have. I just know it wouldn't be there if we did this marriage any other way."

Important as relationship idealogy is, Peer Marriages depend at least as much on coordinating work with home and childraising responsibilities and not letting a higher earner be exempt from daily participation. Previous research had shown me the connection between a husband's and wife's relative income and their likelihood of being egalitarian. So I assumed that most of the couples I interviewed would be working couples, and have relatively similar incomes. This was mostly true, although I was struck by the couples who were exceptions. Four husbands in the study had non-working wives. The men didn't want to dominate those relationships because they felt very strongly that money did not legitimately confer power. For example, one husband had inherited a great deal of money but didn't feel it was any more his than his wife's. She stayed at home with the children, but he took over in the late afternoon and on weekends. He also was the primary cook and cleaner. In another case, a husband who earned a good deal more than his wife put all the money in a joint account and put investments in her name as well as his. Over time, she had assets equal to his. While these triumphs over income differentials were exceptions, it did make me respect the fact that truly determined couples could overcome being seduced by the power of economic advantage.

However, many Peer Marriages had a significant income differential and husbands and wives had to negotiate a lot just to make sure they didn't fall into the trap of letting the higher earner be the senior decision-maker. Even more tricky, according to many, was not letting work set the emotional and task agenda of the household. The couples needed to keep their eyes on what was the tail and what was the dog so that their relationship was not sidetracked by career opportunities or job pressures. Many Peer Couples had gone through periods in which they realized that they were beginning to have no time for each other, or that one of them was more consistently taking care of the children while the other was consumed with job demands. But what distinguished those couples from more traditional marriages was that they had a competing ideology of economic or career success that guided them when their egalitarianism began to get out of kilter.

One husband, who had an architectural practice designing and building airports, had begun to travel for longer and longer periods of time until it was clear that he was no longer a true co-parent or a full partner in the marriage. After long and painful discussions, he quit his job and opened up a home office so he could spend more time with his wife and children. Both partners realized this would cause some economic privations and, in fact, it took the husband five years to get a modestly successful practice going while the wife struggled to support the family. Without minimizing how tough this period had been, the couple felt they had done the right thing. "After all," the husband said, "we saved our marriage."

This attitude helped explain another surprise in this study. I had presumed that most of the Peer Marriages I would find would be yuppie or post-yuppie couples, mostly young or baby boom professionals who were "having it all." In fact, most of them were solidly middle class: small-business owners, social workers, school teachers, health professionals (but not doctors). Apparently, people on career fast tracks were less willing to endanger their potential income and opportunities for promotion. There may be childrearing Peer Marriages out there comprised of litigators, investment bankers and brain surgeons—but I didn't find them. The closest I came to finding fast trackers in a Peer Marriage and family were high-earning women who had husbands who were extremely pleased with their partner's success and were willing to be the more primary parent in order to support her career.

When these women negotiated issues with their husbands in front of me, they seemed more sensitive about their husbands' feelings than men of comparable accomplishment with lower earning wives. For example, they did not interrupt as much as high-earning men in traditional marriages, and they seemed to quite consciously not pull rank when I asked them jointly to solve a financial problem. They told me, however, that they consciously had to work at being less controlling than they sometimes thought they deserved to be. A very successful woman attorney, married to another, significantly-less-prominent attorney, told me that they had some problems because he wasn't used to picking up the slack when she was called away suddenly to represent a Fortune 500 company. She found herself battling her own ambitions in order to be sensitive to his desire for her to let up a bit. As she noted, "We [women] are not prepared to be the major providers and it's easy to want all the privileges and leeway that men have always gotten for the role. But our bargain to raise the kids together and be respectful of one another holds me back from being like every other lawyer who would have this powerful a job. Still, it's hard."

The other fast track exception was very successful men in their second marriages who had sacrificed their first in their climb to the top. Mostly these were men who talked about dependent ex-wives, their unhappiness at paying substantial support and their determination not to repeat the mistakes of their first marriages. One 50-year-old man, who had traveled constantly in his first marriage raising money for pension funds, told me he was through being the high earner for the company and wanted more family time in the second part of his life. As he put it, "I consciously went looking for someone who I could spend time with, who I had a lot in common with, who would want me to stop having to be the big earner all the time. I don't want to die before I've been a real partner to somebody who can stand on her own two feet . . . and I've been a real father."

When I first realized how often the desire to co-parent led couples into an egalitarian ideology, I thought this might also lead couples to prioritize their parenting responsibilities over their husband-and-wife relationship. But these were not marriages in which husbands and wives called each other "Mom" and "Dad." For the most part, these couples avoided the rigidly territorial approach I saw in Traditional and Near Peer marriages. In both of these types of couples, I observed mothers who were much more absorbed in their children, which both partners regarded as a primarily female responsibility. As a result, women had sole control over decisions about their children's daily life and used the children as a main source of intimacy, affection and unshared secrets. They related stories about things the children told them that "they would never dare tell their father." While quite a few of the mothers talked about how "close" their husbands were with their children, they would also, usually in the same story, tell me how much closer their children were with them. What surprised me was that while these traditional moms complained about father absence, very few really wanted to change the situation. Most often, it was explained that, while it would be great to have their husband home, they "couldn't afford it." But of course "afford" is a relative term and I sensed that the women really did not want the men interfering with their control over parenting. Or they would have liked more fatherly engagement but definitely not at the cost of loss of income. One young, working Near Peer Couple with four kids was discussing the husband's lesser parenting responsibilities with me when he said, "You know, I could come home early and get the kids by 3:30. I'd like to do that." The wife's response was to straightforwardly insist that with four kids going to private school, his energies were best used paying for their tuitions. She preferred a double shift to a shared one because her financial priorities and her vision of what most profited her children were clear.

But there was an unexpected downside for the couples who did manage to co-parent. I was unprepared for how often Peer Couples mentioned serious conflict over childrearing. Because each partner felt very strongly about the children's upbringing, differences of opinion were not easily resolved. As one peer wife said, "We are both capable of stepping up to the line and staying there screaming at each other." Another husband said, "If you only talked to us about how we deal with disagreements about the kids, you might think we were a deeply conflicted marriage. We're not. But unfortunately, we have very different ideas about discipline and we can get pretty intense with one another and it might look bad. We went to counseling about the kids and this therapist wanted to look at our whole relationship and we had to say, 'You don't get it. This really is the only thing we argue about like this.' "

Peers may, in fact, have more conflict about children than more Traditional partners because unlike Traditional Marriage, there is no territory that is automatically ceded to the other person and conflict cannot be resolved by one person claiming the greater right to have the final word. I wondered if these arguments threatened the relationship. In the majority of the Peer marriages where such conflicts occurred, the couples talked about how they ultimately, if not in the heat of battle, followed their usual pattern of talking until an agreement was reached. What usually forced them to continue to communicate and reach a joint answer was their pledge to give the other partner equal standing in the relationship. Occasionally, a few people told me, they just couldn't reach a mutually satisfying answer and let their partner "win one" out of trust in his or her good judgment, not because they agreed on a given issue.

The couples that I felt might be in more trouble had recurring disagreements that they were never able to resolve over punishments, educational or religious choices or how much freedom to give kids. Furthermore, in each instance at least one partner said that the other partner's approach was beginning to erode the respect that made their relationship possible. Moreover, this particular kind of conflict was deeply troubling since many of them had organized their marriage around the expectation of being great co-parents. It may be that co-parenting requires that parenting philosophies be similar or grow together. Co-parents may have a particular need for good negotiating and communication skills so that they can resolve their differences without threatening the basis of their relationship.

In contrast with traditional or Near Peer Couples, the partners in Peer Marriages never complained about lack of affection or intimacy in their relationships. What they did mention, that other couples did not, was the problem of becoming so familiar with each other that they felt more like siblings than lovers. Some researchers have theorized that sexual arousal is often caused or intensified by anxiety, fear and tension. Many others have written about how sexual desire depends on "Yin" and "Yang"—mystery and difference. And quite a few women and men I talked to rather guiltily confessed that while they wanted equal partners, all their sexual socialization had been to having sex in a hierarchical relationship: Women had fantasies of being "taken" or mildly dominated; men had learned very early on that they were expected to be the orchestrators of any given sexual encounter and that masculinity required sexual directiveness. For men, sexual arousal was often connected with a strong desire to protect or control.

Peer couples complained that they often forgot to include sex in their daily lives. Unlike Traditional or Near Peers, their sexual frequency did not slow down because of unresolved issues or continuing anger, at least not in any systematic ways. These couples may start to lose interest in sex even more than the other kinds of marriages because sex is not their main way of getting close. Many Traditional and some Near Peer Couples mentioned that the only time they felt that they got through to each other was in bed. Perhaps the more emotional distance couples feel with one another, the larger the role sexuality plays in helping them feel they still have the capacity for intimacy. Being less dependent on this pathway to intimacy, partners in Peer Marriage may be more willing to tolerate a less satisfactory sexual relationship.

One husband, who worked with his wife in their own advertising firm, even talked about having developed "an incest taboo," which had led to the couple entering therapy. They were such buddies during the daytime, he had trouble treating her as anything else in the evening. The therapist this couple consulted encouraged them to assume new personas in the bedroom. For example, he told them to take turns being the dominant partner, to create scenarios where they created new characters and then behaved as they thought the person they were impersonating would behave. He gave them "homework," such as putting themselves in romantic or sexy environments and allowing themselves to imagine meeting there the first time. The wife was encouraged to dress outrageously for bed every now and then; the husband occasionally to be stereotypically directive. The therapist reminded both partners that their emotional bargain was safe: they loved and respected each other. That meant they could use sex as recreation, release and exploration. They were good pupils and felt they had really learned something for a lifetime.

In another couple, it was the wife who mentioned the problem. Her husband had been the dominant partner in his previous marriage and had enjoyed that role in bed. However, she liked more reciprocity and role-sharing in sex, so he tried to be accommodating. However, early on in the relationship he began treating her, as she put it, "too darn respectfully . . . it was almost as if we were having politically correct sex . . . I had to remember that he wasn't my brother and it was okay to be sexually far out with him."

On the other hand, Peer Couples with satisfying sexual relationships often mentioned their equality as a source of sexual strength. These couples felt their emotional security with one another allowed them to be more uninhibited and made sex more likely since both people were responsible for making it happen. Women with unhappy sexual experiences with sexist men mentioned that for the first time in their lives they could use any sexual position without worrying about any larger meaning in the act. Being on the bottom just meant being on the bottom; it was not about surrendering in a more cosmic ways. Being a sex kitten was a role for the evening—and not part of a larger submissive persona.

Many of the Peer Couples I interviewed had terrific sexual lives. The women, especially, felt they had finally met men with whom they could be vulnerable and uninhibited. As one woman said, "I used to be a real market for women's books. I wanted men who fit the stereotype of Clark Gable or Kevin Costner—few words, and when they are delivered, they are real ringers, and there is a lot of eye contact and passion, and that's about as much talking as you get. Maybe it was dating all these guys who were really like that, but even as fantasy objects, I got tired of men who didn't want to explore a feeling or who were only loving when they had a hard-on. I fell in love the first time sharing *Prince of Tides* with the guy I was dating, and fell in love with Eric [her husband] over a discussion of *Eyes on the Prize*. The sexy thing was the conversation and the quality of our minds . . . I can't imagine anything more boring or ultimately unsexy than a man—and I don't care if he looked like Robert Redford and earned like Donald Trump—who had nothing to say or if he did, didn't get turned on by what I was saying."

Equality brings with it the tools to have a great erotic relationship and also, at the same time, the pitfalls that can lead to sexual boredom. If couples learn that their sexual lives need not be constrained by any preconceived idea of what is "egalitarian sex" or appropriate sexual roles, there is no reason that their equality can't work for them. But couples who cannot separate their nights and days, who cannot transcend their identities in everyday life, may need guidance from a knowledgeable counselor.

What enables couples to sustain a style of egalitarian relationship in a world that encourages families to link their economic destiny with the male's career and casts women in an auxiliary worker role so that they can take responsibility for everyday childcare and household chores? In Peer Couples, a sense of shared purpose helps guide the couple back to why they are putting up with all the problems that come from putting together a new model of relationship without societal or familiar supports.

Otherwise it is all too easy for mothers to fall in love with their children and assume primary responsibility for their upbringing or for men to allow their careers to sweep them out of the home, away from their children and back into the more familiar territory they have been trained to inhabit. When this begins to happen, a couple's ideology, almost like an organization's mission statement, helps remind them what their central goal is: the marital intimacy that comes from being part of a well-matched, equally empowered, equally participatory team.

But avoiding traditional hierarchy involves a constant struggle to resist the power of money to define each partner's family roles. Peer Couples continually have to evaluate the role of work in their lives and how much it can infringe on parenting and household responsibilities. If one partner earns or starts to earn a lot more money, and the job starts to take up more time, the couple has to face what this means for their relationship—how much it might distort what they have set out to create.

Peer Couples check in with each other an extraordinary amount to keep their relationship on track. They each have to take responsibility for making sure that they are not drifting too far away from reciprocity. Peer Couples manage to maintain equity in small ways that make sure the balance in their marriage is more than an ideology. If one person has been picking up the kids, the other is planning their summer activities and getting their clothes. Or if one partner has been responsible lately for making sure extended family members are contacted, the other person takes it over for a while. If one partner really decides he or she likes to cook, then the other partner takes on some other equally functional and time-consuming job. There's no reason that each partner can't specialize, but both are careful that one of them doesn't take over all the high-prestige, undemanding jobs while the other ends up with the classically stigmatized assignments (like cleaning bathrooms, or whatever is personally loathed by that person).

Besides monitoring jobs and sharing, couples have to monitor their attitude. Is the wife being treated as a subordinate? Does one person carry around the anger so often seen in someone who feels discounted and unappreciated? Is one person's voice considered more important than the other person's? Is the relationship getting distant and is the couple starting to lead parallel lives? Do they put in the time required to be best friends and family collaborators? Are they treating each other in the ways that would support a non-romantic relationship of freely associating friends?

There is nothing "natural" or automatic about keeping Peer Marriages going. There will be role discomfort when newly inhabiting the other gender's world. That is why some research shows that men who start being involved with a child from prenatal classes show more easy attachment and participation in childrearing activities later. While men become comfortable with mothering over time, some need a lot of help. Children will sense who is the primary parent and that will be the person to whom they run, make demands, and from whom they seek daily counsel. One direct way of helping fathers evaluate how they are doing is to help the partners measure how much the children treat them as equally viable sources of comfort and help.

Likewise, being a serious provider is a responsibility some women find absolutely crushing. Most middle-class women were raised to feel that working would be voluntary. After they have made a bargain to do their share of keeping the family economically afloat, they may regret the pressures it puts on them. The old deal of staying at home and being supported can look pretty good after a bad day at the office. But only the exceptional relationship seems to be able to make that traditional provider/mother deal for very long and still sustain a marriage where partners have equal standing in each other's eyes. Couples have to keep reminding themselves how much intimacy, respect and mutual interest they earn in exchange for learning new roles and sustaining the less enjoyable elements of new responsibilities.

Couples who live as peers often attract others like themselves and the building of a supportive community can modify the impact of the lack of support in the larger world. Like-minded others who have made similar decisions help a lot, especially when critical turning points are reached: such as re-evaluating a career track when it becomes painfully clear that it will not accommodate Peer Family life.

This study yielded no single blueprint for successful Peer Marriage. As in all couples, partners in Peer Marriages require a good measure of honesty, a dedication to fair play, flexibility, generosity and maturity. But most of all, they need to remember what they set out to do and why it is important, at least for them. If they can keep their eyes and hearts on the purpose of it all—if we help them do that—more Peer Marriages will endure and provide a model for others exploring the still-unchartered territory of egalitarian relationships.

R E A D I N G

12

Divorce: Challenges, Changes, and New Chances

E. Mavis Hetherington, Tracy C. Law,
and Thomas G. O'Connor

Studies of the effects of divorce on family members traditionally have centered around the development of problem behaviors subsequent to marital dissolution. Recent findings, however, have emphasized the wide variation in responses to stressful experiences and life transitions, including divorce and remarriage (e.g., Rutter, 1987; Werner, 1987; Hetherington, 1991a). Although debate still exists over the question of the magnitude and duration of the effects of parental divorce on children, work in the past 10 years has converged in suggesting that

---

From *Normal Family Processes*, edited by Froma Walsh. Copyright © 1993 by The Guilford Press. Reprinted by permission of The Guilford Press. pp. 208–217. References have been omitted from end of Reading.

the interaction among individual differences in personal and familial character-istics and extrafamilial factors that support or undermine coping efforts by family members must be examined in order to understand the spectrum of responses to divorce. This spectrum can range from enhanced competence to clinical levels of problem behavior (Hetherington, 1989, 1991a; Stolberg, Camplair, Currier, & Wells, 1987).

In addition, it is becoming increasingly apparent that divorce should be viewed not as a discrete event but as part of a series of family transitions and changes in family relationships. The response to any family transition will depend both on what precedes and follows it. The response to divorce and life in a single-parent household will be influenced by individual adjustment and the quality of family relationships before the divorce as well as circumstances surrounding and following the divorce. In many families, divorce may trigger a series of adverse transactional factors such as economic decline, parenting stress, and physical and psychological dysfunction in family members. For others, it may present an escape from conflict and an unsatisfying marital relationship, a chance to form more gratifying and harmonious relationships, and an opportunity for personal growth and individuation (Gore & Eckenroade, 1992; Hetherington, 1989).

The recognition that divorce is part of a chain of marital transitions and shifting life experiences, and that individual responses to these experiences demonstrate marked variability, has been a powerful influence on recent theo-retical models developed to explain children's adjustment to parental divorce. In understanding these findings, many researchers have adopted a developmental contextual framework (Gore & Eckenroade, 1992; Nock, 1982; Hetherington & Clingempeel, 1992; Hetherington & Martin, 1986). This approach examines adjustment across time, and on multiple levels, including interactions among the overarching social and historical context, changing dynamics within the family system, individual ontogenic characteristics of child and parent, and influences external to the family such as the extended family, peer relationships, and the educational, occupational, mental health, legal, religious, and welfare systems.

The purpose of this chapter is not to present a comprehensive review of research and clinical findings concerning the adjustment to divorce. Selected recent research examples and a developmental, contextual, interactive model will be used as an organizational framework in which to examine factors that contribute to individual differences in the way family members negotiate the changes and challenges associated with divorce. Many of the research findings will be drawn from the longitudinal studies of Hetherington and her colleagues. Before discussing the factors implicated in a developmental, contextual, interac-tive approach, it is important to place the findings in the larger context of demo-graphic and social changes that have occurred in the last 20 years.

THE CHANGING WORLD OF THE FAMILY: DEMOGRAPHIC AND SOCIAL FORCES

Although the divorce rate doubled between 1960 and 1980, it has leveled off and even declined slightly in the past decade (Glick, 1988). Currently, it is estimated that half of all marriages will end in divorce and that approximately 60% of these dissolutions will involve children. Although the percentage of marriages ending in divorce has not changed appreciably since the early 1980s, the number of children affected by parental divorce, as well as the number of children from divorced families now of marriageable age themselves, has continued to increase (Bumpass, 1984). It has been estimated that 38% of white children and 75% of African-American children born to married parents in the United States will experience their parents' divorce before their 16th birthday (Bumpass, 1984). In addition, African-Americans not only have a higher rate of divorce than whites, they are also more likely to separate but not go through a legal divorce procedure, to experience a longer time-lag between time of separation and divorce, and are less likely to remarry (Glick, 1988; Teachman, Polonko, & Scanzoni, 1987). Although families who are poor, African-American, and suffering multiple life stresses are more likely to divorce, the rise in economic independence for well-educated women also has led to a greater likelihood that these women will divorce compared to their less-educated peers. Furthermore, since most divorced men and women remarry, and since the rate of divorce in second marriages is even higher than in first marriages (61% of men and 54% of women go through a second divorce), many children and parents encounter a series of marital transitions and reorganizations in family roles and relationships (Glick, 1988; Chase-Lansdale & Hetherington, 1990). These statistics indicate that divorce, once considered an atypical family event, is now a "normative," even if not a "normal," experience in the life cycle of many contemporary American families (Emery & Forehand, 1992).

Shifting social and historical factors affect patterns of both marriage and divorce (Cherlin, 1981; Teachman et al., 1987; Glick, 1988). Wars, whether the Civil War, World War II, the Korean War, or the Vietnam War, have been associated with hasty marriages followed by increased rates of divorce (Glick, 1988). Current high rates of divorce have also been attributed to greater labor force participation and economic independence of women, improved contraception, the emergence of the welfare system, an increase in the proportion of marriages involving premarital births, changing ideologies associated with the women's movement, and the liberalization of divorce laws. The family is being reshaped in response to transformations in social values and roles. Greater diversity in attitudes and accepted behaviors are found not only in family and gender roles but also in other social systems—in law, politics, religion, education, and the workplace. Divorce and the concomitant experiences of family members are only one reflection of the need for social institutions, such as the family, to adapt to historical and social change.

WHY MARRIAGES FAIL: THE PRECURSORS OF DIVORCE

Neither marital satisfaction nor sheer frequency of disagreements is a good predictor of divorce. Instead, styles of conflict resolution involving disengagement, stonewalling, contempt, denial, and blaming are likely to be associated with divorce (Gottman, 1994; Hetherington, 1989). One of the most common patterns of marital relations leading to divorce is a conflict-confronting, conflict-avoiding pattern where one spouse, usually the wife, confronts areas of concern and disagreements in the marriage and expresses her feelings about these problems, while the other spouse responds with defensiveness, avoidance, withdrawal, whining, and, if prodded, with resentment and anger. A second common marital pattern associated with later divorce is one in which couples have little overt conflict, but have different expectations and perceptions about family life, marriage and their children, and have few shared interests, activities, or friends (Hetherington & Tryon, 1989; Notarius & Vanzetti, 1983).

These patterns of relating in dysfunctional couples means that many children before the divorce are likely to have been exposed to unresolved disagreements, resentment, anger, and ineffective marital problem solving. Prospective studies indicate that troubled marital relations and interparental tension accompanied by unsupportive parenting and high rates of behavior problems in children occur years before the dissolution of the marriage (Block, Block, & Gjerde, 1986, 1988; Cherlin et al., 1991). The inept parenting and behavior disorders usually attributed to divorce and life in a one-parent household may, to some extent, be a continuation of predivorce functioning and be associated with disrupted processes in the nuclear family. Although the popular interpretation of these findings is that marital tension, alienation and conflict cause inept parenting and behavior problems in children, it may be that the stress of dealing with a difficult, noncompliant, antisocial child helps to undermine an already fragile marriage and precipitates divorce.

Recently, another explanation, based on the findings of twin studies, has been proposed. It suggests that divorce and problem behaviors in children are genetically linked, and that this may help to explain the slightly higher rates of divorce found in offspring of divorced parents (McGue & Lykken, in press). Irritable, antisocial behavior in parents may provoke marital problems and be genetically associated with behavior problems in children, with the subsequent marital difficulties of adult offspring of divorced parents, and with the intergenerational transmission of divorce. Whatever the reasons may be for the dysfunctional precursors of divorce, it is against a background of disrupted family relationships and disordered behavior in parents and children that family members move into the changes and challenges associated with separation, divorce, and life in a one-parent household.

CHANGES IN THE LIVING SITUATION

An established family system can be viewed as a mechanism for identifying and framing the roles, activities, and daily life of each family member. When a divorce occurs, it means not only the loss of patterns of everyday family interaction and a family member, but loss of a way of life. Pervasive alterations in expectations, life experiences, and the sense of self in parents and children are associated with the uncertainty, found not only in divorce, but also in other transitions, such as loss of a family member through death (Silverman, 1988) or even with the addition of a family member through remarriage (Hetherington, in press).

Immediately following divorce, household routines and roles break down and parents experience task overload as a single parent attempts to perform the tasks usually assumed by two parents. In such situations, children, especially daughters, in divorced families are often asked to assume responsibility for household chores and care of younger siblings. Many of the interactions between custodial mothers and their children, are instrumental in nature and occur in the context of shared tasks. The problems of overwhelming responsibility for parent and child are often exacerbated when divorced mothers must begin working or increase their workload because of economic necessity (Duncan & Hoffman, 1985).

In the first year following divorce, the average family income of women decreases by almost 40%. Although income relative to needs gradually increases, even 5 years after divorce, the income of divorced mothers remains at 94% of their predivorced income, in contrast to 130% for divorced fathers and 125% for remarried women (Duncan & Hoffman, 1985). This is the result, in part, of partial or intermittent payment, or nonpayment, of child support by 70% of divorced noncustodial fathers. This loss of income following martial dissolution often determines where families live, where children go to school, the quality of neighborhoods and peer groups, and the accessibility of jobs, health care, and support networks. Although income level or loss explains only a small amount of the variance related to children's adjustment following divorce, poverty does increase the probability of encountering these other transactional factors associated with the ability of parents and children to manage stress successfully and with developmental outcomes for children. Negative life stresses are most marked for members of divorced families in the first 2 years following divorce and gradually decline with time; however, they always remain higher than those in nondivorced families (Forgatch, Patterson, & Ray, in press; Hetherington, Cox, & Cox, 1985). An unexpected bill, illness, or a school closing may present a greater emergency for a divorced mother than for parents in a two-parent household with mutual support and greater resources.

In spite of the difficulties encountered by divorced women, by 2 years after divorce, whether or not they initiated the divorce, the vast majority of women report being more satisfied with their family situation than they had been in the last year of their marriage. Furthermore, although divorced mothers report more child-rearing stress than do nondivorced mothers, they also say that parenting is easier without a nonsupportive spouse who undermines or disagrees with their parenting practices. The balance between increased risk and stressors and positive life changes must be considered in examining the response to divorce (Hetherington, in press).

CUSTODY, CONTACT, AND CO-PARENTAL RELATIONS

In the vast majority of divorces, the mother is awarded custody of children; only 13% of fathers are awarded sole custody of their children at the time of divorce (Emery, 1988). In these cases, it is often because mothers are deemed incompetent, do not want custody of their children, or because male or adolescent children are involved. In spite of the overt or covert legal preference for mothers as custodians under the guise of best interests of the child or primary caregivers guidelines, there is no consistent evidence that fathers who seek custody are less competent parents than mothers (Warshak, 1992). In fact, by 2 years after divorce, custodial fathers report better family relations and fewer problems with their children than do custodial mothers (Furstenberg, 1988). This may be because custodial fathers, in contrast to custodial mothers, have higher incomes, more available supports, and are more likely to be caring for older children. In addition, fathers may be less sensitive and responsive than mothers to family dysfunction and behavior problems in children. However, reluctant fathers who assent to assume custody because of their wives' inability or disinclination to care for their children are less involved and able parents. A finding relevant to decisions involving custody is that, although there is some continuity in the pre- and postdivorce quality of parenting for mothers, there is little for fathers (Hetherington, Cox, & Cox, 1982). Some custodial fathers seem to exhibit a *Kramer vs. Kramer* response and develop an involvement and parenting skills they had not had before the divorce, but some intensely attached noncustodial fathers find intermittent parenting painful and withdraw from their children. On the other hand, a substantial number of noncustodial fathers report that their relationship with their children improves after divorce.

On the average, noncustodial fathers become increasingly less available to their children. In the most recent national study using a probability sample, mothers reported that, following divorce, only one-quarter of children see their fathers once a week or more, and over a third do not see their father at all or see them only a few times a year (Seltzer, 1991). Physical distance in residence, low socioeconomic status, remarriage, and having only female rather than male children are associated with less visitation by noncustodial fathers. Noncustodial mothers are more likely to maintain contact with their children than are noncustodial fathers (Furstenberg, 1988; Zill, 1988). This leads to the rather intriguing issue as to whether differences found in children in a mother's custody, and a father's custody are attributable to the relationship with the custodial parent or to differences in the child's contact with the noncustodial parent and additional support in childrearing for custodial fathers provided by noncustodial mothers.

The move toward facilitating visitation and joint custody has been based on the premises that continued contact with both parents is desirable and that noncustodial parents with joint custody will be more likely to maintain contact and financial support. The response to the first premise must be that it depends on who is doing the visiting and on the relationship between the parents. If the noncustodial parent is reasonably well-adjusted, competent in parenting, and has a close relationship with the child, and if the child is not exposed to conflict between the two parents, continued contact can have a salutary effect on the child's adjustment. However, it takes an exceptionally close relationship with a noncustodial parent to buffer a child from the deleterious effects of a conflictual, nonsupportive relationship with a custodial parent (Hetherington et al., 1982). If there is high conflict between the parents, joint custody and continued contact can have adverse effects on the child (Maccoby, Depner, & Mnookin, 1988;

Wallerstein & Blakeslee, 1989). Furthermore, there is some evidence that, after remarriage, although continued involvement of the noncustodial father with the child does not interfere with family functioning in the stepfamily, frequent visits by the noncustodial mother may be associated with negative relations between children, especially daughters, and their stepmothers (Brand, Clingempeel, & Bowen-Woodward, 1988).

Although cooperative, consensual coparenting following divorce is the ideal relationship (Camara & Resnick, 1988), in most cases the best that can be attained is one of independent but noninterfering parental relations. In a substantial group of families, conflict is sustained or accelerates following divorce (Hetherington et al., 1982; Kline, Johnston, & Tschan, 1991; Maccoby, Depner, & Mnookin, 1990). Interparental conflict in the long run is related to diminished contact and fewer child support payments by noncustodial fathers (Seltzer, 1991). In addition, in such conflicted relationships, children may feel caught in the middle as they are sometimes asked to carry messages between parents, to inform each parent of the other's activities, to defend one parent against the other's disparaging remarks, or to justify wanting to spend time with the other parent (Buchanon, Maccoby, & Dombusch, 1991; Hetherington, in press). Being "caught in the middle," rather than divorce per se, or loss of contact with a noncustodial parent, has the most adverse effect on children's behavior and psychological well-being. Parental conflict provides children with an opportunity to exploit parents and play one off against the other, and when they are older, to escape careful monitoring of their activities. However children, especially older children, are able to function well over time in independent, noninterfering households. As long as they are not involved in parental conflict, children are able to cope well even if these households have different rules and expectations. Children are able to learn the differing role demands and constraints required in relating to diverse people in a variety of social situations such as in the peer group, church, the classroom, on the playing field, or at grandmother's house. In view of children's adaptability and differentiated responses to a broad range of social situations, the resistance to recognizing that children can cope with two different home situations is remarkable. Problems in joint custody come when parents interfere in each other's childrearing, and when children don't want to leave their friends, neighborhoods, or regular routines. In the rare cases where joint custody requires shifts between schools, this too may become a burden. Difficulty in visitation under any custody arrangement may emerge as children grow older and want to spend more time with their peers and less with parents.

Joint custody does tend to promote greater contact and financial support by noncustodial parents (Maccoby et al., 1988). Noncustodial fathers or fathers with joint custody are more likely to support children when they feel they have power in decisions relating to their children's life circumstances and activities. However, under conditions of high conflict, the increased contact associated with joint custody can be detrimental to the well-being of the child. Under conditions of low or encapsulated conflict, or emotional distancing between the parents, the effects of contact will be positive or at least neutral. Most children want to maintain contact with both parents and are more satisfied with continued contact. However, if the custodial parent has formed a hostile alliance with the child against the noncustodial parent, if the child feels caught in the middle of the parental conflict, or if the noncustodial parent has been extremely dysfunctional (e.g., abusive), children may seek to limit their contact with the nonresidential parent.

ADJUSTMENT OF DIVORCED PARENTS

Separation and divorce place both men and women at risk for psychological and physical dysfunction (Chase-Lansdale & Hetherington, 1990). In the immediate aftermath of marital dissolution, both men and women often exhibit extreme emotional lability, anger, depression, anxiety, and impulsive, and antisocial behavior, but for most this is gone by 2 years following divorce. However, even in the long run, alcoholism, drug abuse, psychosomatic problems, accidents, depression, and antisocial behavior are more common in divorced than nondivorced adults (Bloom, Asher, & White, 1978). Furthermore, recent research suggests that marital disruption alters the immune system, making divorced persons more vulnerable to disease, infection, chronic and acute medical problems, and even death (Kiecolt-Glaser et al., 1987). Some of these postdivorce symptoms in adults, such as depression and antisocial behavior, seem likely to have been present before divorce and even to have contributed to a distressed marriage and to marital dissolution. Depression and antisocial behavior are related to irritable, conflictual marital interactions. Adults exhibiting antisocial behavior are more likely to have disordered social relationships, to encounter negative life events, and to undergo multiple marital transitions (Forgatch et al., in press). Our own work, examining couples who later divorced, suggests that, especially for women in distant or hostile, conflicted marriages, depression is likely to decline following divorce, whereas antisocial behavior is likely to remain constant or to increase. Continued attachment to the ex-spouse is associated both with health problems and depression (Kiecolt-Glaser et al., 1987). This connection, however, declines with repartnering and the formation of a close meaningful relationship (Hetherington et al., 1982; Forgatch et al., in press).

We spoke earlier of divorce, like death of a spouse, involving loss of a way of life. It also involves loss of aspects of the self sustained by that way of life (Silverman, 1988). Because of this, the early years of separation and divorce offer great opportunity for positive and negative change. In this early phase, separated and divorced men and women often complain of being disoriented, of not knowing who they are or who they want to be, and of behaving in ego alien ways. They speak of having "not me experiences" where previously rational, self-controlled individuals report such things as smearing dog feces on their ex-spouse's face, following them and peering into their bedroom windows, defacing their property, fantasizing and sometimes acting out violent impulses, or whining and begging for reconciliation. "I can't believe I did that" or "That wasn't really me" is repeatedly heard in interviews with divorcing adults. Many noncustodial fathers feel rootless, disoriented, shut out of regular contact with their children and nurture unrealistic fantasies of reconciliation. Others throw themselves into a frenzy of social activity and try to develop a more open, free-living persona.

Conventional women have more problems in adapting to their new life situation than do less conventional, more internally controlled, androgynous, or working women. Nonemployed women in traditional marriages have often organized their identities around the achievements of their husbands and children. One said, "I used to be Mrs. John Jones, the bank manager's wife. Now I'm Mary Jones! Who is Mary Jones?" In spite of the problems with income, housing, inadequate childcare, loneliness, and limited resources and support encountered by many divorced women, our work shows that about 70% in the long run, prefer their new life to an unsatisfying marriage. Most think that divorce and raising children alone have provided an experience of personal growth, albeit sometimes painful growth. Some of these women were competent, autonomous women before the divorce. Others, in coping with the demands of their new situation, discovered strengths, developed skills, and attained levels of individuation that might never have emerged if they had remained in the constraints of a dysfunctional marriage. It should be noted, however, that in comparison to married women, divorced women are overrepresented at both extremes of competence and adjustment. Some are found in a group with high self-esteem and few psychological problems who function ably in social situations, in the workplace, and in the family. Others seem permanently overwhelmed by the losses and changes in their lives, show little adequate coping behavior, and exhibit low self-esteem and multiple problems such as depression, antisocial behavior, substance abuse, and repeated, unsuccessful intimate relationships. Job training, continued education, and professional enhancement play important roles not only in the economic, but also the psychological, well-being of women. Adequate childcare is critical in facilitating these activities (Burns, 1992). Although work satisfaction plays an important role in the self-esteem of divorced adults, most custodial mothers and fathers restrict their social, and to some extent, work activities, and organize their lives around providing and caring for their children. Adequacy in these roles is central to their self-esteem.

Repartnering is the single factor that contributes most to the life satisfaction of divorced men and women; however, it seems more critical to men. Divorced fathers are less likely than divorced mothers to show marked personal growth and individuation while they are single. Men show more positive development in the security of a marriage.

The significance for children of these psychological, emotional, and physical changes in parents is that, in the early years following divorce, children are encountering an altered parent at a time when they need stability in a rapidly changing life situation. A physically ill, emotionally disturbed, or preoccupied parent and a distressed, demanding, angry child may have difficulty giving each other support or solace. Over time, the well-being of the child is associated with the adjustment of the custodial parent, and this is largely an indirect path mediated by parenting behaviors. If parent distress, low self-esteem, depression, or antisocial behavior results in disrupted parenting, behavior problems in children increase (Hetherington & Clingempeel, 1992; Patterson & Bank, 1989; Forgatch et al., in press). If a disturbed parent is able to maintain authoritative qualities, such as responsiveness, warmth, firm control, monitoring, and communication, adverse effects on children are less likely to occur.

R E A D I N G

13

The Remarriage Transition

CONSTANCE R. AHRONS AND ROY H. RODGERS

The family change process set in motion by one marital disruption boggles one's mind. It frequently requires complex computation to chart and understand the kinship relationships. Even though the current remarriage rates show a continuing decline . . . , the vast majority of divorced families will move through the series of stressful transitions and structural changes brought about by the expansion of the family postdivorce. The structural changes in remarriage give rise to a host of disruptions in roles and relationships, and each transition may be mastered with varying amounts of stress and turmoil.

Projections from the current trends indicate that between 40 and 50 percent of the children born in the 1970s will spend some portion of their minor years in a one-parent household. Given the current remarriage rates it is also projected that approximately 25 to 30 percent of American children will live for some period of time in a remarried household. Although we do not have as adequate cohabitation information as we would like, we can assume that many of these children will also live for some period of time in a cohabiting household, which may or may not become a remarriage household. This means that at least 25 to 30 percent of the children will have more than two adults who function simultaneously as parents. Rates of redivorce are also increasing, resulting in even more complex kinship structures.

Consider the following case example of the Spicer/Tyler/Henry binuclear family. . . .

When Ellen was eight and David ten, their parents separated. They continued to live with their mother, Nancy, spending weekends and vacations with their father, Jim. Two years after the divorce their father married Elaine, who was the custodial parent of her daughter, Jamie, aged six. Ellen and David lived in a one-parent household with their mother for three years, at which time their mother remarried. Their new stepfather, Craig, also had been divorced, and he was the joint-custodial parent of two daughters, aged six and 11. His daughters spent about ten days each month living in his household. Within the next four years, Ellen and David's father and stepmother had two children of their own, a son and a daughter.

When Ellen and David are 15 and 17, their family looks like this: They have two biological parents, two stepparents, three stepsisters, a half-brother and a half-sister. Their extended family has expanded as well: They have two sets of step-grandparents, two sets of biological grandparents, and a large network of aunts, uncles, and cousins. In addition to this complex network of kin, they have two households of "family. . . ."

BINUCLEAR FAMILY REORGANIZATION THROUGH EXPANSION: AN OVERVIEW

The expansion of the binuclear family through remarriage involves the addition of new family members in all three generations. The recoupling of one of the formation spouses requires another reorganization of the former spouse subsystem and each of the parent-child subsystems; a recoupling of the other former spouse requires still another reorganization of the whole system. Each of these transitions has the potential of being highly stressful for family members. The way in which the family reorganizes itself will determine whether the binuclear family emerges as a functional or dysfunctional system. . . .

We are very much hindered by the inadequacy of current language in our discussion of the binuclear family in remarriage. For most of the relationships between family members in this expanded system there are no formal labels or role titles. What does one call one's former mate's new spouse? Or the children or parents of the new mate who have a relationship with one's child? Even the former spouse relationship has no current title, which requires that we continue to speak of it as a past relationship. Although ex-spouses with children may refer to each other as "my daughter's (or son's) father (or mother)," this does not capture the ongoing nonparental relationship between the divorced couple. So, of necessity, as we struggle to analyze some of the components of this complex system, our language suffers from being cumbersome and we will occasionally resort to inadequate terms that have emerged in the process of studying these families.

Former Spouse Subsystem

The former spouse relationship, with its many possible relational variations, becomes even more complex when one or both partners remarry. The timing of the remarriage further complicates the dynamics of this highly ambiguous post-divorce relationship. In McCubbin and Patterson's theoretical formulation of the pathways and mediating factors leading from stress to crisis, accumulating stressors, or "pileup," increase the potential for crisis. Consequently, if one of the ex-spouses remarries before the binuclear family has adequate time to establish new patterns for its reorganized structure, the potential for dysfunctional stress is high. Given the statistic that about 62 percent of men and 61 percent of women remarry within two years after divorce . . . , many families will experience the added stress of incorporating new family members in the midst of struggling with the complicated changes produced by the divorce.

Even if remarriage is delayed until the divorced family has had sufficient time to reorganize and stabilize, shifting of roles and relationships is necessary when a new member is introduced into the family system by remarriage. The family has to struggle with the role of the new family member while allegiances, loyalties and daily relationship patterns undergo transition. For many families, just as they are adjusting to one new member, the other ex-spouse remarries, which causes another transition requiring a shift in the family's tentative equilibrium. The length of time between one ex-spouse's remarriage and the second remarriage will influence the severity of stress experienced by all family members as they are required once again to cope with reorganization.

For the single ex-spouse, the remarriage of a former mate irrespective of the timing, may stimulate many of the feelings unresolved in the emotional divorce. If there are any lingering fantasies of reconciliation, the remarriage brings the sharp reality that reunion is no longer a possibility. It is not unusual for the single ex-spouse to feel a temporary loss of self-esteem as he or she makes comparisons to the new partner. Feelings of jealousy and envy are normal, even for those who thought they had worked through these feelings at the time of the divorce. Seeing an ex-spouse "in love" with someone else often rekindles the feelings of the early courtship and romantic phase of the first married relationship and a requestioning of the reasons for divorce. For a single ex-spouse who did not want the divorce, the remarriage has the potential of creating a personal crisis that closely resembles the experiences of the divorce. But even for those ex-spouses who may have initiated the divorce, the remarriage usually stimulates old feelings and resentments.

> Nancy: When Jim told me he was getting married I reacted with a cutting comment, saying I hoped she was better prepared for long evenings alone than I was. But what I was really scared about was that he would be different with her than he was with me. What if he had *really* changed? I realized that I wanted his marriage to fail. Then I would know that I was right in divorcing him.

Jim's remarriage resulted in Nancy's returning to therapy to work through many of the unresolved issues of the divorce. Jim's new wife was younger than Nancy and had one child by a previous marriage. Nancy and Jim had become cooperative colleagues in their divorced parenting relationship and she was fearful that she would have to give up many of the conveniences of their shared parenting as Jim took on the responsibilities of a new family.

The remarriage of one or both of the former spouses might be expected to decrease the amount of coparenting between former spouses, since a person involved in a new relationship may have less time to spend, or interest in, relating to his or her former spouse, or may perhaps feel pressure from the new spouse to decrease his or her involvement with the first spouse. For Jim, the conflicts were many.

> Jim: When Elaine and I decided to get married I felt guilty and like I needed to tell Nancy immediately. I dreaded telling her. When I did tell her she didn't say much but I knew she was feeling upset. I wanted the kids to be part of the wedding and I knew Nancy was going to feel jealous and left out. I'd feel much better if she had someone else in her life. Elaine's relationship with her ex-husband is nothing like my relationship with Nancy and she didn't understand my wanting to ease Nancy's pain by not flaunting my new life at her.

Jim's marriage to Elaine initiates a complex cycle of changes for all participants. Nancy needs to adjust to Jim's sharing of his life with a new partner and a child, while both Jim and Elaine need to cope with two ex-spouses who will continue to be part of their future lives. Six months after Jim's marriage to Elaine, Nancy summarized it this way:

> Nancy: Things have changed a lot since Jim remarried. He's less willing to accommodate when I need to change plans around the kids. He always has to check with Elaine first. I really resent that—the kids should come first. I invited Jim to Ellen's birthday party but he couldn't come because of plans he had made with Elaine and her child. And I feel uncomfortable calling him at home about anything. Elaine usually answers the phone and I feel like she's listening the whole time. Jim has asked to take the kids on a week's vacation to visit Elaine's parents over Easter. I know it's his time with the kids but I think he should give them some special time and not make them spend it with Elaine's family.

For Nancy it is difficult for her to see her children's family extending to include more members not directly related to her. And in these early stages of his remarriage Jim is having difficulty coping with the conflicting demands that his increasing family membership causes.

> Jim: I knew Nancy would be upset about our plans for the Easter vacation. Sometimes I wish I could just go off with the kids skiing like we did the first year after the divorce, but I know Elaine wants to visit her parents. There's no way I can please everyone.

Nancy and Jim's relationship is in the process of undergoing considerable change. They talk less frequently and anger sparks up more often now as they try to make decisions about the kids. Jim feels more anger at Nancy now because she is "not understanding" his new responsibilities, and Nancy feels more anger as she has less access to Jim. They are traveling the bumpy road of this transition as they redefine their relationship again, dealing with the changes brought about by Elaine's entry into the family system.

In Ahrons' Binuclear Family Study a deterioration in coparental relations after remarriage did occur among the respondents. This was especially true if only the husband had remarried. For instance, the number and frequency of childrearing activities shared between the former spouses were highest where neither partner had remarried and lowest if only the husband had remarried. The amount of support in coparental interaction was highest and conflict lowest where neither partner had remarried, while conflict was highest and support lowest if only the husband had remarried. Also, if neither former spouse had remarried, they were most likely to spend time together with each other and their children, and least likely if only the husband had remarried. . . .

Remarried Couple Subsystem

The transition to remarriage after a divorce of one or both partners is markedly different from the transition to a first marriage. Not only do the new spouses bring their families of origin into their extended system, but they also have relationships with their first married families which need to be integrated in some way. Remarried couples overwhelmingly report that they are unprepared for the complexities of remarried life. Their model for remarriage is often based on a first marriage model. In contrast to the relatively impermeable boundary that surrounds a nuclear family, permeable boundaries are needed in households within the binuclear family system. These facilitate the exchange of children, money, and decision-making power. If one of the partners has not been previously married, he or she is particularly vulnerable to the dream of the ideal traditional family. . . .

When Elaine and Jim decided to get married, they talked about their divorce histories and their current relationships with their ex-spouses and brought their respective children together for brief periods of time. They fantasized about their plans for blending their family and perhaps adding a new child of their own to the picture. Although they were both aware of some potential problems, they felt able to cope because of the strong bond they had developed between themselves. But as they actually made the transition to remarriage many of the problems created more stress than they had anticipated.

> Elaine: When Jim and I decided to get married I was surprised by his feeling guilty about Nancy. I didn't have any of those feelings about my ex, Tom. When Tom remarried last year it didn't make much difference in my life. He hadn't seen much of Jamie anyway and he just saw her less after he remarried. It was a relief not to have much to do with him. So, after living alone with Jamie for three years, I was really excited to have a family again and give Jamie more of a dad. But it's not working out that way. Jamie is angry a lot about not having time alone with me, which ends up with Jim and me fighting a lot. Jim feels badly about not spending enough time with his kids and when the kids are together, it just seems to be everyone fighting over Jim. And I feel resentful at not having enough time alone with Jim. Between every other weekend with his kids and the long hours we both work we never seem to have time alone together. Last Friday we were finally spending an evening all alone and, just as I was putting dinner on the table, Nancy called. Jim and I spent the next two hours talking about Nancy. It ended up spoiling our whole evening.

Elaine's feelings are not uncommon for second spouses within a complex binuclear family. The stresses of accommodating the existing bonds of first married relationships into the new stepfamily subsystem often turn the traditional "honeymoon stage" of marriage into an overwhelming cast of characters who share the marital bed. The reorganization required in moving from a one-parent household to a two-parent one often involves more adjustment than the single parent expected. Roles and relationships require realignment and the addition of a new person in some type of parent role is stressful for all the family participants. A frequent complaint in new remarriages is the lack of time and privacy for the newly remarried partners. Jim expressed his disillusionment this way:

> Jim: Maybe we shouldn't have gotten married. When we were dating we made time for each other and spent many days and evenings enjoying things together. But after we got married Elaine felt guilty leaving Jamie with her mother or a babysitter very often. Jamie is very demanding—she always seems to want Elaine to do something for her. And Elaine can't seem to say no. Whenever I try to suggest to Elaine that Jamie should learn to play alone more, Elaine seems to get moody and quiet. Her resentment of the time I spend with my kids is hard for me to deal with. Sometimes I think she wishes I would stop seeing them or see them as little as Tom sees Jamie.

When the remarriage partners have been previously married, it is difficult for them not to compare their respective relationships with their ex-spouses. Their own former spouse relationship becomes the model for their new spouse's former spouse relationship. Elaine's expectation that Jim would have a similar relationship with Nancy as she had with Tom was shattered as she realized that Nancy was still very much a part of Jim's life.

The rise of dual-career marriages has resulted in a time problem for first marriages which is only exacerbated in the dual career remarriage. Add to this children and an ex-spouse or two and the issue of time becomes a very real problem. The usual marital issues of power and regulation of distance and intimacy are multiplied in the complex binuclear family. . . .

As with divorce, and with marriage as well, the first year of remarriage has the most potential for crisis. The rate for divorce after remarriage is even higher than that for divorce in first marriages. Glick calculates that 54 percent of women and 61 percent of men who remarry will divorce. The timing of redivorce also differs from that of a first divorce. Remarriages have a 50 percent greater probability of redivorce in the first five years than first marriages.

Current empirical work also suggests that remarriage satisfaction is highly dependent on stepparent-stepchild relationships. How the crises are handled by the remarriage pair will depend on many past experiences and will define the future functioning of the family. Over time, and perhaps with some professional help, Elaine and Jim may be able to find ways to cope with their overcrowded lives. They will need to devise ways to protect and nourish their relationship without damaging the existing parent-child bonds. This will require developing a new model of familying which includes more flexibility, compromise, and fluidity of boundaries than they may have expected originally. . . .

Sibling Subsystems: Step and Half

The child development literature notes the stresses of adding children to the family with its normalizing of "sibling rivalry." In the remarriage family with children of both partners, the joining of the new sibling subsystems is a difficult transition for the children—acquiring an "instant sibling" can pose a threat to even the most secure child. The new remarriage partners have their marriage at stake and, therefore, need their respective children to like each other. Given a host of factors, such as the age and temperament of the children, the blending of two households of unrelated children requires major adjustments. Few newly blended families resemble the "Brady Bunch," but many have this as their model for this transition!

The usual competitive struggles among siblings often become major battles in remarried families, as children must adapt to sharing household space and parental time with new siblings. . . . [T]he remarriage of Ellen and David's father included a new "kid sister" for them. That was followed a year later by their mother's remarriage, which included two more "kid sisters" who shared their home with them for one-third of every month. And, a few years down the line, they had to incorporate two half siblings when their father and stepmother had a son and a daughter. . . .

Empirical research on the effects of remarriage on children is not as easily summarized as the literature on the effects of divorce. Although research is steadily increasing, we still lack major longitudinal studies identifying the stresses and developmental phases of adding new members to the binuclear family. And sibling relationships in binuclear families have been a sadly neglected area of study. But it is our guess that for many children the transition to remarriage is more stressful than the transition to divorce. The addition of new family members can also mean more loss than gain for many children—if not permanent losses, then at least temporary relationship loss in the transition period. The changes children need to make when a parent inherits new children as part of his or her remarriage are numerous and difficult. And the newly remarried parent, who so frequently feels overwhelmed, may have her or his energies absorbed more in the new mate than in facilitating the child's transition.

Mother/Stepmother–Father/Stepfather Subsystems

Now we are faced with describing baffling relationships with a wordiness created by our current language deficits. We are hampered further in our efforts by the lack of clinical or empirical research on these relationships. Nevertheless, we will attempt here to describe some of the stressful aspects of these relationships, which form such an integral part of the remarriage transition.

In fact, these first and second spouses do have some bearing on each other's lives. For some second spouses, the "ghost" of the first spouse is ever present. For many, the first spouse can be an unwanted interloper, creating conflict between the remarriage pair. In other remarriage couples the first spouse is a uniting force on whom the new spouses place blame for all the problems of a dysfunctional family. This type of scapegoating is the subject of much humor and provides the basis for many of the prevalent negative stereotypes of this relationship.

Obviously, even in one family system, the relationships between current and former spouses can be quite different, depending on the type of relationship between the former spouse pairs and all the individual personalities. . . .

The possibilities and complexities in these types of relationships are vast, and our knowledge of them is almost nonexistent. But clearly the type of relationship style adopted by the former spouses is a major factor determining the relationship between first and second spouses. In many remarried binuclear systems the former spouse relationship is likely to diminish in importance over time, especially when there are no minor children to bind the parents together. As this happens the need for first and second spouses to relate also diminishes. . . .

Functional and Dysfunctional Remarriage Relationships

Our definition of functional and dysfunctional systems in remarriage is very similar to that of functional and dysfunctional divorces. . . . Developing new roles and relationships in remarriage which take into account the existence and losses of divorced family relationships is critical to enhancing remarried family functioning. The addition of new family members can result in dysfunctional binuclear family systems if prior kin relationships are severed. If remarriage subsystems try to model nuclear families—that is, if they insist upon "instant" family and try to establish traditional parenting roles—they will experience resistance and distress. A functional binuclear family system needs to have permeable boundaries which permit children and adults to continue prior family relationships while slowly integrating the new remarried subsystem. This, of necessity, causes transitory stresses and strains created by the conflict between new and old alliances. Remarriage is still another transition, with even more possibilities for stress than divorce.

As we emphasized in the divorce transition, the clear delineation of boundaries is critical to successful functioning. The remarried husband coparent, for example, must clarify his role vis-à-vis his biological and stepchildren, and his first and second spouses. He and his ex-spouse need to renegotiate what is appropriate and inappropriate in his continuing role as coparent. Coparenting agreements that may have been satisfactory prior to his remarriage are likely to have implications for his current spouse. For example, if it has been agreed that he needs to spend more time with his eight-year-old son, who wants and needs his father's attention, this takes time away from his marriage. His responsibilities as a parent and his spousal responsibilities come into conflict. This can be exacerbated by opinions expressed by his current partner that the "boy is spoiled and demanding and needs to learn that his father can't always be there." Or she may feel that the former spouse is using the child as a way of hanging on to her ex-husband. And, of course, she may also be concerned about the time taken away from her and the children she has brought to this new marriage. But the new partner must also be sensitive to the degree that expression of such thoughts violates important boundaries between the new marriage and the old.

While he will be wise not to pass these opinions of his new partner on to the former spouse (these are clearly outside the boundaries of the former spouse relationship), unless the husband coparent is able to deal effectively with his ex-spouse around these conflicting pressures, crisis may result. His former wife may see him as withdrawing from the coparental relationship they have agreed upon. And she, not having remarried, may have a renewed sense of abandonment resulting from the remarriage of her former spouse. Given their agreements concerning coparenting, she has legitimate call upon her former spouse. At the same time, the remarried spouse has equally legitimate expectations related to their marriage. Without explicit negotiation of arrangements and reasonable expectations from both sides, thus establishing clear boundaries for his actions in both subsystems, he is destined to fall short in both.

The single former spouse also may experience considerable distress in adjusting to the expanded system. Noncustodial parents will feel some resentment at losing some of their former responsibilities in both division of labor and decision-making. They may also feel that the new spouse interferes in their relationship with the former spouse and their children. A custodial parent, usually the mother, will often experience a loss of services when her former spouse remarries. She may no longer be able to call on him for help, as many of her demands—except as they are related to the coparenting relationship—begin to fall outside the legitimate boundaries of the former spouse relationship. Clearly, agreements and court orders with respect to financial child support are legitimate. However, expectations that the former husband will perform repairs or maintenance on the home of the former spouse may have to be rejected. This may be difficult, since that home is likely to be his former home, in which he may feel some residual investment, and in some cases may still retain some financial investment. However, resistance from the new partner to continuing such tasks is likely to severely restrict any such activity. All of this may be softened or made more difficult, depending upon the kind of postdivorce relationship style which has developed.

Remarriage restructures the division of labor developed in the postdivision reorganization. New spouses of custodial parents take on many of the day-to-day responsibilities for care of children and household tasks formerly handled alone by the custodial parent or carried out by one of the children from time to time. As we have seen, this may lead to some genuine friction, as children resent the new stepparent's "taking over" or displacing them in some valued responsibility. If the new spouse attempts to assume responsibilities which the noncustodial parent may have continued, this is another source of potential stress. The former spouse may resent it, the stepchildren may resent it, and even the new spouse may have difficulty in accepting it.

Decision-making and the power structure implications carry similar potential stress. This will be especially true around decisions concerning the stepchildren but may be true in other areas as well. If a new spouse has been used to having his or her former spouse participate and be involved in decisions concerning the children, the new spouse can easily be seen as "interfering," both by the other biological parent and the child. For example, as we have seen in the case presented this chapter, Nancy resented Elaine's parenting involvement.

The style of the postdivorce ex-spouse relationship may either ease these adjustments . . . or make them more difficult. . . . If former spouses are insecure and competitive about their parenting relationships with their children, . . . the addition of a new parent figure will intensify those feelings during the transition. An ex-spouse may feel threatened by the "new family" of the remarried spouse, anticipating that the children will prefer this new household to the one-parent household where they currently live.

When parents—both biological and step—are unclear about their roles, children are likely to use the ambiguity to manipulate the new stepparent, their custodial parent, and the noncustodial parent. During the early stages of the remarriage transition it is not unusual for children to play one parent off against another for some personal gain. For example, in the Spicer-Tyler-Henry family, Ellen, after spending a weekend at her father's house, might very well tell her mother that Elaine, her new stepmother, "lets me watch TV until 10 p.m." Ellen's hope, of course, is that her mother will respond by permitting her to stay up later than her usual bedtime. Sometimes, new stepparents will be more lenient with their stepchildren in the hopes of being liked and accepted by them. Consciously, or perhaps unconsciously, the new stepparent is competing with the other biological parent for the child's affections.

Although former spouses may have worked out consistent rules for discipline, etc., during the divorce transition, these are likely to need renegotiation when a new parent enters the family. Only now, the renegotiation is more complicated, as three parents become part of the process instead of the original two. And if another ex-spouse remarries, there may be a replay of some of the issues as the system accommodates to a fourth parent. As we noted earlier, however, this may be an easier transition. Not only are the parents familiar now with many of the problems of adjustment but the system itself is in better balance. There are now two stepfamily households, with each biological parent having an ally.

The remarried binuclear family faces a unique problem in controlling intimacy in the family. Incest taboos, which are assumed between blood kin in first marriage nuclear families (though, as is now being revealed, more often violated than many have known), become an important issue. The function of such taboos, of course, is to maintain unambiguous and appropriate intimate relationships in families. The potential for sexual feelings and possible abuse between non-blood parents and children, as well as between adolescent stepsiblings, is high. Therefore, establishment of clearly defined boundaries in this highly charged emotional area is essential.

A situation observed by one of the authors in family therapy illustrates how dysfunctional failure to establish such boundaries can be. In the course of the session, an adolescent stepdaughter revealed that she had been sexually involved with the son of her stepfather, i.e., her stepbrother. There were indications that this involvement was involuntary on her part. The mother of the young woman became very angry. At this point, the two biological daughters of the stepfather, who no longer lived in the household, confronted their stepmother with their sexual experiences some years before with her son—their stepbrother. They were extremely angry with the stepmother for not having the same reactions to their experiences, of which they believed the stepmother to be aware. These revelations, of course, provided some understanding of the kinds of conflicts in this stepfamily that had prompted the request for therapeutic treatment. The issues extended far beyond the matter of sexual abuse to include the entire range of emotional relationships which had developed in this remarried family over several prior years. Failure to have defined appropriate intimacy boundaries in the reorganization of this binuclear family had contributed to an extremely dysfunctional situation.

Relationships with extended kin find new stresses facing them upon the remarriage of one or both ex-spouses. Children may be particularly puzzled by suddenly finding their access to one set of grandparents or a favored aunt or uncle severely restricted or cut off. The nature of those relationships may also be changed, even if they are continued, by the inability of the extended kin to keep their feelings about the ex-spouse from contaminating their interactions with the children. Further, the introduction of new extended kin can also be confusing and stress-producing for children.

The new relationships with the spouse's extended family are not of the same character as those of first married couples. They often carry residual elements from the former marriage, particularly since these are not just in-laws, but also grandparents, uncles, and aunts. In addition, in many cases there are also associations to be worked out with the former spouse of the new partner. Until new relationships with extended family are established, they tend to be mediated through the new marital relationship.

CONCLUSION

The study of even one remarried subsystem alone presents sufficient complexities to cause many social scientists to return to studying individuals rather than family systems. Our lack of both language and analytic tools, as well as the difficulties in conceptualizing the totality of these complex systems, creates frustration in both the writer and the reader.

All of this brings into sharp relief the importance of developing a new set of meanings for the relationships between former spouses, with the new spouses, between former and current spouses, between stepparents and stepchildren, between step and half siblings, and with extended kin. If the expanded binuclear family structure is to survive and function in an effective manner, then all parties must develop clear understandings of what these meanings are in the new remarriage situation. These meanings are most likely to center on the coparenting responsibilities that the ex-spouses share, but they go well beyond this.

Clearly delineating a precise definition of functional and dysfunctional remarriage binuclear families is not possible, given our current lack of knowledge. Although we can comfortably conclude that remarriage subsystems must be open systems with permeable boundaries, we cannot say what degree of openness is optimal. Remarriage subsystems need to be able to develop their own sense of connectedness and independence, while simultaneously functioning as interdependent units. Stepparents have a confusing and difficult role. In most families they need to develop new parenting type roles that supplement, rather than replace, biological parents. And they need to do so expecting resistance and a long developmental process of integration. What is required is a new model of familying that encompasses an expanded network of extended and quasi-kin relationships.

PART THREE

PARENTS
AND
CHILDREN

INTRODUCTION

No aspect of childhood seems more natural, universal, and changeless than the relationship between parents and child. Yet historical and cross-cultural evidence reveals major changes in conceptions of childhood and adulthood and in the psychological relationships between children and parents. For example, the shift from an agrarian to an industrial society over the past 200 years has revolutionized parent-child relations and the conditions of child development.

Among the changes associated with this transformation of childhood are: the decline of agriculture as a way of life; the elimination of child labor; the fall in infant mortality; the spread of literacy and mass schooling; and a focus on childhood as a distinct and valuable stage of life. As a result of these changes, industrial-era parents bear fewer children, make greater emotional and economic investments in them, and expect less in return than their agrarian counterparts. Agrarian parents were not expected to emphasize emotional bonds or the value of children as unique individuals. Parents and children were bound together by economic necessity: children were an essential source of labor in the family economy and a source of support in an old age. Today, almost all children are economic liabilities. But they now have profound emotional significance. Parents hope offspring will provide intimacy, even genetic immortality.

Although today's children have become economically worthless, they have become emotionally "priceless" (Zelizer, 1985).

No matter how eagerly an emotionally priceless child is awaited, becoming a parent is usually experienced as one of life's major "normal" crises. In a classic article, Alice Rossi (1968) was one of the first to point out that the transition to parenthood is often one of life's difficult passages. Since Rossi's article first appeared over three decades ago, a large body of research literature has developed, most of which supports her view that the early years of parenting can be a period of stress and change as well as joy.

Parenthood itself has changed since Rossi wrote. As Carolyn and Philip Cowan observe, becoming a parent may be more difficult now than it used to be. The Cowans studied couples before and after the births of their first children. Because of the rapid and dramatic social changes of the past decades, young parents today are like pioneers in a new, uncharted territory. For example, the vast majority of today's couples come to parenthood with both husband and wife in the workforce, and most have expectations of a more egalitarian relationship than their own parents had. But the balance in their lives and their relationship has to shift dramatically after the baby is born. Most couples cannot afford the traditional pattern of the wife staying home full time; nor is this arrangement free of strain for those who try it. Young families thus face more burdens than in the past, yet supportive family policies such as visiting nurses, paid parental leave, and the like that exist in other countries are lacking in the United States.

Parents who successfully weather the early years often face another stressful period when their child becomes an adolescent. Reed Larson and Maryse Richards examine a sample of middle-class, two-parent families with a teenager in the home. Tracking the activities of family members throughout the day by means of beepers, they find that mothers, fathers, and children are pulled into separate worlds during the day. The fast-paced but different realities faced by each family member create a minefield of possible misunderstandings and conflict. Some families, however, manage to maintain warm and supporting relationships with one another; they don't get overstressed at work, and they keep "emotional brushfires" from flaring into emotional firestorms.

Mothers are still the principal nurturers and caretakers of their children, but the norms of parenthood have shifted—as the growing use of the term "parenting" suggests. Views of fatherhood in the research literature are changing along with the actual behavior of fathers and children in real life. Until recently, a father could feel he was fulfilling his parental obligations merely by supporting his family. He was expected to spend time with his children when his work schedule permitted, to generally oversee their upbringing, and to discipline them when necessary. Even scholars of the family and of child development tended to ignore the role of the father except as breadwinner and role model. His family participation did not call for direct involvement in the daily round of child rearing, especially when the children were babies. By contrast, scholars expressed the extreme importance of the mother and the dangers of maternal deprivation. Today, however, the role of father is beginning to demand much more active involvement in the life of the family, especially with regard to child rearing. Rosanna Hertz reports on the different ways dual-earlier couples arrange for the care of their young children. In her study, she found three different patterns. In the "mothering approach," the couple agree that it is best for the mother to care for the children in the home; even if the mother must work outside the home, she arranges her schedule so as to maximize her time with the children. In the "parenting approach," both parents share the care of the children, and organize their work lives so as to maximize the time they have with their children. In the "market approach," the couple uses professional caregivers to look after their children. Hertz observes that only the shared parenting approaches challenge traditional gender roles and the traditional demands of the workplace.

Although some fathers are becoming more involved with their children, divorce often means a greatly reduced amount of life with father. In their article, Frank F. Furstenberg and Andrew J. Cherlin take a more detailed look at the effects of divorce on children's adjustment. They find that divorce is a long process, not a single event. They find that much of the negative impact of divorce on children stems from conflict between the parents. Indeed, there is evidence that children from divorcing families begin to have problems well before the parents separate. A key factor in children's well-being after divorce is the quality of the child's relationship with the custodial parent, usually the mother.

REFERENCES

Rossi, A. 1968. Transition to parenthood. *Journal of Marriage and the Family* 30, 26–39.

Zelizer, V. A. 1985. *Pricing the Priceless Child.* New York: Basic Books.

◆

CHAPTER 6

PARENTHOOD

14

Becoming a Parent

CAROLYN P. COWAN AND PHILLIP A. COWAN

Sharon: I did a home pregnancy test. I felt really crummy that day, and stayed home from work. I set the container with the urine sample on a bookcase and managed to stay out of the room until the last few minutes. Finally, I walked in and it looked positive. And I went to check the information on the box and, sure enough, it *was* positive. I was so excited. Then I went back to look and see if maybe it has disappeared; you know, maybe the test was false. Then I just sat down on the sofa and kept thinking, "I'm pregnant. I'm really pregnant. I'm going to have a baby!"

Daniel: I knew she was pregnant. She didn't need the test as far as I was concerned. I was excited too, at first, but then I started to worry. I don't know how I'm going to handle being there at the birth, especially if anything goes wrong. And Sharon's going to quit work soon. I don't know when she's going to go back, and we're barely making it as it is.

Sharon: My mom never worked a day in her life for pay. She was home all the time, looking after *her* mother, and us, and cleaning the house. My dad left all of that to her. We're not going to do it that way. But I don't know how we're supposed to manage it all. Daniel promised that he's going to pitch in right along with me in taking care of the baby, but I don't know whether that's realistic. If he doesn't come through, I'm going to be a real bear about it. If I put all my energy into Daniel and the marriage and something happens, then I'll have to start all over again and that scares the hell out of me.

Sharon is beginning the third trimester of her first pregnancy. If her grandmother were to listen in on our conversation with Sharon and her husband, Daniel, and try to make sense of it, given the experience of her own pregnancy fifty years ago, she would surely have a lot of questions. Home pregnancy tests? Why would a woman with a newborn infant *want* to work if she didn't have to? What husband would share the housework and care of the baby? Why would Sharon and Daniel worry about their marriage not surviving after they have a baby? Understandable questions for someone who made the transition to parenthood five decades ago, in a qualitatively different world. Unfortunately, the old trail maps are outmoded, and there are as yet no new ones to describe the final destination. They may not need covered wagons for their journey, but Sharon and Daniel are true pioneers.

Like many modern couples, they have two different fantasies about their journey. The first has them embarking on an exciting adventure to bring a new human being into the world, fill their lives with delight and wonder, and enrich their feeling of closeness as a couple. In the second, their path from couple to family is strewn with unexpected obstacles, hazardous conditions, and potential marital strife. Our work suggests that, like most fantasy scenarios, these represent extreme and somewhat exaggerated versions of what really happens when partners become parents. . . .

THE FIVE DOMAINS OF FAMILY LIFE

The responses of one couple to our interview questions offer a preview of how the five domains in our model capture the changes that most couples contend with as they make their transition to parenthood. Natalie and Victor have lived in the San Francisco Bay Area most of their lives. At the time of their initial interview, Natalie, age twenty-nine, is in her fifth month of pregnancy. Victor, her husband of six years, is thirty-four. When their daughter, Kim, is six months old, they visit us again for a follow-up interview. Arranged around each of the five domains, the following excerpts from our second interview reveal some universal themes of early parenthood.

Changes in Identity and Inner Life

After settling comfortably with cups of coffee and tea, we ask both Natalie and Victor whether they feel that their sense of self has shifted in any way since Kim was born. As would be typical in our interviews, Mother and Father focus on different aspects of personal change:

> Natalie: There's not much "me" left to think about right now. Most of the time, even when I'm not nursing, I see myself as attached to this little being with only the milk flowing between us.
>
> Victor: I've earned money since I was sixteen, but being a father means that I've become the family breadwinner. I've got this new sense of myself as having to go out there in the world to make sure that my wife and daughter are going to be safe and looked after. I mean, I'm concerned about advancing in my job—and we've even bought insurance policies for the first time! This "protector" role feels exciting *and* frightening.

Another change that often occurs in partners' inner lives during a major life transition is a shift in what C. Murray Parkes (1971) describes as our "assumptive world." Men's and women's assumptions about how the world works or how families operate sometimes change radically during the transition from couple to family.

Natalie: I used to be completely apathetic about political things. I wasn't sure of my congressman's name. Now I'm writing him about once a month because I feel I need to help clean up some of the mess this country is in before Kim grows up.

Victor: What's changed for me is what I think families and fathers are all about. When we were pregnant, I had these pictures of coming home each night as the tired warrior, playing with the baby for a little while and putting my feet up for the rest of the evening. It's not just that there's more work to do than I ever imagined, but I'm so much more a part of the action every night.

Clearly, Natalie and Victor are experiencing qualitatively different shifts in their sense of self and in how vulnerable or safe each feels in the world. These shifts are tied not only to their new life as parents but also to a new sense of their identities as providers and protectors. Even though most of these changes are positive, they can lead to moments when the couple's relationship feels a bit shaky.

Shifts in the Roles and Relationships within the Marriage

Victor: After Kim was born, I noticed that something was bugging Natalie, and I kept saying, "What is bothering you?" Finally we went out to dinner without the baby and it came out. And it was because of small things that I never even think about. Like I always used to leave my running shorts in the bathroom . . .

Natalie: He'd just undress and drop everything!

Victor: . . . and Nat never made a fuss. In fact she *used* to just pick them up and put them in the hamper. And then that night at dinner she said, "When you leave your shorts there, or your wet towel, and don't pick them up—I get furious." At first I didn't believe what she was saying because it never used to bother her at all, but now I say, "OK, fine, no problem. I'll pick up the shorts and hang them up. I'll be very conscientious." And I have been trying.

Natalie: You have, but you still don't quite get it. I think my quick trigger has something to do with my feeling so dependent on you and having the baby so dependent on me—and my being stuck here day in and day out. You at least get to go out to do your work, and you bring home a paycheck to show for it. I work here all day long and by the end of the day I feel that all I have to show for it is my exhaustion.

In addition to their distinctive inner changes, men's and women's roles change in very different ways when partners become parents. The division of labor in taking care of the baby, the household, the meals, the laundry, the shopping, calling parents and friends, and earning the money to keep the family fed, clothed, and sheltered is a hot topic for couples (C. Cowan and P. Cowan 1988; Hochschild 1989). It seems to come as a great surprise to most of them that changes in some of their major roles affect their feelings about their overall relationship.

In a domino effect, both partners have to make major adjustments of time and energy as individuals during a period when they are getting less sleep and fewer opportunities to be together. As with Natalie and Victor, they are apt to find that they have less patience with things that didn't seem annoying before. Their frustration often focuses on each other. For couples who thought that having a baby was going to bring them closer together, this is especially confusing and disappointing.

> Natalie: It's strange. I feel that we're much closer *and* more distant than we have ever been. I think we communicate more, because there's so much to work out, especially about Kim, but it doesn't always feel very good. And we're both so busy that we're not getting much snuggling or loving time.
>
> Victor: We're fighting more too. But I'm still not sure why.

Victor and Natalie are so involved in what is happening to them that even though they can identify some of the sources of their disenchantment, they cannot really make sense of all of it. They are playing out a scenario that was very common for the couples in our study during the first year of parenthood. Both men and women are experiencing a changing sense of self *and* a shift in the atmosphere in the relationship between them. The nurturance that partners might ordinarily get from one another is in very short supply. As if this were not enough to adjust to, almost all of the new parents in our study say that their other key relationships are shifting too.

Shifts in the Three-Generational Roles and Relationships

> Victor: It was really weird to see my father's reaction to Kim's birth. The week before Natalie's due date, my father all of a sudden decided that he was going to Seattle, and he took off with my mom and some other people. Well, the next day Natalie went into labor and we had the baby, and my mother kept calling, saying she wanted to get back here. But my dad seemed to be playing games and made it stretch out for two or three days. Finally, when they came back and the whole period was past, it turned out that my father was *jealous* of my mother's relationship with the baby. He didn't want my mother to take time away from him to be with Kim! He's gotten over it now. He holds Kim and plays with her, and doesn't want to go home after a visit. But my dad and me, we're still sort of recovering from what happened. And when things don't go well with me and Dad, Natalie sometimes gets it in the neck.
>
> Natalie: I'll say.

For Victor's father, becoming a first-time grandfather is something that is happening *to* him. His son and daughter-in-law are having a baby and he is becoming grandfather, ready or not. Many men and women in Victor's parents' position have mixed feelings about becoming grandparents (Lowe 1991), but rarely know how to deal with them. As Victor searches for ways to become comfortable with his new identity as a father, like so many of the men we spoke to, he is desperately hoping that it will bring him closer to his father.

As father and son struggle with these separate inner changes, they feel a strain in the relationship between them, a strain they feel they cannot mention. Some of it spills over into the relationship between Victor and Natalie: After a visit with his parents, they realize, they are much more likely to get into a fight.

Changing Roles and Relationships Outside the Family

Natalie: While Victor has been dealing with his dad, I've been struggling with my boss. After a long set of negotiations on the phone, he reluctantly agreed to let me come back four days a week instead of full-time. I haven't gone back officially yet, but I dropped in to see him. He always used to have time for me, but this week, after just a few minutes of small talk, he told me that he had a meeting and practically bolted out of the room. He as much as said that he figured I wasn't serious about my job anymore.

Victor: Natalie's not getting much support from her friends, either. None of them have kids and they just don't seem to understand what she's going through. Who ever thought how lonely it can be to have a baby?

Although the burden of the shifts in roles and relationships outside the family affects both parents, it tends to fall more heavily on new mothers. It is women who tend to put their jobs and careers on hold, at least temporarily, after they have babies (Daniels and Weingarten 1982, 1988), and even though they may have more close friends than their husbands do, they find it difficult to make contact with them in the early months of new parenthood. It takes all of the energy new mothers have to cope with the ongoing care and feeding that a newborn requires and to replenish the energy spent undergoing labor or cesarean delivery. The unanticipated loss of support from friends and co-workers can leave new mothers feeling surprisingly isolated and vulnerable. New fathers' energies are on double duty too. Because they are the sole earners when their wives stop working or take maternity leave, men often work longer hours or take on extra jobs. Fatigue and limited availability means that fathers too get less support or comfort from co-workers or friends. This is one of many aspects of family life in which becoming a parent seems to involve more *loss* than either spouse anticipated—especially because they have been focused on the gain of the baby. Although it is not difficult for us to see how these shifts and losses might catch two tired parents off guard, most husbands and wives fail to recognize that these changes are affecting them as individuals and as a couple.

New Parenting Roles and Relationships

Natalie and Victor, unlike most of the other couples, had worked out a shared approach to household tasks from the time they moved in together. Whoever was available to do something would do it. And when Kim was born, they just continued that. During the week, Victor would get the baby up in the morning and then take over when he got home from work. Natalie put her to bed at night. During the weekends the responsibilities were reversed.

It was not surprising that Natalie and Victor expected their egalitarian system—a rare arrangement—to carry over to the care of their baby. What is surprising to us is that a majority of the couples predicted that they would share the care of their baby much more equally than they were sharing their housework and family tasks *before* they became parents. Even though they are unusually collaborative in their care of Kim, Natalie and Victor are not protected from the fact that, like most couples, their different ideas about what a baby needs create some conflict and disagreement:

Victor: I tend to be a little more . . . what would you say?

Natalie: Crazy.

Victor: A little more crazy with Kim. I like to put her on my bicycle and go for a ride real fast. I like the thought of the wind blowing on her and her eyes watering. I want her to feel the rain hitting her face. Natalie would cover her head, put a thick jacket on her, you know, make sure she's warm and dry.

Natalie: At the beginning, we argued a lot about things like that. More than we ever did. Some of them seemed trivial at the time. The argument wouldn't last more than a day. It would all build up, explode, and then be over. One night, though, Victor simply walked out. He took a long drive, and then came back. It was a bad day for both of us. We just had to get it out, regardless of the fact that it was three A.M.

Victor: I think it was at that point that I realized that couples who start off with a bad relationship would really be in trouble. As it was, it wasn't too pleasant for us, but we got through it.

Despite the fact that their emotional focus had been on the baby during pregnancy and the early months of parenthood, Victor and Natalie were not prepared for the way their relationship with the baby affected and was affected by the changes they had been experiencing all along as individuals, at work, in their marriage, and in their relationships with their parents, friends, and co-workers—the spillover effects. They sometimes have new and serious disagreements, but both of them convey a sense that they have the ability to prevent their occasional blowups from escalating into serious and long-lasting tensions.

As we follow them over time, Victor and Natalie describe periods in which their goodwill toward each other wears thin, but their down periods are typically followed by genuine ups. It seems that one of them always finds a way to come back to discuss the painful issues when they are not in so much distress. In subsequent visits, for example, the shorts-in-the-bathroom episode, retold with much laughter, becomes a shorthand symbol for the times when tensions erupt between them. They give themselves time to cool down, they come back to talk about what was so upsetting, and having heard each other out, they go on to find a solution to the problem that satisfies both of their needs. This, we know, is the key to a couple's stable and satisfying relationship (Gottman and Krokoff 1989).

Compared to the other couples, one of the unusual strengths in Natalie and Victor's life together is their ability to come back to problem issues after they have calmed down. Many couples are afraid to rock the boat once their heated feelings have cooled down. Even more unusual is their trust that they will both be listened to sympathetically when they try to sort out what happened. Because Natalie and Victor each dare to raise issues that concern them, they end up feeling that they are on the same side when it comes to the most important things in life (cf. Ball 1984). This is what makes it possible for them to engage in conflict and yet maintain their positive feelings about their relationship.

Most important, perhaps, for the long-term outcome of their journey to parenthood is that the good feeling between Victor and Natalie spills over to their daughter. Throughout Kim's preschool years and into her first year of kindergarten, we see the threesome as an active, involved family in which the members are fully engaged with one another in both serious and playful activities.

WHAT MAKES PARENTHOOD HARDER NOW

Natalie and Victor are charting new territory. They are trying to create a family based on the new, egalitarian ideology in which both of them work *and* share the tasks of managing the household and caring for their daughter. They have already embraced less traditional roles than most of the couples in our study. Although the world they live in has changed a great deal since they were children, it has not shifted sufficiently to support them in realizing their ideals easily. Their journey seems to require heroic effort.

Would a more traditional version of family life be less stressful? Couples who arrange things so that the woman tends the hearth and baby and the man provides the income to support them are also showing signs of strain. They struggle financially because it often takes more than one parent's income to maintain a family. They feel drained emotionally because they rely almost entirely on their relationship to satisfy most of their psychological needs. Contemporary parents find themselves in double jeopardy. Significant historical shifts in the family landscape of the last century, particularly of the last few decades, have created additional burdens for them. As couples set foot on the trails of this challenging journey, they become disoriented because society's map of the territory has been redrawn. Becoming a family today is more difficult than it used to be.

In recent decades there has been a steady ripple of revolutionary social change. Birth control technology has been transformed. Small nuclear families live more isolated lives in crowded cities, often feeling cut off from extended family and friends. Mothers of young children are entering the work force earlier and in ever larger numbers. Choices about how to create life as a family are much greater then they used to be. Men and women are having a difficult time regaining their balance as couples after they have babies, in part because the radical shifts in the circumstances surrounding family life in America demand new arrangements to accommodate the increasing demands on parents of young children. But new social arrangements and roles have simply not kept pace with these changes, leaving couples on their own to manage the demands of work and family.

More Choice

Compared with the experiences of their parents and grandparents, couples today have many more choices about whether and when to bring a child into their lives. New forms of birth control have given most couples the means to engage in an active sex life with some confidence, though no guarantee, that they can avoid unwanted pregnancy. In addition, despite recent challenges in American courts and legislatures, the 1973 Supreme Court decision legalizing abortion has given couples a second chance to decide whether to become parents if birth control fails or is not used.

But along with modern birth control techniques come reports of newly discovered hazards. We now know that using birth control pills, intrauterine devices, the cervical cap, the sponge, and even the diaphragm poses some risk to a woman's health. The decision to abort a fetus brings with it both public controversy and the private anguish of the physical, psychological, and moral consequences of ending a pregnancy (see Nathanson 1989). Men and women today may enjoy more choice about parenthood than any previous generation, but the couples in our studies are finding it quite difficult to navigate this new family-making terrain.

Sharon, who was eagerly awaiting the results of her home pregnancy test when we met her at the beginning of this reading, had not been nearly as eager to become a mother three years earlier.

> Sharon: Actually, we fought about it a lot. Daniel already had a child, Hallie, from his first marriage. "Let's have one of our own. It'll be easy," he said. And I said, "Yeah, and what happened before Hallie was two? You were out the door."
>
> Daniel: I told you, that had nothing to do with Hallie. She was great. It was my ex that was the problem. I just knew that for us a baby would be right.
>
> Sharon: I wasn't sure. What was I going to do about a career? What was I going to do about me? I wasn't ready to put things on hold. I wasn't even convinced, then, that I wanted to become a mother. It wouldn't have been good for me, and it sure wouldn't have been good for the baby, to go ahead and give in to Daniel when I was feeling that way.

In past times, fewer choices meant less conflict between spouses, at least at the outset. Now, with each partner expecting to have a free choice in the matter, planning a family can become the occasion for sensitive and delicate treaty negotiations. First, couples who want to live together must decide whether they want to get married. One partner may be for it, the other not. Second, the timing of childbirth has changed. For couples married in 1950–54, the majority (60 percent) would have a baby within two years. Now, almost one-third of couples are marrying *after* having a child, and those who marry before becoming parents are marrying later in life. Only a minority of them have their first child within two years. Some delay parenthood for more than a decade (Teachman, Polonko, and Scanzoni 1987).

Couples are also having smaller families. The decline in fertility has for the first time reduced the birthrate below the replacement level of zero population growth—less than two children per family.* And because couples are having fewer children and having them later, more seems to be at stake in each decision about whether and when to have a child. What was once a natural progression has become a series of choice points, each with a potential for serious disagreement between the partners.

Alice is in the last trimester of her pregnancy. In our initial interview, she and Andy described a profound struggle between them that is not over yet.

> Alice: This pregnancy was a life and death issue for me. I'd already had two abortions with a man I'd lived with before, because it was very clear that we could not deal with raising a child. Although I'd known Andy for years, we had been together only four months when I became pregnant unexpectedly. I loved him, I was thirty-four years old, and I wasn't going to risk the possibility of another abortion and maybe never being able to have children. So when I became pregnant this time, I said, "I'm having this baby with you or without you. But I'd much rather have it with you."
>
> Andy: Well, I'm only twenty-seven and I haven't gotten on track with my own life. Alice was using a diaphragm and I thought it was safe. For months after she became pregnant, I was just pissed off that this was happening to me, to us, but I gradually calmed down. If it was just up to me, I'd wait for a number of years yet because I don't feel ready, but I want to be with her, and you can hear that she's determined to have this baby.

Clearly, more choice has not necessarily made life easier for couples who are becoming a family.

Isolation

The living environments of families with children have changed dramatically. In 1850, 75 percent of American families lived in rural settings. By 1970, 75 percent were living in urban or suburban environments, and the migration from farm to city is continuing.

We began our own family in Toronto, Canada, the city we had grown up in, with both sets of parents living nearby. Today we live some distance from our parents, relatives, and childhood friends, as do the majority of couples in North America. Increasingly, at least in the middle- and upper-income brackets, couples are living in unfamiliar surroundings, bringing newborns home to be reared in single-family apartments or houses, where their neighbors are strangers. Becoming a parent, then, can quickly result in social isolation, especially for the parent who stays at home with the baby.

John and Shannon are one of the younger couples in our study. He is twenty-four and she is twenty-three.

> John: My sister in Dallas lives down the block from our mother. Whenever she and her husband want a night out, they just call up and either they take the baby over to Mom's house or Mom comes right over to my sister's. Our friends help us out once in a while, but you have to reach out and ask them and a lot

---

*There are indications, however, that the birthrate in the United States is now on the rise.

of times they aren't in a position to respond. Some of them don't have kids, so they don't really understand what it's like for us. They keep calling us and suggesting that we go for a picnic or out for pizza, and we have to remind them that we have this baby to take care of.

Shannon: All the uncles, aunts, and cousins in my family used to get together every Sunday. Most of the time I don't miss that because they were intrusive and gossipy and into everybody else's business. But sometimes it would be nice to have someone to talk to who cares about me, and who lived through all the baby throw-up and ear infections and lack of sleep, and could just say, "Don't worry, Shannon, it's going to get better soon."

Women's Roles

Since we began our family thirty years ago, mothers have been joining the labor force in ever-increasing numbers, even when they have young babies. Women have always worked, but economic necessity in the middle as well as the working classes, and increased training and education among women, propelled them into the work force in record numbers. In 1960, 18 percent of mothers with children under six were working at least part-time outside the home. By 1970, that figure had grown to 30 percent, and by 1980 it was 45 percent. Today, the majority of women with children under *three* work at least part-time, and recent research suggests that this figure will soon extend to a majority of mothers of one-year-olds (Teachman, Polonko, and Scanzoni 1987).

With the enormous increase in women's choices and opportunities in the work world, many women are caught between traditional and modern conceptions of how they should be living their lives. It is a common refrain in our couples groups.

Joan: It's ironic. My mother knew that she was supposed to be a mom and not a career woman. But she suffered from that. She was a capable woman with more business sense than my dad, but she felt it was her job to stay home with us kids. And she was *very* depressed some of the time. But I'm *supposed* to be a career woman. I feel that I just need to stay home right now. I'm really happy with that decision, but I struggled with it for months.

Tanya: I know what Joan means, but it's the opposite for me. I'm doing what I want, going back to work, but it's driving me crazy. All day as I'm working, I'm wondering what's happening to Kevin. Is he OK, is he doing some new thing that I'm missing, is he getting enough individual attention? And when I get home, I'm tired, Jackson's tired, Kevin's tired. I have to get dinner on the table and Kevin ready for bed. And then I'm exhausted and Jackson's exhausted and I just hit the pillow and I'm out. We haven't made love in three months. I know Jackson's frustrated. *I'm* frustrated. I didn't know it was going to be like this.

News media accounts of family-oriented men imply that as mothers have taken on more of a role in the world of paid work, fathers have taken on a comparable load of family work. But this simply hasn't happened. As Arlie Hochschild (1989) demonstrates, working mothers are coming home to face a "second shift"—running the household and caring for the children. Although there are studies suggesting that fathers are taking on a little more housework and care of the children than they used to (Pleck 1985), mothers who are employed full-time still have far greater responsibility for managing the family work and child rearing than their husbands do (C. Cowan 1988). It is not simply that men's and women's roles are unequal that seems to be causing distress for couples, but rather that they are so clearly discrepant from what both spouses expected them to be.

Women are getting the short end of what Hochschild calls the "stalled revolution": Their work roles have changed but their family roles have not. Well-intentioned and confused husbands feel guilty, while their overburdened wives feel angry. It does not take much imagination to see how these emotions can fuel the fire of marital conflict.

Social Policy

The stress that Joan and Tanya talk about comes not only from internal conflict and from difficulties in coping with life inside the family but from factors outside the family as well. Joan might consider working part-time if she felt that she and her husband could get high-quality, affordable child care for their son. Tanya might consider working different shifts or part-time if her company had more flexible working arrangements for parents of young children. But few of the business and government policies that affect parents and children are supportive of anything beyond the most traditional family arrangements.

We see a few couples, like Natalie and Victor, who strike out on their own to make their ideology of more balanced roles a reality. These couples believe that they and their children will reap the rewards of their innovation, but they are exhausted from bucking the strong winds of opposition—from parents, from bosses, from co-workers. Six months after the birth of her daughter, Natalie mentioned receiving a lukewarm reception from her boss after negotiating a four-day work week.

> Natalie: He made me feel terrible. I'm going to have to work *very* hard to make things go, but I think I can do it. What worries me, though, is that the people I used to supervise aren't very supportive either. They keep raising these issues, "Well, what if so-and-so happens, and you're not there?" Well, sometimes I wasn't there before because I was traveling for the company, and nobody got in a snit. Now that I've got a baby, somehow my being away from the office at a particular moment is a problem.
>
> Victor: My boss is flexible about when I come in and when I leave, but he keeps asking me questions. He can't understand why I want to be at home with Kim some of the time that Natalie's at work.

It would seem to be in the interest of business and government to develop policies that are supportive of the family. Satisfied workers are more productive. Healthy families drain scarce economic resources less than unhealthy ones, and make more of a contribution to the welfare of society at large. Yet, the United States is the only country in the Western world without a semblance of explicit family policy. This lack is felt most severely by parents of young children. There are no resources to help new parents deal with their anxieties about child rearing (such as the visiting public health nurses in England), unless the situation is serious enough to warrant medical or psychiatric attention. If both parents want or need to work, they would be less conflicted if they could expect to have adequate parental leave when their babies are born (as in Sweden and other countries), flexible work hours to accommodate the needs of young children, and access to reasonably priced, competent child care. These policies and provisions are simply not available in most American businesses and communities (Catalyst 1988).

The absence of family policy also takes its toll on traditional family arrangements, which are not supported by income supplements or family allowances (as they are in Canada and Britain) as a financial cushion for the single-earner family. The lack of supportive policy and family-oriented resources results in increased stress on new parents just when their energies are needed to care for their children. It is almost inevitable that this kind of stress spills over into the couple's negotiations and conflicts about how they will divide the housework and care of the children.

The Need for New Role Models

Based on recent statistics, the modern family norm is neither the Norman Rockwell *Saturday Evening Post* cover family nor the "Leave It to Beaver" scenario with Dad going out to work and Mom staying at home to look after the children. Only about 6 percent of all American households today have a husband as the sole breadwinner and a wife and two or more children at home—"the typical American family" of earlier times. Patterns from earlier generations are often irrelevant to the challenges faced by dual-worker couples in today's marketplace.

After setting out on the family journey, partners often discover that they have conflicting values, needs, expectations, and plans for their destination. This may not be an altogether new phenomenon, but it creates additional strain for a couple.

> James: My parents were old-school Swedes who settled in Minnesota on a farm. It was cold outside in the winters, but it was cold inside too. Nobody said anything unless they had to. My mom was home all the time. She worked hard to support my dad and keep the farm going, but she never really had anything of her own. I'm determined to support Cindy going back to school as soon as she's ready.
>
> Cindy: My parents were as different from James's as any two parents could be. When they were home with us, they were all touchy-feely, but they were hardly ever around. During the days my mom and dad both worked. At night, they went out with their friends. I really don't want that to happen to Eddie. So, James and I are having a thing about it now. He wants me to go back to school. I don't want to. I'm working about ten hours a week, partly because he nags at me so much. If it were just up to me, I'd stay home until Eddie gets into first grade.

Cindy and James each feel that they have the freedom to do things differently than their parents did. The problem is that the things each of them wants to be different are on a collision course. James is trying to be supportive of Cindy's educational ambitions so his new family will feel different than the one he grew up in. Given her history, Cindy does not experience this as support. Her picture of the family she wanted to create and James's picture do not match. Like so many of the couples in our study, both partners are finding it difficult to establish a new pattern because the models from the families they grew up in are so different from the families they want to create.

Increased Emotional Burden

The historical changes we have been describing have increased the burden on both men and women with respect to the emotional side of married life. Not quite the equal sharers of breadwinning and family management they hoped to be, husbands and wives now expect to be each other's major suppliers of emotional warmth and support. Especially in the early months as a family, they look to their marriage as a "haven in a heartless world." Deprived of regular daily contact with extended family members and lifelong friends, wives and husbands look to each other to "be there" for them—to pick up the slack when energies flag, to work collaboratively on solving problems, to provide comfort when it is needed, and to share the highs and lows of life inside and outside the family. While this mutual expectation may sound reasonable to modern couples, it is very difficult to live up to in an intimate relationship that is already vulnerable to disappointment from within and pressure from without.

The greatest emotional pressure on the couple, we believe, comes from the culture's increasing emphasis on self-fulfillment and self-development (Bellah et al. 1985). The vocabulary of individualism, endemic to American society from its beginnings, has become even more pervasive in recent decades. It is increasingly difficult for two people to make a commitment to each other if they believe that ultimately they are alone, and that personal development and success in life must be achieved through individual efforts. As this individualistic vocabulary plays out within the family, it makes it even more difficult for partners to subordinate some of their personal interests to the common good of the relationship. When "my needs" and "your needs" appear to be in conflict, partners can wind up feeling more like adversaries than family collaborators.

The vocabulary of individualism also makes it likely that today's parents will be blamed for any disarray in American families. In the spirit of Ben Franklin and Horatio Alger, new parents feel that they ought to be able to make it on their own, without help. Couples are quick to blame themselves if something goes wrong. When the expectable tensions increase as partners become parents, their tendency is to blame each other for not doing a better job. We believe that pioneers will inevitably find themselves in difficulty at some points on a strenuous journey. If societal policies do not become more responsive to parents and children, many of them will lose their way.

R E A D I N G

15

Healthy Families: Toward Convergent Realities

REED LARSON AND MARYSE H. RICHARDS

In many ways the deck is stacked against contemporary families, including the comparatively privileged two-parent families we studied here. They must struggle to create internal vitality within a society that is massive, fragmented, and often pulls family members in different directions. When a couple gets married and has children, they enter a minefield of problems waiting to happen. Differences between the fast-paced daily realities lived by each family member create endless potential for misunderstanding and conflict.

Against this backdrop, our society has evolved a new ideal for family life: providing warm relationships and a personal haven for all members. Evidence shows that this new gold standard is one we should aspire to. When marital partners are caring toward each other, their well-being is greater, as is their children's. When relations between parent and child are warm, the child grows up to be a healthier adult. Our question has been: What can families do that would allow them to live up to this standard more consistently? How can families maintain internal warmth despite all the daily processes that pull them apart?

Certainly there are no easy answers. One woman said, "If you claim to have gotten through your child's adolescence without problems, you're lying." We have seen that the simplest interactions of daily life can lead family members into discord. Getting haircuts for the children, fixing the humidifier, a phone call between an adolescent and her boyfriend can create individual distress and collective disharmony.

Nonetheless, we feel it useful to look closely at the families in our study that were faring better. Despite the hazards of contemporary life, in some of these families the members usually got through most days feeling warm toward each other and good about themselves. Husbands and wives shared love and mutual respect, most of the time. Their children usually rebounded quickly from setbacks in their lives. Of course, all these families had moments of conflict, stress, and exchange of negative feelings—no one family had solved the Rubik's

From *Divergent Realities: The Emotional Lives of Mothers, Fathers and Adolescents.* Copyright © 1994 by Basic Books. pp. 211–219. References have been omitted from end of Reading.

cube of domestic harmony. But in some families individual members were buoyant and their daily lives were coordinated most of the time.

In this concluding chapter we search for clues to what it was that was working in these healthier families: What daily patterns allowed them to surmount the many challenges of modern life? The conclusions we draw are limited to households sharing the cultural niche of those we studied: European-American, middle- and working-class, two-parent families. Even within this population, our conclusions are tempered by the fallibility of the measures we have used and the restricted size of our sample. Nevertheless, we think these families provide hints about a "wisdom" whereby some households function more smoothly.

DAILY PATTERNS OF HEALTHIER FAMILIES

Equilibrium Between Family and Public Spheres

We have already introduced some of the families that scored high on our index of family well-being: Del and Marlene, whose marital conflict was followed not by cycles of acrimony, but rather by creative thought about how to resolve the underlying source of their misunderstanding; Lorraine and her son, Luke, who appeared to maintain a healthy balance between their lives together and apart; Victor and his daughter, Vicki, who seemed to be more accepting of each other's feelings, including negative feelings, than most fathers and adolescents.

When we examine the daily patterns of these healthier families, a first finding that emerges concerns the equilibrium between the parents' lives at home and away from home. Throughout this book we have noted that both fathers and mothers typically experience an imbalance between these two spheres: men report high rates of distress at work and compensate for it by cultivating happier states at home; women are drained at home and depend on their job or interactions with friends for the happier part of their lives. These imbalances, we observed in the last chapter, make each spouse dependent on a particular part of his or her life for emotional sustenance and, as a result, promote distorted family relationships. In healthier families, however, we find that *fathers and mothers maintain emotional balance between their lives inside and outside the family.* They report comparable levels of emotion at home and away from home.

For fathers, this balance means that they less often burned themselves out at their jobs. Fathers in healthier families reported more favorable moods at their jobs than other fathers did: they were less likely to deplete themselves with frustration and anger. Possibly these fathers have deliberately chosen less stressful jobs. We mentioned one such father, John, who quit a high-pressure job because he was bringing home too much hostility and taking it out on his son. But our data also suggest that the fathers in healthier families took more breaks and paced themselves at work. We suspect they did more to regulate the intensity of their involvement, in order to avoid getting agitated. The important point is that these fathers were less likely to be emotional wrecks when they got home.

A good example of this balance is Erik Schaak, a father of four who worked in a factory as a forklift operator. This affable thirty-eight-year-old man experienced some pressure at work to move so many items a day, and events at the plant could anger him. At one point he got upset and cursed an "SOB." But he was usually able to regain his composure and keep himself from becoming overwrought. Because his wife, Judy, had a stable career, he did not feel as much obligation to be the breadwinning hero for the family as so many other fathers in our study did. The result of Erik's ability to keep stress in check at his job was that he arrived home with less of an emotional debt than many other fathers did and thus felt less need for immediate leisure when he came in the door.

For mothers as well, emotional balance means having sources of buoyancy both away from home and at home. While some mothers are solely invested in activities at home, many of the women in the healthier families in our study had rewarding outside activities: a job, school, volunteer work, or regular contact with friends. At home, they were engaged with their families but also gave themselves permission to relax and take care of their own needs: we found they had more leisure on weekends at home than other mothers did. They described pleasure in family recreation, reading a book by themselves, or taking a long bath, activities that restored their personal well-being.

Judy Schaak, a self-assured first-grade teacher, was a good example of this balance. She encountered stresses both at work and at home, but was able to keep them under control; she also found emotional rewards in both contexts, which she savored. Judy consistently reported looking forward to the next day, emphasizing the value of maintaining a "positive attitude." Because Erik shared responsibility for family work, she was able to disengage at home when she needed to, reporting time on her own for reading and embroidering. Because women in these healthier families had vital lives apart from their family activities, they were less likely to become overinvolved.

One result of this balance is that neither spouse felt like a victim at home. Neither brought home a personal agenda of unmet emotional needs. Each was less dependent on the family experience for emotional sustenance—and neither had to leave home to get needs met. Consequently, a couple like Judy and Erik are more flexible to accommodate each other and negotiate each day according to whatever exigencies arise. When Judy heard on Friday that her job was threatened, she called and got support from Erik, just as he turned to her in other situations.

Another result of this balance is that they were more emotionally available as parents to deal with their children's needs. Fathers who are not preoccupied with work and mothers who have the perspective gained from outside involvements may be better able to provide this even, objective attention. Judy and Erik's sixth-grade son, Calvin, was sometimes angered by the discipline his parents imposed, but he also reported learning from the conversations he had with each of them around these disciplinary incidents. Through steady efforts, Calvin said, his father "finally made me realize that I lose my temper too much," for example. Because Erik's emotions were not continuously raw from events at work, he was better able to maintain an even-keeled dialogue with his son, resulting in an important victory of reason over adolescent passion.

The picturebook image of the happy family is one where everyone feels content when together. Our findings suggest that mothers' and fathers' feelings *away from* home may be nearly as important to a family's well-being. "Part of being a parent," the family educator Michael Popkin writes, "is taking care of the parent." And while this is a complicated topic, evidence throughout this book shows that maintaining a healthy family depends on how members run their lives across all their waking hours.

Containing Emotional Brushfires

We suspect this balance in parents' lives contributes to a second feature we find in healthier families. At various points we have seen that negative emotions can be contagious within families. Most often fathers affect other family members, but it can begin with others as well. In some families this contagion leads to cycles of runaway hostility, such as the quarrel between Jerry and Glenna that went on for three days. Healthier families, we find, show less evidence of this transmission of emotion and fewer of these sustained cycles. *One person's emotional states are less likely to be passed to another.*

The family therapist Robert Beavers reached a similar conclusion from his study of successful families. He found that in such families there are stronger "emotional boundaries" between members: it is easier to distinguish mothers', fathers', and children's feelings. Negative states were less often conveyed through blaming, attacking, or scapegoating.

Rather than spraying negative emotions, members of healthier families seem to find ways to process them. One father tried to get home from work early enough so he could go for a run before dinner to dissipate stress. A mother reported taking thirty minutes to pull herself together before leaving her office, because she knew she would be deluged with demands the minute she stepped in the door at home; and though this meant thirty minutes less with her daughter, she found that the restorative effect this time had on her mood made it worthwhile.

Certainly there were occasions in these families where negative emotions got expressed. Erik Schaak admitted that he was sometimes short-tempered after a hard day's work. But these families seemed to be able to respond to members' emotions without letting one person's emotions dictate or dominate another's, as was demonstrated one evening at the Schaaks'. Events on this evening began much like other conflagrations we have seen that rebounded out of control for hours. At 6:58 P.M. Erik and Judy Schaak both reported intense anger over Calvin's "mouthing off." By 8:52, however, all remaining trace of negative feeling was gone. What happened? First, both parents agreed that Calvin's behavior was unacceptable and presented a united front. They did not allow Calvin to play them off against each other as we have seen in some less healthy families. Second, in a kind of "bad cop, good cop" routine, Erik disciplines Calvin by sending him to his room with a clear explanation of why his behavior is unacceptable, then later, Judy went in and comforted Calvin and discussed what had happened. By communicating about the causes of their negative feelings and listening to each other, these families appeared to keep emotional brushfires from getting out of control. Later Calvin reported feeling respectful of how his parents handled the situation.

At heart, members of these families seemed to have greater understanding and acceptance of their own and each other's emotional patterns. Mothers, fathers, and even some adolescents were able to tell us that, yes, they got irritable in certain situations and those feelings could alter their behavior, but they realized it was a pattern they could work on. Parents of one eighth-grade girl characterized their daughter as emotional, but were aware that her emotions passed quickly. Thus rather than fixating and ruminating on her transgressions, they accepted that she was "a moody adolescent" and avoided being pulled in by her hour-to-hour emotional oscillations.

It was fathers in these healthier families who showed the biggest deviation from typical norms for their gender, more often shedding the cloak of patriarchal authority and relating to their wives and children as equals. They were more aware of their own feelings and thus were less likely to dump their negative emotions onto others. They also appeared less likely to withdraw from difficult situations: we found examples of these fathers sustaining engagement with their wives about marital issues and staying with their children even when emotions were painful.

While such attentiveness is customary for mothers, it is rare among fathers. Yet when it exists, it does much to stop the cycles of negative exchange and create a more favorable environment for all family members. Our findings suggest that the art of family life resides in all members being able to attend to, communicate, and contain negative emotions in ways that do not transmit and perpetuate them.

Averting the 6 O'Clock Crash

The volatility of many of the families in our study and the calm of others lie in what happens during the dicey period around six o'clock on weekday evenings. This is a time when lines are most often crossed, when negative emotions are frequently exchanged. It is during this period that we saw a mother's harsh words lead one girl to thoughts of suicide, an angry stepfather push his daughter against the wall, and a dispute between one husband and wife escalate into the husband being kicked out of the house.

Better-functioning families found ways to get through this crunch period with fewer negative emotions. In healthier families, *everyone's mood during this period was more favorable*. Irrespective of mothers' and fathers' employment situations, they avoided the hostile and explosive feelings that are rife in other families.

Part of the problem, as we have discussed, is that fathers bring home emotional stress from work. The other part of the problem is that, in most families, everything that needs to be done during this period hinges on the mother. This can be especially problematic in dual-earner families, where the mother is coming home tired from work herself. In these families the father often flops down in front of the TV, while the mother, who is equally tired, is forced into labor. The result is often negative feelings all around.

So how did healthier families get through this difficult time? In the Schaak family, it was simply understood that Erik, who usually got home from work around 3:30 P.M., was jointly responsible for the urgent tasks of this period. He reported folding clothes with his wife one late afternoon and changing the baby's diaper on another. On yet another, he cooked dinner for Judy, who had had a particularly rough day.

Unlike most fathers, Erik Schaak refused to see his tiredness as more debilitating than his wife's, and Judy was unambivalent about sharing responsibilities with him. Before the school year started, Judy reported, they "sat down and figured out menus for the week and what days laundry and other housework would be done." Now, whatever needed to be done, Erik pitched right in. At times he would lose his cool with the children—late afternoon could still be a stressful period for all. But the fact that both Erik and Judy were involved made them more flexible to handle whatever combination of pressing needs people brought home.

The Schaak family's solution to the 6 o'clock crunch is more the exception than the rule. Some other families reduced the amount of labor required by making microwave dinners or ordering takeout food. Other families have relaxed the expectation that they share a hot meal at 6 each day; in one, different combinations of family members went to exercise during this time, an activity that was effective in both dissipating the day's stress and giving them a chance to check in with each other. In another, each ate separately; the daily family time was not at 6 over supper, but at 10 when all shared a snack and discussed events of the day.

These findings suggest that the art of cultivating a healthy family resides in finding creative solutions for household work, particularly during the 6 o'clock crunch. Each evening produced its unique vortex of urgencies, but through communication, flexibility, and engagement of all members, these healthier families were *usually* able to get through this challenging period with less conflict and transmission of negative emotion.

In Search of Quality Time

Healthy families, according to some family advocates, require not just the avoidance of destructive emotional exchanges, they require renewing ones. Eating meals or spending other time together is thought to provide the opportunity for a family to replenish themselves and affirm their experience of "we-ness."

But defining what makes for this "quality time" is elusive. Some dysfunctional families eat every breakfast and dinner together and spend enormous amounts of time with each other. Spending time in a dysfunctional family may only make members more dysfunctional. "Togetherness is a grand and wonderful thing," the family therapist Nathan Ackerman has written, "but . . . mere physical togetherness may be worse than none at all."

Clearly, just clocking in hours with each other does not automatically reinvigorate the family. We reported earlier that the amount of time husband and wife spent together is related to better marital adjustment, but the same is not true of shared time between parents and adolescents. You may remember that adolescents often experience family time as slow, boring, and constrained; it is thus easy to see why an increase of this kind of time does not enhance family health. But what kind of time do healthier families share? Is there anything unique about their daily contact that might provide hints about improving families' functioning?

First, we found that *members of these families reported fewer negative states when they were together.* Mothers, fathers, and adolescents in the healthier families we studied reported fewer occasions of feeling irritable and angry in each other's presence. This follows from what we have just discussed above: These families find ways to minimize situations that create and perpetuate negative feelings. They maintain a comfortable, relaxed climate in which sustained anger, hurt, and unhappiness cannot thrive.

Second, we found that *the healthier families spent more time in leisure together.* They were more likely than distressed families to go to the zoo, visit relatives, or, as the Schaaks did frequently, just watch TV together. Part of the reason they had more time for each other is that they apparently limited the net hours of work that family members performed. Families who spent most of their time working were less likely to be healthy; this was true irrespective of family social class or mother's employment, suggesting the pattern is not merely a result of financial pressures. Rather than tying up their weekends working overtime or doing household work, members of healthier families are more likely to be available for shared recreational activities.

The third characteristic is that *these families experienced their time together as more egalitarian.* Fewer of them reported a unilateral power structure among members. For times they were together, they reported no one to be the leader twice as often. This mutuality is evident, for example, on a Sunday night when one family was planning a fishing trip together, and all contributed ideas. It is evident in another when they went out for ice cream cones and shared a calm, low-key mood. In many other instances this mutuality was reported when doing chores together or even watching TV. Parents were able to set aside their impulse to control things. These families appeared more able to relax traditional authority structures and find islands of time when they could interact as equals.

What, then, is quality family time? To define it by any rigid criteria would be mistaken. The activities, topics of conversations, and emotional spirit that rekindle family élan may vary from household to household, occasion to occasion, and even from person to person within a family. The elements we have discussed—shared leisure, egalitarian relationships, and avoidance of negative emotion—are important, but there is surely no simple formula. For some families, quality time might even include fathers and adolescents openly airing negative feelings. What is important, we suspect, is not any singular group activity or mystical state, but a climate of attunement between family members, interactions in which each is able to listen and respond to what others are thinking and feeling, even when there is conflict.

In this and the other properties of healthier families, we see a pattern of relating in which fathers, mothers, and adolescents transcend traditional prescriptions for their behavior. . . .

R E A D I N G

16

A Typology of Approaches to Child Care: The Centerpiece of Organizing Family Life for Dual-Earner Couples

Rosanna Hertz

Author's Note: *I thank Faith I. T. Ferguson, who helped interview some of the couples with me, and I thank Wellesley College for a faculty award for tape transcriptions. I also thank Robert J. Thomas for helpful comments on this manuscript. A version of this article was presented at the British Psychological Society, London, 1996.*

Child rearing tends to be regarded as an individualistic concern for parents in the United States. Society may purport to be so-called profamily but, judging by the small number of policies and programs that pertain to child care, society largely ignores how young children spend their days despite widespread recognition that women's labor force participation has increased dramatically over the past several decades.[1] Indeed, it has become quite popular for political contenders to voice support for family values but to sidestep the sticky questions about how children are being cared for when mothers (and fathers) must work for pay outside the home.

With the exception of Head Start programs, when compared with other industrialized nations, the United States has little government-sponsored or subsidized day care (Benin & Chong, 1993; Kamerman & Kahn, 1991; Zigler, 1990). We lack the extensive system of day care that exists in other industrialized countries (Ferber & O'Farrell, 1991; Moen, 1989) because of ideological

From *Journal of Family Issues*, Vol. 18 No. 4, July 1997 355–385 © 1997 Sage Publications, Inc.

conflicts over the government's involvement in family life (Hartmann & Spalter-Roth, 1994).[2] The invocation of family values to indicate a belief in the strength of families to organize independently their lives to maximize the care and nurturance of the young (and elderly), rings hollow when studies find that affordable good quality day care arrangements would reduce both economic hardships and distress couples face in trying to balance the simultaneous child care and workplace demands (Bird, 1995). The lack of affordable child care in the United States is a serious problem for all social classes (Bianchi & Spain, 1986); but its consequences for low-income families are perhaps the greatest of all (Ferber & O'Farrell, 1991, pp. 74–84).[3]

Child care should be a leading social issue addressed at workplaces, in communities and at the state and federal levels of government. But without an array of good solutions to preschool child care (e.g., quality, affordability, certification, etc.), couples attempt to resolve this work/family dilemma through individual solutions. This article explores in a systematic way the different approaches dual-earner couples implement to care for their children. It also seeks to understand in context the critical factors that explain couples' choice of day care arrangements. The data presented suggest that a combination of a priori beliefs and economic resources explains the choice of child care practice. Only in rare instances do beliefs or resources alone play the determining role in selecting child care practices. However, there is no clear-cut relationship between beliefs and economic resources. In the absence of strong evidence regarding the relationship between beliefs and economic resources, I propose a typology of approaches to child care that reflects the interaction of ideology and economic factors. From a sample of dual-earner couples, I suggest that there are three general approaches to child care: (a) the "mothering" approach, (b) the parenting approach, and (c) the market approach. In addition to exploring diverse views of child rearing that exist in the United States, I will analyze how sentiments about mothering influence the ways couples organize and integrate family and work lives.

THE STUDY AND THE INTERVIEW SAMPLE

This article is part of an in-depth study of 95 dual-earner couples, with the majority (88 couples) having at least one child still living in the home in eastern Massachusetts. Each husband and wife was individually interviewed; the majority of couples were also interviewed simultaneously (Hertz, 1995).[4] Husbands and wives were told that we were interested in studying how couples make decisions about child care, finances, and work. The interviews lasted a minimum of 2 hours, with a smaller number of interviews lasting up to 4 hours. There are two parts to the interview: a longer-in-depth open-ended guide with extensive probes and then a shorter division of labor survey adapted from Huber and Spitzer (1983).

Because the primary focus of the study was looking at how women's labor force participation has altered family life—particularly authority surrounding decision making in the home—I decided to use a stratified quota sample.

Different strategies were used to find different segments of the study's population. In general, access to individual couples was obtained either through other professionals who identified couples fitting the study's parameters or through mailings to day care parents in several communities.

I used a combination of factors to decide who belongs in each social class stratum; these included the income of both spouses combined. Families in the upper middle class had a combined income of at least $100,000 annually and professional or managerial occupations; middle-class couples had a combined income of between $40,000 and $100,000, and most were in white-collar jobs in service professions or middle-management occupations; and working-class couples had incomes that overlapped those earned by the middle class, but these couples were distinguished by their occupations. I tried to locate couples for this segment employed in traditional working-class occupations or trades, such as painter, policeman, nurse, waitress, factory worker.

A total of 36% of the couples are working class; the other three fifths are middle and upper middle class. Within the working class, 30 couples are White and 4 couples are of other races. Within the middle and upper middle class, 35 couples are White and 21 couples are of other races. An additional 5 couples do not share the same race as their spouse; they are all middle- to upper middle-class couples. There are no "cross-class" couples (husbands and wives who differ in occupational prestige). For purposes of this article, social class is only mentioned. Racial differences in the three approaches to mothering appear not to be as important for this article as social class. For instance, upper middle-class African American families were as likely to have a professional approach to child rearing as their White counterparts. Racial differences are relevant when it comes to deciding between types of non-kin care and selecting between settings, which I have discussed in another article (Hertz & Ferguson, 1996). Therefore, I have not used race as a way of identifying respondents; I have instead used occupations as a signifier of the social class of each respondent.

At the time of the interview, each spouse within a couple had a minimum of one job. This does not mean, however, that at the time of having young children (preschool or elementary age) there were two full-time jobs. In most cases, women did not leave the labor force for more than 1 year; but in a small number of cases, women were not employed in the labor force when their children were preschool age or younger. More likely among this small group of couples, women worked outside the home for fewer hours than a full-time job. The decision to stay home longer than a year is not related to social class. That is, regardless of social class, it is possible to organize family life around a mothering approach (discussed below) provided that there are enough economic resources to live on one salary for a period of time. It is questionable whether younger couples can afford to do this today except perhaps among the upper middle and upper classes. At the time of the interviews, just over 60% of the couples were between their late 30s and middle 40s.[5] But there is great variation within this group as to the age when they had their first children. For those couples who had children in early decades, having children may have led to greater economic ability for the wife to stay at home. There were also fewer day care services available then; the growth of day care in the United States has mushroomed in the last 10 years. For those couples who have had children in the last 5 years, most remain in the paid labor force, with wives typically taking only brief maternity leaves.[6]

Independent of what age couples are now, I am interested in the relationship between child care beliefs and practices and social class at the time each couple had young children. At the time of the interview, 63 couples (66%) had at least one child age 5 or younger. An additional 25 couples (26%) had children living at home older than age 5. I indicate age of the respondents and their children's ages as part of the lead-ins to quotes so the reader can assess the historical factors (labor force and day care options) that inform each couple's story. I have deliberately selected quotes and respondents in each type who presently have young children as well as those whose children are older to give the reader information about couples presently undergoing child care decision making and couples who are reflecting back to this period in their family lives.

The focal points of this article are based on an analysis of responses to one open-ended question: "Tell me a history of your child care arrangements." Probes included likes and dislikes about child care arrangements but not anything about motherhood. Other topics emerge from the dialogue between interviewer and interviewee. Demographic facts and information are also used to analyze the responses to this question. Because I am particularly interested in the women's and men's views, I have relied heavily on their words and descriptions of family life to demonstrate the diverse beliefs about caring for young children in the United States today.

THE MOTHERING APPROACH

The mothering approach assumes that the person who is best suited to raise the couple's children is the wife, who should be with them at home. According to this approach, only the family can give its children the right values and moral upbringing. These couples uniformly believe that what will create successful adults is a childhood steeped in love, caring, and nurturing properly provided only by the insular world of the family. In this regard, the child's future is tied to a certain kind of early mothering practice.[7]

To maximize wives' abilities to devote themselves to the upbringing of the children, husbands work either overtime or they supplement a primary job with a second one, sacrificing their own leisure and time with children and spouses. But even the additional work hours were insufficient to pay the bills and keep wives out of the paid labor force. For the few lucky families who 15 years ago could get by financially on his earnings, as men reached their late 30s and early 40s, "burn-out" and being physically forced to slow down commonly occurred. Some worked less overtime; others found less strenuous work with less income. Even these men's wives eventually went back to paid work to take the pressure off him and to make their family's life less of an economic struggle to pay bills on time and to perhaps put a little money aside for a vacation. In 53% of working-class couples at the time of the interview, at least one spouse, typically the husband, worked overtime or held a second part-time job, totaling at minimum 60 hours a week.

This ideological belief about child rearing rarely exists for long in practice. Few couples could economically afford to have wives at home and out of the paid labor force. Yet, this central family belief in mother as the best person to raise children fuels how they arrange their work schedules and jobs to attempt not to compromise their children's upbringing. Child rearing—and keeping children within the family circle—is the priority, and work schedules of wives are critical to meeting this approach. Most of these women were employed even when their children were infants and toddlers, but talk about that only emerges once the conversation shifts to paid employment.

Beyond the early childhood years, even mothers who stayed out of the paid workforce, returned to paid employment at least part-time when the youngest entered kindergarten. In other families, however, wives remained in the paid workforce but changed to working shifts (Presser & Cain, 1983; Presser, 1988). To be available to young children, women worked nights giving the appearance of stay-at-home traditional moms to make highly visible their identities as mothers (Garey, 1995). Wives adjusted their work schedules, changing shifts as their children aged, placing their ability to care for children over spending time with husbands (Hertz & Charlton, 1989). Scheduling of work hours for both spouses to maximize mother care is more important than the wife's job mobility or workplace loyalty.

To permit a continued belief in a division of labor in which wives raise children, couples redefine their circumstances. That is, it is not the husband's fault that he does not earn enough. The economy is to blame. Placing blame on an external force does not damage their views of masculinity as tied to being a good provider. Economic explanations also become more congruent with couples' expectations that wives are picking up overtime because of cutbacks or due to erosion of wages so that families can avoid a decline in their standard of living (Ferber & O'Farrell, 1991). Put differently, locating blame external to the couple exempts husbands from feeling they are not good providers and wives from resenting their husbands for having jobs that do not pay enough, forcing them to seek paid employment.

It is interesting that these couples have yet to adjust their ideal view of family life to the reality they are living. But there is reason for this nested in a set of beliefs about family primacy. Even though these couples speak a language of traditional gender roles whereby spouses share the belief that child rearing is the wife's primary responsibility, their practices contradict these beliefs. For the most part, husbands strongly favor their wives' paid employment. It not only relieves the men of economic pressure but also means that the family is not living as tightly. They continue to live paycheck to paycheck but without worrying—especially for wives who typically pay the bills—about meeting monthly payments. But the ideological emphasis for them is not on gender equality as a larger value; instead, family is the critical variable. As a result of wives' paid employment, couples discuss parenting while emphasizing mothering. In this regard, there has been a shift by White working-class couples with traditional values of exclusive mothering to now resemble more the mother practices of earlier generations of minority working-class couples in this study,[8] now family values are about the family doing for itself in terms of raising its children, and whatever couples can do for themselves (without external supports, including everything from day care to welfare) is achieving family values.

Constructing Family Life to Maximize the Mother at Home

Despite hardship at times, keeping the mother/child dyad together is an organizing principal belief of these families. Sometimes, respondents phrased this belief as the mother's need to be with her child; other times, the belief appears as part of what is essential to so-called good mothering in addition to the glue that keeps the family unit strong. Put differently, the wife's status as mother becomes the pivotal point around which all other statuses (e.g., employee) revolve. Because the work of caring for family members is ignored (DeVault, 1991) or regarded as part of what might be called the invisible work (Daniels, 1988) of family life that women do, women's visible presence elevates mothering and other aspects of household work.

This wife, who once managed an office, thought when she was pregnant that she would return to work full-time. But becoming a mother is different than fantasizing about what it might feel like. Now 42 years old and the mother of two children, ages 1 and 10, she reflects back to how dramatically her beliefs changed about the kind of mother she wanted to be:

> I can remember, I always laugh with a girl friend who had a baby a year before me, and she'd say to me, "Are you still going back [to work]?" I go, "Oh ya, I'm gonna go back. No offense Ann, I really don't mean any offense, I really don't know what you do all day." And then once I had my baby, and was home for a couple of weeks with her, I never went back. (Interviewer: Really?) All of a sudden this thing took over me and it was there was no one in this world that could possibly raise this child like I was going to.

Other couples talked quite candidly about this division of labor as a taken-for-granted aspect of their marriage. Another husband, a policeman, age 44 with three children between the ages of 10 and 17, gave a typical response to why it was essential for mothers to be home:

> She's never worked full-time since we had our children. That's a decision we made. She took a maternity leave and decided not to go back to her job. Raising our children was too important. . . . We had had a firm commitment to my children's being raised by my wife. Because we're firm believers in a strong foundation for children. I mean first through age 6. To me, it's like a building. If the foundation isn't strong, you're asking for trouble later, as you build.

His wife, age 42, who presently works part-time as a secretary and cares for a relative's child in her home 2 days a week, told us that it was an implicit part of their marriage that she stay home when the children were born.

(Interviewer: Why did you make the decision to stay home?)

Oh God. I guess because that was just the way it was. I guess I figured when I had children, I'd stay home with them. I had a great job. And I actually probably made more money than my husband did at the time, but it wasn't a question.

(Was it something the two of you talked about at all?)

Not really, it was just I would stay home. . . .

(Were there any family members who could have watched the children?)

My husband's mother never worked, so she probably could have, if I had decided to ever do that, but I really enjoy being here. I really didn't—I wanted to be with them.

In another family, with children ages 10 and 18, the husband, age 37, had been a factory worker since he was 19 years old. High school sweethearts, he and his 36-year-old wife (presently a medical transcriber who has had a series of different jobs) have both always had to work to make ends meet. He explains the couple's philosophy about raising children even though these beliefs were at times thwarted, as is often the case among working-class couples when the inability to pay bills forces the wife back to work—even part-time—and someone else watches the child, which is less of a concern when older siblings or relatives help out:

It's very important to both of us that one, mainly that she should be—you know, because I was the primary breadwinner, I had the steady job—that she be home with our son [the second child], especially. With our daughter, it was hard because when she was born, I was making a lot less money. . . We always tried to put both our kids first. But when my daughter was a baby we had someone watching her—we've always both felt very strongly that if we're going to have children, that we should be with them, it's as simple as that. Not shuffling him off—it was never a "you have to go here [day care] every single day when you get home from school." . . . My daughter sometimes gets him [the son] in the afternoon, she helps a lot or his grandfather who lives down the street or we try to always have someone home for him in the afternoons.

In a fourth example, this mother, age 37, with three children between the ages of 10 and 16, returned to work waitressing after a 3-month maternity leave. Below, she explains why she shifted from working day hours to night hours:

I really didn't want to leave my kids with someone else. You know . . . I did try to go to work during the day when Eric was about 3 months old. When I decided I want—needed to go back to work for the money. And an old job was available that I had had, and they really wanted me to come back. It was waitressing again. I worked 4 days and couldn't do it. I cried and it was just too much, I just couldn't be away from him during the day. Didn't bother me to go in the evening when I knew he was with Mark [his father], sleeping most of the time and that was fine. Actually I've always liked working, but um . . . no, it wasn't for me. And it was tough when I just went to work a few years ago during the day. You know, because I wasn't here in the morning to get them off to school and it was difficult for my youngest. They've done great.

Night work did not compete with being a good mother in ways that being a day-working mom did (Garey, 1995). To meet the ideology of the stay-at-home mom, women are employed outside the home during hours that do not count:

when children are in school and asleep. This allows these families to meet this kind of mothering expectation without challenging women's primary identities. Further, child care decisions (and the choice to limit paid child care services) define the boundaries of what is necessary for them to retain their sense of being good mothers as well as an important part of their families' lives (Hertz & Ferguson, 1996).

Her husband, age 36, a factory worker who leaves home at 6:00 a.m. and returns at 3:30 in the afternoon, during periods when there is no overtime also works as a custodian for a restaurant before his factory job on Thursdays and Fridays. He simplified all his wife's job arrangements to make his point about their shared beliefs regarding child raising as a family-centered activity. Note that his identity is not tied to fathering but his talk is about what is critical to children's upbringing:

> She got a job at night, I worked during the day. The key to good parenting is one parent being with the child at ALL times. That's what we always thought. . . . Cause kids like to see their parents when they get home. I mean, cause they run through the door and they got so many things to tell you. They just, they don't have anybody to blab it out to.

As their family grew, neighbors watched the children in the transition from mom's leaving to work and dad's returning home from work. Neighbors continue to be a source of help during transition points in the day. At the time of the interview, her oldest children were teenagers and she went back to working the dayshift. Below, she describes why she shifted back:

> Because I always hated . . . I hated when I worked nights and weekends. Um, because it was the weekends. I mean I went to work when everybody else was home, basically. And especially when all of the kids were in school, they would come home, even though it was only a couple nights a week, Thursday and Friday.

She felt like an invisible part of the family. Even though much of the evening and weekend time is devoted to team sports that her husband coaches and that she admits to not really enjoying, it was important to her to be a spectator and cheer the family on rather than work during this time. Being visible represents good mothering. Similarly, the woman above who does secretarial work part-time, in addition to caring for a niece 2 days a week, had just filled out an application to work during the day at a store part-time at the time of the interview. Worried about how they will pay the tuition so their oldest daughter can commute to college to study nursing, she explains why she is applying for this particular job:

> So, I recently put in an application at a candy shop. See if I could sort of have two part-time jobs. I really still want to be home when my youngest gets out of school [elementary]. I FIRMLY believe that somebody needs to be home. As a matter of fact, even as they get older I really want to be around. I'm there for my older two [in high school].

The medical transcriber, who has a skill in high demand, requested hours to complement her children's school schedule. Flexibility in work scheduling allows women to assert the salience of their identity as mothers who place a priority on a particular kind of child rearing. Below, she explains the work arrangement she negotiated:

> Now I work days. But once summer vacation comes, I may end up working second shift again. Once again, I don't want to put him in a day care home. . . . I stressed with my boss that I needed flexibility. [She told her boss,] "Yes, I will go full-time, but school vacations, summer vacations, I may have to completely change my schedule and you'll have to go along with that." And that was fine with him.

Even though couples articulate the importance of the wife's being the central care provider, all the women quoted above worked some hours each week from the birth of the first child. But what they did was leave well-paying jobs, often earning more than husbands, to find work with better hours, meaning hours that allowed their husbands (or if possible another relative) to watch the children for at least part of her shift while she went to her job. Neighbors or acquaintances, often members in the same church, cared for children during transition times as part of the patchwork of child care coverage. These "custodial" caregivers did not compete with the mother as the central nurturer (Uttal, 1996). The woman above, who was once an office manager, never really stayed home. This couple needed her income to qualify for a mortgage, so she took a night job as a tax auditor briefly and since then has worked steadily as a phone service operator during weekend evenings and some week nights. He said,

> I'd get out of work at 3:30. Then she'd leave for work. I think she worked 4 to midnight. We might pass in the driveway or my mother-in-law would take care of the baby until I got home at night.

When their mortgage was approved, he was laid off. Finally, finding work as a truck driver, she needed weekend work hours because he was gone during the week. She took her present job as an answering service operator because she needed both a flexible schedule and some time out of the house. Below, she tells about this and her perfect job hours:

> It's probably the lowest paying job I've ever had and the most abusive in that people who call want to get whomever they want to get, not you. But it's the only thing that fits into my schedule. But my ideal is that I'd like to work for 5 nights a week— Sunday to Thursday night—and I'd like to work 6–11. You know, if I could. That's what I'd like to do.

Work histories for more than one third of the women in this group included several years as child care providers. Economically, couples noted this was a way not to have to place several children in the care of others and, equally important, it continued to position women in the world of the home, not the external labor force (Fitz Gibbon, 1993; Nelson, 1994). Some were licensed as family providers; others, such as the secretary quoted earlier, were paid to care for relatives' or friends' children (and for a brief period, even the medical transcriber watched children). Between shifting from a night schedule to a day one, the waitress above also worked out of her home, a culturally desirable place for her to be, to approximate a full-time homemaker mom caring for her children:

> When my youngest was born, I did day care myself. I did day care for two years. . . . I said to my girlfriend, "I don't know what I'm gonna DO, I don't really want to go back to work with three kids and leaving them. It's just too much." And she said, "Well, you know, I was thinking about getting back into day care and doing it up here. Why don't you get licensed?" So I ended up in day care and ah. It was okay. It served the purpose, you know, with Ann a baby and Eric only 2, being able to be home. But, um, I got burnt out really fast. Really fast, cause I had so many babies. . . . And actually when I gave it up and decided that I wanted to work outside the home, I did keep one little girl and my niece. I kept them and still babysat during the day time and waitressed a couple nights a week. . . . Four years that I babysat. It was the hardest work I ever did.

But it is not simply mothers who do all the nurturing. Fathers are active participants in these households, particularly when it comes to scheduling their work so wives can earn as well. The police officer mentioned earlier followed up his comment about his wife's staying at home with the following comment:

> I work nights now. I've worked days. If she has something to go to, we work it out so one of us is around. I mean, we had babysitters, but there's never been a time when both of us worked that we needed day care.

The waitress described her husband's involvement with the children:

> Mark actually does more of the after-school activities than I do. He is the one who takes them to all their meets and practices and spends afternoons hearing about their day. Since I wasn't home during dinner, he gave them supper but now I do it.

According to the medical transcriber's detailed account, her husband is now doing the thinking work of running their household, instead of simply serving the meals she prepared when she worked nights and her first child was young. When she was asked to commit to full-time hours by her employer, they had a long conversation about how the division of labor between them would change:

> But we did talk about it a lot and he was very well aware of the added responsibility that he would have, not just with my son but with the household things. Because when I was working evenings, I would do everything in the house during the day. . . . I was always the one responsible for the housework, cooking, laundry. And now, especially now that I'm working full-time, my husband does just as much, maybe more sometimes, than I do. . . . In fact, my husband did all the laundry last night. He left it for me to fold and put away, but it was clean and dry . . . . Normally, I work 10:30 to 7:00 at night. He gets home at 3:30 or 4:00. So my husband does the majority of the cooking during the week. . . . But if I'm going to be late, then he'll eat. And him and my daughter play cribbage or yahtze to see who does the dishes. And on the weekends, if the house is a real pit, it's like "let's get up Saturday morning and clean the house." We just all chip in.

Finally, the good mother is juxtaposed to leaving children with strangers. Below, the trucker driver husband explains a common reason why the mother is preferred:

> We feel that we see the difference in the children that are being raised by their parents and children that are being raised by, you know, an outside entity.

(Interviewer: In what ways?) Mostly, I think the way they do it is to let their kids do everything and anything. And ah, my wife is, I have to say, she's home with the children more and she does the disciplinary measures 90% of the time. Only because she's there when it's needed and I have very well-behaved children I am told. I feel they are. I'm not ashamed to take my children anywhere . . . my nephew is in day care and they can't go out to dinner unless there are special provisions because he can't sit in a restaurant. . . . (You think that's because he's in day care?) They, they're not spending, he's not getting the quality motherhood. I don't feel he is, ya. And I don't feel it's the day care people's job to, to instill these things in them. She's being paid to watch this child. She'd gonna do what she has to do to get through her day in a sane manner. She's not going to be a disciplinarian, or she shouldn't be there to, ah, to teach everything . . . my wife places our children in the playpen for several hours each day so she can get things done and the children learn to play by themselves. Other children who are in day care come here to play and they don't know how to entertain themselves.

Beliefs about motherhood remain entrenched in an essentialist argument that the only person qualified to care for young children is either the biological or adoptive mother (Hertz & Ferguson, 1996). Not only are strangers problematic as nurturers but they are less likely, these couples believe, to instill a strong foundation of values they share and believe to be necessary for adulthood. Even though fathers are essential to providing round-the-clock home care for children, it is the mother's visible presence that continues to be at the core of this construction of family life.

THE PARENTING APPROACH

The parenting approach is exemplified in the belief that the family ought to be organized around caring for the children with the critical distinction that both parents are full participants. Couples who adopt the parenting approach create new ways of combining family and work by seeking less demanding jobs or by negotiating more flexible arrangements with present employers (at least during the early years of their children's lives.) Some couples, particularly those who have middle-class occupations, are choosing to push employment in new directions. But for others, particularly those with working-class occupations, underemployment becomes a catalyst for rethinking traditional gender-based divisions of labor. These couples are crafting strategic responses to a shrinking labor market.

Regardless of how they came to share parenting, at the time of the interviews, these couples did not essentialize the mother as the only parent capable of nurturing children. For couples who chose to modify rigid work structures out of a belief that the responsibility for child rearing must be shared between mother and father, they talk about parenting with expectations that both parents are essential as nurturers and providers, though parents are not androgynous. Even among those couples wherein the men have lost full-time jobs and are presently doing less challenging work or working part-time, they also come to admit that men can care for children, throwing into question prior ideological beliefs about the dichotomy that conflates manhood and fatherhood with economic provision and womanhood and motherhood with nurturing activities.

(Even though new practices of work/family divisions emerge, it does not necessarily follow that underemployed men view caring for their children as a substitute for their present employment situations.)

Emphasizing the sharing of child rearing between parents limits the need to use external child care providers. When it is used, they attempt to control the kind of child care that supplements their own involvement with children prior to their children's entry into the public schools. Some use only a few hours a week of day care or babysitters; others find cooperative exchanges between families with young children.

Restructuring Employment to Maximize Parenting

This group of parents shares a belief about parental superiority in raising children. They believe that men and women should work outside and inside the home and also share responsibility for child rearing. Individuals attempt to modify their jobs and employment commitments to regulate on their own terms the demands that paid work makes and thus restore some semblance of control, even if it means loss of income (Hertz & Ferguson, 1996).

Couples emphasize that men have historically been short-changed as nurturers, and they are seeking parity with wives in their desire to experience fatherhood (cf. Coltrane, 1989). Men explained their efforts to modify their work schedules to be actively involved in child care. One man, age 37, employed in a social service agency, explains why he decided to reorganize his work schedule to have 1 day a week at home when his first child was born. He was able to reorganize which 40 hours he worked to not cut back on his pay, to have 1 day a week at home and occasionally to hold staff meetings in his home with his infant daughter present:

> Why did I do it? I think I was a new father, I wanted to spend time with my child, first year of life. I also sort of figured I might not have this opportunity again. I thought this was unique. I knew I wasn't going to forever stay at this job and I just had immense flexibility. I still was working very hard, but I had immense flexibility and control because I was the director, so I could really set the policy, and I did. But it was just important to me to spend some time and not have either a professional caregiver or have it so my wife had some time.
>
> It also worked in terms of our hours. Partly there was some pragmatism here in terms of—we wanted to minimize the day care she was in, maximize our time with her, certainly in that first year.

Another unusual arrangement that highlights the prioritizing of family togetherness over full-time work is a middle-class couple who both work part-time day hours: she as a social worker and he as a patient advocate. The wife, age 33, explains that initially she thought she would remain at home, but they each negotiated part-time work hours in their respective jobs to share child rearing. Understanding her husband's desire to be with their child, she reported that they figured out the following solution:

> I had negotiated, at my job, to go back part-time after my maternity leave, but I thought in my heart that I might not go back at all. Then when Andy went back to

work, he missed Sam so much that he felt like he really wanted to be home more. And what we were able to figure out was that if I went back part-time and he cut back his hours—so he decided he'd work 30 hours and I'd work 20 hours. And we could always be home with him. So that was what we did, and that's what we've done. . . . He worked 3 mornings and 2 afternoons and I worked 3 afternoons and 2 mornings. He worked 6 hours a day and I worked 4 hours a day.

Below, she explains why parental child rearing and part-time jobs better matched their desires:

I don't have criticisms of people who use day care. I just couldn't bear the thought. But it just felt, for me, that I really wanted to be with Sam and I wanted Andy to be with Sam and I feel like I got the absolute best of all possible worlds. Because I think it would have been really hard for me to be home full-time and have Andy work full-time. And working part-time is just the perfect balance. So to be able to work, and to have Sam home with Andy, we just couldn't ask for more. . . . I thought it was better for him to be with one of his parents.

The husband, age 39, explains the price he has paid and the confusion this arrangement has caused at the agency where he is employed:

I felt really stressed out initially. When I started working part-time, it was incredibly difficult because the expectations of myself were that I could do what I used to do just in less time. . . . I think more than anybody else at my office, I have had to scale back my expectations of myself. And I feel like people have been very supportive. . . . But it was frustrating. I'd post my schedule for everybody and give them a list. We'd try to set up a staff meeting and if we're going to do it on a Tuesday, do we do it in the morning or the afternoon? . . . And initially I'd have to scratch my own head and wonder when I was going to be in.

Some middle-class couples find a way to implement even more atypical arrangements, such as mutual exchanges, whereby families swap child care and keep track of hours. Administering part-time two different social services, the couple quoted below, ages 47 and 42, are making ends meet, placing themselves at the economic fringes of the middle class and conscious of their own downward mobility relative to their own parents. They know they could earn more money but as she put it,

We want to maximize as much as possible these first 5 years of being with him. So I would say the first thing is values about the amount of day care. It is also more expensive and it makes you work more. . . . I would say the driving factor was about values. We didn't want him to be in a lot of day care. I figured the longer he had more intimate settings, the better.

Their present arrangements are described below:

Now what we do is on Mondays I take care of a little girl in the morning and then her mom takes care of Mark in the afternoon. On Tuesdays and Thursdays, I bring Mark to a friend's house and that little girl's dad takes care of Mark and walks him to preschool with his little daughter and then picks them up and takes care of him. Then on Wednesdays, I take care of both little girls: the little girl whose mom takes care of Mark on Monday and the little girl whose dad takes care of Mark on Tuesdays and Thursdays. Then on Fridays, I take care of the little girl whose dad walked Mark to preschool. I take care of her on Friday mornings. So that evens out that because we get 2 afternoons and we give a day in the mornings. And then Friday afternoon, I pay the little girl's mother $20 to take care of him.

It is more common in this study sample for women to be the part-time worker or ask for special arrangements for them to combine motherhood and work, trading a solid middle-class standard of living for a more modest one. One woman, age 36, found a job working part-time as a lawyer. Below, she explains why:

> I've seen the way other people's lives had been crazy and I wanted to have a good time with my kids. I just kept hearing from people all the time: "These are the most precious years, don't give them up, hold onto them." . . . there's some truth to that and I really wanted to cherish the time I had with them. . . . I wanted to go back to work because I needed the intellectual stimulation and the respect.

But in many ways, the couples quoted above are labor force elites: They can shift the number of hours they work or change jobs without facing permanent career penalties. Eventually, the men and some of the women in these families shifted back to full-time work when their children entered preschool or grade school. But at least during the early years, they restructured the gender system to make fathering and mothering essential to childhood socialization.

Underemployment as a Route to Shared Parenting

For others, the downward economy and downsizing by corporations beginning in the 1980s (Hodson & Sullivan, 1990) led couples to piece together new work arrangements with active fathering a by-product. These latter couples did not make conscious choices to work less (and earn less) to do more for their children directly. They worry about spiraling downward even further. One father, age 39, with two children and presently working part-time as a home health aid, explains how his employment history has devolved:

> No. I think like MANY of the long-term unemployed, people like me who don't show up in the statistics, life goes on. So you do other things, you work part-time, either delivering pizza, which I did for 3 years, or bundling mail for the post office, whatever. But life goes on, so you have to adjust yourself because first of all, no one's gonna hire you. Once you're over 30, no one's gonna hire you for any real job. So what's the sense? . . . Your buddy who mows lawns for a living is offering you $10 an hour. So you do what you have to do. And you just fall into a whole other world that you forget exists when you worked for a large company, working 9–5 for 6 years.

The wife, age 35, a nurse who typically works the 7:00 P.M. to 7:00 A.M. night shift, worries that if she loses her overtime she will have to find a second nursing job. She added to her husband's comments her thoughts on how underemployment has affected her husband's sense of masculinity: "And of course his ego was all shot to hell. He's not the family provider he wants to be and he's not doing exactly what he wanted, what he set in his mind. All his goals are rearranged."

Couples in which the wife was working full-time and the husband part-time often wished that the wife could opt to work fewer hours. Whereas middle-class

White women continue to think about their lives as having the option of staying at home or working full-time, ideological and structural barriers prevent men from having similar choices (Gerson, 1993). Another mother, age 40, an office manager with two children ages 5 and 9, assumed that there would be two full-time paychecks. She now carries the economic burden and wishes she could have a more flexible work schedule.

> When I decided I would have children, I knew I would always be working, but I thought there would be more flexibility in my work schedule that would allow me to take extended vacations with my children, sometimes come home, be available after school to go to a school function with my son, sometimes be able to go to a soccer practice in the afternoon on a Thursday, be able to go to my daughter's ballet classes with her, that kind of thing. I don't feel like I have that kind of flexibility in my life. . . . In the nicer part of the year, I'll arrive home at 6:30 and they've just come from a baseball practice and they're rosy cheeked and they're laughing about what happened, and I'm not a part of that. So I guess over a period of time you do build up a little resentment. It goes away. But that's what I'm missing.

Another man, age 37, who presently works part-time as a postal worker, was laid off from a factory job after a dozen years at his company. His inability to find a full-time job for the past several years made it necessary for his wife to remain employed full-time. Because she is the carrier of the medical benefits, they feel unable to reduce her wok to part-time because they would lose these benefits. Despite his positive experiences caring for his 3-year-old son since he was an infant, this father describes the deep ambivalence he feels about contributing in atypical ways to family life:

> I was sort of thrust into the role. Thrust into it by job circumstances. . . . Sometimes it does bother me [not to be the main breadwinner]. . . . I just don't feel like I'm with the crowd. Not that I have to be with the crowd. . . . I realize that most men my age are probably established in careers now and I'm not. But, I just have that vague sense that, ah . . . like the world is going on out there and I'm here.
>
> I know it's more accepted now in society, but still I feel like I'm in the vast minority when it comes to my role. . . . I've more or less settled into the routine of taking care of my son. At first, it was quite an adjustment. . . . It's been kind of a metamorphosis for me. I've gone from being scared to death of it, to, ah, being actually quite comfortable now. Maybe that's why I stopped looking for full-time work, I don't know.

His wife, age 31, explains how her fantasies of the kind of family life she thought about have not materialized:

> It's funny because I guess we all have an idea of what's going to happen when you get married and all this. All my friends had it easy, you know, got married and then they did have the kids and then they stayed home. So I figured that would just happen to me, too. But it was tough. The first year that I was at work it was hard. I think we had a lot of arguments. And I didn't think he could do anything right. When we were both with him it was like, "What are we DOING now?" There was no set of instructions or anything that come with a baby. I always felt I was better with him. As an infant, he felt very awkward with him. And actually, he's done very well with him. I can't, you know, knock him now. But you know, at that time I was very resentful.

VERY resentful. And the thing is I had a job I didn't like and I had a manager I didn't like, he was terrible to me, very demanding, and he was very chauvinistic about women.

Even though mothering is a kind of craft or practice (Ruddick, 1980), the ideology that only mothers are really capable of maternal thinking is powerful and, as a result, many women do not necessarily want to share the work of mothering. The last woman quoted admits that mothering does not come naturally and it is only through practice that we learn how to do it. She concedes that her husband has mastered maternal practice; that is, he is engaged in sharing the work of parental love, a kind of work he never imagined himself doing. It is ironic that the couples who are on the cutting edge of transforming maternal thinking are doing so not because of an ideological belief as much as structural constraints of a shrinking labor force that catapult men into learning the work of child rearing. In the process, couples rethink family life, particularly caring for children, as they cobble together identities that are no longer unidimensional. Underemployed couples continue to wish their home and work time could be more evenly divided but not because they wish wives would become full-time mothers.

The Rise of Fathering

Fathering emerges but without a separate language from mothering, although the practice of it is markedly different from the White middle-class breadwinning fathers of a past generation (Bernard, 1981; Goode, 1982). Regardless of the route to sharing child care, the practice of fathering transformed these men into more nurturing and sensitive caregivers who are teaching their young children how to navigate the world (Coltrane, 1989). These men report wanting to be different than their own fathers. The husband of the couple who swap child care put it this way: "I didn't want to be the same kind of father my father had been. I wanted to be a more involved father. So, it seemed to me the way to do that was that I would work less and spend more time with [my child]."

The patient advocate quoted earlier talked about what he feels he has gained by taking care of his child:

When James was born, I was smitten, I was blown away by the strong feelings I had toward him. It was kind of like falling in love with a lover for me. I was really—I was shocked by that feeling, by how strong my feelings are and were. . . . But I also feel that I really—it's been a window for me, it's been watching him learn about the world and how much of an influence I have over that. I feel a tremendous amount of responsibility and I feel really eager to help him explore the world. I want him to do it on his own, but I know that I also have a lot of say in how things get set up, presentations that are made. But it's exciting to be part of that and I really love his discovery of things.

Even though the home health worker quoted above wishes he could return to full-time work to take some of the work pressure off his wife, he also was very eloquent about what it meant to be a father. The detailed response about infants he gives was once reserved for mothers only:

> Let's see. I don't think it's that different than being a mother. It's very stressful, very, at the same time it's very rewarding. And . . . but I think to have a lot of your father's influence is a good experience for a lot of children. Because I would take her places that my wife normally wouldn't take her. Like down to the auto parts store. . . . It got a lot harder when my second was born. It's twice as hard, ya. Especially right now, he is cutting teeth. He can't walk and he can't talk and so he can't TELL you anything. And he's at that time when he's trying to rearrange his clock to sleep at night so he's up, like last night he was up at midnight. So I brought him to bed with me. And I put him back to bed around 2 and he was up at 4, so like 3 or 4 times a night. And lack of sleep more than anything else gets you. Then the older one wakes up. Sometimes ARGGGGHHHH. I feel like a lioness with cubs crawling all around. . . . Fatherhood, it's a lot of hard work but it can also be a lot of fun too. . . . As they get older, you can play more and you can put them in a car and go for a ride and it's a lot easier once they're older.

The father, who presently works part-time as a postal worker, explains that what he feels is most important is making a difference in his child's life:

> Mr. Mom? Um . . . it's frus . . . it's rewarding, but it's also very frustrating. It's, it's ah . . . it seems like after a day of being with my son all day, it's fun and all that, but sometimes, some days it just wears thin, and I need some adult interaction if you know what I mean? . . . But I feel like I'm in the role of teacher and ah . . . which is I think the most fun part. And just watching him develop and learn new things . . . to see the difference that I can sort of shape and mold my son's life it gives me some personal satisfaction. Nobody told me that.

In sum, the members of this group are testing and contesting the limits of their work environments. Whereas there are certainly career costs and unwanted underemployment, these couples are altering the landscape of traditional ways that couples have attempted to integrate work and family and, in the process, altering the gender system that locates women according to a primary identity as mother and men as economic providers. Men's caring work undermines the belief that mothering comes naturally to women. Further, caring for children elevates the status of parenting as a source of primary identity for both mothers and fathers; it even takes priority over workplace goals and job advancement. In short, changing labor force patterns and creating flexible jobs forced new family practices and in the process altered beliefs about child care and nurturing.

THE MARKET APPROACH

The market approach to caring for children involves hiring other people to care for one's own children. Both wife and husband are career oriented and they emphasize professional caregivers who replace mothers. Unlike the two approaches discussed in preceding sections, wherein the use of non-kin child care is minimized, among these couples children spend their days with adult caregivers who are not family members.[9] Often, couples have a combination of care providers[10] and commonly they shift from one type of arrangement to another, ostensibly in response to the child's developmental needs. As I and my coauthor, Faith Ferguson, have argued (Hertz & Ferguson, 1996), regardless of whether children are placed in center-based care or in family day care or a woman is hired to provide individual care, in using day care the mother has hired someone to replace herself at least part of the time and her essential contribution to the family has become *deskilled* (Braverman, 1974). But the new middle-class model for women continues to emphasize the achievements of the individual (i.e., the mother); women achieve this by deskilling motherhood, breaking apart a once presumed holistic pattern of practices.[11] In this study, it is typical for couples in which both are professionals working full-time with more than one child to have multiple child care arrangements. Below is a striking example of deskilling the mother role into several components: the woman who is loving and good with infants and drives the children and the woman who provides developmental stimulation and reads to her children:

> But once the kids were 2 or something, when they like to be read to, that sort of thing, I have sent them to a play group, which is a family day care, really down the street from me. They've each gone there 2 days a week. . . . The reason for this is that my babysitter, as lovely and caring a person as she is, is functionally illiterate, which is the downside of what I have. . . . By the time I figured out that she could barely manage to write a phone message, it was clear that she was so good with my infant that it really didn't matter at that point.
>
> Now, she is driving my daughter to . . . Brownies, ballet, that sort of thing. . . . And we don't have family in the area, so she's sort of a surrogate mother to them in that sense. She has a large family of her own, and my kids know all of the members of her family. . . . I think I have been incredibly lucky. The kids love her and she loves them.

The woman above, pregnant with her third child at age 36 and a doctor with a doctor husband, is quite typical of this group whose caregiving role is tied to finding surrogates. Because the mother remains responsible for patching together child care arrangements, she uses different criteria to select different women to replace herself. The love of one's child becomes the major criteria for how couples select providers, particularly nannies, but also family-based day care settings. These kinds of providers are a substitute for mother love (Hertz, 1986; Hertz & Ferguson, 1996; Wrigley, 1995). Yet, often conflicts emerge around dissimilar values between the provider and the couple because couples tend to hire women of different social class and racial backgrounds to care for their children (Hertz, 1986; Wrigley, 1995). Center-based day care providers (or preschool or nursery school programs) are termed *teachers* and they are expected to expose the child to a first learning environment. This enrichment experience is supposed to supplement parental teaching, though often it is also a substitute for early education the mother once provided. Credentials and professionalism are ways couples assess whether a program shares their views on learning (Hertz & Ferguson, 1963).[12] After-school programs are now the new neighborhoods. These institutional settings provide adult supervision, replacing the mom with milk and cookies but also replacing no-longer-safe neighborhoods where children once freely rode bikes and played pick-up games.

Whereas initially women believe that continuity of care is the best replacement for not being at home themselves, they eventually abandon this idea. In this study and in my prior work (Hertz, 1986), not one family kept the same child care arrangements for the first years of a child's life. Dissatisfaction materializes on either side of the provider/couple relationship: Sometimes the child care provider quits, but other times the reason for a change is couched in a language of child development and the need for a new kind of arrangement, as predicted by the child care professional mother of the woman quoted below:

> At 2 years old, it was clear there was way too much TV. I didn't care about it as an infant, I didn't care about it at 1 year old because they watch some of it but they run around. They are too interested in their own motor stuff. And my mom had told me when she saw Janie [the provider]—a lot of my education about child care has come from my mom [a nursery school director]—I said, "Isn't it great because Janie promised me she'll take care of the kid until she is in kindergarten if I want." And there were kids there until 4 years old. So, I kept thinking that would be continuity I wasn't providing my child by working. And my mom said, "You're not going to want her at Janie's after 2 [years old]." And I didn't know at that time, but how right she was.

Couples speak a new language of quasi-psychology that emphasizes developmentally appropriate educational experiences for preschoolers who are introduced to the rudiments of a structured day, develop positive peer group experiences, and begin to develop a positive relationship to learning. Professionals are looked toward to provide these enrichment experiences. In sum, former child care providers are discarded and new child care workers rationalized on the changing developmental stages of the child.

Women do feel guilty for not being with their child and they worry about the cost to their children. The woman below, age 37, when she had her first child 9 years ago, describes the kind of work hours she was expected to keep.

> I had two people coming in, 6-hour shifts. And then when Kyle was 6 months old, I just sat down with my husband and I just felt like this was really hurting Kyle. So, I decided that my career was interfering with my family. And I actually quit my internship. I came home distraught and I just said, "That's it." At that point I was working 100 hours a week, I would leave at 6:00 one morning and come home at 10:00 the next night if I was on call. I was on call every third to fourth night. It was very hard with a newborn, although I had my husband who was here taking care of the baby at night and other family members. I said to myself, "What are you doing? Is it worth it?"

This woman was lucky because a sister volunteered to come and care for her infant son, which lessened her guilt about not caring for her own child. But when she became pregnant with a second child, the sister said two children was one too many to watch and this couple eventually found non-relative live-in help.

But guilt was not shared by husbands who had similar occupations or male colleagues, as a woman doctor, age 31, reported:

> But you know, I've been a mother for 9 years so I've worked on the guilt a lot. . . . And I used to ask all these men I worked with, I said, "You know, when you go out the door in the morning, do you feel guilty when you say goodbye to your children?" And they would look at me as if to say, "What a dumb question that is." But every time I would go out it would tear me apart. So I've tried to lessen the guilt as the years go by.

Men did not mention feeling guilty about working full-time, which underscores the cultural asymmetry in the emphasis placed on the unique role of the mother/child dyad. The husbands of these women did mention the guilt their wives felt by not being available to their children. A professor with more flexible work hours, married to the doctor quoted above, began his discussion on day care with the following:

> My wife was essentially gone [the first year of the child's life]. I used to take the baby into the hospital in the middle of the night to see her mother. It was a rough year. I had a very free year—on sabbatical—which helped enormously and we had my in-laws close by. But my wife still feels that was a desertion, that she essentially deserted her baby 2 weeks after it was born.

The mothers who exemplify this approach are not the only ones in this study who feel guilty. Women in all three approaches feel guilty when they are unable to match their conception of motherhood and family life: Some try to alter shift scheduling; others try cutting back hours or find another type of work. But the ideal work load is rarely attained. I note the guilt in this section because the most career-oriented women have the least options because their work environments remain entrenched in a male trajectory despite recent claims of organizations' becoming more so-called family friendly (Gilbert, 1985; Hertz, 1986; Hochschild, 1971; Slater & Glazer, 1987). These women report that short of quitting professions in which they have invested heavily through years of school and training, hiring surrogates to replace themselves or deskilling motherhood are the only rational solutions.[13] Most mentioned wishing they could become part-time employees at least for a few years (the added income from their full-time employment was not essential to these families) but few employers agreed to experiment with such work arrangements. Some feel trapped as successful professionals wishing for more leisure time for themselves and time with their children.

Couples who select a market approach to child care also have a division of labor between themselves in which the wife does the work of finding the care, making the arrangements, and thinking through the various possibilities (Hertz, 1986; Hochschild & Machung, 1989; Nock & Kington, 1988). Husbands become sounding boards and only marginal participants in arranging the schedules of children. In this regard, women replace themselves and, in the process, the deskilling of tasks leaves mothers with changed relationships to their children, popularly dubbed "quality time" motherhood. Men's lives remain unaltered in these cases. Of the three approaches to child care, the men in this group are the least involved in child care. Masculinity remains tied to economic achievements and career goals. The mother/child dyad is altered by the insertion of another woman or professional day care setting. However, unlike the mothering approach, women's identities remain split between family and career. Gender relations between spouses are altered only because women buy out family commitments, not because men assume more responsibility (Hertz, 1986). Further, both mothers and fathers become primarily economic providers within their children's lives. During the week, it is others who love, nurture, and care for the children, and on weekends they become a family in which the mother might resume the craft of mothering while the men continue to devote themselves to career advancement.

CONCLUSIONS

Mothering does not mean that wives stop working for pay completely (i.e., they do not necessarily devote 100% of their time to caring for their children). It does mean, however, that a wife's status as mother becomes the pivotal point around which all other statuses (e.g., employee) revolve. Indeed, for many couples the arrival of children creates a paradox: One paid worker leaves the labor force at a time when the family's expenses increase dramatically. To maintain a (pre-child) standard of living, adjustments have to be made: Either (a) the husband increases the number of hours he works (which reduces his ability to share parenting) or (b) the wife continues to work but adjusts her job or hours to accommodate the children. In both instances, the basic parameters of work and family go unchallenged: (a) couples adjust their activities to sustain a pre-child standard of living; (b) they make little claim against employers or ask them to adjust in response to family needs; (c) they invoke mothering as either cause or a correlate of their actions.

The detailed exploration of couples who embrace the mothering approach suggests that the organization of gender conflates motherhood and womanhood. Not only does motherhood supersede all other dimensions of identity, it also allows women to claim a special place in the gender system. Just as couples ignore the wife's permanent labor force employment, they minimize the husband's involvement as co-participant in caring for children. Whereas child care work may be conceptualized as the wife's turf, and therefore the language of mothering dominates these interviews, fathers are not absent from the home nor solely economic providers. The emphasis is on an ideological presentation of family life that masks the present practices and a new division of labor between spouses.

Couples who adopt the parenting approach come to reorganize their work in response to placing family first. They are challenging and restructuring the workplace even if it is only temporary: (a) These couples attempt to restructure work to accommodate their family needs by making demands on employers; (b) both women and men are restructuring their work to be active parents at the expense of job mobility, career success, and economic sacrifice; (c) in the process, they are altering the organization of gender in ways that challenge mothering as the exclusive territory of women. In short, they are crafting new ways of parental thinking about child rearing. These couples personify family values as they attempt to push workplaces to care about families as much as they care about organizational goals.

A smaller group of couples back into the parental approach—forced into this reorganization of family and two jobs due to economic constraints. Decreasing jobs will lead more men to rethink their contributions to family life and to adapt to a shrinking economy by staying home or sharing child care, or both. Although the circumstances of their fathering may not be based on their own choice, these men are potential models for a future in which job uncertainty is likely to increase. On one hand, structural workforce constraints for men may alter motherhood ideals, giving rise to equally compelling arguments for men's greater involvement in sharing the work of child care. On the other hand, these data suggest that gender ideology is a powerful countervailing force to a shrinking labor market. Husbands and wives are not willing to agree that parenting is a substitute for men's paychecks. These couples craft shared parenting models but hope that this is a temporary family/work arrangement.

The market approach in many ways resembles the mothering approach in that couples resolve work/family dilemmas by parceling out the job of mothering. They rationalize this (with ambivalence) by placing a premium on professional child care knowledge over old-fashioned folk wisdom; these couples do not make claims against employers who continue to adhere to a masculine prototype of career trajectories, creating, at best, "mommy tracks"—as the major response to family needs. In this respect, husbands and wives may have more equal marriages but do little to alter the organization of gender between men and women. In fact, they only further inequalities between women whom they hire and themselves (Hertz, 1986; Rollins, 1985).

In addition to giving substance to a typology of alternative approaches to child care, the interviews conducted in this study provide valuable insights into the process through which choices among those alternatives are made. That is, as has been noted repeatedly in recent research on changing gender ideologies and child care (e.g., Hochschild & Machung, 1989; Uttal, 1996), it is vital to better understand the meaning women give to child care practices and the division of labor between spouses. By focusing on meaning (both supportive and contradictory), we are in a better position to assess how durable an approach might be or, if it creates conflicts (e.g., between traditional and nontraditional family gender ideologies), who will have to bend to resolve the conflict. A focus on child care choices helps us see what conflicts arise, how they are given meaning, and how they are resolved.

However, recent research in this area (including Garey, 1995; McMahon, 1995; Uttal, 1996) has overlooked the fact that these choices are rarely made by women alone. Whereas this new research is conceptually interesting, by focusing on the changing meaning of motherhood without considering the possibility of similar changes for the partners of these women, we learn little about the position of the partner as a participant or facilitator for social change in the family or workplace. As I have shown in this article, husbands often play an important role in the decision process. Yet, because most prior studies have tended to neglect husbands (e.g., by not interviewing them), they cannot realistically tell us a great deal about men's involvement in child care choices at either the levels of ideology or practice or about how couples may jointly decide or be forced to alter ideology or practice.

Thus, when we look back at the three different approaches to child care described in this article, it is not surprising that in many respects the parenting approach appears the most novel. Unlike mothering and market approaches, husbands play a visible and different role in child care choice. Their involvement is visible and different because they consciously challenge a traditional familial division of labor and a traditional definition of job and career. Neither the mothering nor the market approaches challenge tradition: The former reinforces tradition and the latter merely integrates another service into the family menu of consumption.

NOTES

1. In 1993, fully 60% of all women with children under 6 were in the paid labor force. For those with children aged 6 to 17 years, 75% of all women were employed, representing a marked increase from 1966 when 44% of women with children this age were employed (Hayghe & Bianchi, 1994). For women between 15 and 44 who have had a child for the year 1994, 53% were in the labor force (Bachu, 1995).
2. Day care is regulated by individual states, which vary in licensing regulations and in enforcement (Benin & Chong, 1993). In Massachusetts, lists exist by town, giving the names of all licensed providers. We have no good information on how many family day care providers are illegal. But this assumes that a family would know enough to request a list from the town or know enough to realize that not all providers are licensed.

   The vast majority of U.S. workplaces do not have child care provisions. Those that do have huge wait lists and most employees must go elsewhere for day care. Families in eastern Massachusetts who use center-based care put their children into either for-profit commercial day care and nonprofit centers housed within religious sites or universities and private nonprofit centers. In this area, after kin, family day care is the most often used type of care (Marshall et al., 1988).
3. Day care is also the second largest cost all couples have in this study after mortgages or rents. In 1995, for a preschooler in full-day center-based care in the greater Boston area, couples could expect to pay $12,000 per year for one child. Infant and toddler center-based care is even more costly.
4. See Hertz (1995) for a lengthy discussion of making sense of separate interviews and the rationale for this method.
5. The majority of couples in this study have been married to their present spouses at least 10 years. For the vast majority of individuals, these are first marriages. I note that I did not select couples on length of present marriage. I did, however, deliberately seek couples who still had children at home,

when possible, so that child care and labor force decisions would not be distant memories.

6. With the exception of the upper middle-class professional women in this study, few women could afford to take a 12-week unpaid leave, which Massachusetts has had for quite some years. Most women did take a leave, but they were able to afford this by using their paid vacation time and sick days. In this study, few couples had enough money to cover the paychecks of a maternity leave. No man in this study took a formal paternity leave, though some men (the parental approach) did work out various arrangements with employers.

7. Because this is a study of dual-earner couples, there are no full time stay-at-home moms at the time of the interview who clearly favor this approach to early childhood care. There are a few women in the middle class who were home for a number of years until their youngest child entered elementary school. It is also possible for professional women to decide to leave the labor force permanently and stay home. I feature, in this section, women in working-class or lower middle-class jobs because they are more likely in this study to advance that approach.

8. White working-class mothers of both husbands and wives were typically in and out of the labor force. Mothers of minority spouses were overwhelmingly always in the labor force. Historically, women of color are more likely to work outside the home (Goldin, 1990, p. 18). In this study, working-class mothers of respondents are essential to the household. In addition to the importance of income contribution to the household for middle-class mothers of respondents, using talents and degrees to advance their race was also essential (Perkins, in press).

9. Children are collectively raised by professionally trained women in kibbutzim, which today resemble full-time center-based U.S. child care. Whereas economic necessity was the catalyst for the creation of the children's collective raising, the historical belief in professional knowledge as the best route to child rearing persists. My point here is two-fold: (a) The professional approach is not always tied to two-earner families, even though in the United States case, the emergence of (and rapidly growing) family and center-based day care is tied to the inability of most families to live on one wage as the family wage eroded; and (b) mothers are not essentialized in the kibbutz as the best caregivers of their own children. Professionally trained women are seen as more knowledgeable and suitable and, until recently, expertise superseded parents' wishes. Categorically, however, women rather than men do this work, gendering the job within the kibbutz and within the U.S. context.

10. Two national surveys indicate that approximately two fifths of preschool children with mothers in the paid labor force had multiple child care arrangements (Folk & Belier, 1993; Hofferth. Brayfield, Diech, & Holcomb, 1991).

11. Hertz and Ferguson (1996) argue that for Black couples in this study, deskilling of motherhood does not promote the same kind of crisis that it

does for their White professional counterparts because historically Black women have always been employed outside the home and have had to work out arrangements for the care of children that did not permit nonexclusive mothering practices (Collins, 1990). However, even in this study Black women felt at times like they were the titular wives and mothers (Hertz & Ferguson, 1996). The woman who solved her child care problems and returned to her internship when her sister volunteered to help was a Black woman whose mother had worked her entire life. The solutions to child care for the first child often included kin for women of color, which was less likely to occur among White women whose mothers (or other immediate relatives) were not willing to leave their own lives if they did not live locally. Even among White women whose mothers lived locally, it was less often in this study that they became the primary child care providers.

12. Regardless of race, the majority of families had multiple arrangements; however, there are differences between White women and women of color in how they found child care providers and how race factors into the selection of a particular arrangement (see Hertz & Ferguson, 1996, for a full discussion).

13. See especially Uttal (1996), who is interested in the meaning mothers assign to caregivers. The women who restructure the dominant cultural ideology of the mother as primary provider conceptualize the child care provider as either a surrogate or they define the child care provider as co-mothering in a coordinated effort that the mother orchestrates between herself and the provider.

REFERENCES

Bachu, A. (1995). *Fertility of American women: June 1994* (P20-482, p. XVII). Washington, DC: U.S. Bureau of the Census.

Benin, M., & Chong, Y. (1993). Childcare concerns of employed mothers. In J. Frankel (Ed.), *The employed mother and the family context* (pp. 229–244). New York: Springer.

Bernard, J. (1981). The good-provider role: Its rise and fall. *The American Psychologist. 36*, 1–12.

Bianchi, S. M., & Spain, D. (1986). *American women in transition*. New York: Russell Sage Foundation.

Bird, C. E. (1995, March). *Gender parenthood and distress: Social and economic burdens of parenting*. Paper presented at the Eastern Sociological Society annual meetings, Philadelphia.

Braverman, H. (1974). *Labor and monopoly capital: The degradation of work in the twentieth century*. New York: Monthly Review Press.

Collins, P. H. (1990). *Black feminist thought: Knowledge, consciousness and the politics of empowerment*. New York: Routledge.

Coltrane, S. (1989). Household labor and the routine production of gender. *Social Problems, 36*, 473–490.

Daniels, A. K. (1988). *Invisible careers: Women civic leaders from the volunteer world.* Chicago: University of Chicago Press.

DeVault, M. L. (1991). *Feeding the family: The social organization of caring as gendered work.* Chicago: University of Chicago Press.

Ferber, M., & O'Farrell, B. (1991). Family-oriented programs in other countries. In M. Ferber, B. O'Farrell, & L. R. Allen, (Eds.), *Work and family: Policies for a changing work force* (pp. 155–178). Washington, DC: National Academy Press.

Fitz Gibbon, H. (1993. August). Bridging spheres: The work of home daycare providers. Paper presented at the American Sociological Association Meetings, Miami.

Folk, K. F., & Beller, A. H. (1993). Part-time work and childcare choices for mothers of preschool children. *Journal of Marriage and the Family, 55,* 146–157.

Garey, A. I. (1995). Constructing motherhood on the night shift: "Working mothers" as "stay at home mom." *Qualitative Sociology, 18,* 415–437.

Gerson, K. (1993). *No man's land: Men's changing commitments to family and work.* New York: Basic Books.

Gilbert, L. (1985). *Men in dual career families.* Hillsdale, NJ: Lawrence Erlbaum.

Goldin, C. (1990). *Understanding the gender gap: An economic history of American women.* New York: Oxford University Press.

Goode, W. J. (1982). Why men resist. In B. Thorne & M. Yalom (Eds.), *Rethinking the family: Some feminist questions* (pp. 131–150). New York: Longman.

Hartmann, H.. & Spalter-Roth. R. (1994, March). A feminist approach to policy making for women and families. Paper prepared for the Seminar on Future Directions for American Politics and Public Policy.

Hayghe, H. V., & Bianchi, S. M. (1994). Married mothers' work patterns: The job-family compromise. *U.S. Department of Labor Bureau of Labor Statistics, Monthly Labor Review. 117,* 24–30.

Hertz, R. (1986). *More equal than others: Women and men in dual-career marriages.* Berkeley: University of California Press.

Hertz, R. (1995). Separate but simultaneous interviewing of husbands and wives: Making sense of their stories. *Qualitative Inquiry, 1,* 429–451.

Hertz, R., & Charlton, J. (1989). Making family under a shiftwork schedule: Air Force security guards and their wives. *Social Problems, 36,* 491–507.

Hertz, R., & Ferguson, F.I.T. (1996). Childcare choices and constraints in the United States: Social class, race, and the influence of family views. *Journal of Comparative Family Studies, 27,* 249–280.

Hochschild, A. (1971). Inside the clockwork of male careers. In F. Howe (Ed.), *Women and the power to change* (pp. 47–80). New York: McGraw-Hill.

Hochschild, A.. & Machung, A. (1989). *The second shift.* New York: Viking.

Hodson, R., & Sullivan, T. (1990). *The social organization of work.* Belmont, CA: Wadsworth.

Hofferth, S. L., Brayfield, A., Diech, S., & Holcomb, P. (1991). *National Childcare Survey 1990* (Urban Institute Report 91–5). Washington, DC: Urban Institute Press.

Huber, J., & Spitzer. G. (1983). *Sex stratification: Children, housework; and jobs.* New York: Academic Press.

Kamerman, S. B.. & Kahn, A. 1. (1991). Trends, issues and possible lessons. In S. B. Kamerman & A. J. Kahn (Eds.). *Childcare, parental leave, and the under three's: Policy innovation in Europe* (pp. 201–224). Westport. CT: Auburn House.

Marshall, N., Witte, A., Nichols, L., Marx, F., Mauser, E., Laws, B., & Silverstein, B. (1988). *Caring for our commonwealth: The economics of childcare in Massachusetts.* Boston: Office for Children.

McMahon, M. (1995). *Engendering motherhood: Identity and self-transformation in women's lives.* New York: Guilford.

Moen, P. (1989). *Working parents: Transformations in gender roles and public policies in Sweden.* Madison: University of Wisconsin Press.

Nelson, M. K. (1994). Family day care providers: Dilemmas of daily practice. In N. Glenn, G. Chang, & L. R. Forcey (Eds.), *Mothering ideology, experience and agency* (pp. 181–209). New York: Routledge.

Nock, S. L., & Kington, P. W. (1988). Time with children: The impact of couples' work-time commitments. *Social Forces, 67,* 59–85.

Perkins, L. M. (in press). For the good of the race: Married African American academics, a Historical perspective. In M. A. Ferber & J. W. Loeb (Eds.), *Academic couples: Problems and promises.* Urbana—Champaign and Chicago: University of Illinois Press.

Presser, H. B. (1988). Shiftwork and childcare among young dual-earner American parents. *Journal of Marriage and the Family, 50,* 133–148.

Presser, H. B., & Cain, V. 5. (1983). Shiftwork among dual-earner couples with children. *Science, 219,* 876–879.

Rollins, J. (1985). *Between women: Domestics and their employers.* Philadelphia: Temple University Press.

Ruddick, S. (1980). Maternal thinking. *Feminist Studies, 6,* 343–367.

Slater, M., & Galzer, P. M. (1987). Prescriptions for professional survival. *Daedalus, 116,* 119–135.

Uttal, L. (1996). Custodial care, surrogate care, and coordinated care: Employed mothers and the meaning of child care. *Gender & Society, 10,* 291–311.

Wrigley, J. (1995). *Other people's children.* New York: Basic Books.

Zigler, E. (1990). Shaping child care policies and programs in America. *American Journal of Community Psychology, 18,* 183–215.

CHAPTER 7

◆

CHILDHOOD

Revolutions in Children's Lives

DONALD HERNANDEZ, WITH DAVID E. MYERS

INTRODUCTION

Revolutionary changes in the life course, the economy, and society have transformed childhood, and the resources available to children, during the past 150
years. A revolutionary decline in the number of siblings in the families of children occurred during the past 100 years. Historically, a substantial minority of
children did not spend their entire childhood in a two-parent family, but this
will expand to a majority for children born during the past decade. The role of
grandparents in the home, as surrogate parents filling the gap left by absent
parents, has been important but limited during at least the past half century.

The family economy was revolutionized twice during the past 150 years,
first as fathers and then mothers left the home to spend much of the day away at
jobs as family breadwinners. With these changes, with instability in fathers'
work, and with increasing divorce and out-of-wedlock childbearing, never
during the past half century were a majority of children born into "Ozzie and
Harriet" families in which the father worked full-time year-round, the mother
was a full-time homemaker, and all of the children were born after the parents'
only marriage.

Corresponding revolutions in child care occurred first as children over age
5 and then as younger children began to spend increasing amounts of time in
formal educational or other settings in the care of someone other than their
parents. Since today's children are tomorrow's parents, the spread of universal
compulsory education led to revolutionary increases in the educational attain-

---

ments of parents during the past half century, to the benefit of successive cohorts of children. But as opportunities to complete at least a high school education became substantially more equal for children during the past century, opportunities to go beyond high school and complete at least one year of college became less equal.

The absolute income levels of families increased greatly after the Great Depression and World War II through the 1960s but have changed comparatively little since then. Meanwhile, childhood poverty and economic inequality declined after World War II through the 1960s, then increased mainly during the 1980s. Most poor children throughout the era lived in working-poor families, and only a minority of poor children were fully welfare-dependent.

FAMILY COMPOSITION

Because siblings are the family members who are usually closest in age, needs, and activities, they may be among a child's most important companions and most important competitors for family resources. The typical child born in 1890 lived, as an adolescent, in a family in which there were about 6.6 siblings, but the typical child born in 1994 is expected to live in a family that is only one-third as large—with 1.9 children.

About one-half of this decline in family size had occurred by 1945, and the typical child born during that year lived in a family that had 2.9 siblings. Subsequently, during the postwar baby boom that occurred between 1945 and 1957, the annual number of births jumped by 55 percent (from 2.7 to 4.3 million births per year) and the Total Fertility Rate jumped by 52 percent (from 2.4 to 3.7 births per woman), but the family size of the typical adolescent increased by only 17 percent (from 2.9 to 3.4 siblings).

Changes in the distribution of adolescents by family size tell a similar story. The proportion living in families in which there are 5 or more siblings is expected to decline from 77 percent for children born in 1890 to only 6 percent for children born in 1994. Again, about one-half of the decline had occurred for children born in 1945, 32 percent of whom as adolescents lived in families in which there were 5 or more children, and again the increase during the baby boom was comparatively small at about 6 percentage points. At the opposite extreme, the proportion of adolescents living in families in which there are only 1–2 children is expected to increase from only 7 percent for children born in 1890 to 57 percent for children born in 1994. Among children born in 1945, about 30 percent lived in such small families, and this fell by 10 percentage points to 20 percent during the baby boom.

Historically, black children have tended to live in families in which there were substantially larger numbers of siblings than did white children, but trends in the family sizes of both black and white children were generally similar between the Civil War and 1925. Then for about 20 years, however, the racial gap expanded, apparently because the comparatively large decline in tuberculosis and venereal disease led to increased family sizes among blacks. Since about

1945, the number of siblings in the families of both black and white children have been converging.

Among children born in 1994, family-size differences between blacks and whites, as well as between Hispanic children (of any race) and non-Hispanic children, are expected to essentially vanish. Of the racial convergence in family size that is expected to occur for children born between 1945 and 1994, more than two-thirds had occurred among children born in 1973 who are now about 18 years old and approaching college age.

What are the consequences of this decline for children? First, children with larger numbers of siblings have greater opportunities to experience caring, loving sibling companionship. Hence, the family-size revolution drastically reduced the number of siblings who were available as potential companions during childhood and through adulthood. On the other hand, childhood family size appears to have little effect on psychological well-being later during adulthood. But because children growing up in large families—especially families with 5 or more siblings—tend to complete fewer years of schooling than do children from smaller families, they are less likely to enter high-status occupations with high incomes when they reach adulthood. Hence, the family-size revolution led to greatly improved opportunities for educational, occupational, and economic advancement among successive cohorts of children. . . .

Most children depend mainly on the parents in their homes for financial support and day-to-day care. Hence, it would be surprising if important differences in current welfare and future life chances were not found when children who do spend their entire childhood in a two-parent family are compared with those who do not.

In the short run, for many children the separation or divorce of their parents brings a sharp drop in family income and substantial psychological trauma. When the lone parent in a one-parent family marries to form a stepfamily, however, the children often experience a sharp jump in family income. Still, children in step-families are more likely to have a low family income than are children in intact two-parent families. In addition, since one parent is absent from the home in one-parent families, children in these families may receive substantially less day-to-day care and attention from parents than do children in two-parent families.

Children in one-parent families are more likely, on average, to be exposed to parental stress than are children in two-parent families, more likely to exhibit behavioral problems, more likely to receive or need professional psychological help, more likely to perform poorly in school, and more likely to have health problems. In addition, on average, stepchildren are virtually indistinguishable from children in one-parent families in their chances of having behavioral, psychological, academic, and health problems.

Over the long run, children who do not spend most of their childhood in an intact two-parent family tend, as they reach adulthood, to complete fewer years of schooling, enter lower-status occupations, and earn lower incomes than do adults who did spend most of their childhood in an intact two-parent family. Some children from one-parent families may finish fewer years of school because fathers who can afford to provide financial support in college do not in fact do so when the child reaches college age. Many of the disadvantages associated with living in a one-parent family may result from the low family incomes of many children who live in such families.

In view of the potential disadvantages of not living with two parents, how typical has it become for children not to spend their entire childhood in a two-parent family? Historically, about 90 percent of newborn children under age 1 have lived with both biological parents. Still, between the late 1800s and 1950, a large and nearly stable minority of about 33 percent spent part of their childhood before age 18 with fewer than two parents in the home. Little change occurred during the first half of the twentieth century, despite the rise in parental separation and divorce, because this rise was counterbalanced by declining parental mortality.

Since about 1950 the link between marriage and the bearing and rearing of children has loosened. Because of the rise in out-of-wedlock childbearing that occurred between 1950 and 1980, the proportion of newborn children under age 1 who did not live with two parents doubled, climbing from 9 to 19 percent. Combined with the rise in separation and divorce, the proportion of children who will ever live with fewer than two parents is expected to increase from about 33 percent for the era between the late 1800s and 1950 to about 55–60 percent of children born in 1980.

Since at least the Civil War, white and black children have been quite different in their chances of spending part of their childhood living with fewer than two parents. For example, in 1940 the proportion of newborn children under age 1 who did not live with two parents was about 25 percent for blacks, compared with 7 percent for whites. Historically, it appears that for children born between the late 1800s and 1940, a majority of blacks (55–60 percent) spent part of their childhood in families in which there were fewer than two parents. For whites born between the late 1800s and 1940, a minority (but a large minority of approximately 29–33 percent) spent part of their childhood in families in which there were fewer than two parents. . . .

FAMILY WORK AND EDUCATION

As children were experiencing a revolutionary decline in family size and a large increase in one-parent family living, they also were experiencing two distinct transformations in parents' work and living arrangements. On the family farm, economic production, parenting, and child care were combined, as parents and children worked together to support themselves. This changed with the Industrial Revolution, however. Fathers became breadwinners who took jobs located away from home in order to support the family, and mothers became homemakers who remained at home to personally care for the children as well as to clean, cook, and perform other domestic functions for the family. Following the Great Depression, parents' work and the family economy were again transformed. Today most children live either in dual-earner families in which both parents work at jobs away from home or in one-parent families.

More specifically, between about 1840 and 1920 the proportion of children who lived in two-parent farm families fell from at least two-thirds to about one-third, while the proportion who lived in breadwinner-homemaker families climbed from 15–20 percent to 50 percent. Although a majority of children lived in breadwinner-homemaker families between about 1920 and 1970, this figure never reached 60 percent.

In fact, even during the heyday of the breadwinner-homemaker family, a second transformation in parents' work was under way. Between 1920 and 1970, as the proportion of children living in two-parent farm families continued to fall, the proportion who had breadwinner mothers working at jobs that were located away from home increased, and after 1960 the proportion living in one-parent families with their mothers also increased. The rise in the proportion of children living in dual-earner or one-parent families was extremely rapid, since the increase from 15–20 percent to 50 percent required only 30 years—about one-third as long as the time required for the same rise in the breadwinner-home-maker family to take place.

By 1980, nearly 60 percent of children lived in dual-earner or one-parent families, by 1989 about 70 percent lived in such families, and by the year 2000, only 7 years from now, the proportion of children living in such families may exceed 80 percent. Equally striking is the fact that even between 1920 and 1970, only a minority of children aged 0–17 lived in families that conformed to the mid-twentieth century ideal portrayed, for example, on the "Ozzie and Harriet" television program (that is, a nonfarm breadwinner-homemaker family in which the father works full-time year-round, the mother is a full-time homemaker, and all of the children were born after the parents' only marriage).

In fact, only a minority of newborn children under age 1 lived in such families in any year between 1940 and 1980. During these years a large majority of newborns (75–86 percent) did live with employed fathers, but only 42–49 percent lived with two parents in families in which the father worked full-time year-round and all of the children were born after the parents' only marriage. Still smaller proportions of newborns lived with two parents in families in which the father worked full-time year-round, all of the children were born after the parents' only marriage, and the mother was a full-time homemaker. Between 1940 and 1960, 41–43 percent of newborns lived in such families, and with rising mothers' labor-force participation this fell to only 27 percent in 1980. By age 17, children were even less likely, historically, to live in such families, as the proportion declined from 31 to 15 percent between 1940 and 1980.

These estimates imply that for children born between 1940 and 1960, an average of 65–70 percent of their childhood years were spent in a family situation that did not conform to the mid-twentieth century ideal. Looking ahead, it appears that children born in 1980 may spend an average of 80 percent of their childhood in families that do not conform to this ideal. In addition, children who lived on farms were likely, historically, to experience a parental death or other parental loss, or the economic insecurity associated with drought, crop disease, collapse of commodity prices, and similar catastrophes. Consequently, it is clear that neither historically nor during the industrial era have a majority of children experienced the family stability, the economic stability, and the home-making mother that was idealized in mid-twentieth century America.

For white children, the chances of living in an idealized "Ozzie and Harriet," breadwinner-homemaker family were only slightly larger than for children as a whole. Among newborn black children at least since 1940, however, no more than 25 percent lived in such idealized families, and this figure fell to only 8 percent for black newborns in 1980. By the end of child-hood, among blacks born in 1922, only 15 percent still lived in such families by age 17, and among blacks born in 1962, only 3 percent still lived in such families by age 17. Looking across the entire childhood experience of black children, the average proportion of childhood years not spent in idealized "Ozzie and Harriet" families increased from about 70–80 percent for the 1920s cohort to at least 95 percent for the 1980s cohort.

In 1980 Hispanic children (of any race) were roughly midway between black and white children in their chances of living in an idealized "Ozzie and Harriet" family. Only 10 percent of Hispanic 17-year-olds (of any race) lived in such families in 1980, only 21 percent of Hispanic newborns (of any race) lived in such families in 1980, and among these newborns more than 85 percent of the childhood years will be spent in families that do not conform to the mid-twentieth century ideal.

With these two historic transformations in parents' work and living arrangements, children simultaneously experienced two revolutionary increases in nonparental care, first among those over age 5 and then among younger children.

As farming became overshadowed by an industrial economy in which fathers worked for pay at jobs located away from home, compulsory school attendance and child labor laws were enacted to ensure that children were protected from unsafe and unfair working conditions, that they were excluded from jobs that were needed for adults, and that they received at least a minimal level of education. Also, as time passed increasing affluence allowed families to support themselves without child labor, and higher educational attainments became increasingly necessary in order to obtain jobs that offered higher pay and higher social prestige.

Hence, in 1870 only 50 percent of children aged 5–19 were enrolled in school, and their attendance averaged only 21 percent of the total days in the year. But 70 years later, in 1940, 95 percent of children aged 7–13 were enrolled in school, 79 percent of children aged 14–17 were enrolled in school, and the average attendance amounted to 42 percent of the days in the year. Even as mothers were increasingly viewed as full-time child care providers and home-makers, the need for them to act as full-time child care providers was diminishing, both because of the revolutionary decline in family size and because of the quadrupling in the amount of nonparental child care provided by teachers in school.

Since a full adult workday amounted to about 8 hours per day, 5 days per week (plus commuting time) after 1940, a full adult work year amounted to about 65 percent of the days in a year. But by 1940, school days of 5–6 hours (plus commuting time) amounted to about two-thirds of a full workday for about two-thirds of a full work year. As of 1940, then, childhood school attendance had effectively released mothers from personal child care responsibilities for a time period equivalent to about two-thirds of a full-time adult work year, except for the few years before children entered elementary school.

By reducing the time required for a mother's most important homemaker responsibility—the personal care of her children—this first child care revolution contributed to the large increase in mothers' labor-force participation after 1940, not only for school-age children but for preschoolers as well. Increasing mothers' labor-force participation and the rise in one-parent families then ushered in the second child-care revolution for preschool children aged 0–5. Between 1940 and 1989, the proportion of children who had no specific parent at home full-time tripled for school-age children (from roughly 22 to 66 percent) and quadrupled for preschoolers (from about 13 percent to about 52 percent).

Today these proportions are probably fairly typical for children in industrial countries, since by 1980 labor-force participation rates for women who were in main parenting ages in the United States were average when compared with other industrial countries. For example, the labor-force participation rates for women aged 30–39 were 70–90 percent in Sweden, Denmark, and Norway, 60–70 percent in the United States, France, and Canada, and 45–60 percent in the United Kingdom, West Germany, Italy, Belgium, Switzerland, Australia, and Japan.[1]

The increase in the proportion of preschoolers who had no specific parent at home full-time effectively reduced the amount of parental time that was potentially available to care for preschoolers and effectively increased the need for nonparental care. Yet the proportion of preschoolers who had a relative other than a parent in the home who might act as a surrogate parent also declined. For preschoolers living in dual-earner families, the proportion with a potential surrogate parent in the home declined from 19–20 percent in 1940 to only 4–5 percent in 1980. Meanwhile, the proportion of preschoolers living in one-parent families in which there was a potential surrogate parent in the home declined from 51–57 to 20–25 percent.

Time-use studies of nonemployed mothers indicate that the actual time devoted to child care as a primary activity probably increased by about 50–100 percent between 1926–1935 and 1943 and may have increased a bit more during the 20 years that followed. But between the 1960s and the early 1980s, the average amount of time that all mothers of preschoolers devoted to child care as a primary activity declined because an increasing number of mothers were employed outside the home and because employed mothers of preschoolers devote about one-half as much time to child care as a primary activity as do nonemployed mothers (1.2 vs. 2.2 hours per day during the mid-1970s).

---

[1]Data from the U.S. Bureau of the Census for the following years: 1985 (Norway), 1984 (France), 1983 (Sweden), 1982 (U.S.), 1981 (Canada, Denmark, United Kingdom, Italy, Australia), 1980 (Japan, West Germany, Switzerland), 1977 (Belgium).

By 1989, then, about 48 percent of preschoolers had a specific nonemployed parent at home on a full-time basis (usually the mother), another 12 percent had dual-earner parents who personally provided for their preschoolers' care (often by working different hours or days), and the remaining 40 percent were cared for by someone other than their parents for a large portion of time. Since the proportion of preschoolers who have a specific parent at home full-time declined from about 80 to about 48 percent during the 29 years between 1960 and 1989, we appear to be halfway through the preschool child-care revolution, and we are probably within 30–40 years of its culmination and will then see a very large proportion of preschool children spending increasingly more time in the care of someone other than their parents.

Overall, black children in 1940 were 24 percentage points less likely to have a specific parent at home full-time than were white children, but this racial gap had narrowed to 12 percentage points by 1980. Essentially all of this convergence occurred among older children, since the racial gap among adolescents declined from 27 to 6 percentage points, while the racial gap among preschoolers remained nearly constant at 18–23 percentage points. In 1980, about one-half of the racial gap among preschoolers was accounted for by differences in parental employment, and about one-half was accounted for by differences in the proportion of preschoolers who have no parent in the home.

Also in 1980, Hispanic children (of any race) were generally quite similar to non-Hispanic white children in their parental working and living arrangements, except that Hispanics (of any race) were somewhat more likely to live in one-parent families in which the parent was not employed and somewhat less likely to live in dual-earner families in which at least one parent worked part-time.

The importance of mothers' employment in contributing to family income is discussed below, but what other consequences do mothers' employment and nonparental care have for preschoolers? Past research suggests, broadly, that mothers' employment and nonparental care are neither necessarily nor pervasively harmful to preschoolers. This research also suggests that nonparental care is not a form of maternal deprivation, since children can and do form attachments to multiple caregivers if the number of caregivers is limited, the child-caregiver relationships are long-lasting, and the caregivers are responsive to the individual child.

Available evidence also suggests that the quality of care that children receive is important, and that some children, especially those from low-income families, are in double jeopardy from psychological and economic stress at home as well as exposure to low-quality nonparental child care. Additional potentially beneficial and detrimental effects of mothers' employment and nonparental care for preschoolers have been identified, but most of the results must be viewed as preliminary and tentative. Overall, research on the consequences of nonparental care for preschoolers is itself in its infancy, and much remains to be done.

The first revolution in child care—that is, the advent of nearly universal elementary and high school enrollment between ages 6 and 17—as well as large increases in high school and college graduation, led in due course to a revolutionary increase in parents' education. For example, among children born during the 1920s, the proportions whose fathers completed only 0–8 years of schooling or 4 or more years of high school were 73 and 15 percent, respectively, but these proportions were nearly reversed (at 5 and 85 percent, respectively) among children born only 60 years later during the 1980s. For the same children, those with fathers who had completed 4 or more or 1 or more years of college climbed from 4 and 7 percent, respectively, to 28 and 47 percent. Increases were generally similar for mothers' education, except for a somewhat smaller rise in the proportion with mothers who were college-educated.

Black children, as well as white children, experienced revolutionary increases in parents' education, but blacks continued to lag behind whites, as the black disadvantage effectively shifted higher on the educational ladder but constricted substantially in size. For example, among the 1920s cohort, the maximum racial disadvantages of 38–43 percentage points were in the proportions whose fathers or mothers had completed at least 7–8 years of schooling. But among the 1980s cohort, the maximum racial gaps were only two-fifths as large at 15–16 percentage points, and were in the proportions whose fathers or mothers had completed 13–15 years of schooling.

Measured in terms of the number of decades by which blacks lagged behind whites, the 2–3 decades by which black children born during the 1940s and the 1950s lagged behind whites in having parents who received at least 8 years of education had essentially vanished for the 1970s cohort. But despite a temporary racial convergence among children born during the 1960s and the 1970s, black children born during the 1980s, like black children born during the 1940s and the 1950s, lagged about 2–3 decades behind whites in the proportion whose fathers and mothers had completed at least 4 years of college.

Old-family Hispanic children (of any race) born during the 1960s and the 1970s were fairly similar to non-Hispanic black children in their parents' educational attainments. But first-generation Hispanic children (of any race) were much less likely (by 32–42 percentage points) to have parents who had completed at least 8 years of schooling, presumably because many of their parents had immigrated from countries in which the general educational levels were much lower than those in the United States.

This revolution in parents' education, and continuing differentials by race and Hispanic origin, are important for children both in the short run and throughout their adult years. In the short run, parents with higher educational attainments are more likely to have higher incomes than those with lower educational attainments. In the long run, children whose parents have comparatively high educational attainments also tend, when they reach adulthood, to complete more years of education and thus obtain jobs that offer higher social prestige and income.

Consequently, successive cohorts of children benefited from increasing parents' education both because it contributed to the large increases in family income for children that occurred between World War II and approximately 1970, as described below, and because it contributed to increasing educational levels among children and therefore to higher prestige and income for successive cohorts of children when they reached adulthood. At the same time, the continuing disadvantage of black and Hispanic children (of any race) in their parents' educational attainments tends to limit their current family incomes and their future chances of achieving occupational and economic success during adulthood. . . .

FAMILY INCOME, POVERTY, AND WELFARE DEPENDENCE

Family income, another major feature of family origins, also has important consequences for children's current well-being and future life chances. On a day-to-day basis, whether children live in material deprivation, comfort, or luxury depends mainly on their family's income level. Of particular interest are children in low-income families because they may experience marked deprivation in such areas as nutrition, clothing, housing, or healthcare.

During the 1940s, 1950s, and 1960s, the absolute income levels of American families increased greatly, as real median family income jumped by 35–45 percent per decade, bringing corresponding decreases in absolute want. Associated with this rapid expansion in the ability to purchase consumer products was an unprecedented proliferation in the number and kinds of products that became available, as well as remarkable increases in the quality of these products. By the 1970s the typical American lived in a world of abundance that Americans 30 years earlier could hardly have imagined. Since the beginning of the 1970s, however, real family income has increased comparatively little, despite the ongoing revolution in labor force participation by wives and mothers, and during the 1970s and the 1980s median family income increased by only 5 and 1 percent, respectively.

Despite large improvements in absolute income levels between 1939 and 1969, however, these statistics tell us little about the extent to which children lived in relative deprivation or luxury compared with the standards of the time in which they grew up, because at a specific point in history, the measure of whether a family is judged to be living in deprivation or luxury is that family's income and whether it is especially low or especially high compared with typical families in the same historical period.

Measuring economic deprivation in comparison with median family income in various years, the "relative poverty rate" for children dropped sharply during the 1940s (from 38 to 27 percent) but then much more slowly (to 23 percent in 1969). Subsequently, the relative poverty rate for children increased—mostly during the 1980s—to 27 percent in 1988, reaching the same level experienced almost 40 years earlier in 1949. . . .

CONCLUSION

America's children experienced several interrelated revolutions in their life course, as the family, economy, and society were transformed during the past 150 years. Family size plummeted. One-parent family living jumped. Family farms nearly became extinct, as first fathers and then mothers left the home for much of the day in order to serve as family breadwinners. Formal schooling, nonparental care for children, and parents' educational attainments have increased greatly, although educational opportunities to go beyond high school have become less equal since the turn of the century.

Absolute family incomes multiplied, but the past two decades brought little change in average income and increasing economic inequality among children, despite increasing mothers' labor-force participation. Relative and official poverty rates for children climbed during the past decade. Welfare dependence increased during recent decades, but most poor children historically and today live in working-poor families.

Currently, it appears that many of these revolutionary changes will be most extreme among children born within a decade of this writing. By historical standards, family size can decline comparatively little below the level expected for children born in the mid-1990s. Divorce, the major contributor to one-parent family living, has changed little since the late 1970s. By the year 2000, a large majority of children will live in dual-earner or one-parent families, a majority of preschoolers will receive substantial nonparental care while parents work, and only a small minority, even among newborns, will live in idealized "Ozzie and Harriet" families. Future changes in parents' education, in real income, poverty, and income inequality, and in welfare recipiency appear less certain, partly because they may be more responsive to specific public policies than are family size, divorce, and whether fathers and mothers work outside the home.

Regardless of future public policies, however, it seems likely that the fundamental transformations that have occurred during the past 150 years in the family, the economy, and the society will not be undone. Today, as throughout America's history, most children live with their parents and rely on them to provide for their economic support and day-to-day care. Yet a majority of children—both historically and today—have experienced either the loss of a parent from the home or economic insecurity, or both. Nevertheless, as a result of 150 years of revolutionary change in parents' work, in the family economy, and in the broader economy and society, America's children have entered a new age.

R E A D I N G

18

Children's Adjustment to Divorce

FRANK F. FURSTENBERG AND ANDREW J. CHERLIN

As Helen watched, Sally, then three, walked over to where her six-year-old brother was playing and picked up one of his toy robots. Mickey grabbed the robot out of her hand, shouted "No!" and pushed her away. The little girl fell

Reprinted by permission of the publishers from *Divided Families: What Happens to Children When Parents Part* by Frank F. Furstenberg and Andrew J. Cherlin, Cambridge, Mass.: Harvard University Press, Copyright © 1991 by the President and Fellows of Harvard College.

backward and began to cry. Helen had just finished another frustrating phone call with Herb, who had told her that he could no longer afford to pay as much child support as they had agreed. She was grateful to her parents for allowing her and the kids to live with them temporarily, but the crowded household was beginning to strain everyone's patience. She rushed over to her daughter, picked her up, and shouted at her son, "Don't you hit her like that!" "But it was mine," he said, whereupon he took another robot and threw it on the floor near his mother's feet. She grabbed his arm and dragged him to his room, screaming at him all the way.

Then she sat down in the living room, with Sally in her lap, and reflected on how often scenes such as this were occurring. Ever since the separation eight months earlier, she had had a hard time controlling Mickey. He disobeyed her, was mean to his sister, and fought with friends in school. And when he talked back to her, she lost her temper. But that just made him behave worse, which in turn made her angrier, until he was sent to his room and she sat down, distraught.

Helen's problems with her son fit a pattern familiar to psychologists who study the effects of divorce on children, an escalating cycle of misbehavior and harsh response between mothers and sons. But not all parents and children become caught up in these so-called coercive cycles after the breakup of a marriage. Studies show a wide range of responses to divorce. Some children do very well; others fare poorly. In this chapter we will examine these differences and inquire into why they occur.

We tend to think of divorce as an event that starts when a husband or wife moves out of their home. But it is often more useful to think of divorce as a process that unfolds slowly over time, beginning well before the separation actually occurs. In many cases it is preceded by a lengthy period of conflict between the spouses. It is reasonable to expect that this predisruption conflict, and the corresponding emotional upset on the part of the parents, may cause problems for children.

For example, when things began to heat up between Mickey and his mother, Helen naturally assumed that the problems between them were largely the result of the divorce. Perhaps she was right. But her guilty feelings made Helen conveniently forget that Mickey had had behavioral problems for several years—ever since the quarreling between his parents became severe. Almost two years before the separation, Mickey's preschool teacher had asked Helen if things were going all right at home. Mickey had displayed unusual fits of temper with his classmates and seemed distracted during play periods. If you had asked Mickey's teacher, she would have predicted that Mickey, although bright enough, was going to have adjustment problems in kindergarten. And so he did. True, Mickey's problems did get worse the year that his parents separated, but it is not obvious that his difficulties in school would have been avoided even if his parents had managed to remain together.

In fact, there is evidence that some children show signs of disturbance months, and sometimes even years, before their parents separate. In 1968 a team of psychologists began to study three-year-olds at two nursery schools in Berkeley, California. The psychologists followed these children and their families, conducting detailed personality assessments at ages four, five, seven, eleven, and fourteen.

When the study started, 88 children were living with two married parents. Twenty-nine of these children experienced the breakup of their parents marriages by the time they were fourteen. Curious as to what the children were like before the breakup, the psychologists paged backward through their files until they found the descriptions of the children eleven years earlier, when they were age three.

The results were quite dramatic for boys. Years before the breakup, three-year-old boys whose families eventually would disrupt were more likely to have been described as having behavioral problems than were three-year-old boys whose families would remain intact. According to the researchers, Jeanne H. Block, Jack Block, and Per F. Gjerde, three-year-old boys who would eventually experience family disruption already were rated as more "inconsiderate of other children, disorderly in dress and behavior," and "impulsive" and more likely to "take advantage of other children." Moreover, their fathers were more likely to characterize themselves as often angry with their sons, and both fathers and mothers reported more conflict with their sons. Much smaller differences were found among daughters.

Had the Berkeley researchers started their study when the children were age fourteen, they surely would have found some differences between the adolescents from the 29 disrupted families and the adolescents from the 59 intact families. And they probably would have attributed these differences to the aftermath of the disruption, as most other researchers do. But because they could look back eleven years, they saw that some portion of the presumed effects of divorce on children were present well before the families split up.

Why is this so? It is, of course, possible that some children have behavioral problems that put stress on their parents' marriages. In these instances divorce, rather than *causing* children's problems, may be the *result* of them. But it is doubtful that inherently difficult children cause most divorces. The Berkeley researchers suggest, rather, that conflict between parents is a fundamental factor that harms children's development and produces behavioral problems. In many families, this conflict—and the harm it engenders—may precede the separation by many years.

There are many other characteristics of divorce-prone families that might affect children. For example, people who divorce are more likely to have married as teenagers and to have begun their marriages after the wife was pregnant. They also are less religious. It is possible that these families may provide a less stable and secure environment and therefore cause children more problems even while the family is intact. But no researcher would suggest that all of the effects of divorce are determined before the actual separation. Much of the impact depends on how the process unfolds after the separation and how the children cope with it. Nearly all children are extremely upset when they learn of the breakup. For most, it is an unwelcome shock. Judith Wallerstein and Joan Kelly found that young children seemed surprised even in families where the parents were openly quarreling and hostile. Although young children certainly recognize open conflict—and indeed may be drawn into it—they usually can't grasp the long-term significance and don't envisage the separation. Moreover, parents typically don't inform their children of the impending separation until shortly before it occurs.

When children do learn of the breakup, their reactions vary according to their ages. Preschool-age children, whose ability to understand the situation is limited, are usually frightened and bewildered to find that their father or mother has moved out of the house. Preschoolers see the world in a very self-centered way, and so they often assume that the separation must be their fault—that they must have done something terribly wrong to make their parent leave. Three-year-old Sally promised never to leave her room a mess again if only Daddy would come home. Older children comprehend the situation better and can understand that they are not at fault. But they still can be quite anxious about what the breakup will mean for their own lives. And adolescents, characteristically, are more often intensely angry at one or both of their parents for breaking up their families.

SHORT-TERM ADJUSTMENT

The psychologists P. Lindsay Chase-Lansdale and E. Mavis Hetherington have labeled the first two years following a separation as a "crisis period" for adults and children. The crisis begins for children with shock, anxiety, and anger upon learning of the breakup. (But as was noted, the harmful effects on children of marital conflict may begin well before the breakup.) For adults, too, the immediate aftermath is a dismaying and difficult time. It is especially trying for mothers who retain custody of the children, as about nine in ten do.

Helen, for example, faced the task of raising her two children alone. Even when she was married, Helen had taken most of the responsibility for raising the children. But Herb had helped out some and had backed her up when the children were difficult. Now responsibility fell solely on her. What's more, she was working full time in order to compensate for the loss of Herb's income. And all this was occurring at a time when she felt alternately angry at Herb, depressed about the end of her marriage, and anxious about her future. Harried and overburdened, she was sometimes overwhelmed by the task of keeping her family going from day to day. Dinner was frequently served late, and Sally and Mickey often stayed up past their bedtime as Helen tried to complete the household chores.

Children have two special needs during the crisis period. First, they need additional emotional support as they struggle to adapt to the breakup. Second, they need the structure provided by a reasonably predictable daily routine. Unfortunately, many single parents cannot meet both of these needs all the time. Depressed, anxious parents often lack the reserve to comfort emotionally needy children. Overburdened parents let daily schedules slip. As a result, their children lose some of the support they need.

A number of psychological studies suggest that the consequences of the crisis period are worse for boys than for girls; but it may be that boys and girls merely react to stress differently. Developmental psychologists distinguish two general types of behavior problems among children. The first—externalizing disorders—refers to heightened levels of problem behavior directed outward, such as aggression, disobedience, and lying. The second—internalizing disorders—refers to heightened levels of problem behaviors directed inward, such as depression, anxiety, or withdrawal. Boys in high-conflict families, whether disrupted or intact, tend to show more aggressive and antisocial behavior. Hetherington studied a small group of middle-class families, disrupted and intact, for several years. She found coercive cycles between mothers and sons, like the ones between Helen and Mickey, to be prevalent. Distressed mothers responded irritably to the bad behavior of their sons, thus aggravating the very behavior they wished to quell. Even as long as six years after the separation, Hetherington observed this pattern among mothers who hadn't remarried and their sons.

The findings for girls are less consistent, but generally girls appear better behaved than boys in the immediate aftermath of a disruption. There are even reports of overcontrolled, self-consciously "good" behavior. But we should be cautious in concluding that girls are less affected. It may be that they internalize their distress in the form of depression or lowered self-esteem. And some observers suggest that the distress may produce problems that only appear years after the breakup.

It is also possible that boys do worse because they typically live with their opposite-sex parent, their mother. A number of studies report intriguing evidence that children may fare better if they reside with a same-sex parent after a marital disruption. Families in which single fathers become the custodial parent, however, are a small and select group who may be quite different from typical families. Until recently, sole custody was awarded to fathers mainly in cases in which the mother had abandoned the children or was an alcoholic, drug abuser, or otherwise clearly incompetent. Until there is more evidence from studies of broad groups of children, we think it would be premature to generalize about same-sex custody.

To sum up, researchers agree that almost all children are moderately or severely distressed when their parents separate and that most continue to experience confusion, sadness, or anger for a period of months and even years. Nevertheless, the most careful studies show a great deal of variation in the short-term reactions of children—including children in the same family. Most of this variation remains unexplained, although differences in age and gender account for some of it. Part of the explanation, no doubt, has to do with differences in children's temperaments. Some probably are more robust and better able to withstand deprivation and instability. They may be less affected by growing up in a one-parent family, and they may also cope better with a divorce. In addition, clinicians have speculated that some children draw strength from adults or even peers outside of the household, such as grandparents, aunts, or close friends. But we are far from certain just how important each of the sources of resiliency is to the child's ability to cope with divorce.

LONG-TERM ADJUSTMENT

Even less is known about the long-term consequences of divorces than about the short-term consequences. Within two or three years, most single parents and their children recover substantially from the trauma of the crisis period. Parents are able to stabilize their lives as the wounds from the breakup heal. With the exception of some difficulties between single mothers and their sons, parent-child relationships generally improve. And the majority of children, it seems, return to normal development.

But over the long run there is still great variation in how the process of divorce plays out. Without doubt, some children suffer long-term harm. It is easy, however, to exaggerate the extent of these harmful effects. In their widely read book that reports on a clinical study of 60 recently divorced middle-class couples from the San Francisco suburbs and their 131 children, aged two to eighteen, Judith Wallerstein and Sandra Blakeslee paint a picture of a perma-nently scarred generation. "Almost half of the children," they write, "entered adulthood as worried, underachieving, self-deprecating, and sometimes angry young men and women." Are these difficulties as widespread among children of divorce as the authors suggest? Despite their claim that the families were "repre-sentative of the way normal people from a white, middle-class background cope with divorce," it is highly likely that the study exaggerates the prevalence of long-term problems. Its families had volunteered to come to a clinic for coun-seling, and many of the parents had extensive psychiatric histories. Moreover, there is no comparison group of intact families: instead, all of the problems that emerged after the break-up are blamed on the divorce.

We do not doubt that many young adults retain painful memories of their parents' divorce. But it doesn't necessarily follow that these feelings will impair their functioning as adults. Had their parents not divorced, they might have retained equally painful memories of a conflict-ridden marriage. Imagine that the more troubled families in the Wallerstein study had remained intact and had been observed ten years later. Would their children have fared any better? Certainly they would have been better off economically; but given the strains that would have been evident in the marriages, we doubt that most would have been better off psychologically.

Studies based on nationally representative samples that do include children from intact marriages suggest that the long-term harmful effects of divorce are worthy of concern but occur only to a minority. Evidence for this conclusion comes from the National Survey of Children, which interviewed parents and children in 1976 and again in 1981. For families in which a marital disruption had occurred, the average time elapsed since the disruption was eight years in 1981. James L. Peterson and Nicholas Zill examined parents' 1981 responses to the question, "Since January 1977 . . . has [the child] had any behavior or disci-pline problems at school resulting in your receiving a note or being asked to come in and talk to the teacher or principal?" Peterson and Zill found that, other things being equal, 34 percent of parents who had separated or divorced answered yes, compared with 20 percent of parents in intact marriages.

Is this a big difference or a small difference? The figures can be interpreted in two ways. First, the percentage of children from maritally disrupted families who had behavior or discipline problems at school is more than half-again as large as the percentage from intact families. That's a substantial difference, suggesting that children from disrupted families have a noticeably higher rate of misbehaving seriously in school. (Although some of these children might have misbehaved even if their parents had not separated.) Second, however, the figures also demonstrate that 66 percent of all children from maritally disrupted homes *did not* misbehave seriously at school. So one also can conclude that most children of divorce don't have behavior problems at school. Both conclusions are equally valid; the glass is either half full or half empty, depending on one's point of view. We think that in order to understand the broad picture of the long-term effects of divorce on children, it's necessary to keep both points of view in mind.

The same half-full and half-empty perspective can be applied to studies of the family histories of adults. Based on information from several national surveys of adults, Sara McLanahan and her colleagues found that persons who reported living as a child in a single-parent family were more likely subsequently to drop out of high school, marry during their teenage years, have a child before marrying, and experience the disruption of their own marriages. For example, the studies imply that, for whites, the probability of dropping out of high school could be as high as 22 percent for those who lived with single parents, compared with about 11 percent for those who lived with both parents, other things being equal. Again, the glass is half-empty; those who lived with a single parent are up to twice as likely to drop out of high school. And it is half-full: the overwhelming majority of those who lived with a single parent graduated from high school.

In addition, the NSC data demonstrate that children in intact families in which the parents fought continually were doing no better, and often worse, than the children of divorce. In 1976 and again in 1981, parents in intact marriages were asked whether they and their spouses ever had arguments about any of nine topics: chores and responsibilities, the children, money, sex, religion, leisure time, drinking, other women or men, and in-laws. Peterson and Zill classified an intact marriage as having "high conflict" if arguments were reported on five or more topics or if the parent said that the marriage, taking things all together, was "not too happy." They found that in 1981, children whose parents had divorced or separated were doing no worse than children whose parents were in intact, high-conflict homes. And children whose parents' marriages were intact but highly conflicted in both 1976 and 1981 were doing the worst of all; these children were more depressed, impulsive, and hyperactive, and misbehaved more often.

To be sure, even if only a minority of children experience long-term negative effects, that is nothing to cheer about. But the more fundamental point—one that all experts agree upon—is that children's responses to the breakup of their parents' marriages vary greatly. There is no ineluctable path down which children of divorce progress. What becomes important, then, is to identify the circumstances under which children seem to do well.

WHAT MAKES A DIFFERENCE?

A critical factor in both short-term and long-term adjustment is how effectively the custodial parent, who usually is the mother, functions as a parent. We have noted how difficult it can be for a recently separated mother to function well.

The first year or two after the separation is a difficult time for many mothers, who may feel angry, depressed, irritable, or sad. Their own distress may make it more difficult to cope with their children's distress, leading in some cases to a disorganized household, lax supervision, inconsistent discipline, and the coercive cycles between mothers and preschool-aged sons that have been identified by Hetherington and others. Mothers who can cope better with the disruption can be more effective parents. They can keep their work and home lives going from day to day and can better provide love, nurturing, consistent discipline, and a predictable routine.

Quite often their distress is rooted in, or at least intensified by, financial problems. Loss of the father's income can cause a disruptive, downward spiral in which children must adjust to a declining standard of living, a mother who is less psychologically available and is home less often, an apartment in an unfamiliar neighborhood, a different school, and new friends. This sequence of events occurs at a time when children are greatly upset about the separation and need love, support, and a familiar daily routine.

A second key factor in children's well-being is a low level of conflict between their mother and father. This principle applies, in fact, to intact as well as disrupted families. Recall the finding from the NSC that children who live with two parents who persistently quarrel over important areas of family life show higher levels of distress and behavior problems than do children from disrupted marriages. Some observers take this finding to imply that children are better off if their parents divorce than if they remain in an unhappy marriage. We think this is true in some cases but not in others. It is probably true that most children who live in a household filled with continual conflict between angry, embittered spouses would be better off if their parents split up—assuming that the level of conflict is lowered by the separation. And there is no doubt that the rise in divorce has liberated some children (and their custodial parents) from families marked by physical abuse, alcoholism, drugs, and violence. But we doubt that such clearly pathological descriptions apply to most families that disrupt. Rather, we think there are many more cases in which there is little open conflict, but one or both partners finds the marriage personally unsatisfying. The unhappy partner may feel unfulfilled, distant from his or her spouse, bored, or constrained. Under these circumstances, the family may limp along from day to day without much holding it together or pulling it apart. A generation ago, when marriage was thought of as a moral and social obligation, most husbands and wives in families such as this stayed together. Today, when marriage is thought of increasingly as a means of achieving personal fulfillment, many more will divorce. Under these circumstances, divorce may well make one or both spouses happier; but we strongly doubt that it improves the psychological well-being of the children.

A possible third key factor in children's successful adjustment is the maintenance of a continuing relationship with the noncustodial parent, who is usually the father. But direct evidence that lack of contact with the father inhibits the adjustment of children to divorce is less than satisfactory. A number of experts have stressed the importance of a continuing relationship, yet research findings are inconsistent. The main evidence comes from both the Hetherington and

Wallerstein studies, each of which found that children were better adjusted when they saw their fathers regularly. More recently, however, other observational studies have not found this relationship.

And in the NSC, the amount of contact that children had with their fathers seemed to make little difference for their well-being. Teenagers who saw their fathers regularly were just as likely as were those with infrequent contact to have problems in school or engage in delinquent acts and precocious sexual behavior. Furthermore, the children's behavioral adjustment was also unrelated to the level of intimacy and identification with the nonresidential father. No differences were observed even among the children who had both regular contact and close relations with their father outside the home. Moreover, when the children in the NSC were reinterviewed in 1987 at ages 18 to 23, those who had retained stable, close ties to their fathers were neither more nor less successful than those who had had low or inconsistent levels of contact and intimacy with their fathers.

Another common argument is that fathers who maintain regular contact with their children also may keep paying child support to their children's mothers. Studies do show that fathers who visit more regularly pay more in child support. But it's not clear that they pay more *because* they visit more. Rather, it may be that fathers who have a greater commitment to their children both visit and pay more. If so, then the problem is to increase the level of commitment most fathers feel, not simply to increase the amount of visiting.

These puzzling findings make us cautious about drawing any firm conclusions about the psychological benefits of contact with noncustodial parents for children's adjustment in later life. Yet despite the mixed evidence, the idea that continuing contact with fathers makes a difference to a child's psychological well-being is so plausible and so seemingly grounded in theories of child development that one is reluctant to discount it. It may be that evidence is difficult to obtain because so few fathers living outside the home are intimately involved in child-rearing. It is also likely that, even when fathers remain involved, most formerly married parents have difficulty establishing a collaborative style of child-rearing. We remain convinced that when parents are able to cooperate in child-rearing after a divorce and when fathers are able to maintain an active and supportive role, children will be better off in the long run. But we are certain that such families are rare at present and unlikely to become common in the near future.

DOES CUSTODY MAKE A DIFFERENCE FOR CHILDREN?

The belief that the father's involvement is beneficial to children was an important reason why many states recently adopted joint-custody statutes. Supporters argued that children adjust better when they maintain a continuing relationship with both parents. They also argued that fathers would be more likely to meet child-support obligations if they retained responsibility for the children's upbringing. Were they correct? Joint custody is so recent that no definitive evidence exists. But the information to date is disappointing.

Joint *legal* custody seems to be hardly distinguishable in practice from maternal sole custody. A recent study of court records in Wisconsin showed no difference in child-support payments in joint-legal-custody versus mother-sole-custody families, once income and other factors were taken into account. The Stanford study found little difference, three and one-half years after separation, between joint-legal-custody (but not joint-physical-custody) families and mother-sole-custody families. Once income and education were taken into account, fathers who had joint legal custody were no more likely to comply with court-ordered child-support awards than were fathers whose former wives had sole legal and physical custody. They did not visit their children more often; they did not cooperate and communicate more with their former wives; and they didn't even participate more in decisions about the children's lives. The investigators concluded that joint legal custody "appears to mean very little in practice."

The handful of other small-scale studies of joint legal custody show modest effects, at most. It appears that joint legal custody does not substantially increase the father's decision-making authority, his involvement in childrearing, or the amount of child support he pays. Why is it so hard to increase fathers' involvement after divorce? For one thing . . . many men don't seem to know how to relate to their children except through their wives. Typically, when married, they were present but passive—not much involved in childrearing. When they separate, they carry this pattern of limited involvement with them; and it is reinforced by the modest contact most have with their children. Uncomfortable and unskilled at being an active parent, marginalized by infrequent contact, focused on building a new family life, many fathers fade from their children's lives.

Less is known about joint physical custody. But a few recent studies suggest that it isn't necessarily better for children's adjustment than the alternatives. Among all families in the Stanford Study in which children still were seeing both parents about two years after the separation, parents in dual-residence families talked and coordinated rules more; but they quarreled about the children just as much as did parents in single-residence families. Several colleagues of Wallerstein followed 58 mother-physical-custody families and 35 joint-physical-custody families for two years after the families had been referred to counseling centers in the San Francisco area. Many of the parents were disputing custody and visitation arrangements. Children from the joint-physical-custody families were no better adjusted than children from the mother-physical-custody families: their levels of behavioral problems, their self-esteem, their ease at making friends were very similar. What did make a difference for the children was the depression and anxiety levels of their parents and the amount of continuing verbal and physical aggression between them, regardless of the custody arrangement. The authors suggest that children whose parents are having serious disputes may have more behavior problems, lower self-esteem, and less acceptance by friends if they shuttle between homes. They are exposed to more conflict, and their movement back and forth may even generate it.

The admittedly limited evidence so far suggests to us that custody arrangements may matter less for the well-being of children than had been thought. It is, of course, possible that when more evidence is available, joint custody will be shown to have important benefits for some families. As with father involvement, the rationale for joint custody is so plausible and attractive that one is tempted to disregard the disappointing evidence and support it anyway. But based on what is known now, we think custody and visitation matter less for children than the two factors we noted earlier: how much conflict there is between the parents and how effectively the parent (or parents) the child lives with functions. It is likely that a child who alternates between the homes of a distraught mother and an angry father will be more troubled than a child who lives with a mother who is coping well and who once a fortnight sees a father who has disengaged from his family. Even the frequency of visits with a father seems to matter less than the climate in which they take place.

For now, we would draw two conclusions. First, joint physical custody should be encouraged only in cases where both parents voluntarily agree to it. Among families in which both parents shared the childrearing while they were married, a voluntary agreement to maintain joint physical custody probably will work and benefit the children. Even among families in which one parent did most of the childrearing prior to the divorce, a voluntary agreement won't do any harm—although we think the agreement likely will break down to sole physical custody over time. But only very rarely should joint physical custody be imposed if one or both parents do not want it. There may be a few cases in which the father and mother truly shared the childrearing before the divorce but one of them won't agree to share physical custody afterward. These difficult cases call for mediation or counseling, and they may require special consideration. But among the vastly larger number of families in which little sharing occurred beforehand and one or both parents doesn't want to share physical custody afterward, imposing joint physical custody would invite continuing conflict without any clear benefits. Even joint legal custody may matter more as a symbol of fathers' ties to their children than in any concrete sense. But symbols can be important, and joint legal custody seems, at worst, to do no harm. A legal preference for it may send a message to fathers that society respects their rights to and responsibilities for their children.

Our second conclusion is that in weighing alternative public policies concerning divorce, the thin empirical evidence of the benefits of joint custody and frequent visits with fathers must be acknowledged. All of the findings in this chapter have implications for the way in which we as a society confront the effects of divorce on children. A question we will examine later is: Which public policies should have priority? What outcomes are most important for society to encourage and support? In some cases, such as the economic slide of mothers and children, the problem is clear, and alternative remedies readily come to mind. In other cases, the problems are complex and the remedies unclear. . . .

. . . [H]owever, we must note that a divorce does not necessarily mark the end of change in the family lives of children. A majority will see a new partner move into their home. A remarriage, or even a cohabiting relationship, brings with it the potential both to improve children's lives and to complicate further their adjustment . . . .

PART FOUR

FAMILIES IN SOCIETY

INTRODUCTION

During the 1950s and 1960s, family scholars and the mass media presented an image of the typical, normal, or model American family. It included a father, a mother, and two or three children living a middle-class existence in a single-family home in an area neither rural nor urban. Father was the breadwinner, and mother was a full-time homemaker. Both were, by implication, white.

No one denied that many families and individuals fell outside the standard nuclear model. Single persons, one-parent families, two-parent families in which both parents worked, three-generation families, and childless couples abounded. Three- or four-parent families were not uncommon, as one or both divorced spouses often remarried. Many families, moreover, neither white nor well-off, varied from the dominant image. White and seemingly middle-class families of particular ethnic, cultural, or sexual styles also differed from the model. The image scarcely reflected the increasing ratio of older people in the empty nest and retirement parts of the life cycle. But like poverty before its "rediscovery" in the mid-1960s, family complexity and variety existed on some dim fringe of semi-awareness.

When discussed, individuals or families departing from the standard model were analyzed in a context of pathology. Studies of one-parent families or work-ing mothers, for example, focused on the harmful effects to children of such situations. Couples childless by choice were assumed to possess some basic

257

personality inadequacy. Single persons were similarly interpreted, or else thought to be homosexual. Homosexuals symbolized evil, depravity, degradation, and mental illness.

Curiously, although social scientists have always emphasized the pluralism of American society in terms of ethnic groups, religion, and geographic region, the concept of pluralism had rarely been applied to the family.

In the wake of the social upheavals of the 1960s and 1970s, middle-class "mainstream" attitudes toward women's roles, sexuality, and the family were transformed. Despite the conservative backlash that peaked in the 1980s, the traditional family did not return. American families became increasingly diverse, and Americans were increasingly willing to extend the notion of pluralism to family life.

The selections in this part of the book discuss not only diversity in families, but also the reality that families are both embedded in and sensitive to changes in the social structure and economics of American life. As Lillian B. Rubin writes in "Families on the Fault Line," words like "downsizing," "restructuring," and "reengineering" have become all too familiar and even terrifying to workers and their families who worry about paying the rent or the next mortgage payment. Through evocative case studies, the selection by Rubin develops three major themes: the impact of downsizing on all families who experience it; the differential outcomes by social class; and, finally, the corrosive effects downsizing has had on relations among racial and ethnic communities in the United States.

In a selection that complements Rubin's, Maxine Baca Zinn focuses specifically on the chronic problems of unemployment that prevail in America's inner cities, and their impact on families. Why over the past three decades have we witnessed the growth of a seemingly permanent "underclass" in America—a population of unmarried mothers, "illegitimate" children, and jobless men? Baca Zinn summarizes and evaluates the leading explanations. Many commentators blame the swelling underclass on a self-perpetuating "culture of poverty"—a value system that rejects hard work and achievement and accepts female-headed families. Cultural explanations come in a number of versions, but they all see family disintegration as the source of poverty.

There is, however, a different causal view. This interpretation, rooted in a large body of theory and research, stresses the importance of transformations in the American economy and its opportunity structure, rather than culture, as the foundation of the poverty of the underclass. Baca Zinn concludes that the evidence best supports the structural explanation. But she also contends that most writers who present the structural view, in emphasizing the need to increase employment opportunities for inner city males, overlook the changes in women's roles in recent years.

The other articles in this chapter discuss the revolution in women's roles that has taken place during the past three decades. The two-parent family in which both parents work is the form that now comes closest to being the "typical American family." In the 1950s, the working mother was considered deviant, even though many women were employed in the labor force. It was taken for granted that maternal employment must be harmful to children; much current research on working mothers still takes this "social problem" approach to the subject.

What happens inside the family as women are expected to contribute to family income? Arlie Hochschild and Anne Machung take a close look at the emotional dynamics inside the family when both parents work full-time and the "second shift"—the work of caring for children and maintaining the home—is not shared equitably. The selection from their book portrays a painful dilemma shared by many couples in their study: The men saw themselves as having equal marriages; they were doing more work around the house than their fathers had done and more than they thought other men did. The women, whose lives were different from their own mothers', saw their husbands' contributions as falling far short of true equality. They resented having to carry more than their share of the "second shift," yet stifled their angry feelings in order to preserve their marriages. Still, this strategy took its toll on love and intimacy.

Chapter nine addresses family diversity along a number of dimensions, including race, ethnicity, life span, and lifestyles. Five authors—Paulette Moore Hines, Nydia Garcia-Preto, Monica McGoldrick, Rhea Almeida, and Susan Weltman—examine intergenerational relations in a variety of ethnic and cultural groups, including African Americans and Latinos, Irish and Italians, Asian Indians and Jews. They make the important point that different groups have different expectations about how children are expected to care for aging parents, and about how different responsibilities accrue to women and men. The authors, who are family therapists, argue that although the push to assimilate and acculturate is strong, family therapists need to understand, appreciate, and integrate the distinctive cultural properties of ethnic groups into their thinking and practice.

In 1992, President and candidate George Bush said that "children should have the benefit of being born into a family with a mother and father." But, as Laura Benkov suggests, although Bush spoke in the nineties, his voice was of an earlier decade. As we approach a new century, Americans are facing a tension between the remembered past when "family" was defined by heterosexual procreative unions sanctioned by the law, and families as defined by the quality of relationships—even when these encompass lesbians and gay men choosing to have children. America, Benkov argues, should not grant more privileges to children raised in traditional family forms than to those reared in families formed with nontraditional structures and gender ties.

African Americans are currently the largest minority group in the United States, but won't be for long. The twenty-first century will see Latinos and their families occupying that position. Like African-American families, those of Hispanic origin differ from white families in a number of ways. But like white families, Hispanic families also reflect a great deal of cultural diversity, says Catherine Street Chilman. Simply because they speak a common language does not mean that Puerto Ricans, Mexican Americans, Cuban Americans, and South and Central American immigrants are culturally unified. Understanding diversity in family life means that we must recognize variation within, as well between, ethnic, racial, and religious groups.

Of course, that understanding holds for African-American families as well. William P. O'Hare, Kelvin M. Pollard, Taynia L. Mann, and Mary M. Kent explore some of that variation for African-American households, which have undergone rather dramatic changes in recent decades. These include an increase in single-parent families and a decline in the proportion of children who live with two parents. Their article also discusses how larger social and economic forces have impacted the family life of African Americans.

Chapter ten discusses another major change in family life occasioned by the fact that people, especially Americans, are living longer than ever before. In the first article in this chapter, Matilda White Riley discusses the new variations of family life resulting from the "revolution in longevity." During this century, life expectancy has risen from under 50 to over 70 years of age—and it continues to rise. This sharp increase in life expectancy has been accompanied by a greatly expanded kinship structure persisting through time. People used to have lots of relatives, but they didn't live long. Now people begin with smaller families, but these persist and grow through marriage, procreation, and remarriage. Kinship structures used to look like short, stubby, ephemeral bushes. Now they have sprouted into long, slender trees, with many branches. Riley argues optimistically that the new kinship structure offers more choice for selecting relationships that can provide emotional support.

In earlier years—the so-called good old days—when death took family members at relatively young ages, grandparents were a rare family species. Young people today, even adolescents and twenty- and thirty-somethings, grow up knowing grandparents, a phenomenon that has developed largely since World War II, as a result of medical advances. The grandfather of one of the editors of this volume had his life saved by the then–miracle drug, penicillin, and he went on to live to 98 years of age. Because grandparenthood is so common today, it should not, as Andrew J. Cherlin and Frank. J. Furstenberg observe, be taken for granted. Widespread grandparenthood is a phenomenon of the last half-century, and as they show, it is having a significant effect on contemporary family relations.

Scientific progress is usually positive, but, as with most things in life, there can be unanticipated and unwanted outcomes. As gender and family roles have changed, and as modern methods of contraception have become available, society has experienced a sexual revolution. Part of it, perhaps the most dramatic part, has been the increasing sexual activity of teenagers, especially of girls. Teenage girls who are having sex are also experiencing more pregnancies. In the first reading in Chapter eleven on family troubles, Kristin Luker argues that, while teenage pregnancy is indeed a problem, its causes are often misinterpreted. It is not, she argues, simply an issue of immorality, of young women out of control. Rather, she argues, it makes far more sense to understand that teenage pregnancy partly reflects limited opportunities for realizing personal achievement, fulfillment, and enhancement of self-esteem; and also results from changed cultural expectations about teenage sex and the limits of applying knowledge about contraception.

Where Lillian Rubin's article (Chapter eight) focuses on working-class and ethnic families, Katherine Newman discusses the dark side of the American Dream—the slide down the economic ladder—for white middle-class families. What happens when a successful breadwinner loses his job and the family must suffer the loss of a formerly comfortable, middle-class lifestyle? The result is often a severe loss of status and self-respect for the father, a radical change in family emotional bonds, and the withdrawal of the family from the rest of the community. For middle-class families, the pain of downward social mobility is not just the loss of status and material comfort; it is also, Newman argues, a broken covenant. It is a profound violation of American cultural expectations that if we work hard we will succeed; that we, not economic forces beyond our control shape our fate and that the future will be rosier than the past.

Whatever the gnawing hurts of downward social mobility, the most dramatic, painful, and pronounced of family troubles is violence within the family, whether between partners or against children. Richard J. Gelles and Murray A. Straus provide us with a "profile" of violent families in three dimensions: first, the social organizational features of home and family that contribute to violence; second, the particular characteristics that put certain families at high risk for violence; and third, where and when violence in the home is likely to occur.

As women increasingly participate in the workforce, argues Sharon Hays, they find themselves caught up in a web of cultural contradictions that remain unresolved and indeed have deepened. There is no way, she further maintains, for contemporary women to get it "just right." Both stay-at-home and working mothers maintain an intensive commitment to motherhood, although they work it out in different ways. Women who stay at home no longer feel comfortable and fulfilled being defined by themselves and others as "mere housewives." Correspondingly, working women are frequently anxious about the time away from children, and the complexities of balancing parental duties with the demands of serious employment.

If cultural contradictions trouble motherhood, these could be seen as a part of the larger "cultural war" over the family. But there are more than two sides in the family wars. Janet Z. Giele carefully diagrams *three* models of the family, the conservative, the liberal, and the feminist. The latter, for Giele, is the most promising for developing public policies that would combine conservative and liberal perspectives. The feminist vision, she argues, appreciates the both the "premodern nature of the family" with the inevitable interdependence of family with a modern, fast-changing economy. Consequently, she claims, the feminist approach affords both a policy challenge and a policy synthesis to the culture wars that bedevil the institution of the family.

♦

WORK

AND

FAMILY

R E A D I N G

19

Families on the Fault Line

LILLIAN B. RUBIN

THE BARDOLINOS

It has been more than three years since I first met the Bardolino family, three years in which to grow accustomed to words like *downsizing, restructuring,* or the most recent one, *reengineering;* three years in which to learn to integrate them into the language so that they now fall easily from our lips. But these are no ordinary words, at least not for Marianne and Tony Bardolino.

The last time we talked, Tony had been unemployed for about three months and Marianne was working nights at the telephone company and dreaming about the day they could afford a new kitchen. They seemed like a stable couple then—a house, two children doing well in school, Marianne working without complaint, Tony taking on a reasonable share of the family work. Tony, who had been laid off from the chemical plant where he had worked for ten years, was still hoping he'd be called back and trying to convince himself their lives were on a short hold, not on a catastrophic downhill slide. But instead of calling workers back, the company kept cutting its work force. Shortly after our first meeting, it became clear: There would be no recall. Now, as I sit in the little cottage

Marianne shares with her seventeen-year-old daughter, she tells the story of these last three years.

"When we got the word that they wouldn't be calling Tony back, that's when we really panicked; I mean *really* panicked. We didn't know what to do. Where was Tony going to find another job, with the recession and all that? It was like the bottom really dropped out. Before that, we really hoped he'd be called back any day. It wasn't just crazy; they told the guys when they laid them off, you know, that it would be three, four months at most. So we hoped. I mean, sure we worried; in these times, you'd be crazy not to worry. But he'd been laid off for a couple of months before and called back, so we thought maybe it's the same thing. Besides, Tony's boss was so sure the guys would be coming back in a couple of months; so you tried to believe it was true."

She stops speaking, takes a few sips of coffee from the mug she holds in her hand, then says with a sigh, "I don't really know where to start. So much happened, and sometimes you can't even keep track. Mostly what I remember is how scared we were. Tony started to look for a job, but there was nowhere to look. The union couldn't help; there were no jobs in the industry. So he looked in the papers, and he made the rounds of all the places around here. He even went all the way to San Francisco and some of the places down near the airport there. But there was nothing.

"At first, I kept thinking, *Don't panic; he'll find something.* But after his unemployment ran out, we couldn't pay the bills, so then you can't help getting panicked, can you?"

She stops again, this time staring directly at me, as if wanting something. But I'm not sure what, so I sit quietly and wait for her to continue. Finally, she demands, "Well, can you?"

I understand now; she wants reassurance that her anxiety wasn't out of line, that it's not she who's responsible for the rupture in the family. So I say, "It sounds as if you feel guilty because you were anxious about how the family would manage."

"Yeah, that's right," she replies as she fights her tears. "I keep thinking maybe if I hadn't been so awful, I wouldn't have driven Tony away." But as soon as the words are spoken, she wants to take them back. "I mean, I don't know, maybe I wasn't that bad. We were both so depressed and scared, maybe there's nothing I could have done. But I think about it a lot, and I didn't have to blame him so much and keep nagging at him about how worried I was. It wasn't his fault; he was trying.

"It was just that we looked at it so different. I kept thinking he should take anything, but he only wanted a job like the one he had. We fought about that a lot. I mean, what difference does it make what kind of job it is? No, I don't mean that; I know it makes a difference. But when you have to support a family, that should come first, shouldn't it?"

As I listen, I recall my meeting with Tony a few days earlier and how guiltily he, too, spoke about his behavior during that time. "I wasn't thinking about her at all," he explained. "I was just so mad about what happened; it was like the world came crashing down on me. I did a little too much drinking, and then I'd just crawl into a hole, wouldn't even know whether Marianne or the kids were there or not. She kept saying it was like I wasn't there. I guess she was right, because I sure didn't want to be there, not if I couldn't support them."

"Is that the only thing you were good for in the family?" I asked him.

"Good point," he replied laughing. "Maybe not, but it's hard to know what else you're good for when you can't do that."

I push these thoughts aside and turn my attention back to Marianne. "Tony told me that he did get a job after about a year," I remark.

"Yeah, did he tell you what kind of job it was?"

"Not exactly, only that it didn't work out."

"Sure, he didn't tell you because he's still so ashamed about it. He was out of work so long that even he finally got it that he didn't have a choice. So he took this job as a dishwasher in this restaurant. It's one of those new kind of places with an open kitchen, so there he was, standing there washing dishes in front of everybody. I mean, we used to go there to eat sometimes, and now he's washing the dishes and the whole town sees him doing it. He felt so ashamed, like it was such a comedown, that he'd come home even worse than when he wasn't working.

"That's when the drinking really started heavy. Before that he'd drink, but it wasn't so bad. After he went to work there, he'd come home and drink himself into a coma. I was working days by then, and I'd try to wait up until he came home. But it didn't matter; all he wanted to do was go for that bottle. He drank a lot during the day, too, so sometimes I'd come home and find him passed out on the couch and he never got to work that day. That's when I was maddest of all. I mean, I felt sorry for him having to do that work. But I was afraid he'd get fired."

"Did he?"

"No, he quit after a couple of months. He heard there was a chemical plant down near L.A. where he might get a job. So he left. I mean, we didn't exactly separate, but we didn't exactly not. He didn't ask me and the kids to go with him; he just went. It didn't make any difference. I didn't trust him by then, so why would I leave my job and pick up the kids and move when we didn't even know if he'd find work down there?

"I think he went because he had to get away. Anyway, he never found any decent work there either. I know he had some jobs, but I never knew exactly what he was doing. He'd call once in awhile, but we didn't have much to say to each other then. I always figured he wasn't making out so well because he didn't send much money the whole time he was gone."

As Tony tells it, he was in Los Angeles for nearly a year, every day an agony of guilt and shame. "I lived like a bum when I was down there. I had a room in a place that wasn't much better than a flop house, but it was like I couldn't get it together to go find something else. I wasn't making much money, but I had enough to live decent. I felt like what difference did it make how I lived?"

He sighs—a deep, sad sound—then continues, "I couldn't believe what I did, I mean that I really walked out on my family. My folks were mad as hell at me. When I told them what I was going to do, my father went nuts, said I shouldn't come back to his house until I got some sense again. But I couldn't stay around with Marianne blaming me all the time."

He stops abruptly, withdraws to someplace inside himself for a few moments, then turns back to me. "That's not fair. She wasn't the only one doing the blaming. I kept beating myself up, too, you know, blaming myself, like I did something wrong.

"Anyhow, I hated to see what it was doing to the kids; they were like caught in the middle with us fighting and hollering, or else I was passed out drunk. I didn't want them to have to see me like that, and I couldn't help it. So I got out."

For Marianne, Tony's departure was both a relief and a source of anguish. "At first I was glad he left; at least there was some peace in the house. But then I got so scared; I didn't know if I could make it alone with the kids. That's when I sold the house. We were behind in our payments, and I knew we'd never catch up. The bank was okay; they said they'd give us a little more time. But there was no point.

"That was really hard. It was our home; we worked so hard to get it. God, I hated to give it up. We were lucky, though. We found this place here. It's near where we used to live, so the kids didn't have to change schools, or anything like that. It's small, but at least it's a separate little house, not one of those grungy apartments." She interrupts herself with a laugh, "Well, 'house' makes it sound a lot more than it is, doesn't it?"

"How did your children manage all this?"

"It was real hard on them. My son had just turned thirteen when it all happened, and he was really attached to his father. He couldn't understand why Tony left us, and he was real angry for a long time. At first, I thought he'd be okay, you know, that he'd get over it. But then he got into some bad company. I think he was doing some drugs, although he still won't admit that. Anyway, one night he and some of his friends stole a car. I think they just wanted to go for a joyride; they didn't mean to really steal it forever. But they got caught, and he got sent to juvenile hall.

"I called Tony down in L.A. and told him what happened. It really shocked him; he started to cry on the phone. I never saw him cry before, not with all our trouble. But he just cried and cried. When he got off the phone, he took the first plane he could get, and he's been back up here ever since.

"Jimmy's trouble really changed everything around. When Tony came back, he didn't want to do anything to get Jimmy out of juvy right away. He thought he ought to stay there for a while; you know, like to teach him a lesson. I was mad at first because Jimmy wanted to come home so bad; he was so scared. But now I see Tony was right.

"Anyhow, we let Jimmy stay there for five whole days, then Tony's parents lent us the money to bail him out and get him a lawyer. He made a deal so that if Jimmy pleaded guilty, he'd get a suspended sentence. And that's what happened. But the judge laid down the law, told him if he got in one little bit of trouble again, he'd go to jail. It put the fear of God into the boy."

For Tony, his son's brush with the law was like a shot in the arm. "It was like I had something really important to do, to get that kid back on track. We talked it over and Marianne agreed it would be better if Jimmy came to live with me. She's too soft with the kids; I've got better control. And I wanted to make it up to him, too, to show him he could count on me again. I figured the whole trouble came because I left them, and I wanted to set it right.

"So when he got out of juvy, he went with me to my folks' house where I was staying. We lived there for awhile until I got this job. It's no great shakes, a kind of general handyman. But it's a job, and right from the start I made enough so we could move into this here apartment. So things are going pretty good right now."

"Pretty good" means that Jimmy, now sixteen, has settled down and is doing well enough in school to talk about going to college. For Tony, too, things have turned around. He set up his own business as an independent handyman several months ago and, although the work isn't yet regular enough to allow him to quit his job, his reputation as a man who can fix just about anything is growing. Last month the business actually made enough money to pay his bills. "I'll hang onto the job for a while, even if the business gets going real good, because we've got a lot of catching up to do. I don't mind working hard; I like it. And being my own boss, boy, that's really great," he concludes exultantly.

"Do you think you and Marianne will get together again?"

"I sure hope so; it's what I'm working for right now. She says she's not sure, but she's never made a move to get a divorce. That's a good sign, isn't it?"

When I ask Marianne the same question, she says, "Tony wants to, but I still feel a little scared. You know, I never thought I could manage without him, but then when I was forced to, I did. Now, I don't know what would happen if we got together again. It wouldn't be like it was before. I just got promoted to supervisor, so I have a lot of responsibility on my job. I'm a different person, and I don't know how Tony would like that. He says he likes it fine, but I figure we should wait a while and see what happens. I mean, what if things get tough again for him? I don't ever want to live through anything like these last few years."

"Yet you've never considered divorce."

She laughs, "You sound like Tony." Then more seriously, "I don't want a divorce if I can help it. Right now, I figure if we got through these last few years and still kind of like each other, maybe we've got a chance."

* * *

In the opening pages of this book, I wrote that when the economy falters, families tremble. The Bardolinos not only trembled, they cracked. Whether they can patch up the cracks and put the family back together again remains an open question. But the experience of families like those on the pages of this book provides undeniable evidence of the fundamental link between the public and private arenas of modern life.

No one has to tell the Bardolinos or their children about the many ways the structural changes in the economy affect family life. In the past, a worker like Tony Bardolino didn't need a high level of skill or literacy to hold down a well-paying semiskilled job in a steel mill or an automobile plant. A high school education, often even less, was enough. But an economy that relies most heavily on its service sector needs highly skilled and educated workers to fill its better-paying jobs, leaving people like Tony scrambling for jobs at the bottom of the economic order.

The shift from the manufacturing to the service sector, the restructuring of the corporate world, the competition from low-wage workers in underdeveloped countries that entices American corporations to produce their goods abroad, all have been going on for decades; all are expected to accelerate through the 1990s. The manufacturing sector, which employed just over 26 percent of American workers in 1970, already had fallen to nearly 18 percent by 1991. And experts predict a further drop to 12.5 percent by the year 2000. "This is the end of the post–World War boom era. We are never going back to what we knew," says employment analyst Dan Lacey, publisher of the newsletter *Workplace Trends*.

Yet the federal government has not only failed to offer the help working-class families need, but as a sponsor of a program to nurture capitalism elsewhere in the world it has become party to the exodus of American factories to foreign lands. Under the auspices of the U.S. Agency for International Development (AID), for example, Decaturville Sportswear, a company that used to be based in Tennessee, has moved to El Salvador. AID not only gave grants to trade organizations in El Salvador to recruit Decaturville but also subsidized the move by picking up the $5 million tab for the construction of a new plant, footing the bill for over $1 million worth of insurance, and providing low-interest loans for other expenses involved in the move.

It's a sweetheart deal for Decaturville Sportswear and the other companies that have been lured to move south of the border under this program. They build new factories at minimal cost to themselves, while their operating expenses drop dramatically. In El Salvador, Decaturville is exempted from corporate taxes and shipping duties. And best of all, the hourly wage for factory workers there is forty-five cents an hour; in the United States the minimum starting wage for workers doing the same job is $4.25.

True, like Tony Bardolino, many of the workers displaced by downsizing, restructuring, and corporate moves like these will eventually find other work. But like him also, they'll probably have to give up what little security they knew in the past. For the forty-hour-a-week steady job that pays a decent wage and provides good benefits is quickly becoming a thing of the past. Instead, as part of the new lean, clean, mean look of corporate America, we now have what the federal government and employment agencies call "contingent" workers—a more benign name for what some labor economists refer to as "disposable" or "throwaway" workers.

It's a labor strategy that comes in several forms. Generally, disposable workers are hired in part-time or temporary jobs to fill an organizational need and are released as soon as the work load lightens. But when union contracts call for employees to join the union after thirty days on the job, some unscrupulous employers fire contingent workers on the twenty-ninth day and bring in a new crew. However it's done, disposable workers earn less than those on the regular payroll and their jobs rarely come with benefits of any kind. Worse yet, they set off to work each morning fearful and uncertain, not knowing how the day will end, worrying that by nightfall they'll be out of a job.

The government's statistics on these workers are sketchy, but Labor Secretary Robert Reich estimates that they now make up nearly one-third of the existing work force. This means that about thirty-four million men and women, most of whom want steady, full-time work, start each day as contingent and/or part-time workers. Indeed, so widespread is this practice now that in some places temporary employment agencies are displacing the old ones that sought permanent placements for their clients.

Here again, class makes a difference. For while it's true that managers and professionals now also are finding themselves disposable, most of the workers who have become so easily expendable are in the lower reaches of the work order. And it's they who are likely to have the fewest options. These are the workers, the unskilled and the semiskilled—the welders, the forklift operators, the assemblers, the clerical workers, and the like—who are most likely to seem to management to be interchangeable. Their skills are limited; their job tasks are relatively simple and require little training. Therefore, they're able to move in and perform with reasonable efficiency soon after they come on the job. Whatever lost time or productivity a company may suffer by not having a steady crew of workers is compensated by the savings in wages and benefits the employment of throwaway workers permits. A resolution that brings short-term gains for the company at the long-term expense of both the workers and the nation. For when a person can't count on a permanent job, a critical element binding him or her to society is lost.

THE TOMALSONS

When I last met the Tomalsons, Gwen was working as a clerk in the office of a large Manhattan company and was also a student at a local college where she was studying nursing. George Tomalson, who had worked for three years in a furniture factory, where he laminated plastic to wooden frames, had been thrown out of a job when the company went bankrupt. He seemed a gentle man then, unhappy over the turn his life had taken but still wanting to believe that it would come out all right.

Now, as he sits before me in the still nearly bare apartment, George is angry. "If you're a black man in this country, you don't have a chance, that's all, not a chance. It's like no matter how hard you try, you're nothing but trash. I've been looking for work for over two years now, and there's nothing. White people are complaining all the time that black folks are getting a break. Yeah, well, I don't know who those people are, because it's not me or anybody else I know. People see a black man coming, they run the other way, that's what I know."

"You haven't found any work at all for two years?" I ask.

"Some temporary jobs, a few weeks sometimes, a couple of months once, mostly doing shit work for peanuts. Nothing I could count on."

"If you could do any kind of work you want, what would you do?"

He smiles, "That's easy; I'd be a carpenter. I'm good with my hands, and I know a lot about it," he says, holding his hands out, palms up, and looking at them proudly. But his mood shifts quickly; the smile disappears; his voice turns harsh. "But that's not going to happen. I tried to get into the union, but there's no room there for a black guy. And in this city, without being in the union, you don't have a chance at a construction job. They've got it all locked up, and they're making sure they keep it for themselves."

When I talk with Gwen later, she worries about the intensity of her husband's resentment. "It's not like George; he's always been a real even guy. But he's moody now, and he's so angry, I sometimes wonder what he might do. This place is a hell hole," she says, referring to the housing project they live in. "It's getting worse all the time; kids with guns, all the drugs, grown men out of work all around. I'll bet there's hardly a man in this whole place who's got a job, leave alone a good one."

"Just what is it you worry about?"

She hesitates, clearly wondering whether to speak, how much to tell me about her fears, then says with a shrug, "I don't know, everything, I guess. There's so much crime and drugs and stuff out there. You can't help wondering whether he'll get tempted." She stops herself, looks at me intently, and says, "Look, don't get me wrong; I know it's crazy to think like that. He's not that kind of person. But when you live in times like these, you can't help worrying about everything.

"We both worry a lot about the kids at school. Every time I hear about another kid shot while they're at school, I get like a raving lunatic. What's going on in this world that kids are killing kids? Doesn't anybody care that so many black kids are dying like that? It's like a black child's life doesn't count for anything. How do they expect our kids to grow up to be good citizens when nobody cares about them?

"It's one of the things that drives George crazy, worrying about the kids. There's no way you can keep them safe around here. Sometimes I wonder why we send them to school. They're not getting much of an education there. Michelle just started, but Julia's in the fifth grade, and believe me she's not learning much.

"We sit over her every night to make sure she does her homework and gets it right. But what good is it if the people at school aren't doing their job. Most of the teachers there don't give a damn. They just want the paycheck and the hell with the kids. Everybody knows it's not like that in the white schools; white people wouldn't stand for it.

"I keep thinking we've got to get out of here for the sake of the kids. I'd love to move someplace, anyplace out of the city where the schools aren't such a cesspool. But," she says dejectedly, "we'll never get out if George can't find a decent job. I'm just beginning my nursing career, and I know I've got a future now. But still, no matter what I do or how long I work at it, I can't make enough for that by myself."

George, too, has dreams of moving away, somewhere far from the city streets, away from the grime and the crime. "Look at this place," he says, his sweeping gesture taking in the whole landscape. "Is this any place to raise kids?

Do you know what my little girls see every day they walk out the door? Filth, drugs, guys hanging on the corner waiting for trouble.

"If I could get any kind of a decent job, anything, we'd be out of here, far away, someplace outside the city where the kids could breathe clean and see a different life. It's so bad here, I take them over to my mother's a lot after school; it's a better neighborhood. Then we stay over there and eat sometimes. Mom likes it; she's lonely, and it helps us out. Not that she's got that much, but there's a little pension my father left."

"What about Gwen's family? Do they help out, too?"

"Her mother doesn't have anything to help with since her father died. He's long gone; he was killed by the cops when Gwen was a teenager," he says as calmly as if reporting the time of day.

"Killed by the cops." The words leap out at me and jangle my brain. But why do they startle me so? Surely with all the discussion of police violence in the black community in recent years, I can't be surprised to hear that a black man was "killed by the cops."

It's the calmness with which the news is relayed that gets to me. And it's the realization once again of the distance between the lives and experiences of blacks and others, even poor others. Not one white person in this study reported a violent death in the family. Nor did any of the Latino and Asian families, although the Latinos spoke of a difficult and often antagonistic relationship with Anglo authorities, especially the police. But four black families (13 percent) told of relatives who had been murdered, one of the families with two victims—a teenage son and a twenty-two-year-old daughter, both killed in violent street crimes.

But I'm also struck by the fact that Gwen never told me how her father died. True, I didn't ask. But I wonder now why she didn't offer the information. "Gwen didn't tell me," I say, as if trying to explain my surprise.

"She doesn't like to talk about it. Would you?" he replies somewhat curtly.

It's a moment or two before I can collect myself to speak again. Then I comment, "You talk about all this so calmly."

He leans forward, looks directly at me, and shakes his head. When he finally speaks, his voice is tight with the effort to control his rage. "What do you want? Should I rant and rave? You want me to say I want to go out and kill those mothers? Well, yeah, I do. They killed a good man just because he was black. He wasn't a criminal; he was a hard-working guy who just happened to be in the wrong place when the cops were looking for someone to shoot," he says, then sits back and stares stonily at the wall in front of him.

We both sit locked in silence until finally I break it. "How did it happen?"

He rouses himself at the sound of my voice. "They were after some dude who robbed a liquor store, and when they saw Gwen's dad, they didn't ask questions; they shot. The bastards. Then they said it was self-defense, that they saw a gun in his hand. That man never held a gun in his life, and nobody ever found one either. But nothing happens to them; it's no big deal, just another dead nigger," he concludes, his eyes blazing.

It's quiet again for a few moments, then, with a sardonic half smile, he says, "What would a nice, white middle-class lady like you know about any of that?

You got all those degrees, writing books and all that. How are you going to write about people like us?"

"I was poor like you once, very poor," I say somewhat defensively.

He looks surprised, then retorts, "Poor and white; it's a big difference."

* * *

Thirty years before the beginning of the Civil War, Alexis de Tocqueville wrote: "If ever America undergoes great revolutions, they will be brought about by the presence of the black race on the soil of the United States; that is to say they will owe their origin, not to the equality, but to the inequality of condition." One hundred and sixty years later, relations between blacks and whites remain one of the great unresolved issues in American life, and "the inequality of condition" that de Tocqueville observed is still a primary part of the experience of black Americans.

I thought about de Tocqueville's words as I listened to George Tomalson and about how the years of unemployment had changed him from, as Gwen said, "a real even guy" to an angry and embittered one. And I was reminded, too, of de Tocqueville's observation that "the danger of conflict between the white and black inhabitants perpetually haunts the imagination of the [white] Americans, like a painful dream." Fifteen generations later we're still paying the cost of those years when Americans held slaves—whites still living in fear, blacks in rage. "People see a black man coming, they run the other way," says George Tomalson.

Yet however deep the cancer our racial history has left on the body of the nation, most Americans, including many blacks, believe that things are better today than they were a few decades ago–a belief that's both true and not true. There's no doubt that in ending the legal basis for discrimination and segregation, the nation took an important step toward fulfilling the promise of equality for all Americans. As more people meet as equals in the workplace, stereotypes begin to fall away and caricatures are transformed into real people. But it's also true that the economic problems of recent decades have raised the level of anxiety in American life to a new high. So although virtually all whites today give verbal assent to the need for racial justice and equality, they also find ways to resist the implementation of the belief when it seems to threaten their own status or economic well-being.

Our schizophrenia about race, our capacity to believe one thing and do another, is not new. Indeed, it is perhaps epitomized by Thomas Jefferson, the great liberator. For surely, as Gordon Wood writes in an essay in the *New York Review of Books*, "there is no greater irony in American history than the fact that America's supreme spokesman for liberty and equality was a lifelong aristocratic owner of slaves."

Jefferson spoke compellingly about the evils of slavery, but he bought, sold, bred, and flogged slaves. He wrote eloquently about equality but he was convinced that blacks were an inferior race and endorsed the racial stereotypes that have characterized African-Americans since their earliest days on this continent. He believed passionately in individual liberty, but he couldn't imagine free blacks living in America, maintaining instead that if the nation considered emancipating the slaves, it must also prepare for their expulsion.

No one talks seriously about expulsion anymore. Nor do many use the kind of language to describe African-Americans that was so common in Jefferson's day. But the duality he embodied—his belief in justice, liberty, and equality alongside his conviction of black inferiority—still lives.

THE RIVERAS

Once again Ana Rivera and I sit at the table in her bright and cheerful kitchen. She's sipping coffee; I'm drinking some bubbly water while we make small talk and get reacquainted. After a while, we begin to talk about the years since we last met. "I'm a grandmother now," she says, her face wreathed in a smile. "My daughter Karen got married and had a baby, and he's the sweetest little boy, smart, too. He's only two and a half, but you should hear him. He sounds like five."

"When I talked to her the last time I was here, Karen was planning to go to college. What happened?" I ask.

She flushes uncomfortably. "She got pregnant, so she had to get married. I was heartbroken at first. She was only nineteen, and I wanted her to get an education so bad. It was awful; she had been working for a whole year to save money for college, then she got pregnant and couldn't go."

"You say she had to get married. Did she ever consider an abortion?"

"I don't know; we never talked about it. We're Catholic," she says by way of explanation. "I mean, I don't believe in abortion." She hesitates, seeming uncertain about what more she wants to say, then adds, "I have to admit, at a time like that, you have to ask yourself what you really believe. I don't think anybody's got the right to take a child's life. But when I thought about what having that baby would do to Karen's life, I couldn't help thinking, *What if...?*" She stops, unable to bring herself to finish the sentence.

"Did you ever say that to Karen?"

"No, I would *never* do that. I didn't even tell my husband I thought such things. But, you know," she adds, her voice dropping to nearly a whisper, "if she had done it, I don't think I would have said a word."

"What about the rest of the kids?"

"Paul's going to be nineteen soon; he's a problem," she sighs. "I mean, he's got a good head, but he won't use it. I don't know what's the matter with kids these days; it's like they want everything but they're not willing to work for anything. He hardly finished high school, so you can't talk to him about going to college. But what's he going to do? These days if you don't have a good education, you don't have a chance. No matter what we say, he doesn't listen, just goes on his smart-alecky way, hanging around the neighborhood with a bunch of no-good kids looking for trouble.

"Rick's so mad, he wants to throw him out of the house. But I say no, we can't do that because then what'll become of him? So we fight about that a lot, and I don't know what's going to happen."

"Does Paul work at all?"

"Sometimes, but mostly not. I'm afraid to think about where he gets money from. His father won't give him a dime. He borrows from me sometimes, but I don't have much to give him. And anyway, Rick would kill me if he knew."

I remember Paul as a gangly, shy sixteen-year-old, no macho posturing, none of the rage that shook his older brother, not a boy I would have thought would be heading for trouble. But then, Karen, too, had seemed so determined to grasp at a life that was different from the one her parents were living. What happens to these kids?

When I talk with Rick about these years, he, too, asks in bewilderment: What happened? "I don't know; we tried so hard to give the kids everything they needed. I mean, sure, we're not rich, and there's a lot of things we couldn't give them. But we were always here for them; we listened; we talked. What happened? First my daughter gets pregnant and has to get married; now my son is becoming a bum."

"Roberto—that's what we have to call him now," explains Rick, "he says it's what happens when people don't feel they've got respect. He says we'll keep losing our kids until they really believe they really have an equal chance. I don't know; I knew I had to *make* the Anglos respect me, and I had to make my chance. Why don't my kids see it like that?" he asks wearily, his shoulders seeming to sag lower with each sentence he speaks.

"I guess it's really different today, isn't it?" he sighs. "When I was coming up, you could still make your chance. I mean, I only went to high school, but I got a job and worked myself up. You can't do that anymore. Now you need to have some kind of special skills just to get a job that pays more than the minimum wage.

"And the schools, they don't teach kids anything anymore. I went to the same public schools my kids went to, but what a difference. It's like nobody cares anymore."

"How is Roberto doing?" I ask, remembering the hostile eighteen-year-old I interviewed several years earlier.

"He's still mad; he's always talking about injustice and things like that. But he's different than Paul. Roberto always had some goals. I used to worry about him because he's so angry all the time. But I see now that his anger helps him. He wants to fight for his people, to make things better for everybody. Paul, he's like the wind; nothing matters to him.

"Right now, Roberto has a job as an electrician's helper, learning the trade. He's been working there for a couple of years; he's pretty good at it. But I think—I hope—he's going to go to college. He heard that they're trying to get Chicano students to go to the university, so he applied. If he gets some aid, I think he'll go," Rick says, his face radiant at the thought that at least one of his children will fulfill his dream. "Ana and me, we tell him even if he doesn't get aid, he should go. We can't do a lot because we have to help Ana's parents and that takes a big hunk every month. But we'll help him, and he could work to make up the rest. I know it's hard to work and go to school, but people do it all the time, and he's smart; he could do it."

His gaze turns inward; then, as if talking to himself, he says, "I never thought I'd say this but I think Roberto's right. We've got something to learn from some of these kids. I told that to Roberto just the other day. He says Ana and me have been trying to pretend we're one of them all of our lives. I told him, 'I think you're right.' I kept thinking if I did everything right, I wouldn't be a 'greaser.' But after all these years, I'm still a 'greaser' in their eyes. It took my son to make me see it. Now I know. If I weren't I'd be head of the shipping department by now, not just one of the supervisors, and maybe Paul wouldn't be wasting his life on the corner."

* * *

We keep saying that family matters, that with a stable family and two caring parents children will grow to a satisfactory adulthood. But I've rarely met a family that's more constant or more concerned than the Riveras. Or one where both parents are so involved with their children. Ana was a full-time homemaker until Paul, their youngest, was twelve. Rick has been with the same company for more than twenty-five years, having worked his way up from clerk to shift supervisor in its shipping department. Whatever the conflicts in their marriage, theirs is clearly a warm, respectful, and caring relationship. Yet their daughter got pregnant and gave up her plans for college, and a son is idling his youth away on a street corner.

Obviously, then, something more than family matters. Growing up in a world where opportunities are available makes a difference. As does being able to afford to take advantage of an opportunity when it comes by. Getting an education that broadens horizons and prepares a child for a productive adulthood makes a difference. As does being able to find work that nourishes self-respect and pays a living wage. Living in a world that doesn't judge you by the color of your skin makes a difference. As does feeling the respect of the people around you.

This is not to suggest that there aren't also real problems inside American families that deserve our serious and sustained attention. But the constant focus on the failure of family life as the locus of both our personal and social difficulties has become a mindless litany, a dangerous diversion from the economic and social realities that make family life so difficult today and that so often destroy it.

THE KWANS

It's a rare sunny day in Seattle, so Andy Kwan and I are in his backyard, a lovely showcase for his talents as a landscape gardener. Although it has been only a few years since we first met, most of the people to whom I've returned in this round of interviews seem older, grayer, more careworn. Andy Kwan is no exception. The brilliant afternoon sunshine is cruel as it searches out every line of worry and age in his angular face. Since I interviewed his wife the day before, I already know that the recession has hurt his business. So I begin by saying, "Carol says that your business has been slow for the last couple of years."

"Yes," he sighs. "At first when the recession came, it didn't hurt me. I think Seattle didn't really get hit at the beginning. But the summer of 1991, that's when I began to feel it. It's as if everybody zipped up their wallets when it came to landscaping.

"A lot of my business has always been when people buy a new house. You know, they want to fix up the outside just like they like it. But nobody's been buying houses lately, and even if they do, they're not putting any money into landscaping. So it's been tight, real tight."

"How have you managed financially?"

"We get by, but it's hard. We have to cut back on a lot of stuff we used to take for granted, like going out to eat once in a while, or going to the movies, things like that. Clothes, nobody gets any new clothes anymore.

"I do a lot of regular gardening now—you know, the maintenance stuff. It helps; it takes up some of the slack, but it's not enough because it doesn't pay much. And the competition's pretty stiff, so you've got to keep your prices down. I mean, everybody knows that it's one of the things people can cut out when things get tough, so the gardeners around here try to hold on by cutting their prices. It gets pretty hairy, real cutthroat."

He gets up, walks over to a flower bed, and stands looking at it. Then, after a few quiet moments, he turns back to me and says, "It's a damned shame. I built my business like you build a house, brick by brick, and it was going real good. I finally got to the point where I wasn't doing much regular gardening anymore. I could concentrate on landscaping, and I was making a pretty good living. With Carol working, too, we were doing all right. I even hired two people and was keeping them busy most of the time. Then all of a sudden, it all came tumbling down.

"I felt real bad when I had to lay off my workers. They have families to feed, too. But what could I do? Now it's like I'm back where I started, an ordinary gardener again and even worrying about how long that'll last," he says disconsolately.

He walks back to his seat, sits down, and continues somewhat more philosophically, "Carol says I shouldn't complain because, with all the problems, we're lucky. She still has her job, and I'm making out. I mean, it's not great, but it could be a lot worse." He pauses, looks around blankly for a moment, sighs, and says, "I guess she's right. Her sister worked at Boeing for seven years and she got laid off a couple of months ago. No notice, nothing; just the pink slip. I mean, everybody knew there'd be layoffs there, but you know how it is. You don't think it's really going to happen to you.

"I try not to let it get me down. But it's hard to be thankful for not having bigger trouble than you've already got," he says ruefully. Then, a smile brightening his face for the first time, he adds, "But there's one thing I can be thankful for, and that's the kids; they're doing fine. I worry a little bit about what's going to happen, though. I guess you can't help it if you're a parent. Eric's the oldest; he's fifteen now, and you never know. Kids get into all kinds of trouble these days. But so far, he's okay. The girls, they're good kids. Carol worries about what'll happen when they get to those teenage years. But I think they'll be okay. We teach them decent values; they go to church every week. I have to believe that makes a difference."

"You say that you worry about Eric but that the girls will be fine because of the values of your family. Hasn't he been taught the same values?"

He thinks a moment, then says, "Did I say that? Yeah, I guess I did. I think maybe there's more ways for a boy to get in trouble than a girl." He laughs and says again, "Did I say *that?*" Then, more thoughtfully, "I don't know. I guess I worry about them all, but if you don't tell yourself that things'll work out okay, you go nuts. I mean, so much can go wrong with kids today.

"It used to be the Chinese family could really control the kids. When I was a kid, the family was law. My father was Chinese-born; he came here as a kid. My mother was born right here in this city. But the grandparents were all immigrants; everybody spoke Chinese at home; and we never lived more than a couple of blocks from both sides of the family. My parents were pretty Americanized everywhere but at home, at least while their parents were alive. My mother would go clean her mother's house for her because that's what a Chinese daughter did."

"Was that because your grandmother was old or sick?"

"No," he replies, shaking his head at the memory. "It's because that's what her mother expected her to do; that's the way Chinese families were then. We talk about that, Carol and me, and how things have changed. It's hard to imagine it, but that's the kind of control families had then.

"It's all changed now. Not that I'd want it that way. I want my kids to know respect for the family, but they shouldn't be servants. That's what my mother was, a servant for her mother.

"By the time my generation came along, things were already different. I couldn't wait to get away from all that family stuff. I mean, it was nice in some ways; there was always this big, noisy bunch of people around, and you knew you were part of something. That felt good. But Chinese families, boy, they don't let go. You felt like they were choking you.

"Now it's *really* different; it's like the kids aren't hardly Chinese any more. I mean, my kids are just like any other American kids. They never lived in a Chinese neighborhood like the one I grew up in, you know, the kind where the only Americans you see are the people who come to buy Chinese food or eat at the restaurants."

"You say they're ordinary American kids. What about the Chinese side? What kind of connection do they have to that?"

"It's funny," he muses. "We sent them to Chinese school because we wanted them to know about their history, and we thought they should know the language, at least a little bit. But they weren't really interested; they wanted to be like everybody else and eat peanut butter and jelly sandwiches. Lately it's a little different, but that's because they feel like they're picked on because they're Chinese. I mean, everybody's worrying about the Chinese kids being so smart and winning all the prizes at school, and the kids are angry about that, especially Eric. He says there's a lot of bad feelings about Chinese kids at school and that everybody's picking on them—the white kids and the black kids, all of them.

"So all of a sudden, he's becoming Chinese. It's like they're making him think about it because there's all this resentment about Asian kids all around. Until a couple of years ago, he had lots of white friends. Now he hangs out mostly with other Asian kids. I guess that's because they feel safer when they're together."

"How do you feel about this?"

The color rises in his face; his voice takes on an edge of agitation. "It's too bad. It's not the way I wanted it to be. I wanted my kids to know they're Chinese and be proud of it, but that's not what's going on now. It's more like . . . , " he stops, trying to find the words, then starts again. "It's like they have to defend themselves *because* they're Chinese. Know what I mean?" he asks. Then without waiting for an answer, he explains, "There's all this prejudice now, so then you can't forget you're Chinese.

"It makes me damn mad. You grow up here and they tell you everybody's equal and that any boy can grow up to be president. Not that I ever thought a Chinese kid could ever be president; any Chinese kid knows that's fairy tale. But I did believe the rest of it, you know, that if you're smart and work hard and do well, people will respect you and you'll be successful. Now, it looks like the smarter Chinese kids are, the more trouble they get."

"Do you think that prejudice against Chinese is different now than when you were growing up?"

"Yeah, I do. When I was a kid like Eric, nobody paid much attention to the Chinese. They left us alone, and we left them alone. But now all these Chinese kids are getting in the way of the white kids because there's so many of them, and they're getting better grades, and things like that. So then everybody gets mad because they think our kids are taking something from them."

He stops, weighs his last words, then says, "I guess they're right, too. When I was growing up, Chinese kids were lucky to graduate from high school, and we didn't get in anybody's way. Now so many Chinese kids are going to college that they're taking over places white kids used to have. I can understand that they don't like that. But that's not our problem; it's theirs. Why don't they work hard like Chinese kids do?

"It's not fair that they've got quotas for Asian kids because the people who run the colleges decided there's too many of them and not enough room for white kids. Nobody ever worried that there were too many white kids, did they?"

* * *

"It's not fair"— a cry from the heart, one I heard from nearly everyone in this study. For indeed, life has not been fair to the working-class people of America, no matter what their color or ethnic background. And it's precisely this sense that it's not fair, that there isn't enough to go around, that has stirred the racial and ethnic tensions that are so prevalent today.

In the face of such clear class disparities, how is it that our national discourse continues to focus on the middle class, denying the existence of a working class and rendering them invisible?

Whether a family or a nation, we all have myths that play tag with reality— myths that frame our thoughts, structure our beliefs, and organize our systems of denial. A myth encircles reality, encapsulates it, controls it. It allows us to know some things and to avoid knowing others, even when somewhere deep inside we really know what we don't want to know. Every parent has experienced this clash between myth and reality. We see signals that tell us a child is lying and explain them away. It isn't that we can't know; it's that we won't, that knowing is too difficult or painful, too discordant with the myth that defines the relationship, the one that says: *My child wouldn't lie to me.*

The same is true about a nation and its citizens. Myths are part of our national heritage, giving definition to the national character, offering guidance for both public and private behavior, comforting us in our moments of doubt. Not infrequently our myths trip over each other, providing a window into our often contradictory and ambivalently held beliefs. The myth that we are a nation of equals lives side-by-side in these United States with the belief in white supremacy. And, unlikely as it seems, it's quite possible to believe both at the same time. Sometimes we manage the conflict by shifting from one side to the other. More often, we simply redefine reality. The inequality of condition between whites and blacks isn't born in prejudice and discrimination, we insist; it's black inferiority that's the problem. Class distinctions have nothing to do with privilege, we say; it's merit that makes the difference.

It's not the outcome that counts, we maintain; it's the rules of the game. And since the rules say that everyone comes to the starting line equal, the different results are merely products of individual will and wit. The fact that working-class children usually grow up to be working-class parents doesn't make a dent in the belief system, nor does it lead to questions about why the written rule and the lived reality are at odds. Instead, with perfect circularity, the outcome reinforces the reasoning that says they're deficient, leaving those so labeled doubly wounded—first by the real problems in living they face, second by internalizing the blame for their estate.

Two decades ago, when I began the research for *Worlds of Pain,* we were living in the immediate aftermath of the civil rights revolution that had convulsed the nation since the mid-1950s. Significant gains had been won. And despite the tenacity with which this headway had been resisted by some, most white Americans were feeling good about themselves. No one expected the nation's racial problems and conflicts to dissolve easily or quickly. But there was also a sense that we were moving in the right direction, that there was a national commitment to redressing at least some of the worst aspects of black-white inequality.

In the intervening years, however, the national economy buckled under the weight of three recessions, while the nation's industrial base was undergoing a massive restructuring. At the same time, government policies requiring preferential treatment were enabling African-Americans and other minorities to make small but visible inroads into what had been, until then, largely white terrain. The sense of scarcity, always a part of American life but intensified sharply by the history of these economic upheavals, made minority gains seem particularly threatening to white working-class families.

It isn't, of course, just working-class whites who feel threatened by minority progress. Wherever racial minorities make inroads into formerly all-white territory, tensions increase. But it's working-class families who feel the fluctuations in the economy most quickly and most keenly. For them, these last decades have been like a bumpy roller coaster ride. "Every time we think we might be able to get ahead, it seems like we get knocked down again," declares Tom Ahmundsen, a forty-two-year-old white construction worker. "Things look a little better; there's a little more work; then all of a sudden, boom, the economy falls apart and it's gone. You can't count on anything; it really gets you down."

This is the story I heard repeatedly: Each small climb was followed by a fall, each glimmer of hope replaced by despair. As the economic vise tightened, despair turned to anger. But partly because we have so little concept of class resentment and conflict in America, this anger isn't directed so much at those above as at those below. And when whites at or near the bottom of the ladder look down in this nation, they generally see blacks and other minorities.

True, during all of the 1980s and into the 1990s, white ire was fostered by national administrations that fanned racial discord as a way of fending off white discontent—of diverting anger about the state of the economy and the declining quality of urban life to the foreigners and racial others in our midst. But our history of racial animosity coupled with our lack of class consciousness made this easier to accomplish than it might otherwise have been.

The difficult realities of white working-class life not withstanding, however, their whiteness has accorded them significant advantages—both materially and psychologically—over people of color. Racial discrimination and segregation in the workplace have kept competition for the best jobs at a minimum. They do, obviously, have to compete with each other for the resources available. But that's different. It's a competition among equals; they're all white. They don't think such things consciously, of course; they don't have to. It's understood, rooted in the culture and supported by the social contract that says they are the superior ones, the worthy ones. Indeed, this is precisely why, when the courts or the legislatures act in ways that seem to contravene that belief, whites experience themselves as victims.

From the earliest days of the republic, whiteness has been the ideal, and freedom and independence have been linked to being white. "Republicanism," writes labor historian David Roediger, "had long emphasized that the strength, virtue and resolve of a people guarded them from enslavement." And it was whites who had these qualities in abundance, as was evident, in the peculiarly circuitous reasoning of the time, in the fact that they were not slaves.

By this logic, the enslavement of blacks could be seen as stemming from their "slavishness" rather than from the institution of slavery. Slavery is gone now, but the reasoning lingers on in white America, which still insists that the lowly estate of people of color is due to their deficits, whether personal or cultural, rather than to the prejudice, discrimination, and institutionalized racism that has barred them from full participation in the society.

This is not to say that culture is irrelevant, whether among black Americans or any other group in our society. The lifeways of a people develop out of their experiences—out of the daily events, large and small, that define their lives; out of the resources that are available to them to meet both individual and group needs; out of the place in the social, cultural, and political systems within which group life is embedded. In the case of a significant proportion of blacks in America's inner cities, centuries of racism and economic discrimination have produced a subculture that is both personally and socially destructive. But to fault culture or the failure of individual responsibility without understanding the larger context within which such behaviors occur is to miss a vital piece of the picture. Nor does acknowledging the existence of certain destructive subcultural forms among some African-Americans disavow or diminish the causal connections between the structural inequalities at the social, political, and economic levels and the serious social problems at the community level.

In his study of "working-class lads" in Birmingham, England, for example, Paul Willis observes that their very acts of resistance to middle-class norms—the defiance with which these young men express their anger at class inequalities—help to reinforce the class structure by further entrenching them in their working-class status. The same can be said for some of the young men in the African-American community, whose active rejection of white norms and "in your face" behavior consigns them to the bottom of the American economic order.

To understand this doesn't make such behavior, whether in England or the United States, any more palatable. But it helps to explain the structural sources of cultural forms and to apprehend the social processes that undergird them. Like Willis's white "working-class lads," the hip-hoppers and rappers in the black community who are so determinedly "not white" are not just making a statement about black culture. They're also expressing their rage at white society for offering a promise of equality, then refusing to fulfill it. In the process, they're finding their own way to some accommodation and to a place in the world they can call their own, albeit one that ultimately reinforces their outsider status.

But, some might argue, white immigrants also suffered prejudice and discrimination in the years after they first arrived, but they found more socially acceptable ways to accommodate. It's true—and so do most of today's people of color, both immigrant and native born. Nevertheless, there's another truth as well. For wrenching as their early experiences were for white ethnics, they had an out. Writing about the Irish, for example, Roediger shows how they were able to insist upon their whiteness and to prove it by adopting the racist attitudes and behaviors of other whites, in the process often becoming leaders in the assault against blacks. With time and their growing political power, they won the prize they sought—recognition as whites. "The imperative to define themselves as white," writes Roediger, "came from the particular 'public and psychological wages' whiteness offered to a desperate rural and often preindustrial Irish population coming to labor in industrializing American cities."

Thus does whiteness bestow its psychological as well as material blessings on even the most demeaned. For no matter how far down the socioeconomic ladder whites may fall, the one thing they can't lose is their whiteness. No small matter because, as W. E. B. DuBois observed decades ago, the compensation of white workers includes a psychological wage, a bonus that enables them to believe in their inherent superiority over nonwhites.

It's also true, however, that this same psychological bonus that white workers prize so highly has cost them dearly. For along with the importation of an immigrant population, the separation of black and white workers has given American capital a reserve labor force to call upon whenever white workers seemed to them to get too "uppity." Thus, while racist ideology enables white workers to maintain the belief in their superiority, they have paid for that conviction by becoming far more vulnerable in the struggle for decent wages and working conditions than they might otherwise have been. . . .

R E A D I N G

20

Family, Race, and Poverty

MAXINE BACA ZINN

The 1960s Civil Rights movement overturned segregation laws, opened voting booths, created new job opportunities, and brought hope to Black Americans. As long as it could be said that conditions were improving, Black family structure and life-style remained private matters. The promises of the 1960s faded, however, as the income gap between whites and Blacks widened. Since the middle 1970s, the Black underclass has expanded rather than contracted, and along with this expansion emerged a public debate about the Black family. Two distinct models of the underclass now prevail—one that is cultural and one that is structural. Both of them focus on issues of family structure and poverty.

THE CULTURAL DEFICIENCY MODEL

The 1980s ushered in a revival of old ideas about poverty, race, and family. Many theories and opinions about the urban underclass rest on the culture-of-poverty debate of the 1960s. In brief, proponents of the culture-of-poverty thesis contend that the poor have a different way of life than the rest of society and that these cultural differences explain continued poverty. Within the current national discussion are three distinct approaches that form the latest wave of deficiency theories.

The first approach—culture as villain—places the cause of the swelling underclass in a value system characterized by low aspirations, excessive masculinity, and the acceptance of female-headed families as a way of life.

The second approach—family as villain—assigns the cause of the growing underclass to the structure of the family. While unemployment is often

From *Signs: Journal of Women in Culture and Society* 1989, vol. 14, no. 4 © 1989 by The University of Chicago. Reprinted by permission.

addressed, this argument always returns to the causal connections between poverty and the disintegration of traditional family structure.

The third approach—welfare as villain—treats welfare and antipoverty programs as the cause of illegitimate births, female-headed families, and low motivation to work. In short, welfare transfer payments to the poor create disincentives to work and incentives to have children out of wedlock—a self-defeating trap of poverty.

Culture as Villain

Public discussions of urban poverty have made the "disintegrating" Black family the force most responsible for the growth of the underclass. This category, by definition poor, is overwhelmingly Black and disproportionately composed of female-headed households. The members are perceived as different from striving, upwardly mobile whites. The rising number of people in the underclass has provided the catalyst for reporters' and scholars' attention to this disadvantaged category. The typical interpretation given by these social commentators is that the underclass is permanent, being locked in by its own unique but maladaptive culture. This thinking, though flawed, provides the popular rationale for treating the poor as the problem.

The logic of the culture-of-poverty argument is that poor people have distinctive values, aspirations, and psychological characteristics that inhibit their achievement and produce behavioral deficiencies likely to keep them poor not only within generations but also across generations, through socialization of the young.[1] In this argument, poverty is more a function of thought processes than of physical environment.[2] As a result of this logic, current discussions of ghetto poverty, family structure, welfare, unemployment, and out-of-wedlock births connect these conditions in ways similar to the 1965 Moynihan Report.[3] Because Moynihan maintained that the pathological problem within Black ghettos was the deterioration of the Negro family, his report became the generative example of blaming the victim.[4] Furthermore, Moynihan dismissed racism as a salient force in the perpetuation of poverty by arguing that the tangle of pathology was "capable of perpetuating itself without assistance from the white world."[5]

The reaction of scholars to Moynihan's cultural-deficiency model was swift and extensive although not as well publicized as the model itself. Research in the sixties and seventies by Andrew Billingsley, Robert Hill, Herbert Gutman, Joyce Ladner, Elliot Leibow, and Carol Stack, to name a few, documented the many strengths of Black families, strengths that allowed them to survive slavery, the enclosures of the South, and the depression of the North.[6] Such work revealed that many patterns of family life were not created by a deficient culture but were instead "a rational adaptational response to conditions of deprivation."[7]

A rapidly growing literature in the eighties documents the disproportionate representation of Black female-headed families in poverty. Yet, recent studies on Black female-headed families are largely unconcerned with questions about adaptation. Rather, they study the strong association between female-headed families and poverty, the effects of family disorganization on children, the demographic and socioeconomic factors that are correlated with single-parent status, and the connection between the economic status of men and the rise in Black female-headed families.[8] While most of these studies do not advance a social-pathology explanation, they do signal a regressive shift in analytic focus. Many well-meaning academics who intend to call attention to the dangerously high level of poverty in Black female-headed households have begun to emphasize the family structure and the Black ghetto way of life as contributors to the perpetuation of the underclass.

The population press, on the other hand, openly and enthusiastically embraced the Moynihan thesis both in its original version and in Moynihan's restatement of the thesis in his book *Family and Nation*.[9] Here Moynihan repeats his assertion that poverty and family structure are associated, but now he contends that the association holds for Blacks and whites alike. This modification does not critique his earlier assumptions; indeed, it validates them. A profoundly disturbing example of this is revealed in the widely publicized television documentary, CBS Reports' "The Vanishing Family."[10] According to this refurbished version of the old Moynihan Report, a breakdown in family values has allowed Black men to renounce their traditional breadwinner role, leaving Black women to bear the economic responsibility for children.[11] The argument that the Black community is devastating itself fits neatly with the resurgent conservatism that is manifested among Black and white intellectuals and policymakers.

Another contemporary example of the use of the culture of poverty is Nicholas Lemann's two-part 1986 *Atlantic Monthly* article about the Black underclass in Chicago.[12] According to Lemann, family structure is the most visible manifestation of Black America's bifurcation into a middle class that has escaped the ghetto and an underclass that is irrevocably trapped in the ghetto. He explains the rapid growth of the underclass in the seventies by pointing to two mass migrations of Black Americans. The first was from the rural South to the urban North and numbered in the millions during the forties, fifties, and sixties; the second, a migration out of the ghettos by members of the Black working and middle classes, who had been freed from housing discrimination by the civil rights movement. As a result of the exodus, the indices of disorganization in the urban ghettos of the North (crime, illegitimate births) have risen, and the underclass has flourished.[13] Loose attitudes toward marriage, high illegitimacy rates, and family disintegration are said to be a heritage of the rural South. In Lemann's words, they represent the power of culture to produce poverty:

> The argument is anthropological, not economic; it emphasizes the power over people's behavior that culture, as opposed to economic incentives, can have. Ascribing a society's condition in part to the culture that prevails there seems benign when the society under discussion is England or California. But as a way of thinking about black ghettos it has become unpopular. Twenty years ago ghettos were often said to have a self-generating, destructive culture of poverty (the term has an impeccable source, the anthropologist Oscar Lewis). But then the left equated cultural discussions of the ghetto with accusing poor blacks of being in a bad situation that was of their own making. . . . The left succeeded in limiting the terms of the debate to purely economic ones, and today the right also discusses the ghetto in terms of

economic "incentives to fail," provided by the welfare system. . . . In the ghettos, though, it appears that the distinctive culture is now the greatest barrier to progress by the black underclass, rather than either unemployment or welfare.[14]

Lemann's essay, his "misreading of left economic analysis, and cultural anthropology itself"[15] might be dismissed if it were atypical in the debate about the culture of poverty and the underclass. Unfortunately, it shares with other studies the problems of working "with neither the benefit of a well-articulated theory about the impact of personality and motivation on behavior nor adequate data from a representative sample of the low-income population."[16]

The idea that poverty is caused by psychological factors and that poverty is passed on from one generation to the next has been called into question by the University of Michigan's Panel Study of Income Dynamics (PSID), a large-scale data collection project conceived, in part, to test many of the assumptions about the psychological and demographic aspects of poverty. This study has gathered annual information from a representative sample of the U.S. population. Two striking discoveries contradict the stereotypes stemming from the culture-of-poverty argument. The first is the high turnover of individual families in poverty and the second is the finding that motivation cannot be linked to poverty. Each year the number of people below the poverty line remains about the same, but the poor in one year are not necessarily the poor in the following year. "Blacks from welfare dependent families were no more likely to become welfare dependent than similar Blacks from families who had never received welfare. Further, measures of parental sense of efficacy, future orientation, and achievement motivation had no effects on welfare dependency for either group."[17] This research has found no evidence that highly motivated people are more successful at escaping from poverty than those with lower scores on tests.[18] Thus, cultural deficiency is an inappropriate model for explaining the underclass.

The Family as Villain

A central notion within culture-of-poverty arguments is that family disintegration is the source and sustaining feature of poverty. Today, nearly six out of ten Black children are born out of wedlock, compared to roughly three out of ten in 1970. In the 25–34-year age bracket, today the probability of separation and divorce for Black women is twice that of white women. The result is a high probability that an individual Black woman and her children will live alone. The so-called "deviant" mother-only family, common among Blacks, is a product of "the feminization of poverty," a shorthand reference to women living alone and being disproportionately represented among the poor. The attention given to increased marital breakups, to births to unmarried women, and to the household patterns that accompany these changes would suggest that the bulk of contemporary poverty is a family-structure phenomenon. Common knowledge—whether true or not—has it that family-structure changes cause most poverty, or changes in family structure have led to current poverty rates that are much higher than they would have been if family composition had remained stable.[19]

Despite the growing concentration of poverty among Black female-headed households in the past two decades, there is reason to question the conventional thinking. Research by Mary Jo Bane finds that changes in family structure have less causal influence on poverty than is commonly thought.[20] Assumptions about the correlation and association between poverty and family breakdown avoid harder questions about the character and direction of causal relations between the two phenomena.[21] Bane's longitudinal research on household composition and poverty suggests that much poverty, especially among Blacks, is the result of already-poor, two-parent households that break up, producing poor female-headed households. This differs from the event transition to poverty that is more common for whites: "Three-quarters of whites who were poor in the first year after moving into a female-headed or single person household became poor simultaneously with the transition; in contrast, of the blacks who were poor after the transition, about two-thirds had also been poor before. Reshuffled poverty as opposed to event-caused poverty for blacks challenges the assumption that changes in family structure have created ghetto poverty. This underscores the importance of considering the ways in which race produces different paths to poverty."[22]

A two-parent family is no guarantee against poverty for racial minorities. Analyzing data from the PSID, Martha Hill concluded that the long-term income of Black children in two-parent families throughout the decade was even lower than the long-term income of non-Black children who spent most of the decade in mother-only families: "Thus, increasing the proportion of Black children growing up in two-parent families would not by itself eliminate very much of the racial gap in the economic well-being of children; changes in the economic circumstances of the parents are needed most to bring the economic status of Black children up to the higher status of non-Black children."[23]

Further studies are required if we are to understand the ways in which poverty, family structure, and race are related.

Welfare as Villain

An important variant of the family-structure and deficient-culture explanations, one especially popular among political conservatives, is the argument that welfare causes poverty. This explanation proposes that welfare undermines incentives to work and causes families to break up by allowing Black women to have babies and encouraging Black men to escape family responsibilities. This position has been widely publicized by Charles Murray's influential book, *Losing Ground*.[24] According to Murray, liberal welfare policies squelch work incentives and thus are the major cause of the breakup of the Black family. In effect, increased AFDC benefits make it desirable to forgo marriage and live on the dole.

Research has refuted this explanation for the changes in the structure of families in the underclass. Numerous studies have shown that variations in welfare across time and in different states have not produced systematic variation in family structure.[25] Research conducted at the University of Wisconsin's Institute for Research on Poverty found that poverty increased after the late sixties due to a weakening economy through the seventies. No support was found for Murray's assertion that spending growth did more harm than good for Blacks because it increased the percentage of families headed by women. Trends in welfare spending increased between 1960 and 1972, and declined between 1970 and 1984; yet there were no reversals in family-composition trends during this period. The percentage of these households headed by women increased steadily from 10.7 percent to 20.8 percent between 1968 and 1983.[26]

Further evidence against the "welfare-dependency" motivation for the dramatic rise in the proportion of Black families headed by females is provided by William Darity and Samuel Meyers. Using statistical causality tests, they found no short-term effects of variations in welfare payments on female headship in Black families.[27]

Other research draws similar conclusions about the impact of welfare policies on family structure. Using a variety of tests, David Ellwood and Lawrence Summers dispute the adverse effects of AFDC.[28] They highlight two facts that raise questions about the role of welfare policies in producing female-headed households. First, the real value of welfare payments has declined since the early 1970s, while family dissolution has continued to rise. Family-structure changes do not mirror benefit-level changes. Second, variations in benefit levels across states do not lead to corresponding variations in divorce rates or numbers of children in single-parent families. Their comparison of groups collecting AFDC with groups that were not, found that the effects of welfare benefits on family structures were small.[29] In sum, the systematic research on welfare and family structure indicates that AFDC has far less effect on changes in family structure than has been assumed.

OPPORTUNITY STRUCTURES IN DECLINE

A very different view of the underclass has emerged alongside the popularized cultural-deficiency model. This view is rooted in a substantial body of theory and research. Focusing on the opportunity structure of society, these concrete studies reveal that culture is not responsible for the underclass.

Within the structural framework there are three distinct strands. The first deals with transformations of the economy and the labor force that affect Americans in general and Blacks and Hispanics in particular. The second is the transformation of marriage and family life among minorities. The third is the changing class composition of inner cities and their increasing isolation of residents from mainstream social institutions.

All three are informed by new research that examines the macrostructural forces that shape family trends and demographic patterns that expand the analysis to include Hispanics.

Employment

Massive economic changes since the end of World War II are causing the social marginalization of Black people throughout the United States. The shift from an economy based on the manufacture of goods to one based on information and services has redistributed work in global, national, and local economies. While these major economic shifts affect all workers, they have more serious consequences for Blacks than whites, a condition that scholars call "structural racism."[30] Major economic trends and patterns, even those that appear race neutral, have significant racial implications. Blacks and other minorities are profoundly affected by (1) the decline of industrial manufacturing sectors and the growth of service sectors of the economy; and (2) shifts in the geographical location of jobs from central cities to the suburbs and from the traditional manufacturing cities (the rustbelt) to the sunbelt and to other countries.

In their classic work *The Deindustrialization of America*, Barry Bluestone and Bennett Harrison revealed that "minorities tend to be concentrated in industries that have borne the brunt of recent closing. This is particularly true in the automobile, steel, and rubber industries."[31] In a follow-up study, Bluestone, Harrison, and Lucy Gorham have shown that people of Color, particularly Black men, are more likely than whites to lose their jobs due to the restructuring of the U.S. economy and that young Black men are especially hard hit.[32] Further evidence of the consequences of economic transformation for minority males is provided by Richard Hill and Cynthia Negrey.[33] They studied deindustrialization in the Great Lakes region and found that the race-gender group that was hardest hit by the industrial slumps was Black male production workers. Fully 50 percent of this group in five Great Lakes cities studied lost their jobs in durable-goods manufacturing between 1979 and 1984. They found that Black male production workers also suffered the greatest rate of job loss in the region and in the nation as a whole.

The decline of manufacturing jobs has altered the cities' roles as opportunity ladders for the disadvantaged. Since the start of World War II, well-paying blue-collar jobs in manufacturing have been a main avenue of job security and mobility for Blacks and Hispanics. Movement into higher-level blue-collar jobs was one of the most important components of Black occupational advancement in the 1970s. The current restructuring of industries creates the threat of downward mobility for middle-class minorities.[34]

Rather than offering opportunities to minorities, the cities have become centers of poverty. Large concentrations of Blacks and Hispanics are trapped in cities in which the urban employment base is shifting. Today inner cities are shifting away from being centers of production and distribution of physical goods toward being centers of administration, information, exchange, trade, finance, and government service. Conversely, these changes in local employment structures have been accompanied by a shift in the demographic composition of large central cities away from European white to predominantly Black and Hispanic, with rising unemployment. The transfer of jobs away from central cities to the suburbs has created a residential job opportunity mismatch that literally leaves minorities behind in the inner city. Without adequate training or credentials, they are relegated to low-paying, nonadvancing exploitative service work or they are unemployed. Thus, Blacks have become, for the most part, superfluous people in cities that once provided them with opportunities.

The composition and size of cities' overall employment bases have also changed. During the past two decades most older, larger cities have experienced substantial job growth in occupations associated with knowledge-intensive service industries. However, job growth in these high-skill, predominantly white-collar industries has not compensated for employment declines in manufacturing, wholesale trade, and other predominantly blue-collar industries that once constituted the economic backbone of Black urban employment.[35]

While cities once sustained large numbers of less skilled persons, today's service industries typically have high educational requisites for entry. Knowledge and information jobs in the central cities are virtually closed to minorities given the required technological education and skill level. Commuting between central cities and outlying areas is increasingly common; white-collar workers commute daily from their suburban residences to the central business districts while streams of inner-city residents are commuting to their blue-collar jobs in outlying nodes.[36]

An additional structural impediment inner-city minorities face is their increased distance from current sources of blue-collar and other entry-level jobs. Because the industries that provide these jobs have moved to the suburbs and nonmetropolitan peripheries, racial discrimination and inadequate incomes of inner-city minorities now have the additional impact of preventing many from moving out of the inner city in order to maintain their access to traditional sources of employment. The dispersed nature of job growth makes public transportation from inner-city neighborhoods impractical, requiring virtually all city residents who work in peripheral areas to commute by personally owned automobiles. The severity of this mismatch is documented by John Kasarda: "More than one half of the minority households in Philadelphia and Boston are without a means of personal transportation. New York City's proportions are even higher with only three of ten black or Hispanic households having a vehicle available."[37]

This economic restructuring is characterized by an overall pattern of uneven development. Manufacturing industries have declined in the North and Midwest while new growth industries, such as computers and communications equipment, are locating in the southern and southwestern part of the nation. This regional shift has produced some gains for Blacks in the South, where Black poverty rates have declined. Given the large minority populations in the sunbelt, it is conceivable that industrial restructuring could offset the economic threats to racial equality. However, the sunbelt expansion has been based largely on low-wage, labor-intensive enterprises that use large numbers of underpaid minority workers, and a decline in the northern industrial sector continues to leave large numbers of Blacks and Hispanics without work.

Marriage

The connection between declining Black employment opportunities (especially male joblessness) and the explosive growth of Black families headed by single women is the basis of William J. Wilson's analysis of the underclass. Several recent studies conducted by Wilson and his colleagues at the University of Chicago have established this link.[38] Wilson and Kathryn Neckerman have documented the relationship between increased male joblessness and female-headed households. By devising an indicator called "the index of marriageable males," they reveal a long-term decline in the proportion of Black men, and particularly young Black men, who are in a position to support a family. Their indicators include mortality and incarceration rates, as well as labor-force participation rates, and they reveal that the proportion of Black men in unstable economic situations is much higher than indicated in current unemployment figures.[39]

Wilson's analysis treats marriage as an opportunity structure that no longer exists for large numbers of Black people. Consider, for example, why the majority of pregnant Black teenagers do not marry. In 1960, 42 percent of Black teenagers who had babies were unmarried; by 1970 the rate jumped to 63 percent and by 1983 it was 89 percent.[40] According to Wilson, the increase is tied directly to the changing labor-market status of young Black males. He cites the well-established relationship between joblessness and marital instability in support of his argument that "pregnant teenagers are more likely to marry if their boyfriends are working."[41] Out-of-wedlock births are sometimes encouraged by families and absorbed into the kinship system because marrying the suspected father would mean adding someone who was unemployed to the family's financial burden.[42] Adaptation to structural conditions leaves Black women disproportionately separated, divorced, and solely responsible for their children. The mother-only family structure is thus the consequence, not the cause, of poverty.

Community

These changes in employment and marriage patterns have been accompanied by changes in the social fabric of cities. "The Kerner Report Twenty Years Later," a conference of the 1988 Commission on the Cities, highlighted the growing isolation of Blacks and Hispanics.[43] Not only is inner-city poverty worse and more persistent than it was twenty years ago, but ghettos and barrios have become isolated and deteriorating societies with their own economies and with increasingly isolated social institutions, including schools, families, businesses, churches, and hospitals. According to Wilson, this profound social transformation is reflected not only in the high rates of joblessness, crime, and poverty but also in a changing socioeconomic class structure. As Black middle-class professionals left the central city, so too did working-class Blacks. Wilson uses the term "concentration effects" to capture the experiences of low-income families who now make up the majority of those who live in inner cities. The most disadvantaged families are disproportionately concentrated in the sections of the inner city that are plagued by joblessness, lawlessness, and a general milieu of desperation. Without working-class or middle-class role models these families have little in common with mainstream society.[44]

The departure of the Black working and middle classes means more than a loss of role models, however. As David Ellwood has observed, the flight of Black professionals has meant the loss of connections and networks. If successfully employed persons do not live nearby, then the informal methods of finding a job, by which one worker tells someone else of an opening and recommends her or him to the employer, are lost.[45] Concentration and isolation describe the processes that systematically entrench a lack of opportunities in inner cities. Individuals and families are thus left to acquire life's necessities though they are far removed from the channels of social opportunity.

THE CHANGING DEMOGRAPHY OF RACE AND POVERTY

Hispanic poverty, virtually ignored for nearly a quarter of a century, has recently captured the attention of the media and scholars alike. Recent demographic and economic patterns have made "the flow of Hispanics to urban America among the most significant changes occurring in the 1980s."[46]

As the Hispanic presence in the United States has increased in the last decade, Hispanic poverty rates have risen alarmingly. Between 1979 and 1985, the percentage of Latinos who were poor grew from 21.8 percent to 29.0 percent. Nationwide, the poverty rate for all Hispanics was 27.3 percent in 1986. By comparison, the white poverty rate in 1986 was 11 percent; the Black poverty rate was 31.1 percent.[47] Not only have Hispanic poverty rates risen alarmingly, but like Black poverty, Hispanic poverty has become increasingly concentrated in inner cities. Hispanics fall well behind the general population on all measures of social and economic well-being: jobs, income, educational attainment, housing, and health care. Poverty among Hispanics has become so persistent that, if current patterns continue, Hispanics will emerge in the 1990s as the nation's poorest racial-ethnic group.[48] Hispanic poverty has thus become a trend to watch in national discussions of urban poverty and the underclass.

While Hispanics are emerging as the poorest minority group, poverty rates and other socioeconomic indicators vary widely among Hispanic groups. Among Puerto Ricans, 39.9 percent of the population lived below the poverty level in 1986. For Mexicans, 28.4 percent were living in poverty in 1986. For Cubans and Central and South Americans, the poverty rate was much lower: 18.7 percent.[49] Such diversity has led scholars to question the usefulness of this racial-ethnic category that includes all people of Latin American descent.[50] Nevertheless, the labels Hispanic or Latino are useful in general terms in describing the changing racial composition of poverty populations. In spite of the great diversity among Hispanic nationalities, they face common obstacles to becoming incorporated into the economic mainstream of society.

Researchers are debating whether trends of rising Hispanic poverty are irreversible and if those trends point to a permanent underclass among Hispanics. Do macrostructural shifts in the economy and the labor force have the same effects on Blacks and Latinos? According to Joan W. Moore, national economic changes do affect Latinos, but they affect subgroups of Latinos in different ways:

> The movement of jobs and investments out of Rustbelt cities has left many Puerto Ricans living in a bleak ghetto economy. This same movement has had a different effect on Mexican Americans living in the Southwest. As in the North, many factories with job ladders have disappeared. Most of the newer Sunbelt industries offer either high paying jobs for which few Hispanics are trained or low paying ones that provide few opportunities for advancement. Those industries that depend on immigrant

labor (such as clothing manufacturing in Los Angeles) often seriously exploit their workers, so the benefits to Hispanics in the Southwest of this influx of industries and investments are mixed. Another subgroup, Cubans in Miami, work and live in an enclave economy that appears to be unaffected by this shift in the national economy.[51]

Because shifts in the subregional economies seem more important to Hispanics than changes in the national economy, Moore is cautious about applying William Wilson's analysis of how the underclass is created.

Opportunity structures have not declined in a uniform manner for Latinos. Yet Hispanic poverty, welfare dependence, and unemployment rates are greatest in regions that have been transformed by macrostructural economic changes. In some cities, Puerto Rican poverty and unemployment rates are steadily converging with, and in some cases exceeding, the rates of Blacks. In 1986, 40 percent of Puerto Ricans in the United States lived below the poverty level and 70 percent of Puerto Rican children lived in poverty.[52]

Family structure is also affected by economic dislocation. Among Latinos, the incidence of female-headed households is highest for Puerto Ricans—43.3 percent—compared to 19.2 percent for Mexicans, 17.7 for Cubans, and 25.5 percent for Central and South Americans.[53] The association between national economic shifts and high rates of social dislocation among Hispanics provides further evidence for the structural argument that economic conditions rather than culture create distinctive forms of racial poverty. . . .

NOTES

1. Mary Corcoran, Greg J. Duncan, Gerald Gurin, and Patricia Gurin, "Myth and Reality: The Causes and Persistence of Poverty," *Journal of Policy Analysis and Management* 4, no. 4 (1985): 516–36.

2. Mary Corcoran, Greg J. Duncan, and Martha S. Hill, "The Economic Fortunes of Women and Children: Lessons from the Panel Study of Income Dynamics," *Signs: Journal of Women in Culture and Society* 10, no. 2 (Winter 1984): 232–48.

3. Daniel P. Moynihan, "The Negro Family: The Case for National Action," in *The Moynihan Report and the Politics of Controversy*, ed. L. Rainwater and W. L. Yancy (Cambridge, Mass.: MIT Press, 1967), 39–132.

4. Margaret Cerullo and Marla Erlien, "Beyond the 'Normal Family': A Cultural Critique of Women's Poverty," in *For Crying Out Loud*, ed. Rochelle Lefkowitz and Ann Withorn (New York: Pilgrim Press, 1986), 246–60.

5. Moynihan, 47.

6. Leith Mullings, "Anthropological Perspectives on the Afro-American Family," *American Journal of Social Psychiatry* 6, no. 1 (Winter 1986): 11–16; see the following revisionist works on the Black family: Andrew Billingsley, *Black Families in White America* (Englewood Cliffs, N.J.: Prentice-Hall, 1968); Robert Hill, *The Strengths of Black Families* (New York: Emerson-Hall, 1972); Herbert Gutman, *The Black Family in Slavery and Freedom* (New York: Pantheon, 1976); Joyce Ladner, *Tomorrow's Tomorrow: The Black*

Woman (New York: Doubleday, 1971); Elliot Leibow, *Talley's Corner: A Study of Negro Street Corner Men* (Boston: Little, Brown, 1967); Carol Stack, *All Our Kin* (New York: Harper & Row, 1974).

7. William J. Wilson and Robert Aponte, "Urban Poverty," *Annual Review of Sociology* 11 (1985): 231–58, esp. 241.

8. For a review of recent studies, see ibid.

9. Daniel Patrick Moynihan, *Family and Nation* (San Diego: Harcourt, Brace, Jovanovich, 1986).

10. "The Vanishing Family: Crisis in Black America," narrated by Bill Moyers, Columbia Broadcasting System (CBS) Special Report, January 1986.

11. "Hard Times for Black America," *Dollars and Sense*, no. 115 (April 1986), 5–7.

12. Nicholas Lemann, "The Origins of the Underclass: Part 1," *Atlantic Monthly* (June 1986), 31–55; Nicholas Lemann, "The Origins of the Underclass: Part 2," *Atlantic Monthly* (July 1986), 54–68.

13. Lemann, "Part 1," 35.

14. Ibid.

15. Jim Sleeper, "Overcoming 'Underclass': More Jobs Are Still the Key," *In These Times* (June 11–24, 1986), 16.

16. Corcoran et al. (n. 1 above), 517.

17. Martha S. Hill and Michael Ponza, "Poverty and Welfare Dependence Across Generations," *Economic Outlook U.S.A.* (Summer 1983), 61–64, esp. 64.

18. Anne Rueter, "Myths of Poverty," *Research News* (July–September 1984), 18–19.

19. Mary Jo Bane, "Household Composition and Poverty," in *Fighting Poverty*, ed. Sheldon H. Danziger and Daniel H. Weinberg (Cambridge, Mass.: Harvard University Press, 1986), 209–31.

20. Ibid.

21. Betsy Dworkin, "40% of the Poor Are Children," *New York Times Book Review* (March 2, 1986), 9.

22. Bane, 277.

23. Martha Hill, "Trends in the Economic Situation of U.S. Families and Children, 1970–1980," in *American Families and the Economy*, ed. Richard R. Nelson and Felicity Skidmore (Washington, D.C.: National Academy Press, 1983), 9–53, esp. 38.

24. Charles Murray, *Losing Ground* (New York: Basic, 1984).

25. David T. Ellwood, *Poor Support* (New York: Basic, 1988).

26. Sheldon Danziger and Peter Gottschalk, "The Poverty of *Losing Ground*," *Challenge* 28 (May/June 1985): 32–38.

27. William A. Darity and Samuel L. Meyers, "Does Welfare Dependency Cause Female Headship? The Case of the Black Family," *Journal of Marriage and the Family* 46, no. 4 (November 1984): 765–79.

28. David T. Ellwood and Lawrence H. Summers, "Poverty in America: Is Welfare the Answer or the Problem?" in *Fighting Poverty* (n. 19 above), 78–105.

29. Ibid., 96.

30. "The Costs of Being Black," *Research News* 38, nos. 11–12 (November–December 1987): 8–10.

31. Barry Bluestone and Bennett Harrison, *The Deindustrialization of America* (New York: Basic, 1982), 54.

32. Barry Bluestone, Bennett Harrison, and Lucy Gorham, "Storm Clouds on the Horizon: Labor Market Crisis and Industrial Policy," 68, as cited in "Hard Times for Black America" (n. 11 above).

33. Richard Child Hill and Cynthia Negrey, "Deindustrialization and Racial Minorities in the Great Lakes Region, U.S.A.," in *The Reshaping of America: Social Consequences of the Changing Economy*, ed. D. Stanley Eitzen and Maxine Baca Zinn (Englewood Cliffs, N.J.: Prentice-Hall, 1989), 168–77.

34. Elliot Currie and Jerome H. Skolnick, *America's Problems: Social Issues and Public Policy* (Boston: Little, Brown, 1984), 82.

35. John D. Kasarda, "Caught in a Web of Change," *Society* 21 (November–December 1983): 41–47.

36. Ibid., 45–47.

37. John D. Kasarda, "Urban Change and Minority Opportunities," in *The New Urban Reality*, ed. Paul E. Peterson (Washington, D.C.: Brookings Institution, 1985), 33–68, esp. 55.

38. William J. Wilson with Kathryn Neckerman, "Poverty and Family Structure: The Widening Gap between Evidence and Public Policy Issues," in *The Truly Disadvantaged*, by William J. Wilson (Chicago: University of Chicago Press, 1987), 63–92.

39. Ibid.

40. Jerelyn Eddings, "Children Having Children," *Baltimore Sun* (March 2, 1986), 71.

41. As quoted in ibid., 71.

42. Noel A. Cazenave, "Alternate Intimacy, Marriage, and Family Lifestyles among Low-Income Black Americans," *Alternative Lifestyles* 3, no. 4 (November 1980): 425–44.

43. "The Kerner Report Updated" (Racine, Wis.: Report of the 1988 Commission on the Cities, March 1, 1988).

44. Wilson, *The Truly Disadvantaged* (n. 38 above), 62.

45. Ellwood (n. 25 above), 204.

46. Paul E. Peterson, "Introduction: Technology, Race, and Urban Policy," in *The New Urban Reality*, ed. Paul E. Peterson (Washington, D.C.: Brookings Institution, 1985), 1–35, esp. 22.

47. Jennifer Juarez Robles, "Hispanics Emerging as Nation's Poorest Minority Group," *Chicago Reporter* 17, no. 6 (June 1988): 1–3.

48. Ibid., 2–3.

49. Ibid., 3.

50. Alejandro Portes and Cynthia Truelove, "Making Sense of Diversity: Recent Research on Hispanic Minorities in the United States," *Annual Review of Sociology* 13 (1987): 359–85.

51. Joan W. Moore, "An Assessment of Hispanic Poverty: Does a Hispanic Underclass Exist?" *Tomás Rivera Center Report* 2, no. 1 (Fall 1988): 8–9.

52. Robles, 3.

53. U.S. Bureau of the Census, *Current Population Reports*, Series P-20, nos. 416, 422 (Washington, D.C.: Government Printing Office, March 1987).

R E A D I N G

21

The Second Shift: Working Parents and the Revolution at Home

ARLIE HOCHSCHILD, WITH ANNE MACHUNG

Between 8:05 A.M. and 6:05 P.M., both Nancy and Evan are away from home, working a "first shift" at full-time jobs. The rest of the time they deal with the varied tasks of the second shift: shopping, cooking, paying bills; taking care of the car, the garden, and yard; keeping harmony with Evan's mother who drops over quite a bit, "concerned" about Joey, with neighbors, their voluble baby-sitter, and each other. And Nancy's talk reflects a series of second-shift thoughts: "We're out of barbecue sauce. . . . Joey needs a Halloween costume. . . . The car needs a wash. . . ." and so on. She reflects a certain "second-shift sensibility," a continual attunement to the task of striking and restriking the right emotional balance between child, spouse, home, and outside job.

When I first met the Holts, Nancy was absorbing far more of the second shift than Evan. She said she was doing 80 percent of the housework and 90 percent of the childcare. Evan said she did 60 percent of the housework, 70 percent of the childcare. Joey said, "I vacuum the rug, and fold the dinner napkins," finally concluding, "Mom and I do it all." A neighbor agreed with Joey. Clearly, between Nancy and Evan, there was a "leisure gap": Evan had more than Nancy. I asked both of them, in separate interviews, to explain to me how they had dealt with housework and childcare since their marriage began.

One evening in the fifth year of their marriage, Nancy told me, when Joey was two months old and almost four years before I met the Holts, she first seriously raised the issue with Evan. "I told him: 'Look, Evan, it's not working. I do the housework, I take the major care of Joey, *and* I work a full-time job. I get pissed. This is *your* house too. Joey is *your* child too. It's not all *my* job to care for them.' When I cooled down I put to him, 'Look, how about this: I'll cook Mondays, Wednesdays, and Fridays. You cook Tuesdays, Thursdays, and Saturdays. And we'll share or go out Sundays.' "

According to Nancy, Evan said he didn't like "rigid schedules." He said he didn't necessarily agree with her standards of housekeeping, and didn't like that standard "imposed" on him, especially if she was "sluffing off" tasks on him, which from time to time he felt she was. But he went along with the idea in principle. Nancy said the first week of the new plan went as follows: On Monday, she cooked. For Tuesday, Evan planned a meal that required shopping for a few ingredients, but on his way home he forgot to shop for them. He came home, saw nothing he could use in the refrigerator or in the cupboard, and suggested to Nancy that they go out for Chinese food. On Wednesday, Nancy cooked. On Thursday morning, Nancy reminded Evan, "Tonight it's your turn." That night Evan fixed hamburgers and french fries and Nancy was quick to praise him. On Friday, Nancy cooked. On Saturday, Evan forgot again.

As this pattern continued, Nancy's reminders became sharper. The sharper they became, the more actively Evan forgot—perhaps anticipating even sharper reprimands if he resisted more directly. This cycle of passive refusal followed by disappointment and anger gradually tightened, and before long the struggle had spread to the task of doing the laundry. Nancy said it was only fair that Evan share the laundry. He agreed in principle, but anxious that Evan would not share, Nancy wanted a clear, explicit agreement. "You ought to wash and fold every other load," she had told him. Evan experienced this "plan" as a yoke around his neck. On many weekdays, at this point, a huge pile of laundry sat like a disheveled guest on the living-room couch.

In her frustration, Nancy began to make subtle emotional jabs at Evan. "I don't know *what's* for dinner," she would say with a sigh. Or "I can't cook now, I've got to deal with this pile of laundry." She tensed at the slightest criticism about household disorder; if Evan wouldn't do the housework, he had absolutely *no* right to criticize how she did it. She would burst out angrily at Evan. She recalled telling him: "After work *my* feet are just as tired as *your* feet. I'm just as wound up as you are. I come home. I cook dinner. I wash and I clean. Here we are, planning a second child, and I can't cope with the one we have."

About two years after I first began visiting the Holts, I began to see their problem in a certain light: as a conflict between their two gender ideologies. Nancy wanted to be the sort of woman who was needed and appreciated both at home and at work—like Lacey, she told me, on the television show "Cagney and Lacey." She wanted Evan to appreciate her for being a caring social worker, a committed wife, and a wonderful mother. But she cared just as much that she be able to appreciate *Evan* for what *he* contributed at home, not just for how he supported the family. She would feel proud to explain to women friends that she was married to one of these rare "new men."

A gender ideology is often rooted in early experience, and fueled by motives formed early on and such motives can often be traced to some cautionary tale in early life. So it was for Nancy. Nancy described her mother:

> My mom was wonderful, a real aristocrat, but she was also terribly depressed being a housewife. My dad treated her like a doormat. She didn't have any self-confidence. And growing up, I can remember her being really depressed. I grew up bound and determined not to be like her and not to marry a man like my father. As long as Evan doesn't do the housework, I feel it means he's going to be like my father—coming home, putting his feet up, and hollering at my mom to serve him. That's my biggest fear. I've had *bad* dreams about that.

Nancy thought that women friends her age, also in traditional marriages, had come to similarly bad ends. She described a high school friend: "Martha barely made it through City College. She had no interest in learning anything. She spent nine years trailing around behind her husband [a salesman]. It's a miserable marriage. She hand washes all his shirts. The high point of her life was when she was eighteen and the two of us were running around Miami Beach in a Mustang convertible. She's gained seventy pounds and she hates her life." To Nancy, Martha was a younger version of her mother, depressed, lacking in self-esteem, a cautionary tale whose moral was "if you want to be happy, develop a career and get your husband to share at home." Asking Evan to help again and again felt like "hard work" but it was essential to establishing her role as a career woman.

For his own reasons, Evan imagined things very differently. He loved Nancy and if Nancy loved being a social worker, he was happy and proud to support her in it. He knew that because she took her caseload so seriously, it was draining work. But at the same time, he did not see why, just because she chose this demanding career, *he* had to change *his own* life. Why should her personal decision to work outside the home require him to do more inside it? Nancy earned about two-thirds as much as Evan, and her salary was a big help, but as Nancy confided, "If push came to shove, we could do without it." Nancy was a social worker because she loved it. Doing daily chores at home was thankless work, and certainly not something Evan needed her to appreciate about him. Equality in the second shift meant a loss in his standard of living, and despite all the high-flown talk, he felt he hadn't *really* bargained for it. He was happy to help Nancy at home if she needed help; that was fine. That was only decent. But it was too sticky a matter "committing" himself to sharing.

Two other beliefs probably fueled his resistance as well. The first was his suspicion that if he shared the second shift with Nancy, she would "dominate him." Nancy would ask him to do this, ask him to do that. It felt to Evan as if Nancy had won so many small victories that he had to draw the line somewhere.

Nancy had a declarative personality; and as Nancy said, "Evan's mother sat me down and told me once that I was too forceful, that Evan needed to take more authority." Both Nancy and Evan agreed that Evan's sense of career and self was in fact shakier than Nancy's. He had been unemployed. She never had. He had had some bouts of drinking in the past. Drinking was foreign to her. Evan thought that sharing housework would upset a certain balance of power that felt culturally "right." He held the purse strings and made the major decisions about large purchases (like their house) because he "knew more about finances" and because he'd chipped in more inheritance than she when they married. His job difficulties had lowered his self-respect, and now as a couple they had achieved some ineffable "balance"—tilted in his favor, she thought—which, if corrected to equalize the burden of chores, would result in his giving in "too much." A certain driving anxiety behind Nancy's strategy of actively renegotiating roles had made Evan see agreement as "giving in." When he wasn't feeling good about work, he dreaded the idea of being under his wife's thumb at home.

Underneath these feelings, Evan perhaps also feared that Nancy was avoiding taking care of *him*. His own mother, a mild-mannered alcoholic, had by imperceptible steps phased herself out of a mother's role, leaving him very much on his own. Perhaps a personal motive to prevent that happening in his marriage—a guess on my part, and unarticulated on his—underlay his strategy of passive resistance. And he wasn't altogether wrong to fear this. Meanwhile, he felt he was "offering" Nancy the chance to stay home, or cut back her hours, and that she was refusing his "gift," while Nancy felt that, given her feelings about work, this offer was hardly a gift.

In the sixth year of her marriage, when Nancy again intensified her pressure on Evan to commit himself to equal sharing, Evan recalled saying, "Nancy, why don't you cut back to half time, that way you can fit everything in." At first Nancy was baffled: "We've been married all this time, and you *still* don't get it. Work is important to me. I worked *hard* to get my MSW. Why *should* I give it up?" Nancy also explained to Evan and later to me, "I think my degree and my job has been my way of reassuring myself that I won't end up like my mother." Yet she'd received little emotional support in getting her degree from either her parents or in-laws. (Her mother had avoided asking about her thesis, and her in-laws, though invited, did not attend her graduation, later claiming they'd never been invited.)

In addition, Nancy was more excited about seeing her elderly clients in tenderloin hotels than Evan was about selling couches to furniture salesmen with greased-back hair. Why shouldn't Evan make as many compromises with his career ambitions and his leisure as she'd made with hers? She couldn't see it Evan's way, and Evan couldn't see it hers.

In years of alternating struggle and compromise, Nancy had seen only fleeting mirages of cooperation, visions that appeared when she got sick or withdrew, and disappeared when she got better or came forward.

After seven years of loving marriage, Nancy and Evan had finally come to a terrible impasse. Their emotional standard of living had drastically declined: they began to snap at each other, to criticize, to carp. Each felt taken advantage of: Evan, because his offering of a good arrangement was deemed unacceptable, and Nancy, because Evan wouldn't do what she deeply felt was "fair."

This struggle made its way into their sexual life—first through Nancy directly, and then through Joey. Nancy had always disdained any form of feminine wiliness or manipulation. Her family saw her as "a flaming feminist" and that was how she saw herself. As such, she felt above the underhanded ways traditional women used to get around men. She mused, "When I was a teenager, I vowed I would *never* use sex to get my way with a man. It is not self-respecting; it's demeaning. But when Evan refused to carry his load at home, I did, I used sex, I said, 'Look, Evan, I would not be this exhausted and asexual every night if I didn't have so much to face every morning.' " She felt reduced to an old "strategy," and her modern ideas made her ashamed of it. At the same time, she'd run out of other, modern ways.

The idea of a separation arose, and they became frightened. Nancy looked at the deteriorating marriages and fresh divorces of couples with young children around them. One unhappy husband they knew had become so uninvolved in family life (they didn't know whether his unhappiness made him uninvolved, or whether his lack of involvement had caused his wife to be unhappy) that his wife left him. In another case, Nancy felt the wife had "nagged" her husband so much that he abandoned her for another woman. In both cases, the couple was less happy after the divorce than before, and both wives took the children and struggled desperately to survive financially. Nancy took stock. She asked herself, "Why wreck a marriage over a dirty frying pan?" Is it really worth it?

UPSTAIRS-DOWNSTAIRS: A FAMILY MYTH AS "SOLUTION"

Not long after this crisis in the Holts' marriage, there was a dramatic lessening of tension over the issue of the second shift. It was as if the issue was closed. Evan had won. Nancy would do the second shift. Evan expressed vague guilt but beyond that he had nothing to say. Nancy had wearied of continually raising the topic, wearied of the lack of resolution. Now in the exhaustion of defeat, she wanted the struggle to be over too. Evan was "so good" in *other* ways, why debilitate their marriage by continual quarreling. Besides, she told me, "Women always adjust more, don't they?"

One day, when I asked Nancy to tell me who did which tasks from a long list of household chores, she interrupted me with a broad wave of her hand and said, "I do the upstairs, Evan does the downstairs." What does that mean? I asked. Matter-of-factly, she explained that the upstairs included the living room, the dining room, the kitchen, two bedrooms, and two baths. The downstairs meant the garage, a place for storage and hobbies—Evan's hobbies. She explained this as a "sharing" arrangement, without humor or irony—just as Evan did later. Both said they had agreed it was the best solution to their dispute. Evan would take care of the car, the garage, and Max, the family dog. As Nancy explained, "The dog is all Evan's problem. I don't have to deal with the dog." Nancy took care of the rest.

For purposes of accommodating the second shift, then, the Holts' garage was elevated to the full moral and practical equivalent of the rest of the house. For Nancy and Evan, "upstairs and downstairs," "inside and outside," was vaguely described like "half and half," a fair division of labor based on a natural division of their house.

The Holts presented their upstairs-downstairs agreement as a perfectly equitable solution to a problem they "once had." This belief is what we might call a "family myth," even a modest delusional system. Why did they believe it? I think they believed it because they needed to believe it, because it solved a terrible problem. It allowed Nancy to continue thinking of herself as the sort of woman whose husband didn't abuse her—a self-conception that mattered a great deal to her. And it avoided the hard truth that, in his stolid, passive way, Evan had refused to share. It avoided the truth, too, that in their showdown, Nancy was more afraid of divorce than Evan was. This outer cover to their family life, this family myth, was jointly devised. It was an attempt to agree that there was no conflict over the second shift, no tension between their versions of manhood and womanhood, and that the powerful crisis that had arisen was temporary and minor.

The wish to avoid such a conflict is natural enough. But their avoidance was tacitly supported by the surrounding culture, especially the image of the woman with the flying hair. After all, this admirable woman also proudly does the "upstairs" each day without a husband's help and without conflict.

After Nancy and Evan reached their upstairs-downstairs agreement, their confrontations ended. They were nearly forgotten. Yet, as she described their daily life months after the agreement, Nancy's resentment still seemed alive and well. For example, she said:

> Evan and I eventually divided the labor so that I do the upstairs and Evan does the downstairs and the dog. So the dog is my husband's problem. But when I was getting the dog outside and getting Joey ready for childcare, and cleaning up the mess of feeding the cat, and getting the lunches together, and having my son wipe his nose on my outfit so I would have to change—then I was pissed! I felt that I was doing *everything*. All Evan was doing was getting up, having coffee, reading the paper, and saying, "Well, I have to go now," and often forgetting the lunch I'd bothered to make.

She also mentioned that she had fallen into the habit of putting Joey to bed in a certain way: he asked to be swung around by the arms, dropped on the bed, nuzzled and hugged, whispered to in his ear. Joey waited for her attention. He didn't go to sleep without it. But, increasingly, when Nancy tried it at eight or nine, the ritual didn't put Joey to sleep. On the contrary, it woke him up. It was then that Joey began to say he could only go to sleep in his parents' bed, that he began to sleep in their bed and to encroach on their sexual life.

Near the end of my visits, it struck me that Nancy was putting Joey to bed in an "exciting" way, later and later at night, in order to tell Evan something important: "You win, I'll go on doing all the work at home, but I'm angry about it and I'll make you pay." Evan had won the battle but lost the war. According to the family myth, all was well: the struggle had been resolved by the upstairs-downstairs agreement. But suppressed in one area of their marriage, this struggle lived on in another—as Joey's Problem, and as theirs.

NANCY'S "PROGRAM" TO SUSTAIN THE MYTH

There was a moment, I believe, when Nancy seemed to *decide* to give up on this one. She decided to try not to resent Evan. Whether or not other women face a moment just like this, at the very least they face the need to deal with all the feelings that naturally arise from a clash between a treasured ideal and an incompatible reality. In the age of a stalled revolution, it is a problem a great many women face.

Emotionally, Nancy's compromise from time to time slipped; she would forget and grow resentful again. Her new resolve needed maintenance. Only half aware that she was doing so, Nancy went to extraordinary lengths to maintain it. She could tell me now, a year or so after her "decision," in a matter-of-fact and noncritical way: "Evan likes to come home to a hot meal. He doesn't like to clear the table. He doesn't like to do the dishes. He likes to go watch TV. He likes to play with his son when he feels like it and not feel like he should be with him more." She seemed resigned.

Everything was "fine." But it had taken an extraordinary amount of complex "emotion work"—the work of *trying* to feel the "right" feeling, the feeling she wanted to feel—to make and keep everything "fine." Across the nation at this particular time in history, this emotion work is often all that stands between the stalled revolution on the one hand, and broken marriages on the other.

HOW MANY HOLTS?

In one key way the Holts were typical of the vast majority of two-job couples: their family life had become the shock absorber for a stalled revolution whose origin lay far outside it—in economic and cultural trends that bear very differently on men and women. Nancy was reading books, newspaper articles, and watching TV programs on the changing role of women. Evan wasn't. Nancy felt benefited by these changes; Evan didn't. In her ideals and in reality, Nancy was more different from her mother than Evan was from his father, for the culture and economy were in general pressing change faster upon women like her than upon men like Evan. Nancy had gone to college; her mother hadn't. Nancy had a professional job; her mother never had. Nancy had the idea that she should be equal with her husband; her mother hadn't been much exposed to that idea in her day. Nancy felt she should share the job of earning money, and that Evan should share the work at home; her mother hadn't imagined that was possible. Evan went to college, his father (and the other boys in his family, though not the girls) had gone too. Work was important to Evan's identity as a man as it had been for his father before him. Indeed, Evan felt the same way about family roles as his father had felt in his day. The new job opportunities and the feminist movement of the 1960s and '70s had transformed Nancy but left Evan pretty much the same. And the friction created by this difference between them moved to the issue of second shift as metal to a magnet. By the end, Evan did less house-work and childcare than most men married to working women—but not much less. Evan and Nancy were also typical of nearly 40 percent of the marriages I studied in their clash of gender ideologies and their corresponding difference in notion about what constituted a "sacrifice" and what did not. By far the most common form of mismatch was like that between Nancy, an egalitarian, and Evan, a transitional.

But for most couples, the tensions between strategies did not move so quickly and powerfully to issues of housework and childcare. Nancy pushed harder than most women to get her husband to share the work at home, and she also lost more overwhelmingly than the few other women who fought that hard. Evan pursued his strategy of passive resistance with more quiet tenacity than most men, and he allowed himself to become far more marginal to his son's life than most other fathers. The myth of the Holts' "equal" arrangement seemed slightly more odd than other family myths that encapsulated equally powerful conflicts.

Beyond their upstairs-downstairs myth, the Holts tell us a great deal about the subtle ways a couple can encapsulate the tension caused by a struggle over the second shift without resolving the problem or divorcing. Like Nancy Holt, many women struggle to avoid, suppress, obscure, or mystify a frightening conflict over the second shift. They do not struggle like this because they started off wanting to, or because such struggle is inevitable or because women inevitably lose, but because they are forced to choose between equality and marriage. And they choose marriage. When asked about "ideal" relations between men and women in general, about what they want for their daughters, about what "ideally" they'd like in their own marriage, most working mothers "wished" their men would share the work at home.

But many "wish" it instead of "want" it. Other goals—like keeping peace at home—come first. Nancy Holt did some extraordinary behind-the-scenes emotion work to prevent her ideals from clashing with her marriage. In the end, she had confined and miniaturized her ideas of equality successfully enough to do two things she badly wanted to do: feel like a feminist, and live at peace with a man who was not. Her program had "worked." Evan won on the reality of the situation, because Nancy did the second shift. Nancy won on the cover story; they would talk about it as if they shared.

Nancy wore the upstairs-downstairs myth as an ideological cloak to protect her from the contradictions in her marriage and from the cultural and economic forces that press upon it. Nancy and Evan Holt were caught on opposite sides of the gender revolution occurring all around them. Through the 1960s, 1970s, and 1980s masses of women entered the public world of work—but went only so far up the occupational ladder. They tried for "equal" marriages, but got only so far in achieving it. They married men who liked them to work at the office but who wouldn't share the extra month a year at home. When confusion about the identity of the working woman created a cultural vacuum in the 1970s and 1980s, the image of the supermom quietly glided in. She made the "stall" seem normal and happy. But beneath the happy image of the woman with the flying hair are modern marriages like the Holts', reflecting intricate webs of tension, and the huge, hidden emotional cost to women, men, and children of having to "manage" inequality. Yet on the surface, all we might see would be Nancy Holt bounding confidently out the door at 8:30 A.M. briefcase in one hand, Joey in the other. All we might hear would be Nancy's and Evan's talk about their marriage as happy, normal, even "equal"—because equality was so important to Nancy.

CHAPTER 9

◆

FAMILY

DIVERSITY

R E A D I N G

22

Intergenerational Relationships
Across Cultures

PAULETTE MOORE HINES, NYDIA GARCIA-PRETO, MONICA MCGOLDRICK,
RHEA ALMEIDA, AND SUSAN WELTMAN

The powerful influence of ethnicity on how individuals think, feel, and behave
has only recently begun to be considered in family therapy training and practice
as well as in the larger human services delivery system.

In our efforts to promote the melting-pot myth and the notion that all individuals are equal, we tend to perpetuate the notion that to be different is to be
deficient or bad. Although similarities exist across individuals and groups in this
country and the push for acculturation is strong, differences among groups need
to be recognized, valued, and integrated into our thinking and practice of family
therapy. Human behavior cannot be understood properly in isolation from the
context in which an individual is embedded.

Ethnicity is a critical, but not sufficient, consideration for understanding
personal development and family life throughout the life cycle. McGoldrick
(1982) defined ethnicity as a sense of commonality transmitted over genera-

tions by the family and reinforced by the surrounding community. Our cultural values and assumptions, often unconscious, influence every aspect of our being, including what we label as a problem, how we communicate, beliefs about the cause of a problem, whom we prefer as a helper, and what kind of solutions we prefer.

The rules governing intergenerational relationships in families throughout the life cycle vary across cultures. For instance, considerable differences exist among ethnic groups as to the degree of intergenerational dependence and sharing expected between adult children and their aging parents. Whereas Italians or Greeks are likely to grow up with the expectation that eventually they will take care of their parents, white Anglo-Saxon Protestant (WASP) parents' worst nightmare might be that eventually they will have to depend on their child for support. Minimal interdependence is expected or fostered so that adult children feel relatively guilt free when they have to put their parents in a nursing home. Conversely, adult children avoid asking their parents for support beyond paying for their education.

Another significant difference among groups is the way in which cultures define responsibilities and obligations according to gender roles. Groups differ profoundly in their expectations of motherhood and fatherhood as well as in their treatment of sons and daughters. Families evolve through the life cycle and encounter conflicts at different developmental phases. Marriage, child rearing, leaving home, and caring for the elderly demand changes in relationships that are inherently stressful, especially when ascribed cultural rules for dealing with these stages are challenged or cease to be functional. When conflict erupts, families usually attempt resolution by drawing on the strengths and legacies passed from one generation to the next.

Needless to say, it is difficult to share personal and clinical observations about our respective ethnic groups without generalizing. Thus, readers should understand that, among other variables, the following portraits of ethnic groups are affected by gender, generation, residence, education, socioeconomic status, and migration as well as by the life experience of the authors. We acknowledge that significant variations exist within groups and that ethnic values and practices are constantly evolving.

Clinicians need to remain open to what families tell us about themselves and take care to enter the therapeutic process without predetermined conclusions about families based merely on ethnic generalizations. Equally important is the fact that clinicians neither formulate theories nor conduct interventions in a vacuum. Our cultural lenses dictate our world view and what we consider "normal." It is also useful to have a point of departure in one's work that is larger than one's own limited experiences; hypotheses are simply starting points from which one proceeds to look for data that support or contradict one's initial notions. In the interests of offering that starting point for practitioners, this article addresses rules for relationships, common conflicts, resources and/or legacies that promote or hinder conflict resolution, and implications for assessment and intervention with African American, Hispanic, Irish, Asian Indian, and Jewish families.

AFRICAN AMERICAN FAMILIES

African traditions, the experience of slavery, assimilation into the American mainstream, the psychological scars of past and current discrimination, age, education, religion, and geographic origins allow for great heterogeneity within African American culture. However, survival issues based on interdependence and oppression due to racism are commonalities that transcend individual and group differences.

Despite conscious and consistent efforts by members of the dominant culture to erase all remnants of African culture from the memories and practices of African slaves and their descendants, a sense of "oneness," as exemplified in the practice of greeting one another as "sister" or "brother," is critical to understanding the dynamics of relationships among African Americans. A general assumption exists among African Americans that regardless of the educational or economic advantages of individuals, the legacy of slavery, racism, and oppression is a common bond.

Family relationships, more so than bank accounts, represent "wealth" and guarantee emotional and concrete support in the face of negative feedback from the larger society. The emotional significance of relationships is not determined solely by the immediacy of blood ties. In fact, "family" is an extended system of blood-related kin and persons informally adopted into this system (Hines & Boyd-Franklin, 1982; Boyd-Franklin, 1989). Extended-family systems tend to be large and constantly expanding as new individuals and their families are incorporated through marriage. Commonly, three or four generations live in proximity, sometimes residing in the same household.

Strong value is placed on loyalty and responsibility to others. This value is reinforced through the belief that everything one does in the public domain reflects on one's family and other African Americans. Similarly, African Americans often believe that one does not succeed just for oneself but for one's family and race as well. In essence, African Americans believe that "you are your brother's keeper."

Among African Americans, respect is shown to others because of their intrinsic worth and character, not for their status or what they have accumulated in material wealth. Personal accomplishments are considered the dual consequence of individual effort and, importantly, also due to the sacrifice of others. Success is to be acknowledged and celebrated but not overemphasized, as positive outcomes cannot be guaranteed despite one's efforts in a racist environment. Furthermore, even when success is achieved, it may be short lived. Intelligence and education without character and "common sense" have little value. Good character involves respect for those who helped one succeed and survive difficult circumstances. Family members are expected to stay connected and to reach out and assist others who are in need (McGoldrick, Garcia-Preto, Hines, & Lee, 1989).

The elderly are held in reverence. Older women, more than men, are called upon to impart wisdom as well as to provide functional support to younger family members. Older adults are testimony to the fact that one not only can survive but can transcend difficult circumstances as well. They serve as models for self-sacrifice, personal strength, and integrity. By example, they show that although suffering is inevitable, one can grow from hardship and adversity. Children and adults are expected to show verbal and nonverbal "respect" to the elderly. Titles such as Mr., Mrs., Aunt, and Uncle are used to convey respect, deriving from the slavery and post-slavery eras during which African American men and women, irrespective of their age, were treated and referred to as objects or children.

Children and adolescents may express their feelings and opinions but are not allowed to argue with adults after a final decision has been made. Although adults have the liberty to voice dissenting opinions to those who are older, younger adults are expected to acknowledge respectfully the older adult's opinion and perspective. To fail to do so shows disrespect for the life experience of the older person. Use of profanity in an intergenerational context is generally not acceptable.

Young adulthood for African Americans is a critical period during which poor decisions and impulsive behavior can have life-long consequences (Hines, 1989). The usual stressors on intergenerational relationships during this phase of the family life cycle can be both eased and complicated by the numerous adults who may be intensely concerned about a young adult's well-being. Young adults with few employment possibilities and who find it difficult to achieve adult status while living at home may move in with relatives until they become economically self-sufficient. They remain subject, however, to older family members' collective efforts to protect them from life hardships that might be avoided.

Some young African American adults fear failure and disappointing significant others. Others fear success as a result of internalizing the older generation's concerns about losing one's cultural connectedness. Some young adults are ambivalent about personal success because they are materially comfortable while significant others, especially parental figures, are struggling for basic survival. Conflicts may arise when younger adults believe that the advice of older adults is not appropriate to the context in which the young adult operates. Sometimes older adults may minimize the concerns and distress of younger people because they feel that such concerns are trivial compared with their difficult life experiences. Consequently, some young adults find it difficult to seek help within their families for fear of being perceived as weak; others are afraid that they will overwhelm family members who are already burdened by other life stresses. Young adults may be reluctant to pursue help from appropriate professionals in the work setting for fear of being negatively labeled as well as adversely affecting opportunities for other African Americans. The consequence of these scenarios is over- or underfunctioning, which may result in or exacerbate internal and intergenerational conflicts.

Similar intergenerational issues may surface in families with young children and adolescents. The role flexibility (exchange of responsibilities) characteristic of African American families allows adults to help children thrive in environments with many "mine fields" (Hines, 1990). The proverb "It takes a village to raise a child" works well as long as roles are clearly defined, rules are consistent, and ultimate authority is clearly established. However, boundaries may not be clearly delineated, which creates confusion. Intergenerational conflicts are most likely to arise as a result of a child's "disrespectful" behavior at home or school, poor academic functioning, and behaviors that may put the youth at risk of compromising his or her personal freedom. The primary concerns are that male adolescents will get into trouble with legal authorities and that female adolescents will act out sexually or, worse, become pregnant. Parents may resort to overfunctioning (i.e., become inflexible) and turn to relatives for help. Male adolescents from female-headed households are particularly inclined to rebel against the power and influence of their mothers and other females in positions of authority (Hines, 1990).

Although African Americans have the capacity to be openly expressive of their feelings, such expression may be held in check in an effort to minimize intergenerational conflicts. Such conflicts threaten unity and diminish energy needed to deal with everyday life. Conflict often occurs when individuals are perceived to have lost hope, self-respect, and/or self-responsibility; when they are perceived to be wallowing in sorrow, engaging in self-destructive behaviors, or pursuing individual interests without concern for significant others, particularly children and older adults.

Intergenerational conflicts may revolve around whether children are being taught traditional values basic to the survival of African American people. Parents who invest in providing material things and opportunities to their children that were not available to them while growing up may be perceived by other family members as "spoiling" their children. Conflicts are likely to focus on how to teach children survival skills without depriving them of the fruits of the previous generation's labor. . . .

American clients are uncomfortable in groups in which, as the sole African American participant, their problems might seem to be "exceptional" or different from everyone else's. Clients should be offered the opportunity to discuss such concerns, and alternatives should be made available. Young adults should also be encouraged to develop and use natural support groups within their work and social environments if they are struggling under the weight of unrealistic family- or self-imposed expectations as well as challenged by the inherent stress of working in a bicultural setting.

HISPANIC FAMILIES

The web of relationships that extends across generations in Hispanic families provides a support network sustained by rules of mutual obligation. These rules are perpetuated by patterns of caretaking that fulfill expectations of emotional, physical, and economic support for those who need it from those capable of providing it. Rules of respect also play an important role in preserving this intergenerational network of close personal relationships. Children, for example, learn to relate to others according to their age, sex, and social class. When the system works, that is, if sacrifices do not border on martyrdom, the support and emotional acceptance provided can be very healthy and nurturing as well as reassuring and validating.

The sense of responsibility and mutual obligation can be so ingrained among Hispanics that individuals with few resources run the risk of self-sacrifice. Women, in particular, are expected to assume caretaking roles in the family and tend to experience more pressure than do men to devote their lives to the welfare of others. Becoming martyrs gives them special status, in that family members often see their sacrifice as exemplary. However, the price they pay for "carrying this cross" is often too high (Garcia-Preto, 1990). This behavior is reinforced by the cultural concepts of *marianismo* and *hembrismo*, which contribute to the complexity of Hispanic gender roles.

Marianismo stems from the cult of the Virgin Mary, whereby women are considered morally superior to men and, therefore, capable of enduring the suffering inflicted by men (Stevens, 1973). *Hembrismo*, which literally means femaleness, has been described as a cultural revenge to *machismo* (Habach, 1972) and as a frustrated attempt to imitate a male. *Hembrismo*, within a historical context, shares common elements with the women's movement in the areas of social and political goals (Gomez, 1982). *Hembrismo*, according to Comas-Diaz (1989), connotes strength, perseverance, flexibility, and the ability to survive. However, she adds that it can also translate into a woman's attempt to fulfill her multiple-role expectations as a mother, wife, worker, daughter, and community member—in other words, the "superwoman" working a double shift at home and on the job. In therapy, many Hispanic women present symptoms related to *marianista* behavior at home and *hembrista* behavior at work (Comas-Diaz, 1989).

Men, on the other hand, are more likely to assume financial responsibility for elderly parents, younger siblings, and nephews and nieces. This behavior, too, is admired and respected. Grandparents and other elderly relatives, although not expected to contribute financially to the family, often do so indirectly by caring for grandchildren and thus enabling parents to work or go to school. In return for this assistance and by virtue of their being in need, it is expected that the elderly will be cared for by their adult children. If such expectations are not met, intergenerational conflicts are likely to occur throughout the family system.

A common source of intergenerational conflict in Hispanic families who enter therapy is the struggle between parents and children who have grown apart while trying to adapt to American culture. Traditionally, Hispanic children tend to have closer relationships with their mothers than with their fathers. Perhaps because women are responsible for holding the family together, they tend to develop very strong relationships with their children and other family members. This central position in the family system gives them a measure of power, which is reflected in their alliances with children against authoritarian fathers, who are perceived as lacking understanding with regard to emotional issues. Relationships between sons and mothers are close and dependent; it is not uncommon for a son to protect his mother against an abusive husband.

Mothers and daughters also have close relationships, but these are more reciprocal in nature. Mothers teach their daughters how to be good women who deserve the respect of others, especially males, and who will make good wives and mothers. Daughters usually care for their elderly parents, often taking them into their homes when they are widowed. Relationships between Hispanic women and their fathers vary according to family structure. In families in which fathers assume an authoritarian position, the father-daughter relationship may be marked by distance and conflict. While attempting to be protective, fathers may become unreasonable, unapproachable, and highly critical of their daughters' behavior and friends. On the other hand, in families in which men are more submissive and dependent on their wife to make decisions, fathers may develop special alliances with their daughters, who in turn may assume a nurturing role toward them.

When Hispanic families arrive in the United States, the children usually find it easier to learn English and adapt to the new culture than do parents. The parents, on the other hand, may find English too difficult to learn and the new culture unwelcoming and dangerous. They may react by taking refuge in the old culture, expecting their children to do the same. When this occurs, children typically rebel against their parents' rigidity by rejecting parental customs, which are viewed as inferior to the American way of life.

Children may become emotionally distanced from their parents, who often feel they have lost control. Parents usually react by imposing stricter rules; corporal punishment may be used. Commonly, parents will demand respect and obedience, cultural values that are traditionally seen as a solution to misbehavior. Parents may become very strict and overprotective of adolescents, especially if the family lives in a high-crime community where drugs are prevalent. Daughters, especially, may be overprotected because they are viewed as being more vulnerable than males in a society with loose sexual mores. Such patterns of overprotection are more characteristic of families who are isolated or alienated from support systems in the community and when extended-family members are not available (Garcia-Preto, 1982).

Children who are caught in the conflict of cultures and loyalties may develop a negative self-image, which can inhibit their chances for growth and accomplishment. Parents, then, may feel thwarted at every turn and consequently give up on their children. In therapy, it may be useful to see adolescents alone if they are unable to speak freely in front of their parents. Issues of respect and fear about their parents' reactions may inhibit adolescents from speaking about sex, drugs, incest, problems at school, or cultural conflicts at home and in the community. In such instances, obvious goals include helping adolescents define and share with their parents personal issues that affect their relationship in an effort to find compromises. Discussing a family's migratory history and acculturation process may help clarify conflicts over cultural values. The therapist can also encourage parents to redefine privileges and responsibilities and to discuss their genuine concern for the child. By encouraging parents to express their love, concern, and fear to their children, therapists help parents and children relate in a more positive manner (Garcia-Preto, 1982). . . .

As stated earlier, intergenerational conflict is often caused by the inability of one generation to provide care for another. Adult children who are unable to care for their elderly parents, especially if the parents are ill, may experience stress and guilt. Conflicts with siblings and other family members may result. Practitioners need to encourage communication among family members in order to help them find ways to contribute to the care of elderly parents. Women who devote themselves to caring for elderly parents may express their stress and resentment through somatic complaints and/or depression. Therapists can help these women express their resentments openly as well as assist them in finding support from other family members or community resources.

Leaving the family system (e.g., through divorce or separation) is extremely risky for both men and women because it implies loss of control, support, and protection. For couples who are still adjusting to American culture, the loss of the family system can be devastating. For example, women usually depend on other women in the extended family for help with child-rearing and domestic tasks, because men are not expected to share these responsibilities. Without the help of their mother, mother-in-law, grandmothers, aunts, or sisters, Hispanic women may become overburdened and begin demanding assistance from their husband. The husband may, in turn, resent these demands and become argumentative and distant, perhaps turning to alcohol, gambling, or extramarital affairs. The extended family can provide a measure of control for aggression and violence by intervening in arguments and providing advice to couples. Helping couples make connections with relatives, friends, or community supports may be the therapist's most crucial task.

IRISH FAMILIES

Intergenerational relationships among the Irish are not generally characterized by intimacy. Unlike many other groups, such as African Americans, Italians, or Hispanics, who tend to view the extended family as a resource in times of trouble, the Irish tend to take the attitude that having a problem is bad enough, but if your family finds out, you have two problems: the problem and your embarrassment in front of your family. It is said of the Irish that they suffer alone. They do not like others to see them when they are in pain. It is not so much a fear of dependence, as with WASPs, but a sense of embarrassment and humiliation at not being able to keep up appearances. Intergenerational secrets are common. The Irish would often rather tell almost anything to a stranger than to a family member, but if they do share it with a family member it is usually told to someone of the same sex and generation as the teller. . . .

Within the family, intergenerational relationships throughout the life cycle are handled primarily by the mother. She cares for both the old and the young. She views caretaking as her responsibility, as does everyone else in the family. Her main supporters are her daughters, though she might also call on her sisters.

The Irish sense of duty is a wonderful resource. Parents want to "do the right thing" for their children; it is not a lack of care, but a lack of attention to detail that most often interferes with appropriate nurturing of their children. The Irish tend to focus more on their children's conformity to rules than on other aspects of their child's development, such as emotional expression, self-assertiveness, or creativity. Should a child be brought to the school principal for misbehavior, a traditional Irish mother's reaction to the child might be: "I don't want to hear your explanations or excuses. Just never let it happen that the principal has to contact me again." Traditionally, the Irish have believed that children should be seen and not heard. They should not bring outside notoriety to the family, especially for bad behavior. Less emphasis is placed on being a star student than on not standing out from the group for misbehavior. Irish parents tend to have a superficial sense of child psychology, hoping that keeping their children clean, out of trouble, and teaching them right from wrong will get them through. When children develop psychological symptoms, Irish parents are often mystified. When children act out, parents tend to blame outside influences, although privately they blame themselves.

During the child-rearing phase, the biggest problem in Irish families occurs if a child gets in trouble with outside authorities such as the school system. When the adults have problems at home during this phase, for example, if the father is an alcoholic, Irish children can be remarkably inventive in developing strategies to obey family rules of denial while appearing to function well. However, they may later pay a high price emotionally for having learned at an early age to suppress unacceptable feelings.

During the adolescent phase and the launching years, heavy drinking may become a major, often unidentified, problem that the parents—primarily the mother—do not know how to handle. It therefore may be ignored, often with disastrous consequences.

Irish fathers play a peripheral role in intergenerational family relationships, whereas Irish mothers are at the center. They are indomitable. But the stereotype of the "sainted Irish mother" is not totally positive (McGoldrick, 1991; Rudd, 1984; McGoldrick, 1982; Diner, 1983; McKenna, 1979; Scheper-Hughes, 1979); she can also be critical, distant, and lacking in affection, less concerned about nurturing her children than about control and discipline. She may worry about their dirty underwear lest they be in an accident and she be called in to claim the body. She can be sanctimonious, preoccupied with categories of right and wrong and about what the neighbors think, consciously withholding praise of her children for fear it will give them "a swelled head." Such attitudes and behaviors make sense in a culture with such a long history of foreign domination, in which Irish mothers sought control over "something" through whatever means were available to them and felt a need to keep their family in line to minimize the risk of members being singled out for further oppression.

Sons and daughters rarely voice resentment toward their mothers. To do so is to risk guilt and to undermine their admiration for her stoic self-sacrifice. For generations, Irish women have held rule in their families, including control of the family money. Children tend to speak of "my mother's house," dismissing the role of the father (Diner, 1983). Irish mothers often fail to recognize their own strength or ability to intimidate their children, whether through teasing, ridicule, a disapproving glance, or a quick hand. One Irish mother in therapy described her son's arrest for a drunken escapade as follows:

> Joey's afraid of me. I know he is, because when he got arrested and I went down there to pick him up, the policeman expected when I walked in there that he'd see a big witch of a woman coming through the door, because Joey had said to him, "Just promise me one thing, just protect me from my mother." But I didn't do anything. When I went in there, I just gave him a smack across the face, because I didn't need that nonsense.

Implicit in her comment are ridicule for her son's fear of her and a bold assertion of her own righteousness.

Perhaps because of their history of oppression, the Irish tend to communicate indirectly, often believing that putting feelings into words only makes things worse. They can also be uncomfortable with physical affection (Rudd, 1984; McGoldrick, 1982; Barrabe & von Mering, 1953) and tend to relate to their children through fixed labels: "Bold Kathleen," "Poor Paddy," and "That Joey." Children are loved, but not intimately known (Rudd, 1984).

As a result of her need for ambiguous communication and ambivalence with regard to self-assertion, a mother may indirectly belittle her child for "putting himself ahead" while in the same breath chide him for not being more aggressive and achievement oriented. Irish mothers tend to dote on their sons, overprotecting them and drawing them into powerful bonds more intense than their marital tie. Conversely, Irish parents tend to underprotect their daughters, treating them like sisters and often not allowing them much of a childhood by raising them to be overresponsible and self-sufficient, just like the mothers (Byrne & McCarthy, 1986). This failure to protect daughters teaches them to repress personal needs and contributes to an ongoing fatalism, emotional repression, and stoicism in the next generation of women.

Irish women have little expectation of or interest in being taken care of by a man. Their hopes are articulated less often in romantic terms than in aspirations for self-sufficiency. They are often reluctant to give up their freedom and economic independence for marriage and family responsibilities.

What about Irish fathers and daughters? One pattern involves the "dutiful daughter," especially if the mother is absent, who becomes the caretaker for her father without much real intimacy in the relationship. In other families, the daughter may become "Daddy's girl," even his companion, who is sent to bring him home from the bar or chosen to work with him, especially if there is no son in the family. Generally, however, father-daughter relationships are distant, possibly because the father fears that closeness will be confused with trespass of sexual boundaries. Moreover, Irish families are not very good at differentiating among anger, sexuality, and intimacy. A father may maintain distance from his daughter, or perhaps be sarcastic and teasing, not because such behavior reflects his true feelings but because he is unsure how to approach her.

With sons a father may share sports, work, and jokes, although the teasing and ridicule that are so common in Irish parent-child relationships may be very painful to a son. Some Irish fathers remain silent, almost invisible, in the family. Another common pattern is the father who is jovial or silent, except when drinking, at which time he becomes a fearsome, intimidating, larger-than-life antagonist, who returns to his gentler self when sober with no acknowledgment of this transformation. Children are kept off guard in such relationships. They may be drawn to the humor and fun, yet terrified of the unpredictable and violent moods. In cultures with less dissociation of self from negative behaviors (such as among Italians or Puerto Ricans), children may fear a parent who drinks, but they will not be as mystified by parents' denial of an out-of-control situation.

Resentment over class differences may surface when Irish children marry. The Irish tend to measure others hierarchically as being "better than" or "inferior to" themselves. Thus, parents may criticize children for "marrying up" and putting on airs (which usually means marrying a WASP) or may criticize them for "marrying down." Both of these parental reactions are deeply rooted in tensions stemming from the Irish history of oppression by the British, which left the Irish with a deep sense of inferiority.

When Irish children reach their mid-20s or more, they may begin to resent the denial and emotional suppression of their childhood. Such resentments may be evident in their young-adult relationships with others. Irish communication patterns are generally characterized by a high degree of ambiguity and confusion. Because Irish parents often control their children via indirect communication, such as humor, teasing, sarcasm, and ridicule, outsiders may not understand why children become so frustrated dealing with their parents and feel a need to distance themselves from the family in order to feel "sane." The resentments that Irish children have buried since childhood often continue into adulthood without realization that resolution is possible.

Resentments and distancing may become more intense throughout the adults' life, especially if parents' subtle disapproval continues or if adult children assume caretaking responsibilities for their parents. Unlike other children—such as African American, Greek, Italian, or Jewish—who are freer to express their resentments, Irish children may be extremely sensitive to perceived slights, such as favors shown to siblings, or other imagined wrongs. They may never confront the parent or the sibling with their feelings, dutifully continuing their caretaking responsibilities while maintaining tense silence with regard to their emotional wounds.

As parents age, intimacy typically does not increase. The mother may maintain her matriarchal role within the family. She may be seen as intimidating and indomitable. She may be unaware of the hold she has on her family because inwardly she feels that hold slipping.

Although unmarried children may continue to be emotionally dependent on their parents (and outwardly deny this dependence), they have no strong sense of filial responsibility. For example, placing a parent in a nursing home when the time comes may be acceptable to both children and parents, who prefer to "suffer alone" and never become a burden to their children. . . .

ASIAN INDIAN FAMILIES

In the past 10 years, Asian Indian immigration to the United States has been opened to nonprofessional classes. Twenty years ago, families immigrating here were primarily of the professional class. Today, however, the influx of uneducated families settling into menial jobs has created many problems similar to those experienced by earlier groups of immigrants from other countries.

Despite the intersecting influences of caste, region, and religion, predictable intergenerational conflicts emerge among family members. Relationships within and across generations are influenced by beliefs in caste and karma. These beliefs are pervasive despite the diversity among Asian Indians in the "old country" and in the United States (Malyala, Kamaraju, & Ramana, 1984). However, the degree to which these beliefs affect adaptation to life in Western society is influenced by level of education and acculturation (Segal, 1991; Matsuoka, 1990). For example, an educated family living in this country for 10 to 20 years will adapt to Western values around education and socialization for their children. However, they frequently revert back to Indian values as the marriage of a child approaches.

The caste system is a stratified social system into which one is born as a result of one's fate or karma. Karma can be changed only through death and subsequent rebirth. It is believed that with each rebirth a person moves from a lower caste (pollution) to a higher caste (purity) until "nirvana" (eternal afterlife) is achieved. These beliefs perpetuate values of passivity and tolerance, suffering and sacrifice. The more accepting one is of one's karma (passivity), the greater assurance one has of achieving spiritual afterlife (tolerance).

Hindu culture portrays women in paradoxical positions. Women are sacred (pure) in the afterlife yet they are devalued (polluted) in present life (Bumiller, 1990; Almeida, 1990; Wadley, 1977). Although men share power with women in the scriptures, in present life the male-centered family system exerts enormous social and economic power over women and children. With its concepts of "purity" and "pollution," the caste system shapes both intragenerational and intergenerational relationships. Prejudices related to lighter vs. darker shades of skin color are deeply embedded within the culture, with light skin symbolizing "purity" and dark skin symbolizing "pollution." These "ideals" are carried into the acculturation process in that Asian Indian immigrants find it easier to connect with white Americans than with non-whites, including other Asians. Asian Indian experiences of racism are generally not talked about, as though acknowledgment of racism might connect them with others who are similarly discriminated against. Although work and educational opportunities are available to all, women and lower-caste men have fewer choices regarding marriage partners. Such contradictions are pervasive and are explained in terms of karma.

Karma focuses on past and future life space. Current life dilemmas are explained in terms of karma. For example, a wife who is mistreated by her in-laws might say, "I must deserve this for something bad I did in a past life. If I endure my current life, I know I will be taken care of by God in a future life." Making choices to alter current life struggles is possible within this belief system. Sacrificial actions may alter one's current life and thus are meaningful. Fasting, praying, somatic complaints, head shaving, and suicide alter "karma" and move one toward a better life. In working with Asian Indian clients, therapists might suggest culturally appropriate constructions of less destructive "solutions" such as limited fasting, praying, meditating, or even haircutting.

Intergenerational patterns are embedded and negotiated within a collective consciousness. Relationships are other-directed rather than self-centered. Spirituality and simplicity are applauded, and family-centered decisions take priority over individual preferences. Within the family of origin, older men assume decision-making authority over all members of the family. Fathers are responsible for the education of their male children and for the care of their elderly parents. Emotional connectedness between sons and fathers, as well as among other extended family members, is not expected. However, intimacy between the son and mother is emphasized. Fathers are responsible for the dowry and marriage of their daughters; uncles or older male siblings take on this responsibility in the event of a father's death. Mothers expect their sons to control their wives with regard to money, work, and social activities. Older women gain status and power through the mother-in-law role. Younger women are socialized by their mothers and sisters to idealize the role of "mother-in-law." The cultural system (i.e., caste and karma with their values of tolerance and passivity) supported by the male-family lineage (endorsing tolerance and passivity) enables this process. In this system, women realize power by exerting control over women of lesser status. Caretaking of grandchildren and food preparation are used as "covert" means of gaining power in family relations. A mother-in-law, in charge of preparing food while the daughter-in-law works, might cook only according to her son's desires. Young children are generally overprotected by grandparents, while being taught to respect their elders. Children are taught to avoid direct eye contact with their elders and to avoid disagreeing with them. Older sisters-in-law assume a degree of power over younger women entering into the male-centered family system.

Education of male children is considered necessary for the economic needs of the entire family, whereas education for female children increases their marketability as brides. Aging parents are cared for within the family by adult married male children and, in rare instances, by female children who have families of their own.

Child rearing is a shared responsibility of the women in the male-extended-family system. These women can be aunts or friends of the family from India who visit for extended periods during the family's initial years of child rearing. When young mothers are forced to parent without this extended-kinship system, children are more at risk, because family conflicts tend to be expressed in the mother-child dyad rather than in the marital dyad.

Power in Western marriages is directly connected to the economic resources of each partner. This notion of power and relationships is less applicable to Asian Indian families, because a couple's economic resources are distributed across the extended male-oriented family system (Conklin, 1988). Unlike the white, American, middle-class nuclear family, in which marriage stands at the center of the family system, men and their mothers are at the center of the Asian Indian family system. The mother-son tie is prominent in both Hindu and Christian Asian Indian families (Almeida, 1990; de Souza, 1975). Sons provide their mothers and grandmothers with the ultimate pride and status afforded women in "this" life (Issmer, 1989). Young wives do not participate in this system of power, even when they contribute economically to the family unit (Chakrabortty, 1978). Marriage is complicated by overarching problems of caste, dowry, and expensive weddings.

Arranged marriages are the norm in the adopted country as well as in India. When the family chooses to emphasize college education over marriage, or if the child asserts his or her personal rights over the parents' choice of mates or chooses career and money over marriage, major conflicts within the family system arise. Parents expect daughters to be married between 18 and 22 years of age and sons between the ages of 22 and 26. When this does not occur, parents lack a clear role in their adult child's life. The process of differentiation of self from family, which has various implications for Asian Indians as a result of their cultural norms, is particularly problematic at this stage. Despite their efforts to create choices for their sons and daughters, cultural expectations for "arranged" marriages take precedence.

> An Asian Indian family entered therapy because of their 21-year-old daughter's difficulty completing her last semester of college. They expressed their helplessness in dealing with her launching. The mother said, "Shiva is very immature and irresponsible; it worries me that she does not know the meaning of money or getting a job, and yet she is about to graduate. I think of her as a selfish brat sometimes. She says she is not ready to think about marriage, and I believe it sometimes, but all of our friends and relatives think I am being neglectful in my responsibility to find her a nice man. If she waits until she is 30, then by the time she is 40, when she should be taking care of us, she and her husband will still have the responsibility of young children. I might be too old to be the kind of grandparent I have to be. Of course, I know that if Shiva gets married, then I will be pushing her to give me grandchildren, so I suppose I have to trust that my husband's and my choice to allow her to be independent will turn out OK."

An Asian Indian woman's status within the family is determined by the gender order of her children. First-born males are preferred. First-born females are vulnerable to conflict between the mother and her in-laws and are perceived as diminishing the father's status with the deities. However, a second-born male child helps normalize the situation. A second-born female child following a first-born female child is at risk for premature death through malnutrition and abuse, even in the United States, if the family does not have sufficient social and economic support. Male children offer the family greater economic support and thereby afford better marital opportunities for the female children in the family. A woman's relationship with her mother-in-law may become strained and the marriage may suffer if she is infertile and thus does not meet the family's role expectations. Sons who are unable to support the elderly family members, widowed mothers, or unmarried sisters extort large dowries from their brides as solutions to this intergenerational legacy (Ramu, 1987).

These intergenerational patterns often conflict with Asian Indian acculturation (Sluzki, 1979). Although most Asian Indians accommodate to the work ethic and value of education, they maintain strong cultural ties to Asian Indian concepts of marriage, child rearing, parenting, and the sharing and allocation of economic resources.

Western values of privacy and individualism conflict with Indian values of collectivity and family-centerdness. In the context of separation, less acculturated families view adolescents' and young adults' struggles with independence as disrespect. When Asian Indians speak of *respect*, they mean *obedience* to the family and culture. Similarly, it is difficult for these family members to understand that the Western ideal of love includes separation and independence from the family of origin. Consequently, the Asian Indian concept of love includes control (Mukherjee, 1991). . . .

JEWISH FAMILIES

Judaism has the unusual distinction of being both a religion and an ethnic identity (Farber, Mindel, & Lazerwitz, 1988). Jews, who have a long tradition of intellectual debate and dialogue, carry on a never-ending discussion about who is a Jew and what it means to be a Jew. This debate has been engendered in part by the Jewish history of exclusion, discrimination, and wandering, culminating in the Holocaust and the founding of Israel. As waves of Jewish immigrants entered the United States, including early settlers from Germany who were relatively wealthy, the poor and less assimilated Eastern Europeans before and after World War I, Holocaust survivors, and, most recently, Russian and Israeli Jews, the question of essential Jewishness has continued to be debated—a legacy that has led to sensitivity over issues of discrimination and a sense of being "other." Although "Jewishness" may not be apparent to the outsider, most Jews are sensitive to interactions that might be perceived as anti-Semitic and thus may adopt a defensive posture that seems inexplicable to non-Jews.

Jews in the United States have been both fearful of and fascinated by assimilation into the mainstream culture (Herz & Rosen, 1982). Many families are overwhelmingly concerned that family members marry within the faith, or, if members marry outside the faith, that they maintain their Jewish traditions. A primary concern for many parents who move to a new community is whether their children will have other Jewish children with whom to play and date. The issue is further complicated by the diversity of Jewish religious practice; acceptable "Jewishness" in one family may be considered "too assimilated" in another.

Families often enter treatment to deal with conflicting feelings with regard to intermarriage, which may be perceived as destroying the integrity of the family and the faith. Generally, the families' most immediate concerns revolve around who, if anyone, will be expected to convert, who will perform the wedding, and how the grandchildren will be raised. Intermarriage is often felt to be a failure on the part of the parents, who, somehow, should have prevented this from happening. Such feelings exist even in families that are "culturally" rather than religiously observant Jews and are not affiliated with a synagogue.

When intermarriage is an issue, it is important that therapists attempt to gather concerned family members together. The parent or grandparent who is most upset may be difficult to engage. Because Jews traditionally have had a high regard for discourse and the transmission of cultural tradition and history, it can be helpful to review family history and to engage the family in searching for other families for whom intermarriage did not result in leaving the faith. Jewish families respond well to information and the sharing of stories; thus, referrals to a support group and/or interfaith classes run by Reform synagogues can be effective.

Regardless of geographic distance among family members, maintaining close family ties is important to Jewish families. It is important that the therapist identify family members who are critical to the treatment process but who are not immediately available. Soliciting these persons' involvement as consultants (through inclusion in family sessions, a joint phone call, or a letter) can help promote change.

Jewish families' focus on children, particularly their education and nurturing, can be a mixed blessing. Children are expected to be a source of pride and pleasure for parents and grandparents. However, children may find it difficult to be the focus of so much attention, with so many people having an expressed point of view. Young people may find it difficult to operate independently in their own interests (Farber et al., 1988). Separation and individuation are difficult to achieve if the family has rigid definitions of acceptable and successful behaviors. Young Jewish men and women often enter treatment because they are having difficulty dealing with enmeshment issues. Parents may perceive themselves as being generous and supportive and feel hurt by their children's efforts to become more independent. Reframing and relabeling their adult children's need to separate as "successful" and productive behavior can be an effective treatment approach.

The changing mores of late 20th century American life have been stressful for Jewish families. Traditionally, Jewish women stayed home, complying with the dictum to "be fruitful and multiply." Jewish law has rigidly defined rules for men's and women's behavior, with women having a minor function in religious ritual. Such traditions are less rigidly observed in Reform and Conservative congregations, where women now can be ordained as rabbis and participate in religious ritual. Despite the fact that many Jewish laws concerning gender roles are neglected in all but Orthodox families, these laws still have a subtle influence on role definition and expectations.

In Jewish families, women have traditionally held power at home while the husband faced the work world. Jewish mothers have been responsible for maintaining traditions and culture. However, because many Jewish women were employed outside the home during the Great Depression in the 1930s, many families remember grandmothers or other female relatives who worked out of necessity. Their daughters were primarily homemakers, and their granddaughters now expect themselves to be "supermoms" (Hyman, 1991). The dilemma faced by all three generations has been how to reconcile social expectations with cultural expectations. Women who saw their mothers helping support the family during the Depression came to value their homemaker role. The granddaughters have aspired to raise their family while participating in the educational and professional world. Issues faced by American women in the 1980s and 1990s have been especially complicated for Jewish women due to the emphasis Jewish culture places on education, social consciousness, and tradition. In such situations, the grandmother may serve as a role model for both working and maintaining a family.

Significant shifts in the role of the Jewish husband/father have also occurred. Jewish men have experienced discrimination and violence in the community. Traditionally, their home has been the place where they achieve respect and authority. Because both spouses may work, the father may be called upon or may wish to be a more active parent. But when he does take an active role, he risks the scorn of his own parents, who see him in an unconventional role. The extended family may not be supportive of these changes.

Religion is another source of intergenerational conflict. The majority of Jews in the United States are affiliated with Reform congregations, which do not follow many of the commandments that Orthodox and Conservative Jews follow. Intergenerational conflict may arise over the perceived religious laxity or conservatism of family members. Parents may be disappointed if their child chooses not to be affiliated with a synagogue and not to have a bar mitzvah for their grandson or a bas mitzvah for their granddaughter.

Conversely, some young people have become more observant of the Jewish faith than their families, perhaps joining an Orthodox congregation and living a life-style that is foreign to their families (keeping a kosher home, not traveling on the Sabbath, not practicing birth control). Conflicts in some families may occur if younger family members emigrate to Israel, thus separating parents from their children and grandchildren. Families may enter treatment to deal with feelings of loss and may need help in understanding that their needs are acceptable even if they differ from those of their parents.

Jewish families tend to seek expert opinions and may ask a therapist many questions about professional degrees and competence. Although such inquiries may make practitioners feel uncomfortable and challenged, they may help clients feel more comfortable in therapy. Directing Jewish families to appropriate reading materials about their problems can be helpful, because many Jewish persons place value on being well-informed. Referrals to self-help groups can also be helpful.

Jews are avid consumers of psychotherapy, in part as a result of their comfort with discourse, their search for solutions, and expectation that family life should follow predefined rules (Herz & Rosen, 1982). However, extensive analysis does not always lead to resolution of problems. . . . Families may need to be reminded that the goal of therapy is not to tell a good story or to be "right" in the eyes of the therapist, but to resolve the conflict or assuage the pain that brought the family to therapy.

REFERENCES

Almeida, R. V. (1990). Asian Indian mothers, *Journal of Feminist Family Therapy*, 2(2), 33–39.

Barrabe, P., & von Mering, O. (1953). Ethnic variations in mental stress in families with psychotic children. *Social Problems, 1*, 48–53.

Boyd-Franklin, N. (1989). *Black families in therapy*. New York: Guilford.

Bumiller, E. (1990). *May you be the mother of a hundred sons: A journey among the women of India*. New York: Random House.

Byrne, N., & McCarthy, I. (1986, September 15). *Irish women*. Family Therapy Training Program Conference, Robert Wood Johnson Medical School, Piscataway, NJ.

Chakrabortty, K. (1978). *The conflicting worlds of working mothers*. Calcutta, India: Progressive Publishers.

Comas-Diaz, L. (1989). Culturally relevant issues for Hispanics. In V. R. Koslow & E. Salett (Eds.), *Crossing cultures in mental health.* Washington, DC: Society for International Education, Training and Research.

Conklin, G. H. (1988). The influence of economic development and patterns of conjugal power and extended family residence in India. *Journal of comparative family studies, 19,* 187–205.

de Souza, A. (1975). *Women in contemporary India.* New Delhi, India: Manohar.

Diner, H. R. (1983). *Erin's daughters in America.* Baltimore, MD: Johns Hopkins University Press.

Farber, B., Mindel, C. H., & Lazerwitz, B. (1988). In C. H. Mindel & R. W. Habenstein (Eds.), *Ethnic families in America: Patterns and variations.* New York: Elsevier.

Garcia-Preto, N. (1982). Puerto Rican families. In M. McGoldrick, J. K. Pearce, & J. Giordano (Eds.), *Ethnicity and family therapy.* New York: Guilford.

Garcia-Preto, N. (1990). Hispanic mothers. *Journal of feminist family therapy, 2* (2), 15–21.

Gomez, A. G. (1982). Puerto Rican Americans. In A. Gaw (Ed.), *Cross cultural psychiatry* (pp. 109–136). Boston: John Wright.

Habach, E. (1972). Ni machismo, ni hembriso. In *Coleccion: Protesta.* Caracas, Venezuela: Publicaciones EPLA.

Herz, F. M., & Rosen, E. J. (1982). Jewish families. In M. McGoldrick, J. K. Pearce, & J. Giordano (Eds.), *Ethnicity and family therapy.* New York: Guilford.

Hines, P. (1989). The family life cycle of poor black families. In B. Carter & M. McGoldrick (Eds.), *The changing family life cycle: A framework for family therapy* (2nd ed.). New York: Gardner Press.

Hines, P. (1990). African American mothers. *Journal of Feminist Family Therapy, 2*(2), 23–32.

Hines, P., & Boyd-Franklin, N. (1982). Black families. In M. McGoldrick, J. K. Pearce, & J. Giordano (Eds.), *Ethnicity and family therapy.* New York: Guilford.

Hyman, P. (1991). Gender and the immigrant Jewish experience, J. R. Baskin (Ed.), *Jewish women in historical perspective.* Detroit, MI: Wayne State University Press.

Issmer, S. D. (1989). The special function of out-of-home care in India, *Child Welfare, 68,* 228–232.

Malyala, S., Kamaraju, S., & Ramana, K. V. (1984). Untouchability—need for a new approach. *Indian Journal of Social Work, 45,* 361–369.

Matsuoka, J. K. (1990). Differential acculturation among Vietnamese refugees. *Social Work, 35,* 341–345.

McGoldrick, M. (1982). Irish Americans. In M. McGoldrick, J. K. Pearce, & J. Giordano (Eds.), *Ethnicity and family therapy.* New York: Guilford.

McGoldrick, M. (1991). Irish mothers. *Journal of Feminist Family Therapy. 2*(2), 3–8.

McGoldrick, M., Garcia-Preto, N., Hines, P., & Lee, E. (1989). Ethnicity and women. In M. McGoldrick, C. Anderson, & F. Walsh (Eds.), *Women in families,* New York: W. W. Norton.

McGoldrick, M., Garcia-Preto, N., Hines, P., & Lee, E. (1991). Ethnicity and family therapy. In A. Gurman & D. Kniskern (Eds.), *The handbook of family therapy* (2nd ed.) (pp. 546–582). New York: Guilford.

McKenna, A. (1979). Attitudes of Irish mothers to child rearing. *Journal of Comparative Family Studies, 10,* 227–251.

Mukherjee, B. (1991). *Jasmine.* New York: Fawcett Crest.

Ramu, G. N. (1987). Indian husbands: Their role perceptions and performance in single- and dual-earner families. *Journal of Marriage and the Family, 49,* 903–915.

Rudd, J. M. (1984). *Irish American families: The mother-child dyad.* Thesis, Smith College School of Social Work.

Scheper-Hughs, N. (1979). *Saints, scholars, and schizophrenics.* Berkeley, CA: University of California Press.

Segal, U. A. (1991). Cultural variables in Asian Indian families. *Families in Society, 72,* 233–241.

Sluzki, C. (1979). Migration and family conflict. *Family Process, 18,* 379–390.

Stevens, E. (1973). Machismo and marianismo. *Transaction Society, 10*(6), 57–63.

Wadley, S. (1977). Women and the Hindu tradition, *Journal of Women in Culture and Society, 3*(1), 113–128.

R E A D I N G

23

Reinventing the Family

LAURA BENKOV

There is a certain distortion that occurs when we look back at the past through the lens of the present. When what once seemed impossible has become reality, it is easy to forget the groping in the dark along an untrodden and sometimes treacherous path. It was with this in mind that in March 1988 I read the clipping a friend had sent me from the *Hartford Advocate.* Underneath the headline "The Lesbian Baby Boom," it said "Even Geraldo's covered it—but the women who are doing it say it's no big deal." Almost a decade had passed since I first dared to ask myself if I, a lesbian, could choose to have children. Now as I read the words

"Choosing Children" from *Reinventing the Family: Lesbian and Gay Parents.* Laura Benkov, Ph.D. New York: Crown Trade Paperbacks. 1994.

"No big deal" I flashed back to those sleepless nights clouded with confusion, shame, trepidation, grief, and longing.

One's perspective on the lesbian baby boom is clearly a matter of whom you talk to. When I finally broke through my isolation and began to speak to lesbians who had chosen to raise children, some— like the women described in the *Hartford Advocate*—told me they had never viewed their desire for parenthood as incompatible with their lesbianism. Andrea, a mother of two, said, "I always knew that I was going to be a mother, and being a lesbian never felt like I was making a choice not to have children. That probably had a lot to do with the fact that I came out during the seventies, amid a sense of all sorts of opportunities for women." Yet Andrea's ease with her status as lesbian mother was only one story. There were many other lesbians who had come to be mothers only after significant personal struggle. It is no wonder that I found myself drawn to their descriptions of arduous journeys. Susan lived years of ambivalence about her sexuality, not because she was uncertain of whom she loved but because she believed that choosing a woman meant giving up her lifelong dream of being a parent. Esther talked of being suddenly overcome by grief on an otherwise ordinary evening as she watched her lover washing her hair, when she recognized for the first time a yearning she could not imagine would ever come to fruition: to raise a child with this person she loved so deeply.

If we were indeed in the midst of a lesbian baby boom, then it *was* a big deal, for it was a painful and often lonely journey past grief that had brought us here.

Somewhere along the way these lesbians stopped assuming they couldn't be parents and began figuring out how to bring children into their lives. As I listened to their tales of transformation, each marked by a unique moment of revelation, the "boom" seemed the social equivalent of spontaneous combustion. So many lesbians struggled to become parents at precisely the same historical moment, yet each experienced herself as unique and alone. Of course, no one was as alone as she might have felt, and the movement certainly hadn't appeared out of the blue. Many social forces had laid the groundwork for its emergence.

As women influenced by second-wave feminism questioned their roles in the traditional family, they discovered possibility where before there had been only closed doors. Raising children without being married emerged as a potentially positive decision, not an unwanted circumstance. It is no accident that the rise of lesbian parenting has coincided with the burgeoning of single heterosexual women choosing to have children. The idea that women could shape their intimate lives according to their own standards and values rather than conform to constricting social norms was powerful in its own right. But the feminist movement was significant beyond the realm of ideas. On a very practical level, women's fight for control over their reproductive capacities created a context in which the choice to bear a child was as significantly opened up as the choice not to bear one; abortion rights and access to reproductive technology such as donor insemination are flip sides of the same coin.

The gay rights movement also contributed greatly to the parenting boom, enabling people to take a less fearful, more assertive stance toward society and yielding more visible communities, with the support and social dialogue that implies. From that supportive base, many began to define the kinds of lives they wanted to live, and to pursue their wish to be parents.

Perhaps most significant of all to what has become known in some circles as the choosing children movement, were the lesbian and gay parents who'd come out of heterosexual marriages. They had stepped out of the shadows, transforming the notion of lesbian and gay parents from a contradiction in terms to a visible reality that society had to contend with.

The fact that in our society women tend more than men to be intensely involved with raising children was reflected in the choosing children movement, just as it had been in the battles of parents coming out of heterosexual marriages. During the late 1970s, the first signs of lesbians choosing to have children were evident. By the mid-1980s, the trend had expanded from its initial West Coast and urban-center origins to throughout the nation. It was not until the late 1980s that a similar movement, smaller in scope, emerged among gay men. Though gay men's efforts overlap in some ways with lesbian endeavors, they are also distinctive. Often societal taboos against homosexuals more strongly burden gay men. And homosexuality aside, the notion of men as primary nurturing parental figures is ill defined in our culture. Many gay men seeking to become fathers, and perhaps to raise children without significant female input, feel out of place simply by virtue of their gender.

Initially, gay men participated in the lesbian baby boom as fathers sought by lesbians who chose to bear children. The advent of AIDS profoundly curtailed the move toward joint parenting arrangements. But in many communities it also brought gay men and lesbians together; and in more recent years, with growing consciousness about HIV prevention and testing available, joint parenting arrangements seem to be on the rise again.

Taking on secondary parenting roles in families headed by lesbians does suit some gay men, but others want, as do their lesbian counterparts, to have a more intensive, primary parental relationship. Increasingly, gay men are choosing to become parents through adoption, surrogacy, or joint parenting arrangements.

Within a decade, the unimaginable became commonplace. This remarkable shift occurred against a backdrop of skepticism and hostility. Society remained fixed on the question of whether homosexuals should be allowed to raise children, even as they were becoming parents in record numbers. The fierce debates that began in the early 1970s only continued as openly gay men and women chose parenthood. By the mid-1980s, a multitude of new controversies clamored for attention. Lesbian and gay parents had pushed Americans to look more closely than ever before at a deceptively simple question: What is a family? If the family is not defined by heterosexual procreative union, then what indeed is it? Perhaps it was the fear of this very question that underlay the hostility toward lesbian and gay parents to begin with. If the capacity to have and raise children does not distinguish heterosexuals from homosexuals, then what does?

In a recent *New York Times* book review, Margaret O'Brien Steinfels posed the following question: Does a married heterosexual couple's "capacity to have children [represent] a differentiating quality in heterosexual relationships?" According to Steinfels:

Our legislatures and our religious faiths may come up with new ways to regulate or recognize erotically bound relationships beyond the traditional form of marriage: the state may devise practical solutions to problems like insurance and shared property, and religious bodies may try to encourage lasting and exclusive intimacy in a monogamous setting. Nonetheless society has a legitimate interest in privileging those heterosexual unions that are oriented toward the generation and rearing of children. That, at any rate, is the widely held conviction that remains to be debated. . . .

Steinfels's suggestion that heterosexual unions are uniquely bound to childrearing rings false at this historical moment. Heterosexual procreation is only one of many means of family making. This is underscored not only by the fact that lesbian and gay unions can include childrearing but also because heterosexual unions often do not. Many heterosexual couples choose not to raise children, and many others, despite their heterosexuality, cannot procreate. Divorce, adoption, and reproductive technology mean that children often aren't raised by their birth parents, and likewise many parents aren't genetically connected to their kids. Steinfels's query embodies a myth our society clings to despite its distance from reality: that heterosexual unions, by virtue of their potential link to procreation, are somehow necessary to the survival of the species and therefore morally superior. Lesbians and gay men choosing to parent are not unique in challenging this myth, but they do so most explicitly, often sparking heated backlash.

During his 1992 campaign for reelection, George Bush said that "children should have the benefit of being born into a family with a mother and a father," thus citing the number and gender of parents as a pivotal aspect of optimal family life and implicitly privileging biological connection between parents and children by the phrase "born into." In short, he held up as the ideal the traditional family, characterized by heterosexual procreative unions and legal sanction.

Eight-year-old Danielle, the daughter of lesbian and gay parents, vehemently disagreed. "I have two moms and two dads," she said. "A family is people who all love each other, care for each other, help out and understand each other."

In defining the ideal family, Bush emphasized structural characteristics while Danielle, in contrast, highlighted emotions and relationships. Their disagreement aptly reflects this moment in American society: the tension between idealization of the traditional family and the reality of families that don't fit that mold is strongly emerging as a key issue of our times. As lesbians and gay men choose to raise children, the many different kinds of families they create reveal the inadequacy of a definition of family that rests on one particular structure. Increasingly, our society must heed Danielle's idea that family is defined by the quality of relationships, which can exist in many forms.

DONOR INSEMINATION: A MIMICRY OF PROCREATIVE UNION

In 1884, according to one of the earliest accounts of donor insemination in America, a woman lay unconscious on an examining table while, without her knowledge much less her consent, a doctor inseminated her with sperm from the "handsomest medical student" in his class. It was only after the insemination that the doctor informed the woman's infertile husband, who, pleased by the news, asked that his wife never be told what had occurred. The insemination resulted in the birth of a baby boy, who, presumably along with his mother, wasn't informed of the circumstances of his conception. A little over a century later, though women who are inseminated are neither unconscious nor uninformed, much of this early account remains salient. Donor insemination has evolved as a medically controlled practice, largely restricted to infertile heterosexual couples and shrouded in secrecy. Where then do lesbians fit in?

In the beginning of its use in this country, donor insemination was seen solely as a solution to infertility among married heterosexual couples. As such, donor insemination practices were structured to produce families that mimicked in every way possible the traditional heterosexual family. Both medical practitioners and the law geared donor insemination toward creating families that looked like, and had the legal status of, a family consisting of a married man and woman and their biological offspring.

This attempt to mimic the traditional heterosexual family included an effort to hide the very fact that donor insemination was used. The appearance of a biological connection was painstakingly constructed by matching the donor's physical traits with the husband's. By and large, the fact that a child had been conceived through donor insemination was rarely disclosed within families and was barely discussed in the larger cultural arena. In one major text of the 1960s, a doctor noted that one of the advantages of donor insemination, as compared to adoption, was that its use need never be revealed. He further suggested that screening criteria for couples receiving donor insemination include an assessment of how well they could keep a secret. Now, thirty years later, donor characteristics are still most often matched to that of the husband and secrecy continues.

The effort to hide the use of donor insemination parallels past approaches to adoption. There, too, great pains were taken to match the physical characteristics of children with those of their adoptive parents, and adoption was held as a secret around which much anxiety revolved. More recently, adoption practices have shifted: there is much less emphasis on matching physical characteristics, and experts encourage parents to speak openly about adoption, with the idea that talking to children about their origins from an early age is key to their overall well-being. Unlike earlier practices, this way values honesty in family life over the appearance of a biological family unit. Along with more honesty within adoptive families has come more open discussion of adoption in society. While much thinking about adoption continues to reflect a cultural bias that elevates biological families over all others, adoption practices have begun to move beyond this ideology by coming out of the closet. In contrast, the secrecy surrounding donor insemination points up the continuing emphasis on the appearance of a biological family unit.

The painstaking attention to appearance and the secrecy surrounding donor insemination stem from an insidious ideology: heterosexual procreation is the ideal basis of a family, one which if not achieved in actuality should at least be aspired to in appearance. With this as an undercurrent, donor insemination is characterized by a contradictory view of genetics. On the one hand, the practice distinguishes genetic and social parent roles, relegating genetics to an inconsequential position by severing all ties between donors and their offspring, and by recognizing those who take on the social role of parenthood as fathers of those children. On the other hand, hiding the fact that this process has occurred reveals an almost superstitious belief in the power of genetics. The implication is that biological connection is such a crucial aspect of parenting that its absence is shameful and should be hidden. The social role of a nonbiological parent is not highly valued in its own right, and instead must be bolstered by the illusion of a genetic connection. In this pervasive view, a "real" parent is the biological parent. If you have to, donor insemination is okay to do, but it's not okay to talk about.

THE LEGAL CONSTRUCTIONS OF FAMILY IN DONOR INSEMINATION PRACTICES

As with the secrecy and matching practices, the laws surrounding donor insemination reinforce efforts to make these families look like the standard nuclear model. Children conceived through donor insemination in the context of a heterosexual marriage are deemed the legal children of the recipient and her husband. Donors, on the other hand, waive all parental rights and responsibilities. The complex reality of such families—that there are both a biological and a social father involved—is set aside in favor of a simpler one. Severing the donor tie and sanctioning the husband's parental relationship serve the purpose of delineating one—and only one—father.

As donor insemination was more widely practiced in this country, legal parameters developed that, like the practices themselves, value the traditional family over all others. Among the first legal questions posed about donor insemination was whether it constituted adultery and, along with that, whether the child so conceived was "illegitimate." As the courts decided these initial cases they exhibited a strong conviction that children need to be "legitimate"— that is, to have fathers. From this premise the law constructed the husbands of inseminated women as the legal fathers of the resulting children. Father status thus hinged on marriage— that is, children were considered to be the "issue of the marriage." This was automatic, with no mediating process such as adoption needed to complete the arrangement. Initially these parameters were outlined only when disputes arose, but as the use of donor insemination grew more widespread, legislation was enacted that explicitly delineated what the courts had implicitly held all along: families that, in fact, were not created through the procreative union of a married heterosexual couple were given the legal status of this traditional unit. The state threw a safety net around the families created through donor insemination when, and only when, those families were headed by married heterosexual couples. On a state-by-state basis, the law carved out a distinction between donors and fathers: donors, in surrendering their sperm to doctors, waived parental rights and responsibilities, while the men married to inseminating women took on the legal rights and responsibilities of father-hood.

Significantly, in many states, the donors' lack of parental status hinges on medical mediation. That is, donors who directly give sperm to women can be, and often are, legally considered parents. Thus, not only is heterosexuality a prerequisite to the legal delineation of families constituted through donor insemination but medical control of the process is built into the law. People creating families through donor insemination do so most safely—that is, with least threat to their integrity as a family unit—if they utilize medical help.

LESBIANS AND SINGLE WOMEN SEEK DONOR INSEMINATION

The extent to which donor insemination practices emphasize the appearance of a procreative heterosexual union has, of course, great implications for lesbians and unmarried heterosexual women—most especially with respect to access to the technology. In conceiving through donor insemination, these women have little possibility of creating "pretend father" relationships that would obscure the fact that donor insemination has occurred. Indeed, when lesbians and single heterosexual women use donor insemination, they bring the practice out of the closet, revealing it to be a way that women can bear children in the absence of any relationship to men. It is no wonder that unmarried women, regardless of their sexual orientation, have been barred from using donor insemination, given the challenge their access poses to deeply held beliefs. To be inseminated as a single straight woman or lesbian is to boldly acknowledge that the resulting child has no father and that women can parent without input from men beyond the single contribution of genetic material. Such inseminations also highlight the separation between social and genetic parenting roles. This last aspect is especially obvious when lesbian couples use donor insemination: a nonbiological mother, clearly not a father, becomes the child's other parent.

For many years, the medical profession would not grant unmarried women access to insemination. A study done in 1979 found that over 90 percent of doctors wouldn't inseminate unmarried women. The doctors gave several reasons for their decision, the most central being their beliefs that lesbians and single women are unfit parents and that all children need fathers. However, some doctors refused to inseminate unmarried women, not out of deep personal conviction, but because they mistakenly believed that it was illegal. Though the statutory language about donor insemination often includes mention of marriage, it does not require it. A number of doctors also feared future wrong-ful-life suits, assuming that children raised by lesbians or single women would ultimately be unhappy enough to sue those responsible for their existence.

In the late 1970s, into the context of medically controlled, heterosexual-marriage–oriented donor insemination practices, came single heterosexual women and lesbians wanting to have children. The technology was an obvious choice for these women, not only in its most basic sense as a source of sperm, but also as a way of forming families whose integrity would be legally protected.

Many want to establish families as couples or individuals without having to negotiate parenting responsibilities with an outside adult. Lesbians choosing to have children are much more vulnerable than married heterosexual couples to disputes about the boundaries of their families. Homophobia in the legal system renders them generally more subject to custody problems. Furthermore, since lesbians are unable to marry, and the female partners of inseminating women by and large can't adopt the resulting children, nonbiological lesbian mothers have no protected legal parent status. In this social context, creating families through known donors poses tremendous legal risks if those donors ever make custody claims. For lesbians, therefore, the legal protection of a family unit created through anonymous donor insemination is crucial.

But since access to the most legally safe source of insemination—that is, medically controlled— was highly restricted in the early days of the lesbian baby boom, many of the first lesbians to have children did so on the margins of mainstream donor insemination practices. Some women created their own alternatives. They inseminated themselves and, in an effort to protect the integrity of their families, created their own systems of anonymity, using go-betweens to conceal the identity of the sperm donors. However, this means of anonymity didn't provide firm protection against the possibility of custody disputes. In practice, the anonymity of donors would often be hard to maintain in small communities, and legally—especially in the absence of medical mediation—an identified donor would have parental rights. Matters became more complicated with the advent of AIDS, which made this way of inseminating a highly risky business. Ultimately, the self-created system gave way to another approach.

Some lesbians moved in a different direction, attempting to change the exclusionary practices themselves. During the late 1970s and early 1980s, as the feminist health-care movement grew and women fought to gain reproductive freedom, unmarried women made headway with demands for access to medically controlled donor insemination. The Sperm Bank of California in Oakland was established in 1982 by women running the Oakland Feminist Women's Health Center in response to the rising number of unmarried women seeking advice about insemination. The Sperm Bank of California led the way in establishing an insemination program that didn't screen out women on the basis of sexual orientation or marital status. Currently there are several such sperm banks throughout the country, and increasingly doctors are willing to inseminate unmarried women. However, access remains restricted in certain areas, and many insurance companies will cover insemination expenses only for married women.

During the last fifteen years, lesbians choosing to be parents have been charting a course through society that began on the margins and has increasingly moved into the mainstream, yielding social changes along the way.

In the realm of donor insemination, the reciprocal influence of heterosexual, nuclear family ideology and lesbian parenthood is strikingly apparent. Lesbians choosing to have children shape their families along parameters stemming from the idealization of the traditional nuclear family, but by the same token they significantly transform many of those parameters. Donor insemination has shifted from a completely medically dominated, heterosexually defined technology to a practice that serves unmarried women, both straight and gay, and thereby yields many different sorts of families. As lesbians and single heterosexual women make more use of donor insemination, the practice itself is changing: by necessity, donor insemination is coming out of the closet. In our culture there are few stories of conception through donor insemination. Despite the fact that approximately a million Americans have been conceived this way, we continue to behave as though conception occurs only through heterosexual union. Ultimately, lesbians will write the stories of donor insemination, as they speak openly to their children about another way that people come into the world.

Choices: Known or Unknown Donors

As the doors to donor insemination opened for lesbians, a new era began. Having access to the technology is not synonymous with wanting to use it. Most lesbian mothers-to-be spend considerable time deciding whether to do so through a known or unknown donor. The complexity of this decision was a theme in many of my talks with lesbian mothers. In December 1991, as I was trying to sort through the many layers of this decision, both for myself and in relation to this book, I decided to visit the sperm bank in Oakland. I was not prepared for the intensity of my response. Barbara Raboy, the director, explained the process of freezing and storing sperm as I stared at hundreds upon hundreds of specimens neatly ordered in dozens of large metal tanks. It was about what I'd expected to see, except for the names scribbled in marker across the outside of the tanks and in smaller letters on the compartments within each tank. In front of me was the Artist tank, with Fuchsia, Chartreuse, and Amber as its subdivisions. Next to it was the Universe tank, with Mars, Pluto, and Jupiter; and behind that, the Landscape tank, with Rocky Mountain, Grand Canyon, and Yellowstone. Barbara noticed my puzzlement and explained: "We thought names would be more fun than a strict number and letter filing system, so the staff take turns naming the tanks and the subdivisions within them—it's how we locate any particular specimen—you know donor number 5003 is in the A row in the Fuschia section of the Artist tank." I was disappointed that the tank names had no more salient correspondence to the sperm inside, but the knowledge freed me from the mind-boggling task of imagining what distinguished a Rocky Mountain sperm specimen from a Jupiter one.

Instead, I began to imagine the people who dreamed up these names: huddled among the slides and test tubes, who had been most pleased by colors, who by mountain vistas or thoughts of intergalactic travel? As the namers became more real to me, so too did the men whose sperm was sequestered in the tiny vials. Several pages listed donor characteristics—no. 2017, Dutch descent, blue eyes, brown wavy hair, 6 feet tall, athletic student of computer technology. If you wanted to know more about a particular donor, there were additional sheets—medical history and some personal information. But when all was said and done, the wish to know would remain just that. To see these vials was to glimpse the unknown. Throughout the country women were waiting—some whose male partners were infertile, some who were single, some who were lesbian. What they had in common was a strong yearning for children. This is what I was thinking as I looked at vial no. 2017. Then my ears rang with the voices of children, and I knew that I was standing in a place of beginnings, surrounded by mystery.

My initial puzzlement about the tank labels was a clue to my state of mind. I'd entered the sperm bank as I would a foreign country, imagining the tank names held some crucial meaning as unintelligible to me as a street sign in China. It struck me as odd that I could feel this way despite the fact that for years I'd thought about becoming a mother through this very process. Donor insemination was potentially a key element of my future, one that would involve my body and my most intimate relationships; yet simultaneously, I experienced it as a strange, foreign, and mystifying process.

I was not alone in this contradictory place. Though donor insemination has been practiced in this country for over a century, as a culture we have barely begun to grapple with the meaning it holds for us. Standing amid the vials of semen at the sperm bank, I could not help but be aware of the unique historical moment in which we are living. The very fact that I, a lesbian, could consider insemination is remarkable. Just ten years earlier I would have been shut out of any insemination program. But choices bring great complexity. Layers of thinking make up the decision about whether to become pregnant through a donor, known or unknown. How do lesbians aspiring to be mothers respond to society's constraints? What ways of forming a family will be safe in a culture that doesn't recognize our primary intimate connections? Because society as yet barely acknowledges donor insemination, an air of mysteriousness pervades the practice. How then do lesbians sort out the meanings donor insemination has for us and may have for our children?

From the language of "illegitimacy" and "bastards" to the tales of adopts searching for their birth parents, we are inundated with ideas that a father's absence is always problematic and knowledge of our genetic roots always essential. What do we accept of these stories? What do we reject? All of this is filtered through our most intensely personal experiences and histories. Ultimately it is from these many layers that lesbians create their families. Self-consciously exploring the meaning of family, each woman writes her own story. But no one writes it alone: each family is shaped by the culture it is embedded in, and in turn, the culture is changed by these emerging families.

The Role of the State

After twelve years together, Jasmine and Barbara agreed they were ready to raise children. Other than the gender of their partners, they envisioned family life in rather traditional terms. Their household would define the boundaries of their family; as a couple, they would jointly share parenting. Jasmine saw their decision to inseminate with an unknown donor as stemming clearly from the surrounding social context.

Jasmine explains: "We were very stuck on the method of conception—a known versus an unknown donor. One of the things that happened around the time we were thinking about this question was the foster-care issue in Massachusetts. We knew women who had adopted young children through foreign adoptions, and I listened to their descriptions of the home-study process. I felt very uncomfortable with the idea that somebody was judging you, and that you in a sense had to give them this little drama that 'I'm the one who's adopting and this woman is my roommate.'

"Not only did we feel angry about the injustice of it, but we also felt frustrated by the fact that as a couple we had so much more to offer in terms of the structure of our lives than this fallacy would indicate. When the foster-care uproar happened, we were very indignant about the idea that we could be judged that way. If we had gone along with the little drama of who we were supposed to be, it wouldn't have barred us from adopting, so it was really our decision that we wanted as few external people as possible out there judging us or making decisions about our lives.

"We didn't want that interference. That spilled over into the issue of the donor. We really needed to feel in control. The thing was, we were the parents and we wanted to make the decisions as the child grew up about other adults in the child's life. It's not that we wanted to shelter the child from other people, but we certainly didn't want an obligation ready-set. So given that we wanted integrity as a family unit, we decided to go with an unknown donor."

The influence of homophobia and heterosexist constructions of the family is apparent in Jasmine's explanation for their decision to use an anonymous donor. Jasmine and Barbara shied away from adoption because they didn't want to be subjected to state scrutiny that would have failed to recognize the value of their relationship. The homophobia unleashed during the Massachusetts foster-care battle was a bitter reminder of their vulnerability. A known donor was also someone who could potentially bring the state to bear on their family life—someone who in the eyes of the law would have parental rights in contrast to the nonbiological mother. Protecting the integrity of their family unit as they defined it meant using an unknown donor.

Though all prospective lesbian parents face the same legal constraint—a definition of family that gives privilege to genetic connection and heterosexual parenting—people see the state's potential role in their lives quite differently. Unlike Jasmine and Barbara, Susan and Dana chose to have a child with a man they knew who would be involved as a parent but in a secondary role. Each had a close relationship with her own father, and they wanted the same for their children. Though concerned about how legally vulnerable the nonbiological mother would be, Susan and Dana proceeded on the assumption that they could work out a trusting relationship with the father, one which would not ultimately bring them face-to-face with the state's ill-fitting definition of family.

Susan, explaining their decision, says: "The legal line obviously is 'don't take risks, therefore don't use a known father who would then have the possibility of having rights.' I agree that that's one way to avoid the particular risk of a custody fight and control issues over the child. But I think it's one of the most personal choices in the world—anything about reproductive issues and how one wants to raise one's children are very intimate and individual, and I think you shouldn't make decisions frankly just on the legal basis.

"You should make them on your whole world view and your values and what you want for your child. Maybe the risk of a custody fight could be minimized by choosing a person carefully and by choosing a gay man rather than a person who would have the gay issue to use against you."

Jasmine and Barbara's thinking diverges from Susan and Dana's along several lines. First, the two couples position themselves very differently in relation to the state. Jasmine and Barbara are acutely focused on the threat the state poses to the integrity of their family unit. Susan and Dana, on the other hand, feel that threat less acutely because they believe that recourse to the state's definition can most likely be avoided through establishing trustworthy relationships. Marie, another lesbian who chose a known donor, explains the position:

> I don't have the kind of fears around the legal stuff that some people do. You have to pick really carefully. Obviously there are certainly men out there whom you could enter into this kind of relationship with and it would be a disaster. But I don't think it's impossible to find a situation where you can have some confidence that this guy will do what he says he'll do. I understand legally you leave yourself open. I think it would be dangerous to do this with a man who is conflicted and who's doing this because he wishes he had kids. Then, ten years down the line he might turn around and say, "I want the child."

These women are grappling with the question of whether you can create a family that defies the state's definition and feel safe that its boundaries will remain as you intended them to be. In part, the different choices lesbians make about family structure stem from different perspectives on the state's ultimate power in their lives.

What Makes a Family?

There is another important dimension to the decision of choosing between known and unknown donors: what should constitute the boundaries of a family? Many women, like Marie and her lover, Jana, choose a donor who will be known to the child but won't take on a parental role. Essentially, except for the fact that the child can know the donor, these families closely resemble families like Jasmine and Barbara's, where the women are the child's sole parents. However, often lesbians choosing known donors draw the boundaries around their families a little differently. Though frequently the men aren't primary parents, they do have a parental role. Susan and Dana created this type of family. While they define their family primarily within the bounds of their own household, their arrangement with their children's father is similar to an extended family. Though at first they were most concerned about maintaining their status as primary parents, as the family became securely established, Susan and Dana wanted the father to be more rather than less involved. They encouraged him to develop a strong relationship with the children. Susan says, "You realize that there are so many things to do. There's never enough time in a day. So additional people to help out is wonderful. We should all have bigger extended families, especially when we're all working. We've been lucky that not just our children's biological father but his choice of partners and his family have been a very rich source of additional good people in the kids' lives."

Opening boundaries in this way can be challenging, however. For a while, Dana, who was to be the nonbiological mother struggled with her lack of society-recognized parent status. "I think for a lot of Susan's pregnancy I was obsessed that this child might be born and this father would have more rights than I would. I had this image that he would never be doing the dirty work of everyday parenting. He'd show up as this knight on a white horse and get all this affection and admiration."

Susan and Dana were deeply committed to the idea that Dana was as much a mother as Susan, and Dana's feelings of doubt dissipated soon after their daughter's birth. "Once Danielle was born it was bizarre to think that. Her father is an important part of her life, but there's a whole 'nother ball game in terms of who her parents are who raise her. My fears were so far from reality. Before Danielle and I had this bond I imagined, in the naiveté of someone who's not a parent, that someone who shows up once a week could be an equal parent to someone who's with you twenty-four hours a day."

Deciding who will be part of one's family is, of course, a highly personal endeavor. The decision regarding a known or unknown donor is partly a decision about what kind of intimate relationships to create. Some are comfortable sharing parenting with people outside a romantic relationship, while others find this a complicated and unrewarding situation.

The Ties that Bind?—the Meaning of Genetic Connections

Beyond thinking about the relationships they want for themselves, lesbians choosing between known and unknown donors must consider how their choice will affect their children. As lesbians think about this, beliefs about the importance of genetic connections take center stage. These beliefs come partly from personal history and partly from ideas that dominate our culture. When women consider whether to use a known or unknown donor, complex, intense, and often conflicting feelings arise. Esther, for instance, originally tried to find a man who would be willing to be a sperm donor but maintain a minimal role in the child's life. The men she approached either wanted more involvement or were worried that they would be asked to take on more responsibility than they bargained for. Esther reconciled herself to conceiving with an anonymous donor, but her feelings about her son Ian's origins intensely color her relationship with him. She says, "I'm consumed by the connections. I look at Ian and see my grandmother's hands. He's an incredible dancer and my father was, too. I don't know if there's a dancing gene. That's why I wanted a Jewish donor. I wanted the history and culture. A known donor would have embodied more of that. Ian's relation to the donor has been a presence for me since he was born. It's hard to sort out my own sadness about my father's death and my sadness for Ian in not having that relationship."

It is hard also to separate Esther's personal history from the culture we are immersed in. As a society, we tend to emphasize intergenerational biological connections and pay scant attention to nonbiological relationships. For example, we continually hear stories about adopted children who feel an absence in their lives and need to search for their birth parents. We rarely hear about the adopted children—of whom there are also many—who don't feel a need for this contact. Hearing these stories of searches for genetic roots, many lesbians are uncomfortable with anonymous donor insemination. As Marie put it, "I don't think an anonymous donor is the best thing for a kid. I'm sure that kids conceived that way will manage and will be okay if their parents handle it levelly and matter-of-factly. But we don't really know. We haven't had a generation of kids growing up without knowing anything about half of their genetic material. What we know about is kids who were adopted and don't have that kind of information. Most of them go through something about it whether they end up searching or not. It just makes sense to me that if you can provide a child with that basic information, then you should."

While many like Marie see children as better off with access to genetic information, even if the donor is uninvolved as a parent, a good case can be made for the opposite decision. Jenny, for instance, chose a sperm bank, in part to protect her child from possibly feeling rejected by a known but uninvolved donor. "I'd rather take responsibility for my choice to have him this way," she said. "He can be angry at me for my decision, rather than feel hurt because there's a man he can identify who doesn't behave as a father."

As important as it is for lesbians to think through their decisions, the reality all ultimately may have to come to terms with is not a singular model. Instead, we must come to recognize and appreciate pluralism: children who are loved and given opportunities to grow can thrive in many different family contexts. Knowing this, we can discard a determination of which family structure is "best" in favor of finding ways to make all the different structures work.

GAY MEN HAVE A DIFFERENT SET OF DECISIONS

Gay men are often in the position of parenting children who are primarily raised by lesbians. This family model fits in a culture in which women are socialized toward primary childrearing and men toward a secondary role. While there are many gay men for whom this arrangement works well, there are also those who, like their lesbian counterparts, want more involvement with their children. But men do not have the same options as lesbians. There is no equivalent of donor insemination. Surrogacy comes the closest, but it is a much more biologically, ethically, legally, financially, and psychologically complex process. Similarly, gay men are considerably less likely to find women willing to be the equivalent of a known donor—that is, to have babies with whom they will be minimally involved (though on occasion people do make such arrangements). For gay men who want to be primary parents, adoption is often a more feasible option than biological parenting. Given all this, the issues faced by gay men who choose to become fathers through biological conception are quite distinct from lesbians' concerns.

Becoming a Father Through Surrogacy

Eric and Jeff were college sweethearts who came out together. Though each had imagined they would get married and have children, it was clear early on in their relationship that their futures were bound together. Jeff never gave up the idea of having children, though he didn't actively pursue it until he hit his thirties. At that point, he approached Eric with the idea of advertising for a surrogate mother. Though he thought about adoption, he wanted to have a child who was biologically connected to him. Eric was doubtful that they would find someone willing to be a surrogate. "Everything you read about surrogacy is these women who are married who have several kids, who want to give this to another couple who can't have kids—it's all portrayed in a straight, heterosexual way."

They discussed the possibility of co-parenting with lesbians, but that wasn't an appealing arrangement. Jeff says, "I wanted this to be our child—for this to be a family of three." Eric says, "We've structured a life for ourselves that we feel very comfortable with, that we like a lot, and we set the parameters for that. We don't let others set the parameters, and that's important to us. A co-parenting relationship would just be way too complicated, and too many people who we know don't approach life the way we do." Jeff adds, "Being dependent on someone else would be very frustrating." They placed an ad that specified they were two gay men wanting to raise a child. They got one response, which they pursued.

Paid surrogacy is a complicated social and personal step. It is fundamentally a financial arrangement through which a child comes into the world. The biological parameters, including a woman's efforts to conceive and nine months of carrying a child, are much more extensive than for donor insemination. For these reasons, the social and psychological issues that surround the process are complex.

One of the most troubling aspects of surrogacy is the class imbalance: Eric and Jeff wanted a child and were well off financially; Donna, who responded to their ad, did not want a child, but needed money. Eric and Jeff hoped that they could work out a friendly arrangement, one that would benefit all concerned. At first it seemed they were on their way to doing just that. An agreement was hammered out with lawyers, and the insemination and pregnancy went smoothly. In less than two years since Jeff first proposed parenting, he and Eric had a baby girl, Leah.

Eric, Jeff, and Donna were on friendly terms and had agreed on limited visitation, but this eventually became a source of strife. Jeff and Eric wanted the visits to be supervised and to occur in their home; Donna wanted to take the baby on her own. Communication broke down when Eric and Jeff refused Donna's request. There was a series of exchanges in letters, through which Jeff and Eric tried to establish ground rules for Donna's visitation. Ultimately, Donna didn't respond and contact ceased.

Despite the problems that arose, Eric feels that, "If there wasn't a whole lot of emotional baggage involved on the part of the mother, contact would be preferable. It would be easier for Leah to understand more of her background and her heritage, and who she is as a person if she had that contact, but I could be wrong."

Jeff doesn't quite agree. "I've changed my opinion. Now I feel that other than curiosity, it would be a lot easier for them to have next to no involvement with each other. We have very little in common with her mother. . . . I think those relationships where a gay man helps out two women and stays involved and all are friends are wonderful, but they're unrealistic in these circumstances. Surrogacy is just this bizarre thing where you're dealing with different financial statuses. Because there's such disparity, there's so little in common to base that kind of friendship on."

Like some women who conceive through unknown donors, Jeff is ambivalent about his wish that there be no contact between his child and her biological mother. "I do worry sometimes, like when I see people on television who've been adopted and haven't seen their biological parents, and are freaked out. But I think that doesn't have to happen—that often those people have a lot of other emotional baggage." Eric points out the different positions of gay men and lesbians. "I feel kind of envious of women who go to sperm banks. Once they make that decision, it's over. They may still agonize over not being able to provide that connection for their child, but it's done." In contrast, surrogacy often involves a process of negotiation and the formation of a relationship. As it was for Eric, Jeff, and Donna, surrogacy can be an intense and complex undertaking. What it will ultimately mean to children like Leah is yet to be seen.

As the nonbiological parent, Eric was in a vulnerable position. Like most lesbian and gay couples raising children, Eric and Jeff had to rely on mutual trust. Jeff says, "We can't conceive of ourselves breaking up. If for some unknown reason we ever did, it would have to be amicable—it's just we can't not be that way. We have a relationship where we talk and communicate better than almost anyone we know." Eric adds, "If you can't work out your differences, I believe you have no right to take this kind of adventure. Because we are trailblazing, we take the responsibility very seriously."

Legally, the surrogacy process is not complete until an adoption has occurred. In the case of heterosexual couples, the biological mother terminates her parental rights, and the spouse of the biological father adopts the child, making the couple the child's only legal parents. In their attempt to "close the circle" of the surrogacy arrangement, Jeff and Eric attempted a second-parent adoption. When Donna agreed to terminate her parental rights, it was Eric who would adopt Leah. The legal question revolved around whether he could do that without Jeff giving up his parental rights. If he had not been able to, the couple considered having Eric become the sole legal parent, as a source of balance. However, shortly before Leah's second birthday, Eric and Jeff were successful in their adoption attempt—their particular circumstances making them a first in the country. When Leah was two years old, Jeff and Eric initiated another surrogacy arrangement through which they had a son.

For the most part, access to surrogacy—like access to other alternative modes of bringing children into one's life—is much more available to heterosexual infertile couples than to gay men. However, surrogacy is much like independent adoption, with access strongly related to financial resources. Surrogacy is far less popular among gay men than donor insemination is among lesbians. Its high cost, along with the social complexity it involves, render it a less frequent approach than adoption or joint-family arrangements.

Surrogacy has been practiced since biblical times—in some informal sense, there have always been women bearing children for friends or family members. But formal, paid contracts for surrogacy arrangements first emerged in this country around 1976, and have been on the rise ever since. Though in any given case surrogacy can work well for all involved, it poses major ethical issues not just for its participants but for society as well. It involves much more than a separation between genetic and social parenting roles, since gestation and birth are processes involving not only a woman's body but also her relation to the child she bears. For the most part, these arrangements involve large sums of money, and bring wealthy people who want children together with poor women in need of money. Out of these issues—the psychological ramifications and the financial exchange—arise many crucial questions.

The major societal quandaries about surrogacy fall into two categories: is it baby selling? and is it exploitative of women? These questions came most vividly to public attention in 1987, when Mary Beth Whitehead, having given birth to the child the courts would refer to as Baby M after signing a surrogacy contract for William and Betsy Stem, changed her mind and wanted to keep the baby. Was she bound by the contract she'd signed? Was the contract, in which there was an exchange of money and an exchange of human life, legal? Was it ethical? And, most important, who should get the child? Mary Beth Whitehead argued that the contract was invalid; she captured the complexity of the surrogacy issue in her statement that she'd "signed on an egg, not on a baby." After a much publicized trial, the Stems were awarded full custody of the one-year-old child. However, along with that decision came a ruling that made surrogacy illegal in the state of New Jersey, where the case had occurred.

While there is little legislation explicitly applying to surrogacy, after the Whitehead case, seventeen states enacted some form of applicable legislation. For the most part, these laws make surrogacy contracts unenforceable. The legal reasoning is drawn from several other areas of law. One argument is that a woman cannot consent to adoption before the birth of a child, and hence cannot be bound by a surrogacy contract drawn up at the time of conception. Another is that in every state baby selling is illegal. Here though, much of surrogacy bypasses this idea, treating compensation not as money in exchange for a human life but as payment for the mother's expenses or for her work in gestation—akin to rent. Some of the laws have focused on money as the key issue, strictly forbidding any exchange other than expenses; a few states prohibit mediators (that is, brokers) from accepting fees. Even with the contracts legally unenforceable, many of the problems that arise when mothers change their minds remain unresolved. Since surrogacy arrangements by and large involve men with substantial resources and women in need of money, if a child is born from such an arrangement and the surrogate changes her mind, most often a typical custody battle ensues, with the best-interests-of-the-child standard applied by the courts. Here, surrogate mothers are at a considerable disadvantage, often not well off enough to pursue a court battle. Surrogacy practices contain a major potential for the exploitation of women in desperate financial circumstances. The guidelines that minimize the risk of such exploitation include making contracts unenforceable (that is, permanently decided only after birth, as in adoption) and giving, as only New York does, the woman custody without a court battle in the event that she changes her mind.

Another Kind of Extended Family

Not all surrogacy arrangements involve a financial exchange. At the other end of the spectrum from the tradition of women as primary and men as secondary parents are the more rare arrangements of women who bear children for men to raise. Such was the case with Kevin, John, and Toni. Kevin had always wanted to be a father and had thought seriously about adopting a child, but he was ultimately discouraged by the foster-care debate in Massachusetts. He was a publicly gay man who would neither have nor want the option of passing as straight in order to adopt a child, so he worried that his chances of getting a child were minimal. Over many years, Kevin had become very close friends with Toni, a single bisexual mother. Kevin had been present at the birth of Toni's second child, and he and John were now like uncles to the children. A close-knit extended-family relation was well established by the time Toni shocked Kevin with the offer to bear a child for him and John to raise. Toni felt she could offer a child no better parents than Kevin and John. For his part, Kevin was overwhelmed by Toni's offer. "I would never have asked a woman to have a baby for me—it's way too much to ask. But I was thrilled."

John was skeptical, feeling strongly still that adopting an existing child was a better way to go. But as the foster-care battle raged, "biological parenting began to seem more appealing because of the legal protection it provided." The three carefully hammered out an agreement, one that included a clear commitment on John and Kevin's part not to challenge Toni if she changed her mind and wanted the baby. For her part, however, Toni was far more worried about the opposite occurrence; she did not want to raise another child, and wanted John and Kevin to have primary responsibility. Her involvement with now two-year-old Amber is substantial, and the group does function as an extended family, with Toni's other children clearly Amber's siblings. Though the arrangement thus bears some resemblance to the familiar family, it is also highly unusual, especially because, simultaneously to being Amber's mother, Toni is not her parent; both the power and the responsibility of parenting fall equally on John and Kevin's shoulders.

JOINT PARENTING—LESBIANS AND GAY MEN TOGETHER

Arrangements such as Kevin and John's with Toni, or Susan and Dana's with their children's father, bring lesbians and gay men together to form families. Most commonly these arrangements involve a division into primary and secondary parenting centered in one household, most often the woman or women involved. These setups resemble amicable custody arrangements in cases of divorce, but they are in reality quite different because they are planned this way and from the outset fall outside of the law's definitions.

Lesbians and gay men also come together in a different family form, that of equally shared parenting. Though it has much in common with the arrangement described above, this particular version deserves separate consideration. Joint-parenting arrangements bring lesbians and gay men together in ways that push even further beyond the nuclear family model, creating an altogether new family form. Truly joint-parenting arrangements decenter family life, creating strong bonds between lesbians and gay men established around parenting itself and independent of primary erotic and romantic unions. Such was the family Barry and Adria established.

"I always say this is the longest pregnancy in the world because it took thirteen years of actively trying to become a dad 'til the time Ari was born," Barry said. He had always seen himself as someone who would have children and, though he didn't know how it would happen, that vision didn't change when he came out at age twenty-two. In his late twenties, he began to discuss the possibility of shared parenting with a heterosexual female friend. But over the course of their conversations, it became clear to Barry that the relationship wouldn't work; much as he wanted a child, he decided not to pursue that possibility.

Then he began to look into adoption as a single man, getting as far as the home-study stage. But at that point he backed away from the process. "It was not a time I wanted to invite the state into my home to scrutinize the way I lived. Also I didn't really want to raise a child alone. I really did want to have another parent."

Shortly after that, he was approached by an acquaintance. "She had had a child when she was really young and felt both trapped in her life and not able to figure out how she could get out of the trap in terms of getting more money and some skills. She had seen me interact with her son who was three at the time, and she knew I was trying to become a father and thought it was really unfair that gay men had such a hard time doing it. She offered to be a surrogate mom if I would help her get some kind of training so that she could get a better kind of job. She still wanted to be friends, and thought maybe an appropriate arrangement would be that she would relate to this child like a distant relative. We hadn't worked out the details, but it was '81 and AIDS was happening. There were no tests, and I didn't feel like I could responsibly inseminate so I decided not to do it."

With his third attempt to become a father failing to pan out, and AIDS on the horizon, Barry put the question of children on the back burner for the next four years. Once the HIV test was available and he tested negative, he decided he could continue his quest.

On New Year's Eve, 1986, Barry was introduced by a mutual friend to Adria, a lesbian who was looking for someone with whom to raise a child. In her early adulthood, Adria had assumed she would adopt children. But as she became focused on her work and community, the idea of becoming a parent faded into the background. Unlike Barry, Adria hadn't spent years engrossed in the pursuit of parenthood. At age forty-two, her world view shifted dramatically when a close friend was diagnosed with AIDS and moved into her home. During the process of caring for him while he was dying, Adria became possessed with an intense desire to be pregnant. What had previously been a source of ambivalence and questioning became definitive. Living through her friend's illness, Adria felt, "If I can do this, I can do anything." The catch was, that Adria had been in a relationship with Marilyn for eight years and Marilyn was not keen on the idea of raising a child. Adria, for her part, wanted her child to have an involved father. This proved to be a good fit, since from Marilyn's perspective it would be more comfortable if Adria had a co-parent other than herself.

Barry describes the tumble of feelings and questions he encountered during their first meetings: "We'd been part of overlapping communities with the same kind of political history, so we knew things about each other and felt very familiar when we actually met, but we had never met before we sat down to ask questions like, 'Would you like to make a commitment for the rest of your life with this stranger and have a very intimate relationship—not sexual, but as close as you can be?' It was very awkward, like going through a series of courting behaviors—checking each other out, putting your best foot forward, and there are these flirtations going on. Our process was that we couldn't say, 'Yes, this is working, let's do it.' It was more like looking for why it wouldn't work until we could find nothing more, then saying, 'Is there any reason why we couldn't do this?' " Adria, on the other hand, immediately impressed by Barry's integrity and level of commitment to parenting, knew at their first encounter that she and Barry would become family.

During the next five months, they let each other into their lives. "It became clear that our sensibility around child-rearing was very similar even though we're very different people," Barry remembers. "Our personalities and backgrounds are very different. Starting this process at an older age, we were both clear about what we wanted and what we didn't want. We wanted to build family with each other. I think we both hoped that ideally that could happen, but if we could find someone close enough, with a similar enough world-view, we knew enough not to expect everything on our list. We introduced each other to our circle of friends, celebrated our birthdays together, gradually doing some of those kinds of family things."

A month after Barry and Adria decided to go ahead with the plan, Barry met Michael. "Here I am, not looking for a relationship, because I'm clear I want kids. You know, if a relationship happens that's fine, that can come later. And then, here's Michael to integrate into this picture. Part of his attraction to me was that I was building a family and he loves children—so we have this dynamic of Michael who is outside wanting in as much as he could, and Marilyn, who is inside wanting to have boundaries as much as she could. And there's Adria and me in the middle, trying to make this happen."

During the next two years, Barry and Adria went through a very intense period that included difficulty conceiving and four miscarriages. The process was particularly discouraging, given Adria's age. One doctor dismissed them completely, chalking up the difficulties to approaching menopause. Adria feared that Barry would abandon the effort to have a baby with her since he so badly wanted a child. But there was never any question in Barry's mind. "We were clear that we really wanted to parent together. That had already been born in this process. We were already really close friends and had this thing that was starting to cross all the traditional lines between gay men and lesbians—building the most physical, intimate relationship you can. Being in the medical part of this process, which was very unpleasant, was really one of the things that pulled us together. Those miscarriages, though I don't recommend this as a strategy, turned out to be a way to find out how you are together. Going through hard times, what we learned is that our instincts pull us together—that's how we deal with hardship. And so that brought us even closer." Barry and Adria supported each other through each episode and were very much partners in the effort. Eventually they saw a fertility specialist, who prescribed Clomid and took over the insemination process. Barry became an expert at assisting the doctor in ultrasound and follicle measuring. At age forty-four, Adria became pregnant and carried to term.

Throughout this process a complicated dynamic developed among the four adults. In many ways Adria and Barry developed a primary intimate relationship, one that had to be balanced with their respective partner relationships. It was the beginning of what was to be their particular sort of family—not a uniform, single entity but more like concentric circles, with four overlapping intimate adult relationships. Though Barry and Adria were at the center of this parenting unit, their approach was inclusive, embracing Michael and Marilyn. This was evident as they moved about the world. Barry remembers the day Adria was late for her first Lamaze class: "So in this room are all these straight couples with very pregnant women, and in walk Barry, Michael, and Marilyn, who is an Olympic athlete, with a very slender toned body—I mean, this woman is not pregnant. It's an awkward threesome. The teacher looks at us and says, "This is the birthing class." And we say, "Great, we're in the right place." Now they're really confused, and we go around the room to introduce ourselves. You have to say your name and the magic due date, so I say 'My name is Barry and I'm the father of this child that Adria, who's not here, is carrying,' and then Michael says, 'My name is Michael and I'm Barry's partner, and I'm going to help parent this child that Adria, who's not here, is carrying,' and then Marilyn, 'I'm Marilyn and I'm Adria's partner.' Their eyes are getting bigger and their mouths are falling open, and finally Adria comes, not having a clue what she was walking into."

Ari was delivered through cesarean section in 1989—Marilyn, Barry, and Michael were all present at his birth. Adria and Barry had agreed to share parenting equally. This is difficult to achieve in the context of two separate households. Each can be with Ari whenever he or she wants and also whenever he is needing one of them. Though they have free access to each other's homes, separation is a key issue in this family. From the very beginning of his life, Ari has gone back and forth between the households almost every other day. Barry and Adria also do a lot of traveling. In the first couple of months, before Ari began to travel back and forth, Barry slept at Adria's house. After that, while Adria was nursing Ari, she would come to Barry's house on the days he wasn't with her. At six months of age, Ari began to take a bottle as well, which somewhat eased the stress.

As they look toward the future, both Barry and Adria have some trepidation about their own feelings regarding separations. They are beginning to feel that Ari, now a preschooler, needs longer stretches in each household. Barry anticipates this. "It's hard for me to imagine him not being home for three days in a row. I just can't—not that I'm not totally comfortable and happy with where he is, because he's at home being loved by his wonderful mother and other parent, and nothing could please me more, but he's not home with me. I find myself wandering into his room a lot when he's not there, looking for him."

Adria has been known to appear at Barry's house in the middle of the night, needing to check in with Ari. Speculating about Ari's responses to the constant comings and goings, Adria says, "I think he suffers as any being would suffer from everything changing all the time. It's the same two houses, it's the same people, and he has everything at both places. He always has his little shopping bag and he carries his blanket with him wherever he goes. I think he'll either grow up to be a person who will only be in one place and will be kind of rigid about it because he's had enough of this, or he'll be someone who any place he hangs his hat will be his home. I think he'll have a certain kind of autonomy and confidence, because he seems to now, but I think he'll also have some issues about being left—people always come back , but they also always leave." One of the issues Barry and Adria are currently trying to address is their desire to have more time together with Ari rather than being on separate shifts.

The complexities of the four-way relationship take a lot of energy to navigate. Though decisions are essentially a matter of consensus, the family's communication about Ari is primarily channeled through Barry and Adria. In a sense, Michael and Marilyn have become the keepers of their respective couple relationships. As Adria sees it, "they watch over the intimacy of the couples— and they help each couple to separate from the other." For Marilyn, Barry's and Michael's involvements with Ari have freed her to be his parent. "The fact that she's not the only other parent besides me, the fact that there's someone else who's fifty percent responsible for him has allowed her a lot of room, to in fact be a very important parent. In our family, because she doesn't want to be a mother, there's not much competition like you'll see in some lesbian couples. And she doesn't want to be his father; there's not competition with Michael and Barry, either. She has her place with Ari. She's the only athlete among us. He's a little talking boy—he's not very athletic. She teaches him how to jump. That's where they live together, in this sort of playful world and he's very close to her."

Michael, unlike Marilyn, has much more interest in a primary parenting role, and has had to grapple with that in the context of a family unit that is clearly centered on Barry and Adria as primary parents. He and Barry think about expanding the family—through having Michael father a child. "When Ari's at our house he's there with both of us and it's fairly equal in terms of day-to-day doing things," Barry says. "Michael has stepped in as the cook. He likes to do it and he cooks for Ari all the time, so he's Ari's best cook and when he's hungry he looks to Michael. I know Michael has felt unseen and unrecognized but not by me or our family. My father, for instance, was watching Michael put Ari to bed one night and he just said 'it's so amazing—he is a father to this child.' But even though Michael gets recognition from our family and community, there's so much in this culture that in basic ways doesn't recognize his role. We try to be especially conscious of it and name it when it's happening."

As with the Lamaze class, as they move about the world this family shakes people's attitudes. Once, Ari closed a car door on his hand. In the emergency room, Barry and Michael met Adria and Ari at the hospital. Barry remembers that day vividly; "So I'm holding Ari and he's telling me the story, saying 'Daddy, I cried a little but it's okay now,' and we go together but they keep trying to separate us all. Then we get to the point of registering, and I'm holding Ari and the clerk is asking me all these questions that I'm answering while Michael and Adria stand behind me. Then the clerk says to me, 'Okay, Michael, so you're the father,' and Michael says 'No, I'm Michael and he's on my plan.' Meanwhile, Ari is pointing to me saying, 'This is the father.' So, okay, this is the father, but Michael learned that in order to get his work to pay these bills—to not raise red flags—he says he's the stepfather. And the clerk must be thinking—well, okay, this is a very friendly divorce—here's the mom, dad, stepfather, and kid. Then he asks Michael for his address. I'd already given him my address as the father and, of course, it's the same address. At this point we're all fidgeting, and Adria says, 'I bet you want to know my address next.' So we have these funny experiences, but we make it work."

Of his family life, Barry says, "It's made us all look at how we do relationships. I think our mode of operating now is basically to act out of the basic goodness that's there in all of these relationships and to let go of a lot of the petty stuff about each other that drives each of us crazy. We pick and choose what we have to deal with. It works incredibly well, and it's also complicated trying to manage these multiple needs." Looking back at his original decision to become a parent in this way, Barry says, "It's important to try to imagine every situation you can before you do something like this, 'cause it gets you thinking, but there's no way to know what the reality will be. No matter how much we talked, there was no way I could be prepared for the instant of Ari's birth, when I went from one primary relationship with Michael to three. And of course it doesn't matter what the adults decide in advance; once the child is born, their needs are going to determine—and should determine—what happens. Sometimes that can bear no relation to all these plans."

Amid all the complexity, Ari seems to thrive. He makes families out of everything, one of his favorites being clothes hangers. The blue one is always himself, and then there is a Mommy, a Daddy, a Marilyn, and a Michael. He wonders why his best friend has no Marilyn or Michael.

THE REINVENTED FAMILY

Lesbian and gay parents essentially reinvent the family as a pluralistic phenomenon. They self-consciously build from the ground up a variety of family types that don't conform to the traditional structure. In so doing, they encourage society to ask, "What is a family?" The question has profound meaning in both the culture at large and the very heart of each of our intimate lives. It is like a tree trunk from which many branches extend: What is a mother, a father, a parent, a sibling? Can a child have two or more mothers or fathers? Is one more "real" by virtue of biological or legal parent status? How does society's recognition (or its absence) foster or impede parent-child relationships? To what extent does the state shape family life? To what extent can nontraditional families alter the state's definition of family?

These questions go well beyond the issue of whether families headed by lesbians and gay men should exist. There emerges a complex reciprocal tension between lesbian and gay family life on the one hand and homophobia and the idealization of the traditional family on the other. Clearly, lesbian and gay parents don't create their families in a vacuum. Their choices are shaped by the institutions that mediate family formation, most notably the legal and medical systems, and adoption agencies. Lesbian and gay parents vary with respect to how they view the state. While some let legal definitions inform their choices, others feel they can probably keep the state out of their lives by relying on trust and goodwill. Sometimes families who've taken this route end up, to their dismay, in the courts, challenging prevailing legal thought.

However they choose to form their families, lesbians and gay men do so in the context of the idealization of the traditional model; their families are inevitably shaped by this fact. Yet at the same time, over the past decade, many changes have been wrought by lesbian and gay family formation itself—ranging from unmarried women's increased access to donor insemination to the particular challenges that lesbian and gay families bring to the law. Though our society is a long way from embracing eight-year-old Danielle's deceptively simple statement that a "family is people who all love each other, care for each other, help out, and understand each other," her words may yet prove to be our most crucial guide to the future.

R E A D I N G

24

Hispanic Families in the United States: Research Perspectives

CATHERINE STREET CHILMAN

The impact of the Hispanic population on American society is enormous and diverse, having many implications for family research, professional practice, and public policies. Scholars and professionals need a deeper understanding of the variety of Hispanic individuals and families in this country.

From Catherine Street Chilman, "Hispanic Families in the United States: Research Perspectives," in *Family Ethnicity: Strength in Diversity*, ed. by Harriette Pipes McAdoo (Newbury Park, CA: Sage, 1993), pp. 141–163.

Although it is common to view all Hispanic families in this country as being similar in values, beliefs, behaviors, resources, and concerns, such sweeping assumptions are seriously erroneous (Andrade, 1982; Cortes, 1980; de Silva, 1981; Frisbie, 1986; Mirandé, 1977; Staples and Mirandé, 1980). These families are far from homogeneous; they represent a number of different national and ethnic origins, vary by social class, speak a variety of dialects, have differing histories, differ in immigration and citizenship status, and live in various regions of this country. . . .

The first part of this chapter provides general immigration and demographic facts about each of the major Hispanic groups in the United States. The second section discusses some of the chief social and psychological research findings regarding these families. . . .

SOME CURRENT ISSUES IN IMMIGRATION

Until 1945, legal immigration to the United States was mainly governed by an act of Congress of 1924, which was amended in 1952. This used the national origin system, which favored Western Europeans over Asians and Pacific peoples. In general, there was a ratio for each nation in the world that limited immigrants to numbers proportional to the population makeup of the United States in 1920 (for example, about one-fourth of immigrants granted entry were from Great Britain). However, the independent countries of the Western Hemisphere were afforded unlimited entry under this act.

In 1965, new legislation abolished restrictions against Asian and Pacific peoples. However, it imposed limits on immigration from the Western Hemisphere, with a quota of 120,000 persons a year being established. Preference was given to those with occupational skills judged to be needed in this country (LaPorte, 1977).

Because of severe economic and political problems in their own countries, larger numbers of Hispanics have sought to enter the United States than provided for under immigration laws. Thus many illegal aliens have recently entered this country, particularly from Mexico and Central and South America. Portes (1979) holds that the current large waves of illegal immigrants, most of whom are Mexicans, could be prevented from entering the United States, but that business and industry do not want this to occur. These workers are a cheap source of labor, and the fact that they are illegal creates an advantage for their employers, because they are highly vulnerable employees.

The Immigration Reform and Control Act of 1986 offered legal status in the United States or amnesty to illegal aliens who could prove they had resided continuously in this country since before January 1, 1982. More liberal amnesty provisions were developed for agricultural workers. The amnesty program includes sanctions against employers who hire illegal aliens and provisions for stepped-up border patrol and immigration service enforcement agents. The goal is to deter further illegal immigration while offering the protection of legal status to aliens who have lived here since before January 1, 1982 (Applebome, 1988).

Aliens applying for jobs had to apply for amnesty by the end of August 1987 to be hired for work that year, but applications were low and only about half of the estimated 2 million illegal aliens in this country had applied for amnesty by January 1, 1988, even though the deadline for such application was May 1, 1988. Most observers agree that the major impediment to this application was fear that families would be broken up, because some members of a number of families lacked documentary proof that they had lived continuously in the United States since before January 1, 1982. In fact, it is probable that many family members did not live in this country before 1982 and that of those who were here at that early date, a number probably had moved back and forth across the border. Attempts were made in Congress in 1987 to amend the legislation to protect family unity and grant amnesty to all family members if some members had gained amnesty or were eligible for it, but these amendments failed to pass.

The family issue is but one difficult aspect of the immigration problem. There are powerful economic and political pressures in countries of origin inducing immigrants to cross the border, whether these immigrants can gain legal entry or not. At the same time, many Hispanics south of the United States yearn to enter this country because of the relative economic gains and personal freedoms it appears to offer. Moreover, the long border between the countries is very difficult to police adequately, and a number of U.S. employers desire the cheap labor provided by illegal immigrants who fear discovery and deportation.

It is essential for family researchers, policy and program personnel, and practitioners to recognize the severe problems families face when they have immigrated to this country illegally. As suggested earlier, they are extremely vulnerable to employer exploitation. They also live in constant fear of discovery and are therefore difficult to reach if they need assistance. Further, they are ineligible for public aid and must rely on private sources for help. Immigration, in and of itself, poses a number of problems for families; illegal immigration severely escalates these problems.

POPULATION CHARACTERISTICS

There are difficulties in defining the term *Spanish origin*. Recognizing that census reports do contain some errors, it is helpful, nonetheless, to consider the data they present. According to these reports, there were more than 12 million persons of Spanish origin in the United States in 1979: 7.3 million Chicanos, 1.7 million Puerto Ricans, 800,000 Cubans, 900,000 Central or South Americans, and more than 1 million persons of other Spanish backgrounds. The total number of Hispanic-origin people in the United States increased by 33 percent between 1970 and 1979, with the fastest-growing group being Mexican—which grew by 62 percent. The majority of Hispanic families live in Arizona, California, Colorado, New Mexico, Texas, Florida, and New York. These families are largely concentrated in 10 of the nation's 305 metropolitan areas, with especially large numbers in New York and Los Angeles.

Age

The median age of the Hispanic population is fairly young when compared with the remainder of the population. This difference in age level is both a result and a cause of the higher fertility rate of Hispanic families. This comparatively youthful age has a number of other implications for public policy, including the likelihood that programs for children and adolescents will have a disproportionate number of Hispanics in them.

Educational Levels

On the average, members of Hispanic families, particularly the elderly, have lower educational levels than any other population group in the United States (U.S. Bureau of the Census, 1980). These lower levels of education for most Hispanics are partly a result of the recent migration of many of them, as well as the poverty and low levels of public education in their former countries. Continuing problems of low educational achievement for many Hispanic-Americans, including children and youth, is a matter of intense concern, especially because it adversely affects their future employment opportunities.

Employment and Income

Racial discrimination is apt to be another important factor in the high rates of unemployment of those Puerto Ricans who have dark skins and are classed as nonwhites—an effect of the African, Indian, and Spanish mix of their native land. Racial discrimination, still present in the United States, often comes as a shock to immigrants who have experienced much less of this in Puerto Rico (M. Delgado, 1987).

Spanish-American men and women are more apt than the rest of the population to be in blue-collar and service occupations. This is especially true for people of Mexican and Puerto Rican origin. Women are more apt than men to be in white-collar occupations. The great majority of Hispanic families live in urban areas today. There has been a massive shift away from farm employment, mostly because of the industrialization of agriculture. However, on average, there has been little advancement in occupational level.

Hispanic women are generally paid at a lower wage level than either white or African-American women. This is also true for those Hispanic men who are in clerical occupations or who are factory operatives. On the other hand, Hispanic men who are in professional or managerial fields earn more, on average, than black men in these occupations but considerably less than white males.

As of the 1980 census, more than 50 percent of all female-headed Hispanic families were below the poverty line, including 72 percent of Puerto Rican families, 49 percent of Chicanos, and 38 percent of other Hispanic families. For all groups, two-parent families with the wife in the labor force had the highest income, and one-parent families had the lowest annual income: about $25,000 for white one-parent families, $15,000 for African-Americans, and $18,000 for Hispanics (U.S. Bureau of the Census, 1983). In general, families with young children had the lowest average annual income in the nation. Overall, a large percentage of the children lived in impoverished families—a shocking and tragic fact. Minority children were in particularly adverse situations: 46 percent of black families with children had incomes below the poverty line. This was the case for 39 percent of Hispanic families and 16 percent of white families. . . .

Marital Stability

The 1980 census data for five southwestern states show that rates of marital stability are about the same for Mexican-Americans, Cuban-Americans, and Anglo-Americans, with divorce and separation rates of about 25 percent for these groups (U.S. Bureau of the Census, 1980). However, both blacks and Puerto Ricans experienced rates of about 40 percent. Mexican-Americans and Cuban-Americans had a far lower remarriage rate than did Anglos, but the reasons for this are unknown. Interestingly, Mexican-American divorce rates rise with higher levels of education for women, though the reverse tends to be true for Anglos (except for those women with graduate educations). Frisbie (1986) speculates that Mexican-American women with higher levels of education tend to become more acculturated to American patterns and are, therefore, more accepting of separation and divorce; however, this may be an overtly simple explanation.

Precise data regarding unmarried parenthood among Hispanic-Americans tend to be missing. However, studies of unmarried adolescent mothers reveal that Hispanic girls are fairly similar to other adolescent women (*Family Planning Perspectives*, 1983). Although premarital chastity has been emphasized within the culture, this norm has been drastically eroded in recent years. Thus nonmarital intercourse and pregnancy have become increasingly common. Although the parents of pregnant teenage girls usually consider illegitimate childbearing a serious problem, they tend to welcome the baby into the family if the young woman decides to keep her child and not get married—a decision she frequently makes.

Fertility

According to the 1980 census, Hispanic women had higher birth rates than did either blacks or Anglos; however, those rates have been declining somewhat in more recent years. For example, only a little more than one-third of the women aged 15 to 44 had three or more children in 1980, compared with almost half of this group in 1970. Estrada (1987) notes that these high rates are caused by a number of factors: the youthful age structure of the Hispanic-American population, large families and high fertility rates of incoming immigrants, and traditional, though fading, negative attitudes toward birth control. These attitudes are partly associated with the fact that the huge majority of Hispanic-Americans are Catholic.

Large families are most likely to be characterized by low levels of employment, education, and income. This is found for such families in most parts of the world. Therefore, although these data can be interpreted as the consequence of high fertility, analyses also show that high fertility is a result of little education, unemployment, and poverty and the hopelessness, alienation, and lack of medical care they often engender (Chilman, 1968, 1983). High fertility also tends to go with low levels of modernization and a predominantly agricultural society (Chilman, 1968). There is evidence that the birth rate for Hispanic-American families is currently declining in association with rising levels of education, urbanization, and employment of Hispanic women. Increased availability of low-cost, high-quality family planning services also has been helpful, although addition of Spanish-speaking personnel to the professional staffs of such service agencies is frequently needed (J. Jones, 1985).

Language

The vast majority of Hispanics in this country are bilingual. Two-thirds of those who speak Spanish report that they also speak English well or very well (Estrada, 1987). A recent Institute of Social Research survey of Mexican-American households in the Southwest and Midwest revealed that the majority of adults interviewed spoke both English and Spanish. There was general consensus among the respondents that the speaking of Spanish was very important. Most thought there ought to be bilingual education in the schools. There was a generally strong feeling of ethnic identity, with many of the younger members of the population showing a particularly enthusiastic movement in this direction (Arce, 1982).

Many of the elderly and recent immigrants speak only Spanish, and many Hispanics, in general, chiefly speak Spanish within the family. As with other immigrant groups, it is common for the children to learn English before the parents do and for family members who are mainly confined to the home (often the elderly and mothers of young children) to speak English far less well than those who are in school or employed. This can create a number of disruptive family problems and is another indication that professionals who seek to work with Hispanic families should be bilingual, so that they can converse directly with all family members (Bernal, 1982; Falicov, 1982; Garcia-Preto, 1982).

Variations by National Origin

In the discussion that follows, emphasis is placed on the family-related cultural patterns of various Hispanic-American groups. There are two reasons for this emphasis: (a) most of the associated research and clinical observations reported in the literature emphasize cultural patterns and (b) these patterns are important in affecting individual and family behaviors, although not as important as much of the literature, including the following discussion, would suggest.

It is essential to recognize that cultural patterns by themselves do not determine an individual's behavior, although they may strongly affect his or her values, attitudes, and norms. Each person's behavior is also strongly affected by her or his temperament, special abilities and limitations, physical condition, age, life situation, and total developmental experience within the family and elsewhere. Moreover, the behavior of families is an outcome of the interaction of the individuals within them, plus the family's size, structure, history, developmental stage, and total situation—as well as cultural patterns.

Thus these patterns constitute one of a number of complex factors that affect familial behaviors and those of family members. For instance, Baca Zinn (1980) perceptively wrote that cultural values are important in family life, but should be studied in social context. They become fully meaningful only when they are related to historical, economic, residential, and other structural factors. Although they are important dimensions of families, they do not by themselves determine, or fully explain, family organization. Rather, one needs to study actual behaviors of families as well as their expressed beliefs (Baca Zinn, 1980, pp. 68–69). One also needs to take into account the economic resources of a family. For instance, members of an extended family may live together out of economic need rather than preference. Younger relatives may provide support for aging kin—again, more because of necessity than because of cultural norms.

The historical background of a people also influences the behavior of its members in a number of subtle and not-so-subtle ways. Among other things, history, including legends, affects the self-image of group members as well as their perceptions of people of other national origins. Thus brief historical sketches of various Hispanic groups are provided below.

Puerto Ricans

Puerto Rico was a Spanish colony from the time of its discovery by Columbus in 1493 until the United States invaded and annexed it in 1898 during the Spanish-American War (Fitzpatrick, 1981; Garcia-Preto, 1982). Although Puerto Rico gained increasing control over its own affairs during the next half century, becoming a commonwealth in 1952, real political control over the island remains in the United States today. This fact has spawned understandable resentment among Puerto Ricans, with some groups agitating for complete independence, some for statehood, and others for continued collaboration with the United States and the resulting benefits of this partnership, perceived by some as outweighing the costs. These varying positions naturally affect the attitudes of Puerto Ricans who come to the United States; it can be expected that a number would continue to harbor antipathy toward this country, with resulting barriers to acculturation.

As a people, Puerto Ricans are of many colors, from completely Negroid to completely Caucasian, and they must face the difficult problem of racial prejudice in the United States (Fitzpatrick, 1981). Poverty has been widespread in Puerto Rico, a central reason for the large migration to the continental United States. Cultural patterns are highly variable, affected by the kind of occupation pursued, the region of the island (such as isolated rural areas, farm villages, or urban areas), and social class status. Fitzpatrick (1981) cites a number of studies of family life and socialization in Puerto Rico, but most of them were carried out during the 1950s and 1960s and are therefore now rather out of date. There seems to be almost no research regarding Puerto Rican family life in this country. Thus in their discussions of the topic, both Garcia-Preto (1982) and Fitzpatrick (1981) tend to rely chiefly on clinical observations.

According to Garcia-Preto (1982), the dignity of the individual and respect for each person, regardless of her or his status, is of basic importance to most Puerto Ricans. This also pertains to respect for authority within the family as well as elsewhere. "The rules for respect are complex. For instance, Puerto Ricans think that a child who calls an adult by his or her first name is disrespectful. To make direct eye contact with strangers, especially women and children, is also unacceptable" (Garcia-Preto, 1982, p. 172). Garcia-Preto writes further that Puerto Ricans strongly favor self-control and an appearance of calm; they tend to attribute stressful situations to external factors and to express stress indirectly through somatic complaints.

Traditionally, Puerto Ricans place a high value on the family's unity, welfare, and honor. Emphasis is on commitment to the group, rather than the individual, and on familial responsibilities, including obligations to and from the extended family.

The double standard of sexual morality has been instilled as a basic value, with emphasis on modesty and virginity in women, sexual freedom among men, and, simultaneously, the obligation of men to protect the honor of the women in the family. This double standard has been considerably eroded in recent years, owing to the impact of changing cultural patterns in the United States and in Puerto Rico itself. Clearly defined sex roles have been common, but this pattern is changing, especially as more and more women find employment outside the home.

Parent-youth conflicts are observed by clinicians to be common among Puerto Rican families in the United States, especially among recent immigrants. As often happens with immigrants, traditional family values and roles are frequently challenged by children and adolescents as they seek to become completely "Americanized" in our highly individualistic, competitive society. As parents feel they are losing control, they often become more authoritarian, emphasizing responsibility, obedience, and respect toward the family. This tends to escalate the conflict, which may become particularly intense and harmful because the support of a homogeneous neighborhood and extensive family network is generally lacking—aids that had been of important assistance in their former island home (for further details, see Fitzpatrick, 1981; Garcia-Preto, 1982).

The above observations concerning Puerto Rican cultural patterns should be viewed with a certain amount of skepticism, especially with regard to Puerto Rican families in this country. As noted earlier, cultural patterns vary from group to group within Puerto Rico and also within the United States. The latter variation is strongly affected by the reasons, timing, and conditions of immigration and the region of the United States to which the immigrants came. For instance, the existence of large Puerto Rican communities within New York City and the constant movement back and forth, to and from the island, tend to reduce ready acculturation and shifts from more traditional family roles. This movement has a deep impact on the family, as it reinforces many links to the island and fosters continuous dismantling and reconstruction of family life (Rodriguez, Sanchez, and Alers, 1980). Puerto Ricans who have moved to other regions, such as in the Midwest, less readily find compatriots and may, therefore, take on American ways, including egalitarian family patterns and individualism, more quickly. However, they may also suffer more from a sense of loneliness and isolation.

As indicated earlier, Puerto Ricans, on the average, tend to have more economic, occupational, familial, and educational problems than other Hispanic groups in this country. The reasons are unclear, but such problems are probably a result of such factors as the poverty in Puerto Rico, from which they have fled; poor economic and social conditions in New York City, where most of them live; racism; lack of facility in the English language; perhaps, in some cases, a search for the more generous public assistance grants in New York as against Puerto Rico; and slow acculturation to this country because of frequent travel back and forth to the homeland.

A large percentage of Puerto Ricans in this country receive public assistance. This is partly a result of their ready eligibility for this aid because they are citizens of the United States, an outcome of Puerto Rico's status as a commonwealth of this country. This status also makes it possible for them to move readily to the U.S. mainland without immigration restrictions. Their citizenship status, in sum, confers certain privileges on them and makes them different from other Hispanic groups seeking entry to, and citizenship in, this country.

Mexican-Americans

Most Mexicans are of mixed Spanish and Indian descent. Their national heritage goes back many centuries to Indian civilizations that existed before the arrival of the Spanish explorers in the early 1500s. During the seventeenth, eighteenth, and nineteenth centuries, Spain extended its rule over the region that is now Mexico, California, and the southwestern United States. Mexico finally obtained its independence from Spain in 1821, but it was a weak country with little control over its vast territory (Kraus, 1959).

The rule by the United States over what is now the American Southwest and was previously part of Mexico dates only from the Mexican War of 1848—a war that ended in victory for the United States and the acquisition of lands that now include Arizona, California, Nevada, Utah, and Wyoming. Texas, which had recently (1835) won its independence from Mexico, was annexed by the United States in 1844. Thus, for a number of Mexicans in this country, their roots in what is now American soil far predate the arrival of the Anglos (Falicov, 1982). It is natural that Indian-Spanish heritage remains strong and that many continue to have feelings of resentment toward the United States. Although some Mexican-Americans have been in this country for many generations, the majority are either first- or second-generation immigrants.

Resentment toward this country has been perpetuated and, at times, strengthened by discriminatory and often exploitative behaviors by some Anglo-Americans toward many Mexicans in the United States and toward Mexico itself

(Alvirez, Bean, and Williams, 1981). However, this resentment is mixed with admiration and envy of this country, which, potentially at least, offers many more opportunities than Mexico does for economic advancement.

At different time periods there have been large waves of Mexican immigration to the United States for political reasons (for example, flight from the violence of the Mexican Revolution of 1910) and for economic reasons (for example, the flight from crushing poverty and unemployment in Mexico in recent years). Most Mexican-Americans in the United States continue to suffer discrimination today, with limited access to good housing, education, and jobs. They are often exploited by employers, especially if they are illegal immigrants. They also have high rates of both unemployment and early school leaving.

Although most Mexican-Americans live in the Southwest, some have migrated to other parts of the country. For instance, some have lived in midwestern cities for three generations or more. As in the case of other immigrant groups, those who live near the borders of their "mother" country are less likely to acculturate readily than those who live far from their native land. For example, Mexicans who live in Chicago are more apt to become Americanized quickly than are those who live in southern Texas.

Much more has been studied and written about the family patterns of Chicanos (the appellation that many of today's Mexican-Americans prefer) than any other Hispanic group in the United States. Earlier research tended to assume that Mexican and Mexican-American life family patterns were essentially the same. It was generally believed that Hispanics were all highly familistic, with authoritarian, patriarchal patterns, including machismo for males and submissiveness for females. It was also held that premarital virginity and high fertility norms were characteristic of these families.

Andrade (1982) has summarized numerous studies and reports that an exaggerated supermother figure emerges from a summary of impressions of Mexican-American women: the unceasingly self-sacrificing, ever-fertile woman without aspirations for herself other than to reproduce. Andrade comments that several of the investigations from which this interpretation emerged were carried out in rural settings by Anglos, many of whom were males, unfamiliar with the culture or the situation they were investigating. Notably, almost all of these studies investigated lower-class samples, thus confounding ethnicity with socioeconomic status. Moreover, samples tended to be small and nonrandom (Andrade, 1982, p. 229).

Both Andrade (1982) and Mirandé (1977, 1979) emphasize that early writings about Hispanic family patterns (especially those about the Chicanos) were quite erroneous in stressing lack of egalitarian behaviors between husbands and wives. Mirandé (1979, p. 474) proposes that the concept of the all-dominant and controlling Chicano male is largely mythical. He criticizes unfounded psychoanalytic interpretations that interpret the machismo concept as a pathological defense against the Mexican-American male's feelings of inadequacy engendered by the adverse effects of discrimination and poverty. Mirandé also stresses that there are many kinds of Mexican-American families, with differing culture patterns. These patterns vary in accordance with recency of immigration, place of residence, socioeconomic status, degree of intermarriage with other ethnic groups, age, urbanization, and employment of women outside the home.

According to Mirandé (1979), more recent studies have shown an egalitarian family pattern in the behaviors of urban as well as rural Chicano families. One Mexican-American study project found, in both Los Angeles and San Antonio, that the families were not patriarchal, as had been frequently assumed (Grebler, Moore, and Guzman, 1973). Rigid differentiation of sex role tasks was lacking, and both men and women shared in homemaking and child rearing as needed. However, fathers tended to have a stronger role outside the family, and mothers were usually the dominant persons in the day-to-day matters of child rearing and homemaking—a point also made by Baca Zinn (1980). See also Cromwell and Cromwell (1978), Hawkes and Taylor (1975), and Staton (1972) for generally similar findings.

Mirandé (1977) describes the Chicano woman as the center of the family and the mainstay of the culture. As with many other ethnic groups, the mother tends to perpetuate the language and values of the "old country" and is usually a source of warmth and nurturance within the home.

The father is seen as the authority figure in many Chicano families. He is usually warm in his relationships with younger children, but more controlling as they get older. He often appears to be aloof and uninvolved in the details of family matters. Although he is seen by himself and others as the family leader who has power, the culture also includes a strong sense of related paternal responsibility.

Children are taught to carry family responsibilities, to prize family unity, and to respect their elders. However, the peer group becomes very important to adolescent boys as they grow older. Traditionally, girls stay at home with their mothers until marriage, but Chicanas (Mexican-American females) today are struggling for greater equality with both men and Anglos. They wish to keep their ethnic identity, but they also desire more flexibility in family and other roles.

The culture also emphasizes the family as a basic source of emotional support, especially for children. Support is provided not only by the parents, but also by grandparents, uncles, aunts, cousins, and friends. For example, although there has been a great deal of rural-urban migration among Hispanic populations, it appears that many Chicanos continue to live in comparatively large, intact kinship units where there are extensive networks of relatives who are helpful and supportive (Arce, 1982). No sharp distinction is made between relatives and friends, with the latter being considered as virtually kin if a close relationship has been formed. The term *compadrazo* is often used for this relationship. However, the pattern of close extended family relationships tends to fade among third- and fourth-generation families and among those who are upwardly mobile (Alvirez et al., 1981).

Bean, Curtis, and Marcum (1977) carried out an analysis of 1969 data from 325 Mexican-American couples who were members of a stratified sample in the Southwest. They found, among other things, that couples with egalitarian relationships were highest in their marital satisfaction—hardly a surprise. In general, the authors found little to support the concept that Mexican-American families have cultural patterns that are different from those of Anglo families and unique, culturally related sources of marital satisfaction. This point is also made by Zapata and Jaramillo (1981), who compared a small sample of Anglo families to Mexican-American ones in two southwestern cities. They found that differences in perceived family roles and alliances pertained far more to differences in socioeconomic status than to ethnicity.

Vega, Patterson, et al. (1986) provided helpful information regarding selected family patterns of a group of southwestern urban Mexican-American and Anglo parents with fifth- and sixth-grade children ($N = 147$ in each group). Using the Family Adaptability and Cohesion Scale II (Olsen, Russell, and Sprenkel, 1982), observers rated these families for the above characteristics. They also used an acculturation scale developed by Cuellar, Harris, and Jasso (1980). As might be expected, Vega, Patterson, et al. (1986) found that levels of acculturation varied for the Mexican-Americans according to their length of residence in the United States and their socioeconomic status.

Cuban-Americans

Cuban-Americans have a rather different background and immigration history than either Puerto Ricans or Mexican-Americans. . . . Cuba had been a colony of Spain for hundreds of years before the intervention of the United States in 1898, following an insurrection of some Cuban groups against oppressive Spanish domination. American motivations for intervention were mixed: Some liberal groups supported the Cuban cause of independence from Spain, but more powerful groups were swayed by their economic and political interests in this strategic island (Dulles, 1959).

After victory in the Spanish-American War, the United States established a strong political hold on Cuba, inducing rebellions, especially on the part of those people who were victims of the one-crop sugar economy and land ownership by the very few. The Cuban revolution of 1959 brought Castro and a predominantly socialist government into power and created fear and resistance in the United States, especially among those who, correctly or incorrectly, equated the Castro government with Soviet intrusion into the Western Hemisphere. At the present time, barely contained conflict between the United States and Cuba continues. One result of this conflict has been differing waves of immigration from Cuba to this country (Bernal, 1982; Dulles, 1959).

Many of the first wave of Cuban immigrants made a poor adjustment to the United States, partly because of their own troubled and disadvantaged backgrounds (Bernal, 1982). A serious public policy issue has arisen concerning government plans to deport some of those Cubans who have criminal records and the resistance of many to being deported. Cuban immigrants have settled chiefly in metropolitan areas such as Miami, New York, and Chicago. Although the different immigrant groups vary enormously in a number of ways, they also share a general cultural heritage.

Although formal research regarding Cuban-American families seems to be lacking, Bernal (1982) presents a summary of largely clinical observations. The traditional Cuban emphasis on familism, including the extended family, appears to be much like that found in other Hispanic countries. According to Bernal, the double standard of sexual morality, along with the concept of male dominance has prevailed in Cuban culture as well. However, as shown above concerning Mexican and Puerto Rican families in the United States, when women work outside the home, egalitarian values and behaviors tend to emerge.

Bernal cites several small studies from the 1970s to the effect that younger and second-generation Cubans become acculturated to the United States more quickly than older or first-generation immigrants. As in reports regarding Puerto Rican families and immigrant families from many countries, the cultural differences between children and their parents often lead to youthful rebellions, authoritarian parental reactions, and considerable family stress. Bernal observes further that Cubans tend to regard themselves as a special people, perhaps because of their homeland's strategic political and economic importance to other nations over the centuries. This sense of being special may lend a feeling of superiority to some Cubans, with allied attitudes of chauvinism, racism, and classism, which may be viewed by some observers as arrogance and grandiosity. However, as in the case of Puerto-Rican Americans, more research about Cuban-American families is needed before much can be said about the ways in which they are like or different from other families in this country.

Immigrants from Central and South America

Very little has been written about the family patterns of other Hispanic immigrants. According to L. Cohen (1977), two-thirds of the immigrants from Central and South America during the 1970s were women. Most had children whom they left behind with their maternal grandmothers. These women often came on student or tourist visas or crossed the border illegally. They frequently had kin and friends who helped them come into this country and find work. They were afraid to bring their young children with them, and often dreaded returns home to visit for fear they could not reenter the United States.

These women were usually never married, separated, divorced, or widowed. They had a harder time than men in getting employment because of both sex and ethnic discrimination (L. Cohen, 1977). Despite low wages, most sent money home to help their families. They found it hard to bring their children to this country because it is difficult to gain permission for immigration of whole families to the United States. Much more needs to be learned about immigrant families in the United States from many parts of Central and South America, but there appears to be limited research about them. . . .

SOME IMPLICATIONS FOR RESEARCH

As we have seen, there has been relatively little research devoted to Hispanic-American families. Most studies have focused on selected marital attitudes and behaviors of Mexican-American couples. The majority of these studies have looked at what significant differences, if any, are to be found between these couples and their Anglo counterparts, especially in matters pertaining to traditional male-dominant behaviors and segregated, rigidly defined sex roles. No significant differences between groups have been found, and it seems that these particular questions do not need further general exploration with respect to Mexican-Americans. However, they might well be asked in studies of particularly problem-laden subgroups, as well as Puerto Rican, Cuban, and other Hispanic families in this country, with the appropriate use of demographic controls.

Research has far from answered a number of other questions that might be raised about Hispanic family relationships, including further exploration of the impact on marital and parent-child relationships of recent immigration, extended families, unmarried parenthood, divorce, remarriage, unemployment, substance abuse, and family violence.

Much more needs to be known about Hispanic child-rearing beliefs, attitudes, goals, and behaviors with respect to the various ethnic and social class groups and in association with child development outcomes in such areas as school achievement, parent and child satisfaction, crime and delinquency, and youth employment. . . .

REFERENCES

Alvirez, D., Bean, F., & Williams, D. (1981). "The Mexican-American Family." In C. H. Mindel and R. W. Habenstein (eds.), *Ethnic families in America: Patterns and variations* (2nd ed., pp. 269–292). New York: Elsevier.

Andrade, S. (1982). "Social science stereotypes of the Mexican American woman: Policy implications for research." *Hispanic Journal of Behavioral Science*, 4, 223–243.

Applebome, P. (1988, January 3). "Amnesty requests by aliens decline." *New York Times*, pp. 11, 12Y.

Arce, C. (1982, March). "Maintaining a group culture." *ISR Newsletter.*

Baca Zinn, M. (1980). "Employment and education of Mexican-American women: The interplay of modernity and ethnicity in eight families." *Harvard Educational Review*, 50, 47–62.

Bean, F. D., Curtis, R., and Marcum, J. (1977). "Families and marital status among Mexican Americans." *Journal of Marriage and the Family*, 39, 759–767.

Bernal, G. (1982). "Cuban families." In M. McGoldrick, J. K. Pearce, and J. Giordano (eds.), *Ethnicity and family therapy* (pp. 186–207), New York: Guilford.

Chilman, C. (1968). "Fertility and poverty in the United States." *Journal of Marriage and the Family*, 30, 207–227.

Chilman, C. (1983). *Adolescent sexuality in a changing american society: Social and psychological perspectives for human services professions.* New York: John Wiley.

Cohen, L. (1977). "The female factor in resettlement." *Society*, 14(6), 27–30.

Cortes, C. (1980). *The Cuban experience in the United States*. New York: Arno.

Cromwell, V. L., and Cromwell, R. E. (1978). "Perceived dominance in decision making and conflict resolution among Anglo, Black, and Chicano couples." *Journal of Marriage and the Family*, 40, 749–759.

Cuellar, I., Harris, L., and Jasso, R. (1980). "An acculturation scale for Mexican American normal and clinical populations." *Hispanic Journal of the Behavioral Sciences*, 2, 199–217.

Delgado, M. (1987). "Puerto Ricans." In *Encyclopedia of social work* (vol. 2, pp. 427–432). Silver Spring, MD: National Association of Social Workers.

de Silva, E. (1981). *Survival and adjustment skills to the new culture: Working with Hispanic women who have settled in the United States*. Paper presented at the National Conference on Social Welfare, San Francisco.

Dulles, F. (1959). *The United States since 1865*. Ann Arbor: University of Michigan Press.

Estrada, L. (1987). "Hispanics." In *Encyclopedia of social work* (vol. 1, pp. 730–739). Silver Spring, MD: National Association of Social Workers.

Falicov C. (1982). "Mexican families." In M. McGoldrick, J. K. Pearce, and J. Giordano (eds.), *Ethnicity and family therapy* (pp. 134–163). New York: Guilford.

Family Planning Perspectives. (1983). vol. 15(4), 197.

Fitzpatrick, J. (1981). "The Puerto Rican family." In C. H. Mindel and R. W. Habenstein (eds.), *Ethnic families in America: Patterns and variations* (2nd ed., pp. 189–214). New York: Elsevier.

Frisbie, W. (1986). "Variations in patterns of marital instability among Hispanics." *Journal of Marriage and Family Therapy*, 48, 99–106.

Garcia-Preto, N. (1982). "Puerto Rican families." In M. McGoldrick, J. K. Pearce, and J. Giordano (eds.), *Ethnicity and family therapy* (pp. 164–186). New York: Guilford.

Grebler, L., Moore, J. W., and Guzman, R. (1973). "The family: Variations in time and space." In L. Duran and H. Bernal (eds.), *Introduction to Chicano studies: A reader.* New York: Macmillan.

Hawkes, G., and Taylor, M. (1975). "Power structure in Mexican and Mexican-American farm labor families." *Journal of Marriage and the Family*, 37, 806–811.

Hetherington, M., Cox, M., and Cox, R. (1978). "The aftermath of divorce." In J. Stevens and M. Mathews (eds.), *Mother-child, father-child relationships.* Washington, DC; National Association for the Education of Young Children.

Jones, J. (1985). "Fertility-related care." In H. P. McAdoo and T. Parkam (eds.), *Services to young families* (pp. 167–206). Washington, DC: American Public Welfare Association.

Kraus, M. (1959). *The United States to 1865*. Ann Arbor: University of Michigan Press.

LaPorte, B. (1977). "Visibility of the new immigrants." *Society*, 14(6), 18–22.

Mirandé, A. (1977). "The Chicano family: A reanalysis of conflicting views." *Journal of Marriage and the Family*, 39, 747–756.

Mirandé, A. (1979). "Machismo: A reinterpretation of male dominance in the Chicano family." *Family Coordinator,* 28, 473–479.

Olsen, D., Russell, C., and Sprenkel, D. (1982). "The circumplex model of marital and family systems: VI. Theoretical update." *Family Process,* 22, 69–83.

Portes, A. (1979). "Labor functions of illegal aliens." *Society,* 14(6), 31–37.

Rodriguez, C., Sanchez-Korrol, V., and Alers, J. (1980). *The Puerto Rican struggle: Essays on survival.* New York: Puerto Rican Migration Research Consortium.

Staples, R. & Mirandé, A. (1980). "Racial and cultural variations among American families: An analytic review of the literature on minority families." *Journal of Marriage and the Family,* 42, 887–904.

Staton, R. (1972). "A comparison of Mexican and Mexican-American families." *Family Coordinator,* 21, 325–329.

U.S. Bureau of the Census. (1980). *Persons of Spanish Origin in the United States: March 1979* (Current Population Reports, Series P-20, no. 354). Washington, DC: Government Printing Office.

U.S. Bureau of the Census. (1983). *Characteristics of the population below the poverty level* (Current Population Reports, Series P-60, no. 138). Washington, DC: Government Printing Office.

Vasquez, M., and Gonzalez, A. (1981). "Sex roles among Chicanos." In A. Baron, Jr. (ed.), *Explorations in Chicano psychology* (pp. 50–70). New York: Praeger.

Vega, W. A., Kolody, B., and Valle, J. (1986). "The relationship of marital status, confidant support, and depression among Mexican immigrant women." *Journal of Marriage and the Family,* 48, 597–605.

Vega, W. A., Patterson, T., Sallis, J., Nader, P., Atkins, C., and Abramson, I. (1986). "Cohesion and adaptability in the Mexican American and Anglo families." *Journal of Marriage and the Family,* 48, 857–867.

Wallerstein, J. (1985). "The over-burdened child: Some long-term consequences of divorce." *Social Work,* 30, 116–123.

Ybarra, L. (1982). "When wives work." *Journal of Marriage and the Family,* 44, 169–177.

Zapata, J., and Jaramillo, P. (1981). "Research on the Mexican-American family." *Journal of Individual Psychology,* 37, 72–85.

R E A D I N G

25

African-Americans in the 1990s

WILLIAM P. O'HARE, KELVIN M. POLLARD, TAYNIA L. MANN,
AND MARY M. KENT

African-Americans—30 million in number in 1991—are the largest and most visible minority group in the United States.[1] Because of their population size, along with their legacy of slavery and legal subjugation, blacks occupy a special niche in U.S. society. We often view the progress of blacks as a litmus test of how open our society really is. Furthermore, as African-Americans become a larger share of the U.S. population, the black experience assumes a greater part of our national character.

Blacks have made significant progress on many fronts since the 1950s and 1960s, when major civil rights legislation was enacted. In general, the education, health, living conditions, and incomes of African-Americans have improved. Many more blacks vote in elections and get elected to public office. But the remarkable progress of the post–World War II era appears to have slowed during the 1980s, even regressed in some areas. And African-American still rank below whites on nearly every measure of socioeconomic status.

The gap between the well-being of blacks and whites is continuing evidence of the second-class status of African-Americans. Black infants are twice as likely to die as are white infants. Black children are nearly three times more likely to live in a single-parent family or to live in poverty than are white children. Blacks are only half as likely to go to college; those who earn college degrees have incomes one-third less than do whites with the same education. And, while the number of affluent blacks has skyrocketed over the past decade, the net wealth of black households is only one-tenth that of whites.

Why has the progress of African-Americans slowed? Many observers feel that Ronald Reagan's presidential administration, which dominated national politics during most of the 1980s, was particularly harmful to black socioeconomic advancement, erasing civil rights gains and promoting a general antiminority climate. Others see a myriad of factors that combined to thwart the progress of blacks. Some of these factors have polarized American society in general, widening the gap between rich and poor and chipping away at the

From William P. O'Hare, Kelvin M. Pollard, Taynia L. Mann, and Mary M. Kent, "African-Americans in the 1990s," *Population Bulletin*, 46, no. 1 (July, 1991).

middle class. Among African-Americans, opportunities continue to open up for the educated middle class while the urban poor appear stuck in a quagmire of unstable families, intermittent employment, welfare dependence, and the temptations of crime.

This view of black Americans as living within two increasingly separate worlds gained wide acceptance during the 1980s. William Julius Wilson, a sociologist at the University of Chicago who emerged as a major analyst of U.S. blacks in the past decade, argues that economic changes, combined with social and demographic forces within the black community, produced these countervailing trends.[2] Wilson contends that the urban poor became more impoverished and more isolated because the decline of manufacturing and the movement of many blue-collar jobs to suburban areas eliminated a source of relatively well-paying, secure jobs for blacks. Joblessness increased among urban blacks, reducing the pool of marriageable men and undermining the strength of the family. Poverty increased as the number of female-headed households grew.

At the same time, new opportunities for middle-class blacks were generated by the expansion of civil rights. But the movement of the middle class out of the ghettos left "behind an isolated and very poor community without the institutions, resources and values necessary for success in modern society."[3]

This interpretation of the origins of urban poverty drew attention away from racial discrimination as the major barrier to the progress of African-Americans and toward the effects of broad economic, demographic, and social welfare trends. But recent studies provide new evidence that racial discrimination continues to undermine the progress of blacks.

Assessing the well-being of blacks is more difficult now than in the past. Only a few generations ago, 90 percent of African-Americans lived in poverty and racial inequities seemed obvious. Today, the root of the disparities between blacks and whites is harder to discern. Is racism dying, or is it still the primary reason for black underachievement? Why are some blacks moving into the middle and upper classes while others remain in poverty? There is no consensus about the answers to these complex questions. We can, however, sketch a portrait of African-Americans in the 1990s using demographic and socioeconomic data, and shed some light on these complex relationships.

AFRICAN-AMERICAN FAMILIES

No change in the black community has been more dramatic or more fundamental than the reordering of families and family relationships. In recent years, these changes have prompted many observers to proclaim a crisis in the black family, generally characterized by the growing numbers of poor, female-headed families.

While the vast majority of the 10 million African-American households are family households (that is, the household members are related by birth, marriage, or adoption), only about half the families were headed by a married couple in 1990, down from 68 percent in 1970 and 56 percent in 1980. A much higher percentage (83 percent) of white families are headed by married couples, although this percentage also has slipped over the past two decades.[4]

African-American households are larger than white households, but are slightly smaller than Hispanic households. The average black household contained 2.9 persons in 1990, compared with 2.6 persons for all whites and 3.5 persons for Hispanics. Both African-American and Hispanic female-headed households have one more person, on average, than households headed by whites females. Black households also are more likely than white to include adults in addition to a married couple or household head. In 1990, about a third of all black households included other adults, compared with only a fourth of white households.[5]

Changing Marriage Patterns

Marriage and divorce statistics since the 1960s record major shifts in the African-American family. In 1960, 65 percent of black women age 30 to 34 were in an intact marriage. In 1990, only 39 percent were married and living with their husbands. Over the same period, the percentage divorced grew from 8 to 12 percent, and the percentage who had never married grew from 10 to 35 percent. While a similar movement away from marriage occurred among white women, the change was much more dramatic among blacks.

Some analysts explain the decline in marriage among blacks in economic and demographic terms, while others cite more fundamental societal changes that have affected all Americans. The rising divorce rates and increase in the number of persons who choose not to marry may indicate that the institution of marriage itself is weakening. The marketplace and public institutions provide many of the goods and services that previously were the domain of the family. Low fertility rates have curtailed the number of years parents have dependent children living at home. The increased job opportunities for women make marriage less of an economic necessity, and, in the more tolerant climate of modern society, less of a social necessity for women. With a fourth of all children born to unmarried women, even childbearing is no longer confined to marriage. The movement away from marriage can also be seen as a consequence of modernization and urbanization, which has fostered individualism, weakening the family.[6]

Many social scientists focus on the relationship between marriage rates and the relative number of men and women. Women are more likely to marry when the ratio of men to women is high than when there is a relative shortage of men. The rapid rise in the number of births during the baby boom created a "marriage squeeze" in the 1970s and 1980s because there were more women than men in the marrying ages. This caused many young Americans to delay or forego marriage and childbearing.[7] This imbalance of the sexes was more extreme for the black than for the white population: On average, the ratio of males to females at birth is lower among blacks than whites,[8] and black male mortality is relatively high in the young adult ages. Even allowing for an undercount of black men in the census, black women outnumber men in the ages when most people marry and start families, age 20 to 49. Following this reason-ing, fewer black women are getting married because there are not enough eligi-ble men available.

In addition to demographic and social factors, economic changes—which eliminated many jobs held by black men in central city areas—and racial discrimination in hiring and firing have pushed many black men to the margins, or completely out, of the labor force. The deteriorating economic position of black men has been blamed for further discouraging the formation of married-couple families. Black men, with low wages and little job security, have difficulty fulfilling the traditional role as the major breadwinner for a family. The rise in female-headed families, whether formed through divorce, separation, or out-of-wedlock childbearing, has been linked to the decline in the ratio of employed black men per black woman.

Several analysts claim that welfare programs designed to aid single-parent families were a disincentive for low-income blacks to marry, although statistical analysis has failed to find a strong association between welfare payment levels and family composition.[9]

Many analysts argue that the modern African-American family has always differed from European-American families and should not be expected to conform to the married-couple pattern. Modern black family structure can be viewed as a legacy of slavery, when marriage among blacks was not recognized legally. Slave families tended to be consanguineal (organized around blood rela-tives) rather than conjugal (built around a married couple). Some trace this family structure back to the social structure in the African countries from which the ancestors of American blacks came.[10]

There is an ongoing debate as to whether the retreat from marriage among black Americans resulted directly from the disruptive effects of slavery; whether it is only indirectly associated with slavery through the continuing economic marginalization of blacks; or whether black culture and social structure, emanating from African roots, lead to different marriage and family patterns. Recently, social scientists have focused on issues related to the social and economic marginaliza-tion of black men to explain the low marriage rates among African-Americans.

Overwhelmingly, blacks still marry other blacks, despite opinion polls show-ing that interracial marriage has become socially acceptable to a growing percent-age of Americans. The percentage of married African-Americans whose spouse is not black has not changed over the past decade. In 1987, only 3 percent of married blacks had a nonblack spouse. In contrast, about 16 percent of married Asians and Hispanics had a non-Asian or non-Hispanic spouse. When African-Americans do marry a nonblack, it is usually the wife who is white, Asian, or of another race.

The Children

African-American children have been most affected by the changes in marital status and family composition that have occurred over the past few decades. The share of black children living with two parents declined from 58 percent in 1970 to 38 percent in 1990.[11] Just over half (55 percent) of black children lived in a

TABLE 9.1 Living Arrangements of Children Under 18 by Race and Ethnic Group, 1990 (numbers in thousands)

	BLACKS		WHITES		HISPANICS[a]	
	Number	Percent	Number	Percent	Number	Percent
Total children	10,018	100.0	51,390	100.0	7,174	100.0
Living with						
Two parents	3,781	37.7	40,593	79.0	4,789	66.8
One parent	5,485	54.8	9,870	192.	2,154	30.0
Mother only	5,132	51.2	8,321	16.2	1,943	27.1
Father only	353	3.5	1,549	3.0	211	2.9
Other relative[b]	654	6.5	708	1.4	177	2.5
Nonrelative	98	1.0	220	0.4	54	0.8

[a]Hispanics may be of any race.

[b]463,000 black children and 452,000 white children lived with a grandparent with neither parent present.

Source: Bureau of the Census, *Current Population Reports* P-20, no. 447 (Washington, D.C.: GPO, 1990), table 4.

single-parent household in 1990, 51 percent with their mother. In contrast, 19 percent of white children lived in single-parent households in 1989—a significant share, but minor compared with the statistic for blacks (see Table 9.1).

Black children are more likely to live with a grandparent than are white or Hispanic children. In 1990, 12 percent of black children lived in households that included their grandparents, compared with only 4 percent of whites and 6 percent of Hispanics.[12]

More than a fourth (27 percent) of all African-American children live with mothers who have never married. The percentage is highest among young children: 39 percent for children under age six.[13] One of the major consequences of living in a female-headed family is that such families generally have fewer economic resources than married-couple families. Nearly two-thirds are poor and live in central cities; over one-quarter live in public housing (see Table 9.2). The 3.8 million black children living in two-parent families appear privileged in comparison. Their parents are more educated, earn nearly four times as much money, and are more than twice as likely to own their own home. These stark differences highlight the two separate worlds inhabited by poor and middle-class black children, and suggest that the African-American population will become more polarized as these children mature.

TABLE 9.2   Characteristics of Black Children and Their Families, 1990

	CHILDREN LIVING IN	
	Two-Parent Households	Female-Headed Households
Median family income (1989)	$31,757	$9,590
Percent of children whose families:		
Are headed by a high school graduate	79.2	66.0
Own their home	55.3	22.3
Live in central cities	49.7	63.6
Live in public housing	6.3	29.8
Have incomes below poverty	18.1	61.1

Source: Bureau of the Census, *Current Population Reports* P-20, no. 450 (Washington, D.C.: GPO, 1991), table 6.

FERTILITY

Black Americans have had higher fertility than white Americans for the past two centuries. At the height of the baby boom in the mid-1950s, blacks were having an average of 4.4 children per woman, compared with 3.6 among whites. Because of their higher birth rates and younger age structure, a disproportionately high share of U.S. births are black. In 1988, the National Center for Health Statistics registered 671,976 African-American births—17 percent of all births that year.[14] The total fertility rate (TFR), or total number of lifetime births per woman, has remained higher for blacks. The TFR, which provides a good barometer of fertility independent of age structure, was 32 percent higher for blacks than for whites in 1988—2.4 children per woman compared with 1.8 per woman for whites.

There has been remarkable stability in the ratio of black to white fertility rates since 1960: the TFR for blacks has remained one-quarter to one-third higher than the TFR for whites. Fertility levels for blacks and whites fell in tandem during the 1960s and 1970s and have fluctuated similarly during the 1980s. The TFRs for both groups have risen slightly in recent years.[15]

Socioeconomic differences between blacks and whites explain much of the difference in their fertility levels. Birth rates are similar among black and white women with the same level of educational attainment, for example. In 1988, the completed fertility rate of black women age 35 to 44 with some college education was only 4 percent higher than that of their white counterparts. The black rate was 11 percent higher among women with less than a college education.[16] And among low-income families in 1985, white women were more likely to have had a child in the previous year than were black women.[17]

Regardless of the reasons, black fertility remains slightly higher than white fertility. In addition, two glaring disparities in the childbearing patterns of blacks

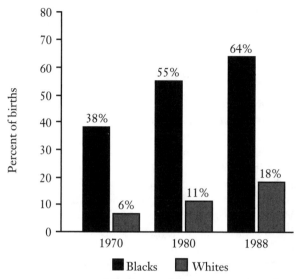

FIGURE 9.1   Babies Born Out-of-Wedlock, by Race, 1970, 1980, and 1988. *Source:* National Center for Health Statistics, *Monthly Vital Statistics Report* 39, no. 4, supplement (1990), table 18, and *Vital Statistics of the United States* 1987 (Washington, D.C.: GPO, 1989), table 1–31.

and whites are cause for concern: compared with whites, black babies are nearly four times more likely to be born to a single mother, and three times more likely to be born to a young teenage mother.

In 1988, 64 percent of black babies were born out-of-wedlock, compared with 18 percent of white babies. Birth rates for unmarried women have soared in the 1980s, as shown in Figure 9.1. In fact, the rates have increased faster among whites than blacks. Still, single black women of every age are more likely to have a child than single white women. The disparity is greatest among teenagers. In 1988, unmarried white teenagers age 15 to 17 bore 17 births per 1,000 girls, while unmarried black teenagers bore 74 births per 1,000.

Birth rates for all teenagers have fallen over the past two decades. Between 1970 and 1985, the fertility rate for teenage black girls age 15 to 17, whether married or single, declined from 101 to 70 births per 1,000 girls; for white teenagers, the rate fell from 29 to 24. In the past several years, however, teenage fertility has edged upward. By 1988, birth rates had increased to 77 for black teenagers and to 26 for white teenagers. Throughout the 1980s, however, the gap between black and white teenage fertility remained fairly constant.

The disproportionately high rate of teen childbearing in the African-American community exacerbates many social problems. Health problems, high infant mortality, educational deficiencies, long-term welfare dependency, and poverty are among the consequences risked by teens who have babies. Teenage mothers are more likely to be unmarried, and therefore without the potential income and support a husband could provide. Many analysts also fear that a "cycle" of teenage childbearing may continue into succeeding generations.[18]

INCOME, WEALTH, AND POVERTY

Black family incomes increased during the 1950s and 1960s, but beginning with the recession in the early 1970s, the income levels for blacks have stagnated. In 1989, the median annual income for black families was $20,200, a 6 percent improvement over 1980 after adjusting for inflation, but slightly below the comparable figure for 1969.[19]

White families, in contrast, continued to increase their incomes during the 1970s and 1980s, albeit at a lower rate than during the expansionary years just after World War II. The ratio of black to white earnings has actually fallen. Black family income was 61 percent that of whites in 1969, but only 56 percent as high as in 1989.

Why have black families lost ground over the past two decades? Demographic factors explain part of the loss. Foremost among them is the growth in female-headed families, which pulled a larger proportion of black families into the lowest income groups. In 1989, black female-headed families had only a third the annual income of black married-couple families, $11,600 compared with $30,700.

Also, the average black family has fewer members in the labor force than white families, 1.51 compared with 1.67 in 1989. This 10 percent difference is explained by the lower participation of blacks in the labor force, higher unemployment rates, and greater percentages of single-parent households among black than white families. Even if blacks and whites held comparable jobs and earned equal pay, the higher number of wage-earners per family for whites would keep their average family income above that for blacks.

Age, Family, and Education Differences

Average income figures also fail to show the vast diversity within the African-American population. While the percentage of low-income families is much greater among blacks, there is also a solid middle class. The plethora of studies on blacks in poverty may give a distorted view of the African-American population.[20] Only a few writers have focused on the middle-class and affluent blacks, yet these groups have increased significantly.[21]

In 1989, 26 percent of black families had incomes below $10,000, 32 percent earned between $10,000 and $25,000, and 42 percent received $25,000 or more per year. Among whites, however, only 8 percent of families had incomes under $10,000, while 69 percent were in the $25,000 or over category.

Income levels differ markedly by educational level, age, and family type. Black married-couple families, for example, increased their earnings during the 1970s and 1980s. By 1989, the median income for blacks had grown to 82 percent that of whites for families in which both husband and wife worked.

In families headed by younger blacks, especially those with a college degree, average income is almost as high for blacks as it is for whites. Among married-couple families where the head of household is 25 to 44 years old and a college graduate, the median income of blacks ($54,400) is 93 percent that of whites ($58,800).[22]

Female-headed families rank at the bottom of the income distribution, but there is considerable diversity even within this group. The extremely low median income of black female-headed households—less than $12,000, compared with nearly $19,000 for white female-headed households—is partially attributable to the lower educational levels and the lower percentages of divorced women among blacks. White women are more likely to obtain a legal divorce, and therefore to receive alimony or child support, an important source of additional income. Among white and black women with similar marital and educational characteristics and who head their families, however, the income differences diminish. Average incomes for families headed by single women who are college graduates are no higher for white than for black families.

While a college education erases some of the income difference between whites and blacks, blacks do not reap the same financial rewards from education as do whites. The average incomes for blacks invariably are lower than for whites, regardless of educational level or geographic area (see Table 9.3). Race differences are somewhat smaller in the South than in the North, especially in nonmetropolitan areas where all incomes are lower.

THE FUTURE OF AFRICAN-AMERICANS

The history of the black population in the United States is fairly well documented, but what does the future hold for these Americans? Many of the forces that will shape the advancement of black Americans have been described above, but it is not clear what the sum of these forces portends.

Many of the trends outlined here suggest that the black population will be more diverse as America moves into the twenty-first century. The economic gap between rich and poor blacks is growing. Many black scholars argue that *race* will lose significance while *class* divisions gain importance. Already, many young blacks who spent most of their lives in post-1960s America see issues differently than their parents, who grew up enduring overt racial oppression.

The middle-class blacks of the future may feel little in common with poor blacks because their experiences will have been dramatically different in so many ways. By the year 2000, every black under age 40 (nearly 60 percent of the black population) will have grown up in the more hospitable post-1960 racial climate.

Yet racism—one of the major forces that led blacks to rely so heavily on one another—is still very much evident. While the attitudes of whites toward blacks have softened a great deal over the past few decades, many still harbor discriminatory attitudes. Indeed, efforts to promote fuller participation of blacks in colleges and the work force have generated claims of reverse discrimination by

TABLE 9.3 Median Income and Poverty Rates by Education in Three Geographic Areas: Blacks and Whites Age 25–44, 1989

	METROPOLITAN NORTH		METROPOLITAN SOUTH		NONMETROPOLITAN SOUTH	
	Black	White	Black	White	Black	White
Median personal income (dollars per year)						
Less than high school	$5,700	$9,800	$6,000	$8,300	$4,900	$8,200
High school only	13,000	17,000	12,500	15,100	10,000	13,000
Some college	18,100	21,800	17,000	19,000	12,600	16,900
College graduate	26,000	30,100	24,000	29,000	20,000	22,500
Poverty rate (percent)						
Less than high school	51	23	41	26	52	25
High school only	24	6	18	8	24	10
Some college	13	3	13	4	23	6
College graduate	4	2	3	1	6	4

Source: Authors analysis of the March 1990 Current Population Survey.

some whites. Furthermore, the actions of many whites in the voting booth, in hiring, and in decisions of where to live are at odds with the benign attitudes expressed in opinion polls. To confound matters, the rapid growth of Hispanics and Asians may imperil black economic advancement, heighten group tensions, and lead to stronger black cohesiveness. While the future of America's black population is uncertain, it is clear that African-Americans will continue to be a highly visible feature of the American social and political landscape.

NOTES

1. The terms "African-American" and "black" are used interchangeably in this report. The term "white" refers to all whites, including Hispanics, unless specifically stated otherwise. Hispanics may be of any race, but the majority are white.

2. William J. Wilson, *The Truly Disadvantaged: The Inner City, the Underclass, and Public Policy* (Chicago: University of Chicago Press, 1987); and William J. Wilson, *The Declining Significance of Race: Blacks and Changing American Institutions* (Chicago: University of Chicago Press, 1978).

3. Douglas Massey and Mitchell L. Eggers, "The Ecology of Inequality: Minorities and the Concentration of Poverty, 1970–1980," *American Journal of Sociology* 95 (March 1990)): 1153–1188.

4. Paul C. Glick, "A Demographic Picture of Black Families," in *Black Families*, ed. Harriette P. McAdoo (Beverly Hills, Calif.: Sage Publications, 1981), p. 108; and Bureau of the Census, "Household and Family Characteristics: March 1990 and 1989," *Current Population Reports* P-20, no. 447 (Washington, D.C.: GPO, 1990), table 1.

5. Bureau of the Census, P-20, no. 447, 1990, op. cit., table 16.

6. Thomas J. Espenshade, "Marriage Trends in America: Estimates, Implications, and Underlying Causes," *Population and Development Review* 11, no. 2 (1985): 193–245; and Charles Westoff, "Fertility Decline in the West: Causes and Prospects," *Population and Development Review* 9, no. 1 (1983): 99–104.

7. Espenshade, op. cit., pp. 232–234.

8. Among white Americans, nearly 106 male babies are born for every 100 female babies, on average. Among African-Americans, 103 males are born for every 100 females. Male mortality is higher than female at every age, further depleting the number of African-American men relative to women. For the 20 to 49 age group, there are only 89 black men for every 100 black women.

9. Wilson 1987, op. cit., pp. 95–100; Jaynes and Williams, op cit., p. 531; see also Reynolds Farley and Walter R. Allen, *The Color Line and the Quality of Life in America* (New York: Russell Sage Foundation, 1987), p. 170.

10. Farley and Allen, op. cit., p. 171; and Floretta Dukes McKenzie, "Education Strategies for the '90s," in *The State of Black America 1991*, ed. Janet Dewart (New York: National Urban League, Inc., 1991), pp. 95–110.

11. Glick, op. cit., p. 110; and Bureau of the Census, "Marital Status and Living Arrangements: March 1990," *Current Population Reports* P-20, no. 450 (Washington, D.C.: GPO, 1991), table 4.

12. Bureau of the Census, P-20 no. 450, 1991, op. cit., table 4.

13. Ibid., tables 4 and 6.

14. National Center for Health Statistics, "Advance Report of Final Natality Statistics 1988," *Monthly Vital Statistics Report* 39, no. 4, supplement (15 August 1990), table 1.

15. Ibid., table 4.

16. Bureau of the Census, "Fertility of American Women: June 1988," *Current Population Reports* P-20, no. 436 (Washington, D.C.: GPO, 1989), table 2.

17. O'Hare 1987, op. cit., p. 46.

18. Reid, op. cit., pp. 12–13.

19. Bureau of the Census, P-60, no. 168, 1990. op. cit., table 8.

20. Wilson 1987, op. cit.; Jencks and Peterson, op. cit.; Ken Auletta, *The Underclass* (New York: Random House, 1982); Fred Harris and Roger W. Wilkins, eds., *Quiet Riots: Race and Poverty in the United States* (New York:

Pantheon Books, 1988); and Nicholas Lemann, *Promised Land: the Great Black Migration and How it Changed America* (New York: Alfred A. Knopf, 1991).

21. Bart Landry, *The New Black Middle Class* (Berkeley, Calif.: University of California Press, 1987); and William P. O'Hare, "In the Black," *American Demographics* 11 (November 1989): 25–29.

22. Bureau of the Census, P-60, no. 168, 1990, op. cit., table 4.

CHAPTER 10

◆

THE

AGE

REVOLUTION

R E A D I N G

26

The Family in an Aging Society: A Matrix of Latent Relationships

MATILDA WHITE RILEY

I am going to talk about families and the revolution in longevity. This revolution has produced configurations in kinship structure and in the internal dynamics of family life at every age that have never existed before.

Over two-thirds of the total improvement in longevity from prehistoric times until the present has taken place in the brief period since 1900 (Preston, 1976). In the United States, life expectancy at birth has risen from less than 50 in 1900 to well over 70 today. Whereas at the start of the century most deaths occurred in infancy and young adulthood, today the vast majority of deaths are postponed to old age. Indeed we are approaching the "squared" mortality curve, in which relatively few die before the end of the full life span. For the first time in all history, we are living in a society in which most people live to be old.[1]

Though many facts of life extension are familiar, their meanings for the personal lives of family members are elusive. Just how is increasing longevity

From *Journal of Family Issues*, Vol. 4, No. 3, September 1983, pp. 439–454. Copyright © 1983 by Sage Publications, Inc. By permission of Sage Publications, Inc.

transforming the kinship structure? Most problematic of all, how is the impact of longevity affecting those sorely needed close relationships that provide emotional support and socialization for family members (see Parsons and Bales, 1955)? To answer such questions, I must agree with other scholars in the conclusion that we need a whole new way of looking at the family, researching it, living in it, and dealing with it in professional practice and public policy.

Indeed, an exciting new family literature is beginning to map and interpret these unparalleled changes: it is beginning to probe beneath the surface for the subjective implications of the protracted and intricate interplay of family relationships. As the kinship structure is transformed, many studies are beginning to ask new questions about how particular relationships and particular social conditions can foster or inhibit emotional support and socialization—that is, the willingness to learn from one another. They are asking how today's family can fill people's pressing need for close human relationships.

From this developing literature, four topics emerge as particularly thought-provoking: (1) the dramatic extension of the kinship structure; (2) the new opportunities this extension brings for close family relationship; (3) the special approaches needed for understanding these complex relationships; and (4) the still unknown family relationship of older people in the future. I shall touch briefly on each of these topics. From time to time I shall also suggest a few general propositions—principles from the sociology of age (see M. W. Riley, 1976; forthcoming) that seem clearly applicable to changing family relationships. Perhaps they will aid our understanding of increasing longevity and the concomitant changes about us. The propositions may guide us in applying our new understanding in research, policy, and practice.

THE CHANGING CONFIGURATIONS OF THE KINSHIP STRUCTURE

I shall begin with the kinship structure as influenced by longevity. The extent and configurations of this structure have been so altered that we must rethink our traditional view of kinship. As four (even five) generations of many families are now alive at the same time, we can no longer concentrate primary attention on nuclear families of young parents and their children who occasionally visit or provide material assistance to grandparents or other relatives. I have come to think of today's large and complex kinship structure as a matrix of latent relationships—father with son, child with great-grandparent, sister with sister-in-law, ex-husband with ex-wife, and so on—relationships that are latent because they might or might not become close and significant during a lifetime. Thus I am proposing a definition of the kinship structure as a latent web of continually shifting linkages that provide the *potential* for activating and intensifying close family relationships.

The family literature describes two kinds of transformations in this structure that result from increasing longevity: (1) The linkages among family members have been prolonged, and (2) the surviving generations in a family have increased in number and complexity.

Prolongation of Family Relationships

Consider how longevity has prolonged family relationships. For example, in married couples a century ago, one or both partners were likely to have died before the children were reared. Today, though it may seem surprising, couples marrying at the customary ages can anticipate surviving together (apart from divorce) as long as 40 or 50 years on the average (Uhlenberg, 1969, 1980). As Glick and Norton (1977:14) have shown, one out of every five married couples can expect to celebrate their fiftieth wedding anniversary. Because the current intricacy of kinship structures surpasses even the language available to describe it (our step-in-laws might not like to be called "outlaws"), it sometimes helps to do "thought experiments" from one's own life. As marital partners, my husband and I have survived together for over 50 years. What can be said about the form (as distinct from the content) of such a prolonged relationship?

For one thing, we share over half a century of experience. Because we are similar in age, we have shared the experience of aging—biologically, psychologically, and socially—from young adulthood to old age. Because we were born at approximately the same time (and thus belong to the same cohort), we have shared much the same historical experiences—the same fluctuations between economic prosperity and depression, between periods of pacifism and of war, between political liberalism and reactionism, and between low and high rates of fertility. We have also shared our own personal family experiences. We shared the bearing and raising of young children during our first-quarter century together; during our second quarter century we adjusted our couplehood to our added roles as parents-in-law and grandparents. The third quarter-century of our married life, by the laws of probability, should convert us additionally into grandparents-in-law and great-grandparents as well. In sum, prolonged marriages like ours afford extensive common experiences with aging, with historical change, and with changing family relationships.

Such marriages also provide a home—an abiding meeting place for two individuals whose separate lives are engrossed in varied extrafamilial roles. Just as longevity has prolonged the average duration of marriage, it has extended many other roles (such as continuing education, women's years of work outside the home, or retirement). For example, Barbara Torrey (1982) has estimated that people spend at least a quarter of their adult lives in retirement. Married couples, as they move through the role complexes of their individual lives, have many evening or weekend opportunities either to share their respective extrafamilial experiences, to escape from them, or (though certainly not in my own case) to vent their boredom or frustration on one another (see Kelley, 1981).

Thus two features of protracted marriages become apparent. First, these marriages provide increasing opportunity to accumulate shared experiences and meanings and perhaps to build from these a "crescive" relationship, as suggested by

Ralph Turner (1970) and Gunhild Hagestad (1981). But second, they also present shifting exigencies and role conflicts that require continual mutual accommodation and recommendation. As Richard Lazarus (DeLongis, et al., 1982) has shown, "daily hassles" can be more destructive of well-being than traumatic family events. And Erving Goffman (1959:132) warns that the home can become a "backstage area" in which "it is safe to lapse into an asociable mood of sullen, silent irritability."

Many marriages, not ended by death, are ended by divorce. The very extension of marriage may increase the likelihood of divorce, as Samuel Preston (1976:176–177) has shown. Returning to my personal experience, I was the only one of four sisters who did not divorce and remarry. But as long as their ex-husbands were alive none of my sisters could ever entirely discount the remaining potential linkages between them. These were not only ceremonial or instrumental linkages, but also affective linkages that could be hostile and vindictive, or (as time passes and need arises) could renew concern for one another's well-being. Whatever the nature of the relationship, latent linkages to ex-spouses persist. Thus, a prolonged marriage (even an ex-marriage) provides a continuing potential for a close relationship that can be activated in manifold ways.

The traditional match-making question—"Will this marriage succeed or fail?"—must be replaced and oft-repeated as the couple grows older by a different question: "Regardless of our past, can we—do we want [to]—make the fresh effort to succeed, or shall we fail in this marriage?"

Here I will state as my first proposition: *Family relationships are never fixed:* they change as the self and the significant other family members grow older, and as the changing society influences their respective lives. Clearly, the longer the relationship endures (because of longevity) the greater the opportunity for relational changes.

If, as lives are prolonged, marital relationships extend far beyond the original nuclear household, parent-offspring relationships also take on entirely new forms. For example, my daughter and I have survived together so far for 45 years of which only 18 were in the traditional relationship of parent and child. Unlike our shorter-lived forebearers, my daughter and I have been able to share many common experiences although at different stages of our respective lives. She shares a major portion of the historical changes that I have experienced. She also shares my earlier experience of sending a daughter off to college, and will perhaps share my experience of having a daughter marry and raise children. Of course, she and I differ in age. (In Alice Rossi's study of biological age differences, 1980, the consequences for parent-offspring relationships of the reciprocal tensions between a pubescent daughter and her older mother who is looking ahead to the menopausal changes of midlife were explored.)[2] Although the relational age between me and my daughter—the 26 years that separate us—remains the same throughout our lives, the implications of this difference change drastically from infancy to my old age.

Number and Stability of Generations

I have dwelt at length on the prolongation of particular relationships to suggest the consequent dramatic changes in the family structure. Longevity has, in addition, increased the stability and the number of generations in a family. A poignant example of this instability (Imhof, 1982) can be found in an eighteenth century parish where a father could spawn twenty-four offspring of whom only three survived to adulthood—a time in which "it took two babies to make one adult." With increased longevity each generation becomes more stable because more of its members survive. For the young nuclear family in the United States, for example, though the number of children born in each family has been declining over this century, increased longevity has produced a new stability in the family structure. In an important quantitative analysis, Peter Uhlenberg (1980) has shown how the probability of losing a parent or a sibling through death before a child reaches age 15 [has] decreased from .51 in 1900 to .09 in 1976. Compared with children born a century ago, children born today are almost entirely protected against death of close family members (except for elderly relatives). To be sure, while mortality has been declining, divorce rates have been increasing but less rapidly. Thus, perhaps surprisingly, Uhlenberg demonstrates that disruptions of marriage up through the completion of child rearing have been declining since 1900. In other words, many marriages have been broken by divorce, but overall more have remained intact because of fewer deaths! Thus the young family as well as each of the older generations becomes more stable through survival.

At the same time, the number of older generations has been increasing. Looking up the generational ladder, increasing numbers of a child's four grandparents survive. Among middle-aged couples, whereas back in 1900 more than half had no surviving elderly parents, today half have two or more parents still alive (Uhlenberg, 1980:318). Conversely looking down the generational ladder, each set of elderly parents has adult children with spouses and children of their own. Meanwhile, the increase in divorce and remarriage (four out of five divorced people remarry) compounds the complexity of this elaborate structure, as Andrew Cherlin (1981) has shown. In my own family, for example, each of our two middle-aged children have their own children, and they also have us as two elderly parents; my daughter's husband also has two parents; and my son (who has married twice) has his ex-wife's parents and his current wife's mother, father, and step-mother in addition to us. A complex array!

Of course, as these surviving generations proliferate and overlap, each generation is continually growing older and moving up the generational ladder to replace its predecessor until ultimately the members of the oldest generation die. Because of longevity, every generation—the oldest as well as the youngest—is increasingly stable and more likely to include its full complement of surviving members.

CHANGING DYNAMICS OF CLOSE FAMILY RELATIONSHIPS

What, then, are the implications of this greatly expanded kinship structure for the dynamics of close family relationships? How does the matrix of latent kinship linkages provide for close ties between particular individual lives, as these lives weave in and out of the intricate and continually shifting kinship network? Under what conditions do some family members provide (or fail to provide) recognition, advice, esteem, love, and tension release for other family members?

The answer, it seems to me, lies in the enlarged kinship structure: It provides many new opportunities for people at different points in their lives to select and activate the relationships they deem most significant. That is, the options for close family bonds have multiplied. Over the century, increased longevity has given flexibility to the kinship structure, relaxing both the temporal and the spatial boundaries of optional relationships.

Temporally, new options have arisen over the course of people's lives because, as we have seen, particular relationships have become more enduring. Particular relationships (even following divorce) are bounded only by the birth and death of members. Now that the experience of losing family members by death is no longer a pervasive aspect of the full life course (and is in fact rare except in old age), people have greater opportunity to plan their family lives. They have time to make mutual adjustments to personal crises or to external threats such as unemployment or the fear of nuclear war. Here we are reminded of my first proposition: Family relationships are never fixed, but are continually in process and subject to change. As family members grow older, they move across time—across history and through their own lives—and they also move upward through the generations in their own families and the age strata of society.[3] As individual family members who each pursue a separate life course, thoughts and feelings for one another are developed; their lives weave together or apart so as to activate, intensify, disregard, or disrupt particular close relationships. Thus the relationship between a mother and daughter can, for example, become close in the daughter's early childhood, her first years of marriage, and again after her children have left home although there may be interim lapses. Or, as current norms permit, couples can try each other out through cohabitation, before deciding whether or not to embark upon marriage.

Just as such new options for close ties have emerged from the prolongation of family relationships, other options have arisen because the number and variety of latent linkages has multiplied across the entire kinship structure. Spatially, close relationships are not bounded by the nuclear households that family members share during their younger lives. Given the intricacy of current kin networks, a wide range of linkages can be activated—between grandchild and grandparent, between distantly related cousins, between the ex-husbands of sisters, or between a child and his or her new step-parent. (Only in Grimm's fairy tales, which reflected the earlier frequency of maternal deaths and successive remarriages, were step-mothers always "wicked.") Aided by modern communication and transportation, affection and interaction can persist even during long periods of separation. On occasion, long-separated relatives or those not closely related may arrange to live together or to join in congregate housing or communes.

Given these options, let me now state a second general proposition: As active agents in directing the course of their own lives, *individuals have a degree of control over their close family relationships.* This control, I submit, has been enhanced because longevity has widened the opportunities for selecting and activating relationships that can provide emotional support and advice when needed.

This part of my discussion suggests a new view of the family. Perhaps we need now to think of a family less as the members of one household with incidental linkages to kin in other households and more as a continuing interplay among intertwined lives within the entire changing kinship structure. The closeness of these intertwined lives and the mutual support they provide depend on many factors (including the predispositions of each individual and the continuing motivation to negotiate and renegotiate their joint lives) but the enlarged kinship structure provides the potential.

NEW APPROACHES TO FAMILY RESEARCH AND PRACTICE

Before considering how the oldest family members—those in the added generation—fit into these intertwined lives, let me pause to ask how we can approach these complex and changing family relationships. If the tidy concept of the nuclear family is no longer sufficient, how can we deal in research and in professional practice with the newly emerging concepts? Clearly, special approaches are required for mapping and understanding the centrifugal and centripetal processes of family relationships within the increasing complexity of the kinship matrix. Such approaches must not only take into account my first two propositions (that relationships continually change, and that family members themselves have some control over this change) but must also consider a third proposition: *The lives of family members are interdependent* such that each person's family life continually interacts with the lives of significant relatives. Though long-recognized by students of the family, this proposition takes on fresh significance in the matrix of prolonged relationships.

As case examples, I shall describe two or three studies that illustrate how we can deal with the family as a system of interdependent lives. These studies are also important as they add to our understanding of emotional support and socialization under current family conditions.

In one study of socialization outcomes, Mavis Hetherington et al. (1977) have shown how parental disruption through divorce has a complex impact on the still-intertwined lives of the spouses and on the socialization of their children. Over a two-year period, detailed investigations were made of nursery school boys and girls and their parents, half of whom were divorced and the other half married. Differences were detected: Divorced parents showed comparatively less affection for their children, had less control over them, and elicited more dependent, disobedient, and aggressive child behavior—particularly in mother-son interactions. But relations between the parents also made a difference in these parent-child relationships: If divorced couples kept conflict low and agreed about child rearing, their ineffectiveness in dealing with children could be somewhat offset. This two-year tracing of the three-way interrelationships among spouses and children in disrupted families yields many insights into the interdependence of life course processes.

As family relationships are prolonged, socialization is more frequently recognized as a reciprocal process that potentially extends throughout the lives of parents and children as well as of marital partners. How can socialization operate across generations that belong to differing periods of historical change? One key mechanism, as Marilyn Johnson (1976) has demonstrated, is normative expectations. Parents can influence offspring by expecting behavior that is appropriate to social change, and can in turn be guided by offspring in formulating these expectations. Such subtleties to intergenerational influence are illustrated in a small study which Johnson and I made of high school students in the early 1960s (see Riley, 1982). Just as women's careers were burgeoning, we found that most girls looked forward to combining a career with marriage, whereas most boys did not anticipate marrying wives who worked. How had these young people been socialized to such sharply conflicting norms? We questioned their mothers and fathers to find out. Indeed we learned that, on the whole, parents wanted self-fulfillment for their daughters both in marriage and in work outside the home, while for their sons they wanted wives who would devote themselves fully to home and children. These slight yet provocative findings did presage the future impact of the women's movement on family lives, but I note them here as another instance of research that fits together the differing perspectives of the several interdependent family members.

Analyzing such studies of close relationships impresses one with the problem of studying families from what is often called the "life course" or "lifespan perspective" (see Dannefer, forthcoming). We are indeed concerned with people moving through life. Yet we are concerned not with a single life or a statistical aggregate of lives, but with the dynamic family systems of interdependent lives. An example I often use in teaching comes from the early work of Cottrell and Burgess in predicting success or failure in marriage. Starting with a case study, Cottrell (1933) saw each partner in a marriage as reenacting his or her childhood roles. He showed how the outcome of the marriage depended upon the mesh between these two different sets of early-life experiences—that is, how nearly they would fit together so that each partner met the role expectations of the other. Unfortunately, however, these researchers subsequently departed from this admirable model by questioning large samples of men and women as individuals and then analyzing the data for separate aggregates of men and women rather than for male-female pairs. Each individual was given a score of likely success in marriage, but without considering the success of a marriage between a particular man and a particular woman! Because the interdependent lives were not examined jointly, the central objective of the project was lost.

This difficulty, which I now call "life-course reductionism," still persists. Although many studies purport to study families as systems, they in fact either aggregate individual lives (as Cottrell and Burgess did) or reason erroneously from the lives of single members about the lives of other family members significant to the relationship. The danger of not considering a key family member is highlighted, for example, in Frank Furstenberg's (1981) review of the literature on kinship relations after divorce. Some studies had suggested that divorce disrupts the relations with parents-in-law (that is, with the parents of the ex-spouse) but these studies failed to include the children of the broken marriage. Only after examining the children's generation was it learned that they, by retaining contact with both sets of their grandparents, could help to link divorced spouses to their former in-laws. Supporting this clue from a small study of his own, Furstenberg found that the ties between grandparents and grandchildren did continue to exist in most cases, even though for the divorced parents (the middle generation) the former in-law relationships were largely attenuated or broken. In reconstituted families, then, grandparents can perhaps serve as "kinkeepers."

Among the studies that pursue close relationships across three generations is a national survey of divorce and remarriage now being conducted by Frank Furstenberg, Andrew Cherlin, Nicholas Zill, and James Peterson. In this era of widespread divorce and remarriage, this study is examining the important hypothesis that new intergenerational ties created by remarriage will balance— or more than balance—the losses incurred as a result of divorce. Step-relationships may replace disrupted natural relationships. The intricacy of interdependent lives within our proliferating kinship structure is dramatized by the design of this study. Starting with a sample of children aged 11 to 16 and their parents (who were originally interviewed five years earlier) the research team will now also question these children's grandparents; note that there can be two sets of grandparents where the parents are in intact first marriages or have been divorced, three sets if one parent has remarried after divorce, and four sets (no less than eight grandparents) if both have remarried. Thus, as surviving generations proliferate, their part in the family system will be explored in this study by questioning the many members of the grandparent generation. Surviving generations cannot be fully understood (as many studies of three generations have attempted) by examining a simple chain of single individuals from each of the generations.

These studies, as models for research, reflect the complex family relationships within which people of all ages today can seek or can give affection, encouragement, companionship, or advice.

OLDER GENERATIONS OF THE FUTURE

About the fourth generation (great-grandparents) that is being contributed by longevity, I want to make three final points.

First, it is too early to tell how an enlarged great-grandparent generation will fit into the kinship structure, or what close family relationships it may form. It is too early because the marked increase in longevity among the old began only in recent decades and are still continuing at a rate far exceeding earlier predictions (Preston, 1976; Manton, 1982; Brody and Brock, n.d.). Will this added generation be regarded as the more familiar generation of grandparents has been regarded—either as a threat to the young adult generation's independence, or as a "social problem" for family and community, requiring care from the mid-generation that is "squeezed" between caring for both young children and aging parents? Or will an added fourth generation mean new coalitions and new forms of personal relationships? And what of five-generation families in which a grandmother can be also a granddaughter (see Hagestad, 1981)? It is still too early to tell what new family norms will develop (see Riley, 1978).

Second, while we do not know how a fourth or even a fifth generation may fit in, we do know that most older family members are not dependent or disabled (some 5 percent of those 65 and over are in nursing homes). For those requiring care or instrumental support, families generally make extraordinary efforts to provide it (see Shanas, 1979). Yet most of the elderly, and especially those who are better educated and more active, are stronger, wiser, more competent, and more independent than is generally supposed. Public stereotypes of old people are far more negative than old people's assessments of themselves (National Council on the Aging, 1981). Healthy members of this generation, like their descendants, must earn their own places in the family and create their own personal ties. They cannot expect obligatory warmth or emotional support.

Third, at the close of their lives, however, old people will need advice and emotional support from kin. This need is not new in the annals of family history. What is new is the fact that terminal illness and death are no longer scattered across all generations but are concentrated in the oldest one. Today two-thirds of all deaths occur after age 65, and 30 percent after age 80 (Brody and Brock, n.d.). And, although most deaths occur outside the home, programs such as the hospice movement are being developed for care of the dying in the home where the family can take part (see J. W. Riley, forthcoming).

In conclusion, I have attempted to trace the impact of the unprecedented increases in longevity on the family and its relationships. In our own time the kinship structure has become more extensive and more complex, the temporal and spatial boundaries of the family have been altered, and the opportunities for close family relationships have proliferated. These relationships are no longer prescribed as strict obligations. They must rather be earned—created and recreated by family members throughout their long lives. Each of us is in continuing need of advice and emotional support from one another, as we contend with personal challenges and troubles, and with the compelling effects of societal changes in the economy, in technology, in culture, and in values. We all must agree with Mary Jo Bane (1976) that the family is here to stay, but in forms that we are beginning to comprehend only now. As members of families and students of the family—whether we are theorists, researchers, counselors, or policy makers—we must begin to realign our thinking and our practice to incorporate the new realities that are being engendered by increasing longevity.

NOTES

1. Note that increasing longevity in a society is not necessarily the same as increasing proportions of old people in the population, a proportion influenced in the long-term more by fertility than by mortality. Longevity affects individual lives and family structures, while population composition affects the total society.

2. Gunhild Hagestad (1982) talks even of menopausal grandmothers with pubescent granddaughters.

3. Of course, divisions between generations are only loosely coterminous with age divisions (see the discussion of the difference between "generations" and "cohorts" in the classic piece by Duncan, 1966, and a definitive formulation of this distinction in Kertzer, forthcoming). As Gunhild Hagestad (1981) puts it, "people do not file into generations by cohorts." There are wide ranges in the ages at which particular individuals marry and have children. In addition to the recognized differences by sex, there are important differences by social class. For example, Graham Spanier (Spanier and Glick, 1980) shows how the later marriage age in upper as compared with lower socioeconomic classes postpones many subsequent events in the lives of family members, thus slowing the proliferation in numbers of surviving generations.

REFERENCES

Bane, M. J. 1976. *Here to Stay: American Families in the 20th Century*. New York: Basic Books.

Brody, J. A., and D. B. Brock, n.d. "Epidemiologic and statistical characteristics of the United States elderly population." (unpublished)

Cherlin, A. J. 1981. *Marriage, Divorce, Remarriage*. Cambridge, MA: Harvard University Press.

Cottrell, L. S., Jr. 1933. "Roles and marital adjustment." *American Sociological Society*, 27, 107–115.

Dannefer, D. Forthcoming. "The sociology of the life course." *Annual Review of Sociology*.

DeLongis, A., J. C. Coyne, G. Dakof, S. Folkman, and R. S. Lazarus. 1982. "Relationship of daily hassles, uplifts, and major life events to health status." *Health Psychology*, 1, 119–136.

Duncan, O. D. 1966. "Methodological issues in the analysis of social mobility," pp. 51–97 in N. J. Smelser and S. M. Lipsett (eds.), *Social Structure and Mobility in Economic Development*. Chicago, IL: Aldine.

Furstenberg, F. F., Jr. 1981. "Remarriage and intergenerational relations," pp. 115–142 in R. W. Fogel et al. (eds.), *Aging: Stability and Change in the Family*. New York: Academic Press.

Glick, P. C., and A. J. Norton. 1977, "Marrying, divorcing, and living together in the U.S. today." Population Bulletin 32. Washington, D.C. Population Reference Bureau.

Goffman, E. 1959. *The Presentation of Self in Everyday Life*. Garden City, NY: Doubleday.

Hagested, G. O. 1982. "Older women in intergenerational relations." Presented at the Physical and Mental Health of Aged Women Conference, October 21–22, Case Western University, Cleveland, OH.

———. 1981, "Problems and promises in the social psychology of intergenerational relations," pp. 11–46 in R. W. Fogel et al. (eds.), *Aging: Stability and Change in the Family*. New York: Academic Press.

Hetherington, E. M., M. Cox, and R. Cox. 1977. "The aftermath of divorce," in J. H. Stevens, Jr. and M. Matthews (eds.), *Mother-Child, Father-Child Relations*. Washington, D.C.: National Association for the Education of Young Children.

Imhof, A. E. 1982. "Life course patterns of women and their husbands—16th to 20th century." Presented at the International Conference on Life Course Research on Human Development, September 17, Berlin, Germany.

Johnson, M. 1976. "The role of perceived parental models, expectations and socializing behaviors in the self-expectations of adolescents, from the U.S. and West Germany." Dissertation, Rutgers University.

Kelley, H. H. 1981. "Marriage relationships and aging," pp. 275–300 in R. W. Fogel et al. (eds.), *Aging: Stability and Change in the Family*. New York: Academic Press.

Kertzer, D. I. Forthcoming. "Generations as a sociological problem." *Annual Review of Sociology*.

Manton, K. G. 1982. "Changing concepts of morbidity and mortality in the elderly population." Milbank Memorial Fund Q. 60: 183–244.

National Council on the Aging. 1981. *Aging in the Eighties: America in Transition*. Washington, D.C.: Author.

Parsons, T., and R. F. Bales. 1955. *Family, Socialization and Interaction Process*. New York: Free Press.

Preston, S. H. 1976. *Mortality Patterns in National Population: With Special References to Recorded Causes of Death*. New York: Academic Press.

Riley, J. W., Jr. Forthcoming. "Dying and the meanings of death: sociological inquiries." Annual Review of Sociology.

Riley, M. W. 1976. "Age strata in social systems," pp. 189–217 in R. H. Binstock and E. Shanas (eds.), *Handbook of Aging and the Social Sciences*. New York: Van Nostrand Reinhold.

———. 1978. "Aging, social change, and the power of ideas." Daedalus 107, 4: 39–52.

———. 1982. "Implications for the middle and later years," pp. 399–405 in P. W. Berman and E. R. Ramey (eds.), *Women: A Development Perspective NIH Publication* No. 82-2298. Washington, DC: Dept. of Health and Human Services.

———. Forthcoming. "Age strata in social systems," in R. H. Binstock and E. Shanas (eds.), *The New Handbook of Aging and the Social Sciences*.

Rossi, A. S. 1980. "Aging and parenthood in the middle years," in P. B. Baltes and O. G. Brim, Jr. (eds.), *Life-Span Development and Behavior 3*. New York: Academic Press.

Shanas, E. 1979. "Social myth as hypothesis: the case of the family relations of old people." *The Gerontologist* 19: 3–9.

Spanier, G. B., and P. C. Glick. 1980. "The life cycle of American families: an expanded analysis," J. of Family History: 97–111.

Torrey, B. B. 1982. "The lengthening of retirement," pp. 181–196 in M. W. Riley et al. (eds.), *Aging from Birth to Death, vol. II: Sociotemporal Perspectives*. Boulder, CO: Westview.

Turner, R. H. 1970. *Family Interaction.* New York: John Wiley.
Uhlenberg, P. R. 1969. "A study of cohort life cycles: cohorts of native born Massachusetts women. 1830–1920," Population Studies 23, 3: 407–420.
———. 1980. "Death and the family." J. of Family History (Fall): 313–320.

R E A D I N G

27

The Modernization of Grandparenthood

ANDREW J. CHERLIN AND FRANK F. FURSTENBERG, JR.

Writing a book about grandparents may seem an exercise in nostalgia, like writing about the family farm. We tend to associate grandparents with old-fashioned families—the rural, extended, multigenerational kind much celebrated in American mythology. Many think that grandparents have become less important as the nation has become more modern. According to this view, the shift to factory and office work meant that grandparents no longer could teach their children and grandchildren the skills needed to make a living: the fall in fertility and the rise in divorce weakened family ties; and the growth of social welfare programs meant that older people and their families were less dependent on each other for support. There is some truth to this perspective, but it ignores a powerful set of historical facts that suggest that grandparenthood—as a distinct and nearly universal stage of family life—is a post–World War II phenomenon.

Consider first the effect of falling rates of death. Much of the decline in mortality from the high preindustrial levels has occurred in this century. According to calculations by demographer Peter Uhlenberg, only about 37 percent of all males and 42 percent of all females born in 1870 survived to age sixty-five; but for those born in 1930 the comparable projections were 63 percent for males and 77 percent for females. The greatest declines in adult mortality have occurred in the last few decades, especially for women. The average number of years that a forty-year-old white woman could expect to live increased by four between 1900 and 1940; but between 1940 and 1980 it increased by seven. For men the increases have been smaller, though still substantial: a two-year increase for forty-year-old whites between 1900 and 1940 and a four-year increase between 1940 and 1980. (The trends for nonwhites are similar.) Consequently, both men and women can expect to live much longer lives than was the case a few decades ago, and more and more women are outliving men. In 1980, the average forty-year-old white woman could expect to live to age eighty, whereas the average forty-year-old white man could expect to live only to age seventy-four. As a result, 60 percent of all the people sixty-five and over in the United States in 1980 were women. Thus, there are many more grandparents around today than just a few decades ago simply because people are living longer—and a majority of them are grandmothers.

This decline in mortality has caused a profound change in the relationship between grandparents and grandchildren. For the first time in history, most adults live long enough to get to know most of their grandchildren, and most children have the opportunity to know most of their grandparents. A child born in 1900, according to Uhlenberg, had a better than nine-out-of-ten chance that two or more of his grandparents would be alive. But by the time that child reached age fifteen, the chances were only about one out of two that two or more of his grandparents would still be alive. Thus, some children were fortunate enough to establish relationships with grandparents, but in many other families the remaining grandparents must have died while the grandchild was quite young. Moreover, it was unusual for grandchildren at the turn of the century to know all their grandparents: only one in four children born in 1900 had four grandparents alive, and a mere one in fifty still had four grandparents alive by the time they were fifteen. In contrast, the typical fifteen-year-old in 1976 had a nearly nine-out-of-ten chance of having two or more grandparents still alive, a better than one-out-of-two chance of having three still alive, and a one-out-of-six chance of having all four still alive. Currently, then, nearly all grandchildren have an extended relationship with two or more grandparents, and substantial minorities have the opportunity for extended relationships with three or even all four.

Indeed, Americans take survival to the grandparental years pretty much for granted. The grandparents we spoke to rarely mentioned longer life when discussing the changes since they were children. *Of course* they were still alive and reasonably healthy; that went without saying. But this taken-for-granted-ness is a new phenomenon; before World War II early death was a much greater threat, and far fewer people lived long enough to watch their grandchildren grow up.

Most people are in their forties or fifties when they first become grandparents. Some observers have mistakenly taken this as an indication that grandparents are younger today than in the past. According to one respected textbook:

> Grandparenting has become a phenomenon of middle age rather than old age. Earlier marriage, earlier childbirth, and longer life expectancy are producing grandparents in their forties.

But since the end of the nineteenth century (the earliest period for which we have reliable statistics) there has been little change in the average age at marriage. The only exception was in the 1950s, when ages at marriage and first birth did decline markedly but only temporarily. With the exception of the unusual 1950s, then, it is likely that the age when people become grandparents has stayed relatively constant over the past century. What has changed is the amount of time a person spends as a grandparent: increases in adult life expectancy mean that grandparenthood extends into old age much more often. In our national sample of the grandparents of teenagers, six out of ten had become grandparents while in their forties. When we interviewed them, however, their average age was sixty-six. Grandparenting has been a phenomenon of middle age for at least the past one hundred years. The difference today is that it is now a phenomenon of middle age *and* old age for a greater proportion of the population. To be sure, our notions of what constitutes old age also may have changed, as one woman in our study implied when discussing her grandmother:

> She stayed home more, you know. And I get out into everything I can. That's the difference. That is, I think I'm younger than she was at my age.

Moreover, earlier in the century some middle-aged women may have been too busy raising the last of their own children to think of themselves as grandmothers. Nevertheless, in biological terms, the average grandparent alive today is older, not younger, than the average grandparent at the turn of the century.

Consider also the effects of falling birth rates on grandparenthood. As recently as the late 1800s, American women gave birth to more than four children, on average. Many parents still were raising their younger children after their older children had left home and married. Under these conditions, being a grandparent often overlapped with being a parent. One would imagine that grandparenthood took a back seat to the day-to-day tasks of raising the children who were still at home. Today, in contrast, the birth rate is much lower; and parents are much more likely to be finished raising their children before any of their grandchildren are born. In 1900, about half of all fifty-year-old women still had children under eighteen; but by 1980 the proportion had dropped to one-fourth. When a person becomes a grandparent now, there are fewer family roles competing for his or her time and attention. Grandparenthood is more of a separate stage of family life, unfettered by child care obligations—one that carries its own distinct identification. It was not always so.

The fall of fertility and the rise of life expectancy have thus greatly increased the supply of older persons for whom grandparenthood is a primary intergenerational role. To be sure, there always have been enough grandparents alive so that everyone in American society (and nearly all other societies, for that matter) was familiar with the role. But until quite recently, an individual faced a considerable risk of dying before, or soon after, becoming a grandparent. And even if one was fortunate enough to become a grandparent, lingering parental obligations often took precedence. In past times, when birth and death rates were high, grandparents were in relatively short supply. Today, as any number of impatient older parents will attest, grandchildren are in short supply. Census data bear this out: in 1900 there were only twenty-seven persons aged fifty-five and over for every one hundred children fourteen and under; but by 1984 the ratio had risen to nearly one-to-one. In fact, the Bureau of the Census projects that by the year 2000, for the first time in our nation's history, there will be more persons aged fifty-five and over than children fourteen and under.

Moreover, technological advances in travel and long-distance communication have made it easier for grandparents and grandchildren to *see* or talk to each other. . . . [T]he grandparents at one senior citizen center had to remind us that there was a time within their memories when telephone service was not universal. We tend to forget that only fifty years ago the *Literary Digest* predicted a Landon victory over Roosevelt on the basis of responses from people listed in telephone directories—ignoring the crucial fact that telephones were to be found disproportionately in wealthier, and therefore more often Republican, homes. As late as the end of World War II, only half the homes in the United States had a telephone. The proportion rose quickly to two-thirds by the early 1950s and three-fourths by the late 1950s. Today, more than 97 percent of all homes have telephones. About one-third of the grandparents in our survey reported that they had spoken to the study child on the telephone once a week or more during the previous year.

Nor did most families own automobiles until after World War II, as several grandparents reminded us:

> I could be wrong, but I don't feel grandparents felt as close to grandchildren during that time as they do now. . . . Really back there, let's say during the twenties, transportation was not as good, so many people did not have cars. Fortunately, I can say that as far back as I remember my father always had a car, but there were many other people who did not. They traveled by horse and buggy and some even by wagons. And going a distance, it did take quite some time. . . .

Only about half of all families owned automobiles at the end of the war. Even if a family owned an automobile, long trips still could take quite some time:

> Well, I didn't see my grandmother that often. They just lived one hundred miles from us, but back then one hundred miles was like four hundred now, it's the truth. It just seemed like clear across the country. It'd take us five hours to get there, it's the truth. It was an all-day trip.

But in the 1950s, the Federal government began to construct the interstate highway system, which cut distances and increased the speed of travel. The total number of miles driven by passenger vehicles increased from about 200 million miles in the mid-1930s to about 500 million miles in the mid-1950s to over a billion miles in the 1980s. Not all of this increase represents trips to Grandma's house, of course; but with more cars and better highways, it became much easier to visit relatives in the next county or state.

But weren't grandparents and grandchildren more likely to be living in the same household at the turn of the century? After all, we do have a nostalgic image of the three-generation family of the past, sharing a household and solving their problems together. Surprisingly, the difference between then and now is much less than this image would lead us to believe. To be sure, there has been a drastic decline since 1900 in the proportion of older persons who live with their adult children. In 1900 the proportion was more than three out of five, according to historian Daniel Scott Smith; in 1962 it was one out of four; and by 1975 it had dropped to one in seven. What has occurred is a great increase in the proportion of older people who live alone or only with their spouses. Yet the high rates of co-residence in 1900 do not imply that most grandparents were living with their grandchildren—much less that most grandchildren were living with their grandparents. As Smith's data show, older persons who were married tended to live with unmarried children only; children usually moved out when they married. It was mainly widows unable to maintain their own households who moved in with married children. Consequently, according to Smith's estimates, only about three in ten persons sixty-five and over in 1900 lived with a grandchild, despite the great amount of co-residence between older parents and their adult children. What is more, because of the relative shortage of grandparents, an even lower percentage of grandchildren lived with their grandparents. Smith estimates that about one in six children under age ten in 1900 lived in the same household with someone aged fifty-five or over. Even this figure overestimates the number of children living with their grandparents, because some of these elderly residents were more distant kin, boarders, or servants.

There were just too many grandchildren and too few grandparents for co-residence to be more common. In the absence of more detailed analyses of historical censuses, however, the exact amount of change since 1900 cannot be assessed. Nor was our study designed to provide precise estimates of changes in co-residence. But it is still worth nothing that just 30 percent of the grandparents in our sample reported that at least one of their grandparents ever lived with them while they were growing up. And 19 percent reported that the teenaged grandchild in the study had lived with them for at least three months. Undoubtedly, some of the grandparents in our study had shared a household with some of their own grandchildren, although we unfortunately did not obtain this information. Thus, although our study provides only imperfect and incomplete data on this topic, the responses are consistent with our claim that the change in the proportion of grandparents and grandchildren who share a household has been more modest than the change in the proportion of elderly persons who share a household with an adult child.

Grandparents also have more leisure time today, although the trend is more pronounced for men than for women. The average male can now expect to spend fifteen years of his adult life out of the labor force, most of it during retirement. (The labor force comprises all persons who are working for pay or looking for work.) The comparable expected time was ten years in 1970, seven years in 1940, and only four years in 1900. Clearly, a long retirement was rare early in this century and still relatively rare just before World War II. But since the 1960s, workers have begun to leave the labor force at younger ages. In 1961, Congress lowered the age of eligibility for Social Security benefits from sixty-five to sixty-two. Now more than half of all persons applying for Social Security benefits are under sixty-five. Granted, some of the early retirees are suffering from poor health, and other retirees may have difficulty adjusting to their new status. Still, when earlier retirement is combined with a longer life span, the result is a greatly extended period during which one can, among other things, get to know and enjoy one's grandchildren.

The changes in leisure time for women are not as clear because women have always had lower levels of labor force participation than men. To be sure, women workers also are retiring earlier and, as has been noted, living much longer. And most women in their fifties and sixties are neither employed nor raising children. But young grandmothers are much more likely to be employed today than was the case a generation ago; they are also more likely to have aged parents to care for. Young working grandmothers, a growing minority, may have less time to devote to their grandchildren.

Most employed grandparents, however, work no more than forty hours per week. This, too, is a recent development. The forty-hour work week did not become the norm in the United States until after World War II. At the turn of the century, production workers in manufacturing jobs worked an average of fifty hours per week. Average hours dropped below forty during the depression, rose above forty during the war, and then settled at forty after the war. Moreover, at the turn of the century, 38 percent of the civilian labor force worked on farms, where long hours were commonplace. Even in 1940, about 17 percent of the civilian labor force worked on farms; but currently only about 3 percent work on farms. So even if they are employed, grandparents have more leisure time during the work week than was the case a few decades ago.

They also have more money. Living standards have risen in general since World War II, and the rise has been sharpest for the elderly. As recently as 1960, older Americans were an economically deprived group; now they are on the verge of becoming an economically advantaged group. The reason is the Social Security system. Since the 1950s and 1960s, Congress has expanded Social Security coverage, so that by 1970 nearly all nongovernment workers, except those in nonprofit organizations, were covered. And since the 1960s, Congress has increased Social Security benefits far faster than the increase in the cost of living. As a result, the average monthly benefit (in constant 1980 dollars, adjusted for changes in consumer prices) rose from $167 in 1960, to $214 in 1970, to $297 in 1980. Because of the broader coverage and higher benefits, the proportion of the elderly who are poor has plummeted. In 1959, 35 percent of persons sixty-five and over had incomes below the official poverty line, compared to 22 percent of the total population. By 1982 the disparity had disappeared: 15 percent of those sixty-five and over were poor, as were 15 percent of the total population. The elderly no longer were disproportionately poor, although many of them have incomes not too far above the poverty line. Grandparents, then, have benefitted from the general rise in economic welfare and, as they reach retirement, from the improvement in the economic welfare of the elderly.

Because of the postwar prosperity and the rise of social welfare institutions, older parents and their adult children are less dependent on each other economically. Family life in the early decades of the century was precarious; lower wages, the absence of social welfare programs, and crises of unemployment, illness, and death forced people to rely on their kin for support to a much greater extent than is true today. There were no welfare checks, unemployment compensation, food stamps, Medicare payments, Social Security benefits, or government loans to students. Often there was only one's family. Some older people provided assistance to their kin, such as finding a job for a relative, caring for the sick, or tending to the grandchildren while the parents worked. Sometimes grandparents, their children, and their grandchildren pooled their resources into a single family fund so that all could subsist. Exactly how common these three-generational economic units were we do not know; it would be a mistake to assume that all older adults were cooperating with their children and grandchildren at all times. In fact, studies of turn-of-the-century working-class families suggest that widowed older men—past their peak earning capacity and unfamiliar with domestic tasks as they were—could be a burden to the households of their children, while older women—who could help out domestically—were a potential source of household assistance. Nevertheless, these historical accounts suggest that intensive intergenerational cooperation and assistance was more common than it is today. Tamara Hareven, for example, studied the families of workers at the Amoskeag Mills in Manchester, New Hampshire, at the turn of the century. She found that the day-to-day cooperation of kin was necessary to secure a job at the mill, find housing, and accumulate enough money to get by. Cooperation has declined because it is not needed as often: social welfare programs now provide services that only the family formerly provided; declining rates of illness, death, and unemployment have reduced the frequency of family crises; and the rising standard of living—particularly of the elderly—has reduced the need for financial assistance.

The structure of the Social Security system also has lessened the feelings of obligation older parents and their adult children have toward each other. Social Security is an income transfer system in which some of the earnings of workers are transferred to the elderly. But we have constructed a fiction about Social Security, a myth that the recipients are only drawing out money that they put into the fund earlier in their lives. This myth allows both the younger contributors and the older recipients to ignore the economic dependency of the latter. The elderly are free to believe that they are just receiving that to which they are entitled by virtue of their own hard work. The tenacity of this myth—it is only now breaking down under the tremendous payment burden of our older age structure—demonstrates its importance. It allows the elderly to accept financial assistance without compromising their independence, and it allows children to support their parents without either generation openly acknowledging as much.

All of these trends taken together—changes in mortality, fertility, transportation, communications, the work day, retirement, Social Security, and standards of living—have transformed grandparenthood from its pre–World War II state. More people are living long enough to become grandparents and to enjoy a lengthy period of life as grandparents. They can keep in touch more easily with their grandchildren; they have more time to devote to them; they have more money to spend on them; and they are less likely still to be raising their own children.

CHAPTER 11

◆

TROUBLE

IN THE

FAMILY

R E A D I N G

28

Why Do They Do It?

KRISTIN LUKER

It's difficult to be the mother of a very young child. It's more difficult still when the mother is a teenager. And if she's not only a teen but unmarried, her life can he even grimmer than the most outspoken opponents of early childbearing can imagine. Many young mothers, when asked about their situation, readily describe how hard it is to raise a child. For some of them, having a baby was a serious mistake.

> I'm not living with my family. I'm living with a friend. It's really bleak and confusing. I miss everything I left behind. (Christina, seventeen, white, Colorado)

> If I thought I didn't have freedom before the baby, I didn't know what freedom was. My parents watch every step I take. After all, they are paying for me and my baby. (Holly, sixteen, white, Colorado)

> After they cut Marquis's umbilical cord, they just put him up on me and I told 'em, "Get that ugly baby off of me!" He was all covered with blood. It upset me. They took him, washed him off, put him back in my arms. I was just so tired. All I could say was, "He look just like William." And I turned my head to the other side. It took me a long time to get use to Marquis. I didn't want to accept at fifteen I have a baby.

From *Dubious Conceptions: The Politics of Teenage Pregnancy*. Copyright 1996. Published by Harvard University Press.

It took me about two months to get use, to get really use to Marquis. (Sherita, fifteen, black, Washington, D.C.)

I was going to have an abortion since I was only fifteen, but my family talked me out of it because of their religion, I love my baby now, but I'm only sixteen. I feel like I'm still a child—and here I have a child. It's completely changed my life. I look at other sixteen-year-olds and know that I can never be like them again. I sometimes wonder if an abortion wouldn't have been better. (Angela, sixteen, white, Colorado)

It's hard to be a parent by yourself. If I had it to do over again, I'd do things really different. When people tell you it's going to be difficult, believe them. My child is with me all the time . . . shopping, school, wherever I go. It's even harder than they say it is. I knew it would be hard, but not this hard.

Why is it that young people have babies, despite these depressing stories in which teens frankly admit how difficult it is for them to be mothers, and despite the national consensus that it's a very bad idea? No one in the United States is in favor of early childbearing: elected officials campaign against it, the public disapproves of it, and professionals warn that it is costly for everyone concerned. Even the group thought to be most accepting of unwed teenage mothers—the African American community—is far more disapproving than most people think. Acceptance of a teenage mother or father is not the same as approval: young mothers, both black and white, often report widespread censure from those around them. Their own mothers, many of whom were once teenage mothers themselves and were hoping for a better life for their daughters, sometimes express a disappointment bordering on rage.

So why do they do it? Why do approximately one million young women get pregnant each year? More than half a million carry their babies to term, and about two-thirds of them will be unmarried when they give birth. Certainly, adolescents live in a world very different from that of adults, but the evidence suggests that age is not the only factor leading teenagers to reject the path those older and wiser would choose for them. Through their actions, teens are trying to come to terms, sometimes ineptly, with the immense social and economic challenges they face in today's world: a shrinking job market, an indifferent community network, and public skepticism about the worth of minorities. Early pregnancy and childbearing are not an isolated problem restricted to a small but growing number of poor, young, and minority women; they are the result of an array of problems in American society—problems that have no easy solutions. Unwed teenage mothers are pioneers on a frontier where increasing numbers of Americans are now settling.

DREAMS AND REALITIES

Today, half of all marriages end in divorce, only half of divorced fathers make their full court-ordered child support payments, and unwed fathers visit their children more often than divorced fathers who have remarried. Even as the cultural meanings of "husband" and "wife" are shifting, men and women are expected to work in the paid labor force for much of their adult lives. Although there are still "men's jobs" and "women's jobs," one can no longer automatically assume that the former are better paid and more secure than the latter. In the tidy world of the 1950s, society expected that women would be virgins when they married (or at least when they got engaged); would remain married throughout their lives to the same man; would stay home, take care of the housework, and raise the children while their husband worked at a stable, well-paid job that he would keep until he decided to retire. This predictable scenario no longer exists for today's teenagers, although many of its cultural ideals live on in their dreams.

What it means to be an adult man or woman is now in constant flux, and we do not yet live in a world of perfect gender equality. Indeed, the sexual revolution seems to have stalled: women have taken on many of the responsibilities of men, but men have yet to assume their fair share of the nurturing and caretaking roles traditionally assigned to women. On the one hard, a young woman can no longer expect that she will have a husband on whom she can be totally dependent, both economically and emotionally. On the other hand, she can't expect a husband to share the burdens of child rearing and homemaking equally. Such changes in gender roles intersect with new uncertainties surrounding the meanings of race and class in American society. Between World War II and 1973, when wages were steadily rising, minorities and blue-collar workers could hope for the same job mobility and financial stability that white professionals enjoyed. But today's young people must compete intensely for jobs that are increasingly scarce, and must strive to meet meritocratic criteria that punish the less advantaged. They confront the future with far less assurance.

Young women in particular are finding life extremely complex. The rules that applied in their mothers' day were simple, at least in theory: do what it takes to get a good man, and keep him happy. Now women are aware of what this formula can lead to: displaced homemakers, divorcees and widows who are unprepared to support themselves, women who think they have no value unless they have a male partner. But dreams die hard. Today's young women say that they want a career in addition to, not instead of, a family life. No teenager hopes to end up as an unmarried mother on welfare. Although many disadvantaged teens do dream of motherhood, they dream of white-picket-fence motherhood, or at least the version of it to which girls from poor neighborhoods can realistically aspire.

> I want to have an average American life, not the average Puerto Rican life with a break-up here and a fight there. (Diane, Hispanic, New Jersey)

> [I see myself] mainly being a housewife, a mother, and probably going to school, trying to get my trade or something like that. I want me a job too, but jobs is so hard to find. I want one through the University. My sister told me, she said, "You can't be picky and choosy." So I told her, "Okay, I guess I just want me a job so bad." (Roberta, eighteen, black, Florida)

> I don't want to be dependent on my parents for the rest of my life. I want to help out, even though my parents aren't putting any pressure on me. (Woman from rural New England, eighteen, white)

I want to live in a two-bedroom apartment with a TV and carpeting. Nice and clean. If I'm older I have a car. I'd rather work at night and have somebody be there or early in the morning and come home by two or three. Other than that I be satisfied. Once I do what I want to do, I don't go back, I keep going. That's what I want to do. Get on my own with my baby and get situated. You know, I be having a good job. (Young woman living in an East Coast city)

I want to be a good mother, giving my kid all, everythin', and makin' my kids go to school, college, somethin' that I can't get.

Unfortunately, the odds against achieving even these modest dreams are getting longer. Young women with limited educational and labor market skills face many more obstacles to a stable relationship and a secure job than they used to, especially when they are members of minority groups and come from poor homes. And the young men in their lives have bleaker employment prospects than ever, making them a slender reed for young women to rely upon. Roberta's sister is right: when it comes to men and jobs, these young women can't be "picky and choosy." But even their willingness to be adaptable may not ensure that they get what they want.

In is hard for young people who have grown up in poverty to figure out how to make their dreams come true, how to negotiate the small steps that get them from one point to another. Moreover, young women of all classes must find a way to balance investments in their own future with commitment to a partner. Women have always had to decide whether and when to make such "selfish" investments, as opposed to devoting their energies to meeting the needs of a partner and children. Today they have to make decisions whose outcomes cannot be known. And teens of both sexes are on radically new terrain when it comes to making choices about sexual activity, marriage, family, and work. The sexual revolution has transformed Americans' values, attitudes, and behavior in ways that are unlikely to be reversed. How do teens—should teens—think and act in this new world, and reconcile its alluring promises with its hard realities? How can they manage the consequences of their sexual freedom?

Many people of all political persuasions think that teenagers should simply stop having sex. Liberals argue that public campaigns have induced teenagers to curtail their drug use and that such campaigns could likewise induce them to abstain from sex; conservatives plead for "a little virginity." Unfortunately both groups are working against the historical tide. Premarital sexual activity has become steadily more common in the twentieth century, throughout the industrialized world. But the sexual revolution has not been fully integrated into people's lives, especially the lives of teenagers. The American public is still unsure whether the tide can or should be turned back. Given society's deep ambivalence about sexual activity among teenagers, young women often find themselves in a state of confusion—a state that is often apparent in the ethnographic accounts. They tell researchers about their decisions concerning sex, conception, and pregnancy. But when we say that teens "decide" on a course of action in such matters, we may be using much too active a verb. On the one hand, young people are told to "just say no"; on the other, their friends, the media, and society at large foster the idea that sexual activity among teenagers is widespread and increasingly commonplace. If a young woman doesn't want to have sex, she has little in the way of support, since sexual activity has come to be expected.

> They looked at a virgin as being something shameful. They were the type of people who would always tell what happened if they made out with a boy or a boy made out with them. I was the only one they never heard from. They would say. "You don't know what you're missing." The more they talked the more curious I got. (Theresa, eighteen, black, Washington, D.C.)

> All of my friends were having sex and I was curious to see what it was all about. I didn't even know the guy very well and I don't even want to know him. It wasn't like it is shown on TV or in the movies. I didn't even enjoy it. (Young woman from Colorado)

> All my friends were doing it and they dared me. After all, I was seventeen and had never had sex. I thought maybe I really was missing something. (I wasn't.)

> Some girls will have sex to get guys to like them. Some girls do it thinking. "Well, I'm going to keep this boyfriend." If I could, I would tell them. "Don't, until you feel they respect and love you. You're too good to be chasing and trying to make someone stay with you." (Robyn, black, Colorado)

The sexuality that young women express in such ethnographic accounts is often curiously passive. Although a few young women brag about their sexual conquests and skills, many simply make themselves available, in part because it seems that everyone else is doing it.

Even as they feel pressure to be sexually active, teens are urged to abstain, or at least to "be careful" and use contraceptives. Thus, in their accounts they describe their first sexual intercourse as an experience remarkably devoid of pleasure. They are anxious, in a hurry to get it over with, eager to cross the Rubicon in a leap before courage fails; or they see it as something that "just happened," without anyone's having made an active decision.

> Then he asked me to have sex. I was scared and everything, and it was like, "What am I gonna do?" The first time I told him no and he understood. We watched TV. And he brought me home. Then a couple of days after that he asked me again, I said okay. I guess I said so because I just wanted to show him I wasn't scared to have sex. I was scared. And he kinda knew I was scared. But I guess I was playing a role. I wanted to show him that I'm not scared. So we had sex . . . and now it's like we don't get along. (Young black woman from Oakland, California)

> We was going together for two years and we didn't do anything. I was like "no" and he was scared also. Finally we just—hurry up and get it over with. We just took off our clothes real quick. Just hurry up and get it over with and we both shaking and crying. (High school student in a midwestern city)

> I didn't talk to my boyfriend about sex, and he didn't talk to me. One day we were together and started hugging and kissing, then we just did it. (Latisha, fifteen, black, Chicago)

And I used to go home and he would call me on the phone and then we were like that for about a month or so and then we just started to get involved. I don't know, he just asked me and I said sure, if that was what you want to do . . . We just did it to do it and then I just got pregnant. (Sally, fifteen, white)

He was someone to lean on. When I was depressed, I figured, I'll lean on him. Next thing you know, I figured I started to listen to him. Then I saw him as more of a friend. Then why not kiss him? Why not touch him? It seemed that one thing led to another. Afterward we never made a big deal out of it like, "Wow, wasn't that great last night." We never even talked much about it . . . We said we shouldn't have let that happen. It won't happen again. And then it did happen again. (Ivy, seventeen, black, Boston)

Not only are many young women confused and indecisive when it comes to their first sexual encounters, but they often know few adults whom they can comfortably ask for guidance. According to their own accounts, even their mothers offer little or no help:

Only thing she said was, "Don't be out there messing with no boys." And that was it. (Sherita, twelve, black, Washington, D.C.)

I love my mother, but she never really talked to me, and I don't feel like I can talk to her about private matters. She acts like we shouldn't talk about sex. She only told me after my period, that I shouldn't go with boys. (Latisha, fifteen, black, Chicago)

She didn't want me to know nothing about sex but "just don't do it." But I was like— I was like, gosh, but everybody is doing this and I wanted to try it, too. (Fourteen-year-old, attending high school in a midwestern city)

The little information available on young men shows that they, too, see themselves as failures if they have not had sex. For them, sexual activity is an indication of maturity and masculinity.

If they haven't [had intercourse] then they are like outcasts. Like, "Man, you never made love to a girl!" Some of them get teased a lot. It's like on the baseball team and they start talking about that and you have got the younger guys out there and you could tell because they are all quiet and stuff and they won't talk. Some of the other people start laughing at them and start getting on them and get them kind of upset. (Male high school student in a midwestern city)

Premarital sexual activity has become increasingly common in the twentieth century. This is partly due to the fact that people are getting married later, but it is also a function of America's transition from a rural, kinship based society to a modern industrial one that tends to disconnect sex from marriage. Some experts argue that the real sexual revolution in the United States occurred in the 1880s and was largely over by 1915. Others maintain that there were two sexual revolutions, one between 1915 and 1925 and the other between 1965 and 1975. All agree, however, that sexual activity among teenagers is not peculiar to the late twentieth century; rather, it is the result of long-term trends shaped by social and economic forces that are probably irreversible. Furthermore, whatever it is about modernity that makes sex independent from marriage, it is present in most of the industrialized nations. Teens all over the developed world are engaging in sex before marriage. When in 1984 the United Nations undertook a survey of adolescent sexual and reproductive behavior, it concluded that "without doubt, the proportion of teenagers who have experienced sex by age nineteen has been increasing steadily over the years among all adolescents." Even conservative Japan—a communitarian society with strongly internalized social controls—has reported increases in sexual activity among its teenagers, as well as a rise in out-of-wedlock childbearing. Surveys conducted by the Japanese government in 1981 found that in Japan about 28 percent of young women and 37 percent of young men were sexually active by the end of their teenage years— figures that were less than half of those for the United States but that, compared with the proportions in 1974, represented an increase of 40 percent for young men and an amazing 150 percent for young women.

According to conservatives, the fact that contraception was made available to teenagers in the late 1960s was the fuel that ignited the explosion of early sex. Prior to 1964 contraceptives were nominally illegal in many jurisdictions, were never mentioned in public (much less advertised), and were difficult to obtain. In pharmacies, condoms were typically kept behind the counter and some pharmacists in small towns refused to sell them to young men they knew to be unmarried. Since out-of-wedlock pregnancy was stigmatized and likely to lead to a clandestine abortion or a hasty marriage, there is a certain logic to the notion that the stunning reversal in the status of contraception—from illegal and unmentionable to widely available at public expense—fostered the spectacular increase in sexual activity among teenagers. And since this increase in activity and the proliferation of low-cost birth control clinics both occurred in the late 1960s and early 1970s, there is at least a temporal connection between the two.

This commonsensical and comforting notion (comforting because it implies that one way to curtail sexual activity among teens is to limit the availability of contraception) has several things wrong with it. First, a great many aspects of American society were changing in the sixties and seventies. Public attitudes shifted radically on issues such as contraception, premarital sex, abortion, and illegitimacy; family planning clinics were only one part of the context surrounding teenagers' behavior. Second, as we have seen, young people throughout the industrialized world have increased their premarital sexual activity, despite the fact that policies regarding contraception vary widely from country to country. Finally, and perhaps most tellingly, in the 1980s federal funding of family planning services dropped sharply—from $400 million in 1980 to $250 million in 1990—but sexual activity among teens continued to increase. The states compensated in some measure for the cutbacks, but they by no means filled the gap entirely. Though it is disappointing not to be able to pinpoint a cause for the increase in sexual activity among the young, historical and international evidence suggests that it is probably the result of a blend of factors. What *is* extremely clear is that the welter of societal changes and conflicting messages surrounding sexual activity has left many young people confused, misinformed, and adrift.

THE PATH TO PREGNANCY

Some teenagers get pregnant for exactly the same reason that older women do: they are married and they want a child. It is true that in the United States marriage rates among teens have declined dramatically and the median age at first marriage is higher than it has ever been. Still, in 1990 about 7 percent of all American teens (about 10 percent of all eighteen- and nineteen-year olds) were married, and about one out of every three babies born to a teen was born to a married mother. It is important to keep in mind that discussions of early pregnancy and childbearing include these married teenagers, whom the public usually does not think of as part of the constellation of problems associated with "teenage pregnancy."

Other teens are unmarried but are using contraception to avoid pregnancy. Stereotypes to the contrary, teenagers are using more contraception, and using it more effectively, than ever before. In 1982 about half of all American teenagers used a contraceptive method the first time they had sex; in 1988 about 70 percent of them did. Of all the sexually active teenage women surveyed in the 1988 National Survey of Family Growth who were currently having sex, who were neither pregnant nor seeking pregnancy, and who had not been sterilized, about 80 percent were using some method of contraception. Among poor teens, those whose family income was less than twice the poverty level, the rate was a little lower (72.5 percent), and among affluent teens it was a little higher. But if teens are using contraception to such an extent, why aren't their pregnancy rates plummeting?

One major reason is statistical. Teens today actually do have a lower risk of getting pregnant: in 1972 the odds that a sexually involved teen would become pregnant were about one in four; by 1990 they had decreased to one in five. (These figures include married teens, who accounted for approximately 26 percent of all sexually experienced teens in 1972, but only about 15 percent in 1984.) Unfortunately, however, the decline in the odds that an individual teen would get pregnant did not lead to a decline in the pregnancy rate for all teenagers: the increase in effective contraceptive use was offset by the fact that so many more unmarried teenagers became sexually involved during this period. In 1972, in a population of approximately 10 million teenage women, about 2.5 million were sexually active—a rate of roughly 25 percent. By 1984 the total number of teenagers had decreased slightly to 9 million, but the number of sexually active teens had grown to 4 million—a rate of about 50 percent. Thus, although an individual teen had a smaller chance of getting pregnant, the fact that there were twice as many teens at risk meant that there were more pregnancies. Still, the two trends balanced each other so that the pregnancy rate among all teenage women remained roughly stable: in 1972 it was 95 per thousand; in 1984 it was 108 per thousand; and in 1988 it was 117 per thousand. This may be even better news than it seems: some observers think that teenagers' rates of premarital sexual activity are leveling off, and since there is no evidence that the propensity to use contraception is declining, some of the incidence of pregnancy among teens may be a lag effect that will persist only while they are learning how to use contraception well. But the pregnancy rates among American teenagers are worrisome. especially when about half of the pregnancies end in abortion. Despite more than two decades' worth of research on the matter, there are no clear answers as to why the rates remain so high in the United States, compared to those in other countries.

Within a general pattern of increased contraceptive use, there are a number of factors that enable one to predict which teenagers will use contraception more consistently and effectively than others. For example, the higher a teen's socioeconomic status and educational aspirations, the more likely he or she is to use contraception. Older teens are more consistent users than younger ones, for two reasons: sexually active teens get better at it over time; and teens who are older when they have their first sexual experience are more careful than those who start at an earlier age. Contraceptive use also tends to be relationship specific. That is, young men and women are not users or nonusers, but change their practice with individual partners. We know that older women (that is women whose teen years are behind them) are likely to get pregnant after the breakup of a relationship: about one-fourth of all babies born out of wedlock are born to women who have left one marriage but have not entered into another. This suggests that when experienced users move out of a stable relationship, the meaning and practice of contraception change. Thus, young women are even more at risk, since their sexual relationships tend to be more short-lived and sporadic. Studies have shown that sexually active teens in fact go through long periods during which they have no sex at all because they are not involved in a relationship and often have relatively low rates of sex even when they are. And when sexual activity is unpredictable, using contraceptives becomes more difficult.

Contraceptive use may also change over the course of a relationship. When young people have sex for the first time, they tend to rely on male protection methods, notably condoms. In 1982, 23 percent of teenage women reported using condoms the first time they had intercourse, and an additional 13 percent said they used withdrawal; in 1988 about 65 percent used condoms and virtually none used withdrawal. After their first sexual encounter, unmarried adolescents tend increasingly to use female contraceptives (diaphragms and the Pill) instead of male methods. In 1982 about 43 percent of sexually active teenage women were on the Pill, 15 percent were using condoms, and almost 30 percent were using no contraception at all. Similarly, in 1988 about 47 percent were on the Pill, 27 percent were using condoms, and 20 percent were using no contraception. Contrary to stereotype, young black women are *more* likely than young white women to use highly effective contraception, mostly because they are much more likely to be Pill users; but they also tend to begin using contraception at a later age, so their overall risk of pregnancy is higher. Poor teens and affluent teens are almost equally likely to be Pill users.

So why do teens get pregnant if so many of them are using contraception? The short answer is that some get pregnant the first time they have sex, because they use no contraception, use relatively ineffective methods, or use methods inadequately. Others get pregnant during transitions—either within a relationship, as they move from male methods to female methods, or between relationships, when they stop using a certain method. (About 70 percent of all sexually active teenage women have had more than one partner by the time they reach their twenties.) Still others get pregnant because they use no contraception: either they have never used it, or they are not presently using a method they used earlier. Finally, a small number get pregnant even though they are using contraception faithfully.

One troubling and rarely acknowledged fact is that teenagers' sexual involvements are not always consensual, particularly in the case of young women. The younger the woman, the more likely this is to be a problem. In one national survey of American teens, about 7 percent answered yes when they were asked, "Was there ever a time when you were forced to have sex against your will, or were raped?" Thirteen percent of the white women and 8 percent of the black women reported having coercive sex before they were twenty; among young men, the figures were 1.9 percent for whites and 6.1 percent for blacks. An astonishing 74 percent of all women who had had sex before the age of fourteen reported that they had had coerced sex; among those who had had sex before the age of fifteen, the figure was 60 percent. Since most experts think that the respondents in such interviews underreport coercive sex, these numbers are probably conservative. And the question used in the survey defined coercive sex rather narrowly: as the national debate on rape and date rape makes clear, it is difficult to draw the exact boundaries of sexual consent.

In the days when premarital sex was considered wrong, young men and women typically negotiated the meaning of each step (the first kiss, the first caress, "petting") and where it fit into the relationship; the woman permitted increasing sexual intimacy in return for greater commitment from the man. Young women today have no such clear-cut rules. Society has become more tolerant of the notion that an unmarried couple may be sexually involved if they are emotionally committed to each other, but the emotional and social context within which sexual encounters take place has become quite fluid.

When sexual activity is coerced, as it is for a small but important subset of American teens, it is extremely unlikely that the victim will have planned ahead to use contraception. But even in consensual situations, young people—especially young women—still face obstacles to effective contraception use. Social pressures concerning gender roles and sexual activity exert some real constraints on the ability to use contraception effectively—constraints that are similar in effect, if not in degree or kind to those of coercive sex.

During the past thirty years, for example, contraceptive use has become increasingly feminized: both men and women tend to think that contraception is the responsibility of the woman and that it's the woman's fault when something goes wrong. This represents a revolution—one so subtle that most Americans have scarcely noticed it. Until 1965 condoms were the most frequently used form of contraception in America, at least among married couples. There was a time when a young man would carry a lone, crumbling condom with him wherever he went, and carry it so long that it would wear its oulines into his wallet. But with the development of the Pill and the IUD, contraception came to be considered something for which women were responsible and accountable. Interestingly, concerns about sexually transmitted diseases (especially AIDS) and the health effects of the Pill have made condoms popular once again, only today they are marketed to both men and women. What this means in practice is that couples often must negotiate which contraceptives to use and when to use them, with little in the way of clear social rules.

In such negotiations, women tend to be culturally handicapped by society's expectations of appropriate female sexual behavior. The first time a woman has intercourse, she is considered to be "giving away" something valuable: her virginity. If she is young and unmarried, she is culturally enjoined from looking too "ready." (This may explain the increasing popularity of the condom, which the man usually provides and which became popular among teens prior to the recent concern with AIDS and other sexually transmitted diseases.) An unmarried woman who is in the early stages of getting involved in a relationship and who must not look too "ready" for sex is therefore forced to rely on the goodwill and motivation of her partner, who may not be as committed to the relationship as she is and who will suffer fewer consequences if something goes wrong. The first time the couple has sex, he is the one who typically takes the contraceptive precautions, yet he has a very different set of incentives and faces a very different set of risks. Many of these pressures at first intercourse recur every time a woman has a new sexual partner. (Most adolescent women are still having sex in serially monogamous relationships.)

The prevalence of premarital sex means that a "nice girl" is no longer defined as a young woman who has never had sex. Rather, it means a young woman who has had sex but not too much of it, or who is sexually active but not promiscuous. Alas, one simple way of showing that one is a "nice girl" is to be unprepared for sex—to have given no prior thought to contraception. Both at first sex and with each new partner, a young woman is thus subject to powerful cultural pressures that penalize her for taking responsibility. To use contraception, a woman has to anticipate sexual activity by locating the impetus within herself, rather than in the man who has overcome her hesitancy. She must plan for sex, must be prepared to speak about contraception frankly with someone she may not know very well (at the time when, according to cultural expectations, her emotions rather than her intellect are supposed to hold sway), and must put her own long-term welfare before the short-term pleasure of the couple, especially of the man.

When young women talk about the obstacles to using contraception, they frequently describe the way in which conflicting social pressures intersect with their own ambivalent and contradictory feelings:

> I went to Planned Parenthood and I had my aunt help me get the diaphragm. I didn't like it, it didn't feel comfortable and I was embarrassed, You know, jump up [during sex] and say, "Um, wait a minute."

Many American teenagers receive at least some information about contraception (often in sex education classes), but this information must be assessed in, terms of a complex set of parameters concerning the way in which a teenager views sexual activity and why he or she is using contraception. Young people often report misunderstandings about contraception—misunderstandings that are shared by those around them.

> I think I was thirteen when I first started having sex. My best friend thought I was crazy 'cause I went to my mother and said, "Well, Mom, I like this boy and I might be doing something with him and would you take me to get birth control?" And she said, "No, because once you start taking these pills, you'll become sterile." See, I love kids, I love 'em and I want 'em. So it scared me . . . but she knew I was going to do something. (Sixteen-year-old)

> I wish 1 had taken the pill. I waited too long. I just kept telling myself, "Well, I can wait a little bit longer." And then I found out it was too late. I wasn't afraid to take it—I just kept putting it off and putting it off, and I put it off too long. (Kimberly, white, Colorado)

In short, the skills a young woman needs in order to use contraception effectively are precisely the skills that society discourages in "nice girls," who are expected to be passive, modest, shy, sexually inexperienced (or at least less experienced than their partners), and dedicated to the comfort of others. A woman who obtains contraception in anticipation of sexual activity is thought to be "looking for sex" (as teens say) and is culturally devalued. More to the point, she risks being devalued within the relationship. When it comes to contraception, she is caught in a net of double binds. She is the one who is supposed to "take care of it," the one at whom most contraceptive programs are aimed, and the one for whose body the most effective methods have been developed. Yet she is expected to be diffident about sex, and interested in it only because love and erotic arousal have spontaneously led her to be "carried away." And if she seems too interested in sex for its own sake, as evidenced by her use of contraception, she is in a weak position to trade sex for commitment and intimacy from the man involved. These pressures are often exacerbated because the woman's partner is older than she is, and presumably more experienced and sophisticated. Scattered data suggest that the partners of teenage mothers are typically older, sometimes significantly older: in 1988, although about 80 percent of teenage mothers had a partner who was within a few years of their own age, 29 percent had a partner who was six or more years older than they were; for very young mothers (fifteen-year-olds), the figure climbed to 30 percent.

A couple may go through a period in which they use no contraception, while they try to work out the meaning of the relationship and how contraception fits into it. Young women who seek contraceptive services sometimes say that they are doing so because their relationship is becoming more serious—meaning they have used no contraception up to that point. Of course, their statistical risk of getting pregnant is just as high in the early months of their relationship as it is later, and may in fact be higher: one study showed that most young women who got pregnant did so in the early, perilous part of their relationship. This suggests that what has changed are not the statistical odds of getting pregnant, but the social cost. Once a relationship is defined as getting serious, it's easier for the young woman to make the commitment to contraception without risking her commitment to her boyfriend. And it may be easier for him to argue for contraception without seeming as if he's "leading her on."

So commitment to and by a partner may counteract some of the pressures that serve as obstacles to contraception. Some young women say that they put off seeking contraceptive services because they are afraid of being found out, particularly by their parents. Yet once their relationship is defined as serious and the young man has demonstrated his commitment, the young woman's sexual desire is transformed from potentially promiscuous into true love, and she is equipped to take the public step of obtaining contraception. Young women whose significant others (parents, partners, and best friends) urge them to get contraception are more likely to obtain it before becoming sexually active and more likely to use it effectively.

Teenagers from different classes and racial groups tend to have different patterns of contraceptive use, both at first intercourse and subsequently. Although there are few studies of the way in which class and race affect the meanings attached to specific contraceptives and to contraception in general, one can make two broad observations. First, when sexual partners come from different social or ethnic groups (as they increasingly do these days), they may have additional problems communicating about contraception. Second, researchers who study sexual and contraceptive decisions in contexts where AIDS is a factor tell us that young women who have a sense of power and efficacy in their lives are more able to protect themselves in their sexual relationships than women who feel weak. Since many poor and minority women lack sources of esteem and power in their lives, they may be more vulnerable in their relationships.

Of course, the desire or lack of desire for a baby plays an important role in the decisions that people make about contraception. The American public often assumes that teenagers have babies simply because they know little about, or ignore, birth control practices. But in many cases this is untrue. In 1984 a sixteen-year-old urban black woman named Tauscha Vaughan made the following comment to *Washington Post* reporter Leon Dash: "Will you please stop asking me about birth control? Girls out here know all about birth control. There's too much birth control out here. All of them know about it. Even when they twelve, they know what birth control is. Girls out here get pregnant because they want to have babies!" This young woman highlights an important fact: that decisions about contraception are intimately related to whether or not one wants a child. But the situation is more complex than this simple statement would make it appear.

When young women talk about their lives, it is clear that their feelings about childbearing exist in a context of numerous shifting assessments. For example, they often describe a partner who does not use contraception or who stops using a contraceptive.

> It [the condom] didn't feel comfortable, and I didn't enjoy it either, so I kept taking my chances on withdrawal. (Reggie, black, Washington, D.C.; father of Tauscha Vaughan's baby)

> We had sex for about a year before I got pregnant. I wasn't using birth control, not at first. Then he said, we'll use something. We didn't really talk about it. The condoms he used hurt him and they irritated me, you know, real bad. I didn't enjoy it and I said, "No, I don't think we'll have it, if it's gonna bother me so bad."

> I knew that it could happen; I just thought I would be lucky and not get caught. We used condoms sometimes, but he said it feels better without them. But when I knew I was pregnant I kept acting like it wasn't real. (Young woman in a Teen Parenting program with black, white, and Hispanic participants)

For many adults, quotes such as these are just one more example of teenagers' fecklessness, of their inability to plan ahead or to see the consequences of their own actions. But when such accounts are read more carefully, many of them reveal that behind the seeming aimlessness are some serious, complex, and often hidden negotiations about the meaning of the relationship—negotiations that teens, like adults, are often reluctant to conduct straightforwardly. In many cases, for example, a young woman thinks that if she and her boyfriend use no contraception, there is a tacit assumption that they are sharing the risk: he must love her so much that he wants to have a child with her and is willing to stand by her if she does:

> I expected the father to be helpful; to take care of the baby. All three of us to go places and have fun. Live together as a family. (Shana, black, Oakland, California)

> I expected commitment of just being a father. Of being there saying "I'm going to help you. I'll be there to take care of Jimmy when you want, when you need to do other things." I expected his support emotionally, financially as much as he could, I expected him to be there for me . . . I expected him to love me because I was the woman who had his baby. But he loves everyone else who didn't. (Diane, black, Oakland, California)

Cynics may ascribe such expectations to wishful thinking; but caught up in a relationship, boys sometimes do make promises—promises that are difficult to keep.

> We were going to be married in April. We didn't want to have a baby right away, but neither of us wanted to use birth control, so when I asked J. if he was ready for the consequences he said yes. He said if I got pregnant he'd want to be with me and the baby always, which is what he said when he found out I was pregnant. Then he changed his mind and split. (Seventeen-year-old, white, rural New England)

> I dated John for about a year. He always told me that if anything happened he would take care of me. When I told him I was pregnant he said that it wasn't his baby. He dropped me and started dating my best friend. It was hard for me to accept that he didn't care as much as he said he did before I got pregnant. (Robyn, black, Colorado)

Although some teenagers try to prevent pregnancy and fail, others get pregnant because they believe pregnancy is not such a bad thing. Young unmarried women, like young married ones, may become pregnant because they want to or at least because they are not sufficiently motivated to avoid it. Experts have long debated whether teenagers want their pregnancies and births. A recent study by the Alan Guttmacher Institute estimated that only 7 percent of all such pregnancies were intended. Does this fully capture what we know about teens and their plans?

It seems at first glance that most young women would prefer not to have a baby. About half of all pregnant teens have abortions, and about 87 percent of those who carried their babies to term in 1988 described their pregnancies as unintended. These findings come from the National Survey of Family Growth (conducted in four cycles: 1973, 1976, 1982, and 1988), which asked a national sample of women the following question: "Was the reason you (had stopped / were not) using any contraceptive method because you yourself wanted to become pregnant?" If a woman answered no, she was asked another question: "It is sometimes difficult to recall these things; but just before that pregnancy began, would you say you probably wanted a(nother) baby at some time or probably not?" This is a rather inflexible way to investigate a fluid, complex, and constantly reexamined decision. The National Center for Health Statistics is revising its methods for the next round of the survey, but we must keep in mind the language of the questions as they were posed if we are to understand the responses fully. Until the 1970s, the typical woman in need of family planning was a woman who had already had all the children she wanted and who was at risk of having additional children she did not want, and the language of the questions reflected the situation of such women. Teens fit into this group awkwardly, if at all. Since teens are just starting to build their families, the questions posed by the survey do not reveal their plans or preferences very well. Few teens have babies that are unwanted in this traditional sense; mostly they say that their babies came earlier than planned. Thus far, the wording of survey questions has not allowed researchers to assess the effects (if any) that early childbearing may have on women's life plans.

The concept of wantedness has been subject to a good deal of criticism. A women may find it very difficult to tell interviewers that she did not want her baby. Moreover, an unwanted pregnancy may well result in a wanted child. And there is a deeper and more philosophical problem with efforts to measure wantedness by means of questionnaires, particularly in the case of teenagers. Surveys assume that people perceive clear choices and that they feel empowered to act on them. Such certainty and confidence can, of course, be deduced in some instances. If a woman and her partner say that they consistently and effectively used birth control up to the date of conception, and then terminate the pregnancy, we can be fairly confident that they did not want the child. Likewise, if a woman tells an interviewer that she deliberately stopped using contraception because she wanted to become pregnant, we can be reasonably certain that she wanted her baby. But for most teenage mothers, these two extremes rarely capture the lived experience. Contraception, particularly among unmarried people and particularly among the young, may be a casualty of unspoken dynamics in the relationship. Say, for instance, a young man complains about using condoms and finally decides not to use one, and his girlfriend interprets this to mean that he will marry her if she gets pregnant. Is her subsequent pregnancy a wanted pregnancy? What complicated negotiations between a woman and a man determine whether a baby is wanted or unwanted?

Still, the information that interviewers glean from women is interesting, especially when it changes over time. In 1973 the National Survey of Family Growth revealed that of all the children that had been born to American wives in the previous five years, 14 percent had been unwanted at the time of conception. In 1982, when the survey included both married and unmarried mothers, it found that only 7.7 percent of the children born in the previous five years had been unwanted. By 1988, the figure had risen again, to 10.3 percent. And the survey revealed significant differences according to age, race, and socioeconomic status: black women, poor women, and older women were all more likely (again, because of the way the question was worded) to tell interviewers that their children had been unwanted.

But the data are most troubling and most opaque in the case of teenagers. Since the survey asked women if they wanted a baby or another baby at some time, it presumably succeeded in reaching teenagers who had definitely not wanted a baby. Prior to 1982 unmarried women were not interviewed unless they had a child living with them, so we have comparative data only from 1982 and 1988. But in 1988, about 15 percent of white teens and about 30 percent of black teens said that they had not wanted their baby at the time of conception. Thus, although many young mothers did find themselves with babies they had not wanted, 85 percent of white teens and 70 percent of black teens told researchers that they had indeed wanted their children. Most, however, were unhappy about the timing of the birth: more than eight out of ten teenagers who said that they had wanted their babies also asserted that they had become pregnant sooner than planned.

In 1988 analysts took a new approach to the data. Previously the survey had made a distinction only between babies that had been wanted at the time of conception and those that had not; and this made sense, given that the women of interest were older and had nearly completed building their families. Wanted babies were then subdivided into those wanted at the time of conception and those wanted later. In 1988, however, the number of unwanted children was combined with the number of wanted children who had arrived sooner than expected. The resulting new category of "unintended" births was probably designed to accommodate the new demographic reality that teens represented. But the concept of unintendedness is just as slippery as the notion of wantedness. From the available data, we just cannot tell when a young woman would have preferred to have the baby that came too soon. In view of the way the survey questions were worded, a teen who was eager to be a mother but who would have preferred to wait a few months cannot be distinguished from a teen who planned eventually to become a mother but who viewed her recent pregnancy as a serious disruption in her life plans.

According to other studies. poor teenagers are more likely than affluent ones to report that a pregnancy was intended, and are more likely to continue their pregnancies to term. Furthermore, those who deliberately become pregnant and who do not seek abortions tend to be less advantaged teenagers. The entire issue of wantedness must thus be considered in the context of teenagers' available choices, which are often highly constrained.

R E A D I N G

29

The Downwardly Mobile Family

KATHERINE S. NEWMAN

Brutal though it can be, the damage downward mobility does to a displaced manager is only the beginning of a longer story. Like a storm gathering force, failure in the work world engenders further havoc, first buffeting relations between breadwinner and spouse, then spreading to the children. Economic foundations are wrenched out from under the family, and emotional bonds are stretched to the breaking point. In the end, even children's values and plans for the future are drawn into the maelstrom as they struggle to reconcile the teachings of meritocratic individualism with their parents' glaring inability to prove their worth in the world.

As unwilling refugees from the middle class, children of downwardly mobile managers offer a unique window into the world they have left behind. Most had taken their old affluent life-style for granted and did not understand the significance of what they had had until after it was gone.

For Penny Ellerby, who was fifteen when the great crash came, the most immediate and troubling impact was the change it wrought upon the father she looked up to:

> The pressure on my Dad was intense. From my point of view he just seemed to be getting irrational. He would walk around the house talking to himself and stay up all night, smoking cigarettes in the dark.
>
> When things started to fall apart no one would tell my sister or me anything about what was happening. So all I perceived is that somebody who used to be a figure of strength was behaving strangely: starting to cry at odd times . . . hanging around the house unshaven in his underwear when I would bring dates home from high school. In

the absence of any understanding of what was going on, my attitude was one of anger and disgust, like "Why don't you get your act together? What's the matter with you?"

Penny's father had been a successful show business promoter. He had invested most of the family's assets in a talent show that ran successfully for four years until its sponsors pulled the plug and sent his career into a tailspin. Penny remembers the spectacular crash that followed:

> We went from one day in which we owned a business that was worth probably four or five million dollars in assets and woke up the next day to find that we were personally probably a half million in debt. Creditors called at the house and started to send threatening notes.
>
> First he started a novel, but that didn't last more than two months. Then he went back into a public relations project, which also didn't work out. Then he tried to put together a series of college film festivals. Nothing worked.

Penny's adolescence came to an abrupt end at that point. Her father was unable to find a professional position of any kind. Tension between her parents rose to unbearable heights. Her dad finally left home, one step ahead of the bill collectors. She had not seen him for nearly ten years; for most of that time he has lived on the streets in San Francisco. Penny's mother managed to find a low-level clerical job but it could not begin to sustain the life-style she had known as the wife of a promoter. Today she lives in one of New York's tougher public housing projects and faces problems familiar to many a marginal wage earner: how to make ends meet and how to face the prospect of poverty-level retirement.

* * *

Downward mobility can occur as the result of a precipitous crash whose effects are felt immediately. Indeed, Penny's story demonstrates how rapidly, and how completely, downward mobility can undermine a family. But for most managerial families, the process is one of gradual erosion. Occupational dislocation may occur suddenly, but its consequences can take six or seven years to become fully evident, depending upon the resources the families can tap.

When occupational disaster strikes, the first impulse is typically to contain the damage to the work world, and to continue as far as possible to maintain a sense of normalcy in the family realm. Hence families continue to pay the mortgage and send the kids off to school. But as months elapse without reemployment, and bank balances plummet, the attempt to maintain a normal life-style falters. What begins as a principled commitment to avoid defeatism and get on with life takes on a new character—the family starts to dissemble and hide its problems from the outside world, starting with small cover stories. Paul Armand instructed his son on how to describe his Dad's unemployment to his friends at boarding school: "In his school, everybody's father is the head of this and that. So I said, 'You just tell them your Dad was VP of a company and he just refused to go on an overseas assignment. . . .' I told him if anybody asks, tell them I started my own firm." This was, at best, a shading of the truth. Paul had created a "firm" on paper, but it was not engaged in any money-making enterprises.

The impetus to conceal, if not lie, sometimes comes from adolescent children. The world of the middle-class adolescent is consumerist, elitist, and exceptionally unforgiving of divergence from the norm. Teenagers want to look like, act like, and think like their friends. The paradox of middle-class adolescents is that they must achieve individuality first and foremost by learning to look and sound just like "everyone else" their own age. Dress style and musical taste are only part of the cultural baggage American adolescents bring to the task of peer consolidation. Children of affluence—the sons and daughters of the managerial middle class—also rely upon their families' social position in seeking peer acceptance. Their fathers' occupation, and the life-style that it makes possible, is part and parcel of a cultural image they attempt to project.

When David Patterson moved his wife and two teenage children from California to Long Island, his children complained at first that they were looked upon, with some degree of suspicion, as "transients." To overcome the ill-will and cultivate new friends, Patterson's son boasted his father's status as an executive. The scheme worked, for local families were highly attuned to occupational prestige. Consequently, when Patterson received his pink slip, it threatened to undermine his teenagers' public identity and put their social acceptance by peers at risk. The children reacted with shame and with secrecy: They stopped bringing acquaintances home; they avoided discussing the family crisis with peers or school counselors. They became overwhelmed by the feeling that if their father's downward mobility became public knowledge, their own social standing would be destroyed.

The downwardly mobile managerial family jealously guards its public face, even if this means that everyone must eat a dreary diet so that the children can have some stylish clothes for school. They cherish central symbols of belonging, like the family home, and families make considerable sacrifices in other domains to hold on to these valued possessions. Large houses are rarely traded in for something more modest until there is no other alternative.

Families avoid bankruptcy, both because they look upon it as the coward's way out of a disaster and as a too-public admission of failure and surrender. Dierdre Miller's father inherited a family firm that ran aground in the late 1960s. By the time Dierdre was a teenager, the firm was near collapse and the creditors began to hound Mr. Miller to pay up on his bills. It was clear to Dierdre's mother that they needed to declare bankruptcy to protect the family's remaining assets. But as Dierdre tells it, this was unthinkable:

> My dad wouldn't hear of the idea of declaring bankruptcy or of selling the family business. He felt he had a reputation to protect and that if he went bankrupt it would be destroyed. He used to tell me that you just have to meet your obligations, that you can just walk out on people and companies you owe money to. I think he felt that if he declared bankruptcy he'd never be able to recover. It would be the end because no one would respect him.

Joan deLancy, a Wall Street lawyer, remembers that her father—whose career as an engineer bit the dust in the wake of defense department cutbacks in the early 1970s—felt the same way:

My father did earn money through various consulting jobs and short-term positions of one kind or another, but we didn't see much of it. It went toward paying off their debts. He could have walked away from them by declaring bankruptcy, but he thought that would really seal his fate. Bankruptcy was too final, too much an admission of failure. Besides, it is not part of his character to walk away from responsibilities. As bad as things were financially, I think my parents were proud of the fact that they didn't take the easy way out.

As the financial slide worsens, the task of keeping up appearances becomes more difficult. Dierdre Miller's family lived in one of California's wealthiest suburbs before their troubles and continued to hold on after the crisis. She remembers that her mother would drive miles out of her way to spend the family allotment of food stamps in neighborhoods where her face was unknown. Though the Miller family was in serious financial trouble, with no money coming in to speak of, the mother's primary concern was maintaining face: "My mother wouldn't go down and apply for the food stamps. She made my father do all of that. She wouldn't have anything to do with [it]. She was real ashamed." Mrs. Miller's strategy worked. For many years, outward appearances provided no clue that her family was poor enough to qualify for public assistance. The Miller children stopped bringing their friends home and virtually never talked about their family troubles to anyone.

Eventually however, most downwardly mobile families find themselves in such financial straits that they can no longer camouflage their situation. Children begin to feel uncomfortable about the increasing visibility of the material differences between themselves and their peers, a problem that exacerbates the stigma of their fathers ending up in low status jobs.

The Boeing company was Seattle's largest employer up until the late 1960s. In 1968, it shut down a large part of its operations, throwing thousands of engineers, draftsmen, and technicians onto a weak labor market. The Boeing slump spread like a wave through the supplier industries in the area, compounding the disaster. Alice Pendergast's father was a sales manager in a firm that made precision tools; their biggest client was Boeing. By the time Alice was thirteen, five years after the crash, the depth of the Pendergast family disaster had become clear, especially by comparison to her more fortunate friends:

> My junior high school was situated right under this big hill where all the Seattle executives lived, and so I started going to school with their kids. It ended up that my best friend's father was the vice president of the biggest bank in town. She lived in this house that seemed like the most beautiful place I'd ever seen. I remember feeling really awful because she had so much stuff.
>
> I guess our standard of living was all right, given the bad money situation. But I always felt we were quite poor because I couldn't go out and buy new clothes like all my friends at school. Instead of shopping at Nordstrom's, the high-class department store, we used to go to K-Mart or Penney's. When I was a kid, trying to impress my peers, it was awful. I remember going to school every day and thinking. "Well, I got this new shirt but I got it because it was on sale at K-Mart."

Alice's dilemma is shared, in part, by all poor kids who rub shoulders with the more affluent. But she suffered an additional humiliation: She used to shop in exclusive stores, and therefore fully understood the disdain the Benetton set have for K-Mart kids.

It took a number of years before John Steinberg's family sank under the weight of prolonged income loss. In the good old days, John had enjoyed summers at the local country club, winter vacations in the Caribbean, and family outings to fancy restaurants. The Steinbergs lived in a magnificent three-story house atop a hill, a stately place fronted by a circular drive. Five years into the disaster, and with no maintenance budget to speak of, it was becoming visibly run down.

John remembers that by the time he was a college sophomore, the paint was peeling badly on the outside. The massive garden, long since bereft of a professional landscaper, was so overgrown he could no longer walk to the back of it. The inside of the house was a study in contrasts. Appliances that were standard issue for the managerial middle class—dishwashers, washing machines, dryers, televisions—stood broken and unrepaired. The wallpaper grew dingy, and the carpet on the stairs became threadbare. The antique chairs in the dining room were stained, the silk seat cushions torn. Chandeliers looked vaguely out of place in the midst of this declining splendor. The whole household had the look of a Southern mansion in the aftermath of the Civil War—its structure reflected a glorious past, but its condition told of years of neglect.

The family car was a regulation station wagon, the kind designed to haul a mob of kids. It aged well, but as John neared the end of high school the car developed signs of terminal mechanical failure. By this time, John's mother had taken a factory job in a nearby town and was dependent on the old wagon to travel to work. The starter motor went out at a particularly bad moment and, for nearly six months, the car could only function by being pushed out of the drive-way and rolled down the hill until it picked up enough speed to jump-start in second gear. John remembers being grateful they lived on such a steep incline.

The Steinberg children had, in years past, accompanied their mother on her weekly shopping trips, for the fun of the outing and to make sure special treats found their way home. They would walk up and down the main street of their Connecticut town, stopping at the various specialty stores lining the prosperous commercial strip. Meat came from a butcher shop, bread from a fancy bakery, treats from the handmade candy shop, and staples from an independent, small grocery store. By the time John was in his late teens, the specialty stores were a thing of the past:

> I remember the first time I went with my mother to a big supermarket, a chain store we hadn't been to much before. She went to the meat counter and there were these precut packages of meat in plastic wrap. I had never seen meat set out of that way before. We had always gone to the butcher and he cut the meat to order for us and wrapped it in small white packages.

There are many people in the United States and around the world who would be more than satisfied to eat at the table of the downwardly mobile managerial family. None of these people were hungry or malnourished. But food has greater significance than the vitamins it provides. That middle-class families can open the refrigerator and eat their fill is a demonstration of their freedom from want. The recent proliferation of "designer" foods and fancy delicatessens reveals the additional role of food as fashion and of gastronomy as tourism. And not least, food is a symbol of social status.

For affluent adolescents wolfing down pizza, the connection between diet and fortune is obscure. They devote little energy to thinking about how the food they see on their own tables compares to the fare consumed by other, less fortunate families. Downwardly mobile children *do* learn about how high income underwrites a refrigerator stocked with goodies—when these items disappear. John Steinberg again:

> My family was the real meat and potatoes type. We used to have roast beef and steak all the time. After a few years we couldn't afford it and it was just hamburger and more hamburger. That didn't bother me or my sisters. We were teenagers and we were perfectly happy with it. But I can remember one time my mother went out and splurged on what must have been a fairly cheap roast. It wouldn't hold up under my Dad's carving knife. It just fell apart. He was so disgusted he just walked out of the dining room, leaving my mother to face the kids. He was mad about having to eat that way.

Food, appliances, vacations, clothes, and cars—these basics of middle-class existence are transformed under the brunt of downward mobility. The loss of these items is not just a matter of inconvenience or discomfort. The lack of wheels whittles down each family member's freedom of movement and underlines a new dependency upon others. Dietary changes symbolize a shrinkage in the family's realm of choice. In a culture that lionizes independence, discretion, and autonomy, these material transformations become dramatic emblems of the family's powerlessness to affect its own fate.

But it is the loss of the home, the most tangible symbol of a family's social status, that is the watershed event in the life cycle of downward mobility. In one act, years of attachment to a neighborhood and a way of life are abruptly terminated. The blow is a hard one to withstand, for at least since the era of the GI mortgage, owning a house has defined membership in the middle class. Home ownership is America's most visible measure of economic achievement. Adults who have lost their homes—to foreclosure or distress sales—have truly lost their membership card in the middle class.

It took nearly eight years from the time John Steinberg's father lost his job to the time they lost the house. But when it finally happened, the family was grief-stricken:

> Letting go of that house was one of the hardest things we ever had to do. We felt like we were pushed out of the place we had grown up in. None of the rental houses my family lived in after that ever felt like home. You know, we had a roof over our heads, but losing that house made us feel a little like gypsies.

Distress sales can free up capital and provide some cash reserves to draw on, but the financial relief is often short lived. The house is usually the last thing to go and debts have ordinarily piled high before that occurs. Hence the profits are already earmarked for debt relief. Moreover, the need to relocate finds the downwardly mobile family facing the same escalating housing costs that enabled them to pull a profit from their own home. Rental accommodations anywhere near the family's original homestead are frequently costly. Indeed, rents can be much higher than the house payments on the old home, simply because it was purchased years ago, in the days of low mortgages and reasonable prices. These market factors ultimately lead the downwardly mobile in the direction of lower-income neighborhoods, where their dollars go farther but where the atmosphere is comparatively déclassé.

The sliding standard of living the downwardly mobile endure constitutes a drift away from normal middle-class expectations and behavior. The family is growing more deviant over time—its resemblance to the "precrisis" era becomes increasingly faint. Some of the slide can be hidden through dissembling, lies, or cover-ups. The whole family goes "into the closet"—hiding the real situation from the outside world, trying to appear "straight" to their neighbors—while behind the scenes its life steadily draws farther and farther away from the middle-class norm. But there is a psychological cost to living in the closet: Relations between family members grow more intense, and new, sometimes arduous, demands are placed upon children.

R E A D I N G

30

Profiling Violent Families

RICHARD J. GELLES AND MURRAY A. STRAUS

Each incident of family violence seems to be unique—an uncontrolled explosion of rage, a random expression of anger, an impulse, a volcanic eruption of sadism. Each abuser seems a bit different. The circumstances never seem to be the same. In one home a child may be attacked for talking back to a parent, in another the precipitating incident may be a broken lamp. Wives have been beaten because the food was cold, because the house was cold, because they were cold.

If we reject the notion that violence and abuse are the products of mental illness or intraindividual pathologies, then we implicitly accept the assumption that there is a social pattern that underlies intimate abuse.[1] The public and the media recognize this underlying pattern. Perhaps the most frequently asked

From pp. 77–97 in *Intimate Violence*. New York: Simon & Schuster Copyright © 1988 by Richard J. Gelles and Murray A. Straus. Reprinted by permission of Simon & Schuster, Inc.

question by the press, public, and clinicians who treat cases of domestic abuse is, "what is the profile of a violent parent, husband, wife, family?" . . . [H]umans have an innate desire for social order. They want to live in a predictable world. Even though violence in the home is more socially acceptable than violence in the street and thus, to a degree, more orderly, people still want to know what to look for. What are the signs, indicators, predictors, of a battering parent, an abusive husband?

A profile of intimate violence must include at least three dimensions. First, we need to examine the social organization of families in general that contributes to the risk of violence in the home. Second, we review the characteristics of families in particular that make certain families high risk for violence. Third, we discuss the temporal and spatial patterns of intimate violence—where and when violence is most likely to occur.

VIOLENCE AND THE SOCIAL ORGANIZATION OF THE FAMILY

The myth that violence and love do not coexist in families disguises a great irony about intimacy and violence. There are a number of distinct organizational characteristics of the family that promote intimacy, but at the very same time contribute to the escalation of conflict to violence and injury.[2] Sometimes, the very characteristics that make the family a warm, supportive, and intimate environment also lead to conflict and violence.

The time we spend with our family almost always exceeds the time we spend at work or with nonfamily members. This is particularly true for young children, men and women who are not in the work force, and the very old. From a strictly quantitative point of view, we are at greater risk in the home simply because we spend so much time there. But, time together is not sufficient to lead to violence. What goes on during these times is much more important than simply the minutes, hours, days, weeks, or years spent together.

Not only are we with our parents, partners, and children, but we interact with them over a wide range of activities and interests. Unless you live (and love) with someone, the total range of activities and interests you share are much narrower than intimate, family involvements. While the range of intimate interactions is great, so is the intensity. When the nature of intimate involvement is deep, the stakes of the involvement rise. Failures are more important. Slights, insults, and affronts hurt more. The pain of injury runs deeper. A cutting remark by a family member is likely to hurt more than the same remark in another setting.

We know more about members of our family than we know about any other individuals we ever deal with. We know their fears, wants, desires, frailties. We know what makes them happy, mad, frustrated, content. Likewise, they know the same about us. The depth of knowledge that makes intimacy possible also reveals the vulnerabilities and frailties that make it possible to escalate conflict. If, for instance, our spouse insults us, we know in an instant what to say to get even. We know enough to quickly support a family member, or to damage him. In no other setting is there a greater potential to support and help, or hurt and harm, with a gesture, a phrase, or a cutting remark. Over and over again, the people we talk to point to an attack on their partner's vulnerabilities as precipitating violence:

> If I want to make her feel real bad, I tell her how stupid she is. She can't deal with this, and she hits me.

> We tear each other down all the time. He says things just to hurt me—like how I clean the house. I complain about his work—about how he doesn't make enough money to support us. He gets upset, I get upset, we hit each other.

> If I really want to get her, I call her dirty names or call her trash.

We found, in many of our interviews with members of violent families, that squabbles, arguments, and confrontations escalate rapidly to violence when one partner focused on the other's vulnerabilities. Jane, a 32-year-old mother, found that criticizing her husband's child-care skills often moved an argument to violence:

> Well, we would argue about something, anything. If it was about our kids I would say, "But you shouldn't talk, because you don't even know how to take care of them." If I wanted to hurt him I would use that. We use the kids in our fights and it really gets bad. He [her husband] doesn't think the baby loves him. I guess I contribute to that a bit. When the baby start's fussin' my husband will say "Go to your mom." When I throw it up to him that the baby is afraid of him, that's when the fights really get goin'.

It is perhaps the greatest irony of family relations that the quality that allows intimacy—intimate knowledge of social biographies, is also a potential explosive, ready to be set off with the smallest fuse.

The range of family activities includes deciding what television program to watch, who uses the bathroom first, what house to buy, what job to take, how to raise and discipline the children, or what to have for dinner. Whether the activities are sublime or ridiculous, the outcome is often "zero-sum" for the participants. Decisions and decision making across the range of family activities often mean that one person (or group) will win, while another will lose. If a husband takes a new job in another city, his wife may have to give up her job, while the children may have to leave their friends. If her job and the children's friends are more important, then the husband will lose a chance for job advancement or a higher income. While the stakes over which television station to watch or which movie to go to may be smaller, the notion of winning and losing is still there. In fact, some of the most intense family conflicts are over what seem to be the most trivial choices. Joanne, a 25-year-old mother of two toddlers, remembers violent fights over whether she and her husband would talk or watch television:

> When I was pregnant the violence was pretty regular. John would come home from work. I would want to talk with him, 'cause I had been cooped up in the house with the baby and being pregnant. He would just want to watch the TV. So he would have the TV on and he didn't want to listen to me. We'd have these big fights. He pushed me out of the way. I would get in front of the TV and he would just throw me on the floor.

We talked to one wife who, after a fight over the television, picked the TV up and threw it at her husband. For a short time at least, they did not have a television to fight over.

Zero-sum activities are not just those that require decisions or choices. Less obvious than choices or decisions, but equally or sometimes more important, are infringements of personal space or personal habits. The messy wife and the neat husband may engage in perpetual zero-sum conflict over the house, the bedroom, and even closet space. How should meals be served? When should the dishes be washed? Who left the hairbrush in the sink? How the toothpaste should be squeezed from the tube, and a million other daily conflicts and confrontations end with a winner and a loser.

Imagine you have a co-worker who wears checkered ties with striped shirts, who cannot spell, whose personal hygiene leaves much to be desired. How likely are you to (1) tell him that he should change his habits; (2) order him to change; (3) spank him, send him to his room, or cut off his paycheck until he does change? Probably never. Yet, were this person your partner, child, or even parent, you would think nothing of getting involved and trying to influence his behavior. While the odd behavior of a friend or co-worker may be cause for some embarrassment, we typically would not think of trying to influence this person unless we had a close relationship with him. Yet, family membership carries with it not only the right, but sometimes the obligation, to influence other members of the family. Consequently, we almost always get involved in interactions in the home that we would certainly ignore or make light of in other settings.

Few people notice that the social structure of the family is unique. First, the family has a balance of both males and females. Other settings have this quality—coeducational schools, for instance. But many of the social institutions we are involved in have an imbalance of males and females. Some settings—automobile assembly lines, for instance—may be predominantly male, while other groups—a typing pool, for instance—may be almost exclusively female. In addition to the fact that intimate settings almost always include males and females, families also typically include a range of ages. Half of all households have children under 18 years of age in them.[3] Thus the family, more so than almost any other social group or social setting, has the potential for both generational and sex differences and conflicts. The battle between the sexes and the generation gap have long been the source of intimate conflict.

Not only is the family made up of males and females with ages ranging from newborn to elderly, but the family is unique in how it assigns tasks and responsibilities. No other social group expects its members to take on jobs simply on the basis of their age or their sex. In the workplace, at school, and in virtually every other social setting, roles and responsibilities are primarily based on interest, experience, and ability. In the home, duties and responsibilities are primarily tied to age and gender. There are those who argue that there is a biological link between gender and task—that women make better parents than men. Also, the developmental abilities of children certainly preclude their taking on tasks or responsibilities that they are not ready for. But, by and large, the fact that roles and responsibilities are age- and gender-linked is a product of social organization and not biological determinism.

When someone is blocked from doing something that he or she is both interested in and capable of doing, this can be intensely frustrating.[4] When the inequality is socially structured and sanctioned within a society that at the same time espouses equal opportunity and egalitarianism, it can lead to intense conflict and confrontation. Thus, we find that the potential for conflict and violence is especially high in a democratic and egalitarian society that sanctions and supports a male-dominated family system. Even if we did not have values that supported democracy and egalitarianism, the linking of task to gender would produce considerable conflict, since not every man is capable of taking on the socially prescribed leadership role in the home; and not every woman is interested in and capable of assuming the primary responsibility for child care.

The greater the inequality, the more one person makes all the decisions and has all the power, the greater the risk of violence. Power, power confrontations, and perceived threats to domination, in fact, are underlying issues in almost all acts of family violence. One incident of nearly deadly family violence captures the meaning of power and power confrontations:

> My husband wanted to think of himself as the head of the household. He thought that the man should wear the pants in the family. Trouble was, he couldn't seem to get his pants on. He had trouble getting a job and almost never could keep one. If I didn't have my job as a waitress, we would have starved. Even though he didn't make no money, he still wanted to control the house and the kids. But it was my money, and I wasn't about to let him spend it on booze or gambling. This really used to tee him off. But he would get the maddest when the kids showed him no respect. He and I argued a lot. One day we argued in the kitchen and my little girl came in. She wanted to watch TV. My husband told her to go to her room. She said, "No, I don't have to listen to you!" Well, my husband was red. He picked up a knife and threw it at my little girl. He missed. Then he threw a fork at her and it caught her in the chin. She was bloody and crying, and he was still mad and ran after her. I had to hit him with a chair to get him to stop. He ran out of the house and didn't come back for a week. My little girl still has a scar on her cheek.

You can choose whom to marry, and to a certain extent you may choose to end the marital relationship. Ending a marital relationship, even in the age of no-fault divorce, is not neat and simple. There are social expectations that marriage is a long-term commitment—"until death do us part." There are social pressures that one should "work on a relationship" or "keep the family together for the sake of the children." There are also emotional and financial constraints that keep families together or entrap one partner who would like to leave.

You can be an ex-husband or an ex-wife, but not an ex-parent or an ex-child.[5] Birth relationships are quite obviously involuntary. You cannot choose your parents or your children (with the exception of adoption, and here your choices are still limited).

Faced with conflict, one can fight or flee. Because of the nature of family relations, it is not easy to choose the flight option when conflict erupts. Fighting, then, becomes a main option for resolving intimate conflict.

The organization of the family makes for stress. Some stress is simply developmental—the birth of a child, the maturation of children, the increasing costs of raising children as they grow older, illness, old age, and death. There are also voluntary transitions—taking a new job, a promotion, or moving. Stress occurring outside of the home is often brought into the home—unemployment, trouble with the police, trouble with friends at school, trouble with people at work. We expect a great deal from our families: love, warmth, understanding, nurturing, intimacy, and financial support. These expectations, when they cannot be fulfilled, add to the already high level of stress with which families must cope.

Privacy is the final structural element of modern families that makes them vulnerable to conflict, which can escalate into violence. . . . The nuclear structure of the modern family, and the fact that it is the accepted norm that family relations are private relations, reduces the likelihood that someone will be available to prevent the escalation of family conflict to intimate violence.

We have identified the factors that contribute to the high level of conflict in families. These factors also allow conflicts to become violent and abusive interchanges. By phrasing the discussion differently, we could have presented these factors as also contributing to the closeness and intimacy that people seek in family relations. People who marry and have families seek to spend large amounts of time together, to have deep and long-lasting emotional involvement, to have an intimate and detailed knowledge of another person, and to be able to create some distance between their intimate private lives and the interventions of the outside world.

There are a number of conclusions one can draw from the analysis of the structural factors that raise the risk of conflict and violence in the family. First, there is a link between intimacy and violence. Second is the classic sociological truism—structures affect people. Implicit in the discussion of these factors is that one can explain part of the problem of violence in the home without focusing on the individual psychological status of the perpetrators of violence and abuse. Violence occurs, not just because it is committed by weird, bad, different, or alien people, but because the structure of the modern household is conductive to violent exchanges.

FAMILY AND INDIVIDUAL CHARACTERISTICS RELATED TO INTIMATE VIOLENCE

The structural arrangement of the family makes it possible for violence to occur in all households. However, not all homes are violent. A profile of intimate violence needs to analyze the characteristics of violent individuals and their families.

Volumes could be written inventorying the characteristics that are thought to be related to family violence. The earliest students of child and wife abuse focused on individual personality characteristics.[6] Abusers were described as sadomasochistic, having poor emotional control, self-centered, hypersensitive, dependent, egocentric, narcissistic, and so on. Later, those who studied violence and abuse examined social and social psychological factors such as income, education, age, social stress, and social isolation.[7] Other investigators focused on experience with and exposure to violence. Still others chose to study violence from the point of view of the family level of analysis, examining family size, family power, and family structure.[8]

Sometimes investigators agree on specific characteristics that are believed to be associated with violence; other times the findings are contradictory. There is one thing that researchers agree on—there are a multitude of factors associated with violence in the home.[9] Despite public clamor for a single-factor explanation, no one factor—not mental illness, not experience with violence, not poverty, not stress, and not alcohol or drugs—explains all or most acts of intimate violence.

Abusive Violence Toward Children

Most people who try to explain and understand individual acts of deviant or aberrant behavior such as child abuse immediately turn their focus on the perpetrator. Our culture has a definite "individual level" bias when it comes to trying to explain seemingly unexplainable acts. When someone does something outrageous, weird, or bizarre, our immediate reaction is to look for the answer within that individual. A full understanding of abusive violence, however, requires an examination of not only the violent parent, but the child and family situation.

If one had to come up with a profile of the prototypical abusive parent, it would be a single parent who was young (under 30), had been married for less than ten years, had his or her first child before the age of 18, and was unemployed or employed part time.[10] If he or she worked, it would be at a manual labor job. Studies show that women are slightly more likely to abuse their children than men. The reason is rather obvious: Women typically spend more time with children. But, even if mothers and fathers spend equal time with children (and this is rare), it is the woman who is typically given the responsibility of caring for and dealing with the children.

Economic adversity and worries about money pervade the typical violent home. Alicia, the 34-year-old wife of an assembly-line worker, has beaten, kicked, and punched both her children. So has her husband Fred. She spoke about the economic problems that hung over their heads:

> He worries about what kind of a job he's going to get, or if he's going to get a job at all. He always worries about supporting the family. I think I worry about it more than he does. . . . It gets him angry and frustrated. He gets angry a lot. I think he gets angry at himself for not providing what he feels we need. He has to take it out on someone, and the kids and me are the most available ones.

We witnessed a more graphic example of the impact of economic stress during one of our in-home interviews with a violent couple. When we entered the living room to begin the interview we could not help but notice the holes in the living room walls. During the course of the interview, Jane, the 24-year-old mother of three children, told us that her husband had been laid off from his job at a local shipyard and had come home, taken out his shotgun, and shot up the living room. Violence had not yet been directed at the children, but as we left and considered the family, we could not help but worry about the future targets of violent outbursts.

Stressful life circumstances are the hallmark of the violent family. The greater the stress individuals are under, the more likely they are to be violent toward their children. Our 1976 survey of violence in the American family included a measure of life stress.[11] Subjects were asked if they had experienced any of a list of 18 stressful events in the last year, ranging from problems at work, to death of a family member, to problems with children. Experience with stress ranged from households that experienced no stressful event to homes that had experienced 13 of the 18 items we discussed. The average experience with stress, however, was modest—about two stressful life events each year. Not surprisingly, the greater the number of stressful events experienced, the greater the rate of abusive violence toward children in the home. More than one out of three families that were unfortunate enough to encounter ten or more stressful events reported using abusive violence toward a child in the previous year. This rate was 100 percent greater than the rate for households experiencing only one stressful incident.

Violent parents are likely to have experienced or been exposed to violence as children. Although this does not predetermine that they will be violent (and likewise, some abusive parents grew up in nonviolent homes), there is the heightened risk that a violent past will lead to a violent future.

One of the more surprising outcomes of our first national survey of family violence was that there was no difference between blacks and whites in the rates of abusive violence toward children. This should not have been the case. First, most official reports of child abuse indicate that blacks are overrepresented in the reports. Also, blacks in the United States have higher rates of unemployment than whites and lower annual incomes—two factors that we know lead to higher risk of abuse. That blacks and whites had the same rate of abusive violence was one of the great mysteries of the survey. A careful examination of the data collected unraveled the apparent mystery. While blacks did indeed encounter economic problems and life stresses at greater rates than whites, they also were more involved in family and community activities than white families. Blacks reported more contact with their relatives and more use of their relatives for financial support and child care. It was apparent that the extensive social networks that black families develop and maintain insulate them from the severe economic stresses they also experience, and thus reduce what otherwise would have been a higher rate of parental violence.[12]

Most of the cases of child abuse we hear about involve very young children. There is nothing that provokes greater sadness and outrage than seeing the battered body of a defenseless infant. The youngest victims evoke the most sympathy and anger, best fit the stereotype of the innocent victim, and are more likely to be publicly identified as victims of abuse. The youngest children are indeed the most likely to be beaten and hurt.

However, the myth that only innocents are victims of abuse hides the teenage victim. Teenagers are equally likely to be abused as children under three years of age. Why are the youngest children and teenagers at the greatest risk of abusive violence? When we explain why the youngest children are likely victims the answer seems to be that they are demanding, produce considerable stress, and cannot be reasoned with verbally. Parents of teenagers offer the same explanation for why they think teenagers as a group are at equally high risk.

Among the younger victims of violence and abuse, there are a number of factors that make them at risk. Low birth weight babies, premature children, handicapped, retarded, and developmentally disabled children run a high life-long risk of violence and abuse.[13] In fact, the risk is great for any child who is considered different.

If you want to prevent violence and abuse, either have no children or eight or nine. This was the somewhat common-sense outcome of our research on family factors related to violence toward children. It is rather obvious that more children create more stress. Why then did we find no violence in the families with eight or nine children? Perhaps people who have the largest families are the kindest, most loving parents. Perhaps they are simply exhausted. A more realistic explanation is that at a certain point, children become resources that insulate a family from stress. A family with eight or nine children probably did not have them all at once. With a two- or three-year gap between children, a family with eight or more children has older children at home to help care for and raise the infants, babies, and toddlers. If there is a truly extended family form in our society, it is the large family with children ranging from newborn to 20 living in the home.

A final characteristic of violent parents is that they are almost always cut off from the community they live in. Our survey of family violence found that the most violent parents have lived in their community for less than two years. They tend to belong to few, if any, community organizations, and have little contact with friends and relatives. This social isolation cuts them off from any possible source of help to deal with the stresses of intimate living or economic adversity. These parents are not only more vulnerable to stress, their lack of social involvement also means that they are less likely to abandon their violent behavior and conform to community values and standards. Not only are they particularly vulnerable to responding violently to stress, they tend not to see this behavior as inappropriate.

Abusive Violence Between Partners

Dale, wife of a Fortune 500 executive, wrote us so that we would know that wife beating is not confined to only poor households. Her husband beats her regularly. He has hurled dishes at her, thrown her down stairs, and blackened her eyes. When her husband drinks, she often spends the night huddled in the back-seat of their Lincoln Continental. Marion lives so far on the other side of the tracks, she might as well be on another planet. She and her husband live five stories up in a run-down tenement. Heat is a luxury that they often cannot afford, and when they can afford it, the heat rarely works. Marion's husband has broken her jaw and ribs, and has shot at her on two occasions. The range of homes where wife beating occurs seems to defy categorization. One can pick up a newspaper and read of wife beating in a lower-class neighborhood and then turn the page and read that the wife of a famous rock musician has filed for divorce claiming she was beaten.

If there is a typical wife beater, he is not a rock musician, actor, football player, or business executive.[14] The typical beater is employed part-time or not at all. His total income is poverty level. He worries about economic security, and he is very dissatisfied with his standard of living. He is young, between the ages of 18 and 24—the prime age for violent behavior in and out of the home—and has been married for less than ten years. While he tries to dominate the family and hold down what he sees as the husband's position of power, he has few of the economic or social resources that allow for such dominance; not only does his neighbor have a better job and earn more money than he does, but often so does his wife.

Researchers have found that status inconsistency is an important component of the profile of the battering husband.[15] An example of status inconsistency occurs when a man's educational background is much higher than his occupational attainment—a Ph.D. who drives a taxicab for a living. Status inconsistency can also result when a husband does not have as much occupational or educational status as his wife. Researchers Carton Hornung, Claire McCullough, and Taichi Sugimoto report that contrary to what is generally believed, violence is less common when the wife is at home than when she works. They suggest that status inconsistency explains this finding. Husbands, they note, can be more threatened when their wives work and have an independent source of income and prestige than when they are home and dependent. Conflict and verbal aggression are frequent occurrences in the wife beater's home. Verbal violence and mental abuse are also directed at his spouse. Perhaps the most telling of all attributes of the battering man is that he feels inadequate and sees violence as a culturally acceptable way to be both dominant and powerful.

There is a great tendency to blame the victim in cases of family violence. Battered women have frequently been described as masochistic. The debate over such presumed masochism has raged to the point where a substantial group of psychologists have called for elimination of the diagnostic category "masochist" from the revision of DSM-III, the official description of psychological diagnostic groupings.

There is not much evidence that battered women as a group are more masochistic than other women. There are, however, some distinct psychological attributes found among battered women. Victims of wife beating are often found to be dependent, having low self-esteem, and feeling inadequate or helpless.[16] On the other hand, battered wives have been found to be aggressive, masculine, and frigid. In all likelihood these contradictory findings are the result of the fact that there is precious little research on the consequence of being battered, and the research that has been conducted frequently uses small samples, without comparison groups. This makes generalizing from such research difficult and contradictory findings inevitable.

Another problem with assessing the psychological traits of battered women is the difficulty in determining whether the personalities were present before the battering or were the result of the victimization. . . .

Pregnant women often report being beaten.[17] Pregnancy, however, does not make women vulnerable to violence and battering.[18] When we analyzed the results of the Second National Family Violence Survey we found that age, not pregnancy, is the best predictor of risk of wife beating. Women between the ages of 18 and 24 are more likely to be beaten, whether they are pregnant or not. Women older than 24 years of age are less likely to be beaten.

Although pregnant women are not more vulnerable to violence, the nature of the violent attack does appear to change when a woman is pregnant. One of the first interviews we ever conducted still stands out in our minds. The subject was a 30-year-old woman who had been beaten severely throughout her marriage. The beatings were more severe, and took on a different tone, when she was pregnant: "Oh, yeah, he hit me when I was pregnant. It was weird. Usually he just hit me in the face with his fist, but when I was pregnant he used to hit me in the belly."

Perhaps the most controversial finding from our 1975 National Family Violence Survey was the report that a substantial number of women hit and beat their husbands. Since 1975 at least ten additional investigations have confirmed the fact that women hit and beat their husbands.[19] Unfortunately, the data on wife-to-husband violence have been misreported, misinterpreted, and misunderstood. Research uniformly shows that about as many women hit men as men hit women. However, those who report that husband abuse is a common as wife abuse overlook two important facts. First, the greater average size and strength of men and their greater aggressiveness means that a man's punch will probably produce more pain, injury, and harm than a punch by a woman. Second, nearly three-fourths of the violence committed by women is done in self-defense. While violence by women should not be dismissed, neither should it be overlooked or hidden. On occasion, legislators and spokespersons like Phyllis Schlafly have used the data on violence by wives to minimize the need for services for battered women. Such arguments do a great injustice to the victimization of women.

As we said, more often than not a wife who beats her husband has herself been beaten. Her violence is the violence of self-defense. On some occasions she will strike back to protect herself; on others she will strike first, believing that if she does not, she will be badly beaten. Sally, a 44-year-old woman married for 25 years, recounted how she used violence to protect herself:

> When he hits me, I retaliate. Maybe I don't have the same strength as he does, but I know how to hold my own. I could get hurt, but I am going to go down trying. You know, it's not like there is anyone else here who is going to help me. So . . . I hit him back . . . I pick something up and I hit him.

Marianne does not wait until she is hit. She says she has learned the cues that her husband is about to hit her:

> I know that look he gets when he gets ready to hit me. We've been married for ten years, and I've seen that look of his. So he gets that look, and I get something to hit him with. Once I hit him with a lamp. Another time I stabbed him. Usually I don't get so bad, but I was real fearful that time.

The violence in Marianne's home is not just one way. She has been hospitalized four times as a result of her husband's beatings. Her fears are very real.

The profile of those who engage in violence with their partners is quite similar to the profile of the parents who are abusive toward their children. The greater the stress, the lower the income, the more violence. Also, there is a direct relationship between violence in childhood and the likelihood of becoming a violent adult. Again, we add the caution that although there is a relationship, this does not predetermine that all those who experience violence will grow up to be abusers.

One of the more interesting aspects of the relationship between childhood and adult violence is that *observing* your parents hit one another is a more powerful contributor to the probability of becoming a violent adult than being a victim of violence. The learning experience of seeing your mother and father strike one another is more significant than being hit yourself. Experiencing, and more importantly observing, violence as a child teaches three lessons:

1. Those who love you are also those who hit you, and those you love are people you can hit.

2. Seeing and experiencing violence in your home establishes the moral rightness of hitting those you love.

3. If other means of getting your way, dealing with stress, or expressing yourself do not work, violence is permissible.

The latter lesson ties in well with our finding that stress also leads to an increased risk of violence in the home. One theory holds that people learn to use violence to cope with stress. If this is correct, then stress would be a necessary, but not sufficient, precondition for family violence. In other words, stress alone does not cause violence unless the family members have learned that being violent is both appropriate and also will not meet with negative sanctions. Another theory is that learning to be violent and stress are two independent contributors to intimate violence and abuse.

The sociologists Debra Kalmuss and Judith Seltzer tested these two theories using the data collected for the First National Family Violence Survey.[20] They found that stress and learning are independent contributions to the risk of abusive violence. Moreover, observing and experiencing violence while growing up was a more powerful contributor to the later risk of intimate violence than was life stress.

Lurking beneath the surface of all intimate violence are confrontations and controversies over power. Our statistical evidence shows that the risk of intimate violence is the greatest when all the decision making in a home is concentrated in the hands of one of the partners. Couples who report the most sharing of decisions report the lowest rates of violence. Our evidence goes beyond the statistics. Over and over again, case after case, interview after interview, we hear batterers and victims discuss how power and control were at the core of the events that led up to the use of violence. Violent husbands report that they "need to" hit their wives to show them who is in charge. Some of the victimized wives struggle against domination and precipitate further violence. Other wives tell us that they will actually provoke their husband to violence because they want him to be more dominant. This is not so much a case of the wife being a masochist as it is another example of the conflicts and struggles that occur as couples confront the traditional cultural expectation that the male should be the dominant person in the household. Some couples fight against this prescription, while others fight to preserve it.

NO PLACE TO RUN, NO PLACE TO HIDE

Eleanor began to prepare dinner for her two children and her husband. It was evening on a Saturday night in January. While she grilled hamburgers, her husband Albert walked in. An argument began over whether Eleanor had taken Albert's shirts to the cleaners. Eleanor protested she had. Albert said she was lying. Eleanor protested, yelled, and finally said that Albert was drunk so often he never remembered whether his shirts were clean or dirty. Albert lunged at his wife. He pushed her against the stove, grabbed the sizzling burgers, and threw them across the room. He stalked out, slamming the front door behind him. Quiet tension reigned in the house through a dinner of tuna fish sandwiches and some television, and then the children were put to bed. Eleanor went to bed at 11:00 P.M., but could not fall asleep. At around 1:00 A.M. Albert returned home. He was quiet as he removed his clothes and got into bed. Eleanor turned over, her back to Albert. This signaled that she was awake, and another argument began to brew. This time it was over sex. Eleanor resisted. She always resisted when Albert was drunk. Tonight she resisted because she was still angry over the dinnertime argument. Albert lay his heavy arms around Eleanor and she struggled to get free. The quiet, almost silent struggle began to build. Angry whispers, angry gestures, and finally yelling ensued. Eleanor knew that Albert kept a gun in his night table drawer. Once, after a fight, Albert had gone to bed by putting the bullets on Eleanor's nightstand and the gun under his pillow. As the midnight fight escalated, Albert made a gesture toward the night table. For whatever reason, Eleanor thought that this would be the time that Albert would try to shoot her. She dove across the bed, pulled the drawer out of the night table, clawed for the gun as it rattled to the floor, and came to her feet with the gun in her hand. The first shot tore through Albert's right arm, the second slammed into the wall, the third tore away the top of his head. Eleanor stopped firing only after she heard three of four clicks as the hammer struck the now empty cylinders.

This could be a story out of a soap opera or a supermarket newsstand magazine. It is, unfortunately, a story repeated 2,000 times a year. We have focused on the family structure and the individual and family characteristics that increase the risk of violence in specific households. Eleanor's and Albert's story illustrates the situational structure of intimate violence.

It goes without saying that intimate violence is most likely to occur in intimate settings. Occasionally couples will strike one another in the car. Husbands sometimes grab their wives at a party or on the street. Husbands or wives rarely slap their partners in public. The majority of domestic combat takes place in private, behind closed doors. We have known men and women to stifle their anger and see the while guests are in the home. As the last guest leaves and the door closes, the fight and the violence erupt.

Eleanor and Albert began their path to their lethal confrontation in the kitchen. When we interviewed couples about the location of violence between partners and toward children, more than half said that the violence occurs in the kitchen. The living room and bedroom were the next most likely scenes. Only the bathroom seemed free from conflict and violence—perhaps because most bathrooms are small, have locks, or most likely because bathrooms are places of individual privacy.

Students of domestic homicide report that the bedroom is the most lethal room in the home. The criminologist Marvin Wolfgang reported that 20 percent of *all* victims of criminal homicide are killed in the bedroom.[21] The kitchen and dining room are the other frequent scenes of lethal violence between family members.

After 8:00 P.M. the risk for family violence increases.[22] This is almost self-evident, since this is also the time when family members are most likely to be together in the home. We found that four out of ten cases of domestic violence occur between 8:00 P.M. and midnight. Eight out of ten domestic fights take place between 5:00 P.M. and 7:00 A.M. Early evening fights occur in the kitchen. The living room becomes the likely setting for evening disputes, and the most violent and most lethal altercations break out in the bedroom, late at night.

The temporal and spatial patterns of intimate violence support our notion that privacy is a key underlying factor that leads to violence. Time and space constrain the options of both the offender and the victim. As the evening wears on, there are fewer places to run to, fewer places to hide. When the first fight broke out between Eleanor and Albert, it was about 5:00 P.M. Albert rushed out of the house in a huff—most likely heading for the neighborhood bar. The bar closed at 1:00 A.M., and that was when Albert went home to his final conflict.

A fight that erupts in the bedroom, in the early morning, constrains both parties. It is too late to stalk out of the home to a bar and too late to run to a friend or family member. The bed and the bedroom offer no protection and precious few places to flee or take cover. It is not surprising that so many of the most violent family fights end there.

Common sense would argue that weekends are the most violent time of the week for families. Common sense would not lead one to assume that the most violent times of the year are Christmas and Easter. When we looked at which day of the week violence was most likely to occur, we found that the empirical evidence was in full support of common sense. Weekends are when families spent the most time together and when the potential for conflicts and conflicts of interest is greatest. Not surprisingly, seven out of ten violent episodes we talked about with family members took place on either Saturday or Sunday. Weekends after a payday can be especially violent. Janice, the mother of an infant daughter, told us about the typical weekend fight:

It starts over money. He gets paid on Friday. So he comes home on Fridays and I ask him for money. I am usually at the stove cooking when he comes home. And I have no money left. So I ask. This last Friday he said he didn't have no money. I got real mad. I mean, its payday and he has no money? He said he borrowed money and had to pay it back. I said he just must be lyin'. He spends it on booze or gambles it. Other times we fight because he gives me only fifty dollars. I can't feed him and the baby with just fifty dollars. So I got mad and started to yell.

Thus, the days of the week that are the most violent are those that combine the most conflict and violence-producing structural components of family life—time together, privacy, and stress.

Common sense would not suggest that violence is most likely to erupt at times of the year when families celebrate holidays and the spirit of family togetherness. Yet, contrary to common sense, it is the time from Thanksgiving to New Year's Day and again at Easter that violence in the home peaks.

As we conducted our interviews with members of violent homes we heard again and again about violence that occurred around the Christmas tree. Even the Christmas tree became a weapon in some homes:

I remember one particularly violent time. When we were first married. He was out drinking and he came home stinking drunk. I suppose I must have said something. Well, he took a fit. He started putting his first through the walls. Finally, he just picked up the Christmas tree and threw it at me.

Another woman recalled her most violent experience:

He hit me just before New Year's Day. I don't really recall what went on. We argue a lot. This time it might have been about money, or maybe the kids. Anyway, he got fierce. He punched me again and again. I was bleeding real bad. He had to take me to the hospital. It was the worst time of the year I ever had.

Perhaps people have a clearer memory of a violent event if it happens around a holiday. While this is a plausible explanation for our findings, it is not the complete answer. We have examined weekly reports of hospital admissions for child abuse and neglect, and found that the peak times of year for admissions were the period from Christmas to New Year's Day, and again in the spring around Easter Sunday.

A number of factors may contribute to the likelihood of domestic violence and abuse during the Christmas season. This is a time when families can assume tremendous financial burdens. Purchasing Christmas gifts can either take a toll on a family's resources or plunge a family into debt. Stress can also come from *not* buying gifts and presents. If a family cannot afford gifts expected by children, loved ones, and others, this can be extremely frustrating. The holiday season offers a stark contrast between what is expected and what a family can afford.

Holidays also create nonfinancial stress. Christmas and Easter holidays project images of family harmony, love, and togetherness. Songs, advertisements, and television specials all play up the image of the caring, loving, and even affluent family. A family with deep conflict and trouble may see these images in sad and frustrating contrast with their own lives. We know that prison riots are more likely to occur during holiday seasons, as prisoners apparently become stressed about being separated from family and friends during times of the year when such closeness is expected. Clearly, being with family and friends, but having unmet expectations for love and warmth, can also be extremely frustrating.

Time of day and time of year analysis supports the notion that privacy and stress are important structural contributors to domestic violence. Conflict frequently erupts over a stressful event, during a stressful time of the day, or around a stressful time of year. If the eruption takes place in a private setting, and at a time and place where it is difficult to flee or back down, the conflict can escalate into violence. The more privacy, the greater the power difference, and the fewer options the victim has in terms of getting help or finding protection, the more the violence can escalate.

The saddest and most frustrating aspect of our analysis of the structural, personal, familial, temporal, and spatial dynamics of intimate violence is that our results seem to say that violence in the home is inevitable. Lessons learned as a child set the stage for using violence as an adult. The structural makeup of the modern family is like a pressure cooker containing and escalating stress and conflict. If violence breaks out late at night, on a weekend, or a holiday, victims often have no place to run, no place to hide.

Our profile of violent families is not quite as bleak as it might seem. First, no one structural factor, personal experience, or situation predetermines that all or any family will be violent. Second, families do not live in a vacuum. Family members and people outside of the home can intervene to turn down the heat under the pressure cooker. We have found that friends, relatives, and neighbors can successfully intervene and reduce the pressure that could lead to violence.

NOTES

1. Two articles that critique the theory that abuse is the product of mental illness or psychopathology are Richard J. Gelles, "Child Abuse as Psychopathology: A Sociological Critique and Reformulation," *American Journal of Orthopsychiatry* 43 (July 1973): 611–21; and J. Spinetta and D. Rigler, "The Child-Abusing Parent: A Psychological Review," *Psychological Bulletin* 77 (April 1972): 296–304.

2. The organizational characteristics of the family that promote both intimacy and conflict were first described in Richard J. Gelles and Murray A. Straus, "Determinants of Violence in the Family: Towards an Integrated Theory," in Wesley Burr, Reuben Hill, F. Ivan Nye, and Ira I. Reiss, eds., *Contemporary Theories About the Family* vol. 1. (New York: Free Press, 1979), 549–81. These ideas were further developed in Murray A. Straus and Gerald T. Hotaling, eds., *The Social Causes of Husband-Wife Violence* (Minneapolis: University of Minnesota Press, 1980); and Richard J. Gelles and Claire Pedrick-Cornell, *Intimate Violence in Families* (Beverly Hills, Calif.: Sage, 1985).

3. U.S. Bureau of the Census, *Statistical Abstract of the United States: 1987*, 107th ed. (Washington, D.C.: Government Printing Office, 1986), chart 45; U.S. Bureau of the Census, *Current Population Report*, ser. P-20, no. 411.

4. This is the classic statement of psychological frustration/aggression theory. The theory has been articulated by J. C. Dollard, L. Doob, N. Miller, O. Mowrer, and R. Sears, *Frustration and Aggression* (New Haven, Conn.: Yale University Press, 1939); and N. E. Miller, "The Frustration-Aggression Hypothesis," *Psychological Review* 48, no. 4 (1941): 337–42. A sociological formulation of the notion that blocked goals can be frustrating can be found in Robert K. Merton, "Social Structure and Anomie," *American Sociological Review* 3 (October 1938): 672–82.

5. This idea was first presented by Alice Rossi in her article, "Transition to Parenthood," *Journal of Marriage and the Family* 30 (February 1968): 26–39.

6. See, for example: Vincent J. Fontana, *The Maltreated Child: The Maltreatment Syndrome in Children* (Springfield, Ill.: Charles C. Thomas, 1971); Richard Galdston, "Observations on Children Who Have Been Physically Abused and Their Parents," *American Journal of Psychiatry* 122, no. 4 (1965): 440–43; Leroy G. Schultz, "The Wife Assaulter," *Journal of Social Therapy* 6, no. 2 (1960): 103–12; Brandt F. Steele and Carl B. Pollock, "A Psychiatric Study of Parents Who Abuse Infants and Small Children," in R. Helfer and C. Henry Kempe, eds., *The Battered Child* (Chicago: University of Chicago Press, 1968), 103–47; and S. R. Zalba, "Battered Children," *Transaction* 8 (July–August 1971): 58–61.

7. See Gelles, "Child Abuse"; and David Gil, "Violence Against Children," *Journal of Marriage and the Family* 33 (November 1971): 637–48.

8. See R. Emerson Dobash and Russell Dobash, *Violence Against Wives: The Case Against Patriarchy* (New York: Free Press, 1979).

9. For a review of the factors related to family violence, see Richard J. Gelles, "Family Violence," in Ralph H. Turner and James F. Short, eds., *Annual Review of Sociology*, vol. 11 (Palo Alto, Calif.: Annual Reviews, Inc. 1985), 347–67; Marc F. Maden and D. F. Wrench, "Significant Findings in Child Abuse Research," *Victimology* 2 (1977): 196–224; and Suzanne K. Steinmetz, "Violence Between Family Members," *Marriage and Family Review* 1 (1978): 1–16.

10. The profile that is presented is a statistical profile. It would be incorrect to assume that someone who does not fit this profile would not be an abuser. Similarly, someone who fit the profile is likely to abuse, but is not always an abuser. The profile was developed in Murray A. Straus, Richard J. Gelles, and Suzanne K. Steinmetz. *Behind Closed Doors: Violence in the American Family* (Garden City, N.Y.: Anchor Books, 1980).

11. The survey is reported in Straus, Gelles, and Steinmetz, *Behind Closed Doors*. The measure of stress was adapted from T. H. Holmes and R. H. Rahe, "The Social Readjustment Rating Scale," *Journal of Psychosomatic Research* 11 (1967): 213–18.

12. Straus, Gelles, and Steinmetz, *Behind Closed Doors;* and Noel Cazenave and Murray A. Straus, "Race, Class, Network Embeddedness and Family Violence: A Search for Potent Support Systems," *Journal of Comparative Family Studies* 10 (Autumn 1979): 281–300.

13. A review of child factors that are related to physical abuse can be found in W. N. Friedrich and J. A. Boriskin, "The Role of the Child in Abuse: A Review of the Literature," *American Journal of Orthopsychiatry* 46 (October 1976): 580–90.

14. The profile of wife beaters is a statistical profile and was first presented in Straus, Gelles, and Steinmetz, *Behind Closed Doors.*

15. C. A. Hornung, B. C. McCullough, and T. Sugimoto, "Status Relationships in Marriage: Risk Factors in Spouse Abuse," *Journal of Marriage and the Family* 43 (August 1981): 675–92.

16. Lenore Walker, *The Battered Woman* (New York: Harper & Row, 1979).

17. Richard J. Gelles, "Violence and Pregnancy: A Note on the Extent of the Problem and Needed Services," *Family Coordinator* 24 (January 1975): 81–86.

18. When we analyzed the results of the Second National Family Violence Survey, we did find that the rates of violence and abuse were higher among pregnant women than women who were not pregnant. However, when we controlled for age, the differences disappeared. Women under the age of 24 years old experienced high rates of violence and abuse, but the rates were the same for pregnant and nonpregnant women. Women over 24 years old experienced lower rates of violence, and again, there were no differences between pregnant and nonpregnant women. Thus, the relationship between violence and pregnancy which we first reported in 1975 (Gelles, "Violence and Pregnancy") and which others have reported, turns out to be spurious.

19. Michael David Allan Freeman. *Violence in the Home: A Socio-legal Study* (Farnborough, England: Saxon House, 1979); Richard J. Gelles, *The Violent Home: A Study of Physical Aggression Between Husbands and Wives* (Beverly Hills, Calif.: Sage, 1974); Morgan E. Scott, "The Battered Spouse Syndrome," *Virginia Medical* 107 (January 1980): 41–43; Suzanne Sedge, "Spouse Abuse," in Marilyn R. Block and Jan D. Sinnott, eds., *The Battered Elder Syndrome: An Exploratory Study* (College Park, Md.: Center on Aging, 1979), 33–48; Suzanne K. Steinmetz, "The Battered Husband Syndrome," *Victimology* 2 (1978): 499–509; Straus, Gelles, and Steinmetz, *Behind Closed Doors;* Mary Warren, "Battered Husbands," in Margaret E. Ankeney, ed., *Family Violence: A Cycle of Abuse* (Laramie, Wyo.: College of Education, University of Wyoming, 1979), 76–78.

20. Debra Kalmuss and Judith A. Seltzer, "A Test of Social Learning and Stress Models of Family Violence." (Paper presented at the annual meetings of the American Sociological Association, New York, 1986).

21. Marvin Wolfgang, *Patterns in Criminal Homicide* (Philadelphia: University of Pennsylvania Press, 1958).

22. This analysis was first presented in Gelles, *Violent Home,* chapter 4.

CHAPTER 12

PUBLIC DEBATES
ON THE FAMILY

The Mommy Wars: Ambivalence,
Ideological Work, and the Cultural
Contradictions of Motherhood

Sharon Hays

I have argued that all mothers ultimately share a recognition of the ideology of intensive mothering. At the same time, all mothers live in a society where child rearing is generally devalued and the primary emphasis is placed on profit, efficiency, and "getting ahead." If you are a mother, both logics operate in your daily life.

But the story is even more complicated. Over half of American mothers participate directly in the labor market on a regular basis; the rest remain at least somewhat distant from that world as they spend most of their days in the home. One might therefore expect paid working mothers to be more committed to the ideology of competitively maximizing personal profit and stay-at-home mothers to be more committed to the ideology of intensive mothering. As it turns out, however, this is not precisely the way it works.

Modern-day mothers are facing two socially constructed cultural images of what a good mother looks like. Neither, however, includes the vision of a cold, calculating businesswoman—that title is reserved for childless career women. If you are a good mother, you *must* be an intensive one. The only "choice" involved is whether you *add* the role of paid working woman. The options, then, are as follows. On the one side there is the portrait of the "traditional mother" who stays at home with the kids and dedicates her energy to the happiness of her family. This mother cheerfully studies the latest issue of *Family Circle*, places flowers in every room, and has dinner waiting when her husband comes home. This mother, when she's not cleaning, cooking, sewing, shopping, doing the laundry, or comforting her mate, is focused on attending to the children and ensuring their proper development. On the other side is the image of the successful "supermom." Effortlessly juggling home and work, this mother can push a stroller with one hand and carry a briefcase in the other. She is always properly coiffed, her nylons have no runs, her suits are freshly pressed, and her home has seen the white tornado. Her children are immaculate and well mannered but not passive, with a strong spirit and high self-esteem.

Although both the traditional mom and the supermom are generally considered socially acceptable, their coexistence represents a serious cultural ambivalence about how mothers should behave. This ambivalence comes out in the widely available indictments of the failings of both groups of women. Note, for instance, the way Mecca, a welfare mother, describes these two choices and their culturally provided critiques:

> The way my family was brought up was, like, you marry a man, he's the head of the house, he's the provider, and you're the wife, you're the provider in the house. Now these days it's not that way. Now the people that stay home are classified, quote, "lazy people," we don't "like" to work.
>
> I've seen a lot of things on TV about working mothers and nonworking mothers. People who stay home attack the other mothers 'cause they're, like, bad mothers because they left the kids behind and go to work. And, the other ones aren't working because we're lazy. But it's not lazy. It's the lifestyle in the 1990s it's, like, too much. It's a demanding world for mothers with kids.

The picture Mecca has seen on television, a picture of these two images attacking each other with ideological swords, is not an uncommon one.

It is this cultural ambivalence and the so-called choice between these paths that is the basis for what Darnton (1990) has dubbed the "mommy wars." Both stay-at-home and paid working mothers, it is argued, are angry and defensive; neither group respects the other. Both make use of available cultural indictments to condemn the opposing group. Supermoms, according to this portrait, regularly describe stay-at-home mothers as lazy and boring, while traditional moms regularly accuse employed mothers of selfishly neglecting their children.

My interviews suggest, however, that this portrait of the mommy wars is both exaggerated and superficial. In fact, the majority of mothers I spoke with expressed respect for one another's need or right to choose whether to go out to work or stay at home with the kids. And, as I have argued, they also share a whole set of similar concerns regarding appropriate child rearing. These mothers have not formally enlisted in this war. Yet the rhetoric of the mommy wars draws them in as it persists in mainstream American culture, a culture that is unwilling, for various significant reasons, to unequivocally embrace either vision of motherhood, just as it remains unwilling to embrace wholeheartedly the childless career woman. Thus, the charges of being lazy and bored, on the one hand, or selfish and money-grubbing, on the other, are made available for use by individual mothers and others should the need arise.

What this creates is a no-win situation for women of child-bearing years. If a woman voluntarily remains childless, some will say that she is cold, heartless, and unfulfilled as a woman. If she is a mother who works too hard at her job or career, some will accuse her of neglecting the kids. If she does not work hard enough, some will surely place her on the "mommy track" and her career advancement will be permanently slowed by the claim that her commitment to her children interferes with her workplace efficiency (Schwartz 1989). And if she stays at home with her children, some will call her unproductive and useless. A woman, in other words, can never fully do it right.

At the same time that these cultural images portray all women as somehow less than adequate, they also lead many mothers to feel somehow less than adequate in their daily lives. The stay-at-home mother is supposed to be happy and fulfilled, but how can she be when she hears so often that she is mindless and bored? The supermom is supposed to be able to juggle her two roles without missing a beat, but how can she do either job as well as she is expected if she is told she must dedicate her all in both directions? In these circumstances, it is not surprising that many supermoms feel guilty about their inability to carry out both roles to their fullest, while many traditional moms feel isolated and invisible to the larger world.

Given this scenario, both stay-at-home and employed mothers end up spending a good deal of time attempting to make sense of their current positions. Paid working mothers, for instance, are likely to argue that there are lots of good reasons for mothers to work in the paid labor force; stay-at-home mothers are likely to argue that there are lots of good reasons for mothers to stay at home with their children. These arguments are best understood not as (mere) rationalizations or (absolute) truths but rather as socially necessary "ideological work." Berger (1981a) uses this notion to describe the way that all people make use of available ideologies in their "attempt to cope with the relationship between the ideas they bring to a social context and the practical pressures of day-to-day living in it" (15). People, in other words, select among the cultural logics at their disposal in order to develop some correspondence between what they believe and what they actually do. For mothers, just like others, ideological work is simply a means of maintaining their sanity.

The ideological work of mothers, as I will show, follows neither a simple nor a straightforward course. First, as I have pointed out, both groups face two contradictory cultural images of appropriate mothering. Their ideological work, then, includes a recognition and response to both portraits. This duality is evident in the fact that the logic the traditional mother uses to affirm her position matches the logic that the supermom uses to express ambivalence about her situation, and the logic that the employed mother uses to affirm her position is the same logic that the stay-at-home mother uses to express ambivalence about hers. Their strategies, in other words, are mirror images, but they are also incomplete—both groups are left with some ambivalence. Thus, although the two culturally provided images of mothering help mothers to make sense of their own positions, they simultaneously sap the strength of mothers by making them feel inadequate in one way or the other. It is in coping with these feelings of inadequacy that their respective ideological strategies take an interesting turn. Rather than taking divergent paths, as one might expect, both groups attempt to resolve their feelings of inadequacy by returning to the logic of the ideology of intensive mothering.

THE FRUMPY HOUSEWIFE AND THE PUSH TOWARD THE OUTSIDE WORLD

Some employed mothers say that they go out to work for pay because they need the income. But the overwhelming majority also say that they *want* to work outside the home. First, there's the problem of staying inside all day: "I decided once I started working that I need that. I need to work. Because I'll become like this big huge hermit frumpy person if I stay home." Turning into a "big huge hermit frumpy person" is connected to the feeling of being confined to the home. Many women have had that experience at one time or another and do not want to repeat it:

> When I did stay home with him, up until the time when he was ten months old, I wouldn't go out of the house for three days at a time. Ya know, I get to where I don't want to get dressed, I don't care if I take a shower. It's like, what for? I'm not going anywhere.

Not getting dressed and not going anywhere are also tied to the problem of not having a chance to interact with other adults:

> I remember thinking, "I don't even get out of my robe. And I've gotta stay home and breast-feed and the only adult I hear is on *Good Morning America*—and he's not even live!" And that was just for a couple of months. I don't even know what it would be like for a couple of years. I think it would be really difficult.

Interacting with adults, for many paid working mothers, means getting a break from the world of children and having an opportunity to use their minds:

> When I first started looking for a job, I thought we needed a second income. But then when I started working it was like, this is great! I do have a mind that's not *Sesame Street!* And I just love talking with people. It's just fun, and it's a break. It's tough, but I enjoyed it; it was a break from being with the kids.

If you don't get a break from the kids, if you don't get out of the house, if you don't interact with adults, and if you don't have a chance to use your mind beyond the *Sesame Street* level, you might end up lacking the motivation to do much at all. This argument is implied by many mothers:

> If I was stuck at home all day, and I did do that 'cause I was waiting for day care, I stayed home for four months, and I went crazy, I couldn't stand it. I mean not because I didn't want to spend any time with her, but because we'd just sit here and

she'd just cry all day and I couldn't get anything done. I was at the end of the day exhausted, and feeling like shit.

Of course, it is exhausting to spend the day meeting the demands of children. But there's also a not too deeply buried sense in all these arguments that getting outside the home and using one's mind fulfill a longing to be part of the larger world and to be recognized by it. One mother made this point explicitly:

> [When you're working outside the home] you're doing something. You're using your mind a little bit differently than just trying to figure out how to make your day work with your kid. It's just challenging in a different way. So there's part of me that wants to be, like, *recognized*. I think maybe that's what work does, it gives you a little bit of a sense of recognition, that you don't feel like you get [when you stay home].

Most employed mothers, then, say that if they stay at home they'll go stir-crazy, they'll get bored, the demands of the kids will drive them nuts, they won't have an opportunity to use their brains or interact with other adults, they'll feel like they're going nowhere, and they'll lose their sense of identity in the larger world. And, for many of these mothers, all these points are connected:

> Well, I think [working outside is] positive, because I feel good about being able to do the things that I went to school for, and keep up with that, and use my brain. As they grow older, [the children are] going to get into things that they want to get into, they're going to be out with their friends and stuff, and I don't want to be in a situation where my whole life has been wrapped around the kids. That's it. Just some outside interests so that I'm not so wrapped up in how shiny my floor is. [She laughs.] Just to kind of be out and be stimulated. Gosh, I don't want this to get taken wrong, but I think I'd be a little bit bored. And the other thing I think of is, I kind of need a break, and when you're staying at home it's constant. It's a lot harder when you don't have family close by, [because] you don't get a break.

In short, paid working mothers feel a strong pull toward the outside world. They hear the world accusing stay-at-home moms of being mindless and unproductive and of lacking an identity apart from their kids, and they experience this as at least partially true.

Stay-at-home mothers also worry that the world will perceive them as lazy and bored and watching television all day as children scream in their ears and tug at their sleeves. And sometimes this is the way they feel about themselves. In other words, the same image that provides working mothers with the reasons they should go out to work accounts for the ambivalence that stay-at-home mothers feel about staying at home.

A few stay-at-home mothers seem to feel absolutely secure in their position, but most do not. Many believe that they will seek paid work at some point, and almost all are made uncomfortable by the sense that the outside world does not value what they do. In all cases, their expressions of ambivalence about staying at home mimic the concerns of employed mothers. For instance, some women who stay at home also worry about becoming frumpy: "I'm not this heavy. I'm, like, twenty-seven pounds overweight. It sounds very vain of me, in my situation. It's like, I'm not used to being home all the time, I'm home twenty-four hours. I don't have that balance in my life anymore." And some stay-at-home mothers feel as if they are physically confined inside the home. This mother, for example, seems tired of meeting the children's demands and feels that she is losing her sense of self:

> There's a hard thing of being at home all the time. You have a lot of stress, because you're constantly in the house. I think having a job can relieve some of that stress and to make it a lot more enjoyable, to want to come home all the time. . . . My outings are [limited]. I'm excited when I have to go grocery shopping. Everything I pick is what they eat, everything they like, or what they should eat. Me, I'm just *there*. I'm there for them. I feel that I'm here for them.

Both of these stay-at-home mothers, like over one-third of the stay-at-home mothers in my sample, plan to go out to work as soon as they can find paid employment that offers sufficient rewards to compensate (both financially and ideologically) for sending the kids to day care. Most of the remaining mothers are committed to staying at home with the children through what they understand as formative years. The following mother shares that commitment, while also echoing many paid working mothers in her hopes that one day she will have a chance to be around adults and further her own growth:

> Well, we could do more, we'd have more money, but that's really not the biggest reason I'd go back to work. I want to do things for myself, too. I want to go back and get my master's [degree] or something. I need to grow, and be around adults, too. I don't know when, but I think in the next two years I'll go back to work. The formative years—their personality is going to develop until they're about five. It's pretty much set by then. So I think it's pretty critical that you're around them during those times.

One mother stated explicitly that she can hardly wait until the kids are through their formative years:

> At least talking to grown-ups is a little more fulfilling than ordering the kids around all day. My life right now is just all theirs. Sometimes it's a depressing thought because I think, "Where am I? I want my life back." . . . I mean, they are totally selfish. It's like an ice cream. They just gobble that down and say, "Let me have the cinnamon roll now."
> . . . [But] I had them, and I want them to be good people. So I've dedicated myself to them right now. Later on I get my life back. They won't always be these little sponges. I don't want any deficiency—well, nobody can cover all the loopholes—but I want to be comfortable in myself to know that I did everything that I could. It's the least I can do to do the best I can by them.

Mothers, she seems to be saying, are like confections that the kids just gobble down—and then they ask for more.

Thus, many stay-at-home moms experience the exhaustion of meeting the demands of children all day long, just as employed mothers fear they might. And many stay-at-home mothers also experience a loss of self. Part of the reason they feel like they are losing their identity is that they know the outside world does not recognize a mother's work as valuable. This woman, committed to staying at home until her youngest is at least three years old, explains:

> You go through a period where you feel like you've lost all your marbles. Boy, you're not as smart as you used to be, and as sharp as you used to be, and not as respected as

you used to be. And those things arc really hard to swallow. But that's something I've discussed with other mothers who are willing to stay home with their kids, and we've formed a support group where we've said, "Boy, those people just don't know what they're talking about." We're like a support group for each other, which you have to have if you've decided to stay at home, because you have so many people almost pushing you to work, or asking "Why don't you work?" You're not somehow as good as anybody else cause you're staying at home; what you're doing isn't important. We have a lot of that in this society.

Another mother, this one determined to stay at home with her kids over the long haul, provides a concrete example of the subtle and not-so-subtle ways in which society pushes mothers to participate in the paid labor force, and of the discomfort such mothers experience as a result:

As a matter of fact, somebody said to me (I guess it was a principal from one of the schools) . . . "Well, what do you *do?* Do you have a *job?*" And it was just very funny to me that he was so uncomfortable trying to ask me what it was in our society that I did. I guess that they just assume that if you're a mom at home that it means nothing. I don't know, I just don't consider it that way. But it's kind of funny, worrying about what you're gonna say at a dinner party about what you do.

And it's not just that these mothers worry about being able to impress school principals and people at cocktail parties, of course. The following mother worries about being "interesting" to other women who do not have children:

I find myself, now that I'm not working, not to have as much in common [with other women who don't have children]. We don't talk that much because I don't have that much to talk about. Like I feel I'm not an interesting person anymore.

In short, the world presents, and mothers experience, the image of the lazy mindless, dull housewife—and no mother wants to be included in that image

THE TIME-CRUNCHED CAREER WOMAN AND THE PULL TOWARD HOME

Stay-at-home mothers use a number of strategies to support their position and combat the image of the frumpy housewife. Many moms who are committed to staying at home with their kids often become part of formal or informal support groups, providing them an opportunity to interact with other mothers who have made the same commitment. Others, if they can afford the cost of transportation and child care, engage in a variety of outside activities—as volunteers for churches, temples, and community groups, for instance, or in regular leisure activities and exercise programs. They then have a chance to communicate with other adults and to experience themselves as part of a larger social world (though one in which children generally occupy a central role).

But the primary way that stay at-home mothers cope with their ambivalence is through ideological work. Like paid working mothers, they make a list of all the good reasons they do what they do. In this case, that list includes confirming their commitment to good mothering, emphasizing the importance of putting their children's needs ahead of their own, and telling stories about the problems that families, and especially children, experience when mothers go out to work for pay.

Many stay-at-home mothers argue that kids require guidance and should have those cookies cooling on the kitchen counter when they come home from school:

> The kids are the ones that suffer. The kids need guidance and stuff. And with two parents working, sometimes there isn't even a parent home when they come home from school. And that's one thing that got me too. I want to be home and I want to have cookies on the stove when they come home from school. Now we eat meals together all the time. It's more of a homey atmosphere. It's more of a *home* atmosphere.

Providing this homey atmosphere is difficult to do if one works elsewhere all day. And providing some period of so-called quality time in the evening, these mothers tell me, is not an adequate substitute. One mother elaborates on this point in response to a question about how she would feel if she was working outside the home:

> Oh, guilty as anything. I know what I'm like after dinner, and I'm not at my best. And neither are my kids. And if that's all the time I had with them, it wouldn't be, quote, "quality time." I think it's a bunch of b.s. about quality time.

And quality time, even if it *is* of high quality, cannot make up for children's lack of a quantity of time with their mothers. This argument is often voiced in connection with the problem of paid caregiver arrangements. Most mothers, whether they work for pay or not, are concerned about the quality of day care, but stay-at-home mothers often use this concern to explain their commitment to staying at home. This mother, for example, argues that children who are shuffled off to a series of day-care providers simply will not get the love they need:

> I mean, if I'm going to have children I want to *raise* them. I feel really strongly about that. Really strongly. I wish more people did that. Myself, I think it's very underestimated the role the mother plays with the child. I really do. From zero to three [years], it's like their whole self-image. [Yet, working mothers will say,] "Well, okay, I've got a caretaker now," "Well, that nanny didn't work out." So by the time the children are three years old they've had four or five people who have supposedly said "I'll love you forever," and they're gone. I think that's really tough on the kids.

Since paid caregivers lack that deep and long-lasting love, I'm told, they won't ever be as committed to ministering to the child's needs as a mom will:

> I don't think anybody can give to children what a mother can give to her own children. I think there's a level of willingness to put up with hard days, crying days, cranky days, whining days, that most mothers are going to be able to tolerate just a little bit more than a caretaker would. I think there's more of a commitment of what a mother wants to give her children in terms of love, support, values, etcetera. A caretaker isn't going to feel quite the same way.

Stay-at-home mothers imply that all these problems of kids who lack guidance, love, and support are connected to the problem of mothers who put their own interests ahead of the interests of their children. A few stay-at-home mothers will explicitly argue, as this one does, that employed mothers are allowing material and power interests to take priority over the well-being of their kids:

> People are too interested in power, they just aren't interested in what happens to their kids. You know, "Fine, put them in day care." And I just feel sad. If you're so interested in money or a career or whatever, then why have kids? Why bring them into it?

Putting such interests ahead of one's children is not only somehow immoral; it also produces children with real problems. The following mother, echoing many stories about "bad mothers" that we have heard before, had this to say about her sister:

> My sister works full-time—she's a lawyer. And her kids are the most obnoxious, whiny kids. I can't stand it. They just hang on her. She thinks she's doing okay by them because they're in an expensive private school and they have expensive music lessons and they have expensive clothes and expensive toys and expensive cars and an expensive house. I don't know. Time will tell, I guess. But I can't believe they're not going to have some insecurities. The thing that gets me is, they don't need it. I mean, he's a lawyer too. Basically, it's like, "Well, I like you guys, but I don't really want to be there all day with you, and I don't want to have to do the dirty work."

These are serious indictments indeed.

It is just these sorts of concerns that leave paid working mothers feeling inadequate and ambivalent about *their* position. Many of them wonder at times if their lives or the lives of their children might actually be better if they stayed at home with the kids. Above all, many of them feel guilty and wonder, "Am I doing it right?" or "Have I done all I can do?" These are the mothers who, we're told, have it all. It is impossible to have it all, however, when "all" includes two contradictory sets of requirements. To begin to get a deeper sense of how these supermoms do not always feel so super, two examples might be helpful.

Angela is a working-class mother who had expected to stay home with her son through his formative years. But after nine months she found herself bored, lonely, and eager to interact with other adults. She therefore went out and got a full-time job as a cashier. She begins by expressing her concern that she is not living up to the homemaking suggestions she reads in *Parenting* magazine, worrying that she may not be doing it right:

> I get *Parenting* magazine and I read it. I do what is comfortable for me and what I can do. I'm not very creative. Where they have all these cooking ideas, and who has time to do that, except for a mother who stays home all day? Most of this is for a mother who has five, six hours to spend with her child doing this kind of thing. I don't have time for that.
>
> So then that's when I go back to day care. And I know that she's doing this kind of stuff with him, teaching him things. You know, a lot of the stuff that they have is on schooling kinds of things, flash cards, that kind of thing. Just things that I don't do. That makes me feel bad. Then I think, "I should be doing this" and "Am I doing the right thing?" I know I have a lot of love for him.

Although she loves her son and believes that this is probably "the most important thing," she also feels guilty that she may not be spending a sufficient amount of time with him, simply because she gets so tired:

> I think sometimes that I feel like I don't spend enough time with him and that's my biggest [concern]. And when I am with him, sometimes I'm not really up to being with him. Even though I am with him, sometimes I want him to go away because I've been working all day and I'm exhausted. And I feel sometimes I'll stick him in bed early because I just don't want to deal with him that day. And I feel really guilty because I don't spend enough time with him as it is. When I do have the chance to spend time with him, I don't want to spend time with him, because I'm so tired and I just want to be with myself and by myself.

Even though Angela likes her paid work and does not want to give it up, the problems of providing both a quantity of time and the idealized image of quality time with her child, just like the challenge of applying the creative cooking and child-rearing ideas she finds in *Parenting* magazine, haunt her and leave her feeling both inadequate and guilty.

Linda is a professional-class mother with a well-paying and challenging job that gives her a lot of satisfaction. She spent months searching for the right preschool for her son and is relieved that he is now in a place where the caregivers share her values. Still, she worries and wonders if life might he better if she had made different choices:

> I have a friend. She's a very good mom. She seems very patient, and I never heard her raise her voice. And she's also not working. She gets to stay home with her children, which is another thing I admire. I guess I sort of envy that too. There never seems to be a time where we can just spend, like, playing a lot. I think that's what really bothers me, that I don't feel like I have the time to just sit down and, in a relaxing way, play with him. I can do it, but then I'm thinking "Okay, well I can do this for five minutes." So that's always in the back of my mind. Time, time, time. So I guess that's the biggest thing.
>
> And just like your question, "How many hours a day is he at preschool and how many hours do you spend per day as the primary caregiver?" just made me think, "Oh my gosh!" I mean they're watching him grow up more than I am. They're with him more than I am. And that makes me feel guilty in a way, and it makes me feel sad in a way. I mean I can just see him, slipping, just growing up before me. Maybe it's that quality-time stuff. I don't spend a lot of time, and I don't know if the time I do spend with him is quality.
>
> [But] if I just stay at home, I'll kind of lose, I don't know if I want to say my sense of identity, but I guess I'll lose my career identity. I'm afraid of that I guess....My friend who stays at home, she had a career before she had her children, but I forget what it was. So that whole part of her, I can't even identify it now.

On the one hand, Linda envies and admires stay-at-home moms and worries about not spending enough quality time with her son, or enough play time. She is also upset that her day-care provider spends more hours with her son each day than she can. On the other hand, Linda worries that if she did stay at home she'd lose her identity as a professional and a member of the larger society. "Time,

time, time," she says, there's never enough time to do it all—or at least to do it all "right."

The issue of time is a primary source of paid working mothers' ambivalence about their double shift. Attempting to juggle two commitments at once is, of course, very difficult and stressful. This mother's sense of how time pressures make her feel that she is always moving too fast would be recognizable to the majority of paid working mothers:

> I can see when I get together with my sister [who doesn't have a paid job] . . . that she's so easygoing with the kids, and she takes her time, and when I'm with her, I realize how stressed out I am sometimes trying to get things done.
>
> And I notice how much faster I move when I shop. . . . She's so relaxed, and I think I kind of envy that.

The problem of moving too fast when shopping is connected to the problem of moving too fast when raising children. Many paid working mothers envy those who can do such things at a more relaxed pace.

For a few employed mothers (two out of twenty in my sample) the problems of quality and quantity time outweigh the rewards of paid work, and they intend to leave their jobs as soon as they can afford to do so. This woman is one example:

> I believe there's a more cohesive family unit with maybe the mother staying at home. Because a woman tends to be a buffer, mediator, you name it. She pulls the family together. But if she's working outside the home, sometimes there's not that opportunity anymore for her to pull everyone together. She's just as tired as the husband would be and, I don't know, maybe the children are feeling like they've been not necessarily abandoned but, well, I'm sure they accept it, especially if that's the only life they've seen. But my daughter has seen a change, even when I was only on maternity leave. I've seen a change in her and she seemed to just enjoy it and appreciate us as a family more than when I was working. So now she keeps telling me, "Mom, I miss you."

When this mother hears her daughter say "I miss you," she feels a tremendous pull toward staying at home. And when she talks about the way a family needs a mother to bring its members together, she is pointing to an idealized image of the family that, like quality and quantity time, weighs heavily in the minds of many mothers.

The following paid working mother also wishes she could stay at home with the kids and wishes she could be just like the television mom of the 1950s who bakes cookies every afternoon. But she knows she has to continue working for financial seasons:

> Yes. I want to be Donna Reed, definitely. Or maybe Beaver Cleaver's mother, Jane Wyatt. Anybody in an apron and a pretty hairdo and a beautiful house. Yes. Getting out of the television set and making the most of reality is really what I have to do. Because I'll always have to work.

But the majority of paid working mothers, as I have stated, not only feel they need to work for financial reasons but also *want* to work, as Angela and Linda do. Nonetheless, their concerns about the effects of the double shift on their children match the concerns of those employed moms who wish they could stay at home as well as mimicking those of mothers who actually do stay at home. This mother, for instance, loves her paid work and does not want to give it up, but she does feel guilty, wondering if she's depriving her kids of the love and stimulation they need, particularly since she does not earn enough to justify the time she spends away:

> Honestly, I don't make that much money. So that in itself brings a little bit of guilt, 'cause I know I work even though we don't have to. So there's some guilt associated. If kids are coming home to an empty house every day, they're not getting the intellectual stimulation [and] they're not getting the love and nurturing that other mothers are able to give their kids. So I think in the long run they're missing out on a lot of the love and the nurturing and the caring.

And this mother does not want it to seem that she is putting her child second, but she feels pressure to live up to the image of a supermom:

> I felt really torn between what I wanted to do. Like a gut-wrenching decision. Like, what's more important? Of course your kids are important, but you know, there's so many outside pressures for women to work. Every ad you see in magazines or on television shows this working woman who's coming home with a briefcase and the kids are all dressed and clean. It's such a lie. I don't know of anybody who lives like that.
>
> There's just a lot of pressure that you're not a fulfilled woman if you're not working outside of the home. But yet, it's just a real hard choice.

This feeling of being torn by a gut-wrenching decision comes up frequently:

> I'm constantly torn between what I feel I should be doing in my work and spending more time with them.... I think I would spend more time with them if I could. Sometimes I think it would be great not to work and be a mom and do that, and then I think, "well?"
>
> I think it's hard. Because I think you do need to have contact with your kid You can't just see him in the morning and put him to bed at night because you work all day long. I think that's a real problem. You need to give your child guidance. You can't leave it to the schools. You can't leave it to churches. You need to be there. So, in some ways I'm really torn.

The overriding issue for this mother is guidance; seeing the children in the morning and putting them to bed at night is just not enough.

This problem, of course, is related to the problem of leaving kids with a paid caregiver all day. Paid working mothers do not like the idea of hearing their children cry when they leave them at day care any more than any other mother does. They are, as we have seen, just as concerned that their children will not get enough love, enough nurturing, enough of the right values, enough of the proper education, and enough of the right kind of discipline if they spend most of their time with a paid caregiver. To this list of concerns, paid working mothers add their feeling that when the kids are with a paid caregiver all day, it feels as if someone else is being the mother. One woman (who stayed at home until her son was two years old) elaborates:

> Well, I think it's really sad that kids have to be at day care forty hours a week. Because basically the person who's taking care of them is your day-care person.

They're pretty much being the mother. It's really sad that this other person is raising your child, and it's basically like having this other person *adopting* your child. It's *awful* that we have to do that. I just think it's a crime basically. I wish we didn't have to do it. I wish everybody could stay home with their kids and have some kind of outlet....

And I think having a career is really important, but I think when it comes time to have children, you can take that time off and spend it with your kid. Because you can't go backwards, and time does fly with them. It's so sad . . . I hear people say, "Oh, my day-care lady said that so-and-so walked today or used a spoon or something." I mean it's just so devastating to hear that you didn't get to see that.

Leaving one's child with a paid caregiver for hours on end is therefore a potential problem not only because that "other mother" may not be a good mother but also because the real mother misses out on the joys that come from just being with the child and having a chance to watch him or her grow. This is a heart rending issue for many mothers who work outside the home.

Once again, the arguments used by stay-at-home mothers to affirm their commitment to staying home are mimicked by the arguments paid working mothers use to express their ambivalence about the time they spend away from their children. And again, though the reasoning of these women is grounded in their experiences, it is also drawn from a widely available cultural rhetoric regarding the proper behavior of mothers.

THE CURIOUS COINCIDENCE OF PAID WORK AND THE IDEOLOGY OF INTENSIVE MOTHERING

Both paid working moms and stay-at-home moms, then, do the ideological work of making their respective lists of the reasons they should work for pay and the reasons they should stay at home. Yet both groups also continue to experience and express some ambivalence about their current positions, feeling pushed and pulled in two directions. One would assume that they would cope with their ambivalence by simply returning to their list of good reasons for doing what they do. And stay-at-home mothers do just that: they respond to the push toward work in the paid labor force by arguing that their kids need them to be at home. But, as I will demonstrate, working mothers do not use the mirror strategy. The vast majority of these women do not respond to the pull toward staying at home by arguing that kids are a pain in the neck and that paid work is more enjoyable. Instead, they respond by creating a new list of all the reasons that they are good mothers even though they work outside the home. In other words, the ideological work meant to resolve mothers' ambivalence generally points in the direction of intensive mothering.

Most paid working mothers cope with they ambivalence by arguing that their participation in the labor force is ultimately good for their kids. They make this point in a number of ways. For instance, one mother thinks that the example she provides may help to teach her kids the work ethic. Another says that with the "outside constraints" imposed by her work schedule, she's "more organized and effective" as a mom. Yet another mother suggests that her second child takes just as much time and energy away from her first child as her career does:

> I think the only negative effect [of my employment] is just [that] generally when I'm overstressed I don't do as well as a mother. But work is only one of the things that gets me overstressed. In fact it probably stresses me less than some other things. I think I do feel guilty about working 'cause it takes time away from [my oldest daughter]. But it struck me that it's acceptable to have a second child that takes just as much time away from the other child. *That* I'm not supposed to feel guilty about. But in some ways this [pointing to the infant she is holding] takes my time away from her more than my work does. Because this is constant.

More often, however, paid working mothers share a set of more standard explanations for why their labor-force participation is actually what's best for their kids. First, just as Rachel feels that her income provides for her daughter's toys, clothing, outings, and education, and just as Jacqueline argues, "I have weeks when I don't spend enough time with them and they suffer, but those are also the weeks I bring home the biggest paychecks," many mothers point out that their paid work provides the financial resources necessary for the well-being of their children:

> How am I supposed to send her to college without saving up? And also the money that I make from working helps pay for her toys, things that she needs, clothes. I never have to say, "Oh, I'm on a budget, I can't go buy this pair of shoes." I want the best for her.

Some mothers express a related concern—namely, what would happen to the family if they did not have paying jobs and their husbands should die or divorce them? One women expressed it this way:

> Well, my dad was a fireman, so I guess there was a little bit of fear, well, if anything happened to him, how are we gonna go on? And I always kind of wished that [my mother] had something to fall back on. I think that has a lot to do with why I continue to work after the kids. I've always just felt the need to have something to hold on to.

The second standard argument given by employed mothers is that paid caregiver arrangements can help to further children's development. With respect to other people's kids, I'm told, these arrangements can keep them from being smothered by their mothers or can temporarily remove them from bad family situations. With reference to their own children, mothers emphasize that good day care provides kids with the opportunity to interact with adults, gives them access to "new experiences" and "different activities," "encourages their independence," and allows them to play with other kids—which is very important, especially now that neighborhoods no longer provide the sort of community life they once did:

> They do say that kids in preschool these days are growing up a little more neurotic, but I don't think that my daughter would have had a better life. In fact I think her life would have been a thousand times worse if I was a low-income mother who stayed home and she only got to play with the kids at the park. Because I think that

preschool is really good for them. Maybe not a holding tank, but a nice preschool where they play nice games with them and they have the opportunity to play with the same kids over and over again. I think that's really good for them. Back in the 1950s, everybody stayed home and there were kids all over the block to play with. It's not that way now. The neighborhoods are deserted during the week.

Third, several mothers tell me that the quality of the time they spend with their kids actually seems to increase when they have a chance to be away from them for a part of the day. Listen to these mothers:

—When I'm with them too long I tend to lose my patience and start yelling at them. This way we both get out. And we're glad to see each other when we come home.
—If women were only allowed to work maybe ten to fifteen hours a week, they would appreciate their kids more and they'd have more quality time with them, rather than having to always just scold them.
—I think I have even less patience [when I stay home with the children], because it's like, "Oh, is this all there is?" . . . Whereas when I go to work and come home, I'm glad to see him. You know, you hear people say that they're better parents when they work because they spend more quality time, all those clichés, or whatever. For me that happens to be true.
—And now when I come home from work (although I wish I could get off earlier from work), I think I'm a better mom. There you go! Because when I come home from work, I don't have *all* day, just being with the kids. It's just that when I'm working I feel like I'm competent, I'm a person!

Getting this break from the kids, a break that reinforces your feeling of competence and therefore results in more rewarding time with your children is closely connected to the final way paid working mothers commonly attempt to resolve their ambivalence. Their children's happiness, they explain, is dependent upon their *own* happiness as mothers. One hears this again and again: "Happy moms make happy children"; "If I'm happy in my work then I think I can be a better mom"; and "I have to be happy with myself in order to make the children happy." One mother explains it this way:

In some ways working is good. It's definitely got its positive side, because I get a break. I mean, now what I'm doing [working part-time] is perfect. I go to work. I have time to myself. I get to go to the bathroom when I need to go to the bathroom. I come home and I'm very happy to see my kids again. What's good for the mother and makes the mother happy is definitely good for the kids.

In all these explanations for why their participation in the paid labor force is actually good for their kids, these mothers want to make it clear that they still consider children their primary interest. They are definitely not placing a higher value on material success or power, they say. Nor are they putting their own interests above the interests of their children. They want the children to get all they need. But part of what children need, they argue, is financial security, the material goods required for proper development, some time away from their mothers, more quality time when they are with their mothers, and mothers who are happy in what they do. In all of these statements, paid working mothers clearly recognize the ideology of intensive mothering and testify that they are committed to fulfilling its requirements.

To underline the significance of this point, let me remind the reader that these paid working mothers use methods of child rearing that are just as child-centered, expert-guided, emotionally absorbing, labor-intensive, and financially expensive as their stay-at-home counterparts; they hold the child just as sacred, and they are just as likely to consider themselves as primarily responsible for the present and future well-being of their children. These are also the very same mothers who put a tremendous amount of time and energy into finding appropriate paid caregiver arrangements. Yet for all that they do to meet the needs of their children, they still express some ambivalence about working outside the home. And they still resolve this ambivalence by returning to the logic of intensive mothering and reminding the observer that ultimately they are most interested in what is best for their kids. This is striking.

CONTINUING CONTRADICTIONS

All this ideological work is a measure of the power of the pushes and pulls experienced by American mothers today. A woman can be a stay-at-home mother and claim to follow tradition, but not without paying the price of being treated as an outsider in the larger public world of the market. Or a woman can be a paid worker who participates in that larger world, but she must then pay the price of an impossible double shift. In both cases, women are enjoined to maintain the logic of intensive mothering. These contradictory pressures mimic the contradictory logics operating in this society, and almost all mothers experience them. The complex strategies mothers use to cope with these contradictory logics highlight the emotional, cognitive, and physical toll they take on contemporary mothers.

As I have argued, these strategies also highlight something more. The ways mothers explain their decisions to stay at home or work in the paid labor force, like the pushes and pulls they feel, run in opposite directions. Yet the ways they attempt to resolve the ambivalence they experience as a result of those decisions run in the *same* direction. Stay-at-home mothers, as I have shown, reaffirm their commitment to good mothering, and employed mothers maintain that they are good mothers even though they work. Paid working mothers do not, for instance, claim that child rearing is a relatively meaningless task, that personal profit is their primary goal, and that children are more efficiently raised in child-care centers. If you are a mother, in other words, although both the logic of the workplace and the logic of mothering operate in your life, the logic of intensive mothering has a *stronger* claim.

This phenomenon is particularly curious. The fact that there is no way for either type of mother to get it right would seem all the more reason to give up the logic of intensive mothering, especially since both groups of mothers recognize that paid employment confers more status than motherhood in the larger world. Yet images of freshly baked cookies and *Leave It to Beaver* seem to haunt mothers more often than the housewives' "problem that has no name" (Friedan 1963), and far more often than the image of a corporate manager with a big office, a large staff, and lots of perks. Although these mothers do not want to be defined as "mere" housewives and do want to achieve recognition in the outside world, most would also like to be there when the kids come home from school. Mothers surely try to balance their own desires against the requirements of appropriate child rearing, but in the world of mothering, it is socially unacceptable for them (in word if not in deed) to place their own needs above the needs of their children. A good mother certainly would never simply put her child aside for her own convenience. And placing material wealth or power on a higher plane than the well-being of children is strictly forbidden. It is clear that the two groups come together in holding these values as primary, despite the social devaluation of mothering and despite the glorification of wealth and power.

The portrait of the mommy wars, then, is overdrawn. Although the ideological strategies these groups use to explain their choice of home or paid work include an implicit critique of those "on the other side," this is almost always qualified, and both groups, at least at times, discuss their envy or admiration for the others. More important, as should now be abundantly clear, both groups ultimately share the same set of beliefs and the same set of concerns. Over half the women in my sample explicitly state that the choice between home and paid work depends on the individual woman, her interests, desires, and circumstances. Nearly all the rest argue that home is more important than paid work because children are simply more important than careers or the pursuit of financial gain. The paid working women in my sample were actually twice as likely as their stay-at-home counterparts to respond that home and children are more important and rewarding than paid work. Ideologically speaking, at least, home and children actually seem to become more important to a mother the more time she spends away from them.

There *are* significant differences among mothers–ranging from individual differences to more systematic differences of class, race, and employment. But in the present context, what is most significant is the commitment to the ideology of intensive mothering that women share in spite of their differences. In this, the cultural contradictions of motherhood persist.

The case of paid working mothers is particularly important in this regard, since these are the very mothers who, arguably, have the most to gain from redefining motherhood in such a way as to lighten their load on the second shift. As we have seen, however, this is not exactly what they do. It is true, as Gerson (1985) argues, that there are ways in which paid working mothers do redefine motherhood and lighten their load—for instance, by sending their kids to day care, spending less time with them than their stay-at-home counterparts, legitimating their paid labor-force participation, and engaging in any number of practical strategies to make child-rearing tasks less energy- and time-consuming. But, as I have argued, this does not mean that these mothers have given up the ideology of intensive mothering. Rather, it means that, whether or not they actually do, they feel they should spend a good deal of time looking for appropriate paid caregivers, trying to make up for the lack of quantity time by focusing their energy on providing quality time, and remaining attentive to the central tenets of the ideology of intensive child rearing. It also means that many are left feeling pressed for time, a little guilty, a bit inadequate, and somewhat ambivalent about their position. These stresses and the strain toward compensatory strategies should actually be taken as a measure of the persistent strength of the ideology of intensive mothering.

To deepen the sense of paradox further, one final point should be repeated. There are reasons to expect middle-class mothers to be in the vanguard of transforming ideas about child rearing away from an intensive model. First, middle-class women were historically in the vanguard of transforming child-rearing ideologies. Second, while many poor and working-class women have had to carry a double shift of wage labor and domestic chores for generations, middle-class mothers have had little practice, historically speaking, in juggling paid work and home and therefore might be eager to avoid it. Finally, one could argue that employed mothers in the middle class have more to gain from reconstructing ideas about appropriate child rearing than any other group—not only because their higher salaries mean that more money is at stake, but also because intensive mothering potentially interferes with their career trajectories in a more damaging way than is true of less high-status occupations. But, as I have suggested, middle-class women are, in some respects, those who go about the task of child rearing with the greatest intensity.

When women's increasing participation in the labor force, the cultural ambivalence regarding paid working and stay-at-home mothers, the particular intensity of middle-class mothering, and the demanding character of the cultural model of appropriate child rearing are taken together, it becomes clear that the cultural contradictions of motherhood have been deepened rather than resolved. The history of child-rearing ideas demonstrates that the more powerful the logic of the rationalized market became, so too did its ideological opposition in the logic of intensive mothering. The words of contemporary mothers demonstrate that this trend persists in the day-to-day lives of women.

R E A D I N G

32

Decline of the Family: Conservative, Liberal, and Feminist Views

JANET Z. GIELE

In the 1990s the state of American families and children became a new and urgent topic. Everyone recognized that families had changed. Divorce rates had risen dramatically. More women were in the labor force. Evidence on rising

From *Promises to Keep: Decline and Renewal of Marriage in America* (1996). David Popenoe, Jean Bethke Elshtain and David Blankenhorn (eds.), Published by Rowman and Littlefield.

teenage suicides, high rates of teen births, and disturbing levels of addiction and violence had put children at risk.

Conservatives have held that these problems can be traced to a culture of toleration and an expanding welfare state that undercut self-reliance and community standards. They focus on the family as a caregiving institution and try to restore its strengths by changing the culture of marriage and parenthood. Liberals center on the disappearance of manual jobs that throws less educated men out of work and undercuts their status in the family as well as rising hours of work among the middle class that makes stable two-parent families more difficult to maintain. Liberals argue that structural changes are needed outside the family in the public world of employment and schools.

The feminist vision combines both the reality of human interdependence in the family and individualism of the workplace. Feminists want to protect diverse family forms that allow realization of freedom and equality while at the same time nurturing the children of the next generation.

THE CONSERVATIVE EXPLANATION: SELFISHNESS AND MORAL DECLINE

The new family advocates turn their spotlight on the breakdown in the two-parent family, saying that rising divorce, illegitimacy, and father absence have put children at greater risk of school failure, unemployment, and antisocial behavior. The remedy is to restore religious faith and family commitment as well as to cut welfare payments to unwed mothers and mother-headed families.

Conservative Model

| Cultural and moral weakening | → | Family breakdown, divorce, family decline | → | Father absence, school failure, poverty, crime, drug use |

Cultural and Moral Weakening

To many conservatives, the modern secularization of religious practice and the decline of religious affiliation have undermined the norms of sexual abstinence before marriage and the prohibitions of adultery or divorce thereafter. Sanctions against illegitimacy or divorce have been made to seem narrow-minded and prejudiced. In addition, daytime television and the infamous example of Murphy Brown, a single mother having a child out of wedlock, helped to obscure simple notions of right and wrong. Barbara Dafoe Whitehead's controversial article in the *Atlantic* entitled "Dan Quayle Was Right" is an example of this argument.[1]

Gradual changes in marriage law have also diminished the hold of tradition. Restrictions against waiting periods, race dissimilarity, and varying degrees of consanguinity were gradually disappearing all over the United States and Europe.[2] While Mary Ann Glendon viewed the change cautiously but relativistically—as a process that waxed and waned across the centuries—others have interpreted these changes as a movement from status to contract (i.e., from attention to the particular individual's characteristics to reliance on the impersonal considerations of the market place).[3] The resulting transformation lessened the family's distinctive capacity to serve as a bastion of private freedom against the leveling effect and impersonality of public bureaucracy.

Erosion of the Two-Parent Family

To conservatives, one of the most visible causes of family erosion was government welfare payments, which made fatherless families a viable option. In *Losing Ground*, Charles Murray used the rise in teenage illegitimate births as proof that government-sponsored welfare programs had actually contributed to the breakdown of marriage.[4] Statistics on rising divorce and mother-headed families appeared to provide ample proof that the two-parent family was under siege. The proportion of all households headed by married couples fell from 77 percent in 1950 to 61 percent in 1980 and 55 percent in 1993.[5] Rising cohabitation, divorce rates, and births out of wedlock all contributed to the trend. The rise in single-person households was also significant, from only 12 percent of all households in 1950 to 27 percent in 1980, a trend fed by rising affluence and the undoubling of living arrangements that occurred with the expansion of the housing supply after World War II.[6]

The growth of single-parent households, however, was the most worrisome to policymakers because of their strong links to child poverty. In 1988, 50 percent of all children were found in mother-only families compared with 20 percent in 1950. The parental situation of children in poverty changed accordingly. Of all poor children in 1959, 73 percent had two parents present and 20 percent had a mother only. By 1988, only 35 percent of children in poverty lived with two parents and 57 percent lived with a mother only. These developments were fed by rising rates of divorce and out-of-wedlock births. Between 1940 and 1990, the divorce rate rose from 8.8 to 21 per thousand married women. Out-of-wedlock births exploded from 5 percent in 1960 to 26 percent in 1990.[7]

To explain these changes, conservatives emphasize the breakdown of individual and cultural commitment to marriage and the loss of stigma for divorce and illegitimacy. They understand both trends to be the result of greater emphasis on short-term gratification and on adults' personal desires rather than on what is good for children. A young woman brings a child into the world without thinking about who will support it. A husband divorces his wife and forms another household, possibly with other children and leaves children of the earlier family behind without necessarily feeling obliged to be present in their upbringing or to provide them with financial support.

Negative Consequences for Children

To cultural conservatives there appears to be a strong connection between erosion of the two-parent family and the rise of health and social problems in children. Parental investment in children has declined—especially in the time available for supervision and companionship. Parents had roughly 10 fewer hours per week for their children in 1986 than in 1960, largely because more married women were employed (up from 24 percent in 1940 to 52 percent in 1983) and more mothers of young children (under age six) were working (up from 12 percent in 1940 to 50 percent in 1983). By the late 1980s just over half of mothers of children under a year old were in the labor force for at least part of the year.[8] At the same time fathers were increasingly absent from the family because of desertion, divorce, or failure to marry. In 1980, 15 percent of white children, 50 percent of black children, and 27 percent of children of Hispanic origin had no father present. Today 36 percent of children are living apart from their biological fathers compared with only 17 percent in 1960.[9]

Without a parent to supervise children after school, keep them from watching television all day, or prevent them from playing in dangerous neighborhoods, many more children appear to be falling by the wayside, victims of drugs, obesity, violence, suicide, or failure in school. During the 1960s and 1970s the suicide rate for persons aged fifteen to nineteen more than doubled. The proportion of obese children between the ages of six and eleven rose from 18 to 27 percent. Average SAT scores fell, and 25 percent of all high school students failed to graduate.[10] In 1995 the Council on Families in America reported, "Recent surveys have found that children from broken homes, when they become teenagers have 2 to 3 times more behavioral and psychological problems than do children from intact homes."[11] Father absence is blamed by the fatherhood movement for the rise in violence among young males. David Blankenhorn and others reason that the lack of a positive and productive male role model has contributed to an uncertain masculine identity which then uses violence and aggression to prove itself. Every child deserves a father and "in a good society, men prove their masculinity not by killing other people, impregnating lots of women, or amassing large fortunes, but rather by being committed fathers and loving husbands."[12]

Psychologist David Elkind, in *The Hurried Child*, suggests that parents' work and time constraints have pushed down the developmental timetable to younger ages so that small children are being expected to take care of themselves and perform at levels which are robbing them of their childhood. The consequences are depression, discouragement, and a loss of joy at learning and growing into maturity.[13]

Reinvention of Marriage

According to the conservative analysis, the solution to a breakdown in family values is to revitalize and reinstitutionalize marriage. The culture should change to give higher priority to marriage and parenting. The legal code should favor marriage and encourage parental responsibility on the part of fathers as well as mothers. Government should cut back welfare programs which have supported alternate family forms.

The cultural approach to revitalizing marriage is to raise the overall priority given to family activities relative to work, material consumption, or leisure. Marriage is seen as the basic building block of civil society, which helps to hold together the fabric of volunteer activity and mutual support that underpins any democratic society. [14] Some advocates are unapologetically judgmental toward families who fall outside the two-parent mold. According to a 1995 *Newsweek* article on "The Return of Shame," David Blankenhorn believes "a stronger sense of shame about illegitimacy and divorce would do more than any tax cut or any new governmental program to maximize the life circumstances of children." But he also adds that the ultimate goal is "to move beyond stigmatizing only teenage mothers toward an understanding of the terrible message sent by all of us when we minimize the importance of fathers or contribute to the breakup of families." [15]

Another means to marriage and family revitalization is some form of taking a "pledge." Prevention programs for teenage pregnancy affirm the ideal of chastity before marriage. Athletes for Abstinence, an organization founded by a professional basketball player, preaches that young people should "save sex for marriage." A Baptist-led national program called True Love Waits has gathered an abstinence pledge from hundreds of thousands of teenagers since it was begun in the spring of 1993. More than 2,000 school districts now offer an abstinence-based sex education curriculum entitled "Sex Respect." Parents who are desperate about their children's sexual behavior are at last seeing ways that society can resist the continued sexualization of childhood. [16]

The new fatherhood movement encourages fathers to promise that they will spend more time with their children. The National Fatherhood Initiative argues that men's roles as fathers should not simply duplicate women's roles as mothers but should teach those essential qualities which are perhaps uniquely conveyed by fathers—the ability to take risks, contain emotions, and be decisive. In addition, fathers fulfill a time-honored role of providing for children as well as teaching them. [17]

Full-time mothers have likewise formed support groups to reassure themselves that not having a job and being at home full-time for their children is an honorable choice, although it is typically undervalued and perhaps even scorned by dual-earner couples and women with careers. A 1994 *Barron's* article claimed that young people in their twenties ("generation X,") were turning away from the two-paycheck family and scaling down their consumption so that young mothers could stay at home. Although Labor Department statistics show no such trend but only a flattening of the upward rise of women's employment, a variety of poll data does suggest that Americans would rather spend less time at work and more time with their families. [18] Such groups as Mothers at Home (with 15,000 members) and Mothers' Home Business Network (with 6,000 members) are trying to create a sea change that reverses the priority given to paid work outside the home relative to unpaid caregiving work inside the family. [19]

Conservatives see government cutbacks as one of the major strategies for strengthening marriage and restoring family values. In the words of Lawrence Mead, we have "taxed Peter to pay Paula." [20] According to a *Wall Street Journal* editorial, the "relinquishment of personal responsibility" among people who bring children into the world without any visible means of support is at the root of educational, health, and emotional problems of children from one-parent families, their higher accident and mortality rates, and rising crime.[21]

The new congressional solution is to cut back on the benefits to young men and women who "violate social convention by having children they cannot support."[22] Sociologist Brigitte Berger notes that the increase in children and women on welfare coincided with the explosion of federal child welfare programs—family planning, prenatal and postnatal care, child nutrition, child abuse prevention and treatment, child health and guidance, day care, Head Start, and Aid to Families with Dependent Children (AFDC), Medicaid, and Food Stamps. The solution is to turn back the debilitating culture of welfare dependency by decentralizing the power of the federal government and restoring the role of intermediary community institutions such as the neighborhood and the church. The mechanism for change would be block grants to the states which would change the welfare culture from the ground up. Robert Rector of the American Heritage Foundation explains that the states would use these funds for a wide variety of alternative programs to discourage illegitimate births and to care for children born out of wedlock, such as promoting adoption, closely supervised group homes for unmarried mothers and their children, and pregnancy prevention programs (except abortion).[24]

Government programs, however, are only one way to bring about cultural change. The Council on Families in America puts its hope in grassroots social movements to change the hearts and minds of religious and civil leaders, employers, human service professionals, courts, and the media and entertainment industry. The Council enunciates four ideals: marital permanence, childbearing confined to marriage, every child's right to have a father, and limitation of parents' total work time (60 hours per week) to permit adequate time with their families.[25] To restore the cultural ideal of the two-parent family, they would make all other types of family life less attractive and more difficult.

Economic Restructuring: Liberal Analysis of Family Change

Liberals agree that there are serious problems in America's social health and the condition of its children. But they pinpoint economic and structural changes that have placed new demands on the family without providing countervailing social supports. The economy has become ever more specialized with rapid technological change undercutting established occupations. More women have entered the labor force as their child-free years have increased due to a shorter childbearing period and longer lifespan. The family has lost economic functions to the urban workplace and socialization functions to the school. What is left is the intimate relationship between the marital couple, which, unbuffered by the traditional economic division of labor between men and women, is subject to even higher demands for emotional fulfillment and is thus more vulnerable to breakdown when it falls short of those demands.

Liberal Model

Changing economic structure	$\rightarrow$	Changing family and gender roles	$\rightarrow$	Diverse effects poor v. productive children

The current family crisis thus stems from structural more than cultural change—changes in the economy, a paired-down nuclear family, and less parental time at home. Market forces have led to a new ethic of individual flexibility and autonomy. More dual-earner couples and single-parent families have broadened the variety of family forms. More single-parent families and more working mothers have decreased the time available for parenting. Loss of the father's income through separation and divorce has forced many women and children into poverty with inadequate health care, poor education, and inability to save for future economic needs. The solution that most liberals espouse is a government-sponsored safety net which will facilitate women's employment, mute the effects of poverty, and help women and children to become economically secure.

Recent Changes in the Labor Market

Liberals attribute the dramatic changes in the family to the intrusion of the money economy rather than cultural and moral decline. In a capitalist society individual behavior follows the market. Adam Smith's "invisible hand" brings together buyers and sellers who maximize their satisfaction through an exchange of resources in the marketplace. Jobs are now with an employer, not with the family business or family farm as in preindustrial times. The cash economy has, in the words of Robert Bellah, "invaded" the diffuse personal relationships of trust between family and community members and transformed them into specific impersonal transactions. In an agricultural economy husbands and wives and parents and children were bound together in relationships of exchange that served each others' mutual interests. But modern society erodes this social capital of organization, trust among individuals, and mutual obligation that enhances both productivity and parenting.[26]

The market has also eroded community by encouraging maximum mobility of goods and services. Cheaper labor in the South, lower fuel prices, and deeper tax breaks attracted first textile factories, then the shoe industry, and later automobile assembly plants which had begun in the North. Eventually, many of these jobs left the country. Loss of manufacturing jobs has had dramatic consequences for employment of young men without a college education and their capacity to support a family. In the 1970s, 68 percent of male high school graduates had a full-time, year-round job compared with only 51 percent in the 1980s. Many new jobs are located in clerical work, sales, or other service occupations traditionally associated with women. The upshot is a deteriorating employment picture for less well educated male workers at the same time that there are rising opportunities for women. Not surprisingly, even more middle income men and women combine forces to construct a two-paycheck family wage.[27]

Changing Family Forms

Whereas the farm economy dictated a two-parent family and several children as the most efficient work group, the market economy gives rise to a much wider variety of family forms. A woman on the frontier in the 1800s had few other options even if she were married to a drunken, violent, or improvident husband. In today's economy this woman may have enough education to get a clerical job that will support her and her children in a small apartment where the family will be able to use public schools and other public amenities.[28]

Despite its corrosive effect on family relations, the modern economy has also been a liberating force. Women could escape patriarchal domination; the young could seek their fortune without waiting for an inheritance from their elders—all a process that a century ago was aligned with a cultural shift that Fred Weinstein and Gerald Platt termed "the wish to be free."[29] Dramatic improvements took place in the status of women as they gained the right to higher education, entry into the professions, and the elective franchise.[30] Similarly, children were released from sometimes cruel and exploitive labor and became the object of deliberate parental investment and consumption.[31] Elders gained pensions for maintenance and care that made them economically independent of their adult children. All these developments could be understood as part of what William J. Goode has referred to as the "world revolution in family patterns" which resulted in liberation and equality of formerly oppressed groups.

The current assessment of change in family forms is, however, mostly negative because of the consequences for children. More parental investment in work outside the family has meant less time for children. According to liberals, parents separate or divorce or have children outside of marriage because of the economic structure, not because they have become less moral or more selfish. Young women have children out of wedlock when the young men whom they might marry have few economic prospects and when the women themselves have little hope for their own education or employment.[33] Change in the family thus begins with jobs. Advocates of current government programs therefore challenge the conservatives' assertion that welfare caused the breakup of two-parent families by supporting mothers with dependent children. According to William Julius Wilson, it is partly the lack of manual labor jobs for the would-be male breadwinner in inner-city Chicago—the scarcity of "marriageable males"—which drives up the illegitimacy rate.[34]

Among educated women, it is well known that the opportunity costs of foregone income from staying home became so high during the 1950s and 1960s that ever increasing numbers of women deserted full-time homemaking to take paid employment.[35] In the 1990s several social scientists have further noted that Richard Easterlin's prediction that women will return to the home during the 1980s never happened. Instead, women continued in the labor force because of irreversible normative changes surrounding women's equality and the need for women's income to finance children's expensive college education.[36] Moreover, in light of globalization of the economy and increasing job insecurity in the face of corporate downsizing, economists and sociologists are questioning Gary Becker's thesis that the lower waged worker in a household (typically the woman) will tend to become a full-time homemaker while the higher waged partner becomes the primary breadwinner. Data from Germany and the United States on the trend toward women's multiple roles suggests that uncertainty about the future has made women invest more strongly than ever in their own careers. They know that if they drop out for very long they will have difficulty reentering if they have to tide over the family when the main breadwinner loses his job.[37]

Consequences for Children

The ideal family in the liberal economic model, according to political philosopher Iris Young, is one which has sufficient income to support the parents and the children and "to foster in those children the emotional and intellectual capacities to acquire such well-paid, secure jobs themselves, and also sufficient to finance a retirement."[38] Dependent families do not have self-sufficient income but must rely on friends, relatives, charity, or the state to carry out their contribution to bringing up children and being good citizens.

Among liberals there is an emerging consensus that the current economic structure leads to two kinds of underinvestment in children that are implicated in their later dependency—material poverty, characteristic of the poor, and "time" poverty, characteristic of the middle class.

Thirty years ago Daniel Patrick Moynihan perceived that material poverty and job loss for a man put strain on the marriage, sometimes to the point that he would leave. His children also did less well in school.[39] Rand Conger, in his studies of Iowa families who lost their farms during the 1980s, found that economic hardship not only puts strain on the marriage but leads to harsh parenting practices and poorer outcomes for children.[40] Thus it appears possible that poverty may not just be the result of family separation, divorce, and ineffective childrearing practices; it may also be the *cause* of the irritability, quarrels, and violence which lead to marital breakdown. Material underinvestment in children is visible not just with the poor but in the changing ratio of per capita income of children and adults in U.S. society as a whole. As the proportion of households without children has doubled over the last century (from 30 to 65 percent), per capita income of children has fallen from 71 percent of adult income in 1870 to 63 percent in 1930 and 51 percent in 1983.[41]

The problem of "time" poverty used to be almost exclusively associated with mothers' employment. Numerous studies explored whether younger children did better if their mother was a full-time homemaker rather than employed outside the home but found no clear results.[42] Lately the lack of parental time for children has become much more acute because parents are working a total of twenty-one hours more per week than in 1970 and because there are more single-parent families. In 1965 the average child spent about thirty hours a week interacting with a parent, compared with seventeen hours in the 1980s. [43] Moreover, parents are less dependent on their children to provide support for them during old age, and children feel less obligated to do so. As skilled craftsmanship, the trades, and the family farms have disappeared, children's upbringing can no longer be easily or cheaply combined with what parents are already doing. So adults are no longer so invested in children's futures. The result is that where the social capital of group affiliations and mutual obligations is the lowest (in the form of continuity of neighborhoods, a two-parent family, or a parent's interest in higher education for her children), children are 20 percent more likely to drop out of high school. [44]

It is not that parents prefer their current feelings of being rushed, working too many hours, and having too little time with their families. Economist Juliet Schor reports that at least two-thirds of persons she surveyed about their desires for more family time versus more salary would take a cut in salary if it could mean more time with their families. Since this option is not realistically open to many, what parents appear to do is spend more money on their children as a substitute for spending more time with them. [45]

Fixing the Safety Net

Since liberals believe in a market economy with sufficient government regulation to assure justice and equality of opportunity, they support those measures which will eradicate the worst poverty and assure the healthy reproduction of the next generation. [46] What particularly worries them, however, is Charles Murray's observation that since 1970 the growth of government welfare programs has been associated with a *rise* in poverty among children. Payments to poor families with children, while not generous, have nevertheless enabled adults to be supported by attachment to their children. [47] Society is faced with a dilemma between addressing material poverty through further government subsidy and time poverty through policies on parental leave and working hours. It turns out that the United States is trying to do both.

Measures for addressing material poverty would stimulate various kinds of training and job opportunities. The Family Support Act of 1988 would move AFDC mothers off the welfare rolls by giving them job training and requiring them to join the labor force. Such action would bring their economic responsibility for supporting their children into line with their parental authority. A whole program of integrated supports for health insurance, job training, earned income tax credits for the working poor, child support by the noncustodial parent, and supported work is put forward by economist David Ellwood in *Poor Support*. [48] An opposite strategy is to consolidate authority over children with the state's economic responsibility for their care by encouraging group homes and adoption for children whose parents cannot support them economically. [49]

Means for addressing time poverty are evident in such legislative initiatives as the Family and Medical Leave Act of 1993. By encouraging employers to grant parental leave or other forms of flexible work time, government policy is recognizing the value of parents having more time with their children, but the beneficiaries of such change are largely middle-class families who can afford an unpaid parental leave.[50] Another tactic is to reform the tax law to discourage marital splitting. In a couple with two children in which the father earns $16,000 annually and the mother $9,000, joint tax filing gives them no special consideration. But if they file separately, each taking one child as a dependent, the woman will receive about $5,000 in Earned Income Tax Credit and an extra $2,000 in food stamps.[51] Changing the tax law to remove the incentives for splitting, establishing paternity of children born out of wedlock, and intensifying child support enforcement to recover economic support from fathers are all examples of state efforts to strengthen the kinship unit.

INTERDEPENDENCE: THE FEMINIST VISION OF WORK AND CAREGIVING

A feminist perspective has elements in common with both conservatives and liberals, a respect for the family as an institution (shared with the conservatives) and an appreciation of modernity (valued by the liberals). In addition, a feminist perspective grapples with the problem of women's traditionally subordinate status and how to improve it through both a "relational" and an "individualist" strategy while also sustaining family life and the healthy rearing of children.[52] At the same time feminists are skeptical of both conservative and liberal solutions. Traditionalists have so often relied on women as the exploited and underpaid caregivers in the family to enable men's activities in the public realm. Liberals are sometimes guilty of a "male" bias in focusing on the independent individual actor in the marketplace who does not realize that his so-called "independence," is possible only because he is actually *dependent* on all kinds of relationships that made possible his education and life in a stable social order.[53]

By articulating the value of caregiving along with the ideal of women's autonomy, feminists are in a position to examine modern capitalism critically for its effects on families and to offer alternative policies that place greater value on the quality of life and human relationships. They judge family strength not by their *form* (whether they have two-parents) but by their functioning (whether they promote human satisfaction and development) and whether both women and men are able to be family caregivers as well as productive workers. They attribute difficulties of children less to the absence of the two-parent family than to low-wage work of single mothers, inadequate child care, and inhospitable housing and neighborhoods.

Feminist Model

Lack of cooperation among community, family, and work	→	Families where adults are stressed and overburdened	→	Children lack sufficient care and attention from parents

Accordingly, feminists would work for reforms that build and maintain the social capital of volunteer groups, neighborhoods, and communities because a healthy civil society promotes the well-being of families and individuals as well as economic prosperity and a democratic state. They would also recognize greater role flexibility across the life cycle so that both men and women could engage in caregiving, and they would encourage education and employment among women as well as among men.

Disappearance of Community

From a feminist perspective, family values have become an issue because individualism has driven out the sense of collective responsibility in our national culture. American institutions and social policies have not properly implemented a concern for all citizens. Comparative research on family structure, teenage pregnancy, poverty, and child outcomes in other countries demonstrates that where support is generous to help *all* families and children, there are higher levels of health and general education and lower levels of violence and child deviance than in the United States. [53]

Liberal thinking and the focus on the free market have made it seem that citizens make their greatest contribution when they are self-sufficient, thereby keeping themselves off the public dole. But feminist theorist Iris Young argues that many of the activities that are basic to a healthy democratic society (such as cultural production, caretaking, political organizing, and charitable activities) will never be profitable in a private market. Yet many of the recipients of welfare and Social Security such as homemakers, single mothers, and retirees are doing important volunteer work caring for children and helping others in their communities. Thus the social worth of a person's contribution is not just in earning a paycheck that allows economic independence but also in making a social contribution. Such caretaking of other dependent citizens and of the body politic should be regarded as honorable, not inferior, and worthy of society's support and subsidy. [55]

In fact it appears that married women's rising labor force participation from 41 percent in 1970 to 58 percent in 1990 may have been associated with their withdrawal from unpaid work in the home and community. [56] Volunteer membership in everything from the PTA to bowling leagues declined by over 25 percent between 1969 and 1993. There is now considerable concern that the very basis that Alexis de Tocqueville thought necessary to democracy is under siege. [57] To reverse this trend, social observers suggest that it will be necessary to guard time for families and leisure that is currently being sucked into the maw of paid employment. What is needed is a reorientation of priorities to give greater value to unpaid family and community work by both men and women.

National policies should also be reoriented to give universal support to children at every economic level of society, but especially to poor children. In a comparison of countries in the Organization for Economic Cooperation and Development, the United States ranks at the top in average male wages but near the bottom in its provision for disposable income for children. In comparison with the $700 per month available to children in Norway, France, or the

Netherlands in 1992, U.S. children of a single nonemployed mother received only slightly under $200.[58] The discrepancy is explained by very unequal distribution of U.S. income, with the top quintile, the "fortunate fifth," gaining 47 percent of the national income while the bottom fifth receives only 3.6 percent.[59] This sharp inequality is, in turn, explained by an ideology of individualism that justifies the disproportionate gains of the few for their innovation and productivity and the meager income of the poor for their low initiative or competence. Lack of access to jobs and the low pay accruing to many contingent service occupations simply worsen the picture.

Feminists are skeptical of explanations that ascribe higher productivity to the higher paid and more successful leading actors while ignoring the efforts and contribution of the supporting cast. They know that being an invisible helper is the situation of many women. This insight is congruent with new ideas about the importance "social capital" to the health of a society that have been put forward recently by a number of social scientists.[60] Corporations cannot be solely responsible for maintaining the web of community, although they are already being asked to serve as extended family, neighborhood support group, and national health service.

Diversity of Family Forms

Those who are concerned for strengthening the civil society immediately turn to the changing nature of the family as being a key building block. Feminists worry that seemingly sensible efforts to reverse the trend of rising divorce and single parenthood will privilege the two-parent family to the detriment of women; they propose instead that family values be understood in a broader sense as valuing the family's unique capacity for giving emotional and material support rather than implying simply a two–parent form.

The debate between conservatives, liberals, and feminists on the issue of the two-parent family has been most starkly stated by sociologist Judith Stacey and political philosopher Iris Young.[61] They regard the requirement that all women stay in a marriage as an invitation to coercion and subordination and an assault on the principles of freedom and self-determination that are at the foundation of democracy. Moreover, as Christopher Jencks and Kathryn Edin conclude from their study of several hundred welfare families, the current welfare reform rhetoric that no couple should have a child unless they can support it, does not take into account the uncertainty of life in which people who start out married or with adequate income not always remain so. In the face of the worldwide dethronement of the two-parent family (approximately one-quarter to one-third of all families around the globe are headed by women), marriage should not be seen as the cure for child poverty. Mothers should not be seen as less than full citizens if they are not married or not employed (in 1989 there were only 16 million males between the ages of 25 and 34 who made over $12,000 compared with 20 million females of the same age who either had a child or wanted one).[62] National family policy should instead begin with a value on women's autonomy and self-determination that includes the right to bear children. Mother-citizens are helping to reproduce the next generation for the whole society, and in that responsibility they deserve at least partial support.

From a feminist perspective the goal of the family is not only to bring up a healthy and productive new generation; families also provide the intimate and supportive group of kin or fictive kin that foster the health and well-being of every person—young or old, male or female, heterosexual, homosexual, or celibate. Recognition as "family" should therefore not be confined to the traditional two-parent unit connected by blood, marriage, or adoption, but should be extended to include kin of a divorced spouse (as Stacey documented in her study of Silicon Valley families), same-sex partnerships, congregate households of retired persons, group living arrangements, and so on. [61] Twenty years ago economist Nancy Barrett noted that such diversity in family and household form was already present. Among all U.S. households in 1976, no one of the six major types constituted more than 15–20 percent: couples with and without children under eighteen with the wife in the labor force (15.4 and 13.3 percent respectively); couples with or without children under 18 with the wife not in the labor force (19.1 and 17.1 percent); female- or male-headed households (14.4 percent); and single persons living alone (20.6 percent). [64]

Such diversity both describes and informs contemporary "family values" in the United States. Each family type is numerous enough to have a legitimacy of its own, yet no single form is the dominant one. As a result the larger value system has evolved to encompass beliefs and rules that legitimate each type on the spectrum. The regressive alternative is "fundamentalism" that treats the two-parent family with children as the only legitimate form, single-parent families as unworthy of support, and the nontraditional forms as illegitimate. In 1995 the general population appears to have accepted diversity of family forms as normal. A Harris poll of 1,502 women and 460 men found that only 2 percent of women and 1 percent of men defined family as "being about the traditional nuclear family," One out of ten women defined family values as loving, taking care of, and supporting each other, knowing right from wrong or having good values, and nine out of ten said society should value all types of families. [65] It appears most Americans believe that an Aunt Polly single-parent type of family for a Huck Finn that provides economic support, shelter, meals, a place to sleep and to withdraw, is better than no family at all.

Amidst gradual acceptance of greater diversity in family form, the gender-role revolution is also loosening the sex-role expectations traditionally associated with breadwinning and homemaking. Feminists believe that men and women can each do both. [66] In addition, women in advanced industrial nations have by and large converged upon a new life pattern of multiple roles by which they combine work and family life. The negative outcome is an almost universal "double burden" for working women in which they spend eighty-four hours per week on paid and family work, married men spend seventy-two hours, and single persons without children spend fifty hours. [67] The positive consequence, however, appears to be improved physical and mental health for those women who, though stressed, combine work and family roles. [68] In addition, where a woman's husband helps her more with the housework, she is less likely to think of getting a divorce.[69]

The Precarious Situation of Children

The principal remedy that conservatives and liberals would apply to the problems of children is to restore the two-parent family by reducing out-of-wedlock births, increasing the presence of fathers, and encouraging couples who are having marital difficulties to avoid divorce for the sake of their children. Feminists, on the other hand, are skeptical that illegitimacy, father absence, or divorce are the principal culprits they are made out to be. Leon Eisenberg reports that over half of all births in Sweden and one-quarter of births in France are to unmarried women, but without the disastrous correlated effects observed in the United States. Arlene Skolnick and Stacey Rosencrantz cite longitudinal studies showing that most children recover from the immediate negative effects of divorce.[70]

How then, while supporting the principle that some fraction of women should be able to head families as single parents, do feminists analyze the problem of ill health, antisocial behavior, and poverty among children? Their answer focuses on the *lack of institutional supports* for the new type of dual-earner and single-parent families that are more prevalent today. Rather than attempt to force families back into the traditional mold, feminists note that divorce, lone-mother families, and women's employment are on the rise in every industrialized nation. But other countries have not seen the same devastating decline in child well-being, teen pregnancy, suicides and violent death, school failure, and a rising population of children in poverty. These other countries have four key elements of social and family policy which protect all children and their mothers: (1) work guarantees and other economic supports; (2) child care; (3) health care; and (4) housing subsidies. In the United States these benefits are scattered and uneven; those who can pay their way do so; only those who are poor or disabled receive AFDC for economic support, some help with child care, Medicaid for health care, and government-subsidized housing.

A first line of defense is to raise women's wages through raising the minimum wage, then provide them greater access to male-dominated occupations with higher wages. One-half of working women do not earn a wage adequate to support a family of four above the poverty line. Moreover, women in low-wage occupations are subject to frequent lay-offs and lack of benefits. Training to improve their human capital, provision of child care, and broadening of benefits would help raise women's capacity to support a family. Eisenberg reports that the Human Development Index of the United Nations (HDI), which ranks countries by such indicators as life expectancy, educational levels, and per capita income, places the United States fifth and Sweden sixth in the world. But when the HDI is recalculated to take into account equity of treatment of women, Sweden rises to first place and the United States falls to ninth. Therefore, one of the obvious places to begin raising children's status is to raise the economic status and earning power of their mothers."[71]

A second major benefit which is not assured to working mothers is child care. Among school-age children up to thirteen years of age, one-eighth lack any kind of after-school child care. Children come to the factoties where their mothers work and wait on the lawn or in the lobby until their mothers are finished working. If a child is sick, some mothers risk losing a job if they stay home. Others are latchkey kids or in unknown circumstances such as sleeping in their parents' cars or loitering on the streets. Although 60 percent of mothers of the 22 million preschool children are working, there are only 10 million child care places available, a shortfall of one to three million slots. [72] Lack of good quality care for her children not only distracts a mother, adds to her absences from work, and make her less productive, it also exposes the child to a lack of attention and care that leads to violent and antisocial behavior and poor performance in school.

Lack of medical benefits is a third gaping hole for poor children and lone-parent families. Jencks and Edin analyze what happens to a Chicago-area working woman's income if she goes off welfare. Her total income in 1993 dollars on AFDC (with food stamps, unreported earnings, help from family and friends) adds up to $12,355, in addition to which she receives Medicaid and child care. At a $6 per hour full-time job, however, without AFDC, with less than half as much from food stamps, with an Earned Income Tax Credit, and help from relatives, her total income would add to $20,853. But she would have to pay for her own medical care, bringing her effective income down to $14,745 if she found free child care, and $9,801 if she had to pay for child care herself. [73]

Some housing subsidies or low-income housing are available to low-income families. But the neighborhoods and schools are frequently of poor quality and plagued by violence. To bring up children in a setting where they cannot safely play with others introduces important risk factors that cannot simply be attributed to divorce and single parenthood. Rather than being protected and being allowed to be innocent, children must learn to be competent at a very early age. The family, rather than being child-centered, must be adult-centered, not because parents are selfish or self-centered but because the institutions of the society have changed the context of family life. [74] These demands may be too much for children, and depression, violence, teen suicide, teen pregnancy, and school failure may result. But it would be myopic to think that simply restoring the two-parent family would be enough to solve all these problems.

Constructing Institutions for the Good Society

What is to be done? Rather than try to restore the two-parent family as the conservatives suggest or change the economy to provide more jobs as recommended by the liberals, the feminists focus on the need to revise and construct institutions to accommodate the new realities of work and family life. Such an undertaking requires, however, a broader interpretation of family values, a recognition that families benefit not only their members but the public interest, and fresh thinking about how to schedule work and family demands of everyday life as well as the entire life cycle of men and women.

The understanding of family values has to be extended in two ways. First. American values should be stretched to embrace all citizens, their children and families, whether they are poor, white, or people of color, or living in a one-parent family. In 1977, Kenneth Keniston titled the report of the Carnegie Commission on Children *All Our Children*. Today many Americans still speak and act politically in ways suggesting that they *disown* other people's children as the next generation who will inherit the land and support the economy. Yet in the view of most feminists and other progressive reformers, all these children should be embraced for the long-term good of the nation.[75] By a commitment to "family values" feminists secondly intend to valorize the family as a distinctive intimate group of many forms that is needed by persons of all ages but especially children. To serve the needs of children and other dependent persons, the family must be given support and encouragement by the state to carry out its unique functions. Iris Young contends that marriage should not be used to reduce the ultimate need for the state to serve as a means to distribute needed supports to the families of those less fortunate.[76] Compare the example of the GI Bill of Rights after World War II, which provided educational benefits to those who had served their country in the military. Why should there not be a similar approach to the contribution that a parent makes in raising a healthy and productive youngster?[77]

At the community level families should be embraced by all the institutions of the civil society—schools, hospitals, churches, and employers—as the hidden but necessary complement to the bureaucratic and impersonal workings of these formal organizations. Schools rely on parents for the child's "school readiness." Hospitals send home patients who need considerable home care before becoming completely well. The work of the church is carried out and reinforced in the family; and when families fail, it is the unconditional love and intimacy of family that the church tries to replicate. Employers depend on families to give the rest, shelter, emotional support, and other maintenance of human capital that will motivate workers and make them productive. Increasingly, the professionals and managers in these formal organizations are realizing that they need to work more closely with parents and family members if they are to succeed.

Feminists would especially like to see the reintegration of work and family life that was torn apart at the time of the industrial revolution when productive work moved out of the home and into the factory. Several proposals appear repeatedly: parental leave (which now is possible through the Family and Medical Leave Act of 1993); flexible hours and part-time work shared by working parents but without loss of benefits and promotion opportunities; home-based work; child care for sick children and after-school supervision. Although some progress has been made, acceptance of these reforms has been very slow. Parental leave is still *unpaid*. The culture of the workplace discourages many persons from taking advantage of the more flexible options which do exist because they fear they will be seen as less serious and dedicated workers. In addition, most programs are aimed at mothers and at managers, although there is growing feeling that fathers and hourly workers should be included as well.[78]

Ultimately these trends may alter the shape of women's and men's life cycles. Increasingly, a new ideal for the life course is being held up as the model that society should work toward. Lotte Bailyn proposes reorganization of careers in which young couples trade off periods of intense work commitment with each other while they establish their families so that either or both can spend more time at home.[79] Right now both women and men feel they must work so intensely to establish their careers that they have too little time for their children.[80] For the poor and untrained, the problem is the opposite: childbearing and childrearing are far more satisfying and validating than a low-paying, dead-end job. The question is how to reorient educators or employers to factor in time with family as an important obligation to society (much as one would factor in military service, for example). Such institutional reorganization is necessary to give families and childrearing their proper place in the modern postindustrial society.

CONCLUSION

A review of the conservative, liberal, and feminist perspectives on the changing nature of the American family suggests that future policy should combine the distinctive contributions of all three. From the conservatives comes a critique of modernity that recognizes the important role of the family in maintaining child health and preventing child failure. Although their understanding of "family values" is too narrow, they deserve credit for raising the issue of family function and form to public debate. Liberals see clearly the overwhelming power of the economy to deny employment, make demands on parents as workers, and drive a wedge between employers' needs for competitiveness and families' needs for connection and community.

Surprising although it may seem, since feminists are often imagined to be "way out," the most comprehensive plan for restoring family to its rightful place is put forward by the feminists who appreciate both the inherently premodern nature of the family and at the same time its inevitable interdependence with a fast-changing world economy. Feminists will not turn back to the past because they know that the traditional family was often a straightjacket for women. But they also know that family cannot be turned into a formal organization or have its functions performed by government or other public institutions that are incapable of giving needed succor to children, adults, and old people which only the family can give.

The feminist synthesis accepts both the inherent particularism and emotional nature of the family and the inevitable specialization and impersonality of the modern economy. Feminists are different from conservatives in accepting diversity of the family to respond to the needs of the modern economy. They are different from the liberals in recognizing that intimate nurturing relationships such as parenting cannot all be turned into a safety net of formal care. The most promising social policies for families and children take their direction from inclusive values that confirm the good life and the well-being of every individual as the ultimate goal of the nation. The policy challenge is to adjust the partnership between the family and its surrounding institutions so that together they combine the best of private initiative with public concern.

NOTES

1. Barbara Dafoe Whitehead, "Dan Qayle Was Right," *Atlantic Monthly* (April 1993): 47. Her chapter in this volume on the "Story of Marriage" continues the theme of an erosion of values for cultural diversity.
2. Mary Ann Glenn "Marriage and the State: The Withering Away of Marriage," *Virginia Law Review* 62 (May 1976): 663–729.
3. See chapters by Milton Regan and Carl Schneider in this volume.
4. Charles A. Murray, *Losing Ground: American Social Policy): 1950–1980* (New York: Basic Books, 1984). Critics point out that the rise in out-of-wedlock births continues, even though welfare payments have declined in size over the last several decades, thereby casting doubt on the perverse incentive theory of rising illegitimacy.
5. U.S. Bureau of the Census. *Statistical Abstract of the United States: 1994*, 114th ed. (Washington, DC: 1994), 59.
6. Suzanne M. Bianchi and Daphne Spain, *American Women in Transition* (New York: Russell Sage Foundation, 1986), 88.
7. Donald J. Hernandez, *America's Children: Resources from Family, Government, and the Economy* (New York: Russell Sage Foundation, 1993), 284, 70; Janet Zollinger Giele, "Woman's role Change and Adaptation. 1920–1990," in *Women's Lives through Time: Educated American Women of the Twentieth Century*, ed. K Hulbert and D. Schuster (San Francisco Jossey-Bass. 1993), 40.
8. Victor Fuchs, "Are Americas Underinvesting in Children?" in *Rebuilding the Nest*, ed. David Blankenhorn, Stephen Bayme, and Jean Bethke Elshtain (Milwaukee: Family Service America, 1990), 66. Bianchi and Spain.. *American Women in Transition*, 141, 201, 226. Janet Zollinger Giele. "Gender and Sex Roles," in *Handbook of Sociology*, ed. N. J. Smelser (Beverly Hills, CA: Sage Publications, 1988), 300.
9. Hernandez, America's Children, 130. Council on Families in America, *Marriage in America* (New York: Institute for American Values. 1995), 7.
10. Fuchs, "Are Americans Underinvesting in Children?" 61. Some would say, however, that the decline was due in part to a larger and more heterogeneous group taking the tests.
11. Council on Families in America *Marriage in America*, 6. The report cites research by Nicholas Zill and Charlotte A. Schoenborn, "Developmental, Learning and Emotional Problems: Health of Our Nation's Children, United States, 1988." *Advance Data*, National Center for Health Statistics,

Publication # 120, November 1990. See also, Sara McLanahan and Gary Sandefur, *Growing Up with a Single Parent* (Cambridge, MA: Harvard University Press, 1994).

12. Edward Gilbreath, "Manhood's Great Awakening," *Christuanity Today* (February 6, 1995): 27.

13. David Elkind, *The Hurried Child: Growing Up Too Fast Too Soon* (Reading, MA: Addison-Wesley, 1981).

14. Jean Bethke Elshtain, *Democracy on Trial* (New York: Basic Books, 1995).

15. Jonathan Alter and Pat Wingert, "The Return of Shame," *Newsweek* (February 6. 1995): 25.

16. Tom McNichol, "The New Sex Vow: 'I won't' until 'I do'," USA Weekend, March 25–27, 1994. 4 ff. Lee Smith. "The New Wave of Illegitimacy." *Fortune* (April 18, 1994): 81 ff.

17. Susan Chira, "War over Role of American Fathers." *New York Times*, June 19, 1994. 22.

18. Juliet Schor, "Consumerism and the Decline of Family and Community: Preliminary Statistics from a Survey on Time, Money, and Values." Harvard Divinity School, Seminar on Families and Family Policy, April 4, 1995.

19. Karen S. Peterson, "In Balancing Act, Scale Tips toward Family," *USA Today*, January 25, 1995.

20. Lawrence Mead, "Taxing Peter to Pay Paula," *Wall Street Journal*, November 2. 1994.

21. Tom G. Palmer, "English Lessons: Britain Rethinks the Welfare State," *Wall Street Journal*, November 2, 1994.

22. Robert Pear, "G.O.P. Affirms Plan to Stop Money for Unwed Mothers," *New York Times*, January 21, 1995, 9.

23. Brigitte Berger. "Block Grants: Changing the Welfare Culture from the Ground Up," *Dialogue* (Boston: Pioneer Institute for Public Policy Research), no. 3, March 1995.

24. Robert Rector, "Welfare," *Issues '94: The Candidate's Briefing Book* (Washington, DC American Heritage Foundation, 1994), chap. 13.

25. Council on Families in America, *Marriage in America*, 13–16.

26. Robert Bellah, "Invasion of the Money World," in *Rebuilding the Nest*, ed. David Blankenhorn, Steven Bayme, and Jean Bethke Elshtain (Milwaukee: Family Service America, 1990), 227–36. James Coleman, *Foundations of Social Theory* (Cambridge, MA: Harvard Univesity Press, 1990).

27. Sylvia Nasar, "More Men in Prime of Life Spend Less Time Working," *New York Times*, December 1,1994, A1.

28. John Scanzoni, *Power Politics in the American Marriage* (Englewood Cliffs. NJ: Prentice-Hall, 1972). Ruth A. Wallace and Alison Wolf, Contemporary Sociological Theory (Englewood Cliffs, NJ: Prentice-Hall, 1991), 176.

29. Fred Weinstein and Gerald M. Platt, *The Wish to Be Free: Society, Psyche, and Value Change* (Berkeley, CA: University of California Press, 1969).

30. Kingsley Davis, "Wives and Work: A Theory of the Sex-Role Revolution and Its Consequenecs," in *Feminism, Children, and the New Families*, ed. S. M. Dornbusch and M. H. Strober (New York: Guilford Press. 1988), 67–86. Janet Zollinger Giele, *Two Paths to Women's Equality: Temperance, Suffrage, and the Origins of American Feminism* (New York: Twayne Publishers, Macmillan, 1995).

31. Vivianna A. Zelizer, *Pricing the Priceless Child: The Changing Social Value of Children* (New York: Basic Books, 1985).

32. William J. Goode, *World Revolution in Family Patterns* (New York: The Free Press, 1963).

33. Constance Willard Williams, *Black Teenage Mothers: Pregnancy and Child Rearing from Their Perspective* (Lexington, MA: Lexington Books, 1990).

34. William Julius Wilson, *The Truly Disadvantaged: The Inner City, the Underclass, and Public Policy* (Chicago: University of Chicago Press, 1987).

35. Jacob Mincer, "Labor-force Participation of Married Women: A Study of Labor Supply," in *Aspects of Labor Economics*, Report of the National Bureau of Economic Research (Princeton, NJ: Univeristies-National Bureau Committee of Economic Research, 1962). Glen G. Cain. *Married Women in the Labor Force: An Economic Analysis* (Chicago: University of Chicago Press, 1966).

36. Richard A. Easterlin, *Birth and Fortune: The Impact of Numbers on Personal Welfare* (New York: Basic Books, 1980). Valerie K. Oppenheimer, "Structural Sources of Economic Pressure for Wives to Work—Analytic Framework" *Journal of Family History* 4, no. 2(1979): 177–99, and Valerie K. Oppenheimer, *Work and the Farnily: A Study in Social Demography* (New York: Academic Press, 1982).

37. Janet Z. Giele and Rainer Pischner, "The Emergence of Multiple Role Patterns Among Women: A Comparison of Germany and the United States," *Vierteljahrshefte zur Wirtschaftsforschung* (Applied Economics Quarterly) (Heft 1–2, 1994). Alice S. Rossi, "The Future in the Making," *American Journal of Orthopsychiatry* 63, no. 2 (1993): 166–76. Notburga Ott, *Intrafamily Bargaining and Household Decisions* (Berlin: Springer-Verlag, 1992).

38. Iris Young, "Mothers, Citizenship and Independence: A Critique of Pure Family Values." *Ethics* 105. no. 3 (1995): 535–56. Young critiques the liberal stance of Williarn Galston, *Liberal Purposes* (New York: Cambridge University Press, 1991).

39. Lee Rainwater and Williarn L. Yancey, *The Moynihan Report and the Politics of Controversy* (Cambridge, MA: MIT Press, 1967).

40. Glen H. Elder. Jr., *Children of the Great Depression* (Chicago: University of Chicago Press, 1974). Rand D. Conger, Xiao-Jia Ge, and Frederick O. Lorenz, "Economic Stress and Marital Relations," in *Families in Troubled Times: Adapting to Change in Rural America*, ed. R. D. Conger and G. H. Elder, Jr. (New York: Aldine de Gruyter, 1994), 187–203.

41. Coleman, *Foundations of Social Theory*, 590.

42. Elizabeth G. Menaghan and Toby L. Parcel, "Employed Mothers and Childrens Home Environments," Journal of Marriage and the Family 53, no. 2 (1991): 417–31. Lois Hoffman, "The Effects on Children of Maternal and Paternal Employment," in *Families and Work*, ed. Naomi Gerstel and Harriet Engel Gross (Philadelphia: Temple University Press, 1987), 362–95.

43. Juliet Schor, *The Overworked American: The Unexpected Decline of Leisure* (New York: Basic Books, 1991). Robert Haveman and Barbara Wolfe, *Succeeding Generations: On the Effects of Investments in Children* (New York: Russell Sage Foundation, 1994), 239.

44. Coleman, *Foundations of Social Theory*, 596–97.

45. Schor, "Consumerism and Decline of Family."

46. Iris Young, "Mothers, Citizenship and Independence," puts Elshtain, Etzioni, Galston, and Whitehead in this category.

47. Coleman, *Foundations of Social Theory*, 597–609.

48. Sherry Wexler, "To Work and To Mother: A Comparison of the Family Support Act and the Family and Medical Leave Act" (Ph. D. diss. draft, Brandeis University, 1995). David T. Ellwood, *Poor Support: Poverty in the American* Family (New York: Basic Books, 1988).

49. Coleman, *Foundations of Social Theory*, 300–21. Coleman, known for rational choice theory in sociology, put forward these theoretical possibilities in 1990, fully four years ahead of what in 1994 was voiced in the Republican Contract with America.

50. Wexler, "To Work and To Mother."

51. Robert Lerman, "Marketplace," National Public Radio, April 18, 1995.

52. Karen Offen, "Defining Feminism: A Comparative Historical Approach," *Signs* 14, no. 1 (1988): 119–51.

53. Young, "Mothers, Citizenship and Independence."

54. Robert N. Bellah et al., *Habits of the Heart* (Berkeley, CA: University of California Press, 1985), 250–71. Gosta Esping-Andersen, *The Three Worlds of Welfare Capitalism* (Princeton, NJ: Princeton University Press, 1990). Susan Pedersen, *Family, Dependence, and the Origins of the Welfare State: Britain and France, 1914–1945* (New York: Cambridge University Press, 1993).

55. Young, "Mothers, Citizenship and Independence."

56. Giele, "Woman's Role Change and Adaptation" presents these historical statistics.

57. Elshtain, *Democracy on Trial*; Robert N. Bellah et al., *The Good Society* (New York: Knopf, 1991), 210. Robert D. Putnam, "Bowling Alone: America's Declining Social Capital," *Journal of Democracy* 4, no. 1 (1995): 65–78.

58. Heather McCallum "Mind the Gap" (paper presented to the Family and Children's Policy Center colloquium, Waltham, MA, Brandeis University, March 23, 1995). The sum was markedly better for children of employed single mothers, around $700 per mother in the United States. But this figure corresponded with over $1,000 in eleven other countries, with only Greece and Portugal lower than the U.S. Concerning the high U.S. rates of

teen pregnancy, see Planned Parenthood advertisement, "Let's Get Serious About Ending Teen Childbearing," *New York Times*, April 4, 1995, A25.

59. Ruth Walker, "Secretary Reich and the Disintegrating Middle Class," *Christian Science Monitor*, November 2, 1994, 19.

60. For reference to "social capital," see Coleman, *Foundations of Social Theory*; Elshtain, *Democracy on Trial*; and Putnam, "Bowling Alone." For "emotional capital," see Arlie Russell Hochschild, *The Managed Heart: The Commercialization of Human Feeling* (Berkeley, CA: University of California Press, 1983). For "cultural capital," see work by Pierre Bourdieu and Jurgen Habermas.

61. Judith Stacey, "Dan Quayle's Revenge: The New Family Values Crusaders," *The Nation*, July 25/August 1, 1994, 119–22. Iris Marion Young, "Making Single Motherhood Normal," *Dissent* (Winter 1994): 88–93.

62. Christopher Jencks and Kathryn Edin, "Do Poor Women Have a Right to Bear Children," *The American Prospect* (Winter 1995): 43–52.

63. Stacey, "Dan Quayle's Revenge": Arlene Skolnick and Stacey Rosencrantz, "The New Crusade for the Old Family," The American Prospect (Summer 1994): 59–65.

64. Nancy Smith Barrett, "Data Needs for Evaluating the Labor Market Status of Women," in *Census Bureau Conference on Federal Statistical Needs Relating to Women*, ed. Barbara B. Reagan (U.S. Bureau of the Census, 1979) Current Population Reports, Special Studies, Series P-23, no. 83, pp. 10–19. These figures belie the familiar but misleading statement that "only 7 percent" of all American families are of the traditional nuclear type because "traditional" is defined so narrowly–as husband and wife with two children under 18 where the wife is not employed outside the home. For more recent figures and a similar argument for more universal family ethic, see Christine Winquist Nord and Nicholas Zill, "American Households in Demographic Perspective," working paper no. 5, Institute for American Values, New York, 1991.

65. Tamar Levin, "Women Are Becoming Equal Providers," *New York Times*, May 11, 1995, A27.

66. Marianne A. Ferber and Julie A. Nelson, *Beyond Economic Man: Feminist Theory and Economics* (Chicago: University of Chicago Press, 1993).

67. Fran Sussner Rodgers and Charles Rodgers, "Business and the Facts of Family Life," *Harvard Business Review*, no. 6 (1989): 199–213, especially 206.

68. Ravenna Helson and S. Picano, "Is the Traditional Role Bad for Women?" *Journal of Personality and Social Psychology* 59 (1990): 311–20. Rosalind C. Barnett, "Home-to-Work Spillover Revisited: A Study of Full-Time Employed Women in Dual-Earner Couples," *Journal of Marriage and the Family* 56 (August 1994): 647–56.

69. Arlie Hochschild, "The Fractured Family," *The American Prospect* (Summer 1991): 106–15.

70. Leon Eisenberg, "Is the Family Obsolete?" *The Key Reporter* 60, no. 3 (1995): 1–5. Arlene Skolnick and Stacey Rosencrantz, "The New Crusade for the Old Family," *The American Prospect* (Summer 1994): 59–65.

71. Roberta M. Spalter-Roth, Heidi I. Hartmann, and Linda M. Andrews,

"'Mothers, Children, and Low-Wage Work: The Ability to Earn a Family Wage," in *Sociology and the Public Agenda*, ed. W. J. Wilson (Newbury Park, CA: Sage Publications, 1993), 316–38.

72. Louis Uchitelle, "Lacking Child Care, Parents Take Their Children to Work," *New York Times*, December 23, 1994, 1.

73. Jencks and Edin, "Do Poor Women Have a Right," 50.

74. David Elkind, *Ties That Stress: The New Family in Balance* (Boston: Harvard University Press, 1994).

75. It is frequently noted that the U.S. is a much more racially diverse nation than, say, Sweden, which has a concerted family and children's policy. Symptomatic of the potential for race and class division that impedes recognition of all children as the nation's children is the book by Richard J. Herrnstein and Charles A. Murray, *The Bell Curve: Intelligence and Class Structure in American Life* (New York: The Free Press, 1994).

76. Young, "Making Single Motherhood Normal," 93.

77. If the objection is that the wrong people will have children, as Herrnstein and Murray suggest in *The Bell Curve*, then the challenge is to find ways for poor women to make money or have some other more exciting career that will offset the rewards of having children, "such as becoming the bride of Christ or the head of a Fortune 500 corporation," to quote Jencks and Edin, "Do Poor Women Have a Right," 48.

78. Beth M. Miller, "Private Welfare: The Distubutive Equity of Family Benefits in America" (Ph.D. thesis, Brandeis University, 1992). Sue Shellenbarger, "Family-Friendly Firms Often Leave Fathers Out of the Picture," *Wall Street Journal*, November 2, 1994. Richard T. Gill and T. Grandon Gill, *Of Families, Children, and a Parental Bill of Rights* (New York: Institute for American Values, 1993). For gathering information on these new work-family policies, I wish to acknowledge help of students in my 1994–95 Family Policy Seminar at Brandeis University, particularly Cathleen O'Brien, Deborah Gurewich, Alissa Starr, and Pamela Swain, as well as the insights of two Ph.D students, Mindy Fried and Sherry Wexler.

79. Lotte Bailyn, *Breaking the Mold: Women, Men and Time in the New Corporate World* (New York: The Free Press, 1994).

80. Penelope Leach, *Children First: What Our Society Must Do and Is Doing* (New York: Random House, 1994).